THE ROUTLEDGE CO.
TO SPATIAL HIST‿ᴜʀᴵ

The Routledge Companion to Spatial History explores the full range of ways in which geographic information systems (GIS) can be used to study the past, considering key questions such as what types of new knowledge can be developed solely as a consequence of using GIS and how effective GIS can be for different types of research.

Global in scope and covering a broad range of subjects, the chapters in this volume discuss ways of turning sources into a GIS database, methods of analysing these databases, methods of visualising the results of the analyses, and approaches to interpreting analyses and visualisations. Chapter authors draw from a diverse collection of case studies from around the world, covering topics from state power in imperial China to the urban property market in nineteenth-century Rio de Janeiro, health and society in twentieth-century Britain to the demographic impact of the Second Battle of Ypres in 1915.

Critically evaluating both the strengths and limitations of GIS and illustrated with over two hundred maps and figures, this volume is an essential resource for all students and scholars interested in the use of GIS and spatial analysis as a method of historical research.

Ian Gregory is Professor of Digital Humanities at Lancaster University, UK. He has worked extensively on using GIS in the Humanities on topics ranging from nineteenth-century infant mortality to Lake District literature. He has published four books and numerous journal articles on the subject. He co-directs Lancaster's Digital Humanities Hub (http://wp.lancs.ac.uk/dighum).

Don DeBats, Head of American Studies at Flinders University, Australia, is also a visiting professor at the University of Virginia, and a Residential Fellow at the Virginia Foundation for the Humanities. His current research on individual level voting by whites and African-Americans in Kentucky from 1870 to the adoption of the

Australian secret ballot in 1891 is supported by the Division of Research Programs of the National Endowment for the Humanities. His interactive data-driven website is: sociallogic.iath.virginia.edu

Don Lafreniere is Assistant Professor of Geography and GIS and Director of the Geospatial Research Facility at Michigan Technological University, USA. His research interests centre on creating GIS methodologies for recreating historical environments and spatializing populations. His recent work includes creating historical spatial data infrastructures for heritage preservation and education and using historical geospatial methods for uncovering the relationships between the built environment and life course health and wellbeing.

THE ROUTLEDGE COMPANION TO SPATIAL HISTORY

Edited by Ian Gregory, Don DeBats, and Don Lafreniere

Routledge
Taylor & Francis Group

LONDON AND NEW YORK

First published 2018
by Routledge

2 Park Square, Milton Park, Abingdon, Oxon, OX14 4RN
605 Third Avenue, New York, NY 10017

Routledge is an imprint of the Taylor & Francis Group, an informa business

First issued in paperback 2020

British Library Cataloguing-in-Publication Data
A catalogue record for this book is available from the British Library

Library of Congress Cataloging-in-Publication Data
Names: Gregory, Ian, 1970- editor. | DeBats, Donald A. (Donald Arthur), 1943- editor. | Lafreniere, Donald, editor.
Title: The Routledge companion to spatial history/edited by Ian Gregory, Don DeBats and Don Lafreniere.
Other titles: Companion to spatial history
Description: Milton Park, Abingdon, Oxon; New York, NY: Routledge, 2018. | Includes bibliographical references and index.
Identifiers: LCCN 2017028318| ISBN 9781138860148 (hardback: alkaline paper) | ISBN 9781315099781 (ebook)
Subjects: LCSH: History–Research–Data processing. | History–Methodology. | Historical geography–Methodology. | Geographic information systems. | Historical geographic information systems.
Classification: LCC D16.12.R68 2018 | DDC 902.85–dc23
LC record available at https://lccn.loc.gov/2017028318

ISBN: 978-1-138-86014-8 (hbk)
ISBN: 978-0-367-73537-1 (pbk)

Typeset in Bembo
by Sunrise Setting Ltd, Brixham, UK

CONTENTS

FIGURES

TABLES

CONTRIBUTORS

Beatrice Alex is a Research Associate at the School of Informatics at the University of Edinburgh. Her research interests focus on information extraction and text mining. She has worked on many projects involving natural language processing of textual documents in different domains such as biomedicine, astronomy, news, recruitment, history and most recently social media and literature. Dr Alex is a member of the Language Technology Group and a co-founder of the Digital Humanities Network Scotland.

Eduard J. Alvarez-Palau is Research Associate at the Cambridge Group for the History of Population and Social Structure, University of Cambridge; and Course Instructor on *City Management and Urbanism* at Universitat Oberta de Catalunya. His research interests are in the frontier between transport modelling, regional planning and history with the aim to better understand the impacts of transport infrastructure in the long term. His recent work focuses on the development of H-GIS databases and the development of computational tools.

Miranda Anderson is a literary scholar at the University of Edinburgh with a particular interest in the cognitive and digital humanities and a focus on exploring notions of the mind and self across disciplinary and chronological spans. She initiated and was a Research Fellow on the Palimpsest project. She also initiated and is now a Research Fellow on the AHRC-funded History of Distributed Cognition project, which explores parallels and contrasts between current notions of the mind as distributed across brain, body and world and the expression of analogous notions in works from classical antiquity to the twentieth century.

Jeremy Atack is Professor Emeritus and Research Professor of Economics at Vanderbilt University where he has taught since 1993. Prior to that he was at the University of Illinois. He is also a Research Associate with the National Bureau of Economic Research in Cambridge, Massachusetts. His undergraduate degree is from the University of Cambridge, his doctorate from Indiana University. He has been

President of the Agricultural History Society, the Business History Conference and the Economic History Association.

Dimitris Ballas is Professor of Economic Geography at the University of Groningen, the Netherlands. He has also previously worked as Associate Professor at the University of the Aegean, Greece, and as a Senior Lecturer at the University of Sheffield, UK. He has held Visiting Research Scholar positions at the University of Cambridge, UK, Harvard University, at the International Institute for Applied Systems Analysis, Austria, and been a Visiting Professor at Ritsumeikan University, Japan. He has published widely in the fields of social and spatial inequalities, regional science and Geoinformatics in the Social Sciences.

Andrew A. Beveridge, PhD, is Professor of Sociology at Queens College and the Graduate School and University Center of the City University of New York. He and his team developed *Social Explorer* (www.socialexplorer.com). It has won six awards, including a Webby in 2016. A volume he edited with David Halle of UCLA, *New York and Los Angeles: The Uncertain Future*, was published in 2013 by Oxford University Press. He has published numerous articles in scholarly journals.

David J. Bodenhamer is (Founding) Executive Director, the Polis Center, Professor of History, and Adjunct Professor of Informatics, Indiana University-Purdue University, Indianapolis. He also is general editor of the Indiana University Press Series on the Spatial Humanities, and is co-editor of *IJHAC: A Journal of the Digital Humanities*. He has written or edited twelve books, including *The Spatial Humanities: GIS and the Revolution of Humanities Scholarship* (2010, with John Corrigan and Trevor Harris), and over 40 journal articles and book chapters.

Douglas H. L. Brown is Senior Lecturer in Geographic Information Systems and Human Geography at Kingston University, UK. His research interests include the historical geographies of poverty, welfare, health and healthcare.

Brian E. Bunker graduated from Brigham Young University with a bachelor's degree in geography and a minor in computer science. He completed a master's degree in geography at the University of Arkansas. Upon graduation he joined ESRI's Professional Services group and currently focuses on applying geographic information technology within agricultural enterprises as a consultant and developer.

N. D. B. Connolly is Associate Professor of History at the Johns Hopkins University, where he holds the Herbert Baxter Adams Chair.

Geoff Cunfer is Professor of History and Founder of the Historical GIS Laboratory at the University of Saskatchewan (www.hgis.usask.ca). He is an environmental historian of agricultural land use and energy on the North American grasslands and the author of *On the Great Plains: Agriculture and Environment* (2005), *As a Farm Woman Thinks: Life and Land on the Texas High Plains, 1890–1960* (2010), and *Bison and People on the North American Great Plains: A Deep Environmental History* (2016).

Don DeBats, Head of American Studies at Flinders University, Australia, is also a visiting professor at the University of Virginia, and a residential fellow at the Virginia Foundation for the Humanities. His current research on individual level voting by whites and African-Americans in Kentucky from 1870 to the adoption of the Australian secret ballot in 1891 is supported by the Division of Research Programs of the National Endowment for the Humanities. His interactive data-driven website is: sociallogic.iath.virginia.edu

Danny Dorling is the Halford Mackinder Professor of Geography at the University of Oxford. He grew up in Oxford and went to university in Newcastle upon Tyne. He has worked in Newcastle, Bristol, Leeds, Sheffield and New Zealand. Much of his work is available open access (see www.dannydorling.org). With a group of colleagues he helped create the website www.worldmapper.org which shows who has most and least in the world. His work concerns issues of housing, health, employment, education, wealth and poverty.

Patrick Dunae is an adjunct associate professor in the History Department at the University of Victoria and Professor Emeritus in History at Vancouver Island University. He is the editor of the Vancouver Island digital archive, viHistory.ca.

Zephyr Frank is Professor of History and Director of the Spatial History Project at Stanford University. He also served as the founding Director of the Center for Spatial and Textual Analysis (2011–2016). His most recent publication is *Reading Rio de Janeiro: Literature and Society in the Nineteenth Century*, Stanford University Press, 2016.

Carol Gelvin-Reymiller was an archaeologist, naturalist, gardener, artist, dog musher, trapper, world traveler and outdoors woman. Her studies included the refinement of methods (phytolith and macroremain extraction from sediments; GIS-based modeling), the relationship of technology to ecology and environment, and human relationships to the environment and ecology of the arctic and subarctic. She conducted fieldwork throughout Alaska (*Daily News-Miner*, 16 April 2013) and in Arizona.

Jason Gilliland is Director of the Urban Development and Professor of Geography at Western University. He is also cross-appointed as a full Professor in the School of Health Studies, Department of Paediatrics, and Department of Epidemiology & Biostatistics at Western and he is a Scientist with the Children's Health Research Institute and Lawson Health Research Institute, two of Canada's leading hospital-based research institutes. His recent research focuses primarily on environmental influences on population health; however, he has a long-standing interest in using GIS to explore historical patterns of social stratification, mobility and urban development.

Ian Gregory is Professor of Digital Humanities at Lancaster University. He has worked extensively on using GIS in the Humanities on topics ranging from nineteenth-century infant mortality to Lake District literature. He has published four books and numerous journal articles on the subject. He co-directs Lancaster's Digital Humanities Hub (http://wp.lancs.ac.uk/dighum).

Claire Grover is a senior research fellow in the School of Informatics, University of Edinburgh. She has a background in computational linguistics and most recently she has focused on the development of XML-based text mining and geo-referencing systems, with applications in digital humanities as well as other domains. She is a lead developer of the Edinburgh Geoparser.

David Harris-Birtill is a Research Fellow at the University of St Andrews, and the creator of the iOS LitLong app; previously he was a researcher in Imperial College London's Department of Surgery and Cancer, and he holds a PhD in Physics from the Institute of Cancer Research, where he used lasers to treat and detect cancer. David is principal investigator on Medical Imaging and Sensing projects within Computer Science, including detecting heart rates using camera-based technology.

Megan Harvey is a PhD candidate in the Department of History at the University of Victoria, British Columbia. Her research focuses on the historical and current-day relationships between Indigenous peoples and the state, the dispossessions and attempted repossessions of land that have been so central to these relationships, and how both can be better understood by exploring their narrative dimensions. She has researched and published on issues of race and colonization, and was co-director of the Colonial Legacies South Africa Field School in 2014.

Justin M. Hays is a registered professional archaeologist and was the study lead of the Susitna Dam Project. He is currently at the University of Alaska. He has been an archaeologist and principal investigator for numerous projects throughout Alaska. He continues to conduct field research designed by GIS modeling. His research interests include: circumpolar anthropology, zooarchaeology and paleoecology. He has done extensive fieldwork throughout Alaska for almost 20 years and resides in Fairbanks.

Richard G. Healey, Professor of Geography, Department of Geography, University of Portsmouth, UK, specializes in the geography of nineteenth-century regional economic development in the USA. He is the author of *The Pennsylvania Anthracite Coal Industry, 1860–1902: Economic Cycles, Business Decision-Making and Regional Dynamics* (University of Scranton Press, 2007) and numerous journal articles on historical GIS and historical census analysis.

Uta Hinrichs is a Lecturer at the University of St Andrews, Scotland, in the SACHI research group. She holds a PhD in Computational Media Design from the University of Calgary. Uta's research is at the intersection of visualization, HCI, design, the humanities and art. Her work focuses on designing and studying the use and experience of interactive systems that facilitate the exploration and analysis of (cultural) data collections from academic, leisurely and artistic perspectives.

James Kari retired from University of Alaska Fairbanks and the Alaska Native Language Center in 1997. Athabascan languages include: Ahtna, Dena'ina, Koyukon, Deg Hit'an, Holikachuk, Tanana, and Upper Tanana. Books include: editor, *Koyukon Athabaskan Dictionary* by Jules Jetté and Eliza Jones; author, *Dena'ina Topical Dictionary*; and co-author, *Shem Pete's Alaska: The Territory of the Upper Cook Inlet Dena'ina*. In addition, he was a co-editor of *The Dene-Yeniseian Connection*, a special edition of the *Anthropological Papers of the University of Alaska*, University of Alaska (2016).

Anne Kelly Knowles, an historical geographer, is Colonel James C. Distinguished Professor of History at the University of Maine. She has written two monographs and edited two of the first books on HGIS: *Past Time, Past Place: GIS for History* and *Placing History: How Maps, Spatial Data, and GIS Are Changing Historical Scholarship*. She was also lead editor of *Geographies of the Holocaust*. Anne's pioneering work was recognized in 2012 by the first annual American Ingenuity Award for Historical Scholarship from *Smithsonian* magazine. In 2015, she was named a Guggenheim Fellow.

Don Lafreniere is Assistant Professor of Geography and GIS and Director of the Geospatial Research Facility at Michigan Technological University, USA. His research interests centre on creating GIS methodologies for recreating historical environments and spatializing populations. His recent work includes creating historical spatial data infrastructures for heritage preservation and education and using historical geospatial methods for uncovering the relationships between the built environment and life course health and wellbeing.

John R. Logan is Professor of Sociology at Brown University, where he has also been director of the initiative on Spatial Structures in the Social Sciences (S4) since 2004. He is co-author (with Harvey Molotch) of *Urban Fortunes: The Political Economy of Place*. He has been working with mapped historical census data on US cities for several years. His Urban Transition Historical GIS Project (www.s4.brown.edu/utp) geocoded 100 percent microdata for thirty-nine cities in 1880. His goal is to complete mapping for most large cities for every decade from 1900 to 1940.

James Loxley is Professor of Early Modern Literature at the University of Edinburgh and was Principal Investigator on the Palimpsest project. He has published widely on many aspects of early modern literature in particular, and has led a number of collaborative AHRC-funded research and public engagement projects in recent years.

John Sutton Lutz is the chair and a professor in the History Department at the University of Victoria with a research focus on Pacific Northwest from the 1770s to the 1970s and has a keen interest in digital tools for research and teaching. He is the author of *Makúk: A New History of Native–White Relations* (UBC Press, 2008), the editor of several volumes including: *Myth and Memory: Stories of Indigenous-European Contact* and *Making and Moving Knowledge: Interdisciplinary and Community Based*

Research in a World on the Edge (McGill-Queen's, 2008), co-director of the award-winning *Great Unsolved Mysteries in Canadian History* internet project and co-director of the Ethnohistory Field School with the Stó:lō.

Richard Marciano is Professor at the College of Information Studies at the University of Maryland and Director of the Digital Curation Innovation Center (DCIC). His research interests center on digital preservation, sustainable archives, cyberinfrastructure and big data.

Jordi Martí-Henneberg has been Professor of Human Geography at the University of Lleida, Spain since 1990, and ICREA-Academia researcher from 2013. He currently leads several research projects, some of which are funded by the European Union (learneurope.eu), the Ministry of Science (europa.udl.cat) and RecerCaixa on Industrial Heritage using GIS applications.

Charles M. Mobley holds a PhD in Anthropology with specialization in archaeology, an MA in cultural resource management/conservation archaeology and a BA in Anthropology. Dr Mobley has spent almost 30 years in Alaska teaching, writing and consulting about Alaska's history and prehistory. He has taught at the University of Anchorage and Sheldon Jackson College, and has written over 100 technical reports, 18 articles, and one book. Dr Mobley's work has included over 100 projects throughout Alaska. charlesmmobley.com.

Ruth Mostern is Associate Professor of History and director of the World History Center at the University of Pittsburgh. She is the author of *Dividing the Realm in Order to Govern: The Spatial Organization of the Song State* (2011), co-editor of *Placing Names: Enriching and Integrating Gazetteers* (2016), and Principal Investigator of the NEH-funded World-Historical Gazetteer project. She has published over two dozen articles and digital works on topics in spatial history methods, imperial Chinese spatial and environmental history, and related fields.

Robert K. Nelson is Director of the Digital Scholarship Lab and affiliated faculty in the American Studies Program at the University of Richmond. He is the editor of two recent digital mapping projects, *American Panorama* and the *Atlas of the Historical Geography of the United States*.

Jon Oberlander holds a chair in Epistemics in the School of Informatics at the University of Edinburgh. He is currently Director of the University's Data Technology Institute, and Co-Director of its Centre for Design Informatics. His research combines computational linguistics and cognitive science, and aims at getting computers to talk (and write) like individual people. He has a long-standing interest in personalization via natural language generation, particularly in the field of cultural heritage.

Sherry Olson, Professor of Geography at McGill University, is a member of the Centre interuniversitaire d'Études québécoises (Laval-UQTR) and co-author with

Patricia Thornton of a social history of Montreal. Her history of Baltimore links the social and environmental challenges. In addition to papers on infant mortality, forest history and street-space, forthcoming book chapters consider urban workhorses, rural children's reports of their tasks on the farm and networking of urban youth a century ago.

Samuel M. Otterstrom is professor of geography at Brigham Young University, where he has taught since 1997. He is married with nine children. Professor Otterstrom specializes in historical and contemporary population and settlement geography, with a focus on the United States, while also maintaining regional teaching and research interests in Latin America and Europe. He enjoyed taking his family with him on assignments to direct university study abroad programs in Madrid, Spain, and London, England.

Corinna Peniston-Bird is a Senior Lecturer in Cultural History in the Department of History at Lancaster University. She has a particular interest in the commemoration of war, and in the relationship between personal testimonies and cultural representations. She has also published widely on gender dynamics in Britain in wartime as well as on historical source methodologies.

Jean-Luc Pinol, Professor of Modern History, Ecole Normale Supérieure, University of Lyon. Member of Laboratoire de Recherche Historique Rhône-Alpes (LARHRA). Specialized in urban history, he is the author and editor of *Histoire de l'Europe urbaine de l'antiquité à nos jours* (6 volumes, Seuil, 2011–12). He used GIS for *Paris de la Révolution à nos jours* (written with Maurice Garden) published in 2009. His interest in spatial history led to his decision to create an interactive map about the deportation of Jewish children in Paris during WWII (http://tetrade.huma-num.fr/Tetrademap_Enfant_Paris/).

Aaron Quigley is the Chair of Human Computer Interaction in the University of St Andrews, where he is director of the St Andrews Computer Human Interaction research group (SACHI). His research interests include surface and multi-display computing, human computer interaction, pervasive and ubiquitous computing and information visualization. He is chair of the ACM MobileHCI steering committee, the ACM SIGCHI Adjunct Chair for Specialized Conferences and board member of ScotlandIS. He has published over 150 internationally peer-reviewed publications, and held appointments in Australia, Japan, USA, Germany, Ireland and the UK.

Kurt Schlichting is the E. Gerald Corrigan '63 Chair in Humanities & Social Sciences and a Professor of Sociology at Fairfield University. His research interests include historic GIS, quantitative history of New York and the city's immigrant neighborhoods, and the Great Migration of African Americans from the south. He is also the author of *Grand Central Terminal: Railroads, Architecture and Engineering in New York*, the basis for the PBS American Experience documentary, *Grand Central*.

Robert M. Schwartz is E. Nevius Rodman Professor of History at Mount Holyoke College, emeritus. Recent publications include 'Agricultural Change and Politics in Late Nineteenth Century Britain: The Enquiries of Two Royal Commissions, 1879–1897', in *The Golden Age of State Enquiries* (Brussels, 2014); 'Digital Partnership: Combining Text Mining and GIS in a Spatial History of Sea Fishing in the United Kingdom, 1860 to 1900', *International Journal of Humanities and Arts Computing* 9(1) (2015); 'Measuring One Century of Railway Accessibility and Population Change in France', *Journal of Transport History* 56 (October 2016).

William E. Simeone is the author and editor of several books related to Athapaskan aspects of life past and present. Major works include *Rifles, Blankets, and Beads: Identity, History, and the Northern Athapaskan Potlatch*; *Han: People of the River*; and *Tannana and Chandalar: The Alaska Field Journals of Robert A. McKennan*.

Humphrey Southall is Professor of Historical Geography at the University of Portsmouth. He has an MA and a PhD in Geography from Cambridge University. Since 1994 he has been leading the development of the Great Britain Historical GIS (Geographical Information System). He contributed to the ESRC's Health Variations Programme, on locality-level mortality since 1920, and to the ESRC HALCyon project ("healthy ageing across the life-course") on area-based characteristics.

Tara Thomson is a Research Fellow on the LitLong: Edinburgh project at the University of Edinburgh, and a Lecturer at Edinburgh Napier University. Her research interests include modernism, feminism and gender studies, everyday life theory and the Digital Humanities. She has edited scholarly editions of Dorothy Richardson's *Pointed Roofs* and *The Tunnel* for Broadview Press, and her monograph *Modernism, Feminism and Everyday Life* is forthcoming from Routledge.

George Vascik is a 1988 graduate of the University of Michigan. He has taught courses in modern history and western civilization at Miami University since 1992. Vascik has published widely on topics in German political and economic history. His book *Antisemitism and Rural Politics in Northwest Germany* is forthcoming from Bloomsbury Press in 2017.

Gustavo Velasco obtained a PhD in Economic History from the London School of Economics. His dissertation studies natural resources exploitation and the formation of the institutions of settler capitalism during the first era of globalization with special interest in the evolution of the Canadian Prairies from the 1850s to 1914 ('Natural Resources, State Formation and the Institutions of Settler Capitalism: The Case of Western Canada, 1850–1914', PhD, London School of Economics and Political Science, 2016. http://etheses.lse.ac.uk/3437). His research interests include Canadian history, economic history, economic geography and Historical GIS.

Nigel Walford is Professor of Applied Geographical Information Systems at Kingston University, London, UK. His research focuses on the application of spatial analytic and geovisualization tools in relation to geodemographics, historical and contemporary rural landscapes and population dynamics.

LaDale Winling is an assistant professor of history at Virginia Tech. His forthcoming book on universities and cities, *Building the Ivory Tower*, will be published by the University of Pennsylvania Press.

Weiwei Zhang is an assistant professor of sociology and Director of the State Data Center at South Dakota State University. Dr Zhang completed her PhD in Sociology at Brown University in 2014. Her research interests include residential segregation, ethnic neighborhood, demographic and spatial methods. Dr Zhang has worked on developing new approaches for population estimation, geocoding and spatial modeling. She is working on projects on the assimilation and integration of Asian and Hispanic groups and historical settlements of immigrant groups in the US.

INTRODUCTION

Spatial history, history, and GIS

Don DeBats, Ian Gregory, and Don Lafreniere

This volume assesses and showcases exemplary research across a wide range of historical fields that have felt the impact of Geographic Information Systems (GIS) technologies and methodologies. The field increasingly referred to as Spatial History encompasses the array of technological and methodological innovations that have revolutionized the relationship between geographical information and historical research.

Historical GIS (HGIS) is a nomenclature within Spatial History that captures developments within geography in GIS and Geographical Information Science (GISc). It became clear that these approaches had much to offer both to historical geographers and to historians more widely. Producing outstanding results within a social sciences framework, as GIS sweeps across disciplinary boundaries, it also impacts historical work in the humanities framework. Spatial History therefore captures the whole of this field of impacted historical research, humanities as well as social sciences.

GIS remains at the core of Spatial History. GIS is ultimately a database technology; it is distinctive because the information in databases developed for GIS includes geographical coordinates in addition to the data found in conventional databases.[1] These coordinates mean that GIS technologies allow information to be displayed on a map (visualized), and GIS methodologies allow dimensions of that spatial display to be measured (analysed). Because of these attributes, GIS is both a map-making technology and a spatial measurement methodology.[2]

Although the terms GIS and GISc are sometimes used interchangeably, technically they refer to something quite different. GISc is a spatial science, with its origins in natural resource management and urban planning. This science has emerged from the realization that GIS is far more than a software package; it is the science of spatial data collection, management, analysis, and dissemination.[3] GIS's appeal stems from its ability to easily manage disparate information about locations on earth with very high precision. Moreover, GIS assists users meeting the challenges of using this information effectively and appropriately.[4]

In somewhat technical terms, HGIS is the creation and use of a relational database of historical geographical information in a GIS. This is what has fuelled 'the spatial turn' in historical studies. HGIS has existed as a scholarly endeavor for fewer than twenty years and the progress of the field in that short space of time has been remarkable.[5] It has indeed proved to be a 'dazzling array of new ways of seeing, and imaging, the past'.[6]

As with any technological change, the reason for such a sudden impact is that many scholars were waiting for this product: there was a pre-existing market of researchers who recognized that databases and maps could be combined. It was just a question of how that would be done. Vector plotters worked but when the Environmental Systems Research Institute (ESRI), headquartered in Redlands, California, released its first GIS software (Arc/Info), the real answer became apparent. Arc/Info, designed to run on mainframe computers with limited graphics capability, gave way to ArcView GIS and then ArcGIS, which provided a new generation of users with powerful graphics capability and a graphical user interface. As ESRI's corporate website notes, its first 'User's Conference' in 1981 had 16 attendees; the 2016 User's Conference had over 16,000 attendees from 138 countries. As Anne Knowles noted, 'people love new tools that enable them to do what they have dreamed of doing'.[7] And so it was with Historical GIS.

In due course the more inclusive notion of Spatial History may replace HGIS as a nomenclature that better recognizes the application of GIS to the humanities in particular.[8] This reflects as well the fact that as GIS rolls over disciplinary boundaries from the sciences to the humanities the importance of technology and methods (GIS) has been reduced, replaced by an emphasis on the applied findings and what they mean to our understanding of the geographies of the past. Spatial History is an inclusive form of historical geography that is largely enabled by its use of GIS but includes other spatial technologies as well. These other technologies include internet mapping technologies such as Google Maps, virtual globes such as Google Earth and location-based mobile apps: in short the technologies that have become part of everyday life. Spatial History is thus closely related to a range of other computing advancements including Spatial Humanities,[9] geohumanities[10] and deep mapping.[11]

This volume is dedicated to presenting the current state of the art in Spatial History. It brings together the work of 50 scholars in 28 chapters. We have subdivided these chapters into six separate fields of historical research to demonstrate the impact of that new knowledge on historical understandings in a diverse collection of fields. These are: 1) population and demography; 2) economic history; 3) urban history; 4) rural and environmental history; 5) political history; 6) the spatial humanities. The first five sections of this volume reflect the traditional and ongoing strengths of HGIS in the social sciences; the final section represents the bridge into the humanities where Spatial History is a more congenial term than HGIS. This is GIS's newest frontier, where spatial historical approaches are based on more conventional qualitative sources and approaches, including literary studies and archaeology.

The work assembled in this volume illustrates the transformative impact of GIS on historical research. The history of GIS in history is remarkably short. It began with four 'potential impact statements', in this century's opening years.[12] If we go back to that point in time, it would have been preposterous to have predicted that a mere 17 years later GIS would have swept across historical research, defining careers, creating scholarly networks and, ultimately, reconfiguring the links between geography and history.

There is much to celebrate in the interdisciplinary success of Spatial History, nurtured to no small degree by the historical geography and GIS network of the Social Science History Association and the spatial and digital history network of the European Social Science History Association. The past does not, however, guarantee the future and we set out below the five problems that we believe require successful resolution if the field is to continue to enjoy this trend-line of growth and development.

First, it is clear that Spatial History is better at creating new knowledge than in problematizing that new knowledge, or explaining how and why that new knowledge matters. Producing knowledge for its own sake can be only part of the guide to the future of Spatial History. If the utilization of GIS in scholarly fields is to continue to expand, practitioners must become more adept at explaining how GIS-generated knowledge provides new answers to old questions and allows new historical insights.

Second, as a field, Spatial History at present concentrates more on visualization of spatial attributes than the measurement of the influence or explanatory power associated with those attributes. Put differently, the outputs of many Spatial History projects depend more on the persuasive power of an image than the generation of measures of the significance of the data creating the image. There is, of course, nothing erroneous in preferencing the former over the latter; nevertheless the dynamics of professional development, especially in the social sciences, will increase the pressure on practitioners to utilize the statistical tools inherent in GIS that are not presently deployed to enhance the explanatory powers of spatial data. Even simple density measurements raise profound problems of scale as do measures of segregation and separation. Such issues may become more important as researchers in Spatial History explore explanations of behaviour. The increasing reach of network analysis as a field of historical inquiry will come in contact with spatial explanations of behavior, so practitioners will confront the need to integrate knowledge of the humanistic ties that create the network with our evidence of the network's spatial dimensions.

Indeed, the third branch point facing Spatial History is the relationship between the quantitative objectives of GIS and the qualitative data central to humanities scholars. As section 6 shows, there is no doubt that GIS handles the former more propitiously than it does the latter and directs research towards that which reflects its capacities. The gap between these two perspectives is, however, bridgeable and recent advances in the demonstration of the capacities of Spatial History to deal with qualitative and textual material provide evidence of that potential.[13] Maintaining this cooperative stance is critical to the mutually beneficial advancement of Spatial History in both quantitative and qualitative areas.

The development of the quantification 'side' of GIS may raise anew the issues of behaviouralism in the 1970s and 1980s that swam into view with the temporary rise of the new social history and the new political history.[14] A similar debate occurred within geography as the discipline confronted its own quantification revolution. The table here is adapted from Anne Knowles and compares the earlier criticisms of quantitative history with recent criticisms of HGIS.[15] These are important critiques but the culture of inclusiveness that has defined the growth of Spatial History may ensure that this time those values rather than a drive toward numeric exclusivity prevails.

Criticisms of quantitative history	Criticisms of GIS
It is a passing fad	Academics are embracing GIS uncritically
The world needs 'essential narrative' works of synthesis, not 'research reports'	GIS is merely a tool
It has not fulfilled its promise. It is dull, local and technical and has confirmed what we already know	Geostatistics are still crude. GIS advocates are recycling the failed approach of 1970s spatial analysis
It examines only questions for which quantitative data exist	GIS handles qualitative data poorly
History must be accessible to all and therefore should not use complex statistics	GIS is too difficult for the masses. Its users are creating a technocracy
Historical information is too imprecise for sophisticated methods and theory	GIS enforces consistency and logic that do not inhere in many data sources
Computer-based analysis is uncreative	GIS too narrowly serves the immediate needs of policy makers
It assumes one can determine truth	GIS divorces information from the context of its social creation

A fifth critical point arises from the fact that Spatial History work is characterized by the creation of large databases which sometimes are deployed in digital, often online, formats. For university practitioners these twin features of their work environment create very substantial problems, of which we will focus on two.

Unlike much social science-based GIS scholarship which can utilize government-created datasets, social surveys or assembled economic data, most Spatial Historians must create their own datasets, a characteristic displayed in nearly every chapter brought together in this volume. An HGIS database can be years or decades in the making. Significant research and methodological expertise is needed before historical sources can be used for spatial or statistical analysis in GIS. Almost always, record linkage is required, joining the handwritten records of a large number of individuals or elements of corporate information across a variety of record types. Almost never do historians discover data bearing the standardized number or ID reference characteristic of modern record-keeping.

Perhaps in time there will be a tradition of secondary analyses of publicly available HGIS datasets and record linkage programs that are more reliable. But at the moment, a self-created HGIS database is the norm: a database constructed by an individual possessing high levels of patience that represents a significant labour and funding investment cost and almost no protection of intellectual property. Compounding that insecurity of access to one's own work are the demands of many granting agencies and high-profile journals for the public release of the data on which a project or article is based: years of work goes to create a database that becomes public property with a single article in a prestigious journal. That places a very low price on high-cost intellectual property.

The centrality of visualization in Spatial Historical research makes publishing in digital format especially attractive: few book or journal publishers would be as generous as Routledge has been in this project where there were no restrictions on the number of maps that could be included. The general trend in historical publication towards digital media projects is accentuated among spatial historians. However, this form of publication, particularly if it is supported by national funding bodies, can generate additional pressure for the full release of the entire database underpinning the project.

The more serious problem is that many university departments and perhaps particularly those related to historical analysis are loath to consider either database creation or the creation of a research-bearing and research-structured website as evidence of scholarly activity. To quote from a recent article in the American Historical Association's (AHA), *Perspectives on History*,

> Digital historians have remediated older forms of scholarship into new media while simultaneously pioneering new forms of scholarly writing, such as the blog post and the knowledge site. In this regard, professional historians share much in common with other disciplines, including the natural sciences, in which scholarship is presented in article and other formats that are much shorter than a book.[16]

These are acute matters for digital historians engaged in Spatial History and for the field of Spatial History: unless its research methods and outputs achieve scholarly recognition, the field cannot continue to attract the interest of young historians for whom promotion and acknowledgement of scholarly productivity are paramount. This will necessitate promoting 'methods of measurement or sets of standards' that compare non-traditional outputs stemming from Spatial History with books and peer-reviewed articles.[17] The continued success of Spatial History will depend not only on cohorts of dedicated scholars, but also the willingness of their many disciplines to take account of scholarly and audience engagement, as well as impact, as proper metrics in ascertaining research activity.[18]

The record of Spatial History in overcoming problems while maintaining an inclusive, cooperative, collegial and multi-disciplinary culture encourages us in the belief that these problems too will be resolved in ways which continue the field's arc toward greater application and impact.

Acknowledgements

Ian Gregory's contribution to this volume received support from the European Research Council (ERC) under the European Union's Seventh Framework Programme (FP7/2007-2013)/ERC grant *Spatial Humanities: Texts, GIS, Places* (agreement number 283850).

Notes

1 Coordinates are expressed as latitude and longitude or in a map projection such as Universal Transverse Mercator (UTM) or British National Grid.

2 Good introductions to GIS include: N. Chrisman, *Exploring Geographic Information Systems*. 2nd ed., New York: John Wiley, 2002; I. Heywood, S. Cornelius and S. Carver, *An Introduction to Geographical Information Systems*, 2nd ed., Harlow, Essex: Prentice Hall, 2002; P.A. Longley, M.F. Goodchild, D.J. Maguire and D.W. Rhind, *Geographical*

Information Systems: Principals, Techniques, Management and Applications, 2nd ed., Chichester: John Wiley, 1999; D. Martin, *Geographic Information Systems and their Socio-economic Applications*, 2nd ed., Hampshire: Routledge, 1996.

3 M.F. Goodchild, 'Geographical Information Science', *International Journal of Geographical Information Systems* 6, 1992, 31–45.

4 P.A. Longley, M.F. Goodchild, D.J. Maguire and D.W. Rhind, *Geographical Information Science and Systems*, 4th ed., Chichester: John Wiley, 2015.

5 For reviews of Historical GIS see: I.N. Gregory and P.S. Ell, *Historical GIS: Technology, Methodology, Scholarship*, Cambridge: Cambridge University Press, 2007; I.N. Gregory and R.G. Healey, 'Historical GIS: Structuring, Mapping and Analysing Geographies of the Past', *Progress in Human Geography* 31, 2007, 638–53; A.K. Knowles, *Placing History: How GIS Is Changing Historical Scholarship*, Redlands, CA: ESRI Press, 2008.

6 D. Holdsworth, 'Historical Geography: New Ways of Imagining and Seeing the Past', *Progress in Human Geography* 27, 2003, 491.

7 A.K. Knowles (ed.), 'Historical GIS: The Spatial Turn in Social Science History', Special Issue, *Social Science History* 24, 2000, 451.

8 I.N. Gregory and A. Geddes, 'From Historical GIS to Spatial Humanities: Deepening Scholarship and Broadening Technology', in I. N. Gregory and A. Geddes (eds), *Toward Spatial Humanities: Historical GIS and Spatial History*, Bloomington: Indiana University Press, 2014, pp. ix–xix.

9 D.J. Bodenhamer, J.Corrigan and T.M. Harris, *The Spatial Humanities: GIS and the Future of Humanities Scholarship*, Bloomington: Indiana University Press, 2010.

10 M. Dear, J. Ketchum, S. Luria and D. Richardson, *GeoHumanities: Art, History, Text at the Edge of Place,* London: Routledge, 2011.

11 D.J. Bodenhamer, J. Corrigan and T.M. Harris, *Deep Maps and Spatial Narratives*, Bloomington: Indiana University Press, 2015.

12 Knowles, 'Historical GIS'; I. Gregory and P.S. Ell (eds), 'Adding a New Dimension to Historical Research with GIS', Special Issue of *History and Computing* 13, 2001; A.K. Knowles (ed.), *Past Time, Past Places: GIS for History,* Redlands: ESRI Press, 2002; Holdsworth, 'Historical Geography'.

13 I. Gregory and D. Cooper, 'Thomas Gray, Samuel Taylor Coleridge and Geographical Information Systems: A Literary GIS of Two Lake District Tours', *International Journal of Humanities and Arts Computing* 3, 2009, 61–84; D. Lafreniere and J. Gilliland, 'All the World's a Stage: A GIS Framework for Recreating Personal Time-Space from Qualitative and Quantitative Sources', *Transactions in GIS* 19, 2015, 225–46.

14 For a critique at the time see S.P. Hays, 'Historical Social Research: Concept, Method, and Technique', *Journal of Interdisciplinary History* 4, 1974, 475–82.

15 Knowles, 'The Spatial Turn in Social Science History', 464.

16 T.J. Gilfoyle, 'The Changing Forms of History', *Perspectives on History* 53(4), 2015, 26–27.

17 Gilfoyle, 'The Changing Forms', 27. See also American Historical Association, 'Redefining Historical Scholarship: Report of the ad hoc Committee on Redefining Historical Scholarship', December 1993.

18 There are promising efforts underway in the Dataverse Project (www.dataverse.org) to provide standards for creating and citing social science datasets.

PART I

Population and demography

INTRODUCTION TO PART I

Don Lafreniere, Ian Gregory, and Don DeBats

The study of population distribution, dynamics of population growth, socio-economic characteristics, and migration have been a long preoccupation of scholars. Traditionally, the study of population fell within two disciplines, with the field of population geography most interested in the spatial distribution and variations of populations (migration, mobility, settlement) while its cognate discipline of demography has focused on the population dynamics of mortality, fertility, and marriage. In recent decades, we see the boundaries between these disciplines blurred, with scholars from anthropology, economics, biology, psychology, and especially history.

Historical demography traces its roots to Louis Henry and his push for the creation of the International Commission for Historical Demography in 1960.[1] Thrust forward by the quantitative revolution in the social sciences in the 1970s and 1980s and the increasing availability of individual-level historical census data, we see the rise of historical population studies such as Stephan Thernstrom's influential writing on social mobility in Newburyport,[2] Tamara Hareven's work on family and kin networks,[3] and Peter Knight's examination of urbanization as a demographic process.[4] In the 1990s and 2000s, historical demographic scholarship led the way in utilizing 'big data' in the social sciences, thanks to the many projects worldwide that began to transcribe, standardize, code and record link population registers such as those in the Integrated Public Use Microdata Series (IPUMS),[5] the North Atlantic Population Project,[6] the Canadian Families Project[7] (later the Canadian Century Research Infrastructure[8]), BALSAC,[9] and the samples archived with the Inter-university Consortium for Political and Social Research (ICPSR)[10] and the European Historical Population Samples Network.[11]

The interdisciplinary interest in historical populations thrived during this period yet despite wide access to GIS in the 1990s, there was little adoption of the methodology. Thanks to the annual cross-fertilization of ideas and methods at the Social Science History Association and biennially at its European counterpart, as well as two workshops, sponsored by the International Union for the Scientific Study of Population[12] (IUSSP) interest in spatializing the big historical population datasets has grown significantly. Among the earliest projects to integrate large census datasets into a GIS was the Great Britain HGIS, started by Humphrey Southall and later joined by Ian Gregory and others.[13] Other national projects started, such as in the US,[14] Ireland,[15] Belgium,[16] and Canada.[17] Others began to use census data at the local scale. The earliest was to study nineteenth-century Montreal, spearheaded by Gilliland, Olson, and Sweeny.[18] Others include Hartford, Connecticut,[19] Victoria, British Columbia,[20] London, Ontario,[21] Alexandria, Virginia, and Newport, Kentucky,[22] and the Urban Transition Historical GIS Project led by John Logan and Weiwei Zhang outlined in section III of this book.[23]

Some of the same leaders who paved the way for using census data in a GIS have contributed their latest work to this collection. The first is by geographer Sherry Olson who using the pre-eminent geodatabases of the *Montréal, l'avenir du passé* presents a dozen experiments using population registers, taxrolls, directories, and fire insurance plans to assess the contributions of women to the industrialization of Montreal. She concludes by outlining the importance of connecting not only disparate demographic datasets to spatial representations of the urban fabric but also to connect scholars who will ask new and fresh questions of past populations. Sam Otterstrom revisits the European migration to America by harnessing the some 800 million names in the FamilySearch genealogical dataset in concert with the spatial analytical tools of an HGIS. Using a generational migration approach, he follows five generations of immigrants forward and backward through their family histories and analyses their migration patterns as well as the level of cultural mixing in different regions of the country. Eduard Alvarez-Palau and Jordi Marti-Henneberg revisit the relationship between the railroad and population distribution. Using a custom HGIS database of the rail network interlinking sixteen European countries and municipal level decennial censuses, the interplay between the accessibility to the rail network and the spatial distribution and intensity of urbanization is explored. Humphrey Southall extends traditional historical geographic and demographic approaches to the study of health and well-being outcomes, a subject of increasing interest among historically minded scholars. Using registrar general reports, census data, and local unemployment data, he reports on a pilot study that investigates the relationship between deprivation and infant mortality. Further, he outlines the important role that historical geographers and HGIS scholars can play on interdisciplinary teams providing expertise in standardizing areal units, geocoding, linking historic datasets, and providing important historical context to data and the interpretation of results. The final chapter of this section is by sociologist Andrew Beveridge. Beveridge interrogates the relationship between population dynamics, economic activity, and the labour force from the 1970s to 2012. Using both global and local measures of spatial autocorrelation, and spatial weighted regressions he finds relationships between the various national economic shifts and population employment change and distribution. These chapters illustrate how an innovative use of old sources can open up new research possibilities to scholars who approach the study of population from a spatial analytical lens.

Notes

1 A. Fauve-Chamoux, I. Bolovan and S. Sogner (eds), *A Global History of Historical Demography. Half a Century of Interdisciplinarity*, Bern: Peter Lang, 2016; P.A. Rosental, 'The

Novelty of an Old Genre: Louis Henry and the Founding of Historical Demography', *Population-E* 58, 2003, 197–29.

2 S. Thernstrom, *Poverty and Progress: Social Mobility in a Nineteenth Century City*, Cambridge, MA: Harvard University Press, 1964.

3 T. Hareven (ed.), *Family and Kin in Urban Communities, 1700–1930*, New York: New Viewpoints, 1977; T. Hareven (ed.), *Transitions: The Family and the Life Course in Historical Perspective*, New York: Academic Press, 1978.

4 P. Knight, *The Plain People of Boston, 1830–1860: A Study in City Growth*, New York: Oxford University Press, 1972.

5 Integrated Public Use Microdata Series. Online. Available HTTP: <www.ipums.org> (accessed 1 May 2017).

6 E. Roberts, S. Ruggles, L. Dillon, O. Garoarsdottir, J. Oldervoll, G. Thorvaldsen, and M. Woollard, 'The North Atlantic Population Project: An Overview', *Historical Methods* 36, 2003, 80–8.

7 E. Sager, 'The Canadian Families Project and the 1901 Census', *Historical Methods* 33, 2000, 179–84.

8 C. Gaffield, 'Conceptualizing and Constructing the Canadian Century Research Infrastructure', *Historical Methods* 40, 2007, 54–64.

9 BALSAC, Online. Available HTTP: <http://balsac.uqac.ca> (accessed 1 May 2017).

10 Inter-university Consortium for Political and Social Research. Online. Available HTTP: <www.icpsr.umich.edu> (accessed 1 May 2017).

11 European Historical Population Samples Network. Online. Available HTTP: <www.ehps-net.eu/> (accessed 1 May 2017).

12 The Workshop on Space and Time was held at the Minnesota Population Center in 2006 and more recently a Spatial Analysis in Historical Demography workshop was held in Quebec City 2015.

13 I. Gregory, C. Bennett, V. Gilham, and H. Southall, 'The Great Britain Historical GIS Project: From Maps to Changing Human Geography', *Cartographic Journal* 39, 2002, 37–49.

14 C. Fitch and S. Ruggles, 'Building the National Historical Geographic Information System', *Historical Methods* 36, 2003, 41–51.

15 P. Ell, 'A Historical GIS for Ireland', *Historical Geography* 33, 2005, 138–40.

16 E. Vanhaute, The Belgium Historical GIS', *Historical Geography* 33, 2005, 140–3.

17 M. St-Hilaire, B. Moldofsky, L. Richard, and M. Beaudry, 'Geocoding and Mapping Historical Census Data: The Geographical Component of the Canadian Century Research Infrastructure', *Historical Methods* 40, 2007, 76–91.

18 J. Gilliland and S. Olson, 'Montreal, l'avenir du passe', *GEOinfo* Jan–Feb, 2003, 5–7; R.C.H. Sweeny and S. Olson, 'MAP: Montréal l'avenir du passé: Sharing Geodatabases Yesterday, Today and Tomorrow', *Geomatica* 57, 2003, 145–54.

19 K. Schlichting, P. Tucker and R. Maisel, 'Residental Segregation and the Beginning of the Great Migration of African Americans to Hartford, Connecticut: A GIS-Based Analysis', *Historical Methods* 39, 2006, 132–44.

20 P. Dunae, J. Lutz, D. Lafreniere and J. Gilliland, 'Making the Inscrutable, Scrutable: Race and Space in Victoria's Chinatown, 1891', *B.C Studies* 169, 2011, 51–80.

21 D. Lafreniere and J. Gilliland, '"All the World's a Stage": A GIS Framework for Recreating Personal Time-Space from Qualitative and Quantitative Sources', *Transactions in GIS*, 2015.

22 D. Debats, 'Using GIS and Individual-Level Data for Whole Communities: A Path toward the Reconciliation of Political and Social History', *Social Science Computer Review* 27, 2009, 313–30.

23 As well see J. Logan, J. Jindrick, H. Shin, and W. Zhang, 'Mapping America in 1880: The Urban Transition Historical GIS Project', *Historical Methods* 44, 2011, 49–60.

1

RE-FOCUS ON WOMEN IN AN INDUSTRIAL REVOLUTION

Montreal 1848–1903

Sherry Olson

How did women contribute to the 'industrial revolution' in Montreal? With the help of an HGIS, can we uncover some roles whose importance we have failed to recognize? The reorganization of production that we still think of as the harnessing of the steam engine, entailed a continual repartitioning by gender, as well as rearrangement of spaces, concentrating workers in large factories, in cities of unprecedented size, and under wider and deeper structures of corporate management. Despite a generation of scholars more alert to the concerns and agency of women, flaws in the 'comprehensive' census make it difficult to get an adequate perspective on the restructuring of work. For more than two-thirds of Montreal women over age 15, the nominal census provides no information about their activities, earnings, or places of work.[1] To gain insight into their roles in the spectacular expansion of an urban economy, we must tap alternative sources, apply more supple concepts of work, and anchor workplaces – domestic and institutional as well as industrial and entrepreneurial – in the urban space. Several chapters of this volume point to the value of an HGIS in the analysis of sites of social change. Along these lines, I shall argue the potential of a well-conceived HGIS for integrating rich local sources as an 'information system'. By coupling additional sources we uncover their complementarities and wring more out of the census itself.

The Canadian metropolis, like other big cities of Europe and North America, attracted more women than men, and textbook accounts of its fast-growth phase 1842–1901 record their increasing presence in factory labour and contemporary concerns about their health, exploitation, abuse, and 'morality'.[2] Designers of the Canadian census, however, in addition to taking a narrow view of women's work, threw up obstacles to any study of spatial dynamics. Every ten years the census-takers redefined their variables, tinkered with the instructions, recreated *de novo* their geographic units, and trashed the documentation of their boundaries. These flaws are not confined to Canada: nineteenth-century censuses did not focus on everyday life, on 'places' filled with pasts and futures, personal experiences and expectations. The census-makers were satisfied to estimate taxables and cannon-fodder, and to project a national glow of 'progress'.[3]

Faced with such gaps, and in response to Mei-Po Kwan's challenge to employ GIS to contextualize women's daily lives,[4] I am proposing the prickly problem of 'women's work' as a demonstration and a test of the HGIS called 'MAP, Montréal l'avenir du passé'. A team of two dozen designed MAP to empower research on nineteenth-century Montreal. As a time frame, we seized upon four high-quality historic maps to bracket the changes that occurred over a suite of three building booms shared throughout North America (see Figure 1.1).[5] The spatial frame was ambitious. Consistent with those maps, we aimed to place each household on the building lot, with a resolution of two or three metres for display of lot lines and building footprints. Since each of us had a different research objective in mind, our design choices reflected a diversity of purposes. We would include all the variables available in four censuses (at 20-year intervals), but we would go well beyond them: we imagined endless extensions, like a Tinkertoy or an inexhaustible supply of Lego bricks, and indeed, in the fifteen years elapsed, a dozen more people have brought forward new sources and used 'MAP' for analyses and displays we did not foresee.[6]

Over the span 1842–1901, we are tracking a census population that increased tenfold, from 30,000 to 350,000. The four sections of this essay all draw upon the 1881 and 1901 layers of MAP to experiment with a dozen different strategies for squeezing clues out of the census material and challenging the bias of the census-makers. What work were the women doing? at what ages? in what settings? in what parts of town? The first step is to examine the gender distribution across the urban space at several resolutions; the second, to explore the temporal variations in work – day and night, summer and winter, from one building boom to the next, or at various

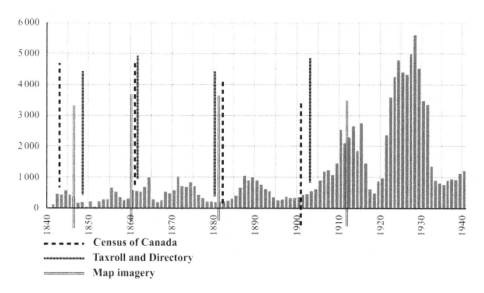

Figure 1.1 Construction cycle, Montreal, 1840–1940, with dates of MAP sources. Construction and in-migration track the continent-wide rhythm of construction, as observed from annual building permits.

Source: Ville de Montréal, Annual reports, Inspector of buildings. Reproduced from S. Olson, 'Setting the Census Household into Its Urban Context', *Demographic Research* 36–46, 2017, 1399–1434.

phases of a life course. Examples featured in the third section point to the advantages of a mix-and-match of information from multiple sources, and confrontation of sources uncovers, in the final section, the shifting nature of our social relations. As gender differences intersected differences of status, race, and cultural identity, they played into moving frontiers of exchange, collaboration, and contention.

Gender distribution across the city

Where in Montreal did the women live and work, and in what proportions or concentrations? To build up a perspective, one step at a time, let me start with the crudest of models. If we take a population, male and female, in proportions close to 50-50 at birth, and scatter them at random across the urban space, we'll find little variation from one district to the next, from one census division to the next, or from one street to the next. But what do the maps tell us? Once we adjust the citywide share of women to a more realistic 53 per cent of adults, the associated age-differences (see Figure 1.2) suggest a gendered logic of migration and high mobility of young people.[7] Western frontiers were attracting more young men to lumbering, mining, and cow-catching, while cities like Montreal attracted young women to fill jobs as servants in wealthy homes, boardinghouses, shops, and hotels.[8] Each building boom was associated with a wave of in-migrants, so that throughout the 60 years of observation, half the adults

Figure 1.2   Population of Montreal by age, gender, and origin, 1901. The bulge of in-migrants is most apparent among people in their early twenties, especially women.

Source: Census of 1901, Canadian Families Project 5 per cent sample.

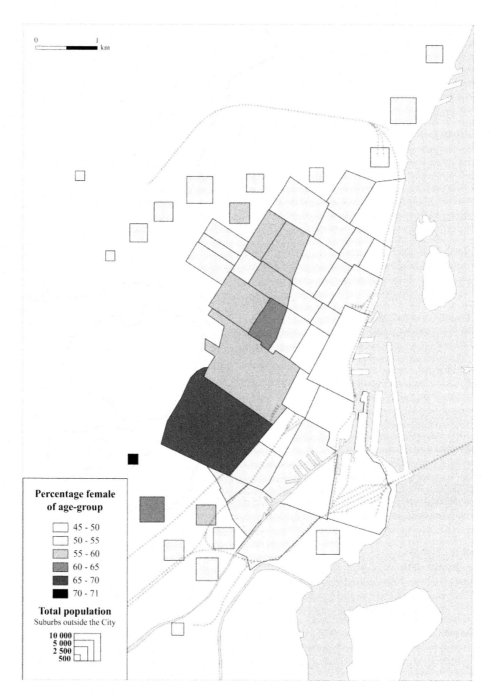

Figure 1.3 Percentage female of population 15–29, by districts of Montreal, 1881 and 1901. The highest concentration of young women reflects the demand for servants in wealthy homes on the slope of Mount Royal. The districts are standardized as identical aggregates of street segments. Suburbs outside the City are sized in proportion to their populations.

Sources: Censuses of 1881 and 1901, 100% index.

were newcomers, born either in the Old World or in rural surroundings of the St Lawrence lowlands. Of 50 districts across the city in 1901, four show women as 60 per cent of the population of young adults 15–29 (see Figure 1.3). The high concentrations identify districts of great wealth, where 44 per cent of households employed a female servant, 22 per cent more than one.

Were women present in all households? As we might suppose, two-thirds of the urban households amounted to a man and a woman and their children – no more no less – and if we allow for a grandma or a sister-in-law, the family nucleus anchored five out of six. Their mean size was only five persons, and three-quarters of them – ranging up to eleven or twelve persons – were housed in dwellings of three, four, or five rooms. But what about households of unusual size or shape? Let us focus for a moment on the single-sex households. Where all the adults were men, most were small groups comprised of three or four laundrymen, teaching brothers, or priests in their presbytery. (Loners were exceedingly rare.) Decidedly more numerous were households where all adults were women – one in six. In addition to mother-led clusters such as a widow and her daughters, they included some hundreds of women deserted by their husbands, and several hundred 'spinsters' on their own. The scatter has little effect on the district-wide ratios of Figure 1.3, but let us zoom into the 662 little strips that routed census-takers through a city of rowhouses. These census divisions capture the differential probabilities of everyday encounters in a 'neighbourhood', and at this finer resolution you might find yourself living in a neighborhood where two-thirds of the grown-ups were women, or two-thirds were men.[9]

For a dozen of these distinctive neighbourhood strips, the profiles of age and gender are warped by the presence of oversized 'households', each with a unique mission (see Figure 1.4). A census household was defined as any group who shared a kitchen and a front door to the street. Over 4 per cent of the city's women were living in institutional settings in 1901, and these households were more specialized than in the past, with as many as a thousand women housed in spaces elaborately designed for controlled circulation, and under the governance of women.[10] In addition to dedicated religious personnel and trainees, they employed female servants and organized the labour of 'inmates' they described as patients, pupils, refugees, penitents, or prisoners. Their unique profiles are compared with divisions composed of families with specialized economic functions, such as the cotton mill workers, garment workers, and the managerial élite.

Many of the large residential communities lived behind stone walls, kept unusual schedules and strict curfew, but they were in fact organized for service in the secular world, and their significance as nodes of communication is seriously underestimated. The communities of religious were conveyor belts of urbanization. In response to needs in the big city, rural parishes supplied vocations to novitiates, administrative motherhouses, hospitals, asylums, and colleges in Montreal. Each community recruited from a distinctive rural catchment, often through schools it operated.[11] Between one quarter and one third of the nuns had a birth-sister, an aunt, or a niece, occasionally a daughter, in the same religious community. Among the Sisters of Charity, for example, the five Gadbois sisters pioneered and successively managed for 50 years the education of the deaf. The nuns' lifelong ties with their rural families of origin, as well as perennial fund-raising campaigns across the diocese, carried

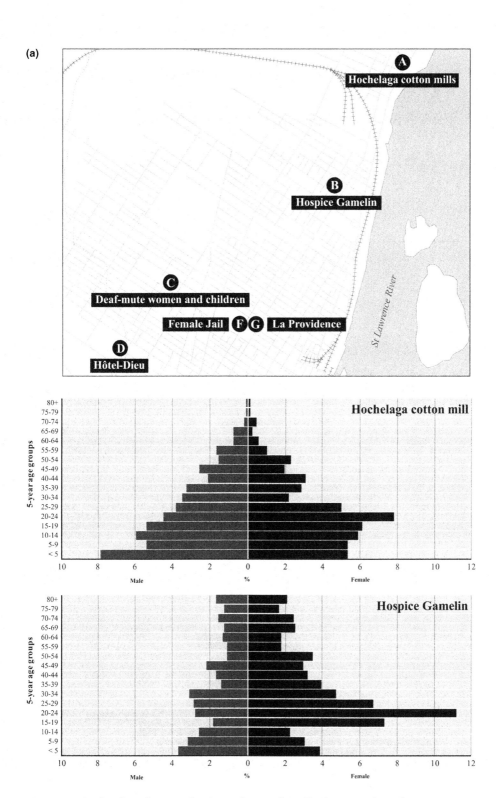

Figure 1.4 (a–d) Selected census divisions of unusual profiles by age and gender, 1901.

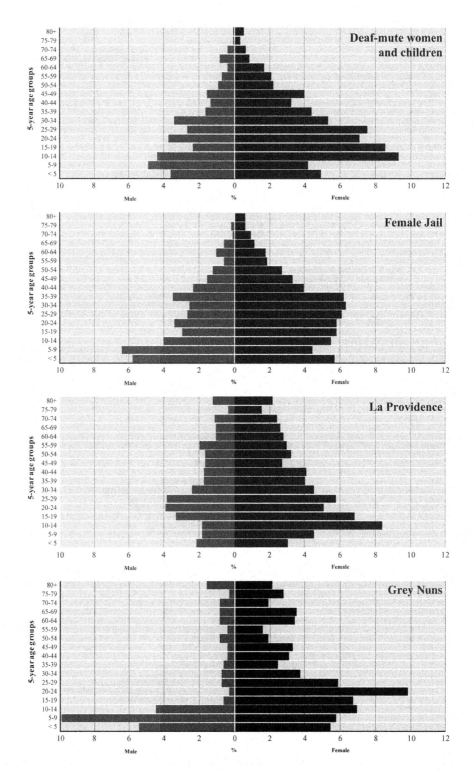

Figure 1.4 (Continued).

(c)

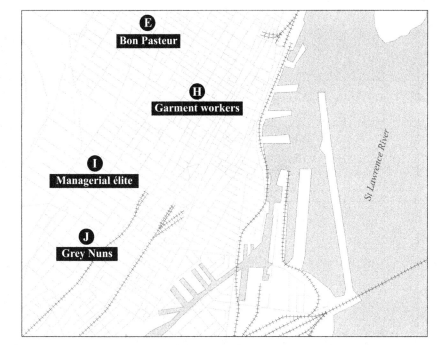

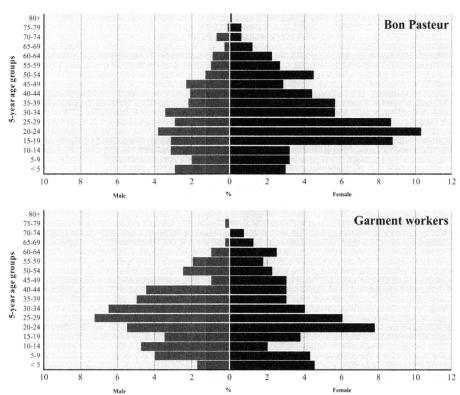

Figure 1.4 (Continued).

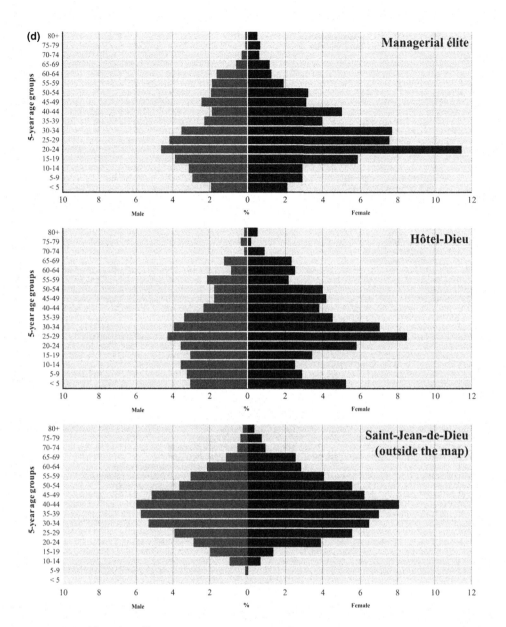

Figure 1.4 (Continued).

Note: Each of the 11 little neighborhoods is affected by the presence of a particular industry or institution dependent on a gendered labour force: the cotton mills, the garment district, a terrace of wealth with live-in servants, and institutions that employed and sheltered women and girls.

Sources: Census of 1901, 100 per cent index, Lovell's directory. Selected census divisions: Saint-Jean-de-Dieu (lpt-c01), Bon Pasteur (lou-b29), Hôtel-Dieu (lau-a36), Female Jail (mar-a45), Hospice Gamelin (mar-a46), Grey Nuns (ant-a47), Deaf mute women and children (jac-b64), La Providence (jac-b27), Hochelaga cotton mills (hch-b11), Garment district (lau-a09), Managerial élite (ant-a20).

incidental messages between village and city: a woman in need of specialized medical care, an unwed mother in need of shelter, a girl seeking a 'place' as a servant, or a young widower seeking a wife to mother his children. The highly formalized communities of religious maintained informal networks by which young people found their way into Montreal.

In the urban habitat, too, the nuns wove neighbourhood ties. In addition to relations they maintained with former patients or pupils and their parents, and with professionals like physicians and parish priests, their teaching and nursing functions took them into homes of the poor; financial pressures led them to take in washing from middle-class families, board rich widows, beg soup-bones from the butchers in the public markets, and sell their embroidery at festivals and charity events. Some communities, seeded from France, maintained correspondence with other 'houses' and exchanged knowhow, such as the Belgian or French system of shorthand, solfège, pharmacopoeia, and educational games for nursery schools. In Montreal they pioneered day care, trained professional musicians, designed mechanisms for publishing books in Braille, and introduced sign languages for the deaf (French and English, functioning on different principles). As early as 1848 communities in Montreal were sending women as teachers and nurses to Alberta, British Columbia, and Oregon, by the 1860s to New England, by the 1890s to South America. The new links contributed to intergenerational and international transfers of knowhow and inquiry, notably in hospital management and record-keeping. As the institutions grew in size and specialization, they developed new layers of management, apprenticeship, and problem-solving. Their elaboration of a division of labour among women was comparable to what was happening in the male-operated railways, civil service, and foundries. Through the intense connectivity, the forbidding stone walls housed hotpoints of innovation.

Although the largest were Catholic, the city's Protestant institutions were likewise intensely networked at the levels of female personnel, dependent families, donors, inmates, and volunteers. The Protestant hospitals and shelters relied on large families of celibate women, for whom they built handsome and closely supervised 'nurses' residences'. The professional sisterhoods, both Catholic and Protestant, were instrumental in reforms as training, registration, antiseptic practices, operating room efficiency, promotion of prenatal care and domestic science.[12]

The simple mapping of gender – straightforward in the HGIS – has brought us directly into the profound contradictions of social life in Montreal. The male clergy, both Protestant and Catholic, in a persistent rehearsal of the sixteenth-century Reformation and Counter-Reformation, aligned all the female communities of care as well-marked nodes of ideological confrontation. Their determination to identify the needy as 'ours' or 'theirs' inhibited the growth of municipal and secular collectives. The segmentation of 'charity' – by gender, religious affiliation, and language – ensured direct interactions between some of the wealthiest women and some of the poorest, between some of the most powerful and some of the most vulnerable. Most of the elaborately segmented structures that mixed relief, social control, and deference were mediated through female leadership, so that a single institution conveyed contradictory images of female dependence and female agency. Debate continues over the degree to which the various communities of women resisted patriarchy and guarded chartered prerogatives;[13] but there is no doubt that the agency of women – at both ends of the scale – was grounded in a crochet of personal relationships.

Night and day, summer and winter, over a lifetime

By tallying people where they sleep, the census of population creates a further challenge to interpreting where they worked and how work was defined. A basic question about the industrial mode of production is the extent to which work moved out of domestic settings; and a basic question about women's work – in every era – is its adaptation over the life-cycle to biologically constrained reproductive demands and culturally normed roles in families.[14] The norms of household structure most often observed in Montreal in 1881 are shown in Figure 1.5, with men usually reported as household head, often as lodger, women more often as spouse, servant, or relative.

Successive stages of the industrial revolution are often defined by transitions from horsepower to waterpower, steampower, and the electric motor; and the timing in Montreal is consistent with other North American cities. In the surge of the 1850s, foundries, locomotive-building, and boilerworks concentrated in particular parts of the city, while other parts of town specialized in textile or shoe manufacture. Each industry mechanized in numerous steps; each step was contested, and gendered

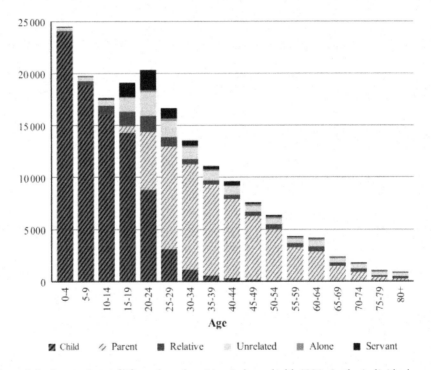

Figure 1.5 Interactions of life-cycle and position in household, 1881. As the individual grows up, gender influences the likelihood of employment outside the home, earnings, pressure to stay or leave home, and status in the household.

Source: Census of 1881, MAP database, 100 per cent of the population. Positions inferred.

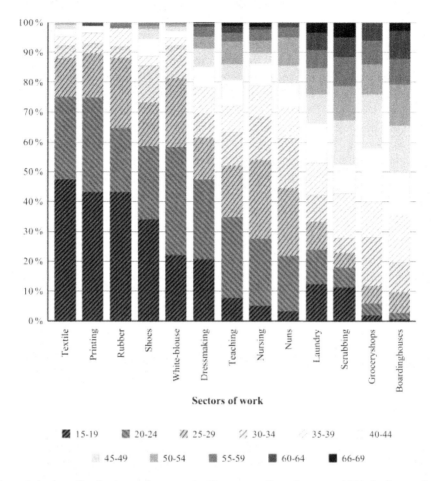

Figure 1.6 Age distributions of women in 12 sectors of employment, 1901. In factory jobs (four columns on the left), three-quarters are under 30 years of age. Their youthful profile contrasts with the four columns on the right. The ages are associated with differences of marital status, job turnover, and home responsibilities.

Source: Census of 1901, MAP sample, 24 per cent.

workplaces exerted a pull on local residential choices, much like the differential attraction of women to cotton mill towns like Lowell, Massachusetts, and of men to the steelworks of Pittsburgh.

By 1860 Montreal women were employed in a great variety of manufactures – nail making, textiles, paper, linseed oil, and manufacture of type. The evidence suggests that the large modernizing firms with a more elaborate division of labour were employing more women and girls; and the largest clumps of female employment we can identify in 1901 are the plants of Canadian Rubber, Macdonald Tobacco, and the cotton mills at Hochelaga and Saint-Henri. Each employed five or six hundred women and four or five hundred men. These clusters figured in the daytime view of the city, in the patterning of the six-days-a-week walk-to-work, and the annual decisions about household moves.[15] Since young women were paid at lower rates than men (of the order of half), concentrations in the vicinity of the cotton mills reflect wage-pressure: their households were composed of more women; more of the households were headed by women; they housed more daughters and more female boarders; and their domestic micro-economies were more fragile, vulnerable to monopoly management and international price-setting.[16]

Between 1881 and 1901 a major trend was a larger female presence in 'waged work' – the jobs best recorded in the census. Use of MAP sources confirmed that the young women of 1901, as compared with young women of 1881, were waiting longer to marry and were spending more years in employment outside the home.[17] Of the younger women in the city (15–29), one third were reported 'at work' and those not yet married accounted for the substantial increase. By postponing marriage by about two years on average, they were 'manning' the industries, and youth, male and female, were now filling half of all the jobs recorded in the census. The relocation and reallocation of the factory labour force was accomplished by adaptation of the life trajectories of women.

Figure 1.6 shows at left the youthful age-distribution of women working in the textile mills in 1901 (cotton, silk, wool), and in printing, rubber, and shoemaking. In these factory jobs, over half were under 25, unmarried, living as daughters or boarders in a family. The factory layout was segregated by gender, and the close work and repetitive gestures, fixed in place and paced by a machine, contrasted dramatically with the work they would subsequently do as housewives – tasks more varied in place, posture, pace, and gesture. At the other end of the scale (the four columns on the right), older women dominated occupations such as laundress, charwoman, grocer, and boardinghouse keeper. Although the census-takers reported only a small share of these, the age-distributions are reliable. Most were married or widowed, and by working in their homes or nearby they were trying to reconcile caring for their children with activities that brought in cash. In the middle range are some curious in-between occupations. The wide range of ages among the nuns (discussed earlier) resulted from lifetime persistence after an initial period of rigorous selection and trial; but we need to bring into sharper focus the dressmakers and the fast-growing ranks of teachers, nurses, and white-blouse occupations who were recruited young, but often withdrew or were fired when they married.

Among dressmakers and milliners, a mix of ages reflects the presence of both factory-based and home-based workers. The census severely underestimates the numbers of seamstresses whose homes were annexes to commercial and manufacturing establishments. In 1887 Hollis Shorey, a large clothing manufacturer,was employing 150 'inside hands' (8am to 6pm at $5 a week) and 450 'outside hands', paid by the piece and doing machine stitching in their homes. On an even larger scale, clothier James O'Brien depended on subcontractors as intermediaries in delivering outwork to families, 'mother and daughters working together'. While a majority of working men were putting in a 60-hour week, the women who were inside hands as milliners and dressmakers worked even longer hours in the fall and spring rush seasons. (In the low season they were subject to unpaid holidays or month-long layoffs.) Female shop clerks worked from 8am till closing time: till 9pm in April, May, and June, on Saturday nights till 1am or 'as long as there is work to do'.[18] Domestic servants, too, 96 per cent of them women, were putting in fourteen-hour days or sixteen hours on call, comparable with the extremes of dock-workers and streetcar motormen.

Despite the imposition of machines and routines for 'dumbing down' work and de-skilling factory shoemakers and boxmakers, there were important counter-trends towards 'sharpening up' skills, ensuring a labour force more literate, more numerate, more disciplined, more mobile, and more versatile. In 1840, fewer than one quarter of Montrealers were able to sign their names as they entered the work force. By 1860 the rate for boys reached 75 per cent, outrunning both urban girls and rural boys. By 1880 both gaps had closed, and the 1901 census reports 90 to 95 per cent of the entire population over age 10 as able to read and write. The literacy revolution essential to the new industrial mode of production was achieved largely by the efforts of rotations of young women teachers, ill-paid and over-qualified.[19]

In addition to the larger female presence in 'waged work' before marriage, the substantial numbers engaged in mass attainment of literacy, and the social services of institutions directed by women, we need to take note of the smaller numbers of stubborn and talented women who between 1881 and 1901 initiated critical 'modern' occupations, the majority of them at the cost of lifelong celibacy. The census of 1901 identifies a hundred trained nurses, a half-dozen graduate physicians, half a dozen female journalists, several photographers, a stammering specialist, the two industrial inspectresses employed by the province, a university lecturer, several librarians and proofreaders.[20]

To interpret the 'housework' of women identifed only as wife or mother, we need to stretch our present-day experience and intuitions. By 1900 the indoor toilet had replaced the outdoor privy, the supply of cold running water was reasonably reliable, and most dwellings had an electric lightbulb in one room. In addition to the hard-to-schedule demands of child care with its 24-hour availability, the housekeeper had to meet the challenge of a rigorous climate by maintaining fires round the clock, moving firewood, coal, and snow, chopping kindling and ice, and mopping out the 'street dirt' – grit, cinders, ashes, and horse manure – continually brought into the house.

The work of reproduction – biological and social – is better acknowledged today, but in the nineteenth century the longer span of birthing and mothering (from menarche to menopause) imposed metabolic demands comparable to the male labourer. High mortality (30 per cent of the babies within twelve months) imposed, in addition to the loss of the investment in gestation and infant care, stresses of grief, guilt, and depression; and a next pregnancy was not a matter of choice. Most of the work of nursing the sick was home-based, handled entirely by women. Spring and fall epidemics of measles, scarlet fever, or diphtheria meant several children sick at once, weeks lost from school or work, and the risk of complications that might lead to permanent deafness or blindness. The sick had little relief or comfort other than the mustard plaster, the cold compress, the dose of alcohol, or the soothing hand and the rockingchair. Women were themselves subject to high rates of tuberculosis and to work injuries, strains, and chronic disabilities.

In response to absence of a 'breadwinner' husband, or cyclical, seasonal, or weather-related layoffs, wives sought short-term or temporary cash opportunities.[21] The intermittency and switching of work modes is at the root of the fundamental mis-conception of work as recorded by census-takers, assessors, and directory agents: they ignored the short-term, unscheduled, unobserved, or concurrent activities, and presumed them 'unskilled' or 'unproductive'. Multi-tasking actually implies a mix of skills for which some men are today well paid: the ability to manage time, evaluate risks, organize a multi-purpose space, handle a changing crew, and restore an interrupted workflow.

In terms of economic growth and capital accumulation attributed to the 'industrial revolution', textbook accounts still fail to recognize the fact that the women and 'unskilled' men and youth were providing the entire margin of flexibility vital to the urban economy as a functional system. Neither the industrial census nor the population census provides straightforward estimates. The expansion of female labour provided the springs for the spectacular acceleration of production between 1880 and 1900, and reallocations of female labour absorbed the impacts of economic recessions (notably 1873–7 and 1893–5), as well as seasonal variations in demand and downtime for rebuilding or retooling. In every branch of the new industrial economy, female shock-absorbers provided the resilience advantageous to employers and investors.

Mix-and-match with multiple sources

To interpret the effects of apparent gaps in work-lives, missing seasons, and unenumerated tasks, we must introduce alternative sources; and in the design of MAP it was the need for addresses to pin the household to the lot that prompted us to turn to the municipal taxroll and the privately published city directory – sources available in many other cities. The matching process was systematic, comprehensive, and laborious; it creates pressure for endless grooming of databases, and the losses (failure to match) are greater for women.[22] All three sources understate the production roles of women, but each, created with a certain objective and bias, provides a new angle from which to view women's work. Our examples are chosen to illustrate some severely neglected activities of women, and to demonstrate the complementarity of taxroll and directory.

A directory entry was a market instrument, and inspection of the 1881 listings shows details unavailable in the census on gender-segmentation of relations of exchange. Catering to female clienteles were 'mumpreneurs' such as corset maker, midwife, 'fashionable milliner', or seller of hair pieces, baby clothes, or fancy goods. The voluminous 1901 directory picks up a thousand women entrepreneurs not recognized as such in the census. Among the female initiatives new since 1881 were schools for teaching job-oriented skills of stenography, type-writing, book keeping, tailoring, dress-cutting, and dress design.[23]

The taxroll reliably recorded women engaged in a taxed or licensed trade such as auctioneer, tavernkeeper, or lessee of a stall in the public markets. Since entries for stallholders are complete in both taxroll and directory, together with home addresses, we can evaluate the journey to work over 60 years. Although some extended families operated over three generations, the trend was to move farther away from the workplace. The women who sold poultry, fish, and vegetables continued, however, to live closer to their workplaces than the men, most of whom were butchers. Linkage of the census, taxroll, directory records, and the leases show that households of the women stallholders were more often mother-led, housed paying boarders, and included teenage daughters who were presumably helping in the market. In other

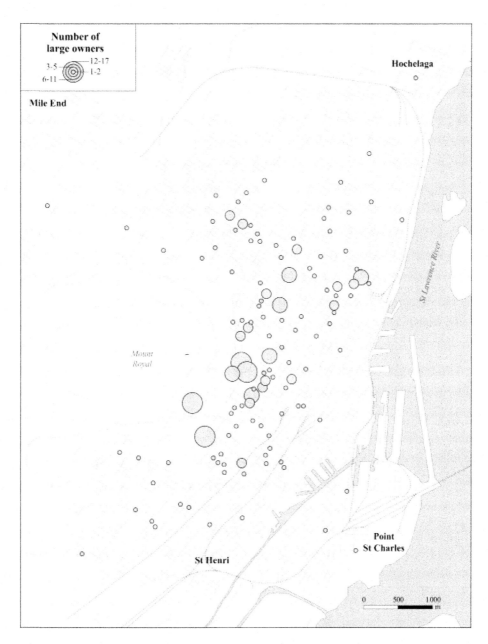

Figure 1.7 Residences of wealth, Montreal, 1903. Represented are the 400 individuals, couples, or personal estates valued at more than $50,000. One quarter were individual women, half of them widows. Not shown are properties beyond the city limits or in the hands of corporations. Most of the corporations were managed by men, but three of the female religious communities ranked among the largest, close to $1 million each.

Sources: Ville de Montréal, Taxroll of June 1903; Census of Canada, 1901.

words, the markets were distinctive social spaces as well as anchors of family networks and relays in the public space.

A still more valuable contribution of the taxroll is to uncover the roles of women as property owners. Possession of real estate is recognized as the key to borrowing power in the nineteenth century, to status and civil participation in governance. Wealth was highly concentrated among a small number with cosy residential proximities among the city's 'one per cent' in 1903 (see Figure 1.7). Using the resources of MAP, Robert Sweeny has demonstrated the large component of female owners (one quarter), geographic clustering of women living on rentier incomes, the emergence between 1825 and 1846 of a market in urban real estate, and a subsequent restriction of women's property rights in order to free up exchange, speculation, and capital accumulation. He proposes a new interpretation of the residential apartheid that emerged in Montreal between 1846 and 1880 as a gendered process of renegotiation of power and status.[24] Property value is theorized as a central feature in urban land use and the urban growth dynamic,[25] and ownership of property is still the cornerstone of municipal finance. It is therefore well-surveyed and registered. At the first step in creation of the vector layers of MAP (when we georegistered the historic maps to modern engineering coordinates), we discovered that the most stable features of the urban environment from 1825 to the present day were the imaginary lines of property. Buildings burned or crumbled, streets were widened, slopes modified, but the lot boundaries and 'back lines' persisted. Despite the importance of real estate in the dynamic of urban growth, and despite its excellent registration, property ownership remains the great secret of the urban economy, understudied in its historical impacts on social mobility, residential segregation, and the segmentation of workplaces.

Alternative sources are especially helpful for exploring the pioneering subset of 'white blouse' workers who in 1901 were still small in numbers but entering into competition with 'white collar' men. Three-quarters of the women were English-speaking, half Protestant and one quarter Irish Catholic, half bilingual, one in five had a sister in the same line of work; most were young, and their earnings were comparable to an illiterate male labourer or laundryman.[26] Mapping the white-blouse occupations reveals an uptown belt of boarding-houses and residences such as the YWCA, and confirms that they were users of the new electric streetcars (1892). Job competition between the sexes was dramatized in races staged between men and women 'type-writers' (promoted by the manufacturers of typewriting machines), petitions and strikes over working hours of telephone operators and access of female stenographers to parliamentary, courtroom, and newspaper services. The city's first telephone directory (1880) listed no women in their own name, but 20 years later included some distinctly female nodes in the expanding communications system, notably widows in high-rent, high-society streets and 74 female-managed institutions, with nominal entries for 99 women in roles as head nurse, sister superioress, or department head in a hotel.[27]

Data-space and social change

Since a GIS is usually defined in terms of its geographic coordinates, we do not always appreciate the range and potential of its social coordinates. The Montreal

MAP tables contain values for each parcel of land, purchasing power of each household, and characteristics of individuals such as their age, sex, language, religion, and marital status. Linked by arbitrary ID numbers and coordinated in data-space, those variables can be recompiled as coordinates of an economic space, a cultural space, a generational space, or a gender space. Central to historical applications, precision of geocoding allows us to drill down through temporal layers to observe changes in any of those social dimensions.

From the data-space structured in MAP, we select a final example – one small story about the scramble to get ahead in the many-dimensioned social space. For centuries, laundering has been the heaviest work consistently reserved for women, and it did not receive an early priority in the industrial mode of production. In Montreal, at the close of the nineteenth century, intense competition emerged among five kinds of suppliers of laundry services. The largest group (a work force of 60,000) was made up of women doing the laundry of their own families; it probably included every married woman in a household without a servant (nine out of ten). Her mechanical assets rarely extended beyond the hand wringer and washboard, wooden tub and boiler; the job occupied at least one full day of her week, and she was washing diapers for about fifteen years of her life.

In the households with a servant – the better-off one in ten – the mother or boardinghouse keeper was likely to hire a laundress by the day or a woman who took washing to her own home. Of several thousands, the hundred who appear as 'laundress' in the directory were situated in a belt of high density, low rents, and mixed ethnicity, sandwiched between the terrace of wealth and the high-rent core. Among them, more centrally located at high-traffic intersections, were half a dozen industrial 'steam laundries', most of them managed by men and staffed by women starchers and ironers, and the first Chinese-managed laundry around which would grow a small 'Chinatown' of groceries and boardinghouses. By 1901 women owned and managed four of the commercial steam laundries, increasingly competitive for handling barbers' towels, sheets for hotels, and linens for Pullman cars.[28] Meanwhile, the large all-female institutions also operated laundries, deploying the labour of the unwed mothers, prisoners, delinquent or 'endangered' girls and orphans they sheltered (recall Figure 1.4). Competing in 1901 were 206 Chinese laundries, constituted as all-male households of three or four persons with minimal capital equipment in small live-and-work premises dispersed along the new network of electric streetcars (see Figure 1.8).

And who were their customers? Since all of us, from birth to death, contribute blood and sweat and shit, I've mapped demand in terms of urban population density. We can add some extra demand from the white-blouse and white-collar workers living in downtown boardinghouses, and from the 'one per cent' who sent out their curtains and tablecloths and their varied costumes for theatre, the dance, the hunt, or the yacht club. At this point we recognize a new strand of racialization that intersected with the gender discrimination. While the Chinese laundries eased the work of some women, they were perceived as invading the economic sphere of others, and threatening the survival of institutions run by women. The steam laundries lobbied vigorously, even viciously, against both institutional and Chinese competitors. When city council set a special tax on the Chinese laundries (about equal to one third of a

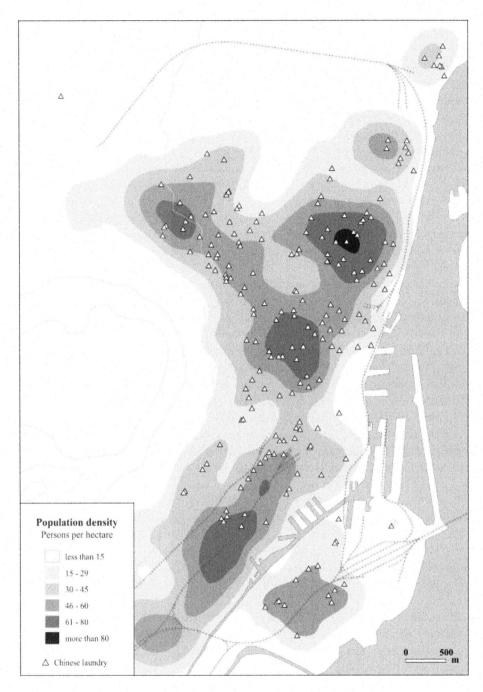

Population density
Persons per hectare

less than 15
15 - 29
30 - 45
46 - 60
61 - 80
more than 80

△ Chinese laundry

0   500
        m

Figure 1.8 Supply and demand for laundry services in Montreal, 1901. Basic demand is suggested by population density per hectare (shaded). White-collar workers such as bank managers and accountants enhanced demand in high-rent areas and boardinghouses close to the centre. The new suppliers were the 206 Chinese laundries.

Sources: Census of 1901, MAP geobases; Chinese laundries confirmed from licensing petition of November 1900, Archives de la Ville de Montréal.

laundryman's yearly earnings), their vocal allies were women's missionary societies, Catholic and Presbyterian, sensitized by their (competing) missions in Guandong, the immigrants' province of origin in China.[29]

Conclusion: The challenge of connections

Peter Gould once remarked that geography is all about connections: 'No connections, no geography.' Certainly cities are all about connections, and Susan Hanson has pointed out that 'Feminist thought fosters seeing connections'.[30] Our recourse to HGIS is an attempt to recognize some of the missing links and rethink our relatedness. As we have just seen in the laundry sector, industrialization rearranged relations between employers and employees, and among competing suppliers of a service. The new relationships stirred public debate over the various dimensions of 'difference' and entailed reassignment of labour among domestic, commercial, and institutional spaces. Each new line of questioning calls for new evidence from the MAP databases, with a reappraisal of the several sources; and each exercise in generating a map, a statistical test, or a model, brings us face to face with social realignment.

As an information system, MAP remains imperfect, unfinished, and full of errors. Access from an appropriate web platform is likely to require funding and entrepreneurship comparable to the investment in its original creation.[31] In retrospect, MAP has, it seems to me, two properties worthy of emulation in the design of any urban HGIS. The first is its high level of resolution, consistent with the household-level precision of census and directory, with the sources available in most cities for geocoding (taxrolls and insurance maps of Goad and Sanborn), and with the urban framework of property.

The second design strength of MAP, more broadly applicable in HGIS ventures, is its versatility as an instrument of exploration. We have seen small examples of exploring a geographic space, exploring a social space, and exploring a data space. Geocoding of the census and integration of local sources into an information system stimulated the framing of new hypotheses. With fifteen years' hindsight, I do not think we could have planned in advance for the full range of applications that emerged. The breadth of research outcomes stems, I suspect, from the messy mix-and-match of people and objectives at the outset. Our tug-of-war promoted a mix-and-match of sources, and Bruce Curtis' argument with respect to census-making in the nineteenth century applies also to HGIS projects of today: 'the logic of design shapes all aspects of reporting'.[32] Creation of so labour-intensive a tool as HGIS demands resources that only a wide collaboration can justify. Other chapters in this volume signal the importance of open-access data, open-source software, interdisciplinarity, and interoperability as ways of sharing resources. To ensure the versatility we have found so rewarding, I would add to those criteria: open-ended design. To ensure a wide-open future of historical research − *l'avenir du passé* − designers must tune their thinking to multiple objectives and leave openings for exploring pathways innumerable and unexpected.

Acknowledgements

Among the many people who have contributed to MAP, this account owes a great deal to Patricia Thornton and Danielle Gauvreau, the Centre interuniversitaire d'Études québécoises (with support of Fonds québécois de recherche sur la société et la culture), the Montreal History Group, and, in particular, Robert C. H. Sweeny, of Memorial University of Newfoundland, for his provocative applications and fastidious work on map links for taxrolls and directories, uninterrupted since 2000. Lisa Dillon contributed an initial database from the Census of 1881; and we have shared in the Census of 1901 samples created in the 1990s under the direction of Eric Sager, Peter Baskerville, Danielle Gauvreau, Peter Gossage, Mary Mackinnon, Chris Minns, and Patricia Thornton, all with support of the Social Science and Humanities Research Council of Canada. Matthew Shields compiled and analysed the stall-holders of the city markets. Émilie Lapierre and Philippe Desaulniers revised maps and figures for publication.

Notes

1 K. Inwood and R. Reid, 'Gender and Occupational Identity in a Canadian Census', *Historical Methods* 32, 2001, 57–70; N.E. Bertaux, 'The Roots of Today's "Women's Jobs" and "Men's Jobs", Using the Index of Dissimilarity to Measure Occupational Segregation by Gender', *Explorations in Economic History* 28, 1991, 433–59.

2 R. Dennis, *Cities in Modernity: Representations and Productions of Metropolitan Space, 1840–1930*, Cambridge: Cambridge University Press, 2008.

3 B. Curtis, 'Expert Knowledge and the Social Imaginary: The Case of the Montreal Check Census', *Histoire sociale/Social History* 28(56), 1996, 313–31; B. Curtis, *The Politics of Population: State Formation, Statistics, and the Census of Canada, 1840–1875,* Toronto: University of Toronto Press, 2001.

4 M.-P. Kwan, 'Re-Envisioning GIS as a Method in Feminist Geograpic Research', *Annals of the Association of American Geographers* 92, 2002, 645–61.

5 J. Adams, *Map of the City and Suburbs of Montreal*, 1825 (1:2400); J. Cane, *Topographic and Pictorial Map of the City of Montreal*, 1846 (1:5100); C. E. Goad, *Atlas of the City of Montreal*, 1881 and 1912; also the Goad 1890 edition; H. W. Hopkins, *Atlas of the City and Island of Montreal*, 1879; and A. R. Pinsoneault, *Atlas of the Island and City of Montreal*, 1906 (1:2400).

6 R. C. H. Sweeny and S. Olson, 'MAP: Montréal l'avenir du passé: Sharing Geodatabases Yesterday, Today and Tomorrow', *Geomatica* 57, 2003, 145–54; S. Olson and P. Thornton, *Peopling the North American City: Montreal 1840–1900*, Montreal: MQUP, 2011; K. Schwartzman et al., 'Geomatics as a Tool for Bridging the Cultures of Research', in N. Chrisman and M. Wachowicz (eds), *The Added Value of Scientific Networking: Perspectives from the GEOIDE Network Members 1998-2012*, Quebec, 2012, pp. 75–100.

7 H. Bras, 'Maids to the City: Migration Patterns of Female Domestic Servants from the Province of Zeeland, the Netherlands (1850–1950)', *History of the Family* 8, 2003, 217–46.

8 S. M. Otterstrom with M. A. Boecke, 'From Wilderness to Megalopolis: A Comparative Analysis of County Level Sex Ratios in the United States from 1790 to 1910 Using a Historical GIS', *Social Science Computer Review* 27, 2009, 297–312.

9 A crude map of the 1901 census divisions was retrieved from Statistics Canada. L. McCann, I. Buck, D. Jordan, and S. Manella, 'Reconstructing the Geographical Framework of the 1901 Census of Canada', *Historical Methods* 33, 2000, 199–205. The MAP team has extended it by matching census addresses from the digital index to taxroll addresses of 1903 and directory cues. Our built-in set of 776 'street segments' which combine opposite block-faces of a street, produces a similar distribution by gender, skewed to higher percentages of women.

10 T. Martin, 'The Mother House of the Grey Nuns: A Building History of the General Hospital', *Journal of the Society for the Study of Architecture in Canada* 24, 1999, 40–9.

11 Louis Rousseau and Céline Payette supplied a database of women who took vows in the diocese of Montreal prior to 1881 (modal age 18 years); see L. Rousseau and F. Remiggi (eds), *Atlas historique des pratiques religieuses: Le sud-ouest du Québec au XIXᵉ siècle,* Ottawa: Presses de l'Université d'Ottawa, 1998.

12 J. Harvey, The Protestant Orphan Asylum and the Montreal Ladies' Benevolent Society: A Case Study in Protestant Child Charity in Montreal, 1822–1900', PhD thesis (history), McGill University, 2003.

13 M. Danylewycz, 'Changing Relationships: Nuns and Feminists in Montreal, 1890–1925', *Histoire Sociale/Social History* 14(28), 1981, 413–34.

14 L. Tilly and J. Scott, *Women, Work and the Family,* New York: Praeger, 1978; P. Hudson and W. R. Lee, *Women's Work and the Family Economy in Historical Perspective,* Manchester: Manchester University Press, 1990; C. Goldin, *Understanding the Gender Gap: An Economic History of American Women,* New York: Oxford University Press, 1990.

15 For 1871 and 1891 only, precision by gender and plant is available from both the industrial census (of employers) and the population census (of householders); see www.canind71. uoguelph.ca/; Elizabeth Bloomfield and G. T. Bloomfield, *Canadian Women in Workshops, Mills, and Factories: The Evidence of the 1871 Census Manuscripts,* University of Guelph, Department of Geography, Research Report no. 11, April 1901; R. D. Lewis, *Manufacturing Montreal, The Making of an Industrial Landscape, 1850 to 1930,* Baltimore, MD: Johns Hopkins University Press, 2000. Employment is reported by gender for large industrial plants 1891 in a local census undertaken by editor of the directory. John Lovell: *Lovell's Historic Report of Census of Montreal, Taken In January 1891,* accessible at http://eco. canadiana.ca/view/oocihm.06065.

16 Barbara J. Austin, 'Life Cycles and Strategy of a Canadian Company: Dominion Textile, 1873–1983', PhD diss., Concordia University, 1985; S. Olson and P. Thornton, *Peopling,* 192–3 and 222–4.

17 S. Olson and P. Thornton, *Peopling,* 198–207.

18 Canada, *Royal Commission on Labor and Capital,* vol. 3, *Quebec Evidence, 1889,* 400.

19 Census of 1901, Canadian Families Project, 5 per cent sample, and MAP databases; earlier data are inferred from the ability to sign the marriage register (S. Olson and P. Thornton, *Peopling,* 85). On gender discrimination in hiring, pay scales, and tax allocation, see M. Danylewycz, 'Sexes et classes sociales dans l'enseignement: Le cas de Montréal à la fin du 19ᵉ siècle', in N. Fahmy-Eid and M. Dumont, *Maîtresses de maison, maîtresses d'école,* Montréal: Boréal Express, 1983, 93–118; M. Danylewycz, *Taking the Veil: An Alternative to Marriage, Motherhood, and Spinsterhood in Quebec, 1840–1920,* Toronto: McClelland & Stewart, 1988; M. Danylewycz and A. Prentice, 'Teachers, Gender, and Bureaucratizing School Systems in Nineteenth Century Montreal and Toronto', *History of Education Quarterly* 24, 1984, 75–100.

20 L. Kay, *The Sweet Sixteen: The Journey that Inspired the Canadian Women's Press Club,* Montreal: MQUP, 2012.

21 B. Bradbury, *Working Families: Age, Gender and Daily Survival in Industrializing Montreal,* Toronto: McClelland & Stewart, 1993; B. Bradbury, *Wife to Widow: Lives, Laws and Politics in Nineteenth-Century Montreal,* Vancouver: University of British Columbia Press, 2011.

22 In 1901 the census-taker designated a household head and for individuals recorded an explicit 'relation to head'; for the nominal census of 1861 or 1881 the relation is inferred; taxroll and directory enter only the name of a head. Consequent ambiguities and match rates are discussed by D. Gauvreau and S. Olson, 'Mobilité sociale dans une ville industrielle nord-américaine: Montréal, 1880–1900', *Annales de démographie historique* 1, 2008, 89–114. On mismatch between nationwide census categories and Montreal dwelling

types, see G. Lauzon, *Pointe-Saint-Charles: L'urbanisation d'un quartier ouvrier de Montréal, 1840–1930*, Montreal: Septentrion, 2015.

23 Of 1901 entries, only 10.5 per cent name women: fewer than 3 per cent spinsters, 7 per cent widows, 0.5 per cent more 'Mrs'. Occupations are listed for 2 per cent of the spinsters, fewer than 1 per cent of the widows and 'Mrs'. On women in business, see M. P. Ryan, *Cradle of the Middle Class: The Family in Oneida County, New York, 1790–1865*, Cambridge: Cambridge University Press, 1981; C. Ekinsmyth, 'Mothers' Business, Work/Life and the Politics of "Mumpreneurship"', *Gender, Place and Culture: A Journal of Feminist Geography* 21, 2013, 1230–48; S. I. Lewis, *Unexceptional Women: Female Proprietors in Mid-Nineteenth-Century Albany, New York, 1830–1885*, Columbus, OH: Ohio State University Press, 2009.

24 R. C. H. Sweeny, *Why Did We Choose to Industrialize? Montreal 1819–1849*, Montreal: MQUP, 2015, 225–310.

25 P. L. Knox, *Urbanization, An Introduction to Urban Geography*, New York: Prentice-Hall, 1985, 175–95; D. R. Denman and S. Prodano, *Land Use, An Introduction to Proprietary Land Use Analysis*, London: George Allen & Unwin, 1972; H. Molotch, 'The City as a Growth Machine: Toward a Political Economy of Place', *American Journal of Sociology* 82, 1976, 309–32; R. Einhorn, *Property Rules: Political Economy in Chicago, 1833–1872*, Chicago: University of Chicago Press, 1991; R. Rodger, *The Transformation of Edinburgh: Land, Property, and Trust in the Nineteenth Century*, Cambridge: Cambridge University Press, 2001; P.-A. Linteau, *The Promoters' City: Building the Industrial Town of Maisonneuve, 1883–1918*, Toronto: James Lorimer, 1985.

26 K. Boyer, 'Place and the Politics of Virtue: Clerical Work, Corporate Anxiety, and Changing Meanings of Public Womanhood in Early Twentieth-Century Montreal', *Gender, Place and Culture* 5, 1998, 261–76; C. Keep, 'Blinded by the Type: Gender and Information Technology at the Turn of the Century', *Nineteenth-Century Contexts* 23, 2001, 149–73.

27 Claire Poitras supplied the Bell Canada Directory for 1880.

28 A. Mohun, *Steam Laundries: Gender, Technology, and Work in the United States and Britain, 1880–1940*, Baltimore, MD: Johns Hopkins University Press, 1999; *Encyclopedia of U.S. Labor and Working-class History*, ed. E. Arnesen, New York: Taylor & Francis, 2007, vol. 1; C. Turbin, *Working Women of Collar City: Gender, Class, and Community in Troy, New York 1864–86*, Urbana, IL: University of Illinois Press, 1992; C. Greenfeld, 'The Identity of Black Women in the Post-Bellum Period, 1865–1885', *Binghamton Journal of History*, Spring 1999.

29 A prolonged dispute over taxing Chinese laundries provides exhaustive confirmation of locations (www2.ville.montreal.qc.ca/archives/500ans/portail_archives_fr/coords.html). Compare P. Dunae, D. Lafreniere, J. Gilliland and J. Lutz, 'Dwelling Places, Social Spaces: Revealing the Environments of Urban Workers in Victoria Using Historical GIS', *Labour/ Le Travail* 72, 2013, 37–73.

30 P. Gould, 'Dynamic Structures of Geographic Space', in S. D. Brunn and T. R. Leinbach (eds), *Collapsing Space and Time: Geographic Aspects of Communication and Information*, London: Harper Collins, 1991, p. 4; S. Hanson, 'Connections', *Gender, Place and Culture* 9, 2002, 301.

31 See https://map.cieq.ca/.

32 B. Curtis, 'Expert Knowledge', 331. See also Sweeny, *Why Did We Choose to Industrialize?*, 273, on research and MAP: 'the process one follows plays a determining role in the results'.

2

GENEALOGICAL GEOGRAPHY AND THE GENERATIONAL MIGRATION OF EUROPEANS TO AMERICA

Samuel M. Otterstrom and Brian E. Bunker

Place, time, and families

Each year thousands of people research their ancestral linkages to reveal their family trees. Those efforts often yield surprising discoveries, expanding the temporal and spatial extent of personal connections with past people and places. Alex Haley's popular novel *Roots*[1] generated tremendous interest in personal history. The vast genealogical resources available on the internet confirm the increasing and enduring following of this open-ended activity. One can never 'finish' building one's family tree.[2]

Genealogy enthusiasts increase the potential of finding commonalities of shared progenitors or identical ancestral origins with others as they discover each new generation of ancestors. Even without a common genealogical link, it becomes apparent to the family historian that past human events are not truly isolated individual experiences. If documented, these events are retained in the memories of descendants, while geographic proximity of ancestors points to shared experiences regardless of family relation.

Genealogical records also illustrate the profound importance of family relationships in fashioning historical migration streams and settlement characteristics.[3] For example, genealogical tracking that follows the diffusion and spread of early northern California family members over multiple generations demonstrates a pattern of proximity for descendants that is likely repeated in many places (Figure 2.1). Impressive growth in the availability of genealogical datasets in digital format has made possible the reconstruction of familial migrations of millions of people. In this chapter, we use a data-intensive method that provides detailed depictions and geographical analyses of the long-term multiple generation migration trends to analyse migration geographies of Europeans to the United States from the 1600s to 1900.

Individuals are tied together in time and space by their biological connections. Migration and marriage patterns are influenced by many factors such as religion,

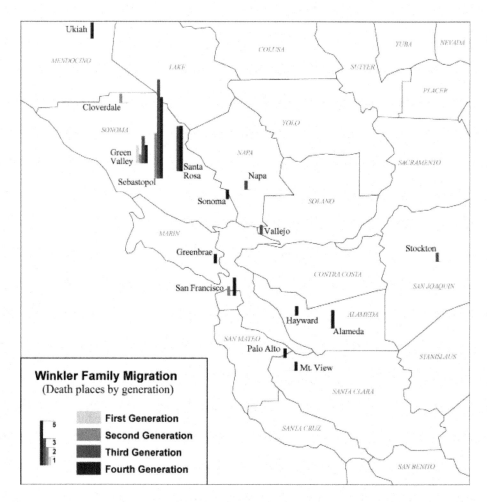

Figure 2.1   Death place of Clayton and Martha Brain Winkler, married 1866 in Green Valley, California, and died there in 1901/1905, along with the death places of their children, grandchildren, and great-grandchildren in Northern California through 2004 (Family genealogical records of Jean Winkler Thomas in the possession of the authors).

gender, ethnicity, historical period, and family proximity.[4] In a specifically genealogical context, people do not make migration and employment decisions in an economically rational manner. This is often because ties to parents, spouses, siblings, and even extended family members, structure, or at the very least influence, their work or career and their location upon the land.[5] Family genealogies are thus firmly entwined within both the temporal and geographical dimensions. In essence, the unveiling of a family history spanning numerous generations reaches out across space and time to reveal the greater historical trends of the world. It also illustrates the friction of distance and our belief that family members tend to cluster together more closely over time compared with the general population.[6] The interconnection of place and people has a most peculiar manifestation in the imprint of families on particular spots over extended periods. Children and grandchildren are also likely to exhibit geographic ties to the homeland of their parents and grandparents. We call this geographic 'stickiness' of families.

In this chapter we highlight a distinct form of migration we term 'generational migration', which when combined with historical GIS helps illustrate large-scale migration trends. Migration analysis over single or multiple generations produces a different set of outcomes than traditional historical migration research because of the distinct time scale involved and the interconnectedness of the migration streams. Specifically, generational migration back in time shows movement of parents to the birthplaces of children so it necessarily involves at least three people, the two parents and child(ren). Thus, the movement measured for each instance is between multiple people over a portion of their lives, and does not illustrate complete life-course migration.[7] Many moves during the period between the birth of a parent and the birth of their child could occur without our method detecting it, while the common occurrence of a person and children being born in the same town would result in a generational migration distance of zero. However, the ability to follow birthplaces through the generations results in a structure that contextualizes other life-course moves in the interim and also displays long-term trends that are completely missed by shorter-term migration studies. Therefore, throughout the chapter 'migration' refers to this generational difference of location from the birthplace of a parent to the birthplace of a child.

Generational migration forward in time has a more varied numerical basis. Each generation size depends on how many children a couple has. The succeeding generations will expand outward from the origin (starting place designated in the search) and the historical geographies of each specifically delimited genealogically tied diaspora can also be analysed.

Descriptive statistics related to generational migration will illuminate an important historical case study. Using the resource of the hundreds of millions of names in the FamilySearch genealogical database allows an extension of analysis beyond the short-term or life-course study scale to one that is tied by kinship and streams over several generations. Any number of other historical migration questions can be answered with the same database extraction and analysis techniques, which is an important contribution of this research.

Genealogy, historical migration, and geography

Geography and genealogy intersect in at least two key ways: first, is the potential of genealogical data to enrich and define geographic research, especially those areas dealing with both small and large-scale historical migration patterns; second is the construction of personal identity that associates one with ethnic origins and family heritage and ancestral homes. The small-scale research focuses on family-centric pedigree connections of a limited number of people, while large-scale approaches collate the mobility data and other characteristics of scores of people with similar geographic paths.

Scholars have long recognized the value and challenges of using genealogical data in analysing historical demographics.[8] As technology and record availability have evolved and expanded rapidly over the last few decades, more opportunities for understanding past people and regions using genealogy are becoming available. Research analysing previous geographies using family history data can be collectively called 'genealogical geography'.[9]

The main interest here in genealogical geography is in what way genealogical data provide means to view past family and community geographies. For example, migration research has revealed the role that factors like kinship or modernization play in whether one decides to migrate.[10] Family genealogies can also illustrate how multiple siblings moved and/or differentially succeeded in relation to each other.[11] Additionally, genealogical records can be used to explain why certain families in pioneer America remained in the settled East while others around them moved to the frontier.[12] Studying basic demographic information such as fertility, marriage status, mortality, and family size and structure is enhanced using published genealogies from certain communities, resulting in detailed local life portraits. These are often overlooked by only using censuses, local church, or government records.[13]

When using genealogical data, geographers and other scholars generally have a broader goal in mind than the professional genealogist who compiles family histories. The academic desires to reveal larger social and environmental processes, while a genealogist is most interested in certain related groups of people with their ancestors and descendants. This contrast suggests that genealogical and family history data are not generally in the format required by scholars, or in sufficiently sizeable collections to be useful. Fortunately, the digital explosion of genealogical data and advances in map use and GIS have made it possible to overcome the traditional limitations of family history data so that genealogies can become powerful resources for those interested in evaluating complicated past geographies.[14]

Technological advances have facilitated the compiling of census enumerated populations. One can potentially gather origins of individuals and many of their parents for whole counties and states in the US from 1850 to 1930. However, locating the same persons in succeeding censuses to see how they moved over time is tedious and requires a considerable investment of resources.[15] Additionally, summaries of these US censuses only show the state or country of birth of each individual and their parents, as the specific city or county of birth is not available in these records.

Using genealogical records that link multiple generations has a different research potential and appeal than using census or other less relationally connected data. They uncover dispersion and convergence of family relations over many generations, which is simply not feasible using other datasets (as illustrated in Figure 2.1). Disadvantages of this type of data include relatively small family compilations and difficulty choosing the geographic area of study. Since one is limited in place and scope using family genealogies, questions must be proffered that pertain to the contents of that particular genealogical database. A notable exception is the research done by Pooley and Turnbull.[16] They sent out thousands of surveys to genealogists in the United Kingdom who replied with detailed migration histories of their ancestors (a sample of some 17,000 ancestors). This data resulted in a book with migration mapping and employment analyses outlining British historical migration over the past two hundred years.

In sum, genealogical geography research can disclose complex generational migration patterns associated with family groups and communities, illustrate past regional ethnic and cultural patterns, and foster redefining or augmenting a person's or community's identity as past relationships and places are revealed. More in-depth geographic research of generational migration patterns requires a distinct paradigm and a searchable database that can explore hundreds of millions of people rather than a few thousand as has been done before. This is the goal of this research.

Methods: generational migration extraction and analysis

To illustrate the research potential of a genealogical geography approach we explain how a large genealogical database can be used to reconstruct the multiple generation origins of migrants to various communities at different time periods. We introduce genealogical migration measures that illustrate generational migration hourglasses. This type of comprehensive analysis has not been feasible until the development of large-scale digital genealogical databases, and the questions we explore and the methods we introduce will add new dimensions to historical migration studies.

FamilySearch

The approach integrates a number of methods to extract straightforward summary measures from the expansive data available in the FamilySearch 'Family Tree' system (http://familysearch.org). The FamilySearch database is a user-contributed, lineage-linked repository of family history information managed by the Church of Jesus Christ of Latter-day Saints.[17] Because authorized users can combine duplicate records, question the veracity of relationships, and add new names that have valid sources, the database is continually improving in quality, which is a step above static published genealogies. All of the searches are performed within this database (we *do not* use other databases in the separate FamilySearch site (www.familysearch.org) such as the historical country censuses).[18]

The FamilySearch database includes over 800 million names, and it will continue to expand as new names are submitted to the system. In the past, the database was populated with ancestors of members of the Church, giving it a historical bias towards the northeast US, Great Britain, Scandinavia, and Germany – the areas from where the largest number of Latter-day Saints originated. Over recent decades, contributions have been added from extracted vital records worldwide from various geographic areas and ethnic groups, greatly increasing the representative nature of the database. Both the geographic and temporal structures of the database vary greatly, so it is important to choose appropriate case studies. Because of the continued high European and North American content in the system, the most robust searches can be made in these areas. It is also best to search for people that were born before about 1900, because the database only includes deceased persons and so it includes far fewer people born in the 1900s than in earlier centuries.[19]

We developed an online query system to use the FamilySearch 'Family Tree' database after being granted access to this database through the application programming interface (API) by FamilySearch. To use the API web service, the city, county, state, and birth or death year are inputted to define a query. The use of the Place API of FamilySearch, which is a separate supporting system of the FamilySearch API, is the important historical GIS component that allows all of the statistic and mapping to work. The Place API has latitude and longitude coordinates for millions of modern and historic places, embedded within their changing geographical jurisdictional levels.

After the Place API helps the user locate the correct place among a list of potential historical locales, the system queries the FamilyTree database and returns a list of 'root' individuals who match the query parameters. This technique makes it possible to sample individuals from a community born during a certain timeframe and then extract their five-generation pedigree information. Each individual with valid birth-place data attached to them is included in the data list with latitudes and longitudes obtained from the Place API. As will be shown, the five-generation query results are then analysed and spatial statistics and indices calculated to display on a webpage template complete with dynamic Google web maps. In this chapter the 'root' generation individuals are those born in the query place and time, the 'first generation' are the parents of the root generation, the 'second generation' are the grandparents of the root, the 'third generation' are the great-grandparents of the root and so forth.

Generational migration themes

Different research threads illustrate genealogically driven analysis' potential. These four themes are *Gathering*, *Genealogical Mixing*, *Diaspora*, and *Community Stability*. To clarify, each location (e.g. city or town) at a certain time functions as the narrow constriction of our conceptual 'Generational Migration Hourglass' (Figure 2.2). Above that narrow opening is the funnel of locations throughout the world from which the people in the constriction were *gathered*, resulting in *genealogical mixing* of ancestral origins. Below is the spreading bottom funnel, which represents the *diaspora* of the succeeding generations. At some places and times, such as during long periods of agricultural *stability* before the industrial revolution, neither the top nor the bottom of the hourglass expand significantly from the point of origin through past or future generations. At these times, migration was mostly local in nature, and it was common that parents and children lived in close proximity.[20] The shaded portion of the hourglass represents the theoretical proportion of the ancestors who lived at the same place as the root generation. This proportion varies by place and time, but usually declines with each generation.

This chapter focuses on *gathering* and *diaspora* with the resulting genealogical mixing at various cities and regions in the United States. Colonization and the industrial revolution in Europe and the subsequent peopling of the Americas, Oceania, and elsewhere significantly changed the migration hourglass.[21] In the United States for example, migration from the Old World and subsequent westward movement across the continent made the top and bottom portions of the Generational Migration Hourglass much more expansive than during the earlier centuries of European feudal rural life.[22] Through succeeding generations, transportation, other technological innovations, and ongoing globalization with its international migration implications have redefined the migration hourglasses of communities worldwide. Within this construct, we illustrate how the various hourglasses of composited migration flows define a set of distinct settlement geographies that underscore the central role of families in the evolution of habitable places.[23]

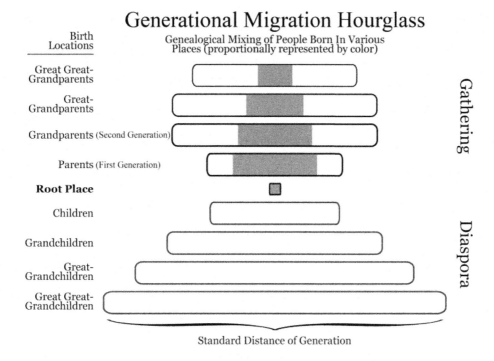

Figure 2.2 Generational migration hourglass depicting various genealogical geography aspects.

Figure 2.3 gives an example of the top part of the migration hourglass for two communities in California, Grass Valley and Oakland, beginning in 1900. The figure illustrates the standard distances (SD) of each generation from the weighted mean centre of that generation of ancestors. Ancestors of those born in Grass Valley in 1900 were more dispersed in each generation in comparison to Oakland, meaning that Grass Valley ancestors were more widely separated and likely more international in nature in comparison to Oakland, which may be explained by the earlier world-wide Gold Rush appeal of that smaller city in the Sierras.

Many different scales of genealogical migration analysis are available. Here, we use the community scale that springs from the personal/family scale. First, we are interested in the variations in the shape of the personal Generational Migration Hourglass, which is a person's genealogical geography. Second, we expand outward toward the composite hourglass that is created from collating large numbers of records from the same local area, which results in a distinctive community genealogical geography.

Each of the four main generational migration themes underscores important migration processes at the aggregate multi-person level. Hourglass genealogical geographies are useful in illustrating the geographic persistence or 'stickiness' related to family migration, and to the unique differences of communities' population stability and migration origin fields. Basic descriptive spatial statistics are necessary to describe the underlying movements of people and to calculate other migration measures. We developed and adapted a number of generational migration measures to help quantify and describe the Generational Migration Hourglass, but we will use just

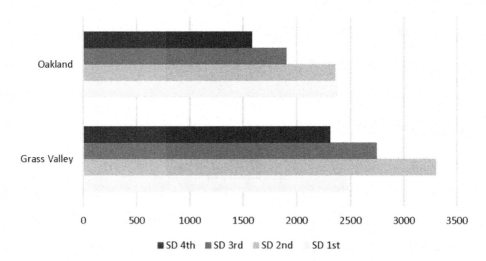

Figure 2.3 Top half of the generational migration hourglass for children born in Grass Valley and Oakland, California in 1900. Each bar represents an earlier generation's standard distance in kilometres (i.e. SD 1 = the standard distance of the parents' birthplaces around the weighted mean centre of children born in 1900 in the respective cities).

simple Genealogical Mixing Ratios (GMR) (proportion of ancestors from various source regions/countries) and Standard Distance of a generation (SD) (the standard distance around the weighted mean centre of birth locations in one generation) in this chapter to illustrate community ethnic origins and heritage.[24]

Ethnic community composition

People may classify their ethnic heritage according to known percentage origins of ancestors or generalized statements of ethnic identity. These descriptions may not always consistent. A more standardized measurement of heritage can be given by using genealogical data. We assume here that national cultural character dissipates over time, even when people identify with some national or ethnic antecedent.[25] This is the time decay factor, which means that more recent birthplaces in the family tree have a greater assumed relative effect on the ethnic identity of an individual or group of people born at about the same time in the same community. Scholars have studied how long cultural assimilation takes. With the Irish in the United States, for example, it took approximately four or five generations to be integrated into American society.[26]

Additionally, settlement stability reinforces local cultural attributes. On the other hand, migrants build new societies or refashion old ones. In other words, greater numbers of in-migrants increase the potential for cultural change in a community. Generational migrants, then, transfer traditions, languages, religion, and other characteristics from their personal and ancestral places of origin to these continually evolving locales. Thus, a concentrated study of migration over multiple generations intertwines cultural geographies of one place and time with those of another through genealogical ties that can be as thin as a single thread or as thick as a heavy rope depending on the size of the generational migration.

To analyse the genealogical identity of a place we compute Genealogical Mixing Ratios (GMR) from the distribution of birthplaces for each generation out of the total group of individuals born at a certain time and place for those who have genealogical links in the database. This measure considers the percentage of ancestors from one or a group of countries as one factor and time decay for how many generations the ancestors resided in the US (taking into account the differences of known versus unknown ancestors) as the second factor.

Calculating and then aggregating the GMR for hundreds born at about the same time in one community yields composite ratios of various regional or national origins that characterize the community at that period. Over time the same percentages can demonstrate how the identity of a community changes and becomes more related to foreign nations rather than the US depending on migration patterns. This is a more far-reaching analysis then what can be done with US Censuses even in the late 1800s and early 1900s because the identity of grandparents and great-parents are brought into the equation. Additionally, this analysis can be used for earlier periods in American history. In this research, we calculate the ancestral background for whole communities of people so we compute percentages of people born in each region (state/country/etc.) within each generation. These calculations are valuable to historians, geographers, and genealogists because they reveal the ethnic character of towns or country subregions in a comprehensive way at many different time periods.

Colonial America: mixed-up pathways

In this research, we use genealogical genealogy's GMR statistics to analyse David Hackett Fischer's *Albion's Seed*[27] work. Fischer makes a strong argument for the Englishness of American culture through an analysis of the historical development of four specific cultural 'pathways' from the British Isles during the colonial period. This genealogical data method helps one delimit the ethnic character of different regions of the nation and confirms how English subregions or other European elements fuse together.

We performed an analysis of Fischer's four main cultural pathways in America to determine whether the origins of these different groups of people are as strongly clustered in his stated respective areas of the British Isles, or if there are other areas that should be classified as origin hearths. Because these migrations to America have already been extensively studied by Fischer and others, it allows us to assess the quality and usefulness of our method compared with traditional archival research of migration origins and destinations. Additionally, it permits us to highlight how next generations back in time either were focused in a relatively small origin area or were more spread out than indicated by the point of departure of the emigrants to America.

We queried the genealogical database at ten-year intervals for numerous communities in the 1600s and 1700s in the four general American regions that corresponded with the British Isles in terms of Fischer's migration origins. The first region comprised the East Anglians emigrating to Massachusetts (1629–40); the second encompassed the south and west Englanders who moved to Virginia (1642–70); the third were those from the north Midlands who gathered in the Delaware Valley

(1675–1715); and the fourth group was from the more varied 'Borderlands' of the British Isles who ended up in the backcountry of the American colonies (1717–75). We included birthplaces of the first four generations back in time from those born in their respective regions in each study year (Figures 2.4 and 2.5).

Our hypothesis is that these American regions did have strong ties to certain cultural areas in the British Isles during the designated periods, but that there was a much broader overall origin geography than Fischer alludes to in his research. Beginning at the first point of time in the cultural pathways analysis and moving back through the generations, we observe some continuity among the various generational origin regions, but there is an understandable significant decline from the first generation to the second of people born in the Americas. Although the 'Unknown' category (unspecified or not placeable location) is large, it is interesting that this category's share of the total does not become much larger by the fourth generation. Typically, this 'Unknown' category includes between 30 and 40 per cent of the sample, which is not surprising due to the spotty genealogical records from this time period. Although cautious in our conclusions, due to the large size of our sample we believe that the 'Unknown' people were likely fairly proportionately distributed within the other origin categories according to those known percentages.

The first stream of migrants to Massachusetts was strongly East Anglian according to Fischer, but also had a significant minority (some 40 per cent) coming from other counties in England.[28] From our 1630 and 1640 samples, East Anglia was the most common specific origin (about 18 per cent shown in Figure 2.6). Even so, East Anglia does not dominate as one might suspect. Southern England was a strong second as the origin of parents and other ancestors (13–14 per cent), which is supported by the fact that southeastern England was the most densely populated area of Britain.[29]

Virginia received many migrants from south and east England in the mid-1600s, with East Anglia being slightly more important by 1665 (4.3 per cent compared with 3.6 per cent). Virginia itself figures prominently in the first generation of birthplaces for all four sample years, meaning that the international migration happened a generation earlier in many cases (26–36 per cent range). Also, with the 1665 and 1675 sample years, by the fourth generation back (great great-grandparents) East Anglia was an even more pronounced origin than Southern England for descendants later migrating to Virginia (about 2–3 per cent higher for East Anglia) (Figure 2.6).

In the third migration stream identified by Fischer as the English Midlands to the Delaware Valley (1675–1715), the results were even more mixed. Besides the Midlands, East Anglia and Southern England were important contributors to the Delaware Valley migration (Figure 2.7).[30] The Midlands did not stand out, except in the 1705 sample, but still it was only 1–3 per cent higher than other England regions. Indeed, the East Anglia and Southern England areas were more important origins for fourth-generation ancestors than the Midlands in all the years excepting 1685, where the Midlands was higher than East Anglia, but not Southern England. What this indicates is internal migration within Britain over the period between generations that might also help explain the lower numbers of people coming from the Midlands in our samples (i.e. they may have been born elsewhere and then departed from the Midlands).

Figure 2.4 Great Britain and Ireland source regions for colonial American migration (as defined by Fischer, *Albion's Seed*).

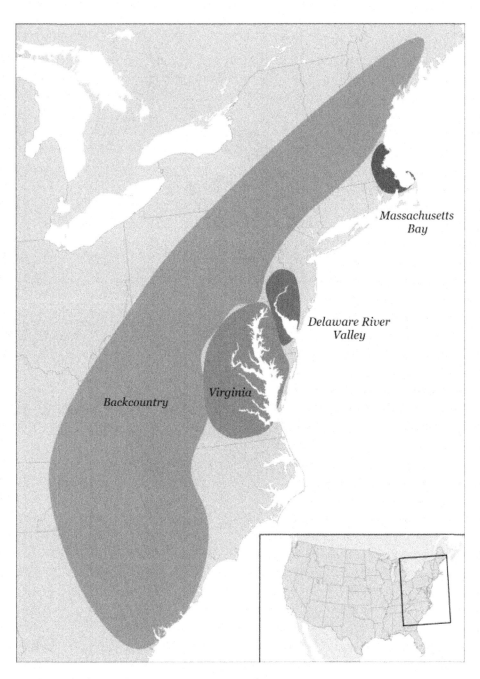

Figure 2.5 Colonial America destinations for British Isles migrants (as defined by Fischer, *Albion's Seed*).

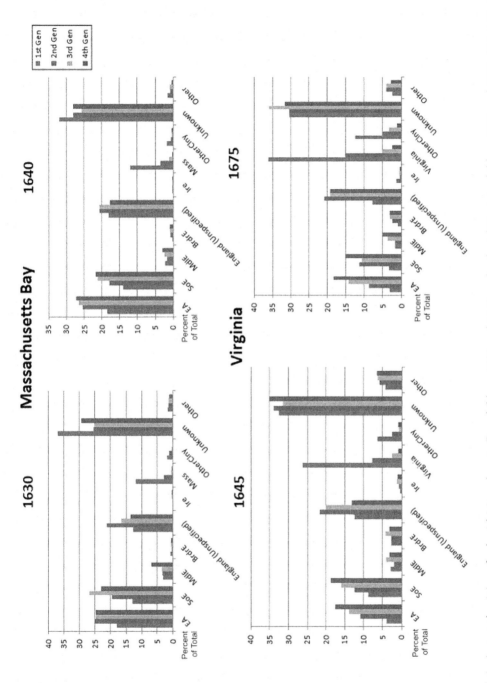

Figure 2.6 Ancestral origins of colonial Massachusetts Bay children, 1630 and 1640, and colonial Virginia children, 1645 and 1675. (EA = East Anglia, SoE =Southern England, MdlE = Middle England, BrdrE = English Borderlands, and Ire = Ireland). Genealogical Mixing Ratios (per cent of total).

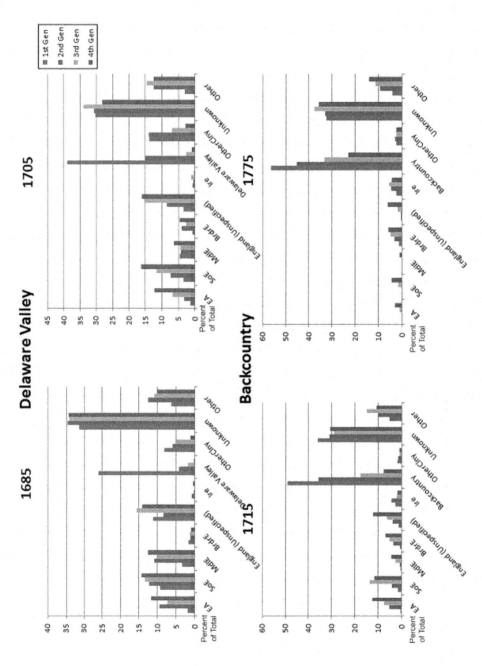

Figure 2.7 Ancestral origins of Delaware River Valley children, 1685 and 1705, and Backcountry colonial America children, 1715 and 1775. Genealogical Mixing Ratios (per cent of total).

To the west of the original settlement areas was the Backcountry. Fischer's origin area of the Borderlands of Great Britain and Northern Ireland (and by our extension, the rest of Ireland) shows some substance, especially from 1735–65, but the numbers are small. However, what is more significant is the fact that large numbers of ancestors of each sample were born in the Backcountry itself, possibly descended from migrants who came first to places like the Virginia Chesapeake or the Delaware Valley a century before and had migrated westward through the generations.[31] For example, over 40 per cent of the 1715–45 parents and over 50 per cent of the 1755–75 parents had been born in the Backcountry, and over 40 per cent of the 1765 and 1775 great-great grandparents originated in the Backcountry. As this migration flow is later in time compared with the earlier major seventeenth-century migrations into North America, it is clear that the Backcountry's population had a greater relative cultural connection and proximity with those of Backcountry heritage themselves, and not with those from the Borderland of Great Britain and Ireland (Figure 2.7).

Fischer's *Albion's Seed* thesis and supporting evidence for the impact of certain British culture areas on the development of specific American regions are quite impressive and can stand on their own. However, our analysis of the four cultural pathways highlighted in his book reveal that the pattern of migration is quite nuanced in its structure, and that probing more generations back in time illuminates the shifting geographic origins of the antecedents of American-bound migrants. Although the cultural impact of these many migrants on parts of North America can be tied to certain prominent European locales, we have revealed that the sources of regional populations in America were more diverse than previously believed. Additionally, it is noteworthy that with our methods we can examine migration trends and cultural diffusion at more refined geographical scales, which can enlighten our understanding of the impacts of the British Isles or other regions on America's culture.

Genealogical geography and historical GIS

Genealogical geography can rewrite the map of historical migration patterns and relationships around the world. The conceptual generational migration hourglass of communities illustrates underlying diasporic and gathering geographies, which show the relative areal pull of diverse cities and towns during different historical periods. In our case study, we presented how historical migration processes are encompassed within the larger scale of our work. We have illustrated how generational migration reveals different migration processes than basic life-course migration studies, as our approach only measures one segment of potential individual movement – birthplace to place of a child's birth. Generational migration thus encompasses a more expansive time scale that is connected by blood over many decades. This allows us to highlight transmission of people and culture over space through intertwined streams of familial relations. The value of our approach, then, is its ability to analyse long-term migration patterns around the world and to describe their character through the means of our varied statistical measures in order to compare, explain, and reveal past diasporas and gatherings.

In this chapter we have only considered a few migration facets of generational genealogical geography. Other applications include obtaining the ethnic composition of cities (GMR statistics) from 1900 backward in time for four generations (in a similar way to our case study, but using a more refined scale of single cities or single counties or state) to show how the ancestry varies by cities. With that analysis we could designate the appropriate ratio cutoff for a community to be considered 'American' (considered here as the percentage of first-generation parents both born in the US) than another nationality because of the parental or grandparental percentages of their origins. However, a set ratio is a tentative marker as it cannot determine the relative cultural influence of certain European hearth regions on a person or region as Fischer argued in his book.

More options abound. We could derive a Birth/Death migration index to measure the stability or 'stickiness' of people at a more immediate individual scale. This index uses the average distance a group of people migrated from their birthplace to their death place during their lives, and can link cities, regions, and/or genders, which index could strengthen an 1800s Irish outmigration study, for example. We may also compare differential migration patterns of men and women to see whether males or females in a generational migration hourglass tended to move the farthest. Additionally, weighted mean centres of a generation's birthplaces can show generational migration streams. Furthermore, at this point FamilySearch's descendancy function is becoming operational, so future analyses will incorporate descendancy linkages, represented by the bottom half of the generational migration hourglass. Thus, there are many possibilities by which we can analyse these past generational migrations.

Crucial to the success of genealogical geography is the historical GIS database system that includes accurate place coordinates, within changing jurisdictions and shifting place names. The FamilySearch Place API forms the foundation to the ability to analyse the varying patterns of migration at different time periods, which allows for descriptive statistics and historical maps that illustrate these important historical patterns. Without this underlying spatial technology, this type of research would be difficult at best. Additionally, historical GIS data structures make searching for ancestors on websites such as Ancestry.com and FamilySearch.org much more successful and efficient as names and dates are matched with places that are spatially associated within the database structure. Thus, genealogical geography pursuits cannot be reasonably robust without using an historical GIS structure.

The focus of the genealogical geography of this chapter has been on migration patterns over several generations. As the tools and data of this historical GIS are improved, other historical demography avenues will be open to analysis. These include examining changing fertility rates within families in multiple generations, examining life expectancies based on family location and generation, and constructing life-course migration flows using integrated birth, death, marriage, and children birthplaces.

In summary, a significant facet of this research avenue is its ability to sort out how family relatedness connects to the migrations of larger clusters of people. None of us is an independently random participant in the world around us. Our migration tendencies and cultural identity are influenced by our parents, siblings, and extended family in a multitude of ways.[32] When we move from one place to another, our culture comes with us, and refines and redefines the place where we go. When multiplied numerous times for thousands of people, it is apparent how past cultural flows are inextricably connected within a strong, but often underappreciated, familial structure. To this end, by using a genealogical database that contains hundreds of millions of names, we have expanded the scope of migration analyses to a consideration of the migration behaviour of multiple generations in contrast to individual movements.

The *Diaspora* corresponding to the bottom half of the generational migration hourglass, the *Gathering* represented by the top half of the hourglass, *Community Stability* illustrated by shared locations of births between adjacent generations of the hourglass, and *Genealogical Mixing* characterized by the fusion of many people from diverse origins, are all available for investigation (Figure 2.2). This reveals a new and dynamic dimension of population geography that sheds many of its longstanding academic limitations. Additionally, an historical GIS that pins down locations of places by latitude and longitude allows for the illustration and analysis of these ideas. Migration is geographically and genetically interconnected, and our retreat into genealogical history helps explain the past march of people and their culture across the landscapes of the world.

Notes

1 A. Haley, *Roots*, New York: Dell, 1977.

2 This chapter is a shortened and revised version of S. M. Otterstrom and B. Bunker, 'Genealogy, Migration, and the Intertwined Geographies of Personal Pasts', *Annals of the Association* 103, 2013, 544–69. Reprinted by permission of The Association of American Geographers (http://www.aag.org).

3 J. Kok, 'The Family Factor in Migration Decisions', in J. Lucassen, L. Lucassen, and P. Manning (eds), *Migration History in World History: Multidisciplinary Approaches*, Leiden: Brill, 2010, 215–50.

4 L. P. Moch, *Moving Europeans: Migration in Western Europe since 1650*, 2nd ed., Bloomington, IN: Indiana University Press, 2003.

5 P. Manning, *Migration in World History*, New York: Routledge, 2005, 120–4.

6 R. E. Bieder, 'Kinship as a Factor in Migration', *Journal of Marriage and the Family* 35, 1973, 429–39.

7 J. W. Adams, A. B. Kasakoff, and J. Kok, 'Migration over the Life Course in XIXth Century Netherlands and the American North: A Comparative Analysis Based on Genealogies and Population Registers', *Annales de Démographie Historique* 2, 2002, 5–27.

8 L. Henry, *Anciennes Familles Genevoises: Étude démographique: XVIe–XXe siècle*, Paris: Presses Universitaires de France, 1956; B. Dyke and W. T. Morrill (eds), *Genealogical Demography*, New York: Academic Press, 1980; J. Dupâquier, E. Hélin, P. Laslett, M. LiviBacci, and S. Sogner, *Marriage and Remarriage in the Past*, London: Academic Press, 1981; W. J. Dennis and K. A. Lynch (eds), 'Genealogies and Population Registers', *Sources and Methods of Historical Demography*, New York: Academic Press, 1982, 109–31; A. B. Kasakoff and J. W. Adams, 'The Effect of Migration on Ages at Vital Events: A Critique of Family Reconstitution in Historical Demography', *European Journal of Population* 11, 1995, 199–242; E. A. Wrigley, R. S. Davis, J. E. Oeppen, and R. S. Schofield, *English Population History from Family Reconstitution 1580–1837*, Cambridge: Cambridge University Press, 1997; Z. Zhao, 'Chinese Genealogies as a Source for Demographic Research: A Further

Assessment of their Reliability and Biases', *Population Studies* 55, 2001, 181–93; L. R. Planta and P. A. Rosental, 'Methods of Historical Demography', in G. Caselli, J. Vallin, and G. Wunsch (eds), *Demography Analysis and Synthesis: A Treatise in Population Studies* 4, Boston: Academic Press, 2006, 597–618.

9 S. M. Otterstrom, 'Genealogy and Family History', in R. Kitchin and N. Thrift (eds), *International Encyclopedia of Human Geography* 4, Oxford, UK: Elsevier, 2009, 4–40; see also D. Gillmor and A. Barry, 'Family Histories and Geographies: Interrelationships between Genealogy and Geography', *Geographical Viewpoint* 40, Ireland, 2012, 15–23.

10 A. G. Macpherson, 'Migration Fields in a Traditional Highland Community, 1350–1850', *Journal of Historical Geography* 10, 1984, 1–14. M. Umezaki and R. Ohtsuka, 'Changing Migration Patterns of the Huli in the Papua New Guinea Highlands: A Genealogical Demoraphic Analysis', *Mountain Research and Development* 22, 2002, 25–62.

11 Schurer, *Migrants*. J. W. Adams and A. B. Kasakoff, 'The Farm Family Economy in the American North, 1775–1875: An Exploration of Sibling Differences', *Continuity and Change* 7, 1992, 357–68.

12 J. W. Adams and A. B. Kasakoff, 'Wealth and Migration in Massachusetts and Maine: 1771–1798', *Journal of Economic History* 45, 1985, 363–8.

13 B. Dyke and W. T. Morril, *Genealogical Demography*. E. A. Wrigley, R. S. Davis, J. E. Oeppen, and R. S. Schofield, *Population History*. A. B. Kasakoff and J. W. Adams, 'The Effect of Migration, Place, and Occupation on Adult Mortality in the American North, 1740–1880', *Historical Methods* 33, 2000, 15–30.

14 M. Kashuba, ed. D. Timothy and J. Guelke, 'The Unfolding Tale of Using APS in Genealogical Research', *Geography and Genealogy: Locating Personal Pasts*, Burlington, VT: Ashgate, 2008, 124–35. M. B. Ruvane and G. R. Dobbs, 'Genealogy, Historical Geography, and GIS: Parcel Mapping, Information Synergies, and Collaborative Opportunities', in D. Timothy and J. Guelke (eds), *Geography and Genealogy: Locating Personal Pasts*, Burlington, VT: Ashgate, 2008, 43–62. M. Shular, 'Turning Genealogists onto GIS', *Journal of Map and Geography Libraries* 5, 2009, 55–71. L. He, M. Chen, G. Lu, H. Lin, L. Liu, and J. Xu, 'An Approach to Transform Chinese Historical Books into Scenario-Based Historical Maps', *The Cartographic Journal* 50, 2013, 49–65.

15 D. P. Davenport, *Population Persistence and Migration in Rural New York 1855–1860*, New York: Garland Publishing, Inc., 1989. J. P. Ferrie, 'Up and Out or Down and Out? Immigrant Mobility in the Antebellum United States', *Journal of Interdisciplinary History* 26, 1995, 33–55. J. P. Ferrie, 'A New Sample of Males Linked from the Public Use Micro-data Sample of the 1850 U.S. Federal Census of Population to the 1860 U.S. Federal Census Manuscript Schedules', *Historical Methods* 29, 1996, 141–56. I. Rosenwaike, M. E. Hill, S. H. Preston, and I. T. Elo, 'Linking Death Certificates to Early Census Records', *Historical Methods* 31, 1998, 65–74.

16 C. G. Pooley and J. Turnbull, *Migration and Mobility since the Eighteenth Century*, London: Routledge, University College London, 1998.

17 S. M. Otterstrom, 'Genealogy of Religious Ritual: The Doctrine and Practice of Family History in the Church of Jesus Christ of Latter-day Saints', in D. Timothy and J. Guelke (eds), *Geography and Genealogy: Locating Personal Pasts*, Burlington, VT: Ashgate, 2008, 137–51.

18 R. Crume, 'Star Search', *Family Tree Magazine* 12, 2011, 42–7.

19 In 2011 the system contained over 155 million names from North America, 219 million from the British Isles, 81 million from Germany, 19 million from Sweden, 15 million from Norway, and 98 million from Mexico. On the other hand, there were less than 2 million from Africa, and less than 4 million originating in China. Also, there was an estimated 15 per cent duplication in the genealogical records (thus, we give numbers of 'names'

rather than people in the database). About 89 per cent of the people with life event dates were born before 1875, with an additional 8.4 per cent born between 1875 and 1900, leaving 2.7 per cent with birthdates after 1900. These total numbers of names by region were sent to the author via email from Gordon Clarke of FamilySearch on 26 June 2011.

20 E. G. Ravenstein, *The Laws of Migration*, New York: Arno Press Inc., 1885, 1889, 182–3.

21 D. Hoerder, *Cultures in Contact: World Migrations in the Second Millennium* Durham, NC: Duke University Press, 2002.

22 D. Hoerder and L. P. Moch, *European Migrants: Global and Local Perspectives*, Boston, MA: Northeastern University Press, 1996; Moch, *Moving Europeans*; R. King, (ed.), *Atlas of Human Migration*, Buffalo, NY: Firefly Books, 2007.

23 K. Schurer, 'The Role of the Family in the Process of Migration', in Colin G. Pooley and Ian D. White (eds), *Migrants, Emigrants, and Immigrants: A Social History of Migration*, New York: Routledge, 1991, 106–42.

24 S. M. Otterstrom and B. Bunker, *Intertwined Geographies*.

25 J. Lucassen and L. Lucassen, 'Migration, Migration History, History: Old Paradigms and New Perspectives', in J. Lucassen and L. Lucassen (eds), *Migration, Migration History, History: Old Paradigms and New Perspectives*, Bern: P. Lang, 1999, 9–38. C. Nash, 'Genealogical Identities', *Environment and Planning D: Society and Space* 20, 2002, 2–52.

26 R. Byron, *Irish America*, Oxford: Clarendon Press, 1999. P. L. Kilbride and N. J. Farley, 'Irish Diaspora', in Melvin Ember, C. R. Ember, and I. A. Skoggard (eds), *Encyclopedia of Diasporas: Immigrant and Refugee Cultures Around the World*, New York: Springer, 2005, 124–35.

27 D. H. Fischer, *Albion's Seed: Four British Folkways in America*, New York: Oxford University Press, 1989.

28 D. H. Fischer, *Albion's Seed*, 34.

29 P. K. O'Brien (ed.), *Atlas of World History*, New York: Oxford University Press, 2003.

30 J. Florin, *The Advance of Frontier Settlement in Pennsylvania, 1638–1850: A Geographic Interpretation*, Papers in Geography #14, University Park, PA: Department of Geography, Pennsylvania State University, 1977.

31 R. D. Mitchell, 'The Shenandoah Valley Frontier', *Annals of the Association of American Geographers* 62, 1972, 461–86. W.S. Robinson, *The Southern Colonial Frontier, 1607–1763*, Albuquerque, NM: University of New Mexico Press, 1979. D. H. Fischer, *British Folkways*. 227. D. H. Fischer and J. C. Kelly, *Bound Away: Virginia and the Westward Movement*, Charlottesville, VA: University Press of Virginia, 2000.

32 J. Kok, 'The Family Factor in Migration Decisions'.

3

RAILROADS AND POPULATION DISTRIBUTION

HGIS data and indicators for spatial analysis

Eduard J. Alvarez-Palau and Jordi Martí-Henneberg

Introduction

This work looks at the impact that the railroad network has had on the distribution of population and urbanization. It fits into what constitutes quite a wide space for reflection about how transport infrastructure has shaped territorial change throughout history.[1] The analysis of the railroad network is particularly relevant in this respect given its rapid expansion throughout Europe from the mid-nineteenth century onwards. The transport network established was completely different from any previous (road, navigable waterways and ports) infrastructure and its efficiency for transporting passengers and goods over long distances left it without any direct competition. In fact, this remained the case until the appearance of the automobile, whose hegemony was not definitively established until the 1950s. There was therefore a significant period (1840–1940) during which the railroad served as the main means of transport wherever it had been introduced.

It is generally accepted that the railroad is essential for understanding the current geography of population and production. Indeed, a number of classical contributions have convincingly shown this interrelationship. In general, academic works coincide in the belief that the provision of rail services facilitated commerce, helped to specialize production, and promoted phenomena such as the integration of markets, movement of people, urbanization and tourism, all of which are elements that have been important in the configuration of our modern society.[2]

Along these lines, we explain what GIS can add to traditional approaches to the analysis of transport networks. In this chapter, we show that new georeferenced databases can help consolidate the geographical scope of historical studies of transport networks, due to their capacity to integrate data relating to various themes, and provide relevant analyses. This territorial dimension can be used to complement the temporal dimension as the datasets used often cover the last 150 years. In this way, it is possible to propose new perspectives from which to study history and to develop a field that is central to the digital humanities.

In this chapter, we present the indicators that we have developed to analyse both the network itself and its interrelationship with population. In this way, we seek to open new lines of work that complement, but do not seek to replace, traditional approaches to these subjects. It is still, however, necessary to carry out archive work, undertake local monographic studies and make global reflections. Only in this way will it be possible to study interaction between the different dimensions of the global railroad network and other disciplines such as architecture, literature, engineering, and art. Within this context, it will be possible to give meaning to the quantitative results provided by Historical-GIS (HGIS).

The aim of our research is to improve our understanding of the relationship between railroads and the distribution of population in Europe. We have done this by analysing case studies referring to specific geographical areas and periods and by using a number of different methodologies. To achieve this, it has been necessary to enter the field of HGIS and to incorporate new databases that permit quantitative and comparative studies conducted at different scales. This has made it possible to show the complex and diverse interrelationship between increases in population and access to rail services.

The following section includes the state of the art and the most important results obtained from other studies. This is the starting point for obtaining a better understanding of what the use of HGIS databases can contribute to the analysis of phenomena that have a long tradition in the study of the humanities and social sciences.

State of the art

We discuss two different questions in this section. First, we examine databases that provide information about railroads and population in Europe from a national and historical perspective. Secondly, we refer to the most significant work that has been undertaken in order to try to quantify the impact of the railroad network on population and urbanization. Both approaches focus on the use of HGIS for spatial analysis; the bibliography cited is therefore relatively recent. Before evaluating the potential contribution of this new approach, we should perhaps first consider some of the earlier contributions to this line of research. The work of Paul Bairoch is particularly relevant as it considers improvements in supplies to major cities using the railroad as a main factor explaining their growth since the nineteenth century.[3] Although economic historians have tried to measure the impact of the railroad in terms of the social savings that it offered the societies into which it was introduced, they have often come to different conclusions about its relevance. It has only been since the emergence of the new economic geography (initiated by Krugman[4] in 1991) that the influence of transport has assumed a clearer role within the field of econometrics. In this field, the growth and distribution of population (the market) and the capacity to access transport are seen as two key explanatory factors.

It should be underlined that many countries have recently made important investments in the creation of HGIS databases at the national scale that are of great relevance. From a demographic perspective, these databases tend to contain information derived from national censuses referring to the nineteenth and twentieth centuries. It is, however, preferable to georeference these data with respect to the administrative boundaries corresponding to each historical period as these have undergone numerous changes over the past two centuries. It should be underlined that this is quite a difficult task and one that, to date, has only really been accomplished at a detailed scale for England and Wales. For the moment, the resulting datasets only tend to show the reality during each specific historical period. However, undertaking long-term comparative studies is much more challenging.[5] For this reason, significant effort has been dedicated to designing approaches that allow the use of existing data as part of a prior approach for exploring long-term change.

In this article, we have resisted the temptation to make a detailed analysis of the monographic studies of railroads that have been carried out to date, as this has already been done in several earlier publications.[6] These publications provide explanations of such aspects as: the initial cartographic databases; how the different elements and their attributes were georeferenced; the digital layers contained in the homogenized information; and the descriptive analyses of the main results obtained relating to the evolution of the railroad network from 1830 until 2015. Other networks, such as that of navigable waterways, have already been identified and georeferenced for specific periods.[7] In the future, it would be relevant to add further information relating to main roads, ports, and airports in order to maximize the explanatory potential of these models.

In the academic arena, the influence of railroads on modern society and economic development has mainly been studied by economists, geographers, and historians and from a predominantly national and regional perspective.[8] In these studies, discussion has mainly centred on determining whether the influence of railroads on territory has been more or less beneficial and on finding new models for obtaining variables that would make it possible to quantify these interrelationships.[9]

In contrast, the influence of railroads on the geography of population has remained relatively forgotten. Although several interesting initiatives have already been undertaken, more analytical studies will be required if we are to obtain significant results. Georeferenced GIS databases and modelling instruments are now available and it will soon be possible to exploit the potential that they offer.

Studies like these require us to combine two different GIS elements: the railroad network and the distribution of population at the municipal level. As we shall see, the results obtained clearly show the impact that railroads had during the period immediately prior to the large-scale development of private, motorized forms of transport. In territorial terms, the results obtained also reveal the positive influence that railroads had on areas that were well-served by the rail network in comparison with those with deficient levels of accessibility.

The acquisition of new databases has facilitated the appearance of many new lines of research and presented different approximations and results. To date, the majority of such studies have focused on European countries: Finland,[10] Sweden,[11] France,[12] Wales,[13] and the UK.[14]

In Spain, comparable population databases exist for the municipal level and allow very accurate HGIS and econometric analyses. Franch et al. used these data to compare and contrast accumulated population growth during the period 1900–2001 within areas served by rail transport.[15] The results obtained show that urban areas directly influenced by railroads either grew more, or declined less, than others and that rural areas suffered important losses of population. Barquín et al. also studied the influence of railroads on population during the period 1860–1910, taking into account a number of other variables that included industry, mining, and distance from the coast.[16] They concluded that areas of Spain with rail connections grew by up to 60 per cent more than those without.

More recently, new work has begun which focuses on Europe as a whole. Caruana and Martí-Henneberg carried out an econometric analysis related to the density of the railroad network at the regional level, substituting GDP for population as an indicator of development.[17] This study also demonstrated a positive correlation between the variables analysed.

Along the same lines, but this time outside Europe, this approach has contributed to methodological discussions that have made it possible to explore existing knowledge in greater depth. Works referring to the USA[18] and South America[19] have compared the availability of rail services to the growth of GDP, following the approach established by the economist G. Solow. They again highlight how railroads made a positive contribution to sustained growth in GDP.

Historical databases on railroads and population

The next section presents the most innovative aspects of compiling historical databases. This is a key consideration because the research currently underway and its potential depend on their scope and precision.

The data described refer to the European railroad network and to population trends in different European countries. All of this information was compiled within the framework of a wider HGISe project. It includes a compendium of different research projects that have been carried out in recent years in collaboration with various European universities.[20]

Railroad data at the European scale

Of the different types of transport infrastructure available, that relating to railroads is probably the easiest to document as it is relatively easy to identify the routes that trains follow and have followed in the past. The fact that stations act as nodes of connection with settlements means that it is possible to locate the exact points at which passengers and goods enter and leave the railroad system. Furthermore, the need for powerful locomotives to move carriages and wagons means that the railroad can only operate as a collective form of transport. We can therefore identify two types of infrastructure that characterize the railroad from the perspective of it offering a transport service: the routes followed by the tracks and the locations of the stations.

The quality of railroad databases will depend on their capacity to include both of these variables. The more precise the data we possess, the more powerful will be the calculation models that we work with and the more reliable the indicators that constitute the study variables.

A first approximation to railroad databases at the European scale can be found within the framework of the HGISe project. This presents an exhaustive compilation of all the wide gauge railroads that have been operational in Europe from the 1830s through to the present day (Figure 3.1). Each line has been digitalized and georeferenced in order to facilitate its visualization and also to obtain certain key attributes via simple spatial calculations. A number of other attributes have also been incorporated, including the number of years that each line has been operative, the type of transport provided (for passengers, freight, or a mixture of the two), and other variables, such as the gauge of the track. This has facilitated the subsequent task of making spatial calculations.

(a)

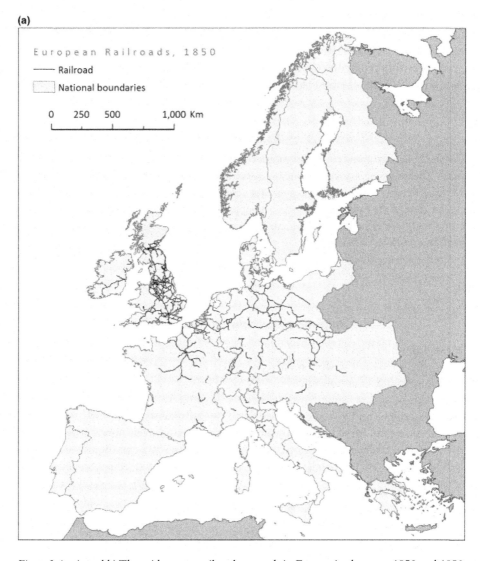

Figure 3.1   (a and b) The wide gauge railroad network in Europe in the years 1850 and 1950.

(b)

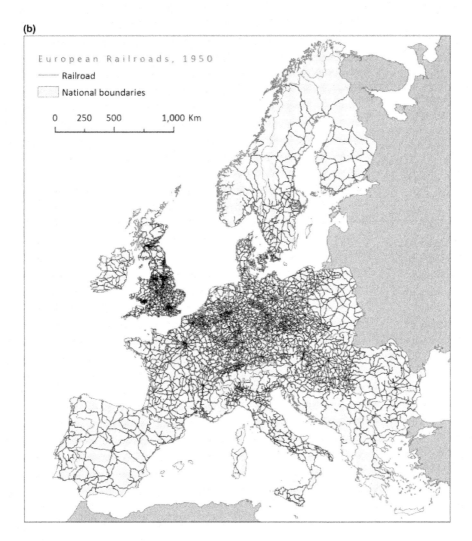

Figure 3.1 (Continued).

Source: Morillas (2014), based on HGISe data (University of Lleida).

The population variable from a historico-spatial perspective

Population is the second main subject studied here and considerable time and effort have been invested in obtaining new, updated datasets. Total population and population density are the only two variables that are perfectly comparable over time, with basic population data being available from official censuses. The majority of European countries began to collect population data at ten-year intervals in the middle of the nineteenth century. Although these databases have often been based on different systems of collection and classification, they have a common denominator: they include information about total population at the municipal level. This concept varies slightly from country to country, but always refers to the smallest local unit. It constitutes a single indicator of human activity as it includes geographically and

Table 3.1 Sources and availability of population data at the municipal level for the countries of Western Europe.

Country	Name of units	Number of units	Period
Austria*	Gemeinde	2,357	1869–2011
Belgium*	Commune / Gemeente	589	1831–2011
Denmark (2)	Byer	1,451	1896–2011
England/ Wales (1)	Civil parish	11,847	1801–1861
England/ Wales**	Civil parish	11,847	1871–2001
Finland*	Kunta	336	1880–2011
France*	Commune	36,570	1801–2011
Germany (3)	Stadt / Gemeinde	11,710	1870–2011
Italy*	Comune	8,100	1920–2011
Luxembourg*	Commune	116	1821–2011
Netherlands(1)	Gemeente	441	1830–2011
Norway*	Kommune	430	1769–2011
Portugal*	Cidades / Freguesias	4,042	1864–2011
Spain*	Municipio	8,114	1877–1911
Sweden*	Stad / Församling	1,646	1810–1911
Switzerland (1)	Commune	2,624	1870–2011
Scotland (2)	Civil parish	870	1841–2011

Source: Own research based on primary sources available via municipal institutes of statistics.

historically comparable data for all of the different states considered. It is therefore possible to transfer this information to an HGIS, using georeference systems, and to assign attributes corresponding to each municipality.

Table 3.1 presents the primary sources for the countries of Western Europe that can be used for this type of analysis. These data have been collected and digitalized within the frameworks of different research projects.

The primary sources used in our HGIS were homogenized decade by decade, based on years ending in '0'. The total number of municipalities has constantly changed over time. Municipal data have been assigned to georeferenced points on maps based on their spatial coordinates. (*) The data presented have been both georeferenced and homogenized. (**) Only georeferenced data or only homogenized data. (1) Data in dataset format. (2) Data only available from original censuses. (3) Data in publishable format, but only for urban areas.

The contents of Table 3.1 will serve as the basis for future work requiring the use of HGIS. Total population figures serve as a comparable reference over time. Significant changes can be interpreted as indicators of economic and social transformations; these can then be examined in detail at a later stage. As can be seen from the section referring to our case studies, it is necessary to have detailed data (at least at the municipal level) in order to obtain relevant results. The problem is that this generally implies a great effort in terms of data collection and exploitation and constitutes an important methodological challenge.

The main indicators used to refer to population are its territorial distribution, whether expressed in absolute terms or as density per unit area, and its percentage increases, which are always contemplated at ten-year intervals. These can then be used to create new variables that can be correlated with railroad indicators of different types. One variable that is intimately related to population and which assumes special relevance in this type of analysis is urbanization. The growth of cities, both in terms of their populations and urban areas, is something that can be shown and measured spatially. This is of particular interest when it comes to providing transport infrastructure to serve a city and its different neighbourhoods.

Based on all of these data and the different possibilities for their analysis, we propose moving on from merely describing the evolution of the geography of population in order to try to determine the factors that explain it. We have sought to do this based mainly on the railroad variable but we have also tried to integrate other indicators at the municipal level that are capable of capturing complementary information. In terms of geographical information, it is possible, for example, to incorporate variables that provide estimates of the altitude and ruggedness of the terrain and of distances from the coast. In terms of political data, we can also incorporate such variables as distances from national borders and/or whether settlements are located near to local or national capitals. Some of these factors have already been used as control variables in previous statistical analysis.

Spatial interactions between railroads and population: case studies

The main objective of this research is to identify population patterns in areas served by railroad networks. This requires the creation of detailed databases and the use of quantitative methods to demonstrate the relationships between the two variables.

In the present study, we identify four major groups of indicators. The first three are based on railroad infrastructure and the fourth on urbanization. First, we detail the classical indicators: length, density, and per capita stock of the railroad network. These can all be calculated quite easily, without the need for GIS, although georeferenced databases greatly facilitate both the calculation and presentation of the results obtained. Secondly, we characterize the indicators of railroad coverage. This dichotomous variable indicates whether a territory is covered by rail services. Thirdly, we describe the indicators of accessibility, which measure the time and/or cost required to travel between each pair of nodes within a given network. These indicators can be presented in an aggregated form, at the state level, or in a disaggregated way, relating to each individual city. However, this is quite complicated to calculate and may require the development of complex spatial models. Finally, there is another group of indicators that can be used in the opposite direction. They consider railroad infrastructure as an invariant and try to quantify urban growth in order to see whether it has been conditioned by either the route taken by a railroad or the presence of a particular station.

Simple indicators: the length, density, and per capita stock of the railroad system

The simplest and most commonly used indicator for determining the availability of railroad infrastructure is the *total length* of the network. This indicator is calculated by summing the total length of track in a given territory. It also makes it possible to observe the evolution of this infrastructure over time. At the European level, the

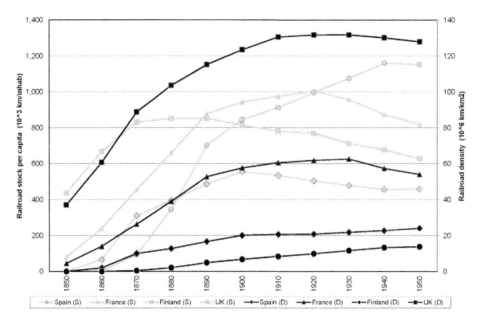

Figure 3.2 Comparative study of railroad density and per capita railroad stock in several European countries: 1850–1950.

previously cited HGISe database has made it possible to calculate this indicator immediately and then to use it as a variable in later analyses.

However, if the aim is to compare results for different territories, it is evident that the length indicator is not sufficient on its own. European regions are very different in terms of their surface areas, populations, and economies and this complicates any form of direct comparison. As a result, there is a tendency to normalize the length of the network with respect to the total surface area of the region being studied (*railroad density*) and its population (*per capita stock*). This could also be done using economic indicators such as GDP (stock in railroad in relation to GDP). Adopting this approach has enabled us to make more precise and focused comparisons.[21]

Figure 3.2 shows the considerable divergence between the two indicators. Railroad density reveals very different provisions of infrastructure between one country and another. The United Kingdom exhibits very high densities in all of the periods studied; this differs notably from what can be observed in all the other countries. France is the next country in terms of performance with respect to this indicator, despite the difference in surface area. Finally, more peripherally located countries, such as Spain and Finland, exhibit relatively low densities. What is interesting here is the fact that, in terms of density, we observe few variations in the rank position of each country over time; this therefore appears to be quite a stable indicator.

The second indicator shows a very different situation. Although the United Kingdom presents high per capita stock during the initial decades of railroad construction, by the end of the twentieth century it has been overtaken by both France and Finland. This could be explained by Britain's strong demographic growth and by a more intense use of its network. We must also consider the physical dimensions of

Finland and its low density of population; this largely explains the major growth observed. Finally, Spain exhibits much lower and more constant levels of growth.

Indicators of railroad coverage

The coverage models seek to offer an index that permits a qualitative and qualitative classification of the distance between a given point within a territory and a particular piece of transport infrastructure. First, we can visualize whether this point is covered by the mode of transport in question. Then we can estimate the corresponding access time and the resulting utility for users. In recent literature, there has been a tendency to calculate coverage by drawing concentric circles around elements of infrastructure, such as railroad stations.[22] The surface area, or population, located within this buffer is then considered to be covered by the network. The sum of all of these surfaces constitutes the total area with coverage within a given country or region and this is contrasted with that without coverage.

A railroad network is generally considered to provide coverage to a territory when it provides it with rail services. This occurs when it satisfies the following mathematical relationship:[23]

$$P_i \in C_{pf} \text{ if } \exists\, E_j \text{ so that it serves } P_i$$

Where:
P_i represents the population of node i.
C_{pf} is a group that includes the total population receiving railroad coverage.
E_j represents station j.

The authors have developed an alternative way to approach this calculation. They did this by testing a coverage model for civil parishes for the whole of England and Wales from 1871 to 1931 (Figures 3.3a and 3.3b). In this case, five different levels of coverage were identified: 1) no railroad station within a two–hour walk from the parish centroid, 2) a nearby station, between one and two hours away, 3) a station less than one hour away, 4) one available station, 5) two or more stations available to the civil parish.

The interesting aspect of this case is the correlation between the indicator of coverage shown here and the variable relating to the increase in population (Table 3.2). In England and Wales, our analysis of parishes that did not experience any changes in coverage during the four decades between 1891 and 1931 shows that those with initially low levels of coverage (1, 2, and 3) tended to lose population (with average values of -0.62, -0.38,and -0.01 per cent, respectively). On the other hand, those with intermediate levels of initial coverage (4) tended to gradually gain population (0.34 per cent), while those initially covered by two or more stations gained population at considerably higher rates (1.07 per cent).

The main problem with this approach is that, to date, very few European countries have HGIS databases providing information about the opening and closing of rail stations. In the case of Spain, for example, there are only registers of the opening and closing of lines, but not of stations. It has therefore been necessary to introduce a number of simplifications when using this indicator. Franch et al. therefore used

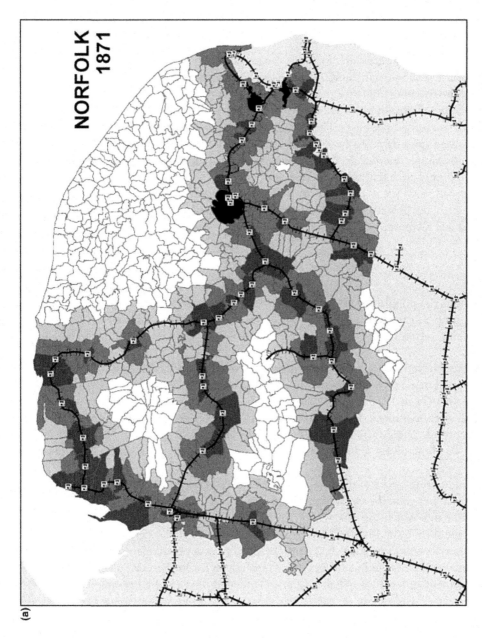

Figure 3.3 (a and b) Spatial distribution of the adapted indicator of railroad coverage for the English county of Norfolk between 1871 and 1931.

Source: Alvarez-Palau et al. (2013).

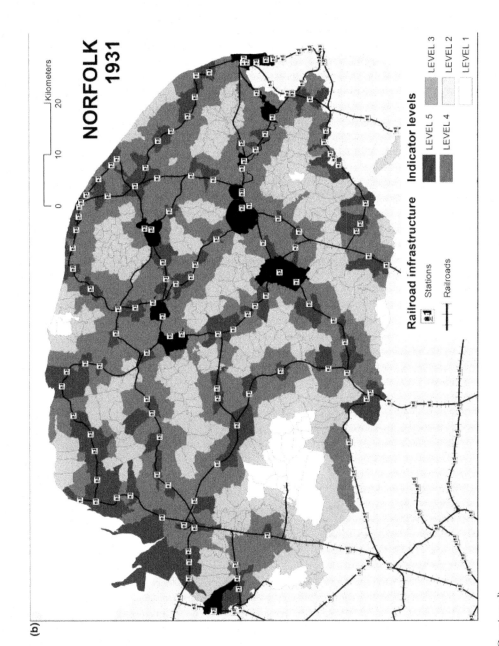

(b)

NORFOLK
1931

Kilometers

0   10   20

Railroad infrastructure   Indicator levels

Stations   LEVEL 5   LEVEL 3
1   LEVEL 4   LEVEL 2
Railroads   LEVEL 1

Figure 3.3   (Continued).

Table 3.2 Evolution of the average cumulative annual growth rate in E&W parishes, according to their respective levels of coverage, 1871–1931.

Year	Level 1	Level 2	Level 3	Level 4	Level 5
1871–81	-0.69%	-0.48%	0.01%	0.52%	1.79%
1881–91	-0.68%	-0.53%	-0.16%	0.44%	1.23%
1891–1901	-0.94%	-0.76%	-0.53%	-0.06%	0.75%
1901–11	-0.25%	0.09%	0.47%	0.74%	1.26%
1911–21	-0.54%	-0.32%	0.00%	0.23%	0.70%
1921–31	-0.64%	-0.26%	0.14%	0.14%	0.66%
AVERAGE	**-0.62%**	**-0.38%**	**-0.01%**	**0.34%**	**1.07%**

Source: Alvarez-Palau et al. (2013).

the physical distance from the railroad as the base from which to estimate coverage.[24] This approach permits an initial approximation when few data are available. However, in this case, it is necessary to carefully define the distance that is considered to denote coverage.

Indicators of railroad accessibility

Models of accessibility seek to generate indicators that incorporate the travel time required for trips undertaken within the railroad network. These are calculated by summing the total time required to make the complete journey. This includes the time required to access the railroad network, any possible waiting time, and the time required to make the journey. The mathematical formulation used to obtain this indicator is presented here:

$$I_{GA_j} = \frac{\sum_{i=1}^{n} C_{ji}}{n-1}$$

Where:

IGA$_j$ is the Index of General Accessibility calculated for node j.

N is the sum of the number of locations included in the study (universe).

C$_{ji}$ is the cost matrix of the cheapest way of travelling from node j to node i.

Where:

$$C_{ji} = t_{origin} + t_{waiting} + t_{travel} + t_{destination}$$

$$t_{travel} = t_{trip\ 1} + t_{transfer\ 1} + \ldots + t_{transfer\ k-1} + t_{trip\ k}$$

The result of the calculation for each pair of nodes is saved in a cost matrix C$_{ji}$ with *n* origins and *n* destinations (*general accessibility*). The average value of each row is represented by a discrete value that determines the average cost, or time, needed to access a particular node from the rest of the territory (*specific accessibility*).

(a)

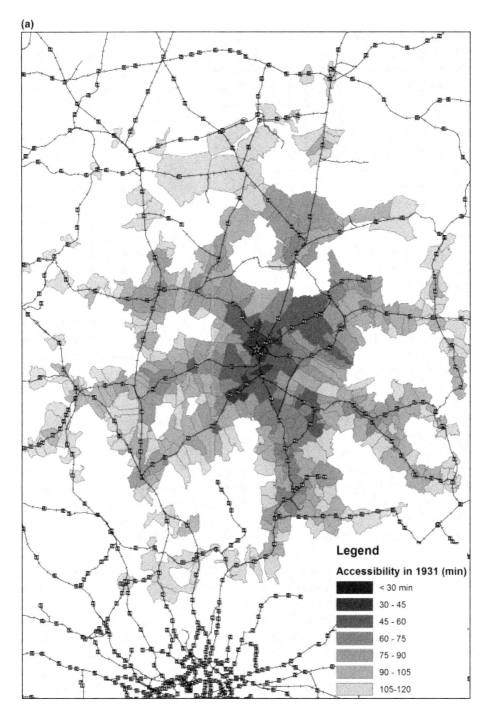

Legend

Accessibility in 1931 (min)

	< 30 min
	30 - 45
	45 - 60
	60 - 75
	75 - 90
	90 - 105
	105-120

Figure 3.4   (a and b) Index of specific accessibility calculated for the urban centre of Cambridge (for trips taking up to two hours) in 1931. On the right, it is possible to see the distribution of population in the same civil parishes.

Source: Own work. See HGIS for railways and Gregory et al. (2011).

(b)

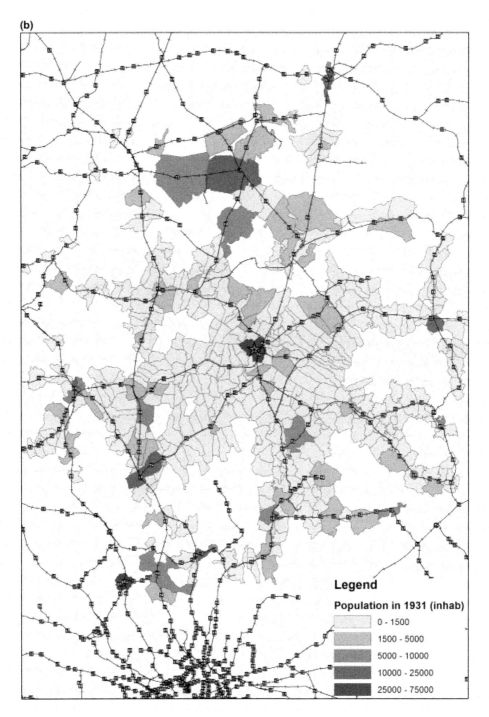

Legend

Population in 1931 (inhab)

	0 - 1500
	1500 - 5000
	5000 - 10000
	10000 - 25000
	25000 - 75000

Figure 3.4   (Continued).

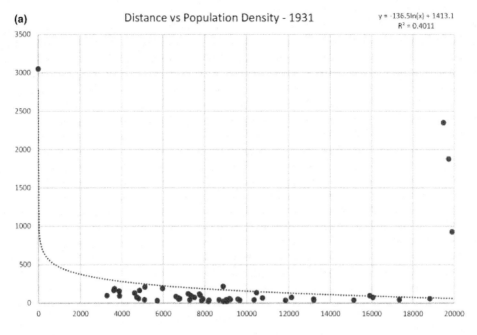

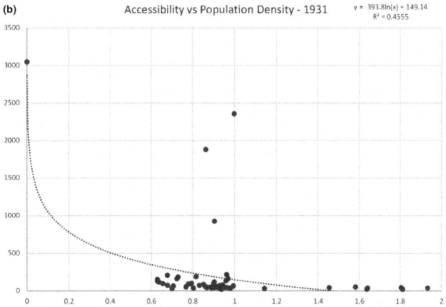

Figure 3.5 (a and b) Correlation between distance from the centre of Cambridge and density of population in 1931. In (b), it is possible to observe the correlation between the index of specific accessibility and the density of population.

Source: Own research.

When we analyse historical data rather than current data, it is not always possible to appropriately calculate all of the terms in the equation and it is therefore necessary to introduce several simplifications. For example, it is not possible to calculate the access time to the station using surveys. Instead, it is necessary to estimate the average journey time from each location. Waiting time is a completely random variable as it depends on each individual and on the number of train services available. In current studies, authors have tended to use half of the frequency time, but when adopting a historical perspective, there is a tendency to remove this item from the equation. Travel time can be estimated with the help of rail timetables, but these are not always available; as a result, average values must also be used. The commercial speed, type of locomotion, and number of tracks per line also vary and are difficult to estimate. It is therefore necessary to propose approximate methods of calculations until current HGIS databases can be improved.

The indicator for the local scale has been adapted in order to capture the spread of accessibility from any specific node to its periphery. Figures 3.4a and 3.4b present a graphic representation of the index of *specific accessibility* of the English city of Cambridge. In this case, it is evident that municipalities with rail coverage exhibit lower travel time values than those lacking coverage.

As expected, it can be clearly observed how the nearest parishes concentrate the highest accessibility values. However, if we observe the grading of the different colours around the railroad infrastructure, there is evidence of induced territorial anisotropy. Parishes with railroad coverage have good levels of accessibility to the central node. In contrast, unconnected locations may be geographically closer, but could be considered to lack coverage and to be spatially marginalized.

What is interesting about this case is the cross between the railroad and spatial population indicators. As a central city, Cambridge exhibits much higher levels of population than the settlements on its periphery, where it is possible to detect a clear decline with distance from the centre. This phenomenon is shown in the first graph in Figure 3.5. However, if we use the accessibility variable instead of the distance from the centre, it is possible to observe how the logarithmic correlation increases the level of significance from 0.401 to 0.456. We also begin to detect examples of territorial polynuclearism as the most important locations become better interconnected.

This correlation makes it possible to study the spatial distribution of population within the territory resulting from the provision of railroad services. The resulting anisotropy of accessibility and population decay can both be clearly observed. However, this situation could be reversed by applying appropriate urban planning and transport policies favouring greater territorial homogeneity. Whatever the case, the contrast between accessibility and population remains a vital instrument for understanding such aspects of day-to-day life as urban mobility, the management of public services, and urbanism itself. Although the railroad does not have the same importance today as it did in the past, the same analysis could be applied to consider other transport infrastructure and the results obtained would probably be quite similar.[25]

Indicators that refer to the urbanization process

The previous section identified the main indicators that can be applied when analysing the railroad network. This one focuses on indicators that can be related to the

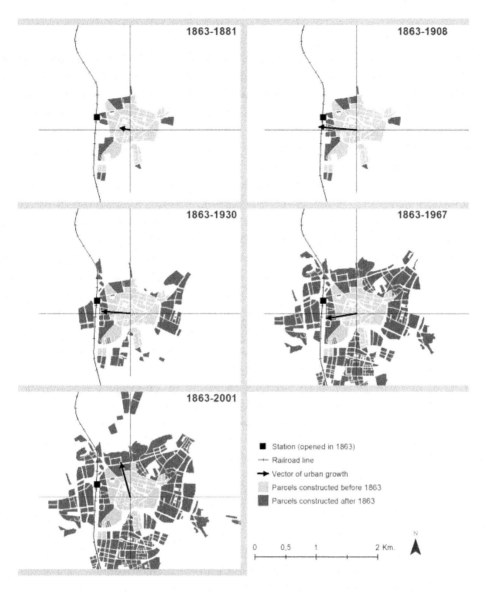

Figure 3.6 Graphic representation of the indicator showing the direction of accumulated urban growth in the city of Vic.

Source: Solanas et al. (2015).

urbanization variable in order to analyse how its evolution has been influenced by railroad infrastructure. In other words, we here use the railroad as an invariant to examine the spatial growth of cities. To do this, it is necessary to work with a powerful HGIS containing information relating to the process of urban expansion. Georeferencing historic urban maps has opened up an important line of new research. It is not difficult to document and measure urban growth if enough comparable maps are available to chart urban development over time.

Focusing on urban reconstruction, the HGIS makes it possible to measure urban growth using spatial vectors. By doing this, it is possible to establish the position of the geographic centre of a city prior to the arrival of the railroad and to calculate how the city has subsequently grown. It can show the location of each new area of a city and its total surface area. This indicator is calculated according to the following formula:

$$\vec{I}_c = \frac{\sum_{i=1}^{n}(\vec{v}_i \cdot S_i)}{\sum_{i=1}^{n} S_i} \quad \text{for i} = 1, 2, ..., n$$

Where:
V_i is the vector between the urban centroid and the area of growth.
S_i is the surface area of each area of growth.

Applying this indicator to the Spanish city of Vic between 1860 and 2001 gives a set of results covering the period prior to the opening of its urban station and for the subsequent period (Figure 3.6).

It can clearly be observed how the accumulated growth of the city is aligned with the vector between the city centre and the station from the creation of the railroad network until the 1930s. In fact, the differences in the angle between the two vectors (accumulated growth and distance from the city to the station) during the first four periods are 10.62, 15.83, 16.80, and 29.5 degrees (over 180 degrees), respectively. From this moment onwards, growth becomes less dependent on the railroad. This can be shown by the emergence of autonomous sectors during the final phase that have more links with the use of the automobile than with other modes of transport. In this last stage, the difference in angle grows by up to 54.10 degrees. This shows the dissociation between urban growth and railroad infrastructure in the city.

In summary, once the railroad had been constructed, it was possible to observe how this infrastructure had a great influence on the city's urban growth. The majority of the cities analysed by Solanas et al. showed clear growth towards their respective stations.[26] As urban land was used up, due to this growth, there was a tendency for the city to expand around the track until the necessary crossings were provided.[27] Finally, when society adopted individual forms of motorized transport, such as the private automobile, the continuous city model was broken and new areas of growth began to appear in the form of isolated polygons of constructed territory.

Synthesis and final reflections

The examples presented here demonstrate the important contribution that HGIS can make to understanding spatial phenomena from a historical perspective. The present contribution focuses on different interrelationships between railroad infrastructure and the distribution of population and demonstrates a strong spatial link between the two variables. To achieve this, we identified a series of indicators that can be applied to railroads in order to obtain explanatory variables and facilitate the understanding of the phenomena studied. Based on these results, accessibility to the railroad highlights the territorial anisotropy created by transport networks and has consequently been revealed as a predictive variable for population concentration. At the same time, railroad coverage could also explain differential growth between locations related to their level of connection. However, this is not all. An analysis of urban growth in relation to infrastructure also shows how the urban fabric of cities has also been influenced by the routes taken by railroads and the locations of rail stations.

Even so, there still remain many improvements to be made. Associating the locations of stations with attributes relating to the years in which they opened (and possibly closed) would be of great interest and would help us to understand the interaction between the railroad network and the territory. Having more information relating to railroad timetables and the frequency of services would also provide us with knowledge of such aspects as the speed at which commercial services circulate (or once circulated) and the carrying capacities of different lines. Adding narrow gauge[28] lines to this study would also represent an important milestone in the development of regional studies, as would the addition of data relating to metropolitan tram and subway train networks. It would similarly be interesting to incorporate information referring to the demand for transport within the network, relating to both passengers and freight. Such indicators would also provide the basis for an initial approach to assess the economic profitability of each railroad system.

By the way of some final reflections, we should underline that the development of HGIS and its application has opened up new possibilities for understanding urban and demographic evolution in relation to transport infrastructure. The current work exclusively focuses on railroad and population, considering a number of specific indicators. The analyses presented here could, however, also be extended to other transport networks, such as highways, navigable waterways, ports, and airports. The study of each network requires appropriate databases, specifically designed indicators and the creation of tailor-made spatial models. The level of precision of HGIS therefore depends on the subsequent adaptation of its indicators and the possibility of providing reasonable simplifications. Having said that, ongoing improvements to databases mean that in the short to medium term it should be possible to apply much more sophisticated models. The data obtained from analyses can then be statistically or cartographically crossed with other spatial variables in order to establish correlations, contrasts, and/or econometric models. These should then allow us to establish relationships between different variables in our search for the maximum significance. It is necessary to continue working on this approach and to improve its results iteratively.

Notes

1 D. Turnock, *An Historical Geography of Railways in Great Britain and Ireland*, Aldershot: Ashgate, 1998. J. Atack and R. A. Margo, 'The Impact of Access to Rail Transportation on Agricultural Improvement: The American Midwest as a Test Case, 1850–1860', *Journal of Transport and Land Use* 4(2), 2011, 5–18. I. Gregory and J. Martí-Henneberg, 'The Railways, Urbanization and Local Demography in England & Wales, 1825–1911', *Social Science History* 43, 2010a, 199–228.

2 P. K. O'Brien, *Railways and the Economic Development of Western Europe, 1830–1914*, London: Macmillan, 1983. S. P. Ville, *Transport and the Development of the European Economy*,

1750–1918, London: Macmillan, 1990. R. D. Knowles, 'Transport Shaping Space: Differential Collapse in Time–Space?', *Journal of Transport Geography* 14, 2006, 407–25.

3 P. Bairoch and G. Goerth, 'Factors of Urbanisation in the Nineteenth Century Developed Countries: A Descriptive and Econometric Analysis', *Urban Studies* 23, 1986, 285–305. P. Bairoch, *Cities and Economic Development*, London: Mansell, 1988.

4 P. Krugman, *Geography and Trade*, Cambridge, MA: MIT Press, 1991.

5 I. N. Gregory, C. Bennett, V. L. Gilham, and H. R. Southall, 'The Great Britain Historical GIS: From Maps to Changing Human Geography', *The Cartographic Journal* 39, 2002, 37–49. J. Martí-Henneberg, 'The Map of Europe: Continuity and Change in Administrative Boundaries (1850–2000)', *Geopolitics* 10(4), 2005, 791–815. I. N. Gregory, J. Martí-Henneberg and F. J. Tapiador, 'Modelling Long-Term Pan-European Population Change from 1870 to 2000 by Using Geographical Information Systems', *Journal of the Royal Statistical Society: Series A* 173(1), 2010b, 31–50.

6 M. Morillas-Torné, 'Creation of a Geo-Spatial Database to Analyse Railways in Europe (1830–2010): A Historical GIS Approach', *Journal of Geographic Information System* 4, 2012, 176–87. J. Martí-Henneberg, 'European Integration and National Models for Railway Networks (1840–2010)', *Journal of Transport Geography* 26, 2013, 126–38.

7 See: http://vps63872.ovh.net/projects/inland-waterways/.

8 R. Roth and M. N. Polino, *The City and the Railway in Europe.* Historical Urban Studies, Aldershot: Ashgate, 2003. G. Dupuy, 'Network Geometry and the Urban Railway System: The Potential Benefits to Geographers of Harnessing Inputs from "Naive" Outsiders', *Journal of Transport Geography* 33, 2013, 85–94.

9 R. W. Fogel, *Railroads and American Economic Growth: Essays in Econometric History.* Baltimore, MD: Johns Hopkins Press, 1964.

10 O. Kotavaara, H. Antikainen, and J. Rusanen, 'Urbanization and Transportation in Finland, 1880–1970', *Journal of Interdisciplinary History* 42(I), 2011, 89–109.

11 T. Berger and K. Enflo, 'Locomotives of Local Growth: The Short- and Long-Term Impact of Railroad in Sweden', *EHES Working Papers* (42), 2013, 43.

12 R. Schwartz, I. Gregory, and T. Thévenin, 'Spatial History: Railways, Uneven Development, and Population Change in France and Great Britain, 1850–1914', *Journal of Interdisciplinary History* 42(1), 2011a, 53–88.

13 R. Schwartz, I. N. Gregory, and J. Martí-Henneberg, 'History and GIS: Railways, Population Change, and Agricultural Development in Late Nineteenth-Century Wales', in *GeoHumanities: Art, History, Text at the Edge of Place*, Abingdon: Routledge, 2011, 251–66.

14 I. N. Gregory, C. Bennett, V. L. Gilham, and H. R. Southall, 'The Great Britain Historical GIS: From Maps to Changing Human Geography', *The Cartographic Journal* 39, 2002, 37–49. M. Felis-Rota, J. Martí-Henneberg and L. Mojica Gasol, 'A GIS Analysis of the Evolution of the Railway Network and Population Densities in England and Wales, 1851–2000', In *EHA Annual Meeting,* Vancouver: EHA,, 2012, 16.

15 X. Franch-Auladell, M. Morillas-Torné, and J. Martí-Henneberg, 'Railways as a Factor of Change in the Distribution of Population in Spain, 1900–1970', *Historical Methods* 46(3), 2013, 144–56. X. Franch-Auladell, M. Morillas-Torné, and J. Martí-Henneberg, 'The Railway Network and the Process of Population Concentration in Spain, 1900–2001', *Revista de Historia Económica* 32(03), 2014, 351–79.

16 R. Barquín, P. Pérez, and B. Sanz, 'La influencia del ferrocarril en el desarrollo urbano español (1860-1910)', *Revista de Historia Económica* 30(03), 2013, 391–416.

17 P. Caruana-Galizia and J. Martí-Henneberg, 'European Regional Railways and Real Income, 1870–1910: A Preliminary Report', *Scandinavian Economic History Review* 61(2), 2013, 167–96.

18 J. Atack, F. Bateman, M. Haines, and R. A. Margo, 'Did Railroads Induce or Follow Economic Growth? Urbanization and Population Growth in the American Midwest, 1850–1860', *Social Science History* 34(2), 2010, 171–97. J. Atack and R. A. Margo, 'The Impact of Access to Rail Transportation on Agricultural Improvement: The American Midwest as a Test Case, 1850–1860', *Journal of Transport and Land Use* 4(2), 2011, 5–18.

19 A. Herranz-Loncán, 'Transport Technology and Economic Expansion: The Growth Contribution of Railways in Latin America Before 1914', *Revista de Historia Económica* 32(01), 2014, 13–45.

20 This was based on different research projects led by J. Martí-Henneberg, which included: 'HGISe: A Platform Analysing Transport, Population and Socioeconomic Data for Europe (1850–2010). The case studies of England & Wales and the Iberian Peninsula' and 'The Development of European Waterways, Road and Rail Infrastructures: A Geographical Information System for the History of European Integration'.

21 J. Martí-Henneberg, 'European Integration and National Models for Railway Networks (1840–2010)', *Journal of Transport Geography* 26, 2013, 126–38.

22 S. Derrible and C. Kennedy, 'Network Analysis of World Subway Systems Using Updated Graph Theory', *Transportation Research Record: Journal of the Transportation Research Board* 2112, 2009, 17–25.

23 E. J. Alvarez-Palau, X. Franch and J. Martí-Henneberg, 'Evolution of the Territorial Coverage of the Railway Network and Its Influence on Population Growth: The Case of England and Wales, 1871–1931'. *Historical Methods* 46(3), 2013, 175–91.

24 Ibid.

25 M. Herce, 'Barcelona: Accessibility Changes and Metropolitan Transformations', *Built Environment* 30, 2004, 127–38.

26 J. Solanas, E. J. Alvarez-Palau and J. Martí-Henneberg, 'Estación ferroviaria y ciudades intermedias: lectura geo-espacial del crecimiento urbano mediante indicadores SIG vectoriales. El caso de Cataluña (1848–2010)', *GeoFocus* 16, 2015, 253–80.

27 E. J. Alvarez-Palau, M. Hernández and A. Tort, 'Modelo morfológico de crecimiento urbano inducido por la infraestructura ferroviaria. Estudio de caso en 25 ciudades catalanas', *Scripta Nova* 20(527), 2016, 1–38.

28 The majority of the railroad network was designed using Standard Gauges (1,435 mm in Europe, except in some countries where is slightly wider). Narrow Gauge lines (1,000 mm or less) tended to be used for regional purposes and were rarely integrated into the main railroad network.

4

ENHANCING LIFE-COURSES

Using GIS to construct 'new' aggregate and individual-level data on health and society in twentieth-century Britain

Humphrey Southall

The elucidation of ill-health, disease, and death through spatial analysis has a long history. Most accounts start with Dr John Snow and the London cholera epidemic of 1854: Snow showed cholera deaths to be clustered around a particular water pump in Broad Street, Soho; removing the pump handle ended the epidemic. However, while effective in this particular episode, Snow's analysis failed to overturn the prevailing miasmic theory that illness was caused by 'bad air'. Snow's map provided no direct evidence that the germs he blamed for the deaths even existed, while the sanitary improvements urged by the leading proponents of the miasmic theory, such as Florence Nightingale and William Farr, were highly and generally effective. The miasmic theory was only supplanted by the germ theory following Pasteur's work in the 1860s, directly demonstrating the existence of micro-organisms (Gilbert, 2004, especially part 2).

Proverbially, 'correlation is not causation', and although mapping rates of illness and death from particular causes may suggest explanations, even the most formal cross-sectional statistical analyses cannot verify them. As discussed below, area-based analyses with a time dimension do begin to provide explanations but still run large dangers of ecological fallacies. Including data on individual people rather than just areas gets us closer to explanation. Ultimately medical science is about what happens inside people's bodies and no purely statistical analysis can extend it. GIS practitioners must accept that their role is ultimately a supporting one, working within a multi-disciplinary team, but that supporting role can enable new analyses which would otherwise be simply impossible.

This chapter describes two major collaborations between the Great Britain Historical GIS and medical researchers, funded by the UK's Economic and Social Research Council under their 'Health Variations' and 'New Dynamics of Aging' programmes. Required to be policy-relevant, they dealt with the relatively recent past: the lifetimes of today's elderly, in practice running back to the 1921 census. Most British historical demographic research using GIS focuses on the period from c.1850 to 1911, when most data were reported by a relatively stable system of Registration Districts, so the next section describes the evolution of the quite different geography of local government districts created in 1894. The second section discusses alternative approaches taken to creating time series for consistent geographical areas. The final substantive section describes how individual-level information from the Office of National Statistics Longitudinal Study and the National Survey of Health and Development, generally known as the 1946 Birth Cohort, were linked to area data and a GIS framework. The conclusion returns to the role of historical GIS.

The statistical reporting geography of England and Wales, 1911–1973

What follows relates specifically to England and Wales: the other components of the United Kingdom, Scotland and (Northern) Ireland, have always had quite separate systems of local administration and demographic reporting, but until 2007 Wales was fully integrated into England. Our work always includes London, but its distinctive administrative geography is not detailed here. Lastly, please understand that any government with a majority in the Westminster parliament had complete freedom to change the country's administrative geography as it saw fit; and often did.

In consequence, there has been a series of complete transformations. First, in the 1830s and 1840s an 'ancient' system with roots before 1066, which varied substantially between different parts of the country, was supplemented by a new set of areas defined initially to administer poor relief. These Poor Law Unions generally combined market towns with their surrounding rural parishes, and almost exactly the same set of c.630 areas also served as Registration Districts, the primary geography for vital registration and the census. The Unions/Districts were grouped in statistical reports into Union/Registration Counties, which mostly had the same names as the Ancient Counties but quite different detailed boundaries. However, this mattered little as none of these kinds of county had any significant administrative function.

That changed with the Education Act of 1870 and a new set of Administrative Counties started to matter, more similar to Ancient than to Registration Counties. Similarly, the Public Health Act of 1872 defined a more detailed geography of Sanitary Districts, consisting by 1891 of 576 Rural Sanitary Districts and 1,067 broadly urban ones. As poor relief, education, and sewerage were quite separate functions, the more detailed districts were not subsidiary to the counties, and there was no requirement that one set of boundaries should nest inside another. The 1894 Local Government Act replaced Rural and Urban Sanitary Districts by, mostly, Rural and Urban Districts, but some towns were Municipal or County Boroughs, the last being completely independent of their Administrative County.

Although demographic reporting in England and Wales has always been based on units with some administrative function, the use made of particular administrative geographies by the census and vital registration reports evolved somewhat independently. Up to 1841, the census reported on ancient units and, as these were not mapped and often disputed, listings are often confused. Vital registration data used the new Registration Districts from the outset, as did the census from 1851. Statistics for Sanitary Districts first appeared in the 1881 census. However, the key change was

1911: that census reported on both Registration Districts and Local Government Districts in considerable detail; later censuses reported only on the latter.

Our research concerned the lifetimes of today's elderly, and the next major *legal* change in the *system* of local government outside London was in 1974, roughly contemporaneous with systematic availability of 'born digital' demographic and boundary data, so this Local Government District geography from 1911 to 1973 was our main focus. However, that geography poses several additional challenges as compared to the Registration District geography between 1851 and 1911.

First, there were more than twice as many units, and they were far more variable in size. Throughout the period, the largest single unit was Birmingham, with a 1931 population of 1,002,603, with almost no data available for any internal subdivisions. The smallest 1931 unit was 'Newcastle upon Tyne Rural District', bizarrely consisting solely of the Moot Hall in central Newcastle and with a population of 5, while 113 districts had populations under 2,000.

Secondly and in consequence, demographic reports do not provide the same level of detail for all units, and the selectivity varied. Data on industry, occupations, and consequently social class were listed by the census in much greater detail for County Boroughs and other towns over 50,000 population. The Registrar General's reports generally provided cause of death data only for the County Boroughs and the county aggregates of all other urban units and of all Rural Districts, which means that small country towns and suburban areas within conurbations are grouped together.

Thirdly, although the legal framework was static over this period the actual geography was not. There was a constant trickle of boundary changes, driven especially by urban growth, but in addition the early 1930s saw a systematic programme of County Reviews. Figure 4.1 plots all boundary changes we know of by year, showing the concentration into the 1930s, and that changes were spread over a series of years. Table 4.1 summarizes inter-censal changes specifically affecting Local

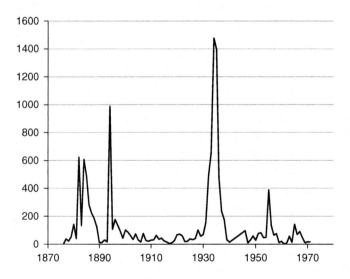

Figure 4.1 Boundary changes at all levels per year, 1881–1973.

Sources: Census reports; Registrar General's *Annual Reports*; Registrar General's *Statistical Reviews*.

Table 4.1 Inter-censal changes to Local Government Districts in England and Wales, 1921–61.

	1921–31		1931–51		1951–61	
	N	%	N	%	N	%
Total no of LGDs at end	1797		1470		1467	
Labelled as 'New Area'	1	0.1	108	7.3	1	0.1
New, or boundary change affecting more than n% of population:						
50%	21	1.2	139	9.5	1	0.1
25%	47	2.6	244	16.6	3	0.2
10%	98	5.5	418	28.4	15	1.0
5%	136	7.6	546	37.1	27	1.8
1%	209	11.6	767	52.2	67	4.6
Any change at all	265	14.7	970	66.0	162	11.0

Government Districts: even in 1931–51, the number of completely new creations was small, but most districts experienced some changes. As discussed in the next section, this programme of rolling changes immensely complicated analysis of the 1930s, and we grasped its extent only after the research project started.

Before discussing specific analytic issues, one very general issue of 'geography' needs to be discussed. Our research analyses change over time, and all available analytic techniques require data for different dates to be presented for the same set of units, so that we can compute rates of change. The methods discussed below enable us to convert between geographies. However, this raises the question of which *analytical geography* should we convert our data from various dates to. Demographic researchers without access to GIS tools generally attempt to finesse the problem away: the very largest changes are handled by merging the units affected and the remainder are ignored as 'small'. This approach may work for the pre-1911 Registration District system, but cannot handle change on the scale of the County Reviews.

Once it is accepted that redistricting rather than ad hoc aggregation is necessary, three approaches are possible, the trade-off being between statistical accuracy and 'impact'. The former criterion argues for using the least detailed reporting geography as the analytic geography. Where the modern data are downloaded small area counts, for census tracts or Output Areas, or individual-level data, historical data taken from published tables will almost always have a less detailed geography. For example, in *Death in Britain* Dorling (1997) compares mortality rates for 1950–3 reported for County Boroughs and for county urban and rural aggregates, as discussed above, with data on all individual deaths in Britain 1990–2, geo-referenced by final place of residence: clearly, the newer data could be precisely assigned to the earlier geography but not vice versa, and in this case 'impact' was not compromised as publication led to mortality rates in the Metropolitan Borough of Shoreditch, abolished in 1965, featuring on the BBC TV news (see also Shaw et al., 1998).

Even so, the impact of research, especially on policy makers, may be greater if research findings are presented for the units which exist today, and while it is clearly invalid to redistrict data for mid-twentieth-century local government districts to modern Output Areas, much of our research involves data redistricted to the 348 current Local Authority Districts of England and Wales. As well as increasing policy impact, this approach is arguably better than working with any particular historical geography when using data from a series of past years, each with substantially different reporting geographies (Gregory et al., 2001). Lastly, Davey Smith and Dorling (1996) argue for maximizing impact on politicians by redistricting mortality data to an unrelated geography, the constituencies those politicians represent, although here we enter the realm of polemic unless our reporting geography is much more detailed than the analytic geography: their raw data are again individually located deaths, but historical data are rarely so flexible.

Aggregate analysis of infant mortality, 1911–1973

The overall aim of all the research described here was to better understand the impact of poverty and hard times on people's health. The next section discusses research into long-term effects, especially of childhood deprivation on health in old age, but this required analysis of individual life histories. Our area-based analyses focused on infant mortality, i.e. the proportion of children dying before their first birthday, usually reported as deaths per thousand live births. In the nineteenth and early twentieth century infant mortality rates were high and generally seen as highly sensitive to deprivation, although more recently much lower rates mean that small number effects complicate analysis.

In particular, we had assembled a large dataset, from the Registrar General's *Annual Report* for 1911–20, and then from the *Registrar General's Statistical Review of England and Wales, Tables. Part I. Medical* for 1921–73, listing annual vital event counts in every local government district in England and Wales, a total of over 120,000 rows of data. The variables listed varied over time and generally increased, but every report listed total births and deaths under 1.

Initial work for the Health Variations Programme focused on the impact of the deep recession of the 1930s, and Figure 4.2 presents the most obvious analysis, plotting infant mortality during 1931 against unemployment as recorded by the 1931 census. Although the data are here aggregated by county, both variables were reported by district, 1931 being the first UK census to gather unemployment data. The correlation is clearly significant ($N=62$), and the three counties with highest unemployment also have the highest infant mortality: Durham, Glamorgan, and Monmouth.

However, Figure 4.3 presents national time series and shows that this cross-sectional correlation may be misleading: infant mortality continued to decline even as unemployment rose spectacularly. What was therefore required was a more complex analysis combining cross-sections and time series, and including other explanatory variables. This is presented in Congdon and Southall (2004).

Data were taken from three distinct sources. First, infant mortality rates for the local government districts of England and Wales for each year 1927 to 1936, from the Registrar General's *Statistical Reviews*. Secondly, data for the same districts was taken from several different tables we had computerized from the 1931 census,

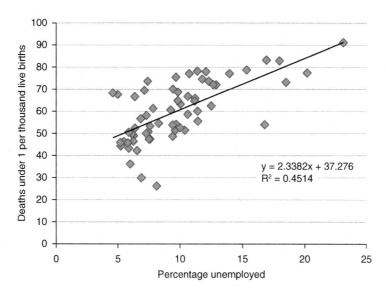

Figure 4.2 County-level unemployment and infant mortality in England and Wales in 1931.

Sources: Census of England and Wales, 1931, *Occupation Tables*, Tables 16 and 17; Registrar General's *Statistical Review*.

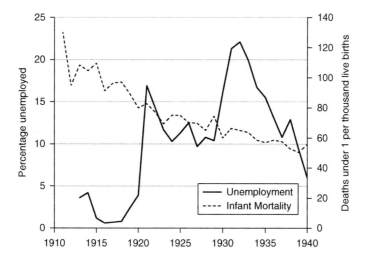

Figure 4.3 Unemployment and infant mortality in England and Wales, 1911–39.

Sources: Department of Employment and Productivity (1971) *British Labour Statistics: Historical Abstract 1886–1968* (London: HMSO), tables 159 (1911–12) and 160 (1913–26); Ministry of Labour *Local Unemployment Index* (1927–39); Registrar General's *Annual Report* (1911–19); Registrar General's *Statistical Review*.

selecting variables which had been highlighted in existing studies. Given the emphasis on urban–rural differences, we included crude population density but also housing overcrowding, defined as the proportion of households with more than 1.5 persons per room; data on 'amenities' such as water supplies and lavatories was not gathered until 1951. The very detailed occupation tables provided a vast range of potential variables but the literature on infant mortality led us to focus on miners as a percentage of occupied males, textile workers as a percentage of occupied females, the overall economic activity rate among females aged 15 to 64, and a categorization of areas into 'Agricultural', 'Professional/Services', 'Staple Industry', and 'Light Industry' developed by the ESRC Cambridge Group (Garrett et al., 2001).

Lastly, the 1931 occupation tables included the number of occupied workers who described themselves as unemployed, but of course only for a single date in the spring of 1931. Given that this was all long before the introduction of regular large-sample surveys such as the Labour Force Survey, the only other source of unemployment data was the National Insurance system. Our analysis began in 1927 because this was when the Ministry of Labour began publishing the Local Unemployment Index (LUI). This listed numbers of insured workers and the number who were unemployed for a changing set of towns which seem to have broadly corresponded to the locations of the Employment Exchanges where the unemployed were required to 'sign on', and had no particular relationship with the local government geography used by our other data. We therefore aggregated the LUI data to create time series for Administrative Counties.

The final dataset therefore contains a mixture of cross-sectional and time series evidence, and two different geographical levels, while the variable being analysed, infant mortality, cannot be assumed to be continuous due to small number effects. Conventional regression analysis was therefore inappropriate. Full details are in Congdon and Southall (2004), but a Bayesian analysis was carried out in which explanatory variables were converted to categorical data, and a series of different models was fitted.

Overall, multiple significant relationships were found between infant mortality and different aspects of industrial structure: areas focused on service sector employment had lower mortality; areas with high female activity rates, such as those dominated by textiles, had higher mortality; so too did mining areas, despite their generally low female activity rates. Overcrowded housing was much more important than overall population density, and it may be that by the inter-war period the latter impacted health primarily through low rural population densities limiting access to medical provision, rather than through the negative effects of crowding people into towns. However, what was strikingly absent was any evidence that rising unemployment rates over the period raised infant mortality. This is an important finding, and may indicate that government and charitable initiatives to limit the impact of the recession on mothers and children, especially supplementary feeding programmes, actually worked (Webster, 1985).

By ending that analysis in 1936 and accepting that some areas were lost from the final years of the analysis due to boundary changes, we were able to carry out a short-term analysis of the impact of the 1929 Crash and subsequent recession on people's health based on the geography of the 1931 census, but a longer term analysis required systematic redistricting. This was the focus of Congdon and Southall (2005), which was limited to 414 local government districts in the north of England by data entry constraints but covered the whole period from 1921 to 1973, using annual data from almost the full run of the Registrar General's *Statistical Reviews* and data from the 1931, 1951, 1961, and 1971 censuses.

As discussed in the previous section, there were very substantial boundary changes over this period and the original intention was to use the detailed boundary GIS systems we were constructing for both local government districts and the more detailed Civil Parish system: by combining the latter boundary data with computerized versions of the census parish-level population counts, the problematic assumption that population was evenly distributed across each district could be relaxed. That approach has been taken in more recent work, but delays in GIS construction coupled with the timetable of the ESRC Health Variations Programme forced us to develop an alternative methodology.

Figure 4.1 shows that the majority of boundary changes in the overall period happened in the early to mid-1930s due to the County Reviews, while Table 4.1 shows that most of the changes to local government districts that did happen outside the 1930s affected relatively small parts of their populations: they were minor adjustments rather than wholesale redistricting. There was in fact another wholesale reorganization of certain counties in 1965, but almost entirely in southern England and therefore not affecting our analysis of the north. We therefore based our analysis on the geography of the 1951 census, which was essentially that created by the County Reviews, put considerable effort into redistricting from 1931 geography to 1951, ignored minor changes between 1921 and 1931, and between 1951 and 1973, and dealt with a small number of major changes in those periods by excluding the affected districts from the relevant end of the time series analysis: this led to the loss of only one district from the 1920s, but thirteen from the late 1960s and 1970s, mainly due to the reorganization of Teesside in 1967–8.

Our methodology for redistricting from 1931 to 1951 was based not on boundary mapping but on the very detailed lists of boundary changes published in the Registrar General's *Statistical Review*, which included the population of each area transferred as enumerated in 1931, as well as the districts it was transferred from and to, plus the total populations of districts in 1931 as listed by the 1931 census, plus the data given in the report of the 1939 National Registration (General Register Office, 1944), discussed in the next section, on the 1931 populations of the districts as defined in 1939: clearly, given that all three sources deal with populations as counted in 1931, taking the 1931 census population of a district and adding or subtracting the populations listed as transferred should result in the population as listed in 1939. So it proved, after very careful checking and correction of these transcriptions, and this enabled us to construct a 'geography conversion table' (Simpson, 2002) providing, for each combination of 1931 and 1939 district which had some overlap, the proportion of the 1931 district's population or other data which should be allocated to the 1939 district.

Although this was not our first choice of methods, it had real merits relative to GIS-based vector overlay. First, it was often more accurate because it drew on detailed information about the actual populations of the areas transferred in boundary changes, rather than assuming they had the same density as either the rest of the area gaining or the area losing: many boundary changes occur on the edges of growing towns, and the areas transferred generally have much higher population densities than the rest of the rural districts they are coming out of, but less than the average density of the town they were joining. Secondly, once the conversion table has been built, the actual calculation of the redistricted data is almost instant, whereas more sophisticated GIS-based approaches, attempting for example to model population density at urban fringes, can involve very lengthy computation and are hard to include in the work flows of substantive research projects. Thirdly, these methods are easy to explain and justify to non-specialists.

Although only small numbers of districts were lost at the beginning and end of the overall study period due to boundary changes, early versions of the analytic dataset were completely missing several years while the County Reviews were being carried out. However, further elaboration of the redistricting procedures enabled us to completely eliminate these gaps.

We again used Bayesian statistical methods assuming a Poisson distribution for infant deaths. Our explanatory variables included housing overcrowding at all four census dates, and housing 'amenities' for the last three, although the amenities listed varied over time: in 1951 they counted households without piped water, while by 1971 they were counting baths and showers. Numbers in each of the Registrar-General's five social classes were included for all four censuses, which required us to assign data from the 1931 occupational classification to the classes as the first census to tabulate class was 1951. Levels of education, measured by the age at which employed persons had terminated their education, was included only for 1951. We also used industrial structure data only for 1951, partly on the grounds these change only relatively slowly, and focused specifically on numbers of males and of females employed in each of agriculture, mining, and textiles. Lastly, we included the unemployment rate for all censuses, although for 1961 data were available only for the larger districts and had to be imputed elsewhere.

One initial finding was that geographical inequalities in infant mortality declined fairly steadily from 1921 until the early 1960s, but then started to rise; this meshes with other evidence of rising inequality since the 1960s. Secondly, in the early part of this long period, variations in infant mortality seem to have been most affected by social class, but by the early 1970s the type of industrial base and housing density were more important; unemployment rates had only a limited impact, as in our earlier analysis of the inter-war period. Despite the rise in inequality, our period of course saw a steady decline in overall infant mortality, rates in the north of England as a whole dropping from 97 deaths per 1,000 live births in 1921 to 19 in 1973.

Individual-level analysis of childhood poverty and health in later life

Our aggregate analyses try to draw conclusions relevant to the present from a historical period, albeit relatively recent. However, the 1930s and 1940s are directly relevant to demands on the modern National Health Service because those come mainly from those over the retirement age, all of whom were born before 1950. There is by now abundant evidence that conditions in childhood have a large impact on health in later life, the paradigmatic study being Barker's analysis of ischaemic heart disease (Barker & Osmond, 1986; Barker, 1992), but here analysis must be at the individual level: in our mobile society it would be absurd to assume that elderly people were children in their area of current residence.

The analyses discussed in this section therefore take their dependent variables from sources which track individuals over long periods of time. However, there was still a substantial role for our aggregate historical data, because the earliest parts of the individual-level longitudinal data sets were inevitably not constructed to support the particular analyses, and lacked explanatory variables.

Although the 1946 birth cohort discussed below was the first planned British longitudinal study, and one of the first in the world, cunning data manipulations have enabled longer life-course data to be assembled. Bristol University researchers located individual-level data on 4,999 babies originally gathered in 1937–9 from sixteen districts across Britain by the Carnegie United Kingdom Trust's study of Family Diet and Health, directed by Sir John Boyd-Orr. Because this was medical research, the researchers were able to collaborate with the National Health Service Central Register, within which 4,397 subjects from the Boyd-Orr Survey could be identified; 3,182 agreed to be contacted; and 1,648 actually returned questionnaires (Martin et al., 2005).

A similar methodology was employed in an analysis based on records of all births in Hertfordshire between 1911 and 1948 (Syddall et al., 2005). However, sample sizes are too small for some purposes and there are obvious issues of selection bias. The Office of National Statistics Longitudinal Study ('the LS') is much larger, including everyone living in England and Wales with one of four birthdays, and drawing information from every census since 1971 plus deaths, births of their children, and certain other information known to the government. One limitation is very tight confidentiality controls: which particular four birthdays are used is secret, and researchers cannot access the data, only submit specific approved queries. Another limitation is, of course, that going back only to 1971 is insufficient for our purposes. However, LS members are identified internally by their National Health Service numbers, and Strachan et al. (1995) discovered that, for those persons already alive on 30 September 1939, their NHS number identified the local government district they were then resident in. This is because on that date, following the start of the Second World War, the government carried out a National Registration which both served as a simplified census, replacing that planned for 1941, and provided everyone with new identity cards with identifying numbers. One significant caveat, given the historical context, is that anyone who subsequently served in the armed force had their number changed.

Strachan used this piece of cunning to assign LS members to just fourteen broad regions. He concluded that region of residence in later life was more important to health, but region of residence in childhood had some independent effect. However, we realized that there were large potentials for further analysis if the LS data were linked to actual area characteristics from inter-war sources. Very little statistical data is available for the local government geography of 1939, the National Registration report reporting only on gender and age (General Register Office, 1944). The obvious alternative source was the 1931 census, especially if our focus was the impact of the inter-war recession on its children. The local government geography of 1931 was very different from that of 1939, due to the County Reviews, but the previous section explained how we redistricted from one to the other.

Another problem of historical context was that the National Registration was made after the mass evacuation of children from cities in the summer of 1939, challenging any simple equation of place of registration with 'where individuals grewup'. Fortunately, the National Registration report itself provided significant information about evacuation. England and Wales was divided into three types of area: 110 districts were classified as *evacuation areas*, 8 per cent of all districts containing 31 per cent of population, these including all London boroughs and the five largest provincial cities; 18 per cent of districts with 25 per cent of population were *neutral*, neither sending nor receiving evacuees, these being outer London and smaller provincial cities; and 75 per cent of districts containing 44 per cent of population were *reception areas* for evacuees. Interestingly, 51 per cent of LS members, who were of course mostly children, were in reception areas compared to 44 per cent of the overall population, suggesting that evacuation had had a substantial effect.

The LS provided two dependent variables, whether the sample member lived or died between 1981 and 1991 and, if they lived, whether they reported 'limiting long-term illness' in 1991. Independent variables included their age and gender; their personal socio–economic characteristics in 1981, including social class, housing, and marital status; characteristics of their area of residence in 1981 as summarized by the Carstairs Index (Carstairs and Morris, 1991); and characteristics of their area of residence in 1939, mostly redistricted from the 1931 census, including population density, the proportion living in overcrowded housing, the unemployment rate, and the proportion doing unskilled or semi-skilled manual work. However, the number of variables which could be included in any given analysis was limited by the LS's disclosure control rules.

Despite various caveats, the study concluded that, even after making full allowance for sample members' current circumstances, conditions in their area of residence in childhood had a measurable association with health outcomes later in life. In particular, those who had lived in areas classified in 1934 as 'depressed areas' had a relative risk of dying or reporting long-term limiting illness 14–15 per cent higher than those living elsewhere. So, while the research described above into the immediate impact of the inter-war recession on infant mortality showed limited effects, in the long-term the 'children of the depressed areas' have experienced significantly worse health.

The obvious limitation of this analysis of the LS is that we know nothing of individual circumstances in childhood, and the mass evacuations of the summer of 1939 limit what we know about the area sample members were actually brought up in. Those limitations were removed in the final study discussed here, where we worked as part of the HALCyon ('Healthy Ageing across the Life Course') project led by the Medical Research Council's Unit for Lifelong Health and Ageing. This research team is remarkable for having been in continuous existence since 1946, managing the National Survey of Health and Development (NSHD), often known as the '1946 Birth Cohort'. The overall findings of the HALCyon project are presented in Kuh et al. (2014).

The NSHD originally targeted the 16,695 children born in England, Wales or Scotland between 3 and 9 March 1946, data being gathered on 13,687 of these births and 5,362 being selected for follow-up research, including all single births to women with husbands in non-manual and agricultural employment, and one in four of the remainder. Members of that sample were then repeatedly contacted at age 2, age 4, and so on, each 'collection' gathering somewhat different data as cohort members aged. Inevitably each collection covered somewhat fewer than the previous, mainly due to loss of contact or unwillingness to participate rather than death, but the project worked to minimize this attrition by sending birthday cards and, in later years, by involving cohort members in the management of the project. Our work focused on collections representing childhood (age 4 in 1950, sample size 4,707), early adulthood (age 26 in 1972, 3,750), and midlife (age 53 in 1999, 3,035), partly because these years were close to censuses (Wadsworth et al., 2006; Murray et al., 2013).

We made two technical contributions as historical geographers. First, assisting with geo-referencing the data. One preliminary problem was that the database containing life histories contained little information on locations, but it was quickly realized that a separate 'Contacts Database' used to send the birthday cards did, of course, include postal addresses. The addresses where sample members were living from 1999 and, with 40 exceptions, 1972 included the postcodes, easily converted to coordinates. However, the UK postcode system was introduced only in 1959 so addresses from 1950 needed systematic geo-referencing. Of course, most streets and buildings from 1950 still exist, so it was initially assumed that most addresses could be matched programmatically against modern address files. However, the separate team charged with that work were able to match only 53 per cent so our role substantially expanded.

The main focus of our geo-referencing work was the relatively small number of addresses from 1950 which had totally disappeared, meaning the buildings and streets no longer existed. Although few, simply dropping them from the analysis would have severely biased the results as these were generally areas of 'comprehensive redevelopment', i.e. the results of government 'slum clearance' programmes targeted at the worst housing and, generally, the most deprived households. These addresses were turned into coordinates by downloading geo-referenced images of Ordnance Survey 1:10,560, 1:2,500, and 1:1,250 scale *County Series* maps from the 1940s and 1950s from the EDINA Digimap service, these showing streets by name, and indicating house numbers in longer streets. One complication with this work was that the data from the cohort, even though they were only addresses rather than cohort members' personal characteristics, could be stored only on an encrypted memory stick, which had to be returned along with the coordinates to the MRC Unit once the research was complete (Murray et al., 2012). In 1951 and 1971, cohort members were living in over half the local government districts of England and Wales, and almost all the counties of Scotland.

Our second contribution was to provide statistical data from the 1951 and 1971 censuses, mostly from our existing collection but involving some new data entry; and then to link these to the individual-level data using the coordinates created from 1950 and 1972 addresses and our existing digital boundary datasets for local government districts. As in our other projects, the variables included were measures of deprivation: the percentages of persons in unskilled and semi-skilled manual work; the unemployment rate; the percentages of households lacking amenities, such as water supplies and their own toilets; the percentages living at densities over one person per room; the percentages of persons either with university degrees or terminating their education at age 20 or above. The justification for including these variables was partly to measure area versus individual-level effects, but also to supplement the slightly limited data gathered in 1950 about family circumstances in what was at the time a project very focused on child health.

One great strength of the 1946 cohort, especially in an analysis trying to identify factors leading not just to longevity but to a *healthy* old age was that it provided objective measures of physical health gathered by medical professionals visiting cohort members, not just a subjective assessment, via tick box, of whether one's life was 'limited' by long-term illness. Our analysis looked at three measures of physical capacity in the 1999 data: 'chair rises', or the number of seconds needed to rise from a chair and sit down again, repeated ten times; 'standing balance', or how long someone can stand on one leg with eyes closed; and 'grip strength', measured using an electronic handgrip dynamometer. 2,566 participants provided all three measures.

A variety of explanatory models were fitted and results varied somewhat between the three measures of physical capacity used as dependent variables. For all measures, there were significant effects from area of residence in all three time periods, and these effects were in addition to the effects of individual socio-economic position, so once again geography matters. The strongest effects were on 'standing balance', which is interesting as this is arguably the capacity with a significant mental as well as physical component. Our conclusions noted that fully disentangling the interactions between individual and area effects at multiple time periods really requires larger samples, which may become possible once the larger birth cohorts started in 1958 and 1970 become old enough for similar analyses (Murray et al., 2013).

Conclusion

This chapter is clearly not a detailed presentation of the research, but rather a guide to the research aimed at GIS practitioners. I hope that readers will explore the references, but what they will find are highly technical papers with no maps, relatively few graphs, a great many tables consisting not of data but parameter estimates plus associated confidence limits and similar, plus many equations. They may find themselves a little baffled; they are not alone!

Even when I was the project's principal investigator, the lead author of each paper was a medical statistician, and my contribution to the writing mainly concerned sources and initial data manipulations, plus some material on historical contexts. However, the overall expertise of the GB Historical GIS team and myself was quite critical to the research, and arguably at least as hard to replace as that of our statistical collaborators. That expertise has four distinct components.

First, technical expertise in GIS and especially in GIS-based redistricting. Statisticians are used to working with geographically organized statistics, and most statistical techniques require them, but most statisticians expect there to be a single reporting geography, or at worst multi-level geographies which nest neatly inside one another. However, over the 80-year spans of people's lives reporting geographies inevitably undergo significant change so the type of health research described here requires either individual-level data which can be geo-referenced from addresses, or some methodology for converting aggregate statistics from one reporting geography to another. This is outside the experience of medical statisticians and absolutely requires knowledge of GIS tools.

One caveat is necessary: although our vector overlay techniques can in principle work from any geography to any other, if the output geography is more detailed than the original reporting one, the apparent accuracy is spurious; and if the output geography contains a similar number of units to the reporting one, but with few shared boundaries, the redistricting process works as a spatial moving average, suppressing variance and therefore reducing the explanatory power of the statisticians' models. We consequently have a strong preference for seeking out detailed historical statistics enabling the redistricting to work from more to less detailed geographies.

Secondly, detailed knowledge of changing statistical reporting geographies. Much of this knowledge is of course embodied in the historical GIS systems we have built which can be downloaded from multiple online sites, without collaborating with us. However, it is by now very obvious that our work on the pre-1911 Registration District geography is much more widely used than our work on the more complex local government geography of the mid-twentieth century, even though the latter covers at least as long a period and has greater contemporary relevance. I suspect that part of the reason is its greater complexity: not just many more units but a need to understand the different kinds of district, and to work with the various simplified versions of the local government geography used in statistical reporting. I hope this chapter will encourage more historical GIS researchers working with British demographic data to venture later than 1911; our medical collaborators would have had no interest in working with us on the earlier period.

Thirdly, a large and diverse library of computerized historical statistics, systematically linked to that geographical framework: it was essential to the research that most of the data were already to hand and well-organized, and also that we were familiar with its structure and content, so the complex analytic datasets we were assembling could be constantly guided both by our collaborators' knowledge of which explanatory variables were theoretically relevant and our own knowledge of what data existed. The research described here was funded through directed research programmes with fixed timetables, so it was seldom practical to stop for new data digitization work, from paper reports or scanned images of them.

Finally, and maybe least obviously, general knowledge of the historical period. Two specific examples noted in this chapter are the existence and impact of the mass evacuation of children in the summer of 1939, before the National Registration, and the effects of slum clearance programmes, especially in the 1960s, on addresses. Everyone involved in this research was conscious that, even though limited to the life spans of today's elderly, we were going back far enough into the past as foreign country for things to be done differently there. Given that we were exploring the relationships between evolving socio-economic structures and health, my own particular background researching historical labour markets and the origins of Britain's north–south divide was often relevant (Gilbert and Southall, 2000).

Overall then, our primary contribution was not as GIS technicians but as historical researchers: the potential of various datasets and the implications of historical context took up far more time in project meetings than did discussion of redistricting techniques. Working with health researchers took us well outside our comfort zone, and we were often pushed to somehow conjure up the data needed to test specific theoretical ideas, rather than just use whatever explanatory variables were most easily available. One reward for this effort is simply that the resulting publications achieve substantially higher citation counts than purely historical studies. However, the larger personal satisfaction comes from engaging with a very different research community, and with directly policy-relevant research.

References

D. Barker, *Fetal and Infant Origins of Adult Disease*, London: British Medical Journal Publishing Group, 1992.

D. J. P. Barker and C. Osmond, 'Infant Mortality, Childhood Nutrition, and Ischaemic Heart Disease in England and Wales', *The Lancet*, May 1986 327(8489), 1077–80.

V. Carstairs and R. Morris, *Deprivation and Health in Scotland*, Aberdeen: Aberdeen University Press, 1991.

P. Congdon and H. R. Southall, 'Small Area Variations in Infant Mortality in England and Wales in the Inter-War Period and their Link with Socio-Economic Factors', *Health and Place* 10, 2004, 363–82.

P. Congdon and H.R. Southall, 'Trends in Inequality in Infant Mortality in the North of England, 1921–1971, and their Association with Urban and Social Structure', *Journal of the Royal Statistical Society, Series A, Statistics in Society* 168, 2005, 679–700.

G. Davey Smith and D. Dorling, '"I'm All Right, John": Voting Patterns and Mortality in England and Wales, 1981–92', *British Medical Journal* 313(7072), 1996, 1573–7.

D. Dorling, *Death in Britain: How Local Mortality Rates have Changed: 1950s–1990s*, Report published by the Joseph Rowntree Foundation, 1997.

E. Garrett, A. Reid, K. Schürer, and S. Szreter, *Changing Family Size in England and Wales: Place, Class and Demography, 1891–1911*, Cambridge: Cambridge University Press, 2001.

D. M. Gilbert and H. R. Southall, 'The Urban Labour Market', in M. Daunton (ed.), *Cambridge Urban History of Britain,* vol. 3, *c.1840–1950*, Cambridge: Cambridge University Press, 2000, 593–628.

P. Gilbert, *Mapping the Victorian Social Body*, Albany, NY: State University of New York Press, 2004.

I. N. Gregory, D. Dorling, and H. R. Southall, 'A Century of Inequality in England and Wales Using Standardized Geographical Units', *Area* 33(3), 2001, 297–311.

D. Kuh, R. Cooper, R. Hardy, M. Richards, and Y. Ben-Shlomo, *A Life Course Approach to Healthy Aging*, Oxford: OUP, 2014.

R. M. Martin, D. Gunnell, J. Pemberton, S. Frankel, and G. Davey Smith, 'Cohort Profile: The Boyd Orr Cohort—An Historical Cohort Study Based on the 65 Year Follow-Up of the Carnegie Survey of Diet and Health (1937–39)', *International Journal of Epidemiology* 34(4), 2005, 742–9.

E. Murray, H. R. Southall, P. Aucott, K. Tilling, D. Kuh, R. Hardy, and Y. Ben-Shlomo, 'Challenges in Examining Area Effects across the Life Course on Physical Capability in Mid-Life: Findings from the 1946 British Birth Cohort', *Health and Place* 18(2), 2012, 366–74.

E. Murray, Y. Ben Shlomo, K. Tilling, H. R. Southall, P. Aucott, D. Kuh, and R. Hardy, 'Area Deprivation across the Life Course and Physical Capability in Mid-Life: Findings from the 1946 British Birth Cohort', *American Journal of Epidemiology* 178(3), 2013, 441–50.

General Register Office, *National Register. Statistics of Population on 29 September 1939 by Sex, Age and Marital Condition. Report and Tables*, London: HMSO, 1944.

M. Shaw, D. Dorling, and N. Brimblecombe, 'Changing the Map: Health in Britain 1951–91', *Sociology of Health and Illness* 20(5), 1998, 694–709.

L. Simpson, 'Geography Conversion Tables: A Framework for Conversion of Data between Geographical Units', *International Journal of Population Geography* 8(1), 2002, 69–82.

D. P. Strachan, D. A. Leon, and B. Dodgeon, 'Mortality from Cardiovascular Disease among Interregional Migrants in England and Wales', *British Medical Journal* 310(6977), 1995, 423–7.

H. E. Syddall, A. Aihie Sayer, E. M. Dennison, H. J. Martin, D. J. P. Barker, C. Cooper and the Hertfordshire Cohort Study Group, 'Cohort Profile: The Hertfordshire Cohort Study', *International Journal of Epidemiology* 34(6), 2005, 1234–42.

M. Wadsworth, D. Kuh, M. Richards, and R. Hardy, 'Cohort Profile: The 1946 National Birth Cohort (MRC National Survey of Health and Development)', *International Journal of Epidemiology* 35(1), 2006, 49–54.

C. Webster, 'Health, Welfare and Unemployment during the Depression', *Past and Present* 109(1), 1985, 204–30.

5

RELATING ECONOMIC AND DEMOGRAPHIC CHANGE IN THE UNITED STATES FROM 1970 TO 2012

A preliminary examination using GIS and spatial analysis techniques with national data sources[1]

Andrew A. Beveridge

Background

Social scientists and historians have long been interested in the spatial structures of changes in economic activity, population, and the labour force. Does the development of a skilled and proficient labour force in one area lead to greater economic activity? For the same reason, does the increase in jobs and other opportunities in a specific area lead to population growth? What sorts of lags exist? To what extent are population and labour force changes impervious to changes in the local economic context? Yet, these questions have not been directly addressed, at least at the national level.[2] Using a variety of newly arrayed material, this chapter sets out to do just that. The recent development of Geographic Information Systems (GIS) techniques, as well as the expansion of a variety of spatial analysis methods, makes this work possible. GIS has become a popular, widespread way to make thematic maps. Using these techniques, along with materials that are created to be comparable over time, makes it possible to visualize changes in population, employment, average wages, as well as many other variables. To do this requires creating materials that are broadly comparable across decades.

As with virtually all historical GIS efforts, one must confront the fact that the materials used were not created with the aim of supporting comprehensive uses, much less relating them to other materials. This analysis used census data, including data from the most recent American Community Survey, for each of the roughly

3,150 counties in the United States, along with County Business Patterns data from 1970 to the most recent survey.[3] This chapter will analyse the changes in the United States labour force and population at the county level, and relate them in a descriptive and suggestive manner to national and local shifts in the economy, changes in the participation rates of men and women in the labour force, and other factors. The 1970s bust and stagflation, the 1990s boom, the internet bubble and bust, and the recent housing boom and financial crisis will set the context.

Most analyses using the County Business Patterns data plus other data provided by the economic division of the US Census Bureau do not explicitly consider spatial relationships, nor do they analyse data over time. Due to changes in boundaries and variable definitions from year to year and decade to decade, few analyses have tracked spatial relationships. This has remained true despite the fact that there is intense interest in the national economy and its relationship to local economic factors for businesses and governments alike. Plainly, the factors that affect labour and business conditions are extremely important for political leaders, and are analysed constantly by planners, business economists, government officials, and others. This chapter will begin to analyse these spatial relationships in a systematic manner.

Most domestic demography relies in whole or in part upon data from the decennial census and, increasingly, from multiple-year files from the American Community Survey (ACS). Starting in 2005, the ACS replaced the long-form decennial census as the source for information beyond very simple demographic categories. Some analyses, including several by this author, have examined changing spatial structures of population and ethnic distribution.[4] However, the data collected by the Census and the American Community Survey do not make serious use of economic data, nor does the economic data explicitly reference the population data. Indeed, even for something as simple as the vintage of county boundaries, the economic division of the US Census Bureau follows different standards than the population division. The same holds for the adjustment of monetary data for change in purchasing power.[5] For these reasons and other limitations, there are very few analyses that draw on data from both the economic and population divisions of the Census and combine them for analyses either spatially or (even rarer) across time. The few prior studies found rely upon very complex spatial and temporal regression models, and do not use data for the entire United States, but rather focus on a small area for a short duration.[6]

This chapter represents the beginning of a project to integrate data and findings on the spatial, economic, and other determinants of the changing population, labour force, and economic shifts in the United States over the last four decades. Based upon the preliminary work reported here, this project will continue and expand at a Census Research Data Center. This will make it possible to use and analyse data and materials much closer to the original detailed records, which include much better geographic information (including census blocks for demographic data and street address for business enterprises) and many of the original responses to questions or register files compiled by the Census Bureau[7]. In addition, using the original data will make it possible to make the analyses more comparable over time, both geographically and in terms of the classification of activities.[8]

However, it is important to note some constraints on the utility of using such available data combined with GIS and spatial techniques. Many historical GIS projects focus on one or two local areas, and painstakingly build an important repository or archive of material at costs as high as years of labour with many assistants. Agencies such as the Census Bureau and its counterparts in other countries have created massive amounts of difficult to parse data at great expense for decades or even centuries. Of course, work is required to use such data, especially to create files from it that are generally comparable both spatially and temporally (not to mention substantively). Much of this data could assist with research problems, but remains underutilized. With the advent of the National Historical Geographic Information System (NHGIS) and other similar projects, it is now possible to begin to exploit such materials and make progress on important, and unanswered, research questions.[9]

This chapter will begin to work out the relationship between economic and demographic change. It will also demonstrate the valuable utility of using such data sources together. Simply put, this analysis will begin to integrate population and economic data, and make it possible to understand demographic change in the context of economic change, and changing economic conditions in the context of population change. In a sense, the goal is to examine the missing link that ties economics and demographics together using the tools of GIS and spatial analysis.

It is critical to do these analyses in a spatial framework because there is often spatial autocorrelation among the variables. For example, if there is strong population growth and employment growth in Santa Clara County, California (the home of Silicon Valley), then there could also be growth in the other San Francisco Bay area counties. Explicitly using spatial techniques brings in such patterns, while not using spatial techniques may mean relationships, such as those between employment and population, are not properly analysed. Indeed, there are examples of apparent relationships reversing when spatial autocorrelation is taken into account.[10]

The *County Business Patterns* datasets include an extract of data from the Business Register, which includes number of employees, wages paid, industrial classification, and location of each enterprise. The Census updates them yearly. They include data on employment, wages paid, hierarchical industrial classification, and the number of establishments by county. This analysis presents data only from the overall summary for total employment, total wages, and average wages paid by county. However, building on this preliminary work, we plan to use data from various broad classifications, including manufacturing and services. In this way, we will also be able to analyse the decline and rise of various lines of business (at least generally). This chapter constitutes only an overview.[11]

The decennial censuses and the American Community Survey include about 50 questions covering basic demographic profiles and a large number of social characteristics (including migration status, birthplace, education, current occupation, and employment). This analysis includes only total population from the census files, since the basic objective here was to see if it were possible to array data into comparable geographic units for the period under study, and demonstrate if there were basic relationships between the County Business Patterns data and the Census/ACS data.

All the data were at the county level, which for the United States is a region that varies from under 100 people (Loving County, Texas) to about 10 million

(Los Angeles County, California). Though the county is not an ideal unit for spatial analysis because of this variability in size, it is nonetheless a popular choice for researchers since it is often the only easily available geographic unit. For the purposes of this chapter and the ensuing research, if results can be found based upon the county, it is quite likely that such results would hold using finer geographic measures such as tracts or other custom areas, which can be created inside the Census Research Data Center.

Over the decades examined, some county names and boundaries have changed. Thus, to ensure generally comparable counties for this study, the small counties (dubbed independent cities) in Virginia were often combined with the larger county in which they were embedded. New counties, mostly created by splitting older counties, were recombined following the older boundaries. These strategic adjustments made the geographic units largely comparable. Indeed, one of the major objectives of this chapter is to see if building a useful dataset combining demographic and economic data over the period 1970 to the present is possible.

The 1990, 2000, and 2012 County Business Patterns data came from the Census Bureau website (United States Census Bureau, 1990–2012), while the 1970 and 1980 data came from the National Archives (United States Census Bureau, 1970–80). The coding of business types also changed several times during the period under review, but the results presented here are not dependent upon that classification. Crosswalks, which link one version of industrial classifications to another, do exist that make it possible to examine change within the broad grouping of the lines of business activity. Future work will explore such further analyses.

Analyses to be presented

First, this chapter presents data on the distribution of several variables and their change over time. A descriptive spatial analysis will set the stage for a preliminary examination of the relationship between population change and employment change. This will include the Moran's I, which is a basic measure of spatial autocorrelation.[12] It behaves very much like any correlation and takes on the range from 0.0 (no autocorrelation) to 1.0 (complete autocorrelation). Analyses performed using the Local Indicator of Spatial Autocorrelation (LISA)[13] make it possible to see where clusters of either employment change or population change exist. Then, a simple spatial regression analysis will ascertain the relationship of population change on employment change and the relationship of employment change on population change decade by decade.[14] We expected to find a strong relationship between changing employment and changing population. We expected to find a positive, though weaker relationship between population change and change in employment. We will then ascertain the presence and location of any clusters of counties that do not follow the model by mapping residuals and examining where they cluster. This will be done for both the model of population change and the model of employment change. Thus, we can see where more or less population growth (or loss) and employment growth (or loss) than would be expected occurred by analysing residuals and determining the extent to which they cluster spatially. These residual clusters can be mapped for each of the decades being examined.[15]

The materials presented in maps and charts are a concept demonstration. These materials and analyses show the following:

1   Consistent definitions (at least consistent enough) of counties exist to make it possible to look at patterns across counties for each decade, and it is possible to examine differences from year to year.
2   The changes from decade to decade and area to area are generally consistent with what is known about the patterns of change.
3   That spatial structure exists within several of the most important variables, including average wages, employment patterns, and population.

Figure 5.1 shows a map of the **average wage** by county in the United States for 2012. This map makes it plain that average wages showed large variation throughout the country in that year. As is well known, average wages in the United States have not shown a large degree of growth from 1970 through 2012. Indeed, wages plummeted from 1970 to 1980, with the recession and stagflation resulting from the OPEC oil cartel. Similarly, there has been very little gain in average wages since 1990, in part due to the fallout from the 2007 financial crisis with effects reaching well into 2011. Using inflation adjustments for average wages shows that there has been only about an 8 per cent gain in average wage between 1970 and 2012, and that the average wages were lower in 1980 than in 1970. Table 5.1 presents the Moran's I for the average wages. The results show that for every decade there were large degrees of spatial autocorrelation in the distribution of average wages. This is true despite the fact that the county is not a particularly homogeneous geographical unit, either in urban or rural areas, and that it varies greatly by state. At the same time, if the average wage in a county were higher than that elsewhere, it might lead individuals and families to migrate for economic opportunities. The size of the labour force in a given county could also have an effect on the results.

Figures 5.2 through 5.9 examine the change in average wages by county from decade to decade, while Table 5.2 presents Moran's I for each decade. The first map for each decade displays the average wage change, while the second presents the manner in which such changes cluster by county using a local Moran's I clustering analysis (often called a LISA or Local Indicator of Spatial Autocorrelation). As the findings show, average wages declined between 1970 and 1980, and roughly one-fifth of all counties were in a cluster where wages declined including the Northeast,

Table 5.1 Moran's I for average wage by county in the United States for selected years 1970 through 2012 based on County Business Patterns.

Year	Moran's I
1970	0.43
1980	0.37
1990	0.38
2000	0.39
2012	0.32

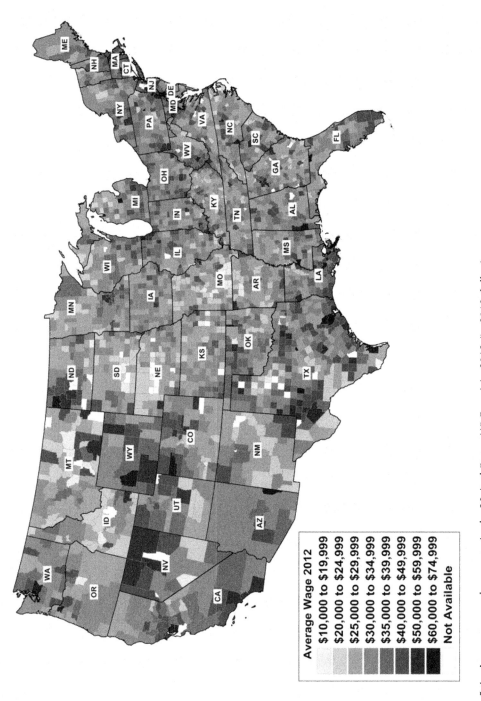

Figure 5.1 Average wages by county in the United States (48 States) in 2012 (in 2012 dollars).

Average Wage 2012
- $10,000 to $19,999
- $20,000 to $24,999
- $25,000 to $29,999
- $30,000 to $34,999
- $35,000 to $39,999
- $40,000 to $49,999
- $50,000 to $59,999
- $60,000 to $74,999
- Not Available

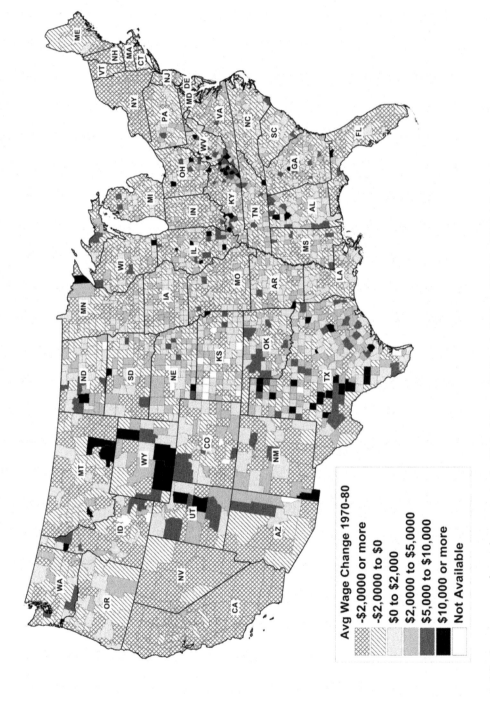

Figure 5.2 Average wage change by county in the United States (48 States), 1970 to 1980 (in 2012 dollars).

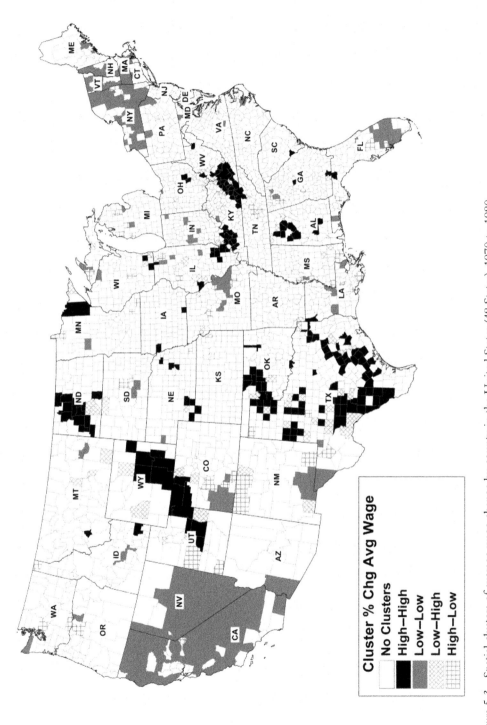

Figure 5.3 Spatial clusters of average wage change by county in the United States (48 States), 1970 to 1980.

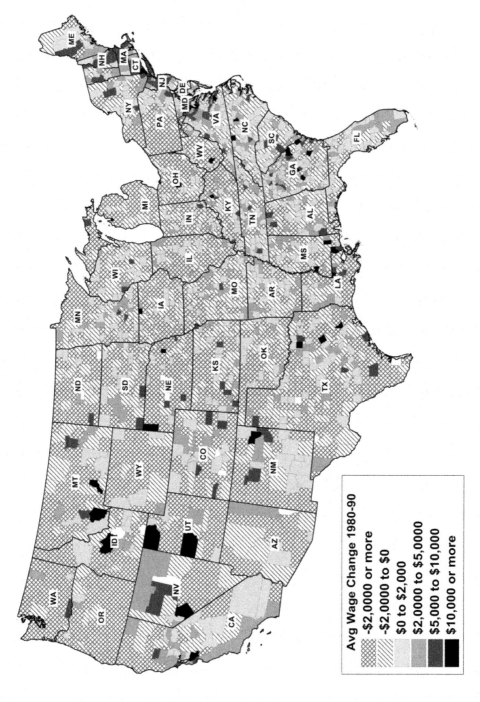

Figure 5.4 Average wage change by county in the United States (48 States), 1980 to 1990 (in 2012 dollars).

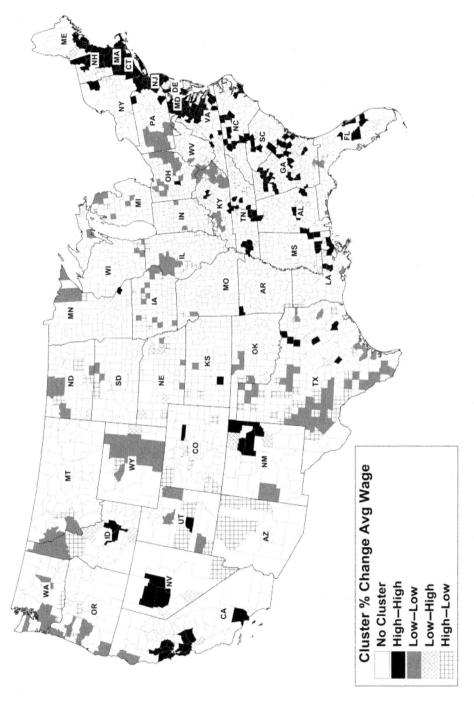

Figure 5.5   Spatial clusters of average wage change by county in the United States (48 States), 1980 to 1990.

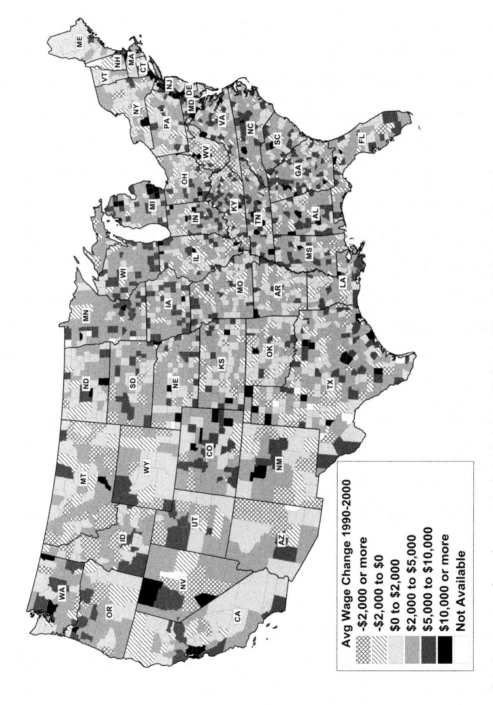

Figure 5.6 Average wage change by county in the United States (48 States), 1990 to 2000 (in 2012 dollars).

Avg Wage Change 1990-2000

-$2,000 or more
-$2,000 to $0
$0 to $2,000
$2,000 to $5,000
$5,000 to $10,000
$10,000 or more
Not Available

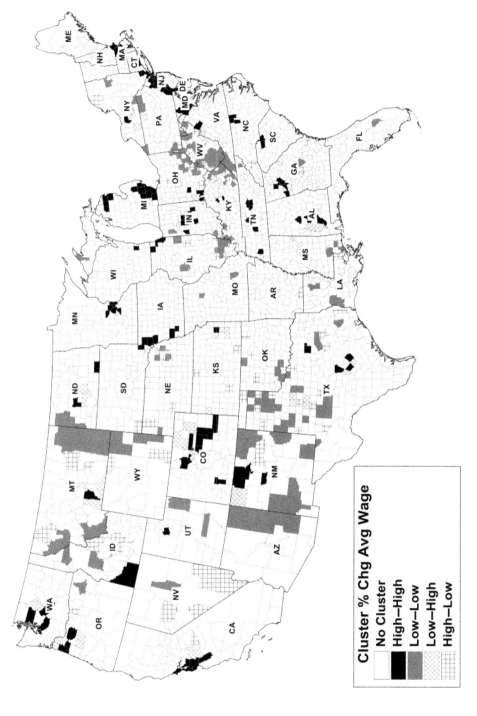

Figure 5.7   Spatial clusters of average wage change by county in the United States (48 States), 1990 to 2000.

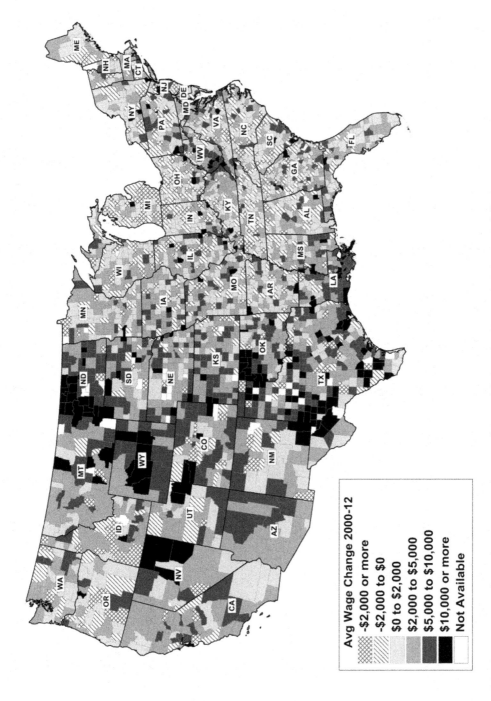

Figure 5.8 Average wage change by county in the United States (48 States), 2000 to 2012 (in 2012 dollars).

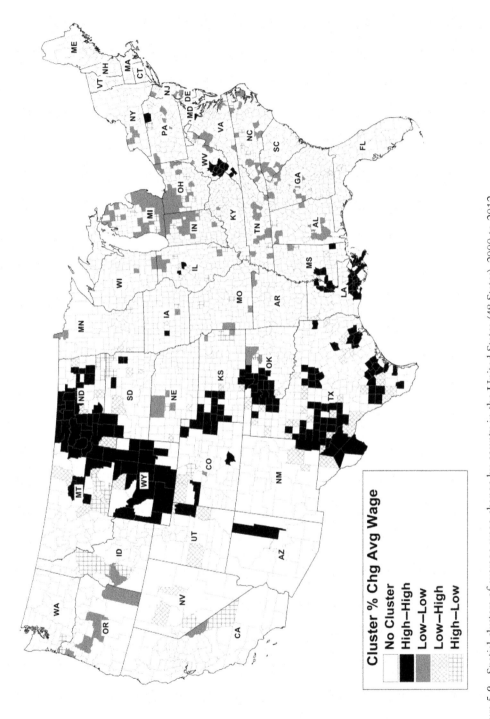

Figure 5.9 Spatial clusters of average wage change by county in the United States (48 States), 2000 to 2012.

Table 5.2 Moran's I for percentage change in various variables by county in the United
States for selected years 1970 through 2012 based on County Business Patterns.

	1970–1980	*1980–1990*	*1990–2000*	*2000–2012*
% Change in Population	0.30	0.41	0.36	0.31
% Change in Average Wage	0.13	0.19	0.12	0.21
% Change in Employment	0.17	0.30	0.16	0.19

the West (including California), an area in Central Florida, and an area around
St. Louis. Wage increases occurred in areas including Texas, Wyoming, Colorado,
and Utah. Of course, some of these areas are centres of oil and gas extraction, which
grew rapidly during the period dominated by the petroleum cartel formed by OPEC.
The figures and table illustrate further decline in wages for 1980 to 1990, but the
patterns are different. The Northeast (especially near the cities) and California cities
gain, while there are clusters of decline in many other parts of the United States. The
internet boom and the explosion of the finance sector and the Wall Street boom
marked the 1990 to 2000 decade. The areas of Silicon Valley, around Denver, and
throughout the New Jersey-New York-Connecticut metro, where the tech, finance,
and (to some extent) pharmaceutical industries are dominant, showed gains, as did
some other areas. At the same time, an area of Kentucky, Ohio, and Western Pennsylvania showed decline, as did some of Texas and some of the upper West.

The twelve years from 2000 through 2012 showed clusters of relative wage gains
in Texas, Wyoming, Montana, Western North Dakota, and Oklahoma. At the same
time, the county including Detroit (Wayne) and other areas including so-called Rust
Belt cities in Ohio, Michigan, and Indiana showed clusters of declines in wages.
Understanding what happened will require more information about the businesses
located in these various areas, but the increase in natural gas and oil drilling is likely
one factor, while the continued collapse of manufacturing in some areas is another.

The change in wages still shows a spatial structure when one examines the Moran's I
in Table 5.2. Though the spatial structures exhibited by the LISA clusters can be suggestive of large areas of similar patterns, the large variation in both density and size of counties means that some of the clusters may not actually affect that many employees, and so,
though statistically and spatially correct, may not be indicative of general patterns.

Maps of the change in overall employment for each decade are displayed in
Figures 5.10 through 5.17. These include a map showing change in employment for
each decade, followed by a map demonstrating how the percentage change is clustered. The period from 1970 to 1980 shows increasing employment but decreasing
average wages. It was during this period that women began to increase their labour
force participation substantially. Figure 5.11 shows clear patterns of increase in the
West, Florida, and Texas, as well as a few other areas. Meanwhile, Western New York
declined. From 1980 to 1990, employment did not increase at the same pace it did
in the earlier decade. Here, relative declines appear in the inter-mountain West and
Texas, and increases in Florida and California, and some other areas, including near

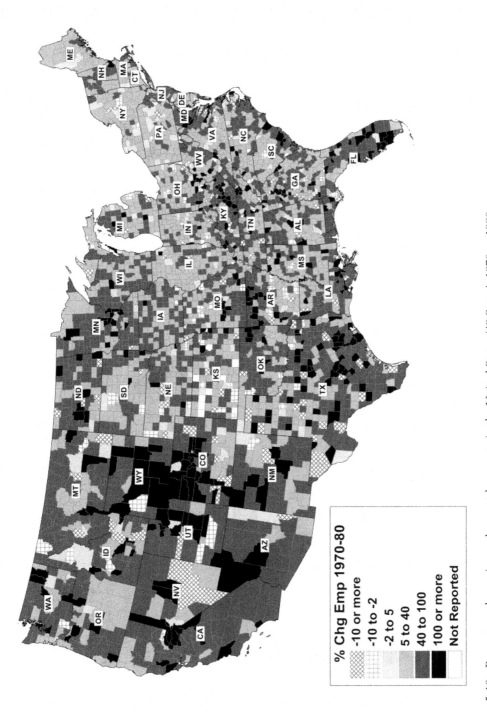

Figure 5.10 Percentage change in employment by county in the United States (48 States), 1970 to 1980.

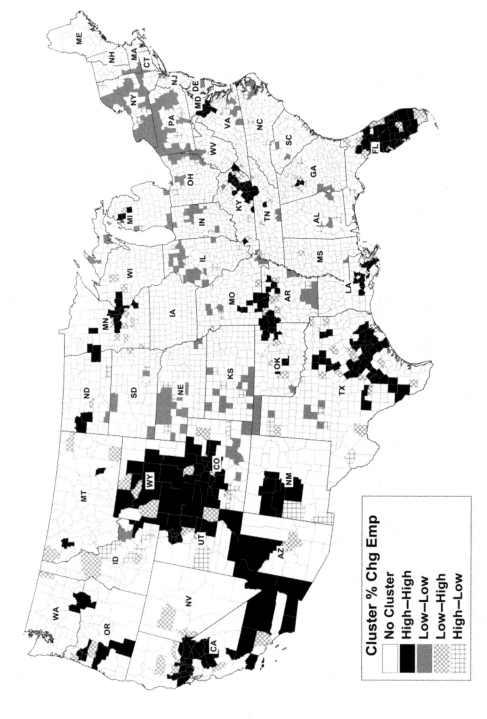

Figure 5.11 Spatial clusters of percentage change in employment by county in the United States (48 States), 1970 to 1980.

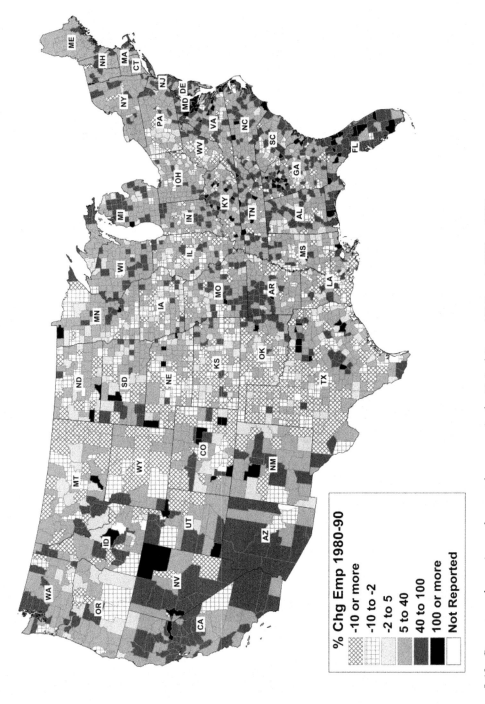

Figure 5.12 Percentage change in employment by county in the United States (48 States), 1980 to 1990.

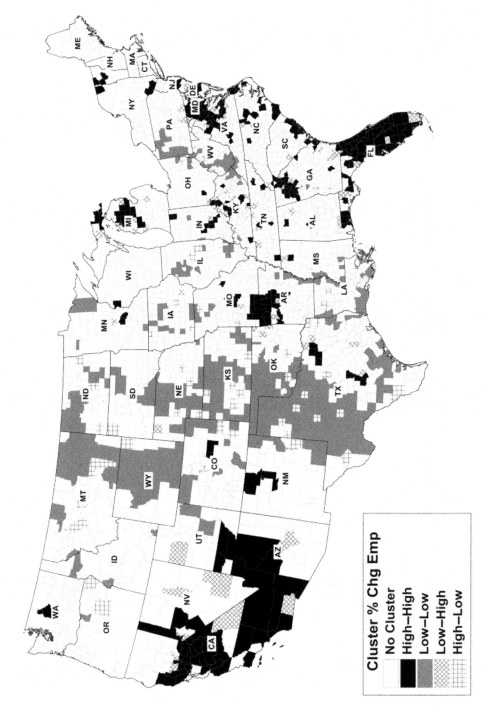

Figure 5.13 Spatial clusters of percentage change in employment by county in the United States (48 States), 1980 to 1990.

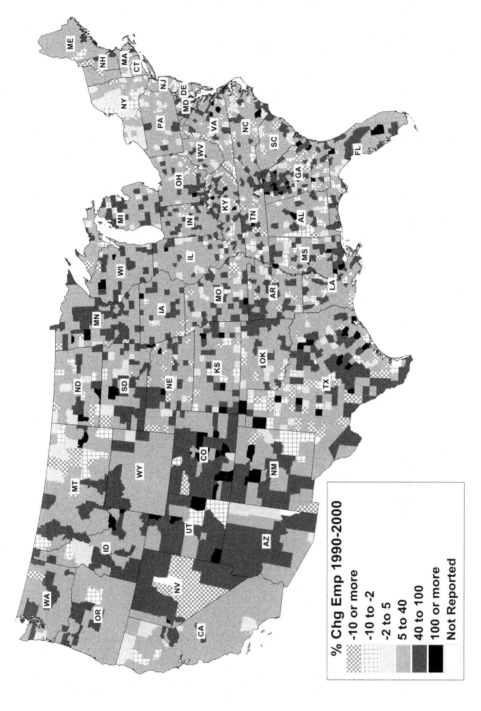

Figure 5.14 Percentage change in employment by county in the United States (48 States), 1990 to 2000.

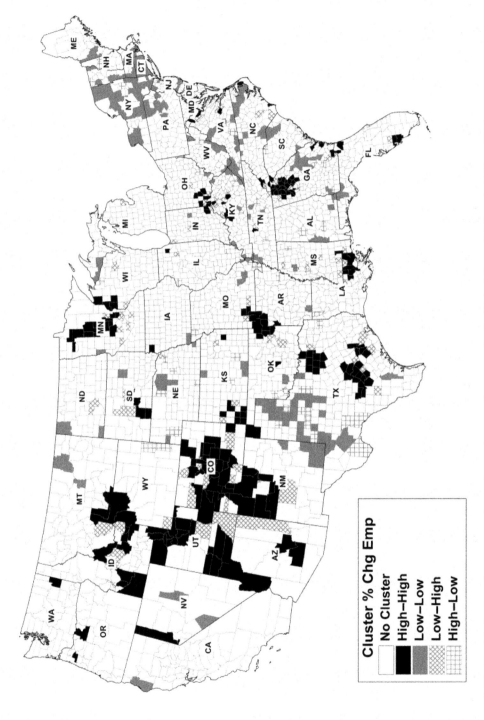

Figure 5.15 Spatial clusters of percentage change in employment by county in the United States (48 States), 1990 to 2000.

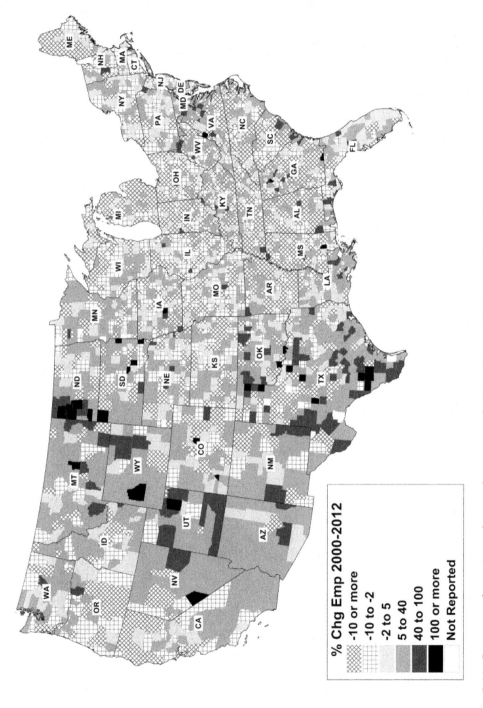

Figure 5.16 Percentage change in employment by county in the United States (48 States), 2000 to 2012.

Legend:

% Chg Emp 2000-2012
- -10 or more
- -10 to -2
- -2 to 5
- 5 to 40
- 40 to 100
- 100 or more
- Not Reported

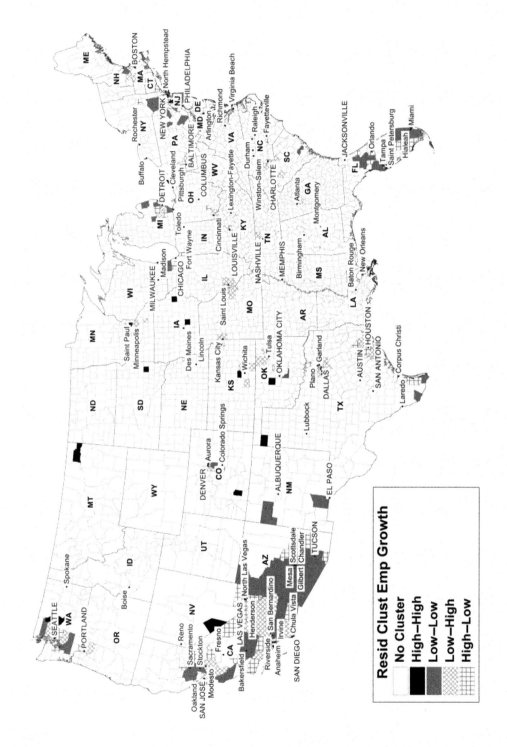

Figure 5.17 Spatial clusters of percentage change in employment by county in the United States (48 States), 2000 to 2012.

Washington, DC. Employment does increase in the period from 1990 to 2000, especially in the inter-mountain West, but not in the Northeast or around the New York City metropolitan area. The final decade also shows some clustering of growth and decline, with growth once again in the Southwest, parts of Texas, and the inter-mountain west. The Moran's I show a large spatial effect in the percentage change in employment from the first three decades, but less so for 2000 to 2012. The change in population is also very strongly spatially structured. Similar patterns exist for population growth, which are not shown here, but the general relationships are presented in Table 5.2.

The relationship between population change and employment change

Analyses for each of the four decades assess the relationship between population growth and employment growth. These used very simple spatial regression models. The dependent variables (actually response variables) for each decade were the total growth in population and the total growth in employment since the first year in the decade. In this way, we ran eight models: one for each decade of interest for each of our two variables of interest. The model included average wage at the beginning of the decade, population and employment at the beginning of the decade, and the change in the average wage. The model predicting employment included the change in population during the decade. The model predicting population included the change in employment. All of the models had a measure of spatial autocorrelations, and ran the appropriate spatial regression, either the lag model or the error model.[16]

Table 5.3 reports a reduced form of the model for each decade, eliminating the spatial term and constant. All the parameters can be interpreted in terms of the number of additional persons based upon a change of one of the various variables. The first models indicate that every increase of one employed person leads to a population increase of 1.329 more persons in that county for the decade 1970 to 1980, while a one-person increase in the population leads to a 0.511 increase in the number employed. Average wages and change of wages are based upon dollars (adjusted for inflation) while population and employment are all based upon either persons or persons employed. The cluster maps (Figure 5.18 and 5.19) of the employment change residuals and population change residuals show that more growth occurred in areas of California, Florida, and some of the Northeast than would have been expected, and some areas of low growth are located near areas of high growth. Meanwhile, some Rust Belt areas experienced lower than expected employment growth. This was during a period of relative decline of wages, and the recession and stagflation brought on by the 1973 oil embargo.

Table 5.3, panel B, shows the patterns for 1980 and 1990. The only strong and positive variable found to lead to increased population growth is increasing employment. However, wages or increased wages have substantial negative relationships to employment. By contrast, they do have a positive impact on population growth. Population growth is higher than expected in clusters in California, Florida, Texas, Seattle, and a few other areas. It is lower than expected in parts of the Northeast and some of the Rust Belt. Once again, several of those areas experienced lower than expected employment growth, while areas in the Northeast experienced

Table 5.3 Regression parameter for decade-by-decade regressions for change in employment and change in population.

A.	Change 1970 to 1980	
	Change in Population	Change in Employment
Change in Employment	1.329	NA
Change in Population	NA	0.511
Average Wage	0.131	−0.032
Change in Wage	−0.136	0.114
Population	−0.121	0.099
Employment	0.149	−0.120

B.	Change 1980 to 1990	
	Change in Population	Change in Employment
Change in Employment	1.422	NA
Change in Population	NA	0.366
Average Wage	−0.534	0.230
Change in Wage	−0.705	0.441
Population	0.020	0.020
Employment	-0.069	0.034

C.	Change 1990 to 2000	
	Change in Population	Change in Employment
Change in Employment	1.162	NA
Change in Population	NA	0.528
Average Wage	−0.401	0.321
Change in Wage	−0.414	0.457
Population	0.113	−0.057
Employment	−0.165	0.110

D.	Change 2000 to 2012	
	Change in Population	Change in Employment
Change in Employment	1.969	NA
Change in Population	NA	0.310
Average Wage	0.141	0.036
Change in Wage	−0.216	0.153
Population	0.031	0.001
Employment	0.151	−0.086

employment growth beyond what would be expected. Figures 5.20 and 5.21 show these patterns.

Table 5.3, panel C, makes it plain that from 1990 to 2000, change in employment fuels population growth, and that most other effects are quite modest or negative. Indeed, average wages and change in average wages both have a negative relationship to population change. At the same time, the strongest variable for change in employment is change in population. However, in 1990, wages and change in average wages relate positively to change in employment.

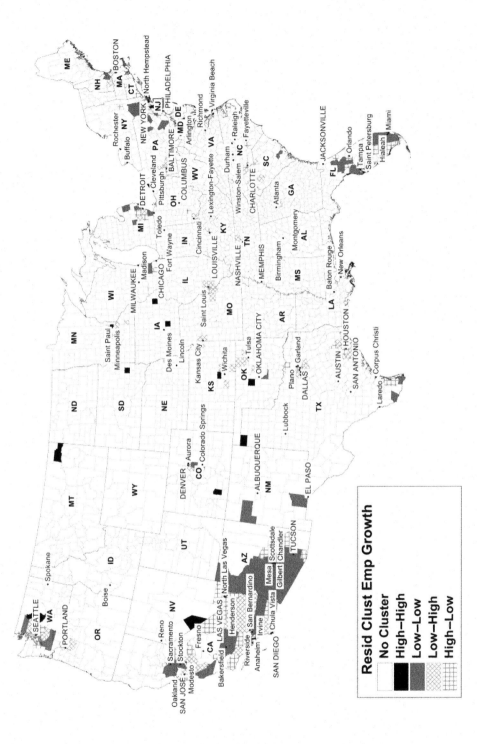

Figure 5.18 Spatial clusters of residuals of regression model of change in employment by county in the United States (48 States), 1970 to 1980.

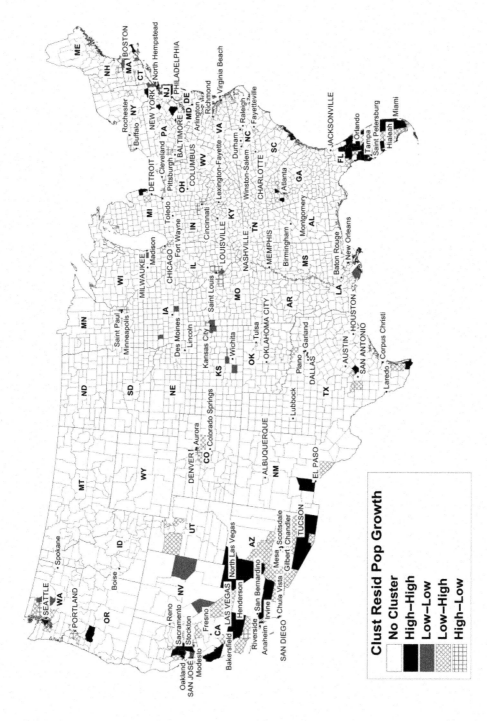

Figure 5.19 Spatial clusters of residuals of regression model of change in population by county in the United States (48 States), 1970 to 1980.

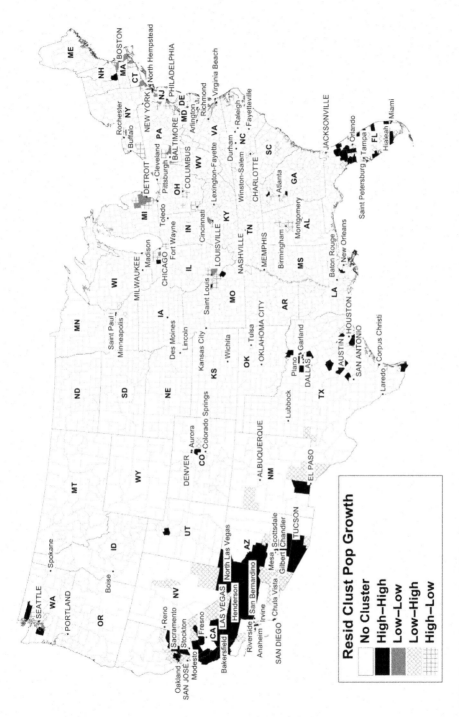

Figure 5.20 Spatial clusters of residuals of regression model of change in employment by county in the United States (48 States), 1980 to 1990.

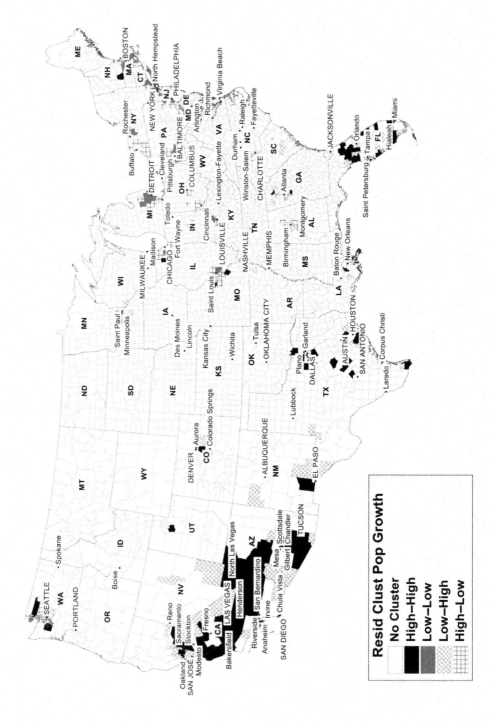

Figure 5.21 Spatial clusters of residuals of regression model of change in population by county in the United States (48 States), 1980 to 1990.

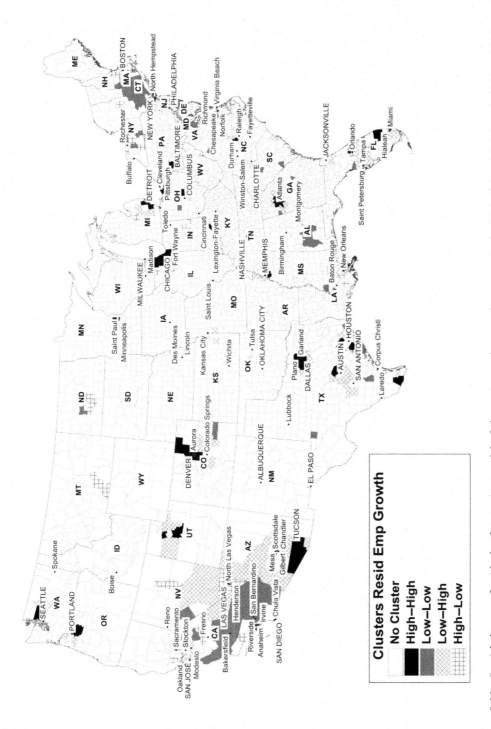

Figure 5.22 Spatial clusters of residuals of regression model of change in employment by county in the United States (48 States), 1990 to 2000.

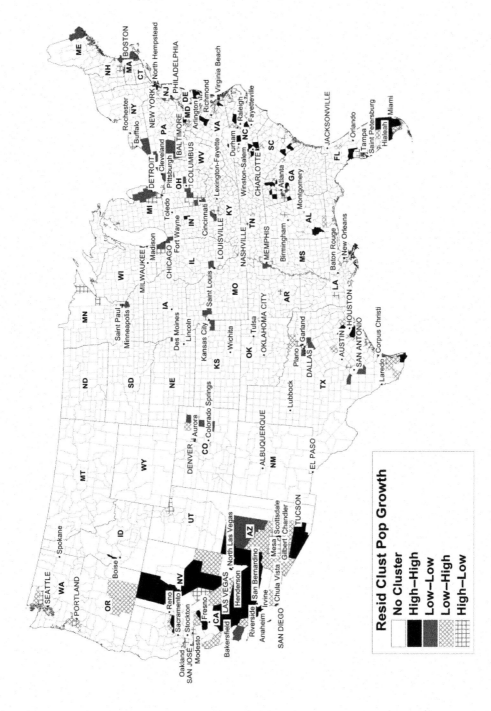

Figure 5.23 Spatial clusters of residuals of regression model of change in population by county in the United States (48 States), 1990 to 2000.

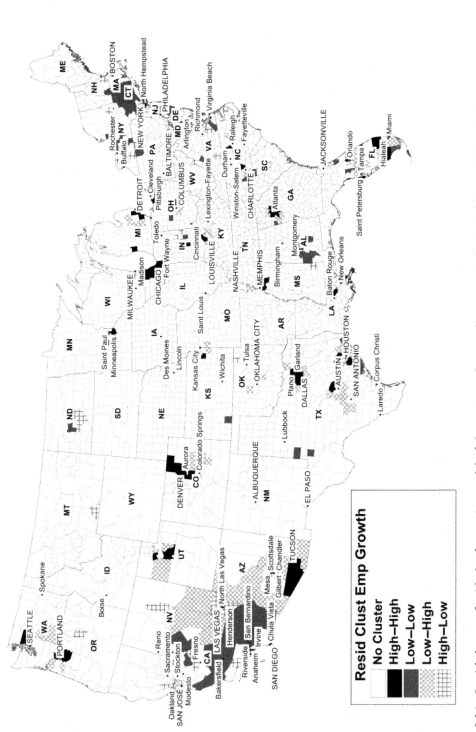

Figure 5.24 Spatial clusters of residuals of regression model of change in employment by county in the United States (48 States), 2000 to 2012.

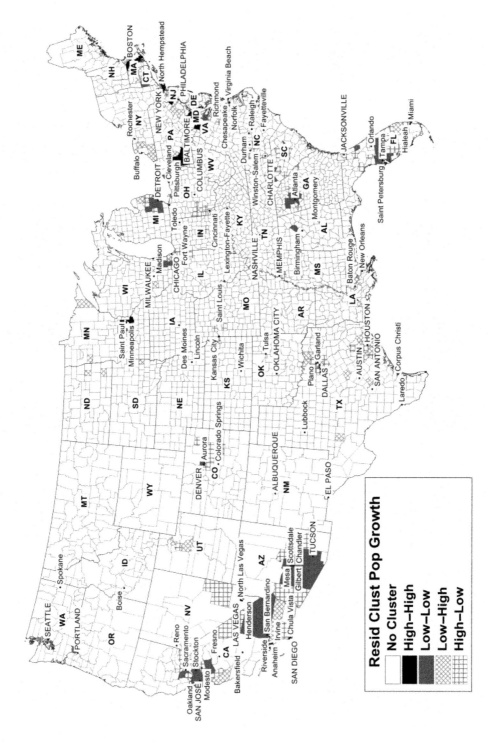

Figure 5.25 Spatial clusters of residuals of regression model of change in population by county in the United States (48 States), 2000 to 2012.

Clusters of less than expected population growth and employment growth are evident in California, the Northeast, and Alabama (see Figures 5.22 and 5.23). Some other areas do have higher than expected growth, including areas around Dallas, Seattle, and Portland.

For the decade from 2000 to 2012, employment has by far the strongest relationship to population growth; the other variables have very small effects. At the same time, few variables have much relation to change in employment (see Table 5.3, panel D). The areas with residual clusters related to population growth have some mixed areas or lower than expected change.

These include California, Connecticut, parts of Florida, and elsewhere (see Figure 5.24). Those clusters related to employment are for the most part in or near similar locations. However, Denver, Seattle, outside of Cleveland, Dallas, Salt Lake City, Atlanta, and a few other exceptions exhibit strong employment growth (see Figure 5.25).

Summary

This first preliminary analysis using the County Business Patterns, Census, and ACS data yields four conclusions.

1   It is possible to develop datasets that can shed light on the relationship between economic growth, employment, and population. When using a finer grained classification, it should be possible to move from simple characterizations of the relationship of employment growth on population to an analysis that contextualizes it based upon specific industries.
2   It is plain that strong spatial relationships exist within the variables of interest, including population and employment.
3   The overall models clearly indicate that at least a large fraction of population change is related to employment change. Consideration of the various components of population change could reveal that this relationship is even stronger. However, this analysis suggests that a main driver of population growth is economic growth, which leads to employment.
4   Finally, it seems obvious that, beyond observing and analysing the main effects, spatial approaches can help formulate better models and shed light on areas where the models do not work as well.

In short, applying spatial approaches to the growth of population and employment is a fruitful research area. It both clarifies patterns, and allows better modelling of phenomena by taking in the spatial structure of relationships. Using the data available in the US Census Research Data Centers will make it possible to develop such analyses more precisely with better geographic information both for the population and for businesses. This will make the modelling and the conclusions much more powerful.

Conclusion

Beyond the specific set of problems that this chapter addresses, the reader should see that the use of spatial approaches with appropriate data could significantly improve the understanding of important social phenomena of change and development. This analysis offers one important example of how GIS with spatial statistical methods can shed new light on age-old problems that have not been systematically addressed, both for lack of appropriate data arrayed spatially and for lack of proper methods to examine and model those problems. Here the subject is the effect of economic activity on the changing population, and vice versa. However, there are many other fruitful topics for the application of these methods. As more and more data become available to do this work, it will be possible to understand better the underpinnings of a variety of historical changes in the economic, social, political, and even the cultural realm. Planned further work should make this even more apparent. Nonetheless, the fact remains, bringing in location and spatial analytic methods leads to a better understanding of the interplay of various factors, and can be revealing. In short, the use of geographic data and spatial analysis techniques greatly aids in understanding the developments examined here.

Notes

1 We acknowledge the support of the National Science Foundation for this work: #0647902 Collaborative Research: The National Historical Geographic Information System; #0919993 Creating and Disseminating Tools to Teach with Demographic Data Maps and Materials; #9950369 Mapping and Exploring New York City Change, 1905-2000: A Set of Interactive Web Based Tools; #0226279 Collaborative Research: A Digital Library Collection for Visually Exploring United States Demographic and Social Change; #1248052 INSPIRE: Studying and Promoting Quantitative and Spatial Reasoning with Complex Visual Data Across School, Museum, and Web-Media Contexts; #0088657 Collaborative Research--Visualizing and Exploring United States Urban and Rural Social Change, 1790-2000: Interactive Multimedia and Web Based Tools; #0088704 Collaborative Research – Visualizing and Exploring United States Urban and Rural Social Change, 1790-2000 – Interactive Multimedia and Web Based Tools; and #0618456 Collaborative Research – Creating Exemplary Curricula and Supporting Faculty Development in Using Social Explorer to Teach with Demographic Data Maps.

2 It should also be noted that despite extensive search in the literature, except for some very complex modelling in local areas, I could find no published or working paper literature that focused on the spatial structure at the level discussed here.

3 The American Community Survey (Five-Year File for 2008–2012) data used and the Census Data from 1970, 1980, 1990, and 2000 were downloaded from Social Explorer (www.socialexplorer.com). Full documentation from the Census Bureau is presented there.

4 A. A. Beveridge, 'Commonalities and Contrasts in the Development of Major United States Urban Areas: A Spatial and Temporal Analysis from 1910 to 2000', in M. P. Guttman, G. D. Deane, E. R. Merchant, and K. M. Sylvester (eds), *Navigating Time and Space in Population Studies*, Amsterdam: Springer for the International Union for the Scientific Study of Population, 2011, 185–216. A. A. Beveridge and S. J. Beveridge, 'The Big Picture: Demographic and Other Changes', in D. Halle and A. A. Beveridge (eds), *New York and Los Angeles: The Uncertain Future*, New York, NY: Oxford University Press, 2013, pp. 33–78. A. A. Beveridge, H. David, T. Edward and B. L. Dufault, 'Residential Diversity and Division: Separation and Segregation among Whites, Blacks, Hispanics, Asians, Affluent and Poor', in H. David and A. A. Beveridge (eds), *New York and Los Angeles: The Uncertain Future*, New York: Oxford University Press, 2013, 310–42. A. A. Beveridge,

'The Development and Persistence of Racial Segregation in United States Urban Areas: 1880 to 2010', in I. Gregory and A. Geddes (eds), *Towards Spatial Humanities: Historical GIS and Spatial History*, Bloomington, IN: Indiana University Press, 2014, 35–61.

5 The economic division of the Census Bureau uses the county vintages that are current when the last economic census was taken, while the geography division updates counties yearly, and the population division uses those vintages. Though not a major problem, this has the effect of making the counties not exactly comparable. Furthermore, the economic division eschews adjustment for inflation, while the population division does adjust for inflation. In short, two massive data collections both related to the same underlying areas are not truly comparable. The analysis presented here, which is really a first step in trying to analyse the relationship between employment and population growth, apparently was not contemplated by the Census Bureau, and the data to conduct it must be modified in many ways before analysis can begin.

6 See, for one example, F. C. Billari, 'Integrating Macro- and Micro-Level Approaches in the Explanation of Population Change', *Population Studies: A Journal of Demography* 69 (supp1), 2015, S11–S20.

7 The economic division of the Census Bureau maintains a business register based upon filings from businesses of social security taxes. This serves as the universe of businesses, which is used for the Economic Census, conducted every five years, and various economic surveys.

8 The Census Research Data Centers allow researchers to use materials much closer to the original census records for analyses, and are the equivalent of having sworn Census Bureau security status. See www.census.gov/fsrdc.

9 It should be noted that the counties from the NHGIS (www.NHGIS.org) were used for this project, along with the data collected by the Census Bureau. Until 1990, the Bureau's maps were paper, and it took an outside-funded project to create comparable electronic boundary files stretching back to 1790 (the beginning of the United States and the first decennial census). Once such files existed, analyses that could not have been contemplated when the data were first collected become possible. The recent donation by Ancestry.com and the Church of the Latter-day Saints of the complete census records spanning the entire period from 1790 through 1940 (with the exception of 1890, which were destroyed in a fire) means that many projects will be possible using both individual- and aggregate-level data in the future. Not only do these data have enough geography to locate them by county, but also enumeration districts are available in many cases and have been mapped for some of the years for some of the urban areas. Indeed, I have used these for other work in the past. See Beveridge in the References.

10 For a seminal example see: P. R. Voss, D. D. Long, R. B. Hammer, and S. Friedman. 'County Child Poverty Rates in the US: A Spatial Regression Approach', *Population Research and Policy Review* 25(4), 2006, 369–91.

11 Going beyond broad classifications will be difficult due to the many changes that have occurred in the industrial classifications used from the addition of new types to the subdividing of existing ones. Eventually, work will include the so-called crosswalks that make it possible to make broadly comparable such classifications (currently there are over 3,000 industrial classifications). For the time being, only major classifications will be used. Here we used total employment and average wages for all workers. However, in the future it will be possible to work at a more fine-grained level.

12 For a discussion of the Moran's I, a very good place to start is the GeoDa workbook, which was developed by Luc Anselin and his colleagues: L. Anselin, *Exploring Spatial Data with GeoDa™: A Workbook, Revised Version*, Champaign, IL: Spatial Analysis Laboratory, Department of Geography, University of Illinois, 2005. It and other materials on spatial

analysis are now available at http://geodacenter.github.io/index.html. The GeoDa Center, originally at the University of Illinois, then at Arizona State University, has recently moved to the University of Chicago https://spatial.chicago.edu.

13 See Anselin, *Exploring Spatial Data*, for a discussion of LISA and the identification of clusters. Using such clusters makes it possible to identify areas that are either high or low in a particular variable, where these information clusters are, and how various areas that are either high or low are related. It should be noted that only a few possible spatial methods have been used to understand how change in population and change in employment may be related and clustered for the four decades under review for this preliminary analysis. The goal here really is descriptive.

14 For all of the analyses presented, GeoDa was used, which is a package developed by Luc Anselin, *Exploring Spatial Data*. It provides the ability to create spatial weights, and compute Moran's I, cluster indices for LISA, and spatial regression. For this preliminary analysis, a very simple approach was taken to see the extent to which changes in employment are associated with changes in population and how changes in population are associated with changes in employment. In further work with more years from the County Business Patterns and estimated population data (or data from the ACS) that gives better information from non-Census years, it will be possible to look at models more deeply at a time series level. Here, the basic effort is to see if a relationship exists that requires further elaboration. As the results show, there are strong relationships.

15 It should be emphasized that the diversity of county size (in both area and population) will make whatever relationships we find weaker than they would otherwise be if more homogeneous spatial units were used. Furthermore, such county diversity might bias the findings of the spatial modelling and the clustering in unknown ways.

16 See Anselin, *Exploring Spatial Data*, 165–210, for discussion of Lag and Error models in spatial regression.

References

L. Anselin, *Exploring Spatial Data with GeoDa™: A Workbook, Revised Version*, Champaign, IL: Spatial Analysis Laboratory, Department of Geography, University of Illinois, 2005.

A. A. Beveridge, 'Commonalities and Contrasts in the Development of Major United States Urban Areas: A Spatial and Temporal Analysis from 1910 to 2000', in M. P. Guttmann, G. D. Deane, E. R. Merchant, and K. M. Sylvester (eds), *Navigating Time and Space in Population Studies*, Amsterdam: Springer for the International Union for the Scientific Study of Population, 2011, 185–216.

A. Beveridge, and S.J. Beveridge, 'The Big Picture: Demographic and Other Changes', in H. David and A.A. Beveridge (eds), *New York and Los Angeles: The Uncertain Future*, New York: Oxford University Press, 2013, 33–78.

A. A. Beveridge, D. Halle, Ed. Telles, and B. Leavenworth Default, 'Residential Diversity and Division: Separation and Segregation among Whites, Blacks, Hispanics, Asians, Affluent and Poor', in D.Halle and A. A. Beveridge (eds), *New York and Los Angeles: The Uncertain Future*, New York: Oxford University Press, 2013, 310–342.

A. A. Beveridge, 'The Development and Persistence of Racial Segregation in United States Urban Areas: 1880 to 2010', in: I. Gregory and A. Geddes (eds), *Towards Spatial Humanities: Historical GIS and Spatial History*, Bloomington, IN: Indiana University Press, 2014, 35–61.

F. C. Billari, 'Integrating Macro- and Micro-Level Approaches in the Explanation of Population Change', *Population Studies: A Journal of Demography* 69 (supp 1), 2015, S11–S20.

Social Explorer, Files for American Community Survey and Long Form Census Data, 2007–16. Data and documentation available at www.socialexplorer.com.

United States Census Bureau, *County Business Patterns Data*, 1990–2012. Online. Available HTTP: www.census.gov/econ/cbp/historical.htm> (accessed April 2014).

United States Census Bureau, *County Business Patterns Data*, National Archives Catalog, 1970–80. Online. Available HTTP: https://catalog.archives.gov/search?q=*:*&rows=20& offset=0&tabType=all&facet=true&facet.fields=oldScope,level,materialsType,fileFormat, locationIds,dateRangeFacet&highlight=true&f.parentNaId=613576&f.level= fileUnit&sort=naIdSort%20asc (accessed April 2014).

Voss, P. R., D. D. Long, R. B. Hammer, and S. Friedman, 'County Child Poverty Rates in the US: A Spatial Regression Approach', *Population Research and Policy Review* 25(4), 2006, 369–91.

PART II

Spatial economic history

INTRODUCTION TO PART II

Don DeBats, Ian Gregory, and Don Lafreniere

Historical GIS impacted the wider scholarly world at the start of this century with the publication of exploratory volumes in four consecutive years: 2000, 2001, 2002, and 2003.[1] Along with urban history, economic history was an 'early starter' in the adoption of GIS technologies and methodologies, with an emphasis more on the former (visualization) than the latter (measurement). This early and enthusiastic take-up stemmed from the fact that several economic historians, especially those associated with the transportation revolution, were already pushing on the mapping front prior to the arrival of GIS, wrestling with vector plotters and trying to calculate distances and proximities. The arrival of GIS was the answer they had long sought.

Within spatial economic history, the impact of railroads on regional economic growth became an immediate and important theme, moving a traditional area of inquiry initially defined by George Taylor's *Transportation Revolution,* into (quite literally) a new space.[2] GIS made the analysis of locational effects of railroad development far easier: the field boomed.[3] *Social Science History* devoted a section to the transportation theme in 2010 as did the *Journal of Interdisciplinary History* with a special issue in 2011.[4]

Spatial economic history also quickly developed the interdisciplinary perspective so characteristic of analyses based on GIS, demonstrating the wide-ranging consequences of economic change over a wide societal span including specific impacts on population growth, urbanization, and on national as well as regional agricultural development. HGIS also proved adept at explaining the spatial and temporal dimensions of technological change.[5]

The five chapters in this section continue and expand several of these themes. Anne Knowles reflects on the impact and utility of GIS in her efforts to master the evolution of the US iron industry and to explain with new data why American iron producers lagged behind their British competitors in adopting coal-fired refining technology, a longstanding issue in the field. GIS again provided the evidence for a new and powerful explanatory variable: the very different geographical circumstances of the iron industry in the United States compared to Britain in terms of access to mineral resources and markets. The result is a new story of innovation and of scholarly discovery.

Also using GIS to examine spatial change over time are two chapters on the transportation revolution. Focusing on the US railroad industry at its height in the early nineteenth century, Richard Healey addresses the importance of careful database construction to enable GIS to advance beyond providing answers to old questions. He moves forward to the development of new questions (and answers) covering such critical issues as the efficacy of management strategies in gaining control of territories to enhance a company's long-term economic success. GIS technologies are central to his creation of a general-purpose HGIS of the railroad network in the American Manufacturing Belt, the utility of which is demonstrated by a case study of the leasing arrangements of the Pennsylvania Railroad in the 1870s in pursuit of a spatial control strategy.

Following a similar strategy of comprehensive database design, but across transportation sectors, Jeremy Atack uses GIS to trace the evolution and spatial distribution of competing (and complementary) modes of transportation across the US prior to WWI. The result is a series of databases that locate, with high levels of spatial accuracy, canal, steamboat, and rail networks across the US from first use to 1911. Much of this transportation network has since disappeared and been lost, including 100,000 miles of railroad track.[6] The painstaking restoration of past water and rail routes provides a new research resource, characterized by a high level of geographic accuracy, for understanding economic change in the nineteenth century and the often central role played by transportation infrastructure.

The final two chapters explore wealth at the two ends of that spectrum. Douglas Brown uses GIS to map at the local level the distribution of poor relief across Wales in the mid-nineteenth century. As in Anne Knowles' project, this use of GIS reveals a new explanation for a long recognized feature: Brown demonstrates with a case study how the uneven distribution of assistance in the Welsh workhouses was associated with the intersection between locally controlled relief expenditure and the locally supplied provisions of goods and services. Workhouses were sizeable local institutions, whose residents (on average 154 residents in 1851) consumed high levels of local products and services; the result is a new measure of the local social networks revealed by and utilized in the process of provisioning the local workhouse.

Dimitris Ballas and Dany Dorling use small area analysis to locate where people are very poor (core poor) and where there are concentrations of the very wealthy (exclusively wealthy) in Manchester, in the UK, and worldwide, now and over long spans of time. Their work allows these extremes to be visualized and trends estimated: Britain and Manchester appeared to be headed towards ever greater extremes at the time this data was gathered whereas at a global scale the division between the 'core poor' and the 'exclusively wealthy' appeared finally to be closing.

As all these chapters suggest, GIS and economic history are journeying together: mapping, creating, and understanding the organization and manifestation of space in an ever expanding range of explanatory frameworks.

Notes

1   A. K. Knowles (ed.), 'The Spatial Turn in Social Science History', Special Issue of *Social Science History* 24, 2000; I. Gregory and P. S. Ell (eds), 'Adding a New Dimension to Historical

Research with GIS', Special Issue of *History and Computing* 13, 2001; A. K. Knowles (ed.), *Past Time, Past Places: GIS for History*, Redlands, CA: ESRI Press, 2002; I. N. Gregory, *A Place in History: A Guide to Using GIS in Historical Research*, London: Oxbow, 2003.

2 G. Taylor, *The Transportation Revolution, 1815–1860*, New York: Rinehart & Co., 1951.

3 J. Atack, 'On the Use of Geographic Information Systems in Economic History: The American Transportation Revolution Revised', *Journal of Economic History* 73, 2013, 317–18.

4 'Railways and Political Economy in Britain, France, and the United States, 1840–1950', Special Section of *Social Science History* 34, 2010; J. M. Henneberg (ed.), 'Railways, Population, and Geographical Information Systems', Special Issue of *Journal of Interdisciplinary History* 42, 2011.

5 See e.g. A. K. Knowles and R. G. Healey, 'Geography, Timing, and Technology: A GIS Based Analysis of Pennsylvania's Iron Industry, 1825–1875', *Journal of Economic History* 66, 2006, 608–34.

6 Atack, 'On the Use of Geographical Information Systems', 320.

6

MAPPING THE AMERICAN IRON INDUSTRY

Anne Kelly Knowles

My study of the antebellum US iron industry, *Mastering Iron*,[1] would have been unthinkable without GIS. Of the geographic methods available when I began the project in 1995, only iterative mapping with GIS could unlock the historical and geographical meaning immured in my chief source, a detailed directory of iron works published in 1859. The ability of GIS to answer data-dense research questions in the form of maps supported my inductive visual approach to historical research.[2] For me, historical research always begins as a map that I want to fill in. I do not mean this metaphorically. When a question piques my interest, the first thing to rise in my mind's eye is a map whose features are indistinct, as if viewed through a fog. The more I learn about the subject, the more clearly I imagine the maps I need to see spatial relationships, compare physical and social conditions, trace movement, or analyse events. Visualizing the geography of history is the chief means I know to discover the extent to which geographical factors may have influenced the past.[3]

When I began research for *Mastering Iron*, Pennsylvania's iron industry was well known and there were a few excellent company histories for antebellum iron works. A handful of book-length studies of the steel industry included significant coverage of the antebellum industry. Historians of steel generally treated iron as a prelude to the main event. They also focused on the Mid-Atlantic region, particularly Pennsylvania, as the productive core of the industry. I wondered whether Pennsylvania's was the only important story and whether it should stand as the era's representative for iron production. Every state in the union had iron works before the Civil War. How could we say we really understood the industry unless someone analysed them all? Given that this would involve hundreds, if not thousands, of sites of production, a national study would have to involve use of GIS to gather and analyse large amounts of information. And because I needed maps to visualize the extent, distribution, patterns of production, and changes over time in the industry, I very much hoped that I would be able to build an historical GIS of antebellum iron.

The main historiographic question I hoped to answer was why American iron producers lagged far behind British competitors until the late 1860s, particularly in the volume of production. At the simplest level, the explanation was obvious. In the late eighteenth century, British inventors and iron masters developed methods to smelt and refine iron using coal rather than charcoal as fuel. Because coal is much harder and burns at a higher heat than charcoal, coal-fired blast furnaces could smelt much more ore in a single 'charge', and so produce much more pig iron, than could charcoal furnaces. Innovations in coal-fired refining technology also led to a leap in the scale of finished iron production. The more complicated question was why American entrepreneurs were slow to implement coal-fired technologies despite knowledge of the new British processes in centres of US iron-making by the early nineteenth century, and the wealth of coal deposits in the United States.

Economic and industrial historians who had studied the antebellum iron industry before me argued that the lag was caused by three broad factors. First, the higher cost of labour in the United States enabled British manufacturers to undercut American prices, which made US firms unwilling to invest in costly new technologies. Tariff legislation twice created periods of protection that stimulated innovation in some places, but when tariffs lapsed, British imports again flooded the American market. Second, the poor or unproven quality of American coal deposits necessitated years of testing and technological adaptation before iron smelted with coal was good enough, or of sufficiently consistent quality, to compete with the established quality of British imports. These arguments mirrored commentary by industry observers in the antebellum period, which similarly focused on the cost of inputs, market prices, and cheap imports. Third, some of my predecessors argued that the hesitance or refusal of many American entrepreneurs to try coal-fired British technologies reflected at least a conservative, and at worst an anti-capitalist, attitude that hindered modernization of the industry. The early adopters of British methods, such as the Lehigh Crane Iron Works and the Bethlehem and Cambria iron companies, all in Pennsylvania, and the Trenton and Burden companies in New Jersey and New York, respectively, were run by forward-thinking iron masters whose businesses anticipated the rise of American steel-making and the corporatization and agglomeration of American industry after the Civil War. This argument was part of a much larger historiographic debate in British, European, and North American cultural and economic history from the 1970s into the 1990s. That debate focused on when, and to what extent, capitalist values and market forces came to dominate social relations in Western societies.[4]

In developing these arguments, scholars gave only passing attention to the geographical circumstances of iron production in Britain and the United States. This seemed to me a crucial oversight. In the heaviest of heavy industries, the many dimensions of distance − distance to resources, distance to markets, cost of available modes of transportation, and access to skilled labour, to name a few − must have figured prominently in the economic and social calculus of risk and in an iron company's chance of turning a profit. I also thought that geographic context was bound to have influenced social relations between labour and management. Histories of a few exceptionally well-documented iron companies give a great deal of attention to this facet of social geography, yet it was almost entirely missing from regional and national studies, which focused on trade, prices, or economic *mentalité*. I wanted to understand the world of iron-making on the ground, company by company, place by place, from workers' and managers' points of view. A deeply situated study could provide a fuller explanation of why the American industry lagged so far behind the

British in the early nineteenth century. An HGIS of the industry would help me contextualize the case studies that I intended to use to examine labour–management relations and to determine why some firms failed and others succeeded in implementing British technologies.

Historical GIS is an excellent method for revealing spatial change over time. It works best when the researcher has longitudinal data from one detailed source, or several linked sources, that are sufficiently consistent over the period of study to support meaningful comparison among various locations and scales of geographical analysis. Census data from Western nations in the nineteenth and twentieth centuries perfectly fit these criteria. While researching Welsh immigration to antebellum Wisconsin and Ohio in my graduate studies, I learned how revealing census data could be, particularly when connected to contemporaneous maps of settlement and land ownership.[5] For the iron industry, I was extremely fortunate to have a superbly suitable source, a book titled *The Iron Manufacturer's Guide to the Furnaces, Forges, and Rolling Mills of the United States* (1859). It became the basis for the HGIS that undergirds much of the geographical analysis in *Mastering Iron*.[6]

An ideal source

J. Peter Lesley, who compiled and wrote *The Iron Manufacturer's Guide*, was a man very much after my own heart – someone who made sense of the world through mapping and the collection of data. Lesley learned geology and surveying as a field assistant with the First Geological Survey of Pennsylvania from 1837 to 1841. In the early 1850s, while conducting surveys for coal companies in the state, he became familiar with the domestic iron industry in its two basic and quite different forms. Lesley greatly admired the big new anthracite-fuelled iron furnaces and large rolling mills that had been built since 1840 along the lower Lehigh, Schuylkill, and Susquehanna rivers. Those companies most nearly replicated the British models that inspired American envy, notably companies in south Wales where coal-fired iron-making technologies had been perfected around the turn of the nineteenth century. Lesley was less impressed by the much smaller and more numerous charcoal-fuelled furnaces, which still provided the majority of high-grade pig iron for American industry, and the rural forges and foundries that met local demand for household wares and agricultural implements.

Lesley was ambitious for the United States to become a self-sufficient industrial nation. He joined leading East Coast iron company owners to form the American Iron Association (AIA) in 1855. Lesley proposed carrying out a survey of all iron companies in the country to determine the state of the American industry and to identify modern firms that other American producers should emulate. Drawing on his experience as a surveyor and cartographer, Lesley planned to include detailed maps of iron works' locations, so that owners could more easily visit and inspect one another's operations. The AIA funded Lesley's exploratory survey. He and two young assistants spent almost three years canvassing the Eastern United States by rail, stage coach, canal barge, and paddle wheeler, on horseback and on foot. *The Iron Manufacturer's Guide* was the result of their efforts. Lesley compiled the information they collected into entries ranging from a single sentence to a dense paragraph, depending on how many questions he and his assistants were able to answer by quiz-zing local informants (see Figure 6.1). He also had several maps produced to show the location of blast furnaces and rolling mills in major iron-making regions.

The most complete entries provide information about a company's geographic location, management, dates of construction and renovation, kinds of equipment and production processes, amount and types of iron produced, and the location and nature of raw materials. Other scholars had mined this information in very limited ways in local or regional studies. Geographers John K. Wright and Kenneth Warren used Lesley's maps to plot the location of blast furnaces and rolling mills for particular regions and the Eastern United States as a whole.[7] No one had comprehensively analysed the 1,500 furnaces, rolling mills, forges, and foundries that Lesley docu-mented. The consistent structure of entries in the *Guide* made the book terribly boring to read, but fairly easy to parse into a relational database. Because Lesley wanted to facilitate communications among iron masters, he described the geographic loca-tion of iron works as accurately as he could. This made it possible to map most iron works to within a mile or better of their probable location.[8] I know of no other individual source that provides so much information about a major nineteenth-century industry.[9] The *Guide* was, in essence, an industrial gazetteer. Like many

33. 34. 35. 36. 37. The Lehigh Crane Iron Company's Anthracite Steam Furnaces, Nos. 1, 2, 3, 4, 5, stand in one pile, at Catasauqua, Lehigh county Pennsylvania, three miles above Allentown on the opposite or eastern side of the river, on the banks of the canal, and in front of the bridge. David Thomas who introduced the successful anthracite make of iron into this country, first at Pottsville and then here, is still the agent and manager of these great works. He built the first stack in 1840, the second in 1842, added a third in 1846, and the remaining two in 1850. The first three are 47 feet high, but of different bosh widths, namely, 11, 13, and 16 feet. The last two are 18 feet wide by 55 feet high, blown by one great blast cylinder, furnishing each of them with 9,500 cubic feet of air per minute, at a pressure of 5½ lbs. to the inch, and made in 1857, No. 4, 10,122 tons, and No. 5, 10,262 tons of metal in the fifty-two weeks, thus not only reaching but exceeding the yield of the Thomas Iron Company stacks next to be discussed. The ores used at the works are obtained from the brown hematite deposits to the east of the river, mixed with magnetic ores from New Jersey.

Figure 6.1 Entry for the Lehigh Crane Iron Company in J. Peter Lesley, *The Iron Manufac-turer's Guide* (1859). This is one of the longest, most complete entries in the *Guide*, reflecting Lesley's admiration for this company, the first American firm to success-fully replicate the Welsh method of smelting iron ore with anthracite coal, begin-ning in 1840. Figure 73 in Knowles, *Mastering Iron* (2013), 250.

other gazetteers, its greatest value lay not in its maps but in its textual descriptions, provided their content and meaning could be extracted for thorough analysis.[10]

What I learned from the Lesley HGIS

Lesley's *Guide* made the HGIS of the American iron industry possible. The process of constructing the relational database, entering the attribute data, geolocating iron works, and then interrogating the database through iterative mapping, gave me a deep understanding of the material and the historical geography of the industry that it describes.

The first task – database design – was itself an act of historical interpretation. I needed to understand how the contents of the survey reflected Lesley's conception of the industry. It became apparent that not all entries fell neatly into one of his primary categories (furnaces, mills, forges, foundries). For example, some rolling mills also functioned as foundries or forges or both. A good portion of smelting operations not only had one or more blast furnaces but also produced castings, the main business of a foundry. This was my first inkling that the antebellum industry included many hybrid forms of business organization and industrial production. Miriam Neirick, the Wellesley College undergraduate who entered the data for most of the blast furnaces and rolling mills, also noticed other inconsistencies that had to be resolved.

We were not far into the project when I realized that historical data entry, even from an exceptionally good source, forces one to confront a host of problems related to data quality, including inaccuracy, incompleteness, internal contradictions, dupli-cation, and information whose quality is difficult or impossible to assess. Manuscript research revealed problems of bias as well. Letters exchanged among Lesley and his two assistants revealed their prejudice in favour of firms that used the latest technol-ogies. This helped me understand why the entries for such firms tended to be the longest and most detailed. Furthermore, the disdain that Lesley and his assistants expressed for what they regarded as backward regions made them unwelcome visitors in the South and rural West. In the most glaring case, iron masters in Richmond, Virginia, soon to become the centre of iron-making for the Confederacy, found no time to meet with Lesley's nephew, a highly educated young Yankee who thought Southerners did not understand their own business. These issues gave me pause. I wondered if I should do additional research on regions that the *Guide* stinted or may have misrepresented. I learned from a colleague that Lesley omitted as many as 30 charcoal furnaces in rural western Virginia. Should the HGIS be a machine to visualize and analyse only *The Iron Manufacturer's Guide*, or should I invest more time to make it a definitive representation of the antebellum iron industry?

I decided not to try to fill all the holes or fact-check all entries in the *Guide*. Life was too short, and I feared that adding information from other sources could actually worsen the skew of the database, given the uneven historical documentation of ante-bellum iron works. Two shortcomings in the *Guide*, however, could be remedied fairly expeditiously. I was able to find opening and closing dates for most of the approximately 30 per cent of entries which lacked that information, mainly in local histories at the Library of Congress. Dates were crucial for analysing the dynamics of growth, longevity, and failure in the industry. It was also important to know where

American firms obtained their raw materials, in order to compare the geography of industrial inputs in Britain and the United States. Thanks to Lesley's impulse to publish everything he knew, further information about ore mines, limestone quarries, and sources of coal was available in the AIA *Bulletin*, which Lesley edited for some years.[11]

Confronting data quality issues in this project taught me several valuable lessons. Any claims based on HGIS analysis have to be qualified by the limits of what one actually knows and how far one can trust the data. Manuscript research was essential for understanding my key source and its creators. This is probably always true. What may be less obvious to those who have not built an HGIS from scratch is that database construction can be a very revealing way to get to know one's sources. Too often I have heard scholars lightly say that the 'grunt work' of data entry can be done by lesser mortals such as graduate students or undergraduate assistants. Although I hired a number of student research assistants for various parts of the iron study, I was able to answer their questions and resolve the problems they raised because my own hands were dirty from wrestling with the data in Lesley's *Guide* and other sources. Data entry brought deep engagement with the material. Time after time, the act of translating running text into categorical fields required decisions, which as often as not sent me back into the secondary literature, a locale's population census, or my archival notes. Literary scholar Franco Moretti has popularized the distinction between distant and close reading.[12] Moretti argues, as HGIS scholars have, that viewing data from the distance afforded by GIS, graphics programs, and statistical packages reveals telling patterns that we cannot perceive when reading texts up close, word for word.[13] Yet, far from distancing me from the data, my experience creating the Lesley HGIS and interrogating the data cartographically deepened my immersion in the source. Database construction became a new kind of close reading for me and my assistants. We came to know the human imperfections of Lesley's *Guide* and recognized its silences. (The almost complete absence of information about labour in the *Guide* was one reason I had to do case studies of companies with extensive employment records and correspondence.) The methodical practice of constructing the database transformed a dreadfully dull, repetitive text into a corpus of unparalleled value.

Placing iron works in their historical locations was another intimate task, one that taught me a great deal about the spatial logic of the industry. Fellow historical geographer Richard G. Healey, an expert on the anthracite coal industry, and his research team took on the task of mapping iron works in Pennsylvania.[14] Meanwhile, I spent the first half of a sabbatical year on my laptop, toggling back and forth between Lesley's locational descriptions, online scans of US Geological Survey topographic quadrangles, and historical maps to place iron works from Maine to Alabama. (This was in 2005, before GoogleEarth.) A few urban rolling mills had street addresses or such precise references to enduring landmarks that I could place them to within a few hundred feet of their historical location. Some iron works were noted as historic sites on the topographic quadrangles, or as a hollow square (meaning an abandoned or ruined structure) with 'iron works' beside it.[15]

The greater challenge was deducing the location of operations that left no obvious trace on any map. These required studying topographic quadrangles for physical clues and indicative human structures, such as roads in steep terrain, small dams, and railroad spurs that ended mysteriously at the foot of a hill or the end of a narrow valley. Through iterative, remotely sensed, yet close reading, comparing unknown locations to those of which I was certain, I learned to recognize settings that could have supported an iron works of one kind or another. For example, the confluence of a mountain stream (to provide water power) with a smattering of small buildings (possibly workers' houses) and a nearby railway bed formed a likely geographical scenario for a charcoal iron furnace and forge. Looking over and over at the landscapes where iron works of various kinds were located helped me realize how similar Northern and Southern charcoal iron operations were in their physical circumstances. Placing iron works became a meditation on the importance of geographical context. Visiting iron works in the field meant more to me for having spent months gazing from an abstract distance at the landscapes of hundreds of iron-making settlements.

Then came the mapping. Geographers are wont to say that, in GIS research, preparing the system to deliver results takes 95 per cent of researchers' time and effort. Once again, my experience was rather different in this case. I spent nearly as much time exploring the spatial and temporal distributions, relationships, and change contained within Lesley's information as I did in building the database. This was partly because my first goal was to describe the iron industry in detail, which meant chipping away at the dumb block of data until its inner shape and characteristics emerged. Iterative data visualization also, inevitably, raised questions that further mapping and additional research helped me refine and eventually answer.

Working with the Lesley HGIS in this way led to a new interpretation of the antebellum American iron industry. My research showed that the large iron-making companies that were early and successful adopters of British technologies constituted a small minority of the industry until after the Civil War. They were all located in the geographically and geologically most favourable region for replicating British methods – the Mid-Atlantic – where mineral resources and transportation were most similar to those in south Wales, Shropshire, and the Scottish Lowlands, where large-scale iron-making developed in the late eighteenth and early nineteenth centuries. The American industry, by contrast, was heterogeneous, full of hybrid operations. I found many examples of American owners and managers taking significant financial risks and trying to adapt British methods to US conditions, often without success. Eventually the analysis revealed seven social-industrial-geographical formations (regions), plus two smaller districts, each distinguished by dominant kinds of technology, scales of production, means of transportation, types of products and markets, historical development, and labour–management relations. Each of those factors was influenced in part by local conditions, including mineral geology, terrain, land cover, drainage, weather, and the historical geography of settlement. European scholars found similar complexity in continental Europe, where most countries also lagged behind the British in the early nineteenth century.[16]

The Lesley HGIS also proved very useful for compiling draft maps. Having worked with the data very closely, I had strong ideas about which spatial summaries were central to my argument, but I needed cartographers' graphic articulateness to make the geographical evidence clear and interesting. Michael Hermann created maps for the first article based on the HGIS analysis, which I co-wrote with Healey.[17] Chester Harvey designed the maps and other graphic figures for *Mastering Iron*. In addition, several of my research assistants at Middlebury College made signal contributions by carrying the HGIS analysis and visualization further than I could myself. Brooke Medley, then an undergraduate Geography major, created GIS layers of topography and antebellum transportation in Pennsylvania, using digital orthographic quarter-quads (DOQQs) and historical maps. In combination with the Lesley HGIS, these layers made it possible for Healey and me to determine how significant distance to rail, canal, and river transportation was for the success or failure of American iron works during the volatile 1840s and 1850s. I went to Garrett

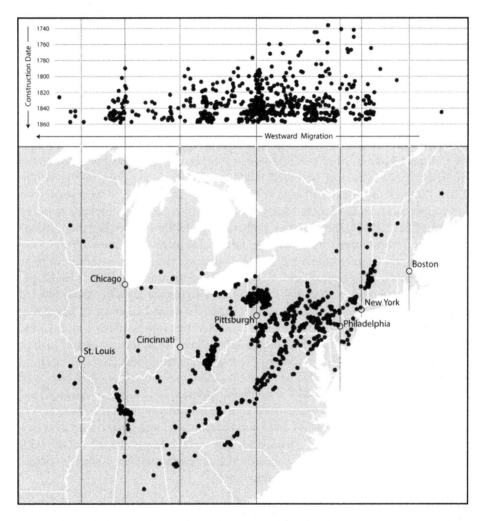

Figure 6.2 Blast furnace construction correlated with location in space and time, 1736–1858. The figure shows only furnaces with a known date of construction. Designed by Garrett Kuzzy, using the Lesley HGIS; final rendering by Chester Harvey. Figure 9 in Knowles, *Mastering Iron* (2013), 35.

Kuzzy, another undergraduate geographer, with an idea I could not quite visualize. I knew generally that the iron industry had moved westward while production became increasingly concentrated in particular urban areas, such as Philadelphia and Pittsburgh, and along transportation corridors, including the Cumberland River in western Tennessee and the Hudson and Shenandoah valleys. Could Garrett find a way to display the simultaneous spatial and temporal dimensions of change? His brilliant answer was to plot the longitude of iron works against their dates of construction (see Figure 6.2).

Strengths and weaknesses of HGIS

The visual aspects of researching and creating *Mastering Iron* – iterative data exploration, collecting and studying historical maps, digitally compiling maps, and working with cartographers to create the final graphics – consumed at least one-quarter of my time. Add to that construction of the database, and the GIS-based research may have claimed half of the project. We should always ask ourselves whether the benefits of a given method outweigh its drawbacks. Although creating and fully exploiting the Lesley HGIS may seem to have required disproportionate effort (I explicitly discuss it in only one chapter), what I learned in the process infused every part the book. For example, while researching two companies that struggled to smelt iron with coal on the industrial frontier, I had in mind scores of other companies whose more or less favourable circumstances I observed while plotting their locations in the HGIS. When I learned of Lesley's flirtation with the notion of investing in Minnesota iron and copper mines in the 1860s, I knew how far they lay on the periphery of heavy industry. The HGIS also provided a solid background for understanding the Confederates' great disadvantage for conducting industrial warfare (see Figure 6.3).

GIS is a tremendously valuable method for empirical research in economic history. Locating people, places, ideas, and events in the context of the physical landscape, with all its constraints, is essential for grounded economic analysis. Multi-layered contextualization is also the springboard for spatial thinking. I know of no better way to contextualize the past; no framework for analysis that is as flexible or as amenable to augmentation; and no analytical method that allows for as many scales of analysis while maintaining essential connections between scales. Economic historians seem to agree. As far as I have been able to determine, they more than any other branch of historians have embraced HGIS as a useful method for empirical research and hypothesis testing. A scan of three major economic history journals (*Economic History Review, American Economic Review*, and *Journal of Economic History*) turned up over two hundred articles published in the last decade that make at least some use of GIS, with particularly strong representation in historical demography, studies of spatially differentiated markets, and historical epidemiology.

As for weaknesses, I have alluded to a few already. Any bespoke historical GIS takes time to build and usually requires assistance from others who possess skills and talents that historical researchers rarely possess. Brian Donahue is one of the very few historians I have met who built, analysed, and mapped a major historical-geographical database on his own, in a project that took him twenty-five years to complete.[18]

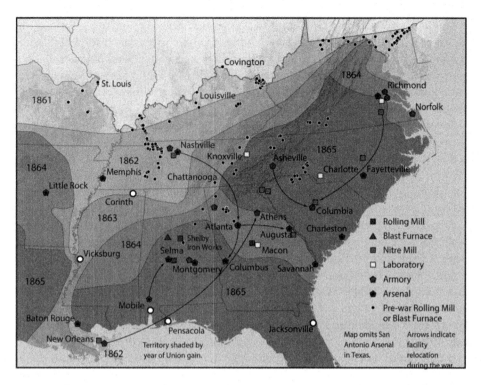

Figure 6.3 The generalized territorial conquest of the South by Union forces (in shades of gray) combined with the location, types, and relocation of Confederate iron works and ordnance manufacturing plants. Map design by Chester Harvey and Anne Knowles. Data derived from the Lesley HGIS and a map of Union gains in Charles O. Paullin, *Atlas of the Historical Geography of the United States*, ed. John K. Wright (1932). Figure 64 in Knowles, *Mastering Iron* (2013), 207.

Many scholars working with HGIS feel the tension between wanting to build a machine to answer particular historical questions and building a bigger machine to answer all the questions that emerge during research. I ran into this problem several times during the iron project. There is something peculiarly beguiling about GIS and cartography. Graphic interfaces suck us in; we lose track of time. Add to that the impulse to chase historical details and to add layer upon layer of possibly relevant data, and one can become obsessed with minutiae. I have seen others become so engrossed in building their HGIS that they forget the question it was meant to answer. When justifying one's use of GIS devolves to the mantra, 'See, you can do this, and this, and this', you know you have lost your way.

Generally, I side with fellow historical geographer Carville Earle's argument that contributing to historiography is the most important work we can do as historical geographers.[19] The way we interpret history filters into public discourse, education, how textbooks and cinema depict the past, and more. I remain dubious about the lasting value of HGIS infrastructure projects, which can be breathtakingly expensive to build, though some, such as the National Historical GIS based at the Minnesota

Population Center at the University of Minnesota, have supported a great deal of substantive research.[20] One can also ask what value lies in a tailor-made HGIS such as mine for the iron industry. Couldn't its usefulness extend beyond *Mastering Iron* to assist scholars' research? Surely it could be included in public history websites and museum exhibitions. Shouldn't I make the database available for others to use as they see fit?

I built the Lesley HGIS to answer my own research questions. Part of the argument of my book, however, was that the iron industry should be considered a fundamental part of American industrialization. I have been pleased to be asked by a number of scholars to share the database, and I had hoped that a state university with strong collections in industrial history would provide a permanent home for the Lesley data. To date, however, I have provided only one partial copy of the HGIS and have yet to prepare a complete set of files that are sufficiently documented and internally consistent to meet my own standards for data quality (though as I write this I have fresh hope of being able to donate the data to a long-term digital archive, with the help of an encouraging colleague). It has certainly been embarrassing not to have made the data publicly available. Such exclusive possession of data developed with federal funding is unacceptable under current requirements for digital research.[21] I confess this problem confident that I am not alone in being very slow to complete the final stage of data preservation and access after a monographic study. The materials that go into non-digital research are rarely published. We box up our notes and stash them in the attic, or gleefully torch them to celebrate the end of a grueling project. The new expectations that databases meet metadata standards, and be designed for others to use, add time and effort to already demanding work. For historical scholars working mainly on their own, without assistance from digitally skilled graduate assistants or university support staff, delivering tidy datasets can be very difficult.[22] This is not a weakness of GIS, but a human weakness that the methodology of GIS throws into sharp relief.

The last weakness of HGIS and its practitioners is familiar to all of us who have tried to straddle the boundary between history and geography. Because of its native categorical structure and mathematical architecture, GIS plays best to social scientific, quantitative inquiry. However many good ideas it may stimulate, GIS is not designed to generate story lines, except perhaps for the skeletal stories of change that numbers or visible stages of environmental change can provide. Stories and people are hard to convey through GIS analysis, nor is attempting to do so part of the social science tradition in which HGIS developed and continues to thrive. Maps created out of GIS layers exacerbate the problem because the usual aesthetics of digital cartography have none of the irregularity, imperfection, texture, ambiguity, or complexity of human experience.[23] One critic of *Mastering Iron* observed that the book was neither fish nor fowl; it does not follow a single narrative arc, nor does it focus entirely on analysing economic and technological issues that hampered development of the iron industry.[24] It is both narrative and thematic, visual and textual, concerned with place and time. The polyglot, relational nature of historical geography – the traits that draw many of us to the hybrid subdiscipline – often make our work less than satisfying for scholars trained in other traditions. We can but keep trying to craft visual texts that convey our spatial understanding of the past.

Conclusion

Environmental historian William Cronon told me years ago that what distinguishes historians from other scholars is their love of sources and the care they invest in the craft of storytelling.[25] I have heard many other historians pair these two as the gifts, or the ideals, of professional history. The best historians winkle the most powerful or revealing or memorable stories from primary sources. They are wizards who can make the past seem to speak for itself. Cronon recently urged historians of all tribes, including historical geographers, to reclaim their special role as storytellers. Stories, he said, capture the imagination. They can still hold young people's attention and they have broad public appeal in our digital age.[26]

I agree. But I part company with Mr Cronon on the definition of storytelling. If it means writing a narrative with a beginning, middle, and end, as most historians I have met would define it, then very few historical geographers qualify as storytellers. Nor does Cronon, in fact. His most famous book, *Nature's Metropolis*, is not a conventional narrative. Its mighty chapters are thematic, each a deep dive into a complex subject that he works his way through, not as piecemeal as Melville's explanation of whaling and the whale, but much more like a grand historical geography than a story. I see *Nature's Metropolis* as an operatic work by a writer in love with his sources and with the ideas and methods he had found to make sense of them: geographic concepts of core and periphery, Von Thünen's model of land use in relation to rent, mapping, statistics, visual analysis of photographs, textual analysis of boosters' claims, and much more. I doubt that a conventional narrative about the growth of Chicago in the nineteenth century would have been half as interesting. Cronon's geographical perspective and his impassioned dance with sources are what entrance readers and make sense of the sprawling story of complex relationships.

So I take a different lesson from Cronon's great work than I do from his advice. We should not hide our process of discovery behind the veil of scholarly performance. Writers using GIS for history should strive to convey the *eureka!* moments that they experience. Those are the human element in scholarship, far more interesting than the dreary social science habit of spelling out methodological details, and potentially more personal than taking the lofty high road that reveals nothing at all about how one cracked sources to release their succulence.[27]

One of the themes running through digital humanities scholarship today is that digital technologies invite interaction, or the further step of enabling people to engage directly in creating their own visualizations, meanings, and stories based on what scholars provide. How can we share the excitement of encountering history through mapping? This raises different issues than providing access to well-documented data in interoperable formats. In my case, it means asking what was most interesting about the struggle to modernize the American iron industry, and how could I share those insights visually? Another way to approach this is to ask, What in my research might seem cool to a 14 year old? Could some combination of digital terrain modelling, historical landscape rendering, oral narration, and maps showing the growth and collapse of the industry, telling the story in a way that is both viscerally geographical and historically meaningful? To recast

Cronon's challenge, how can HGIS and mapping help us become better visual storytellers? That is what today's intensely visual audience would love for us to figure out.

Notes

1 A. K. Knowles, *Mastering Iron: The Struggle to Modernize an American Industry, 1800–1868*, Chicago: University of Chicago Press, 2013.

2 On inductive visualization, see A.K. Knowles, L. Westerveld, and L. Strom, 'Inductive Visualization: A Humanistic Alternative to GIS', *GeoHumanities* 1(2), 2015, published online 11 Dec. 2015.

3 A. K. Knowles, 'Why we Must Make Maps: Historical Geography as a Visual Craft', *Historical Geography* 42, 2014, 3–26.

4 See, among others, A. Kulikoff, *The Agrarian Origins of American Capitalism*, Charlottesville, VA: University Press of Virginia, 1992; W.B. Rothenberg, *From Market-Places to a Market Economy: The Transformation of Rural Massachusetts, 1750–1850*, Chicago, IL: University of Chicago Press, 1992; J.A. Henretta, 'Families and Farms: *Mentalité* in Pre-industrial America', *William and Mary Quarterly* 35, 1978, 3–32 and 'The Protestant Ethic and the Reality of Capitalism in Colonial America', in H. Lehmann (ed.), *Weber's Protestant Ethic: Origins, Evidence, Contexts*, Cambridge: Cambridge University Press, for the German Historical Institute, Washington, DC, 1993, 327–46; and C. Clark, *The Roots of Rural Capitalism: Western Massachusetts, 1780–1860*, Ithaca, NY: Cornell University Press, 1990. The debate over the timing and character of America's transition to a capitalist economy was preceded and informed by E. P. Thompson's studies of Britain, collected in *Customs in Common*, New York: New Press, 1991.

5 A. K. Knowles, 'Welsh Settlement in Waukesha County, Wisconsin, 1840–1873', MSc thesis, Geography, University of Wisconsin-Madison, 1989; Knowles, 'The Making of Ethnic Capitalists: Welsh Iron Makers in Southern Ohio', PhD thesis, Geography, University of Wisconsin–Madison, 1993. The latter was subsequently somewhat revised and published as *Calvinists Incorporated: Welsh Immigrants on Ohio's Industrial Frontier*, Chicago, IL: University of Chicago Press, 1997.

6 J. P. Lesley, *The Iron Manufacturer's Guide to the Furnaces, Forges, and Rolling Mills of the United States*, New York: John Wiley, 1859. A.K. Knowles, *Mastering Iron: The Struggle to Modernize an American Industry, 1800–1868*, Chicago, IL: University of Chicago Press, 2013.

7 The maps appear in 'Iron and Steel Works, 1858', in C.O. Paullin, *Atlas of the Historical Geography of the United States*, ed. John K. Wright, pub. no. 401, Washington, DC: Carnegie Institution of Washington and the American Geographical Society, 1932, plate 135D; and K. Warren, *The American Steel Industry, 1850–1970: A Geographical Interpretation*, Pittsburgh, PA: University of Pittsburgh Press, 1973.

8 The plotting of iron works was done by myself and, in Portsmouth, UK, by Richard G. Healey and his assistants, Paul Carter, Trem Stamp, and David Kidd.

9 Knowles, *Mastering Iron*, 250.

10 Chinese historian and spatial scholar Ruth Mostern has written extensively on gazetteers as rich sources for spatial history and on the utility and limitations of GIS for capturing, representing, and analysing the geographic information that gazetteers contain. See Mostern, 'Historical Gazetteers: An Experiential Perspective, with Examples from Chinese History', *Historical Methods* 41(1), 2008, 39–46; Mostern and I. Johnson, 'From Named Place to Naming Event: Creating Gazetteers for History', *International Journal of Geographic Information Science* 22(10), 2008, 1091–1108; and M.L. Berman, R. Mostern,

and H. Southall (eds), *Placing Names: Enriching and Integrating Gazetteers*, Bloomington, IN: Indiana University Press, 2016.

11 Fellow historical geographer Michael P. Conzen kindly provided complete copies of the AIA *Bulletin* from the University of Chicago's Regenstein Library.

12 F. Moretti, *Graphs, Maps, Trees: Abstract Models for Literary History*, London: Verso, 2005; Moretti, *Distant Reading*, London: Verso, 2013.

13 See e.g. I. N. Gregory and P. S. Ell, *Historical GIS: Technologies, Methodologies and Scholarship*, Cambridge: Cambridge University Press, 2007; and A. K. Knowles (ed.), *Placing History: How Maps, Spatial Data, and GIS Are Changing Historical Scholarship*, Redlands, CA: ERSI Press, 2008.

14 R. G. Healey, *The Pennsylvania Anthracite Coal Industry, 1860–1902: Economic Cycles, Business Decision-Making, and Regional Dynamics*, Scranton, PA: University of Scranton Press, 2007.

15 USGS topographic quadrangles in the 1:24,000 series, like 1:25,000 British Ordnance Survey maps, contain a great deal of information about the cultural and historical landscape.

16 C. Evans and G. Rydén, *The Industrial Revolution in Iron: The Impact of British Coal Technology in Nineteenth-Century Europe*, Aldershot: Ashgate, 2005.

17 A. K. Knowles and R. G. Healey, 'Geography, Timing, and Technology: A GIS-Based Analysis of Pennsylvania's Iron Industry, 1825–1875', *Journal of Economic History* 66(3), 2006, 608–34.

18 B. Donahue, *The Great Meadow: Farmers and the Land in Colonial Concord*, New Haven, CT: Yale University Press, 2005. The estimate of years from conversations with Brian c. 2006, when he was writing an essay for my edited volume *Placing History: How Maps, Spatial Data, and GIS are Changing Historical Scholarship*, Redlands, CA: ESRI Press, 2008.

19 C. Earle, *Geographical Inquiry and American Historical Problems*, Stanford, CA: Stanford University Press, 1992.

20 See the website at www.nhgis.org.

21 My iron research was supported by a number of grants and fellowships, including a Research Fellowship from the National Endowment for the Humanities in 2005–6.

22 I could not have completed the Lesley HGIS analysis as quickly or as well without the excellent support provided by Bill Hegman, GIS Specialist and Teaching Fellow in the Middlebury College Geography Department, his assistants, and my Middlebury research assistants, who were taught fairly advanced GIS and cartography in Geography courses. Even with that support, *Mastering Iron* took me altogether sixteen years to complete.

23 Knowles et al., 'Inductive Visualization'.

24 W. G. Thomas, Critic in the author-meets-critics session on *Mastering Iron*, Social Science History Association annual meeting, Chicago, 2013.

25 This comment came in a personal conversation with Bill during his visit to Wellesley College in fall 1998.

26 W. Cronon, 'Who Reads Geography or History Anymore? The Challenge of Audience in a Digital Age', British Academy Geography Lecture, International Conference of Historical Geographers, London, 7 July 2015.

27 While writing *Mastering Iron* I struggled with whether, and how much, to reveal my methodology in constructing the HGIS and visualizing the data. In the end, I took my publisher's advice and relegated explanation of the Lesley HGIS to a brief appendix. This essay is the first time I have written anything more about the methodological heart of the iron project.

References

M. L. Berman, R. Mostern and H. Southall (eds), *Placing Names: Enriching and Integrating Gazetteers*, Bloomington, IN: Indiana University Press, 2016.

C. Clark, *The Roots of Rural Capitalism: Western Massachusetts, 1780–1860*, Ithaca, NY: Cornell University Press, 1990.

W. Cronon, 'Who Reads Geography or History Anymore? The Challenge of Audience in a Digital Age', British Academy Geography Lecture, International Conference of Historical Geographers, London, 7 July 2015.

B. Donahue, *The Great Meadow: Farmers and the Land in Colonial Concord*, New Haven, CT: Yale University Press, 2005.

C. Earle, *Geographical Inquiry and American Historical Problems*, Stanford, CA: Stanford University Press, 1992.

C. Evans and G. Rydén, *The Industrial Revolution in Iron: The Impact of British Coal Technology in Nineteenth-Century Europe*, Aldershot: Ashgate, 2005.

I. N. Gregory and P. S. Ell, *Historical GIS: Technologies, Methodologies and Scholarship*, Cambridge: Cambridge University Press, 2007.

R. G. Healey, *The Pennsylvania Anthracite Coal Industry, 1860–1902: Economic Cycles, Business Decision-Making, and Regional Dynamics*, Scranton, PA: University of Scranton Press, 2007.

J. A. Henretta, 'Families and Farms: *Mentalité* in Pre-industrial America', *William and Mary Quarterly* 35(1), 1978, 3–32.

J. A. Henretta, 'The Protestant Ethic and the Reality of Capitalism in Colonial America', in H. Lehmann (ed.), *Weber's Protestant Ethic: Origins, Evidence, Contexts*, Cambridge: Cambridge University Press, for the German Historical Institute, Washington, DC, 1993, 327–46.

A. K. Knowles, 'Welsh Settlement in Waukesha County, Wisconsin, 1840–1873', MSc thesis, Geography, University of Wisconsin–Madison, 1989.

A. K. Knowles, 'The Making of Ethnic Capitalists: Welsh Iron Makers in Southern Ohio', PhD thesis, Geography, University of Wisconsin–Madison, 1993.

A. K. Knowles, *Calvinists Incorporated: Welsh Immigrants on Ohio's Industrial Frontier*, Chicago, IL: University of Chicago Press, 1997.

A. K. Knowles (ed.), *Placing History: How Maps, Spatial Data, and GIS are Changing Historical Scholarship* (digital supplement edited by Amy Hillier), Redlands, CA: ERSI Press, 2008.

A. K. Knowles, *Mastering Iron: The Struggle to Modernize an American Industry, 1800–1868*, Chicago, IL: University of Chicago Press, 2013.

A. K. Knowles, 'Why we Must Make Maps: Historical Geography as a Visual Craft', *Historical Geography* 42, 2014, 3–26.

A. K. Knowles and R. G. Healey, 'Geography, Timing, and Technology: A GIS-Based Analysis of Pennsylvania's Iron Industry, 1825–1875', *Journal of Economic History* 66(3), 2006, 608–34.

A. K. Knowles, L. Westerveld, and L. Strom, 'Inductive Visualization: A Humanistic Alternative to GIS', *GeoHumanities* 1(2), 2015, 233–65.

A. Kulikoff, *The Agrarian Origins of American Capitalism*, Charlottesville, VA: University Press of Virginia, 1992.

J. P. Lesley, *The Iron Manufacturer's Guide to the Furnaces, Forges, and Rolling Mills of the United States*, New York: John Wiley, 1859.

F. Moretti, *Graphs, Maps, Trees: Abstract Models for Literary History*, London: Verso, 2005.

F. Moretti, *Distant Reading*, London: Verso, 2013.

R. Mostern, 'Historical Gazetteers: An Experiential Perspective, with Examples from Chinese History', *Historical Methods* 41(1), winter 2008, 39–46.

R. Mostern and I. Johnson, 'From Named Place to Naming Event: Creating Gazetteers for History', *International Journal of Geographic Information Science* 22(10), 2008, 1091–1108.

C. O. Paullin, *Atlas of the Historical Geography of the United States*, ed. J. K. Wright, pub. no. 401, Washington, DC: Carnegie Institution of Washington and the American Geographical Society, 1932.

W. B. Rothenberg, *From Market-Places to a Market Economy: The Transformation of Rural Massachusetts, 1750–1850*, Chicago, IL: University of Chicago Press, 1992.

E. P. Thompson, *Customs in Common*, New York: New Press, 1991.

K. Warren, *The American Steel Industry, 1850–1970: A Geographical Interpretation*, Pittsburgh, PA: University of Pittsburgh Press, 1973.

7

DE GEER REVISITED

Changing territorial and organizational control in the railroad network of the American manufacturing belt, 1850–1900

Richard G. Healey

Introduction

Sten De Geer's classic monograph-length geographical interpretation of the American Manufacturing Belt (AMB)[1] published in 1927 concludes with a major section on the importance of 'railroad lines and systems'.[2] Although rich in descriptive content and categorization of these systems, as of his time of writing, in-depth explanation either of the geographical or economic rationale for their original development and subsequent evolution is rather limited. This is hardly surprising, given the complexity of the dynamics of the transportation network of the AMB, at a variety of spatial and temporal scales, to serve a growing population and a rapidly expanding urban-industrial base.

Linear prose and static manual cartography, however well executed,[3] can scarcely capture such a complex phenomenon, where numerous interacting processes are taking place in parallel across large areas of geographical space. Since the 1920s, attempts to render the problem more manageable for explanatory purposes have mainly resulted in a burgeoning literature on individual railroad companies,[4] and much less frequently, studies of groups of railroads, which have some shared characteristic, such as all being anthracite coal carriers.[5] Only a few brave souls have gone beyond De Geer and attempted a much broader synthesis, either focused solely on the railroad sector or on setting it within the broader context of US economic development since the mid-nineteenth century.[6]

In the past, geographers, in particular, would have understood the quest to link local, regional, and national-scale economic and geographical processes in terms of regional synthesis or regional integration.[7] However, such grand intellectual aims were not matched at the time by the powerful analytical tools and extensive data processing that would have been required to raise the level of such investigations above the often mediocre quality narrative exposition that comprised old-style regional geography.

The advent of GIS technology, enhancements to database functionality, and rapid advances in web-based cartography and visualization techniques have progressively removed the impediments to improved methods of analysis and digital dissemination of findings, as other contributions to this volume bear ample testimony. However, for these new technologies to be deployed to maximum effect, they still require patient and detailed work to create properly structured and accurate datasets relevant to the specific class of research problems at hand. Equally, however, it is not simply a matter of applying new methods to old problems. One of the striking aspects of railroad literature over a number of past decades is the very limited articulation of any guiding research agenda, resulting in rather directionless, though interesting, travel across poorly connected branches of social, economic, and technological history.[8] It could even be argued that railroad research was in a comparatively healthier state over 100 years ago, when railroad-related debates were important aspects of contemporary public policy.[9]

It is therefore appropriate to ask whether the availability of novel analytical approaches, based wholly or in part on historical GIS methodology, will allow researchers not merely to re-examine old problems, but to pose entirely new sets of questions. These might include the efficacy of individual railroad system management within broader interconnected networks of railroads, the impact of territorial control strategies on investment returns or profit margins, the relationships between slowly evolving networks of lines and rapidly fluctuating traffic patterns, and the wider impacts of railroad development on regional economic growth. An unequivocally affirmative answer can be given to the general question, though we are clearly at the very beginning of an immense long-term research endeavour, given the vastness of railroad enterprises over time and space, in the Americas, Europe, and beyond.

If such new research questions are to be posed, what types of historical GIS resources will be needed to support investigations of the required kind? It is helpful in this context to distinguish more general-purpose resources, usable by a large proportion of investigators, from special purpose resources, of value for certain types of studies but not others. Also, under the general-purpose heading, should priority be given to the creation of definitive and comprehensive datasets, which once created, never need to be revisited? An alternative perspective on this would be the establishment of standards for dataset creation, such that incremental work by many researchers would lead to a growing body of consistently structured data resources. Again, although this may be attractive in theory, in practice it may be very difficult to agree widely accepted standards.[10]

Several general-purpose resources can be identified. The first is a digital representation of the railroad network as lines on the ground. The second is a database of the changing organizational structure of the railroad sector as new companies were incorporated, existing companies merged, and ailing companies, in some cases, disappeared altogether. The third is the record of the dynamic relationships, in terms of ownership and control, between the organizational structure of railroad companies and stretches of lines forming the physical network. While these three types of resource may seem to be straightforward and involve separate issues, in fact they are partially interdependent, because of the complex range of control arrangements, sometimes involving disconnected sections of track, coupled with evolution and change in the network of rails on the ground.

Numerous operational questions also arise in relation to the actual building of the GIS and its associated databases. For example, what is the most appropriate scale for digitizing? The answer to this question will affect whether a single digitized line represents the railroad connection between two places, or whether we can also distinguish double or quadruple tracks, and short side tracks. Similarly, are railroad repair shops, depots, and track-side furniture to be included, or can these be ignored? For both lines and depots, temporal change must be accounted for, as new lines were constructed, old ones abandoned, or realigned and new depots were built to cope with expanding traffic.

For companies, which of the many types of change in organization or control need to be recorded? For example, do we need to know about receiverships and bankruptcies, and can we ignore trackage rights, as being only a weak control mechanism? Lengthy experience shows that there is no short-cut to identifying and capturing the dynamic relationships, in terms of ownership and control, between the organizational structure of railroad companies and stretches of lines forming the physical network. Without this resource-intensive stage of the work, many of the questions that geographers, in particular, would wish to ask about the temporal evolution of the railroad system simply cannot be answered effectively across large numbers of individual companies or extensive areas of geographical space. As will be indicated below, historical GIS techniques are essential to making this undertaking operationally feasible.

Ideally the linkage between organizational data and the network on the ground should be undertaken only once in a systematic and standardized manner, to provide a general-purpose GIS that can serve a multiplicity of uses at a variety of scales, excluding only very local studies where a ground survey level of accuracy is required.

There is also a qualitative difference between these general-purpose GIS requirements and the needs of other studies related to the railroad industry. These might include railroad architecture and engineering works, freight and passenger flows, freight rates, military uses of railroads, accounting policies, management approaches, investment strategies, interlocking directorates, labour issues, and technological developments in locomotives and rolling stock. The first four of these headings clearly have a direct relationship to the structure of the railroad network, which includes what might be termed 'organizational topology', as well as physical network connectivity, since the latter cannot be assumed to imply free movement of traffic between actively competing companies. The second set of headings has a much looser set of linkages to the detailed structure of the network. To date, in the absence of accurate GIS datasets for particular areas and time periods derivable from a general-purpose GIS, very little research has been undertaken on the wealth of depot-related freight and passenger flow data available in nineteenth-century railroad annual reports. This suggests a general-purpose resource could 'unlock' major new research avenues, just in this regard.

It is not feasible to propose any standardized approaches that would cover all railroad topics, because the range is simply too wide and data reporting is too inconsistent over time and between companies. That said, increasing use of date-specific 'authority lists' for railroad companies,[11] branch lines, and depots, again derivable from a general-purpose GIS, would greatly facilitate comparability between different studies.

In the light of these extended opening remarks, the remainder of this chapter has two aims. The first is to examine the operational issues involved in the construction of a general-purpose historical GIS of the US railroad network, by means of a study of the part of that network within the AMB. The second is to outline briefly how a more specific study might be undertaken that utilizes both the general-purpose GIS and specific accounting data derived from annual reports. This specific study aims to evaluate the short- and medium-term effectiveness, in financial terms, of the geographical control strategy of railroad leasing, for a particular group of railroads leased by the Pennsylvania Railroad in the 1870s.

The AMB has been chosen because its density of lines, depots, and repair shops was much greater during the nineteenth century than elsewhere in the USA. This greater line density is immediately apparent from examination of published historical atlases of American railroads.[12] The industry in this region also had a very complex organizational history, since most of the earliest short lines were built in the AMB and many of these were subsequently merged into what became known as the Eastern Trunk Lines.

The general-purpose Railroad Historical GIS (RHGIS) of the AMB: background

The RHGIS forms part of a wider, long-term project to investigate the industrial development of the north-east USA in the second half of the nineteenth century. Other sectors of interest include coal mining (anthracite and bituminous), oil, and iron and steel. Phase I of the project dates back to 1996.[13] Subsequent recent funding from the UK Economic and Social Research Council and the JISC/NEH Digging into Data Challenge has enabled Phase II to be initiated. This takes advantage of new software developments and major recent improvements in access to a wide range of online textual and cartographic data sources.

RHGIS: design issues

When the work commenced, it was extremely difficult to envisage the full extent of the possible relationships between different companies and the subtleties of different types of control they exerted through time over rapidly changing track configurations. Experience also showed that seemingly for every proposed rule to guide database design, unexpected and often complex counter-examples would emerge that did not fit the expected pattern.

The first key problem was to establish the basic building blocks for both the company side of the overall linked GIS/database structure, and the physical network side, in such a way that subsequent data capture and querying of both attribute and digital cartographic data would be facilitated. Since acts of incorporation specified the charter start and endpoints of most railroads, these acts were used as the basis for defining individual 'railroad lines' in the database. It was originally assumed that this would cover the vast majority of cases, and that the smaller lines would simply aggregate into the larger lines, as the processes of merger and takeover proceeded over the years. Unfortunately, in the later years of the nineteenth century, this assumption broke down, since parts of the network infrastructure of earlier lines could be taken over by different companies incorporated at a later date, which might themselves be broken up subsequently. As a result, the same identifiable stretch of track might also be labelled differently over time in the literature or in company reports, depending on who controlled it and the type of control being exercised (see below). Therefore it became necessary to generalize the concept of a rail line into a named stretch of track operated by one or more companies as an identifiable unit for a specified period.

Since named track stretches could be shortened or extended over time, e.g. to reach new coal mining operations, the second problem, viewed more from a digitizing than an organizational perspective, was to identify the shortest meaningful lengths of physical railroad line that could be used as the components of track stretches. Using depots and junctions to define these stretches was found to be the best method, as these had operational significance for the running of trains. Unfortunately, neither the pattern/location of depots, nor the configuration of junctions was necessarily static. In increasingly populous areas, new depots would be added over time or the location (and names) of existing depots might be changed. In declining mining areas, on the other hand, freight depots might be abandoned. Likewise, junctions could be moved, as a result of track relocation.

While recognizing these issues, there is no simple GIS solution, since there is no source where all such changes are systematically recorded for all lines over long periods of time. The approach adopted, therefore, was to start from the end of the period of interest in 1900, identify depots and junctions as of that date, and work backwards through sources relevant to each line in turn to identify earlier changes. By working back from 1900, the problem became almost exclusively the identification of the few abandoned depots, rather than the addition of many new depots. There is a distinction here between what might be termed the 'digitizing problem' and the database problem. In ArcGIS parlance, the depots (and junctions) became nodes with attributes, which divided the railroad lines into track segments, the lowest level of cartographic building block in the system. By starting with as many known depots as possible, the segmentation of the network in digitizing terms could be very largely completed at the outset, thereby minimizing the number of subsequent modifications required to the digital cartographic component of the GIS. On the database side, abandonment date is one of the depot attributes, held in a depot chronology table structure that also manages changes in name and function. This means that GIS queries for specific dates will return only operational depots and the apparent track segments between them, even though some apparently single segments on the output map may actually be multiple segments separated by abandoned depots that are not displayed.

Once the inter-depot segments had been identified and digitized, their basic network attributes could be added to the database, including construction-related dates, and date of abandonment, if appropriate. Each segment was then assigned to a specific railroad line or track stretch, as required, so entire named lines/stretches could be displayed based on their component segments.

Separately, and in addition to this, specific lines/stretches were linked to railroad companies by control relationships of a variety of kinds. These relationships are crucial to understanding the combined organizational and geographical evolution of the overall railroad system, but they were the most time-consuming to identify and codify within the GIS/database structure. However, they also provided essential checks on the accuracy of all the information present in that structure, since the results of queries based on them could be directly compared against reliable known sources.

A number of different kinds of control relationships could be identified. The first of these was simple ownership, where a company built a railroad line and continued to operate it thereafter. More complex forms of ownership would include cases where a company purchased the assets of another, including lines already built, either directly or via a more complex legal process of consolidation and merger. These types of control were generally straightforward to document, since they generated a legal 'paper trail'. A more difficult kind of control resulted from majority stock ownership, where stock purchases may not have entered the public record, or been deliberately concealed from it. For these reasons, the GIS adopted a conservative approach of only including control events of this kind if at least one reputable nineteenth-century source could be found to 'confirm' them.

One of the most important types of control strategy by railroads was to lease other lines by formal legal agreements. These agreements were generally long-lasting with terms of 99 or even 999 years. They guaranteed the payment of dividends to stock-holders of the lessor company, often at quite a high rate of 6 or 8 per cent per annum. Such provisions were enormously attractive to stockholders, since they removed the uncertainty in future dividend income streams. Hence if the lessee defaulted on the payments, the lease would be abrogated and control would revert to the lessor company. The converse of acquired financial certainty for the lessor was the transfer of risk and the placing of additional financial obligations on the lessee. The annual rental to cover the lease obligations had to be met regardless of whether the leased line actually paid its way, thereby adding to the fixed charges on the lessee's accounts. The perceived benefits to the lessee were justified in terms of preventing competitors from securing the line and diverting traffic away from the main railroad of the lessee,[14] and the hope of obtaining new tributary traffic and achieving new economies of scale in operation. After the Civil War, the leasing of railroads became such an important part of the long-term process of consolidation and system-building[15] that it is extremely surprising that the literature over the last 150 years contains very few attempts to evaluate its effectiveness as a strategy for organizational and geographical control. The GIS, in conjunction with financial datasets on railroad performance, will enable this major potential research area to be developed progressively. To this end, the brief case study at the end of this chapter aims to provide an indication of how this kind of investigation might be undertaken.

In terms of the GIS, abrogation of a lease would trigger the end of one control event and the start of another, when operational control was returned to the lessor. A good example of this was the ending of the lease of the Lehigh Valley Railroad to the Philadelphia and Reading Railroad in 1893 after the latter road failed to meet the financial obligations of the lease.[16] A somewhat similar change in control, though not necessarily lease-related, could ensue if a railroad passed into receivership, as a result of legal action by bondholders or creditors. A variety of financial vicissitudes could therefore affect any given railroad, large or small, over a period of time, resulting in numerous different control events being recorded. An excellent example of this is provided by the Atlantic and Great Western Railway, a major route running across Ohio. It was eventually renamed the New York, Pennsylvania and Ohio RR, operating within the orbit of the Erie Railway.[17]

The last group of control strategies comprised a range of different operating agreements that allowed the passage of rail traffic, without necessarily conferring any interest in the actual track infrastructure to the party making the agreement with the owning railroad. One common type of agreement provided trackage rights, to allow the cars of one company to pass over track belonging to another, on payment of a suitable fee. Another type might involve two companies sharing both traffic earnings and expenses on a stretch of line.

From the foregoing it is apparent that the complex network of lines on the ground was also intricately connected to an equally, if not more complex, superstructure of time-varying organizational linkages and constraints that had to be negotiated on a continuous basis by train service employees to keep traffic on the move. Little wonder then that a burgeoning cadre of railroad clerks, administrators, and managers was required to handle the financial and legal aspects of intra- and inter-company relationships, resolve disputes, and respond to the ever increasing competitive pressures that characterized the 'nation's first big business'.[18]

RHGIS: implementation

Since the GIS was always intended to be a multi-purpose resource, eventually to be made widely available to a variety of academic users, it needed to support integration with a range of different datasets, e.g. from the mining or metal manufacturing sectors. This implied that the GIS should be of the highest achievable accuracy and be digitized at the largest scale compatible with a realistic prospect of completion across an area as large as the AMB. In practice this meant developing GIS data that could be used down to the sub-township scale, but without guaranteed alignment with detailed geological or hydrological features.[19] Likewise within urban areas, precise alignment with the mid-point of city streets on large-scale plans was not to be expected.

Scanned US Geological Survey historical 15 and 30 minute quadrangle maps met these requirements.[20] The great advantages of these maps lie in the comparatively large scale (approx. 1 inch to the mile for the 15 minute series) and the fact that they contain very detailed railroad track information for the date of survey, often including main line railroad and branch names, in addition to rivers, contours, and depiction of the extent of settlements, large and small. The disadvantages stem from the variable dates of survey (from the late 1880s into the 1940s), and from the use of the polyconic projection on a sheet by sheet basis, which cannot be readily replicated within a GIS, though any resulting small errors can be localized to the areas covered by individual sheets. Absence of the location of railroad depots is also a serious omission.

Variable survey dates and absence of depot information meant that, although the bulk of the required digitizing could be undertaken from a single source, many further tasks were then required before even the basic structure of the GIS could be assembled for any given area. The first of these was comparison of the initial digitized network of lines with other maps from earlier/later dates, to identify further lines that were either abandoned before the survey date or were built after it, but prior to 1900 (for maps with nineteenth-century survey dates). Once the network of lines was established, the sequence of depots had to be identified, followed by their locations. In most cases, the January 1901 *Official Railway Guide* has been used to provide the named sequence of depots as of the end of 1900.[21] However, depot locations were more problematic. If the *Guide* provided mile marker information in relation to depots, this could be utilized within the GIS to measure distances along the tracks. Other sources included the 1900 *Atlas of the State of Pennsylvania*, which gives a good indication of where many depots were located in relation to specific settlements.[22] Most depot locations are accurate to within half a mile or less and were tagged with the degree of exactitude in their currently digitized position, to facilitate possible future improvements based on new data.

Once the depots were in place, the division of each line into inter-depot/junction segments could proceed. After these segments had unique identifiers assigned, the next stage of work on the time-dependent structures of ownership and control could take place.

Sources of information on railroad ownership and control

Despite the vast academic and popular literature on the history of individual railroads, and a wealth of variable quality websites, identification of reliable sources, of the kind required for the GIS, was difficult. Also, metadata were required for all items of data in the organizational database, so any questions about accuracy could quickly be resolved by reference to the original sources. A 'preference hierarchy' of source reliability was also established. The most reliable sources are legal documents, such as company charters, closely followed by printed works that are essentially legal compendia, such as official corporate histories.[23] Archival sources such as company records, printed railroad annual reports, and State Railroad Commission reports are also generally reliable (with some accounting exceptions), though sometimes subject to selective reporting. The same applies to the voluminous ICC Valuation Reports, though these only include subsidiary railroads still owned by larger corporations at the valuation date in the early twentieth century.[24] Newspapers and trade journals may also be useful, though prone to typographical errors and inaccuracies. The secondary literature may be valuable provided suitable caution over the quality of referencing is exercised.

Although corporate takeovers and leases have accompanying legal paper trails that could usually be followed, identifying depot chronologies was much more difficult. Company annual reports may or may not contain such information and maps may confirm the presence of depots (but not necessarily absence) reasonably reliably. Other sources included surviving timetables, the 1850s and early 1860s American Railway Guides, the subsequent Official Railway Guides and the later Rand McNally

Shippers' Guides. Systematic comparison of multiple cartographic and textual sources with careful recording of metadata proved to be the only way of reaching a serviceable first approximation to depot chronologies.

Although such work is labour-intensive and very time-consuming, the combined GIS and database approach adopted here has many key advantages that cannot be replicated by other methods. The first is that queries run against the system provide an extremely powerful mechanism for checking the accuracy, completeness, and internal consistency of the three main components, namely the digitized network, the organizational/control database, and the linkages between the two. Gaps in the connectivity of the output network, e.g. for lines controlled by a given trunk line at a specified date, are immediately identifiable, so they can be checked for correctness.

Secondly, since the system is being built using many types of documentary sources other than historical maps, it can be used to assess the accuracy or otherwise of the latter, in ways previously impossible. Application of this process, to the 1850 Phelps map showing the New York and Erie RR and the section of the 1861 Lloyd map for Ohio, has already demonstrated the shortcomings of the former map and the reliability of the latter.[25] Also, nineteenth-century map annotations, in terms of railroad name labelling, were not always kept fully up to date. This variability in the accuracy of historical mapping also implies caution is needed when utilizing maps from secondary publications, as their sources are rarely given in a systematic manner.

Finally, as milestones are reached in different aspects of the system development, it increasingly becomes possible to provide very flexible outputs in map form, as database lists, or as a combination of both. These include both detailed chronologies of track ownership and control for user-defined areas and dates, and more familiar maps of railroads in operation in specific states, similar to the manual and substantially accurate cartography of Paxson, a century ago.[26] However, the list of possible outputs also extends to much more taxing requirements, such as maps at specific dates of partially built railroads, or of railroads in receivership, or indeed animations of the much grander dynamics of the changing track networks and subsidiary companies controlled by the major trunk lines. Tracing such dynamics utilizes voluminous data in ways that would be almost inconceivable using manual methods.

Work to date on the eastern trunk lines has focused on the Baltimore and Ohio, the Erie, and the Pennsylvania, with additional work on other major systems. An earlier progress report on the project identified different levels of comprehensiveness in data structuring, depending on whether chronologies of subsidiary companies were traced as well as those for the main railroad company.[27] Work on the Baltimore and Ohio and Erie is currently most advanced and examples of outputs for the former can be viewed online.[28] Despite its enormous complexity, work on the Pennsylvania system (including Pennsylvania Company lines west of Pittsburgh to the Indiana border) has progressed to the point where at least 99 per cent of all branch lines in 1900 can be identified by name – this particular undertaking was immensely more difficult than originally anticipated. Figure 7.1 provides an example map showing the current extent of work on the Pennsylvania system.

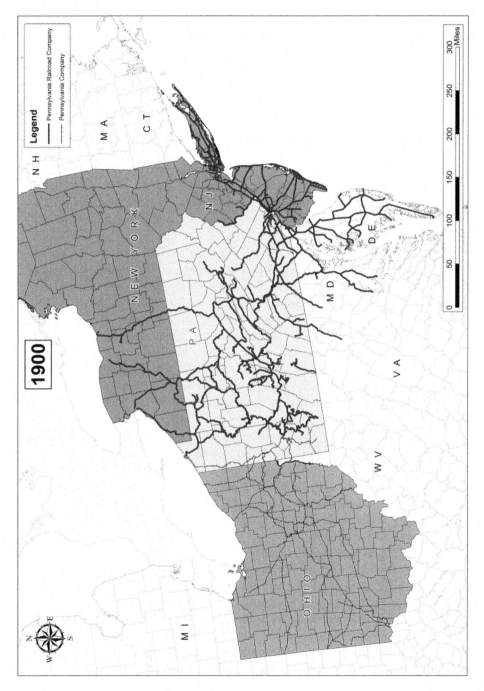

Figure 7.1   Current coverage in the RHGIS of the Pennsylvania Railroad system as of 1900.

Case study: analysis of the commercial success of leasing as a control strategy

As previously noted, the literature is surprisingly silent about the long-term commercial merits, or otherwise, of leasing as a strategy for extending control, both in the territorial and organizational domains. Although a thorough legal assessment is available, this does not extend to operational considerations.[29] Klein's broad study on strategic decision-making by the southern railroads is perhaps most relevant, though it pertains to a section of the national network that is much less complex than that of the AMB.[30]

The potential of using the GIS in conjunction with additional datasets on financial and operational performance to evaluate leasing strategies will now be demonstrated, using the example of the lease of the United Railroad and Canal Companies of New Jersey (URCCNJ) to the Pennsylvania Railroad from 1 December 1871.[31] This important lease provided the Pennsylvania Railroad with a direct outlet to New York Harbor at South Amboy, NJ. It was also one of the most expensive of all nineteenth-century railroad leases.

The URCCNJ comprised three main railroad lines and the Delaware and Raritan canal, which ran across New Jersey. The three lines were the Camden and Amboy Railroad from Camden opposite Philadelphia to South Amboy; the New Jersey Railroad and Transportation Company from near New Brunswick, NJ, to Jersey City; and a line connecting the previous railroad to Trenton, NJ. Other shorter railroads in which the URCCNJ held an interest allowed the connection with the Pennsylvania to be made in West Philadelphia. The resulting configuration of leased lines is shown in Figure 7.2. The lease was for 999 years at 10 per cent per annum on the capital stock, amounting to an annual rental of $1,948,500. The Pennsylvania also assumed the financial obligations of the bonded debt of the URCCNJ.[32] Although the Pennsylvania regarded the terms as 'onerous', it justified the lease to its stockholders on the grounds of the 'great importance . . . of securing a line terminating on the Hudson River'.[33] The company was also candid in pointing out two additional issues to its stockholders. First, while the URCCNJ had been paying 10 per cent dividends up to 1871, its recent earnings had only justified a 7 per cent dividend, the remainder being made up from now exhausted Civil War surpluses. Secondly, the Pennsylvania needed to make significant future investment in new terminal facilities, following execution of the lease.[34]

Hence it might be expected that even if costs were high in the early years of the lease, increased traffic would quickly bolster earnings of the leased line thereafter, such that the lease payments could be easily met. Unfortunately, such expectations could not anticipate the extended business contraction after the 1873 banking panic. In consequence, the financial outcome of the lease was much less satisfactory and for a far longer period than could have been imagined in 1871. This can be seen from Figure 7.3 which shows the net profit or loss on the lease 1872–87. The apparently anomalous 1876 data reflected the boost to passenger revenues from the 1876 Centennial Exhibition in Philadelphia. While losses did eventually begin to taper downwards in the mid-1880s, over the entire sixteen-year period a huge deficit had accumulated, totalling nearly $8.4 million. Taking a more positive view than the

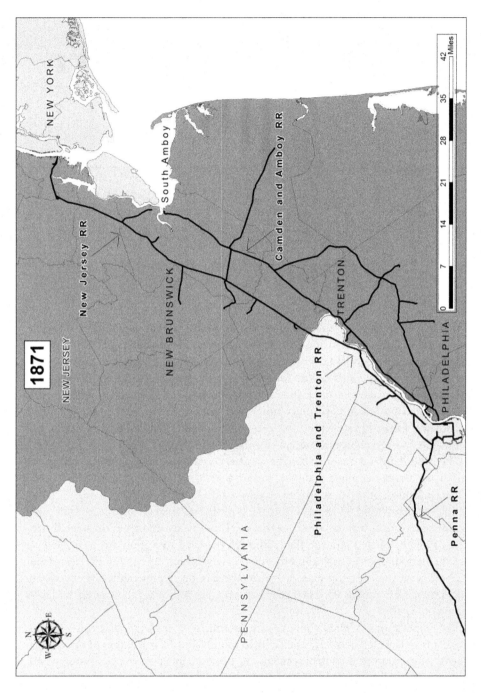

Figure 7.2 Railroad network of the leased URCCNJ and its Pennsylvania Railroad connections in 1871.

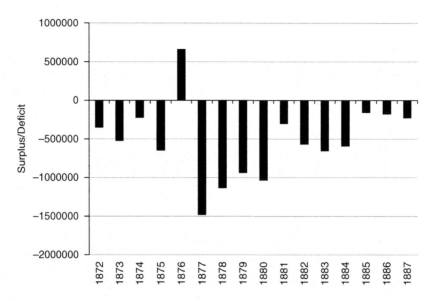

Figure 7.3 Annual deficits and surpluses on the Pennsylvania Railroad lease of the URCCNJ, 1872–87.

narrow accounting loss, despite the cost, the Pennsylvania had invested very heavily both in track infrastructure improvements between Philadelphia and New York[35] and in the major terminal facilities on the Hudson River at Harsimus Cove. Some $9.7 million was expended on the former during the period and $3.3 million on the latter (including real estate and right-of-way purchases).[36] The majority of these costs were covered by issuance of new bonds and stock, but the remaining unfunded $3.7 million formed part of the accumulated lease deficit, while the new stocks and bonds added to the recurrent burden of annual lease charges.

The other hard-to-quantify benefit was the possible increase in traffic offered to the railroad on its main line and branches west of New Jersey, specifically as a result of the availability of these improved transportation facilities to New York. Detailed waybill records would be needed to make a proper assessment of this, so only very general observations can be made in this brief case study. Statistics on overall ton-miles of freight carried indicate that, although the total rose from 1.6 to 5.2 billion over the period, the vast majority of this increase was concentrated in the years from 1879–87, so if the lease did have a beneficial effect on freight traffic, its effect only really became substantial after a lengthy time-lag, i.e. following the end of the 1870s depression in 1879.

The implications of these findings are several. It is apparent that this is a case where it may have taken decades rather than months for the full extent of operational benefits of geographical control strategies to become apparent in accounting terms. However, the counterfactual case, where the lease did not take place is very difficult to evaluate. Existing traffic interchange arrangements *might* have continued, though the weaker financial position of the New Jersey railroads could well have prevented the required investment in new terminal facilities. Alternatively, the Philadelphia and

Reading Railroad *might* have attempted to make a similar lease of the URCCNJ, instead of the later lease of the newly constructed Delaware and Bound Brook Railroad (D&BBRR) that it secured in 1879, for the same purpose of reaching New York Harbor. The extent of the competition and antipathy between the Reading Railroad and the Pennsylvania should not be doubted, as evidenced by the determined attempts of the latter railroad to prevent completion of the construction of the D&BBRR.[37] An interesting irony of this conflict is that the D&BBRR lease, and the resulting improvement in network connectivity to New York, seemingly brought an immediate 100 per cent uplift in the overall freight shipments of the Reading Railroad.[38] This was a much greater and more rapid positive effect on traffic than the Pennsylvania was able to demonstrate from its own lease during the 1870s.

Conclusion

Even from this very brief survey of the issues involved in development of an historical GIS of railroads in the AMB, it is abundantly clear that without extensive deployment of GIS technology, a project designed to meet the needs of multiple types of potential users, by providing a controllable description of a geographically vast and temporally rapidly varying transportation system, would be inconceivable. Even with such technology, capturing the changing network and detailed chronologies for every depot and small section of track is one of the most substantial of current historical GIS (and scholarly) endeavours.

However, to extend beyond this first major step of accurate digital representation of the infrastructure, to evaluation of the associated economic agency, in the form of strategic and operational decision-making at a range of geographical scales, where action and eventual system response may be rapid or may be separated by years, if not decades, will require a whole new order and intensity of research activity. For this, surviving company records, shipment books, even rarely preserved waybill records, will be needed, in addition to the increasingly accessible, though under-utilized, reports of hundreds of railroads, to obtain evidence which has a sufficiently high level of spatial and temporal disaggregation to enable causes and spatially dispersed effects to be accurately linked across multiple temporal scales.

Acknowledgements

I am grateful to Michael Johns for his assistance with the preparation of the map figures.

Notes

1 The AMB was constituted by the swathe of northern industrial states running westwards from Boston to St. Louis.

2 S. De Geer, 'The American Manufacturing Belt', *Geografiska Annaler* 9, 1927, 233–359.

3 G. R. Taylor and I. D. Neu, *The American Railroad Network 1861–1890*, Cambridge, MA: Harvard University Press, 1956, provides a good example.

4 E.g. J. D. Dilts, *The Great Road: The Building of the Baltimore and Ohio, The Nation's First Railroad, 1828—1853*, Stanford, CA: Stanford University Press, 1993.

5 J. I. Bogen, *The Anthracite Railroads: A Study in American Railroad Enterprise,* New York: Ronald Press, 1927.

6 E.g. J. F. Stover, *American Railroads,* Chicago, IL: Chicago University Press, 1961; J. E. Vance Jr., *The North American Railroad: Its Origin, Evolution and Geography,* Baltimore, MD: Johns Hopkins University Press, 1995.

7 R. Hartshorne, *Perspective on the Nature of Geography,* London: John Murray, 1959.

8 See observations on this point in B. Rieger, 'Review', *Albion* 32, 2000, 530–1.

9 H. T. Newcomb, 'The Concentration of Railway Control', *Annals of the American Academy of Political and Social Science* 19, 1902, 89–107.

10 See interesting comments on this issue in http://web.stanford.edu/group/spatialhistory/cgi-bin/site/pub.php?id=23 (accessed November 2016).

11 Authority lists are used to provide standardized lists of names, originally intended to facilitate library catalog searching, see Library of Congress, http://id.loc.gov/authorities/names.html (accessed October 2016) for details of the Library of Congress Name Authority File that includes many railroad company names and variants; W. D. Edson, *Railroad Names: A Directory of Common Carrier Railroads Operating in the United States 1826–1982,* Potomac, MD: Self Published/William D. Edson, 1984.

12 E.g. J. F. Stover, *The Routledge Historical Atlas of the American Railroads,* New York, London: Routledge, 1999.

13 For details of this early work see: R. G. Healey and T. Stamp, 'Historical GIS as a Foundation for the Analysis of Regional Economic Growth: Theoretical, Methodological and Practical Issues', *Social Science History* 24(3), 2000, 575–612; R. Healey and M.D.H. Johns, 'Development of an Historical GIS of Railroads in the North East USA 1826–1900: Phase II', in A. McCants, E. Beira, J. M. Lopes Cordeiro, and P. Lourenco (eds), *Railroads in Historical Context: Construction, Costs and Consequence, Proceedings of the 2011 Foz Tua International Conference,* Oct. 7–9, 2011, Foz Tua, Alto Douro, Portugal, vol. 1, 2012, 193–206.

14 This justification was used e.g. by the Pennsylvania Railroad in leasing the Philadelphia and Erie Railroad in 1862, see H. W. Schotter, *The Growth and Development of the Pennsylvania Railroad,* Philadelphia, PA: Allen, Lane & Scott, 1927, 59.

15 A. D. Chandler, *The Visible Hand: The Managerial Revolution in American Business,* Cambridge, MA, London: Harvard University Press, 1977.

16 Bogen, *The Anthracite Railroads,* 132.

17 New York, Pennsylvania, and Ohio Railroad, *First Annual Report, for the Year Ending December 31st 1880,* Cleveland, OH: J. B. Savage, 1881, 7.

18 A. D. Chandler, *The Railroads: The Nation's First Big Business: Sources and Readings,* New York: Harcourt, Brace & World, 1965.

19 Healey and Johns, 'Development of an Historical GIS of Railroads'.

20 It should be noted that work with these scans commenced some years before the USGS themselves completed their programme of scanning these map series comprehensively – see United States Geological Survey, http://nationalmap.gov/historical/ (accessed October 2016). This limited the scope of the work initially to states eastwards from Ohio, as scans were only available for these areas. Many hundreds of scans were geo-referenced and mosaicked, covering part or all of the states of Delaware, Maryland, New York, Ohio, Pennsylvania, Virginia, and West Virginia.

21 Official Railway Guide, *Travelers' Official Railway Guide for the United States, Canada and Mexico,* New York: National Railway Publication Co., Jan. 1901.

22 J. R. Bien, *Atlas of the State of Pennsylvania,* New York: Julius Bien & Co., 1900.

23 E.g. S. H. Church, *Corporate History of the Pennsylvania Lines West of Pittsburgh, Series A,* vol. 1, Baltimore, MD: Friedenwald Co., 1898.

24 H. W. Rice, *Index of the Interstate Commerce Commission Valuation Reports*, Washington, DC: Association of American Railroads, 1951.

25 For further details, see W. G. Thomas III, R. G. Healey, and I. Cottingham, *Railroads and the Making of Modern America*, http://railroads.unl.edu/views/item/mapping?p=3 (accessed October 2016); H. Phelps, *Phelps's Travellers' Guide Through the United States*, New York: Ensign & Thayer, 1850.

26 F. L. Paxson, 'The Railroads of the "Old Northwest" before the Civil War', *Transactions of the Wisconsin Academy of Sciences, Arts, and Letters* 17(1), 1914, 247–74.

27 Healey and Johns, 'Development of an Historical GIS of Railroads'.

28 W. G. Thomas III, R. G. Healey, and I. Cottingham, *Railroads and the Making of Modern America*, http://railroads.unl.edu/views/item/borr?p=2 (accessed October 2016).

29 J. F. Meck, Jr. and J. E. Masten, 'Railroad Leases and Reorganization: I', *Yale Law Journal* 49(4), 1940, 626–59.

30 M. Klein, 'The Strategy of Southern Railroads', *American Historical Review* 73(4), 1968, 1052–68.

31 Schotter, *Growth and Development*, 97.

32 Schotter, *Growth and Development*, 94–7.

33 Pennsylvania Railroad, *25th Annual Report of the Board of Directors, February 20, 1872*, Philadelphia: E. C. Markley & Son, 1872, p. 14.

34 Pennsylvania Railroad, *25th Annual Report*, 15–16.

35 New Jersey, *Annual Statements of the Railroad and Canal Companies of the State of New Jersey, for the Year 1882*, Jersey City, NJ: M. Mullone, 1883, 5. These improvements were deemed essential for the efficient handling of through freight from the interior.

36 New Jersey, *Annual Statements of the Railroad and Canal Companies of the State of New Jersey, for the Year 1887*, Camden, NJ: Sinnickson Chew, 1888, 15.

37 J. L. Holton, *The Reading Railroad: History of a Coal Age Empire,* vol. 1, *The Nineteenth Century*, Laury's Station, PA: Garrigues House, 1989, 260–61.

38 See R.G. Healey, *The Pennsylvania Anthracite Coal Industry 1860–1902: Economic Cycles, Business Decision-Making and Regional Dynamics*, Scranton, PA: University of Scranton Press, 2007, fig. 6.12. The latter figure and the railroad maps in that volume are derived from the RHGIS and associated data tables.

Bibliography

J. R. Bien, *Atlas of the State of Pennsylvania*, New York: Julius Bien & Co., 1900.

J. I. Bogen, *The Anthracite Railroads: A Study in American Railroad Enterprise*, New York: Ronald Press, 1927.

A. D. Chandler, *The Railroads: The Nation's First Big Business: Sources and Readings*, New York: Harcourt, Brace & World, 1965.

A. D. Chandler, *The Visible Hand: The Managerial Revolution in American Business*, Cambridge, MA, London: Harvard University Press, 1977.

S. H. Church, *Corporate History of the Pennsylvania Lines West of Pittsburgh, Series A*, vol. 1, Baltimore, MD: Friedenwald Co., 1898.

S. De Geer, 'The American Manufacturing Belt', *Geografiska Annaler* 9, 1927, 233–359.

J. D. Dilts, *The Great Road: The Building of the Baltimore and Ohio: The Nation's First Railroad, 1828–1853*, Stanford, CA: Stanford University Press, 1993.

W. D. Edson, *Railroad Names: A Directory of Common Carrier Railroads Operating in the United States 1826–1982*, Potomac, MD: Self Published/William D. Edson, 1984.

R. Hartshorne, *Perspective on the Nature of Geography*, London: John Murray, 1959.

R. G. Healey, *The Pennsylvania Anthracite Coal Industry 1860–1902: Economic Cycles, Business Decision-Making and Regional Dynamics*, Scranton, PA: University of Scranton Press, 2007.

R. G. Healey and M. D. H. Johns, 'Development of an Historical GIS of Railroads in the North East USA 1826–1900: Phase II', in A. McCants, E. Beira, J. M. Lopes Cordeiro, and P. Lourenco (eds), Railroads in Historical Context: Construction, Costs and Consequence, Proceedings of the 2011 Foz Tua International Conference, Oct. 7–9, 2011, Foz Tua, Alto Douro, Portugal, vol. 1, 2012, 193–206.

R. G. Healey and T. Stamp, 'Historical GIS as a Foundation for the Analysis of Regional Economic Growth: Theoretical, Methodological and Practical Issues', *Social Science History*, 24(3), 2000, 575–612.

J. L. Holton, *The Reading Railroad: History of a Coal Age Empire, vol. 1, The Nineteenth Century*, Laury's Station, PA: Garrigues House, 1989.

M. Klein, 'The Strategy of Southern Railroads', *American Historical Review* 73(4), 1968, 1052–68.

Library of Congress, http://id.loc.gov/authorities/names.html (accessed October 2016).

J. F. Meck, Jr. and J. E. Masten, 'Railroad Leases and Reorganization: I', *Yale Law Journal* 49(4), 1940, 626–59.

H. T. Newcomb, 'The Concentration of Railway Control', *Annals of the American Academy of Political and Social Science* 19, 1902, 9–107.

New Jersey, *Annual Statements of the Railroad and Canal Companies of the State of New Jersey, for the Year 1882*, Jersey City, NJ: M. Mullone, 1883.

New Jersey, *Annual Statements of the Railroad and Canal Companies of the State of New Jersey, for the Year 1887*, Camden, NJ: Sinnickson Chew, 1888.

New York, Pennsylvania, and Ohio Railroad, *First Annual Report for the Year Ending December 31st 1880*, Cleveland, OH: J. B. Savage, 1881.

Official Railway Guide, *Travelers' Official Railway Guide for the United States, Canada and Mexico*, New York: National Railway Publication Co., 1901.

F. L. Paxson, 'The Railroads of the "Old Northwest" before the Civil War', *Transactions of the Wisconsin Academy of Sciences, Arts, and Letters* 17(1), 1914, 247–74.

Pennsylvania Railroad, *25th Annual Report of the Board of Directors, February 20, 1872*, Philadelphia: E. C. Markley & Son, 1872.

H. Phelps, *Phelps's Travellers' Guide through the United States*, New York: Ensign & Thayer, 1850.

H. W. Rice, *Index of the Interstate Commerce Commission Valuation Reports*, Washington, DC: Association of American Railroads, 1951.

B. Rieger, 'Review', *Albion* 32, 2000, 530–1.

H. W. Schotter, *The Growth and Development of the Pennsylvania Railroad*, Philadelphia, PA: Allen, Lane & Scott, 1927.

J. F. Stover, *American Railroads*, Chicago, IL: Chicago University Press, 1961.

J. F. Stover, *The Routledge Historical Atlas of the American Railroads*, New York, London: Routledge, 1999.

G. R. Taylor and I. D. Neu, *The American Railroad Network 1861–1890*, Cambridge, MA: Harvard University Press, 1956.

W. G. Thomas III, R.G. Healey, and I. Cottingham, *Railroads and the Making of Modern America*, http://railroads.unl.edu/views/item/mapping?p=3 (accessed October 2016).

W. G. Thomas III, R. G. Healey, and I. Cottingham, *Railroads and the Making of Modern America*, http://railroads.unl.edu/views/item/borr?p=2 (accessed October. 2016).

United States Geological Survey, http://nationalmap.gov/historical/ (accessed October 2016).

J. E. Vance Jr., *The North American Railroad: Its Origin, Evolution and Geography*, Baltimore, MD: Johns Hopkins University Press, 1995.

8

CREATING HISTORICAL TRANSPORTATION SHAPEFILES OF NAVIGABLE RIVERS, CANALS, AND RAILROADS FOR THE UNITED STATES BEFORE WORLD WAR I

Jeremy Atack

Inland transportation in early America was slow and expensive, handicapping trade and communication. Before 1830, for example, many parts of the interior were weeks away from New York City in terms of travel time (Paullin, 1932). This was a reflection, in part, of the continental scale of the country, its sparse settlement, and the challenge to travel posed by its terrain and dense forests. It also reflected the poor state of the country's transportation infrastructure. Rivers and lakes provided the easiest means of travel and were heavily used but did not reach from coast to coast. Moreover, they were often obstructed, seasonably unreliable, and discontinuous, each necessitating frequent transshipment.

The nineteenth century, however, witnessed dramatic declines in transport costs and sharp increases in the speed of travel. These were the result of the spread of new and better modes of transportation and a steady flow of technological improvements within each mode that raised productivity. These changes would have a profound effect upon the spatial distribution of people and economic activity across the nation. But, while their history is well-described, for example by Taylor (1951), the temporal evolution and spatial distribution of these improved modes of transportation is not well documented.

In this chapter, I describe how I have used geographic information systems (GIS) to produce shapefiles (SHP) that show the location and extent, year-by-year, of canal, river steamboat and rail transportation in the contiguous United States from their inception through 1911.[1] GIS not only provides the tools to precisely locate these features relative to one another but it can also be used to generate quantitative information for analysis. These data, for example, reveal the wide-ranging impact of transportation improvements on US growth rates, trade, and GDP

(Donaldson & Hornbeck, 2016), agricultural land values and ownership rates (Atack & Margo, 2011, 2012), urbanization (Atack et al., 2010), and the location and operation of banks (Atack et al., 2014, 2015). Moreover, the effects of transportation on local and regional growth and development persist long after that transportation mode has ceased to be important (Bleakley and Lin, 2012, 2015).

Recognition of these impacts is not new. George Rogers Taylor (1951) referred to them as the 'Transportation Revolution'. Much earlier, though, Thomas Jefferson's Secretary of the Treasury, Albert Gallatin, argued to Congress that 'good roads and canals will shorten distances, facilitate commercial and personal intercourse, and unite, by a still more intimate community of interests, the most remote quarters of the United States' (US Senate, 1808). While it would take decades to realize Gallatin's plan, those transportation changes, when they came, made it possible to settle much of the country's interior, brought new and cheaper products (including agricultural products and minerals) to people around the world, and integrated markets as never before. For example, wheat prices in New York and Chicago converged at an average annual rate of about 1 percent per year from the 1840s to approximately equality by the end of the century (Boyle, 1922; Atack, 2013). As a result, producers and consumers everywhere increasingly responded to the same market price signals.

Others have recognized the importance of the spatial distribution of these changes and have tried to capture it through the visual examination of contemporary maps (Fogel, 1964; Fishlow, 1965; Craig et al., 1998). The inaccuracy of maps and the difficulty of visually correlating the immense amount of information across multiple sources lacking clear and consistent reference points (like county boundaries), however, confounded such efforts (Craig et al., 1998) before GIS software became more widely available and useable by the non-specialist around 2000.

GIS is a relatively recent technology dating from the late 1960s (Tomlinson, 1968). Consequently, most available GIS data are also contemporaneous. Others have demonstrated the value of GIS data to understanding our past (Healey and Stamp, 2000; Knowles, 2002; Knowles and Healey, 2006; Healey, 2007; Knowles and Hillier, 2008). Developing such data is often difficult because the passage of time may have erased the evidence. However, an abundance of such information appears on early maps, but these are often spatially inaccurate. They may also contain what Ovenden (2011) has called 'cartografibs'—mistakes. Some of those are willful such as the failure to place Oak Ridge on maps during the Second World War. Some, however, simply reflect over-optimism regarding anticipated changes. This is especially true of man-made features like railroads and canals that take time to complete.

Increasingly sophisticated surveying techniques, including satellite imagery and global position, now make it is possible to produce extraordinarily accurate maps of current features. I have endeavored to bring that level of spatial accuracy to my historical SHP files even though the historical information itself often appears on spatially inaccurate historical maps. Those sources simply inform me regarding the existence of a particular mode of transportation at a given date, but the specific geographic locations of that transportation infrastructure in my files were determined from relevant United States Geological Survey (USGS) topographic maps, NHGIS boundary files, and satellite imagery and have been approximated as closely as possible by polylines. Some of these I created from scratch; others were modified as necessary from publicly available sources (like the US Department of Transportation National Transportation database, 2012).

When a map source was not already geo-referenced (i.e. not spatially located), I geo-referenced it using ESRI's ArcGIS tools against the University of Minnesota National Historical Geographical Information System (NHGIS) 2008 TIGER-based historical state and county boundary files and the US National Atlas database of cities and towns (2012). I began with points distributed evenly around the perimeter of the historical map images. I added points to the interior of the map images only when the initial geo-referencing was unsatisfactory (i.e. seemed to have large errors as one moved away from the reference points). Fit between the historical map and the geo-located data was made using the ESRI's spline function. Since these historical map images were used only to inform the 'existence', not the specific location, of features, I had no hard-and-fast standard regarding goodness-of-fit. Care was taken to ensure that polylines were 'snapped' end-to-end or edge-to-edge where those lines were continuous.

Water-borne transportation

From earliest times, water has provided the most efficient and cheapest means of transportation. It remains so today. Moreover, it has been so important to commerce that a distinct set of rules and customs – Admiralty law – governs its conduct.[2] These laws were extended to America through colonization and carried over into American jurisprudence via Article III, Section 2 of the US Constitution and also into states' laws.[3] Central to all of these laws is the principle of navigation whereby navigable waterways become imbued with the character of a public highway and to which the public thereby has the right of access and passage.

Rivers

As originally conceived in English jurisprudence, navigability applied to waters subject to 'the ebb and flow of the seas' (Story, 1833),– that is, to the oceans and the tidal reaches of rivers. This is sometimes referred to as the 'salt water test' of navigability. While that criterion worked well for a small island like England, it proved less suitable in a country of continental proportions like the United States (US Supreme Court, 1870). Consequently, even before the US Constitution was adopted, new rules were applied to the interior of the country declaring 'the navigable waters leading into the Mississippi and St. Lawrence, and the carrying places between the same, shall be common highways and forever free' (US Continental Congress, 1787).

Unfortunately, there was (and is) no specific definition of what constitutes navigability. Instead, it has been left to the courts to decide. Various tests have been used. One test is whether or not United States government surveyors had 'meandered' a waterway and declared it to be navigable. Another looks to past legal decisions (i.e. *stari decisis*) such as in the *Daniel Ball* case, where the US Supreme Court ruled that waterways that were 'navigable in fact' were 'navigable-in-law' (US Supreme Court, 1870). The Court would subsequently find that evidence of early fur traders using canoes on the Fox River was sufficient to make that waterway 'navigable in law' (US Supreme Court, 1874). Indeed, federal statutes declares that navigable waters 'are those waters that are subject to the ebb and flow of the tide and/or are presently used, or have been used in the past, or may be susceptible for use to transport interstate or foreign commerce' *at the time of statehood* (33 USC § 329.4). Individual states, however, can adopt their own rules provided that these are at least as permissive as the US Constitution. As a result, there are almost as many state definitions of navigability as there are common law states and these continue to evolve (Kanneberg, 1946).

Waterways have always been barriers to overland transportation. Where they could not be forded, goods and people had to detour around them, be ferried across, or the waterway had to be bridged. Each option was costly. Moreover, where the waterway was also navigable, bridges potentially impaired that navigation. They thus led to litigation and the courts eventually adopted a pragmatic stance favoring the rights of those wishing to cross the waterways over those using them for transportation.[4]

Because of the profusion of legal standards regarding navigability, I have adopted a single, uniform definition for my river SHP files: stretches of a river are 'navigable' wherever steamboats *regularly* operated for some time during the nineteenth century based upon steamboating histories (such as (Chittenden, 1903; Hunter, 1949; Jacobus, 1956)) and representations to Congress by the Army Corp of Engineers. Absent any evidence of regular steamboat traffic, waterways are treated as non-navigable even when minor improvements might have rendered them useable.[5]

My mapping also takes into account changes in the rivers themselves. Floods, for example, can suddenly create new watercourses as, when in April 1881, the Mississippi River broke through an oxbow to the north of its confluence with the Kaskaskia River and took over the lower 10 miles of the Kaskaskia river for its new channel. Silt, gravel, and other waterborne debris can also gradually shift a river's flow and course. Different legal rules apply to each of these situations. Accretion and erosion through the normal action of water leaves boundaries unchanged – generally in the middle of the stream regardless of wherever that might be at any moment.[6] On the other hand, sudden changes resulting from flooding, landslips, and the like, leave the boundary fixed in its original location. Moreover, man, in an effort to improve upon nature and render rivers more useful, has straightened and dammed them (Paskoff, 2007). These changes have generally shortened point-to-point distances and reduced travel times – for example, the Mississippi River in the nineteenth century was about 10 percent longer than it is today. Collectively this means that SHP files of currently navigable rivers are of limited usefulness in reconstructing accurate courses for nineteenth-century rivers.[7]

In many cases, a river's earlier course can be recovered from political boundaries, most of which were determined during settlement in the nineteenth century. The natural barriers created by waterways which made delivering locally supplied services such as police protection or schooling across those barriers inconvenient at best and dangerous or impossible at worst thus determined many boundaries. Moreover, court decisions held that changes in water courses left *political* boundaries, including those between states, unchanged regardless of what might happen to the private property rights from erosion or accretion. Consequently, I approximate their nineteenth-century navigable river courses using the political boundaries from antebellum NHGIS boundary files.

Some rivers have also been 'improved' to enhance their carrying capacity and regulate their flow by systems of locks and dams. Historically, these were called 'Navigations' as in the Muskingum, the Monongahela, and the Youghiogheny Navigations. As a general rule, I have treated these as rivers rather than as canals (i.e. they are included in my rivers SHP file rather than in the canals SHP file) because the waterway generally lay within the river's banks.[8] By the same criterion, I classify the Susquehanna and the Juanita Divisions of the Pennsylvania Mainline as canals since barges operating along them paralleled the natural watercourse but spent very little time in the rivers themselves except to switch banks.

Some rivers, like the Connecticut and Ohio rivers, required short canals around particularly troublesome spots (Harte, 1938; Trescott, 1958). These are treated as short breaks in the river since they (generally) forced traffic out of the natural water-course and into a man-made one, although they did not necessarily require trans-shipment provided that the vessel could fit in the lock chambers.

For each navigable river, I have placed the head of navigation where the historical record indicates steamboats would often travel for at least a part of most years rather than at the highest point ever reached.[9] The downstream limit of rivers is less easily specified. At some point, all rivers that flow into the oceans become subject to the ebb and flow of the tides and are thus navigable *per se* under the English Common Law definition. However, it is not necessarily the same point where rivers (and river navigation) end and the seas (and ocean or coastal navigation) begin. There is no legal definition of what constitutes the coastline or shoreline. Consequently, I generated coastlines for the West Coast, the East Coast and Gulf and the Great Lakes.[10] My navigable river features terminate at these coasts.

One consequence of this decision, however, is that neither the Delaware nor the Potomac rivers appear as navigable rivers in my SHP file since the entire lower reaches of these rivers appear on the ocean side of the coastline.[11] To deal with such problems, I generated a second river SHP file: 'Tidal Reaches'. This connects to the navigable portions of rivers and to canals that terminated at the coastline and traces out the river channels of those navigable rivers as shown on USGS topographical maps. It has been merged with the 'Navigable Rivers' SHP file to create the 'Steamboat Navigated River' SHP file in which tidal and non-tidal portions are identified although some river steamboats, depending upon design, may have ranged further into coastal waters.

Canals

Virtually all of the earliest canals have now vanished.[12] Their prisms (the canal's cross-section) have silted up and become overgrown. Moreover, several canals have been repurposed in ways that have obliterated much of the archaeological evidence of their existence. For example, several railroads were built along canal rights of way, including the Pennsylvania Mainline, the Whitewater, and the Framingham canals. Many railroad rights of way would subsequently meet similar fates as highways have been built atop them.[13]

Construction of my SHP file for canals therefore began with relatively inaccur-ately drawn maps of canal routes. Some of these were more or less contemporaneous (Tanner, 1830; Tanner, 1840; Poor, 1860; Whitford, 1906); others are retrospective

(Goodrich, 1961) but they only serve to determine the existence of a canal and its general location. The precise location of each canal comes, instead, from features like 'abandoned canal' noted on 7.5 minute USGS topographical maps (see the left-hand panel of Figure 8.1 for the Wabash and Erie Canal).[14] These features were then approximated by polylines in ArcGIS.

In a few instances, the tracings of abandoned canals on the USGS maps were discontinuous. In these cases, I approximated their paths by using satellite imagery of vegetation differences and the elevation data encoded in the topographical maps, or by maintaining a fixed relationship to other features on the topographical map. In urban areas, however, urban renewal and road construction have eliminated virtually all of the remnants of early canals. Nevertheless, they live on in street names

Figure 8.1   Locating abandoned canals on USGS topographical maps and in satellite imagery.

Note: Arrows indicate the location of the long silted-up Wabash and Erie Canal.

Sources: USA Topo Maps – Copyright:© 2013 National Geographic Society, i-cubed. World Imagery – Source: Esri, DigitalGlobe, GeoEye, Earthstar Geographics, CNES/Airbus DS, USDA, USGS, AEX, Getmapping, Aerogrid, IGN, IGP, swisstopo, and the GIS User Community. Used with permission. Copyright © 2017 Esri. All rights reserved.

like 'Canal' and 'Basin' street that were associated with canals and which are recorded in Street Views and similar urban maps and these have been used when necessary to approximate the canal's original route.

Since virtually none of these nineteenth-century canals remain evident today, my GIS mapping of their original routes is a crucial element in documenting their economic and social effects in the areas through which they passed and the communities that they linked.

Railroads

Railroads are easily defined and recognized but the railroad network that grew during the nineteenth century shrank during the twentieth century. Fortunately, the vast majority of a railroad's investment went into securing the right of way, grading, cuts and fill to minimize grade, constructing drainage ditches and culverts, bridges, railroad crossings as well as actual costs of the roadbed, sleepers, and rails (US Census Office, 1883). Much of this was literally a sunk cost and, once built, many of these features have remained visible even when the railroad has been abandoned or repurposed.

Like my earlier railroad SHP files (Atack, 2013), digitized state-level maps showing the rail network in 1911 provide evidence of the *existence* of a railroad connecting points in that year. The precise spatial location of the railroad, however, comes from the union of the National Atlas database and the USGS 7.5 minute topographical maps from the late nineteenth century onwards. These topographical maps show active railroad track as well as abandoned lines.

Beginning with the railroad SHP file from the National Atlas database, I first deleted as many tracings of multi-tracking, sidings, turnouts for trains to pass one another, and large switching yards as possible as there is no readily available information indicating when these were built.[15] This modified SHP file was then overlaid on the geo-referenced state-level maps from the *New Century Atlas* for 1911 and I deleted those railroad lines that did not match up by origin, route, and destination with those shown on the 1911 maps since these were, presumably, built later.

There were also railroads on the 1911 maps for which there was no corresponding railroad in the modern data by origin, route, or destination. In these cases, I carefully examined the USGS topographical maps for the area in question. They invariably showed an 'old railroad grade' feature in the expected general location and between the expected origin and destination. In the process, I also examined the registration between the modern active railroad lines and those shown on the topographical maps, including those from late nineteenth and early twentieth centuries. When satisfied, I approximated the route of the old railroad grade using polylines. Such omissions of pre-1911 track from modern railroad maps were expected as tens of thousands of miles of railroad were abandoned (and often torn up) from the 1920s onwards (Carter et al., 2006).

Where there were gaps in 'old railroad grade' features, I looked for roads and trails that might have been built atop the track. I also examined satellite imagery for variations in vegetation that might reveal the drainage provided by old railroad bed and boundary lines (including fences and trees) that might indicate an earlier right of way. I even looked for evidence of railroad-related structures like bridge piers remaining in river and streambeds.

The result of all of these efforts was my best estimate of the railroad SHP file for 1911. This was then copied and used as an overlay for the next earlier digitized railroad map. Choosing maps that were closer together (in terms of copyright date) would seem to offer the promise of a more continuous time series of railroad construction and operation but it comes at the cost of more inconsistent information between successive maps. I eventually settled on an approximately five-year interval between mappings as a reasonable balance between these conflicting forces although other considerations also impinged upon my choices. For example, there was a major railroad building boom during the 1850s concentrated in the Midwest for which detailed, annual data are available for several states (Paxson, 1914). Consequently, I was able to map the railroad network at two-year intervals during the 1850s. Moreover, wherever possible, I made a conscious effort to locate consecutive maps from similar sources. For example, the six map series covering 1877 through 1903 were produced by Rand McNally for use by commercial shippers. Where conflicts between successive maps emerged, efforts were made to resolve them by consulting other sources from a year or two before or after. In some cases, this led me to review and adjust the 1911 mapping if it appeared that I had picked the 'wrong' line(s) between particular origins and destinations from among several possibilities.

These procedures generated a total of sixteen different railroad SHP files between 1850 and 1911. The map sources for these are shown in Table 8.1 (and also in the metadata (XML) files that are a part of the SHP files).[16]

Maps prior to the Civil War are noticeably less accurate than later maps (Modelski, 1987). Moreover, earlier railroad maps tended to be regional or national and their (relatively) small scale may have obscured some details and rail links, especially in more compact and densely settled such as the Northeast Corridor. For this reason, before 1850, I have relied upon the work of railroad enthusiasts and historians, in particular, the work of Milton C. Hallberg who created a comprehensive database of early railroad construction.[17]

Map scale also poses a serious challenge with regard to cities, most of which appear as a dot on maps where several lines converge. We do, however, know that many early railroads did not originally interconnect but rather operated out of separate railroad stations and yards. Boston, for example, had railroad stations at six different locations in the city in 1854, two of which were next door to one another but some (connecting to points south) were across the city, several miles away (Williams, 1854). Work documenting early city rail routes has been completed for four Middle Atlantic cities (Baltimore, New York, Philadelphia, and Washington) (Baer et al., 1981) and is in progress for other cities.[18]

The individual SHP files for each benchmark date were subsequently merged into a single SHP file covering the entire period using the 'Erase' command in ArcGIS to determine what track was added between each successive pair of years. The resulting files were then merged back into a single SHP file. The gain from this seemingly roundabout procedure was that publication (copyright) date for the later of each pair of maps is used to provide a rough dating for the construction of each stretch of line after 1850. Before then, the Hallberg database provides an exact date when each stretch of track was built.

Table 8.1 Map sources used to determine the existence of rail links in each specific year.

Year	Map source used to determine the existence of a rail link in a particular year
1911	William D. Whitney and Benjamin E. Smith (eds) *The Century dictionary and cyclopedia, with a new atlas of the world*, New York: Century Co., 1911. State maps.
1903	Rand McNally, Rand McNally & Co., *Enlarged Business Atlas And Shippers' Guide . . . Showing In Detail The Entire Railroad System . . . Accompanied By A New And Original Compilation And Ready Reference Index . . .*, Chicago, IL: Rand McNally & Co., 1903.
1898	Rand, McNally & Co.'s *New Business Atlas Map of the United States. . .*, Chicago, IL: Rand McNally & Co., 1898. Regional maps.
1893	Rand McNally & Co., *Rand, McNally & Co.'s Enlarged Business Atlas and Shippers Guide; Containing Large-Scale Maps of All the States and Territories in the United States, of the Dominion of Canada, the Republic of Mexico, Central America, the West Indies and Cuba*. Chicago, IL: Rand McNally, 1893. State maps. Louisiana, Maryland/Delaware, Michigan, and Mississippi from Rand McNally, *Universal Atlas of the World*, Chicago, IL: Rand McNally, 1893. Texas: Rand McNally & Co. *Indexed County and Railroad Pocket Map and Shippers' Guide of Texas: Accompanied by a New and Original Compilation and Ready Reference Index, Showing in Detail the Entire Railroad System . . .* Chicago, IL: Rand McNally & Co., 1893.
1889	Rand McNally, *Rand, McNally & Co.'s Enlarged Business Atlas and Shippers Guide . . .*, Chicago, IL: Rand McNally & Co., 1889. State maps.
1881	Rand McNally, *New Indexed Business Atlas and Shippers Guide*, Chicago, IL: Rand McNally & Co., 1881. State maps.
1877	Rand McNally & Co., *Rand McNally & Co's Business Atlas*, Chicago, IL: Rand McNally & Co., 1877. State maps.
1872	Warner & Beers, *Atlas of the United States*, Chicago, IL: Warner & Beers, 1872. Regional maps.
1868	J. T. Lloyd, *Lloyd's New Map of the United States The Canadas and New Brunswick From The Latest Surveys Showing Every Railroad & Station Finished . . . 1868*, New York: J. T. Lloyd, 1868. National map.

Table 8.1 (continued).

Year	Map source used to determine the existence of a rail link in a particular year
1863	J. T. Lloyd, *Lloyd's New Map of the United States The Canadas And New Brunswick From the latest Surveys Showing Every Railroad & Station Finished to June 1863*, New York: J. T. Lloyd, 1863. National map.
1861	G. R. Taylor and Irene D. Neu, *The American Railroad Network 1861–1890*, Cambridge, MA: Harvard University Press, 1956. Regional maps.
1858	Hugo Stammann, *J. Sage & Son's New & Reliable Rail Road Map Comprising All the Railroads of the United States and Canadas with their Stations and Distances*, Buffalo, NY: J Sage & Sons, 1858. National map.
1856	Richard S. Fisher, *Dinsmore's Complete Map of the Railroads & Canals in the United States & Canada Carefully Compiled from Authentic Sources by Richard S. Fisher, Editor of the American Rail Road & Steam Navigation Guide*, New York, 1856. National map.
1854	E.D Sanford, *H. V. Poor's Rail Road Map Showing Particularly the Location and Connections of the North East & South West Alabama Rail Road*, by E. D. Sanford, Civil Engineer, n.p.: 1854. National map.
1852	J.H. Colton, *Colton's Map of the United States, The Canadas &c. Showing The Rail Roads, Canals & Stage Roads: With Distances from Place to Place*, New York: J. H. Colton, 1852. National map.
1850	Curran Dinsmore, *Dinsmore & Company's New and Complete Map of the Railway System of the United States and Canada; Compiled from Official Sources, under the direction of the editor of the 'American Railway Guide.'*, New York: 1850. National map.

Notes: See also the SHP file metadata which is a part of the archived file packet at https://my.vanderbilt.edu/jeremyatack/files/2016/05/RR1826-1911Modified0509161. zip for the specific source(s) (such as a URL or the library collection) of individual maps.

Although I deliberately eliminated multiple tracking, there are exceptions to this rule. For example, in 1861, we know (Taylor & Neu, 1956) that the broad gauge (72″) Delaware, Lackawanna and Western railroad connected to the Central Railroad of New Jersey, a standard gauge road, near Hampton, New Jersey. Rather than break gauge at that point or build an entirely separate right of way, the Lackawanna Railroad continued on to Jersey City via the New Jersey Railroad (a 'New Jersey' gauge line—58″) by means of a third rail attached to the outer edge of the Jersey Central's railroad ties. Broad gauge trains thus used the outer pair of rails while standard and New Jersey gauge trains used the inner rail and the appropriate outer rail. I have represented this arrangement in my SHP files by the creation of parallel tracks, one of each gauge. I used the same procedure in southeastern Indiana and southwestern Ohio where the broad gauge Ohio and Mississippi line met up with the standard gauge Indianapolis and Cincinnati line into Cincinnati. In that case, however, the historical record is silent on whether a third rail was added or two tracks with separate gauges were laid along the right of way.

Prior to the Civil War, I have also tried to identify the operator of each stretch of track. During the 1850s, this was taken to be the name of the operator assigned by Taylor and Neu for that track in 1861. The operators of earlier track are those listed in Hallberg's database. This scheme, however, is imperfect and these data should be used with care. For example, early on, railroads typically changed names at state borders. They also changed name frequently as construction plans changed (many names were intended to be broadly descriptive as to route, as in 'Baltimore and Ohio' and 'Missouri Pacific') or bankruptcy or merger forced corporate reorganization.[19] The SHP file also identifies track gauge prior to 1861 (Taylor & Neu, 1956).[20]

Beside breaks in railroad gauge, others often occurred at major rivers, especially where those waterways were navigable, for example, the Ohio River (Kleber, 2001). To determine when a particular waterway was bridged, I have made considerable use of internet resources, particularly www.bridgehunter.com, a 'database of historic or notable bridges in the United States, past and present' (although this sometimes proved incomplete or wrong). I also made use of http://cs.trains.com/trn/f/507/t/42151.aspx listing Mississippi River crossings. Where I found a specific date for a particular bridge, I incorporated that information in my SHP file.

Concluding remarks

Transportation infrastructure has played and continues to play a vital role in economic growth and development by linking supply with demand and integrating spatially separated markets. Certainly, study after study (e.g. Atack et al., 2010; Atack & Margo, 2011, 2012; Atack et al., 2014, 2015), confirms Taylor's (1951) description of the improved means of transportation (and especially the railroad) as a 'Revolution', that had a significant and positive impact upon measures of economic growth and development. Consequently, the historical SHP files detailing the location and temporal evolution of rail and water transportation in the contiguous United States whose construction I have described here, in conjunction with the various analytical tools of GIS, are a vital new resource that provides new insight into economic change during the nineteenth century.

They can, however, be improved upon and modified. For example, the dating of rail construction could be more accurate by using the annual reports of individual railroads, accounts in the press at the time (including trade journals such as the *American Railroad Journal*), and railroad schedules (e.g. Appleton and Company, 1847; Disturnell, 1847; Doggett, 1848; Cobb, 1853; Rand McNally and Company et al., 1879) but I am leaving this to others!

Nevertheless, there remains one huge transportation unknown: the web of roads (and their quality) linking farm and factory to town to city and to ports. They also connected these to the modes of transportation represented in my SHP files. However, they are largely undocumented in the historical record beyond their (generally) poor quality until sometime after the First World War, their lack of productivity change and their inferiority to each of the transportation modes whose evolution I have mapped with my SHP files.

Notes

1 These GIS files, along with a more extended documentation in PDF format, may be downloaded from my website at https://my.vanderbilt.edu/jeremyatack/data-downloads/. They are also archived at the Inter-University Consortium for Political and Social Research at the University of Michigan (www.icpsr.umich.edu/icpsrweb/landing.jsp) ICPSR 36353 and are being incorporated into the National Historical Geographic Information Systems data from the University of Minnesota Population Center (https://nhgis.org/).

2 These laws can be traced back to ancient Roman times and many of its rules still apply worldwide – e.g. for example, the right of innocent passage outside of a country's territorial waters and rules denying any country monopoly rights over critical waterways like the Straits of Gibraltar, Hormuz and Malacca or the English Channel.

3 Specifically, 'The judicial power shall extend . . . to all cases of admiralty and maritime jurisdiction . . .' https://www.law.cornell.edu/constitution/articleiii#section2.

4 Indeed, this was precisely Abraham Lincoln's winning argument in the Rock Island Bridge case (US District Court for Northern Illinois, 1857), although all the transcripts of that trial were destroyed in the Chicago fire of 1871 – see www.archives.gov/publications/prologue/2004/summer/bridge.html. The debate dragged on to 1867 (US Supreme Court, 1867).

5 The Conecuh River, for example, is not included in my SHP file of navigable rivers because, although the historical evidence indicates that flatboats were regularly used on the river, only one steamboat, the *Shaw*, ever made it up the river from Pensacola. It was sunk by a snag shortly after reloading with a cargo of cotton at Brooklyn Landing in 1845 bringing a premature end to experiments with steam navigation on that river. See Riley (1881). I also exclude those waterways that could have been made navigable (but which were not – at least until sometime after the First World War); see e.g. Fogel (1964) or the Eleventh Census of the US (US Census Office, 1898).

6 An exception is the Ohio River as the Northwest Ordinance places the boundaries on the northern/western bank of the river.

7 A similar point is made in another context by a recent *New York Times* article (Robbins, 2016).

8 This generalization, however, requires qualification as I do treat two waterways each with the term 'Navigation' in their names – the Schuylkill Navigation and the Bald Eagle and Spring Creek Navigation – as canals rather than rivers because for most of their distance these waterways lay outside of their rivers' banks.

9 Thus e.g. Hunter (1949) lists Fulton, AR, as the head of navigation on the Red River but contemporary local newspaper advertisements (Wright, 1930) list more than a dozen steamboat landings above the Oklahoma line by 1854 with service stopping at Fort Towson.

10 The process, however, is non-trivial. I converted the NHGIS TIGER-based polygon state boundary SHP files to lines and dissolved the vectors fronting the ocean or Great Lakes. This procedure generates coastlines that are coincident with the NHGIS TIGER-based historical county boundary used as reference points in all my work. However, these SHP files initially contained (seemingly random) extraneous polylines interior to the coast. These have been deleted from the coastline SHP files.

11 For example, the Delaware River estuary is only closed in the coastline shapefile above Trenton. The same is true of the Columbia River in the Pacific Northwest which appears as an estuary below Crima Island, approximately 50 miles from the mouth of the river on the Oregon–Washington coast.

12 At least two canals were built in the United States during the twentieth century and are still in operation: the New York Barge Canal, completed in 1918 (replacing the Erie Canal) and the Tennessee-Tombigbee waterway which opened in 1984. Moreover, most of the intercoastal waterway is a twentieth-century creation. None are included in my canal SHP except for some early bits of what becomes the intercoastal waterway, like the Albemarle and Chesapeake canal. See e.g. www.carolana.com/NC/Transportation/albemarle_and_chesapeake_canal.html.

13 The portion of Southern Pacific railroad right of way between Katy, TX, and Tower 13 (in northwest Houston), abandoned in 1997, became a part of a widened I-10 (the Katy Freeway). See www.abandonedrails.com/Houston_to_Katy. Even the original Erie Canal could not escape and a stretch near Port Byron is now a part of the New York Thruway.

14 Available from http://ims.er.usgs.gov as gda_5285424.zip. The USGS maps published through the late twentieth century (including earlier USGS historical topo maps from the late nineteenth and early twentieth centuries) are available as overlays in ArcGIS through http://historicalmaps.arcgis.com/usgs, although they are relatively slow to load and render. Unfortunately, as of the time of writing, these maps are not yet implemented as overlays in the much speedier ArcPro. Instead, ArcPro uses more recent, but much less detailed 7.5 minute maps from 2009, which do not mark abandoned canals (see e.g. http://nationalmap.gov /ustopo/quickstart.pdf).

15 For this reason (if no other), track mileage estimates from my SHP file will differ from those given by other sources, such as Carter et al., 2006. Moreover, in some years, many thousands of miles of track were built during the year – some linking new destinations and making timing critical, while other construction was for double (or triple) tracking, sidings, turnouts, etc.

16 In particular, I wish to acknowledge the generosity of Murray Hudson (Antiquarian Books, Maps, Prints & Globes, 109 S. Church Street, Halls, TN 38040) who scanned and provided me with copies of most of the state maps used for my 1893 railroad SHP file. See www.antiquemapsandglobes.com.

17 Hosted at http://oldrailhistory.com. When I produced my earlier SHP files, detailed individual maps of each railroad showing when specific sections of track were built were also a part of the WWW site. Unfortunately, these are no longer available and I have not been able to locate them in any of the WWW archives. The Hallberg database has been supplemented by various published railroad histories, online Google search results, and the Wikipedia entries for specific railroads appearing in the database.

18 See Christian Hung, doctoral dissertation in Economics in progress at Vanderbilt University.

19 For example, the Pendleton and Indianapolis Railroad, organized in 1848, was quickly renamed the Indianapolis and Bellefontaine Railroad when it joined up with an Ohio railroad

from Bellefontaine in January 1853 at Union City, Indiana (Bogle, 1962) and became the first railroad in Indiana to connect to East Coast cities through those Ohio links. In 1855, it was restyled the Bellefontaine and Indiana Railroad which was shortened to the Bellefontaine Railway in 1864, becoming the Cleveland, Columbus, Cincinnati and Indianapolis Railway in 1868, and finally the Cleveland, Cincinnati, Chicago and St. Louis Railway in 1889.

20 Many of the non-standard gauges (i.e. those other than 4′ 8.5″) changed in the decades that followed. See Puffert (1991, 2000). However, I have made no effort to track these changes. By assigning pre-1861 gauges based upon the gauge in use in 1861, I am implicitly assuming that the choice of gauge was non-random since changing it was expensive and that once a railroad had adopted standard gauge they did not switch again since this would dissipate positive network externalities.

Bibliography

33 Usc § 329.4. U.S. Code: Title 33 – Navigation and Navigable Waters.

Appleton and Company, *Appletons' Illustrated Railway and Steam Navigation Guide*, New York: D. Appleton & Co., 1847.

J. Atack, 'On the Use of Geographic Information Systems in Economic History: The American Transportation Revolution Revisited', *Journal of Economic History* 73(02), 2013, 313–38.

J. Atack and R. A. Margo, 'The Impact of Access to Rail Transportation on Agricultural Improvement: The American Midwest as a Test Case, 1850–1860', *Journal of Transport and Land Use*, 4(2), 2011, 5–18.

J. Atack and R. A. Margo, 'Land Ownership and the Coming of the Railroad in the American Midwest, 1850–1860', in A. Mccants and E. Beira (eds), *Railroads in Historical Context: Construction, Costs and Consequences*. Portugal: Foz Tua/EFP/MIT, 2012.

J. Atack, F. Bateman, M. Haines, and R. A. Margo, 'Did Railroads Induce or Follow Economic Growth? Urbanization and Population Growth in the American Midwest, 1850–1860', *Social Science History* 34(2), 2010, 171–97.

J. Atack, M. Jaremski and P. L. Rousseau, 'American Banking and the Transportation Revolution Before the Civil War', *Journal of Economic History*, 74(4), 2014, 943–86.

J. Atack, M. Jaremski, and P. L. Rousseau, 'Did Railroads Make Antebellum US Banks More Sound?', in W. J. Collins and R. A. Margo (eds), *Enterprising America: Business, Banks and Credit Markets in Historical Perspective*. Chicago, IL: University of Chicago Press for the NBER, 2015.

C. T. Baer, G. Porter, W. H. Mulligan, M. E. Amstutz, and A. E. Webster, *Canals and Railroads of the Mid-Atlantic States, 1800–1860*, Wilmington, DE: Regional Economic History Research Center, Eleutherian Mills-Hagley Foundation, 1981.

H. Bleakley and J. Lin, 'Portage and Path Dependence', *Quarterly Journal of Economics*, 127(2), 2012, 587–644.

H. Bleakley and J. Lin, 'History and the Sizes of Cities', *American Economic Review*, 105(5), 2015, 558–63.

V. M. Bogle, 'Railroad Building in Indiana, 1850–1855', *Indiana Magazine of History*, 58(3), 1962, 211–32.

J. E. Boyle, *Chicago Wheat Prices for Eighty-One Years, Daily, Monthly and Yearly Fluctuations and their Causes*, Ithaca, NY: Cornell University Press, 1922.

S. B. Carter, S. S. Gartner, M. R. Haines, A. L. Olmstead, R. Sutch, G. Wright and L. P. Cain (eds), *Historical Statistics of the United States Millennial Edition Online*, New York: Cambridge University Press, 2006.

H. M. Chittenden, *History of Early Steamboat Navigation on the Missouri River: Life and Adventures of Joseph La Barge*, New York: F. P. Harper, 1903.

C. Cobb, *American Railway Guide, and Pocket Companion for the United States . . . Together with a Complete Railway Map*, New York: C. Dinsmore & Co., 1853.

L. A. Craig, R. Palmquist, and T. Weiss, 'Transportation Improvements and Land Values in the Antebellum United States: A Hedonic Approach', *Journal of Real Estate Finance and Economics*, 16(2), 1998, 173–89.

J. Disturnell, *Disturnell's Guide through the Middle, Northern, and Eastern States Containing a Description of the Principal Places, Canal, Railroad, and Steamboat Routes, Tables of Distances, etc.: Compiled from Authentic Sources.* New York: J. Disturnell, 1847.

J. Doggett, *Doggett's Railroad Guide and Gazetteer for–1848–with Sectional Maps of the Great Routes of Travel*, New York: John Doggett Jr., 1848.

D. Donaldson and R. Hornbeck, 'Railroads and American Economic Growth: A "Market Access" Approach', *Quarterly Journal of Economics*, 131(2), 2016, 799–858.

A. Fishlow, *American Railroads and the Transformation of the Antebellum Economy*, Cambridge, MA: Harvard University Press, 1965.

R. W. Fogel, *Railroads and American Economic Growth: Essays in Econometric History*, Baltimore, MD: Johns Hopkins Press, 1964.

C. Goodrich (ed.), *Canals and American Economic Development*, New York: Columbia University Press, 1961.

C. R. Harte, *Connecticut's Canals*, New Haven, CT: C. R. Harte, 1938.

R. G. Healey, *The Pennsylvania Anthracite Coal Industry, 1860–1902: Economic Cycles, Business Decision-Making and Regional Dynamics*, Scranton, PA: University of Scranton Press, 2007.

R. G. Healey and T. R. Stamp, 'Historical GIS as a Foundation for the Analysis of Regional Economic Growth: Theoretical, Methodological, and Practical Issues', *Social Science History*, 24(3), 2000, 575–612.

L. C. Hunter, *Steamboats on the Western Rivers: An Economic and Technological History*, Cambridge, MA: Harvard University Press, 1949.

M. W. Jacobus, *The Connecticut River Steamboat Story*, Hartford, CT: Connecticut Historical Society, 1956.

A. Kanneberg, 'Wisconsin Law of Waters', *Wisconsin Law Review* 1946.

J. E. Kleber, *The Encyclopedia of Louisville*, Lexington, KY: University Press of Kentucky, 2001.

A. K. Knowles, *Past Time, Past Place: GIS for History*, Redlands, CA: ESRI Press, 2002.

A. K. Knowles and R. G. Healey, 'Geography, Timing, and Technology: A GIS-Based Analysis of Pennsylvania's Iron Industry, 1825–1875', *Journal of Economic History*, 66, 2006, 608–634.

A. K. Knowles and A. Hillier, *Placing History: How Maps, Spatial Data, and GIS Are Changing Historical Scholarship*, Redlands, CA: ESRI Press, 2008.

A. M. Modelski, *Railroad Maps of North America: The First Hundred Years*, New York: Bonanza Books, 1987.

M. Ovenden, *Railway Maps of the World*, New York: Viking, 2011.

P. F. Paskoff, *Troubled Waters: Steamboat Disasters, River Improvements, and American Public Policy, 1821–1860*, Baton Rouge, LA: Louisiana State University Press, 2007.

C. O. Paullin, J. K. Wright, Carnegie Institution of Washington, and American Geographical Society, *Atlas of the Historical Geography of the United States*, Washington, DC: Carnegie Institution, 1932.

F. L. Paxson, 'The Railroads of the "Old Northwest" Before the Civil War', *Transactions of the Wisconsin Academy of Sciences, Arts, and Letters* 17(1), 1914, 247–74.

H. V. Poor, *History of the Railroads and Canals of the United States of America*, New York: J. H. Schultz & Co., 1860.

D. J. Puffert, 'The Economics of Spatial Network Externalities and the Dynamics of Railway Gauge Standardization', PhD microform, Stanford University, 1991.

D. J. Puffert, 'The Standardization of Track Gauge on North American Railways, 1830–1890', *Journal of Economic History*, 60(4), 2000, 933–60.

Rand McNally & Co., National General Ticket Agents' Association, and National Railway Publication Co., *The Rand-McNally Official Railway Guide and Handbook*, Chicago, IL: National Railway Publication Co., 1879.

B. F. Riley, *History of Conecuh County, Alabama*, Columbus, GA.: T. Gilbert, printer, 1881.

J. Robbins, 'In Napa Valley, Future Landscapes Are Viewed in the Past', *New York Times*, 25 January 2016.

J. Story, *Commentaries on the Constitution of the United States: With a Preliminary Review of the Constitutional History of the Colonies and States, before the Adoption of the Constitution*, Cambridge, MA: Brown, Shattuck, & Co., 1833.

H. S. Tanner, *Map of the Canals & Rail Roads of the United States Reduced from the Large Map of the U.S. by H. S. Tanner*. Philadelphia: J. Knight, 1830.

H. S. Tanner, *A Description of the Canals and Railroads of the United States*, New York: T. R. Tanner & J. Disturnell, 1840.

G. R. Taylor, *The Transportation Revolution 1815–1860*, New York: Holt, Rinehart & Winston, 1951.

G. R. Taylor and I. D. Neu, *The American Railroad Network, 1861–1890*, Cambridge, MA: Harvard University Press, 1956.

R. F. Tomlinson, 'A Geographic Information System for Regional Planning', in G.A. Stewart (ed.), *Land Evaluation; Papers of a CSIRO Symposium, Organized in Cooperation with UNESCO 26–31 August 1968*, [Melbourne]: Macmillan of Australia, 1968.

P. B. Trescott, 'The Louisville and Portland Canal Company, 1825–1874', *The Mississippi Valley Historical Review*, 44(4), 1958, 686–708.

US Census Office, *United States census of transportation*, 1880, Washington, DC: Govt. Print. Office, 1883.

US Census Office, *Statistical Atlas of the United States Based Upon the Results of the Eleventh Census*, Washington, DC: GPO, 1898.

US Continental Congress, *An Ordinance for the Government of the Territory of the United States, North-west of the River Ohio*, New York: s.n, 1787.

US Department of Transportation, *National Transportation Atlas Database* [Online], Washington, DC: US Department of Transportation Bureau of Transportation Statistics, 2012. Available: www.rita.dot.gov/bts/sites/rita.dot.gov.bts/files/publications/national_transportation_atlas_database/2012/index.html [Accessed February 2013].

US District Court for Northern Illinois, Hurd v. Rock Island Bridge Company, 1857. (The court's papers were all destroyed in the Chicago fire of 1871. See www.archives.gov/publications/prologue/2004/summer/bridge.html).

US Senate, 'Roads and canals', communicated to the Senate, 6 April 1808.

US Supreme Court, The Galena, Dubuque, Dunleith, and Minnesota Packet Co. v. The Rock Island Bridge. *71 U.S. 4 Wall 435*, 1867.

US Supreme Court, The Daniel Ball. *77 U.S. 10 Wall*, 1870.

US Supreme Court, The Montello. *87 U.S. 20 Wall*, 1874.

N. E. Whitford, *History of the Canal System of the State of New York, Together with Brief Histories of the Canals of the United States and Canada. Supplement to the Annual Report of the Engineer and Surveyor of the State of New York*, Albany, NY: Brandow Printing Co., 1906.

A. Williams, *Telegraph and Rail Road Map of the New England States*. Boston, 1854.

M. H. Wright, 'Early Navigation and Commerce along the Arkansas and Red Rivers in Oklahoma', *Chronicles of Oklahoma* 8(1), 1930, 65–88.

9

GEOGRAPHIES OF WELFARE IN NINETEENTH-CENTURY ENGLAND AND WALES

Douglas H. L. Brown

The new poor law

From 1834 the destitute of England and Wales had a new environment of rights, responsibilities and hazards to navigate, in the form of the Poor Law Amendment Act.[1] Since the end of Elizabeth's reign, some 15,535 parishes had been responsible for the distribution of relief.[2] Each had its own practices and policies, and reformers pointed to the social and economic ills which resulted from this patchwork of administration.[3] Under the new poor law – the framework for poor relief in England and Wales which persisted until the early twentieth century – parishes were encouraged to come together as poor law unions run by elected guardians. The object was to ease the tax burden for local ratepayers by reducing the number of paupers through deterrence and by cutting costs through economies of scale.

The local administration of relief was brought under unprecedented central government scrutiny with the formation of the Poor Law Commission and its successors, the Poor Law Board and the Local Government Board. The use of payments in cash or in kind ('outdoor' relief), for able-bodied males at least, was to be discouraged in favour of relief inside the workhouse ('indoor' relief). To encourage this class of person to find employment, rather than apply for relief, indoor relief was to be governed by the principle of 'less eligibility': that conditions in the workhouse should be no better than those enjoyed by the lowest-paid independent labourer. In other words, the poor would exhaust all other options before 'throwing themselves on the parish' and becoming paupers. This, reformers believed, would reduce applications for relief and therefore overall expenditure.

The new poor law guardians, elected by ratepayers, had much less discretion over relief practices under the new law than the local officials who had formerly administered relief. However, it was not the purpose of the central authority to ensure every aspect of relief was identical across the country. Expenditure and types of relief varied widely between unions throughout the life of the new poor law.

Historians have so far explained differences primarily by local divergence in policy and by the uneven demand for poor relief.[4] But this research project adds a new layer of analysis, made possible by GIS: it investigates how far variations in local relief expenditure and policy were linked to the local provision of goods and services. Prices had an effect both on the buying power of poor law unions, and on the decisions guardians made about the extent and types of relief they made available. There were complex links between prices and relief provision: high commodity prices could force many people to seek relief, or could arise from the same economic circumstances that caused destitution. High prices in some circumstances could lead to stricter entitlement regimes, through unions' budgetary constraints. More important, however, were the relationships between unions and their suppliers. An institution like a workhouse could have had a significant impact on a local economy by creating demand that would otherwise not have existed. Workhouses were considerable institutions: the median number of indoor paupers maintained by unions on 1 January 1851 was 154, and all needed three meals a day, bedding, clothing and heating. Suppliers might in some cases have owed their existence to the local workhouse consuming their goods. Furthermore, individual unions were dependent on markets with varying degrees of competition, flexibility, organisation and size.

Boards of guardians took decisions based on their local circumstances and these national and regional contexts. Guardians had little power in the face of economic cycles, regional trade depressions, local outbreaks of infectious diseases and the like. However, they could exercise a certain amount of discretion when it came to contracting for the supply of goods and services to the union. Regulations issued by the central authority could circumscribe guardians' activities, but they could not bind the independent traders who sold goods to the unions. Rather, these interactions were subject to existing contract law. This gave boards of guardians flexibility in their financial management and thereby their local relationships, putting social structures and processes at the heart of poor law economies.

To map supplier networks is, therefore, to map social relationships – and here we see the usefulness of historical GIS in creating new knowledge about society. These relationships formed a significant part of poor law guardians' strategies for controlling costs: the demand for goods from poor law unions was considerable as workhouses consumed very great amounts of food, fuel and clothing. Take, for example, Wandsworth & Clapham union's workhouse, which accommodated around 450 people: it held in its store on 22 March 1851 some 443 lb of cheese, 280 lb of oatmeal, 956 pints of porter, 351 pints of ale, 70 tons of coal, 1,680 lb of potatoes and over a mile of cloth.[5] Guardians therefore had substantial bargaining power.

Despite this, in many respects it was the large suppliers who had the advantage in dictating prices, and guardians' procurement practices were not always efficient. Workhouse inmates suffered the consequences of unions' efforts to reduce costs, with suppliers delivering poor-quality and sometimes adulterated food. Guardians had the dual priorities of keeping costs down, while wanting to spend the rates (the local tax funding poor relief) within their unions. They were also constrained by the number of potential suppliers.

For reasons of availability and cost, therefore, relatively remote unions – such as Llanfyllin, Wales, which is examined here – had to rely on cheap suppliers from major towns outside their unions. Yet there was also space in the market for more minor traders to gain business from poor law supply, and unions gave some trade to local businesses on an *ad hoc* basis.

The research described in this chapter therefore has three intertwined strands. One is the mapping and analysis of poor relief itself. This provides context for the second strand: the charting of the prices paid for certain key commodities by poor law unions. The third strand is the mapping of supplier locations and networks, which enables a deeper understanding of the social relations underpinning poor law supply.

Data sources

Historians have tended to aggregate poor law data by county or region, partly as a result of the necessity of making the data manageable. This approach loses the intra-regional variation which characterises the poor law landscape, however. And at the same time, historians have lamented that the sheer volume of material on the poor law makes it necessary to illustrate chiefly by example, and that it is impossible to know how representative any such example might be.[6] Variations in poor relief must be considered with more granularity, and this chapter therefore uses disaggregated data from all individual poor law unions in Wales, manually digitised from British Parliamentary Papers. Looking at the data at union level shows that it is possible to understand both individual unions and the contexts of their wider regions. The poor law, after all, was a local institution and was treated as such by paupers, guardians, local officials, ratepayers, central government and policymakers.

By 1850, the Poor Law Board (PLB) had been in place for three years and was operating what might be termed a 'mature' system of relief. The early 1850s were also an important demographic turning-point. The 1851 census revealed for the first time that more people in England lived in urban areas than in rural, as a result both of direct migration to towns and of those new urban dwellers increasing local birth rates.[7] This period also has the advantage of data availability as 1850 is the earliest year for which a daily pauper count (held on 1 January) was published nationally for all unions.[8] A population census was held in 1851, permitting demographic analysis; moreover rateable value (the local tax base) was recorded for the period.

Records of the prices paid by individual unions for goods and services on a national scale are not uniformly available, as guardians were very rarely required to make returns of their contract prices. Data are available for 1850 and 1851, published in an 1852 parliamentary paper which gives data for two six-month periods ending 25 March 1850 and 1851 respectively.[9] Details of the suppliers to poor law unions were never systematically recorded centrally, so local archives form the basis of that part of the analysis for Llanfyllin, a case-study union in this chapter.

Most of the centrally collected data, including the annual poor rate return, is found in parliamentary papers published by the Poor Law Commission, Poor Law Board or Local Government Board (Table 9.1). The central authority in all its forms was characterised by a focus on enumerating poor relief expenditure and on quantifying pauperism. The operation of the poor laws had been a subject of statistical inquiry well before their amendment in 1834, but a central government department created by the new law with specific responsibility for poor relief administration had an unprecedented ability to gather, publish and analyse information on national and

Table 9.1 Selected poor law union data sources.

Data type	Source
Population, 1851.	British Parliamentary Papers (PP) 1876 LXIII 1.
Indoor and outdoor paupers, 1 Jan 1850.	*Paupers.*
Area in acres, 1854.	PP 1854 LVI 1. *Poor rates, &c.*
Rateable value of property assessed to the poor rate, 1852.	
Relief expenditure, year to 25 Mar 1850.	PP 1851 XXVI 1. *Third annual report of the Poor Law Board. 1850.*
Provisions prices, 1850 and 1851.	PP 1852 XLV 7: *Poor relief.*
Supplier records, Llanfyllin, 1844–80.	Powys County Archives, M/G/B/8/1.

local practice.[10] In part, this activity was aimed at holding poor law unions to account. It also can be seen in the context of increasing interest in methodologically rigorous approaches to data collection, evident in the close connections between poor law personnel and the Statistical Society of London, which existed to gather and disseminate quantitative data about the state.

Edwin Chadwick was appointed auditor to the society in 1835, within months of its establishment, and fellows included Frederick Purdy, who became head of the PLB's statistical department, and William Golden Lumley, the PLC's Assistant Secretary.[11] The first article published in the society's journal proper was by Assistant Poor Law Commissioner James Phillips Kay.[12] The sheer bulk of information collected by the poor law authorities presented many analytical difficulties, and indeed the 1834 *Report* began with a description of the problems the commissioners had encountered: the replies to their circulated queries were 'so numerous, that it became a question how they should be disposed of'.[13] Modern scholarship has also found the volume of data to be a barrier to research.[14] However, the quantity and detail of available information should be treated as an opportunity, rather than an obstacle.

The PLB from 1848 asked unions to report their respective pauper numbers in and out of the workhouse on 1 January and 1 July.[15] The relationship between these day-counts and total numbers of paupers relieved in the whole year is a difficult one to ascertain, given the flaws in the six-month counts, though some historians have attempted to 'correct' the day-counts by multiplying their averages by certain constants.[16] In this study, unless otherwise specified, only the 1 January count is used, without any attempt at 'correction'. 1 January is an arbitrary date for the collection of the figures – chosen for its administrative convenience by the Poor Law Board – and the numbers of paupers on that date do not represent the same proportion of paupers relieved for the whole year for every union. Figures for 'expenditure per pauper', for example, therefore should be read as expenditure *for the full year* divided by the number of paupers *on 1 January of that year*. This ensures that all the figures are comparable. Figures for expenditure per pauper should therefore be treated as indicative only, as they do not represent actual sums spent per individual pauper.

The digitised quantitative data from Parliamentary Papers were visualised and analysed using shapefiles created by EDINA UKBorders.[17] Joining the data was a fairly straightforward procedure, using unique identifying numbers for each poor law union. The raw shapefiles were available only for 1840 but the quantitative data to be joined to them were for 1850, making necessary some manual editing of the shapefile to reflect boundary changes in the intervening years.

Geo-referencing supplier locations was somewhat more challenging. Identities of winners of contracts were recorded in the minutes of individual unions' boards of guardians, which are usually in local archives if they have survived. Street addresses tended to be noted when the supplier was located within the union, especially within the town in which the workhouse stood. In many cases, though, just parishes, villages or towns were named, especially when the supplier was outside the union or in a village elsewhere in it. For example, a record such as 'James Smith, Baker, High Street' would most likely have indicated the high street in the town containing the union workhouse. For a supplier outside the town, 'John Brown, Butcher, Newtown' would have been the usual record. Many records were more vague, especially when a long-standing supplier was well known to the board. Archival cross-referencing provided more detail, but in most cases contemporary business directories were most useful in narrowing down identities when there were multiple possibilities for the supplier.[18] Business directories could also provide addresses when they were missing from guardians' minutes.

Using historic and modern maps, suppliers were each assigned a modern equivalent street address. This had to be done manually in the absence of reliable gazetteers capable of parsing historic addresses. These addresses were then run through Esri's ArcGIS geocoding database to provide mappable coordinates. Inevitable gaps in the resulting data were filled manually by entering coordinates identified by cross-referencing historic and modern maps. Addresses could not reliably be identified for a handful of suppliers and these were omitted from the final database.[19]

Geographies of poor relief

North Wales's poor law unions in 1850 had among the highest percentage of the population defined as paupers in all of England and Wales. Pauperism cannot necessarily be seen a direct proxy for poverty, as paupers were people the guardians and their officers *chose* to relieve from among the individuals and families who applied for relief (though pauperism rates cannot be divorced from local poverty entirely). Low numbers of paupers, therefore, might not always indicate low levels of poverty in a given union: the guardians might have been keen to keep the poor rates down and thus declined many applications. Though there was a regional trend towards higher pauperism in the north of Wales, clearly there was a good deal of intra-regional disparity between neighbouring unions nonetheless (Figure 9.1).

This variability underlines the importance of preserving local granularity in spatial analysis, a fact not lost on contemporaries: The guardians of individual unions did not like being treated as part of a single bloc, especially when it came to implementing policies seen as being a London solution to a problem inherent in the labour market of south-eastern England. Unions in Wales tended to use much more outdoor relief compared to their English counterparts, because of the expense of running workhouses in rural and remote areas – and no Welsh unions were classed as urban

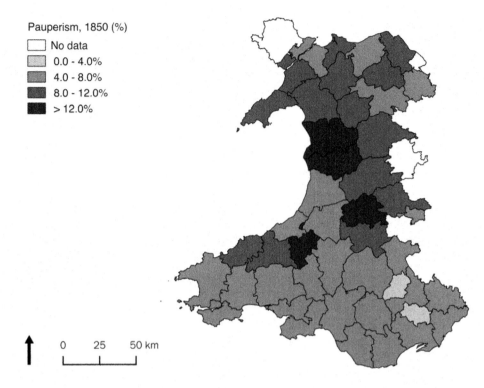

Pauperism, 1850 (%)

☐ No data
▨ 0.0 - 4.0%
▨ 4.0 - 8.0%
▨ 8.0 - 12.0%
■ > 12.0%

0   25   50 km

Figure 9.1 Percentage of paupers in populations in poor law unions, Wales, 1 January 1850.
Source: See Table 9.1.

by the contemporary measure of containing more than one person per acre on average (Figure 9.2).

Between 1850 and 1870 most regions increased their use of the workhouse or were already using it to a significant degree. But in Wales, indoor pauperism increased over the 20-year period by just one percentage point from a very low 5 per cent (Table 9.2).

Why did so many unions in Wales resist using the workhouse? Wales had among the lowest indoor pauperism rates, and was typified by resistance to the principles of the new poor law. The experiences of William Day, an assistant poor law commissioner from 1835 to 1843, suggest some characteristics of the unions in Wales under his superintendence which contributed to their low indoor pauperism rate. From his perspective, the area was rife with abuses and intractable opposition to investing in workhouses, stemming from a combination of misconceptions about the new system and the vested interests of landowners. The ratepayers and guardians of the poor in many unions were stubbornly opposed to adopting the policies advocated by Day and the PLC, such as replacing their old and (in Day's view) inadequate workhouses with expensive modern institutions. In 1839 he told the PLC: 'I cannot but feel that the question henceforth whether you or the Guardians are to be masters in Wales is now in peril. I have been repeatedly told by the Guardians that you *dare* not enforce your orders, & in the confidence of this it is that they dare to disobey them.'[20]

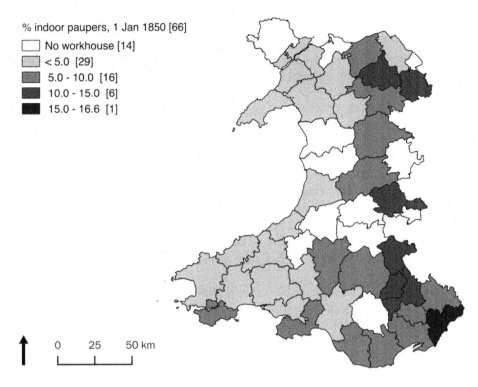

% indoor paupers, 1 Jan 1850 [66]

☐ No workhouse [14]

☐ < 5.0 [29]

▨ 5.0 - 10.0 [16]

▨ 10.0 - 15.0 [6]

■ 15.0 - 16.6 [1]

0   25   50 km

Figure 9.2   Percentage of paupers relieved in the workhouse, 1 January 1850.

Source: See Table 9.1.

Table 9.2 Mean spend per pauper type by relief and location-type of union, 1850 and 1870 (at 1850 values).

Location type	Spend per indoor pauper			Spend per outdoor pauper			Indoor pauperism %		
	1850 (£)	1870 (£)	Change (%)	1850 (£)	1870 (£)	Change (%)	1850 (%)	1870 (%)	Change (%)
London	8.92	9.75	+9	2.94	2.85	−3	23	26	+13
Northern rural	6.10	7.50	+23	3.97	3.95	−1	12	13	+14
Northern urban	6.12	7.60	+24	3.12	3.16	+1	11	17	+59
Southern rural	5.65	6.97	+23	3.90	3.76	−4	16	14	−8
Southern urban	6.36	8.20	+29	3.44	3.29	−4	19	19	+1
Wales	5.80	7.31	+26	3.65	4.08	+12	5	6	+15

Source: PP 1851 XXVI 1; PP 1876 LXIII 1.

He wrote to fellow assistant commissioner Sir John Walsham in 1840: 'You cannot know the miseries of thirty or forty Welsh Guardians who *won't* build a Workhouse, and consequently meet in the parlour of a pot house twelve feet by fourteen and keep all the windows shut and spit tobacco on your shoes – to say nothing of knowing not a word of what they are talking of in an unknown tongue.'[21]

Day's confrontational style might have contributed to the guardians' resistance, and after his forced resignation in 1843 the PLC suggested he 'was wanting not in activity but in discretion'.[22] Here was entrenched resistance to expensive central government policies seen to be designed for the south of England, reinforced by a personality clash.

Goods and suppliers

Guardians acted locally, but they bought goods and services that were subject to national, regional and local markets and supply networks. Local variations in price were key to some of the differences visible in relief practices, not simply because prices affected relief costs but because they were a product of the relationships between unions and suppliers in local economies. Understanding geographies of supply, therefore, is important in developing a clearer grasp of the factors that influenced the overall costs of poor relief. GIS enables the visualisation and analysis of such networks.

Buying low-quality goods in bulk usually meant that unions paid prices at the bottom end of the range. However unions' buying practices were also shaped by the nature of production costs, supply chains, local demand and competition – all of which varied by commodity and by location. Regions with low prices did not necessarily produce regions of low relief expenditure, but relief practices were strongly influenced by the nature of the wider markets for particular goods, whether local, regional or national. The sources of workhouse supplies must therefore be seen as a field of management that was subject not just to administrative activity but also to market forces.

Bread was the staple food of the general population and of paupers in particular.[23] When outdoor relief was given in kind, it tended to be wholly or partly in bread. It was also consumed in the workhouse, frequently with tea and butter for breakfast, as an accompaniment to soup or broth, as a substitute for potatoes with meat, or with cheese or butter for supper.[24] Bread for paupers was renowned in popular culture for its poor quality, and *Punch* parodied the commercial prices columns in the likes of *The Economist* by reporting on 'mysterious transactions in sawdust by the baker who liberally deals with the workhouse'.[25]

The purchasing of bread and flour by poor law unions clearly demonstrates the significance of price in guardians' procurement decisions. Unions had to supply bread to paupers and could choose between baking their own or buying from an external supplier (or a combination of both). In areas where high bread prices prevailed, unions tended to buy flour instead and baked their own loaves. Welsh unions almost entirely made their own, leading to large gaps in mapping the contract prices of bread agreed by poor law unions (Figure 9.3). It can also be seen in the low percentage of Welsh unions reporting their contract prices to the central authority compared to reports from the other regions (Table 9.3).

In many parts of England, unions gave a good deal of outdoor relief in kind – usually bread. In Wales, though, outdoor relief was not usually given in kind: bread was not especially cheap, and we have seen that Welsh guardians defended their long-standing policies of giving outdoor paupers cash (Figure 9.4). There were fewer workhouses,

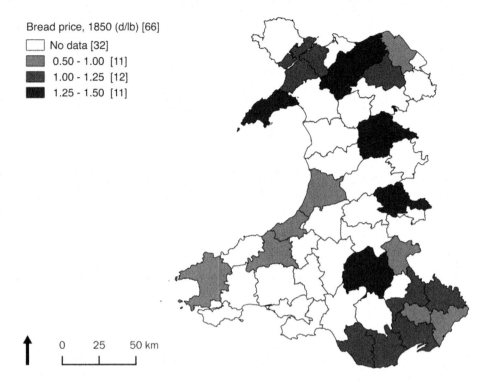

Figure 9.3 Price paid by poor law unions in Wales for bread, 1850.

Source: See Table 9.1.

Table 9.3 Mean prices paid for bread by unions, by location type.

	Mean price, d/lb	% returning prices
London	1.19	92.6
Northern Rural	1.15	65.0
Northern Urban	1.13	66.0
Southern Rural	1.09	89.7
Southern Urban	1.06	96.0
Wales	1.11	59.5
All	1.11	78.5

Source: PP 1852 XLV 7.

and fewer paupers in them. But those workhouses that were in place were, at the very least, obliged to buy flour for their indoor paupers to bake into bread themselves. Hence the map of flour prices has far fewer gaps than that of bread prices (many gaps being because of the absence of a workhouse), and we can also see much more regional uniformity in flour prices (Figure 9.5).

Where flour prices were high, so too were bread prices. The districts with fewer bread-buyers were therefore those districts with high flour prices too – and the

193

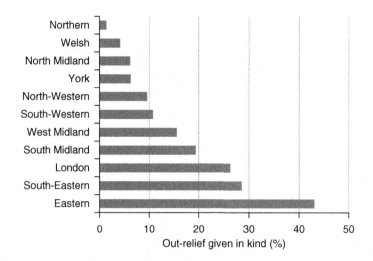

Figure 9.4 Percentage of outdoor relief given in kind, 1881, by Local Government Board poor law union divisions.

Source: PP 1882 XXX Pt. I 1.

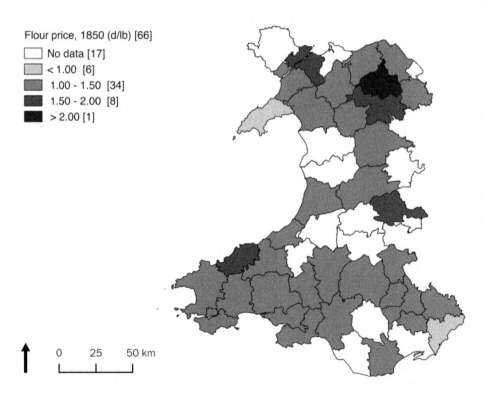

Figure 9.5 Price paid by poor law unions in Wales for flour, 1850.

Source: See Table 9.1.

Table 9.4 Mean prices paid for flour by unions, by location type.

	Mean price, d/lb	% returning prices
London	1.38	96.3
Northern Rural	1.36	94.4
Northern Urban	1.36	90.6
Southern Rural	1.28	96.2
Southern Urban	1.26	100.0
Wales	1.42	94.6
All	1.32	95.2

Source: PP 1852 XLV 7.

unions within them had little option but to buy flour. Wales had the highest flour prices, yet nearly 95 per cent of Welsh unions with workhouses returned prices (Table 9.4).

Mapping the local prices of goods, and in this case flour rather than bread, therefore enables us to see how costs directly affected unions' purchasing decisions and relief policies.

Case study: Llanfyllin poor law union

The geography of the supply of goods to poor law unions was of fundamental importance to boards of guardians, to paupers and to the suppliers themselves. For guardians, knowledge of potential contracting partners was essential for achieving a suitable balance of cost and quality for ratepayers and paupers, and for maintaining good terms with those ratepayers who sold to unions. For suppliers, institutions such as workhouses, schools, infirmaries and asylums could be vital sources of income, and it was in suppliers' interests to form connections with the officials responsible for allocating contracts. Poor law supply was therefore constituted socially, in the relationships between guardians and local business.

These relationships potentially diminished with distance, however.[26] Guardians were more likely to know businesses well if they were within their own unions – and especially in the same town – compared to those further away. Small traders were most likely to supply only the unions in which they were located, first because the ability to send goods cheaply over any greater distance was a function of scale, and second because the opportunities to form essential selling relationships were more present locally. Larger enterprises were therefore better able to supply distant unions. Over the second half of the nineteenth century, these larger businesses took on a greater role in poor law supply.

Business was increasingly given to suppliers further from the workhouse – including some based in London. By around 1880 unions bought more from larger businesses which supplied a wider variety of goods, compared to 30 years earlier when smaller local specialised traders had more poor law business. Nonetheless there were still, in 1880, opportunities for the smaller traders to supply unions, and the poor law remained a key source of revenue for these small businesses. Poor law unions could

Table 9.5 Locations of suppliers to Llanfyllin union, 1844 and 1880.

Year	Suppliers identified	Suppliers in union		<10 miles from WH	
		N	%	N	%
1844	53	32	60.4	33	62.3
1880	34	23	67.6	24	70.6

Source: Minutes of Board of Guardians.

represent very stable and long-lasting sources of business for local suppliers who were capable of meeting their requirements.

Llanfyllin was a large and mountainous union with a fairly small population, with Llanfyllin town connected by road and, from 1863, a branch rail line to the market towns of Oswestry and Shrewsbury. The majority of its workhouse's suppliers in the 1840s were inside the union, but a significant minority were outside (Table 9.5). Several suppliers from outside Llanfyllin town, but within the union's boundaries, provided goods such as straw, shoes, dairy produce, brushes and some groceries. The workhouse was supplied by a wide range of businesses from outside the union, including grocers, chandlers and potato merchants in Oswestry, stationers and shoemakers in Shrewsbury, and two dairy farmers in Llandidloes. Some goods had to bought from suppliers at a greater distance: glass from Birmingham, drapery from Manchester, stationery from London and slate from Pontrhydyfen, near Port Talbot. Because of the town's remoteness, Llanfyllin's traders did not have direct access to goods on the scale that the workhouse required, whereas those in Oswestry and Shrewsbury did.

By 1880 there was a similar number and variety of suppliers from within the union as in 1844, but patterns of distribution from outside the union had changed. There were fewer suppliers in total, and fewer suppliers from outside the union, in 1880 compared to 1844 (Figure 9.6). Much of its provisions now came from a single, out-of-union supplier: Joseph Evans of Oswestry, who sold the union oatmeal, split peas, coffee, sugar, candles, soap and soda. This business was performing the functions which 30 years earlier were carried out by individual mealmen, grocers, chandlers and oilmen. As well as a few specialist suppliers (such as a shoemaker and cheesemonger in Shrewsbury, and a clock repairer in Corwen), there were now some larger enterprises supplying a greater range of goods. Because the region was increasingly well connected, Llanfyllin union was able to seek goods from distant suppliers, though it was still not a hub in itself: rather than buying from businesses in Neath, Birmingham, Manchester and so on, therefore, it could buy more from the growing towns of Oswestry and Shrewsbury.

Llanfyllin's workhouse was a substantial consumer of goods from outside the union in the 1840s, despite not getting a rail link until 1863. In this respect, Llanfyllin resembled other Welsh unions that were hampered by poor communications. Merthyr Tydfil, for example, imported flour from Ireland to avoid high internal transport costs.[27] Furthermore, mid and north Wales did not have an effective internal market, and farmers tended to export to the Midlands and northern counties of

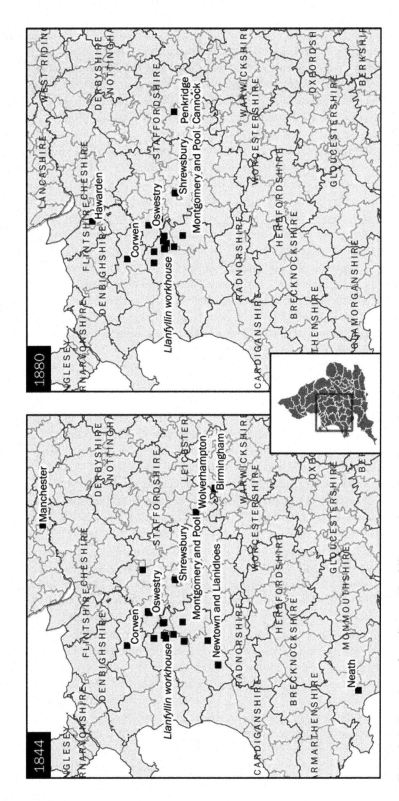

Figure 9.6 Locations of suppliers to Llanfyllin poor law union, 1844 and 1880.

Source: Minutes of board of guardians.

England rather than finding buyers closer to home.[28] This trade, and presumably the trade that brought goods into Llanfyllin, was frequently conducted on waterways.[29] Nearby Newtown and Welshpool were on a branch of the Ellesmere canal which linked to the navigable Severn at Llanymynech, not far from Oswestry.[30] Both the Severn and the Montgomeryshire Canal were used for freight transport.[31] Those businesses which supplied Llanfyllin with goods from further afield would have used waterways such as these.

Businesses did not simply interact with their customers: they also existed in relation to their competitors and colleagues and in the context of wider society. These relations constituted, and were a product of, the business environment. Contractual arrangements made by poor law unions were characterised by a reliance on reputation and reliability, as well as on price, and Rose points to the 'informal networks of mutual trust and interest' in local business communities which kept transaction costs 'comparatively low'.[32] This is borne out by poor law contracting, which was indeed a combination of formal and informal networks and arrangements, enabling well-placed small local businesses to participate. There were low barriers to entry for traders, but the ability to supply on a large scale was still restricted to those who had the required capital. Using GIS to place both local suppliers and those further afield demonstrates that the ease of supply from a large, distant business could trump local connections if the price was right.

Nonetheless, local suppliers tended to have the advantage. A contract to supply a poor law union could be highly lucrative over the long term, though it was not easy to maintain a working relationship over many years when contracts were re-advertised every three or six months. This is clear from examining the longevity of supply relationships over the period 1850 to 1880. According to the guardians' minutes, Llanfyllin bought from 75 individually named suppliers in that period, 24 of whom only held a contract for a single quarter. A relationship, once formed, could be fruitful for many years, underscoring the importance of social processes in the market economy. Many suppliers won poor law business frequently, if not continuously, and a few suppliers held contracts for very long periods: James Fox supplied Llanfyllin with milk and butter, and occasionally shoes, for nearly the full 30 years (110 quarters). Charles Jones supplied the workhouse with shoes for 90 quarters.

Businesses attempting to gain the custom of the Llanfyllin guardians may well have found it very hard to gain a contract in the first place, but easier to maintain it once won (Figure 9.7). There were six periods of more than a year when no new suppliers were given any business. Furthermore, Llanfyllin's guardians tended to award only one new supplier with a contract in any given period. The advantages to suppliers of bidding for poor law business were clear: income was not just relatively secure over the course of one contract but also very likely to be repeated in future contracts. This was dependent on the supplier proving his or her reliability by meeting the expectations of the union.[33] Winning the initial contract was the more difficult task, therefore, as the competition was between the known suppliers who potentially dominated the tendering process and the newcomers who relied on reputations built elsewhere and on lower bids. Guardians were wary of the ability of a low-bidding newcomer to deliver reliably, yet they could not afford to ignore low bidders because of their responsibility to their ratepayer electorates.

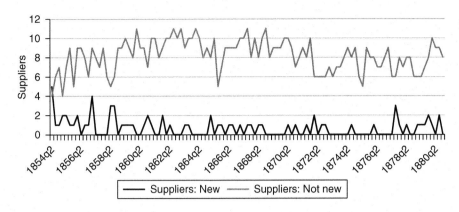

Figure 9.7   Number of new and not new suppliers to Llanfyllin union, 1854–80.

Source: Minutes of board of guardians.

The choice of poor law supplier can be seen as something akin to the exercise of patronage by union boards at those times and places where guardians knew their local pool of suppliers. Guardians relied on information about price and reliability which, in an open market and with all else being equal, would enable them to make the most appropriate decision for their ratepayers. Yet all else could not be equal as long as guardians had the discretion to choose arbitrarily: trust – a social feature – was an integral part of poor law supply. The auditors who scrutinised contractual arrangements were concerned only with whether the deal was legal, not whether it was good value for money, and guardians were largely left to get on with the business of procurement by the central authority.[34]

Social relationships were integral, and can be seen operating in different ways as bigger firms with a longer reach entered the market between the 1840s and 1880s. Boards of guardians formed business relationships with these bigger and more distant suppliers, but continued to work with smaller local suppliers too. As a relatively remote union, Llanfyllin had to buy from somewhat distant suppliers: its local businesses were comparatively poorly connected to wider markets, so it was obliged to buy from firms further afield (such as in Oswestry) which were higher up the supply chain. But contractors were ratepayers wherever possible, and guardians relied on continuity and reliability. Suppliers therefore ranged from individual shopkeepers and dealers to large industrial enterprises. However, *ad hoc* purchases may have been made in small quantities from local traders who were not ratepayers and who might have had incomes at the smaller end of the scale.

The changes between the 1850s and 1880s can be attributed to a number of factors. Railway communications were important in reducing the cost of transporting goods, though existing infrastructure such as waterways was vital for relatively remote places earlier in the period. On a wider scale, developments such as telegraphy and cheaper steel allowed information and goods to be distributed in greater quantities and at longer distances.[35] Poor law supply was therefore, for the most part, characterised by local knowledge networks and relationships, and this persisted even with the gradual introduction of bigger enterprises capable of supplying on a greater scale.

Spatial thinking in socio-economic history

The relative independence of guardians in their contracting practices means that the local geography of supply, and hence the spatial dimension of poor law activity, must be a vital consideration for economic and social historians, just as it was for union boards. Unions did not have to award contracts based on the lowest tender, and a supplier could be chosen on the basis of a reputation for reliability, a personal relationship, or even a bribe. Poor law economies were thus emphatically embedded in social structures rather than adhering rigidly to the dictates of market prices. Geographic information systems are central to developing this understanding. By mapping and analysing poor relief, prices of goods and supplier locations we can begin to see how the social and the economic were intertwined.

The findings discussed here demonstrate the importance of mapping and visualising local, granular, data for identifying trends, with the potential for more multifaceted analysis in the future. Until now, little effort has been made to address Humphrey Southall's 'tentative' suggestion, made in 1991, that 'the general neglect of the spatially disaggregated national statistics in existing studies of the Poor Law is not altogether justified'.[36] This research shows that GIS is capable of answering this call.

Notes

1 4 & 5 Will. IV, c. 76. An Act for the Amendment and Better Administration of the Laws relating to the Poor in England and Wales (1834).

2 43 Eliz., c. 2. An Acte for the Reliefe of the Poore (1601).

3 British Parliamentary Papers (*PP*) *1834 XXVII 1–XXXIX 1: Report . . . into . . . the Poor Laws*.

4 M. MacKinnon, 'Poor Law Policy, Unemployment and Pauperism', *Explorations in Economic History* 23(3), 1986, 229–336; S. King, *Poverty and Welfare in England, 1700–1850: A Regional Perspective*, Manchester: Manchester University Press, 2000; K. Williams, *From Pauperism to Poverty*, London: Routledge & Kegan Paul, 1981; L. H. Lees, *The Solidarities of Strangers: The English Poor Laws and the People, 1700–1948*, Cambridge: Cambridge University Press, 1998.

5 Minutes of Board of Guardians, London Metropolitan Archives (LMA) WABG/010, 22 March 1851.

6 M. A. Crowther, *The Workhouse System 1834–1929: The History of an English Social Institution*, London: Batsford Academic & Educational, 1981, 6; King, *Poverty and Welfare*, 7.

7 Urban and rural as defined by the 1851 census. See C. M. Law, 'The Growth of Urban Population in England and Wales, 1801–1911', *Transactions of the Institute of British Geographers* 41, 1967, 125–43, 125; J.G. Williamson, 'Migrant Selectivity, Urbanization, and Industrial Revolutions', *Population and Development Review* 14(2), 1988, 289 ff.

8 PP 1876 LXIII 1: *Paupers*.

9 PP 1852 XLV 7: *Poor Relief*.

10 S. King, '"In These You May Trust": Numerical Information, Accounting Practices and the Poor Law, c.1790 to 1840', in T. Crook and G. O'Hara (eds), *Statistics and the Public Sphere*, London: Routledge, 2011, 51–6.

11 *Proceedings of the Statistical Society of London* 1(2), 19 January 1835, 9–11.

12 J. P. Kay, 'On the Establishment of County or District Schools, for the Training of the Pauper Children Maintained in Union Workhouses. Part I', *Journal of the Statistical Society of London* 1(1), 1838, 14–27.

13 PP 1834 XXVII 1–XXXIX, 2.

14 H. R. Southall, 'Poor Law Statistics and the Geography of Economic Distress', in J. Foreman-Peck (ed.), *New Perspectives on the Late Victorian Economy*, 1991, 213.

15 PP 1850 XXVII, *Second Annual Report of the Poor Law Board*, 1849, 8–9.

16 See e.g. Lees, *Solidarities of Strangers*, 180–1; Williams, *From Pauperism to Poverty*, 158–62; S. Webb and B. Webb, '*English Local Government,* vol. 9, *English Poor Law History,* part II, *The Last Hundred Years*', London: Longmans, Green & Co, 1929.

17 This work is based on data provided through EDINA UKBorders with the support of the ESRC and JISC and uses boundary material which is copyright of the Great Britain Historic GIS Project, Portsmouth University. Prof. Ian Gregory, Lancaster University, also kindly supplied shapefiles. Historic boundary shapefiles are downloadable at http://census.edina.ac.uk/ but poor law unions were no longer available at the time of writing.

18 *Pigot & Co's Royal National and Commercial Directory and Topography of the counties of Berkshire, Buckinghamshire, Cornwall, Devonshire, Dorsetshire, Gloucestershire, Hampshire, Herefordshire, Monmouthshire, Oxfordshire, Somersetshire, Wiltshire, and North and South Wales*, London and Manchester: Isaac Slater, 1844; *Royal National Commercial Directory of North and South Wales*, Manchester: Isaac Slater, 1880.

19 For Llanfyllin's 1842 records, four out of 58 suppliers could not be located, for example.

20 TNA MH32/14, Day to PLC, 15 August 1839.

21 National Library of Wales, Day MSS 3146 F, Day to Sir John Walsham, 9 August 1840, in R. A. Lewis, 'William Day and the Poor Law Commissioners', *University of Birmingham Historical Journal* 9(1), 1963, 180.

22 TNA HO45/1611, PLC to Sir William Somerville, 5 October 1846.

23 D. J. Oddy, 'Working-Class Diets in Late Nineteenth-Century Britain', *Economic History Review* NS 23(2), 1970, 318.

24 PP 1866 XXXV 321, 6–13.

25 *Punch, or the London Charivari* 3 (64), 1843, 141.

26 As per the 'first law of geography' articulated by Waldo Tobler: 'Everything is related to everything else, but near things are more related than distant things'. W. R. Tobler, 'A Computer Movie Simulating Urban Growth in the Detroit Region', *Economic Geography* 46(2), 1970, 236.

27 D. W. Howell, *Land and People in Nineteenth-Century Wales*, London: Routledge & Kegan Paul, 1978, 120.

28 Ibid. 121–2.

29 Ibid. 121.

30 E. Paget-Tomlinson, *Illustrated History of Canal and River Navigations*, Sheffield: Sheffield Academic Press, 1994, map 10.

31 A. S. Davies, 'The River Trade of Montgomeryshire and its Borders', *Collections Historical and Archaeological Relating to Montgomeryshire and its Borders* 43(1), 1934, 35.

32 M. B. Rose, 'The Family Firm in British Business', in M. W. Kirby and M. B. Rose (eds), *Business Enterprise in Modern Britain from the Eighteenth to the Twentieth Century*, London and New York: Routledge, 1994, 75–6.

33 Women named as suppliers to the workhouse in the Guardians' minutes in 1880 included ironmonger Margaret Jones, earthenware supplier Martha Evans and grocers Jane Edwards and Ann Thomas.

34 See D. H. L. Brown, 'Pauperism and Profit: Financial Management, Business Practices and the New Poor Law in England and Wales', Unpublished PhD thesis, King's College London, 2014, ch. 3.

35 O. M. Westall, 'The Competitive Environment of British Business, 1850–1914', in M. W. Kirby and M. B. Rose (eds), *Business Enterprise in Modern Britain from the Eighteenth to the*

Twentieth Century, London and New York: Routledge, 1994, 213; D. S. Landes, *'The Unbound Prometheus: Technological Change and Industrial Development in Western Europe from 1750 to the Present*, Cambridge: Cambridge University Press, 1969.

36 Southall, 'Poor Law Statistics', 212.

Bibliography

Anon., *Proceedings of the Statistical Society of London* 1(2), 1835, 9–11.

Anon., *Punch, or the London Charivari* 3(64), 1843.

D. H. L. Brown, 'Pauperism and Profit: Financial Management, Business Practices and the New Poor Law in England and Wales', Unpublished PhD thesis, King's College London, 2014.

M. A. Crowther, *'The Workhouse System 1834–1929: The History of an English Social Institution*, London: Batsford Academic & Educational, 1981.

A. S. Davies, 'The River Trade of Montgomeryshire and its Borders', *Collections Historical and Archaeological Relating to Montgomeryshire and its Borders* 43(1), 1934, 33–46.

D. W. Howell, *Land and People in Nineteenth-Century Wales*, London: Routledge & Kegan Paul, 1978.

J. P. Kay, 'On the Establishment of County or District Schools, for the Training of the Pauper Children Maintained in Union Workhouses. Part I', *Journal of the Statistical Society of London* 1(1), 1838, 14–27.

S. King, *Poverty and Welfare in England, 1700–1850: A Regional Perspective*, Manchester: Manchester University Press, 2000.

S. King, 'In These You May Trust: Numerical Information, Accounting Practices and the Poor Law, c.1790 to 1840', in T. Crook and G. O'Hara (eds), *Statistics and the Public Sphere*, London: Routledge, 2011, 51–66.

D. S. Landes, *The Unbound Prometheus: Technological Change and Industrial Development in Western Europe from 1750 to the Present*, Cambridge: Cambridge University Press, 1969.

C. M. Law, 'The Growth of Urban Population in England and Wales, 1801–1911', *Transactions of the Institute of British Geographers* 41, 1967, 125–43.

L. H. Lees, *The Solidarities of Strangers: The English Poor Laws and the People, 1700–1948*, Cambridge: Cambridge University Press, 1998.

R. A. Lewis, 'William Day and the Poor Law Commissioners', *University of Birmingham Historical Journal* 9(1), 1963, 163–97.

M. MacKinnon, 'Poor Law Policy, Unemployment and Pauperism', *Explorations in Economic History* 23(3), 1986, 229–336.

D. J. Oddy, 'Working-Class Diets in Late Nineteenth-Century Britain', *Economic History Review* NS 23(2), 1970, 314–22.

E. Paget-Tomlinson, *Illustrated History of Canal and River Navigations* Sheffield: Sheffield Academic Press, 1994.

Pigot & Co's Royal National and Commercial Directory and Topography of the Counties of Berkshire, Buckinghamshire, Cornwall, Devonshire, Dorsetshire, Gloucestershire, Hampshire, Herefordshire, Monmouthshire, Oxfordshire, Somersetshire, Wiltshire, and North and South Wales, London and Manchester: Isaac Slater, 1844.

PP 1834 XXVII 1–XXXIX 1. *Report from His Majesty's Commissioners for Inquiring Into the Administration and Practical Operation of the Poor Laws*.

PP 1850 XXVII 1. *Second Annual Report of the Poor Law Board, 1849*.

PP 1851 XXVI 1. *Third Annual Report of the Poor Law Board, 1850*.

PP 1852 XLV 7. *Poor Relief*.

PP 1854 LVI 1. *Poor Rates, &c.*

PP 1866 XXXV 321. *Dietaries*.

PP 1872 LI 599. *Workhouses, Metropolis (supply of provisions)*.

PP 1876 LXIII 1. *Paupers*.

M. B. Rose, 'The Family Firm in British Business', in M.W. Kirby and M.B. Rose (eds), *Business Enterprise in Modern Britain From the Eighteenth to the Twentieth Century*, London and New York: Routledge, 1994, 61–87.

Royal National Commercial Directory of North and South Wales, Manchester: Isaac Slater, 1880.

H. R. Southall, 'Poor Law Statistics and the Geography of Economic Distress', in J. Foreman-Peck (ed.), *New Perspectives on the Late Victorian Economy*, Cambridge:: Cambridge University Press, 1991, 180–217.

W. R. Tobler, 'A Computer Movie Simulating Urban Growth in the Detroit Region', *Economic Geography* 46(2), 1970, 234–40.

S. Webb and B. Webb, *English Local Government, vol. 9, English Poor Law History, part II, The Last Hundred Years*, London: Longmans, Green & Co., 1929.

O. M. Westall, 'The Competitive Environment of British Business, 1850–1914', in M. W. Kirby and M. B. Rose (eds), *Business Enterprise in Modern Britain from the Eighteenth to the Twentieth Century*, London and New York: Routledge, 1994, 207–35.

K. Williams, *From Pauperism to Poverty*, London: Routledge & Kegan Paul, 1981.

J. G. Williamson, 'Migrant Selectivity, Urbanization, and Industrial Revolutions', *Population and Development Review* 14(2), 1988, 287–314.

10

SPATIAL DIVISIONS OF POVERTY AND WEALTH

Dimitris Ballas and Danny Dorling

Introduction

In this chapter we describe how GIS has been used in recent years to understand why, locally, nationally in Britain and worldwide, the bulk of the population seems destined to live in 'under-performing' regions; as they do so, more are poor, and the rich are becoming ever more separate from the rest. This chapter traces changes over time: decades, centuries and in one case millennia; all involve inequality, poverty and wealth.

Poverty and wealth are not two sides of the same coin. Many people are neither poor nor wealthy. There are thus more sides than two options in how we are divided by our access to resources (income) and the uses to which we put those resources (expenditure). The very poorest are poor no matter how counted: they have low income, wealth, inadequate possessions and know they are poor and are unambiguously known as poor by others. With colleagues we have termed this group 'Core Poor' in Britain.[1]

In the United States the concept of core poor equates best to the eighth of the population living below the nation's miserly official poverty line. Worldwide the concept equates best to the measure of those living on a couple of dollars a day. The Core Poor in Britain, and those beneath the line in the United States, and those on less than $2 a day in the poor world only just survive. Even attempts at enumerating absolute measures of poverty have to be relative to be meaningful across all of the world, even at the same point in time. Quantifying the very richest is more difficult. To a man (it is usually still a man) with access to $1billion, a man with only $1 million appears a pauper. In between the extremes of core poverty and unimaginable riches runs the gamut of inequity along which most of us are strung.

Being poor or wealthy are, however, qualitatively different experiences from being a little bit better or worse off along a continuum. Both involve social exclusion from the norms of society. Furthermore, neither could exist without the other, but they are better described as very different sized facets on a many sided dice rather than opposite side of the coin.

This chapter shows some examples of how GIS has been used to explore the geography of people living at, and between, these extremes. To do this in we start with a city, then move out to the country and end with the world.

Manchester: so much to answer for

We start the analysis at the city level, focusing on Manchester, the first city in the world to be industrialized. It was the first city in which mass human labour was put to work in a way that so thoroughly dehumanized people. 'Manchester so much to answer for' were originally the lyrics to a popular song that very few of its younger listeners realize concerned the killers of children known as the 'Moors Murderers'.[2] But, as the song implies, Manchester – or rather the way of treating human beings first seen in Manchester – has much more to answer for than that.

The University of Manchester has the date of its founding now inscribed in the logo of the new unified mega-university: 'Manchester 1824'. This is roughly a well-lived lifetime (75 years) older than other provincial English cities. It is not by chance that the city boasts of being something special. Take a trip to the Manchester Museum of Science and Industry and one walks into a giant warehouse established as a warehouse just a decade after the University. A couple of decades later and Friedrich Engels' 'Conditions of the Working Class' was published.[3] In the 1850s, the expectation of life's length from birth in Manchester was just 32 years, falling to 31 years in the 1860s.[4] In the central district of that city it was as low as 29 by then, exceeded – as worse – only by an all-time life-expectancy low of 25 years in those same years in nearby Liverpool.[5] Human life has rarely been valued lower outside of times of war, genocide or in the worse of famines.

The urban experience of systemic poverty that can be wrought through capitalism began in Manchester. By the turn of twentieth century standards of living in North West England were little better than during the middle of the nineteenth. In fact the long hot summer of 1904 saw infants die in Manchester close to the rates (one in four before their first birthday) that they still die in the poorest places on earth a century later. And it was in Manchester that it was first realized that those deaths were not an act of God, but due to the squalor that accompanies poverty – squalor that was quantified in the numbers of flies living around new-born infants:

> By means of a number of beer-traps Dr Niven contrived to count the flies in some dozen houses in Manchester during the summer months of 1904, and from these data he concluded that the advent of the house-fly in numbers precedes by a short time the increase in the number of deaths from diarrhoea. In the fortnight ending August 13th, for instance, the number of flies caught in these traps was 37,521, the maximum in any fortnight, and in the fortnight following the maximum number of deaths from diarrhoea occurred – namely, 192.[6]

In the century that followed the long hot summer of 1904, life in Manchester changed, for most, almost beyond recognition. Nevertheless, the City of Manchester is still the district of England with the lowest male life expectancy from birth, despite its centre now containing one of the most dynamic business districts in the country. The city also now again contains some extremely affluent enclaves, including high-rise luxurious apartment blocks with penthouses that cost a fortune.

The current local authority district of the city of Manchester stretches long and thin from north to south and so it is possible to chart a route – a journey – that covers most of it and does not look too contrived. Journeys have long been a way in which geographical inequalities in Britain were studied.

A journey through Manchester and out into leafy Macclesfield district is described in Figure 10.1, which is shown on a map with areas shaded according to the average incomes of those who live there. Average incomes in the centre of the city were less than half the average in the rural hinterland of Manchester. Many of those (who can) tended to get out but still usually drive in for work. These are just the inequalities

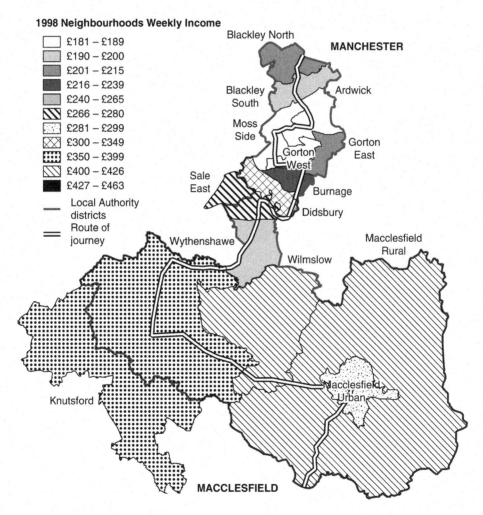

Figure 10.1 A journey from less than £200 a week to more than £400 a week to live on.

Source: Dorling et al., 2004 (details given in endnote 7 of this chapter).

between averages, not extremes, and between a measure already greatly redistributed before it is counted (it is income plus entitlements rather than earned income alone that is shown). The methodology used to draw Figure 10.1 involved the division of Manchester and its neighbouring district of Macclesfield up into a series of areas for which averages could be calculated. More information on the data and methods can be found in a detailed technical report to the UK Office for the Deputy Prime Minister.[7]

It should be noted that, if we had shown inequalities in wealth, rather than income, along this journey the differences would be manifoldly far higher. Had we taken a related measure, but of something very rare – the murder rate – the differences would not be possible to calculate as in places within the city the rate is amongst the highest in England whereas it is practically zero in parts of the outskirts. It is not just in the United States that such extremes occur. Almost all else in life changes along with the trend in inequalities in incomes along this journey through Manchester.

The average incomes shown in Figure 10.1 were estimates which were produced by the UK Office for National Statistics. They almost certainly underestimate the extent of income inequalities along the route, as they are the products of a statistical model based on relatively limited information.

For instance, one of the variables upon which these income estimates are based is the proportion of households in each geographical area which are classified as 'professionals and intermediate', masking the considerable income variation within this group.

From the above discussion it becomes obvious that in order to properly analyse socio-economic inequalities and their spatial manifestations it is necessary to have good-quality small area data on income and wealth. Despite strong arguments of the utility of measures of income in small areas, the UK government has been avoiding the inclusion of such a question in Census questionnaires, on the grounds that it could negatively affect the response rates, as a lot of the respondents would object to being asked this question or find it hard to complete. However, it should be noted that almost all government social surveys, as opposed to the Census, in Britain ask this question and it is also successfully asked in other national censuses. A further argument against the inclusion of an income question in the Census is that it could breach confidentiality rules by making it possible to identify individual respondents. Yet it should be noted that individual answers to census questions, unlike other government surveys, are confidential and cannot be released from ONS for 100 years under the census legislation.[8]

Given the lack of good-quality geographical income data that would allow a thorough investigation of the spatial distribution of poverty and wealth, there have been considerable efforts within the social sciences to estimate income (rather than wealth) for geographical areas that are smaller than the levels at which published data exist.[9]

Similar issues arise when analysing social and spatial inequalities in wealth, as this is also something not asked in the census. Social scientists deal with this lack of wealth data by combining information from a wide range of sources including the Census of population (number of households and socio-economic characteristics), Building Societies and Land Registry (house price data). A recent study in Britain

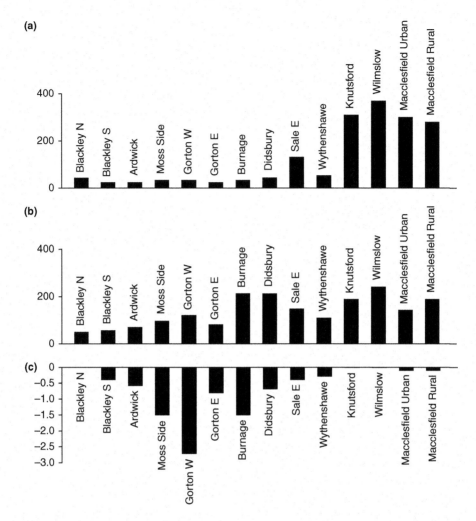

Figure 10.2 (a) Mean detached house price in £s ('000s), 2001: Blakely North to Macclesfield Rural. (b) Mean detached house price in £s, 1995–2003: Blakely North to
Macclesfield Rural. (c) Change in % of population born in Republic of Ireland,
1991–2001: Blakely North to Macclesfield Rural.

published for Shelter, the housing charity, used such methods, revealing the emergence of an unprecedented housing wealth gap.[10] More recent studies[11] extended
such methodologies and estimated and visualized the size and geographical distribution of household wealth.

Just as it is possible to produce a profile of the changing income distribution along
a journey once area data has been estimated, so too can many other aspects of life
related to poverty and wealth be measured and visualized. Figure 10.2a–c shows
three different transects from north Manchester through to the rural southern hinterland as illustrations of this possibility.

First, Figure 10.2a shows how detached property (free-standing residential dwelling) is much more highly valued in the suburbs and rural parts of the route. Figure 10.2b shows that this type of property increased in estimated value much more in recent years as compared to that in the city centre. Figure 10.2c shows how the decline in a particular migrant group – those born in Ireland – occurs in rough tandem with these trends in income and wealth distributions and redistributions and how the socio-economic status and power of residential population may affect the price of property. The centre of Manchester is an area that has been typified by immigration since the first industrial buildings were raised. Figure 10.2c shows the decline of the Irish born due to death in old age and out-migration: it charts the decline of a group which came in large numbers both in the 1840s and 1960s (and often in between) – but no longer.

Manchester was the first modern example of how income, poverty, wealth and inequality tends to be distributed around a city when much of the market in housing, transportation and wages is unregulated.

Spatial divisions in Britain

The journey into Manchester and out into rural Macclesfield is a journey between extremes, although it is one of very many possible such journeys and is certainly not the most extreme that could be taken: Figures 10.3 and 10.4 show that journey drawn with three small arrows upon two maps of all of Britain. These are population cartogram maps and each hexagon is a parliamentary constituency.

Population cartograms differ from conventional maps of places which show areas as they might appear from space, ignoring population distribution. Looking at a country or a city without regard to population distorts economic and social geography. Population cartograms show each area of the country drawn roughly in proportion to the size of its population and thus representing the area in social and economic terms as it would be represented politically: they give the people a 'fairer' representation.[12]

Here we use such cartograms to study the economic geography of Britain and in particular the geographical distribution of people that can be described as 'core poor' and 'exclusive wealthy' according to a study of poverty and wealth that was originally funded and published by the Joseph Rowntree Foundation[13] (also see discussion below). In this section we draw on this work and also highlight the geography of poverty and wealth in the areas covered by the journey from Manchester to leafy Macclesfield that we described above (see annotated arrow in Figures 10.3 and 10.4). In particular, the first of those maps (Figure 10.3) shows the proportion of the population that makes up the 'core poor' in each small part of the country and the second map (Figure 10.4) shows how many of those in each place were 'exclusive wealthy' by the year 2000. The journey we described in the previous section passes through some of the areas containing the highest proportions of 'core poor' folk – and then into places that contain some of the highest proportions of exclusively wealthy households living in the north of England. However, as Figure 10.4 shows, the British 'exclusive wealthy' almost all live in a ring of areas to the west of London in the south of England.

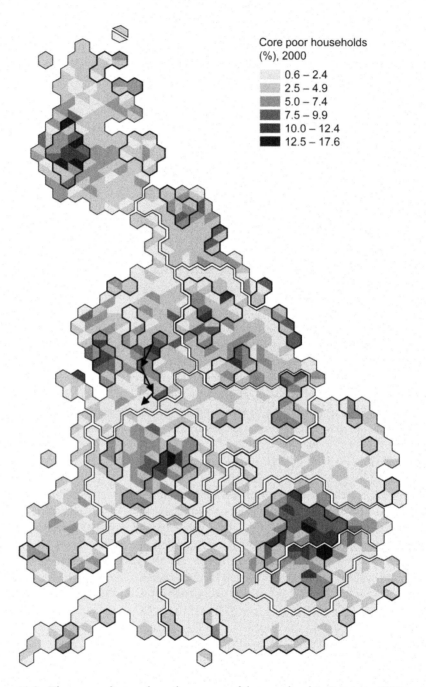

Figure 10.3 The geography to where the poorest of the poor lived in Britain in 2000.

Source: B. Thomas and D. Dorling, *Identity in Britain: A Cradle-to-Grave Atlas*, Bristol: Policy Press, 2007, 290.

Core poor households
(%), 2000

	0.6 – 2.4
	2.5 – 4.9
	5.0 – 7.4
	7.5 – 9.9
	10.0 – 12.4
	12.5 – 17.6

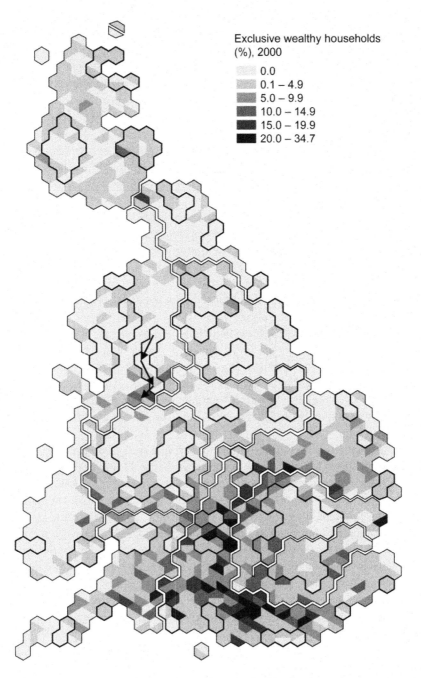

Figure 10.4 The geography of where the exclusively wealthy lived most in Britain in 2000.
B. Thomas and D. Dorling, *Identity in Britain: A Cradle-to-Grave Atlas*, Bristol:
Policy Press, 2007, 290.

Research into the extent and trends in poverty in Britain has generally failed to produce measures for relatively small areas that can be compared over time. To overcome this problem we extended the so called and well-established 'Breadline Britain' methodology which takes into account the public's perception and the extent to which households have access to what are considered to be publicly perceived necessities[14] to produce estimates for small areas across the country around the time of the 1971, 1981, 1991 and 2001 censuses of population.[15] Because we mix these data with that from surveys usually taken a few years earlier (1968, 1983, 1990 and 1999) we will use the dates 1970, 1980, 1990 and 2000 to describe these points in time for which we have estimated measures of poverty and wealth. We also use information of housing prices and consumption by affluent individuals to produce estimates for the same areas of the numbers of households that were asset-wealthy and exclusively wealthy.

Our definition of exclusive wealth is the theoretical opposite of what is normally seen in defining poverty as relative deprivation. Peter Townsend's standard definition of poverty is that the poor lack the opportunities to enjoy a standard of living commensurate with societal norms, and are thus deprived from participating as full citizens of their society.[16] Exclusive wealth in contrast confers privilege through being able to secure benefits by dint of wealth not generally available to the public at large (and certainly not to the poor).

The 'exclusive wealthy' can thus be defined as those living above a high wealth line. This has to be a line sufficiently high that people living above it are able to exclude themselves from participating in the norms of society (if they so wish), moving 'as far from the life of the average citizen as the addict in a blanket under Waterloo Bridge' and no longer inhabiting 'the same planet as the rest of us, hermetically sealed in smoke-windowed limo, private jet, private island, private everything'.[17]

To operationalize this definition of a wealth line, we used data from the Family Expenditure Survey (FES) in combination with the Households Below Average Income (HBAI) adjustments to the incomes of the very 'rich'.[18] The HBAI adjustments account for household size and type when considering household disposable (i.e. after tax and including welfare payments) income, and are the same as those used in the Breadline Britain methodology.[19] The adjusted FES data were then used to define the average level of income at which the following exclusive activities tend to occur, such as children going to independent schools, the use of private health care, second home ownership, having a boat and paying for private club membership fees. To estimate the geographical distribution of exclusively wealthy households, housing data were used to estimate the equivalent asset wealth accompanying this exclusive behaviour.

The group that is the mirror image of the exclusively wealthy in theoretical terms is living below the relative poverty line: the breadline poor. However, at any one time, just as for every person who is rich there is a subset who are extremely rich, for all who experience poverty, there is a subset who are extremely poor. The group termed the core poor here are those who are suffering from a combination of all of normative, felt and comparative poverty. That is, they are people who are simultaneously income poor (normative), subjectively poor (felt) and necessities/deprivation poor (comparatively poor): they are a subset of those who are comparatively poor but do not necessarily feel poor or are normatively poor: the breadline poor. Finally there are those who are neither poor nor wealthy. Table 10.1 shows the proportion of households in Britain we estimate to be in each group at the start of each decade from 1970 to 2000.

Table 10.1 shows that we estimate that only half of all households are neither poor nor wealthy (50.4%) – however two-thirds are generally included in the norms of society. That two-thirds is the non-poor non-wealthy plus the asset wealthy less the exclusive wealth (50.4+22.6–5.6=67.4%). Note that the middle three columns of Table 10.1 sum to one hundred and that the proportion who are excluded from the norms of society either by dint of their breadline poverty or their exclusive wealth can be calculated by summing the second and fifth column of data in the table. Over 30 years the socially excluded (rich and poor) have grown from 30.5% (23.1%+7.4%) to 32.6% (27.0%+5.6%). The extremes were were only a quarter of households in 1980 (when the poor were at a minima) and 1990 (when recession in the southern part of England decreased the wealth of the rich).

Note also that we have no estimate of the asset wealthy in 1970 and so can derive no estimate of those households that are non-poor and non-wealthy in that year. Finally it should be noted that there were fewer core poor in 2000 as compared to 1990 – almost certainly due to social innovations such as the introduction of a minimum wage and tax credits for families in lower paid work. However, it should also be noted that the definition of 'core poor' used here is perhaps excessively strict.

It could well be argued that a robust definition of poverty would be anyone who satisfied any two of the following three conditions: 1) they think they are poor; 2) they have a low income; 3) they have low wealth. The low wealth criteria might be that they are among the 'breadline poor', or simply that they have almost no savings.

The precise definitions of poverty lines become less important when two out of three criteria are used. Most folk understand that someone is poor if they have low

Table 10.1 Poverty and wealth measures for Great Britain, 1970 to 2000.

Year	% core poor*	% breadline poor	% non-poor, non-wealthy	% asset wealthy	% exclusive wealthy*
1970	14.4	23.1	n/a**	n/a**	7.4
1980	9.8	17.1	66.1	16.8	6.9
1990	14.3	21.3	55.7	23.0	3.5
2000	11.2	27.0	50.4	22.6	5.6

Source: D. Dorling et al., *Poverty, Wealth and Place in Britain, 1968 to 2005*, Bristol: Policy Press, 2007.

* Note that 'core poor' and 'exclusive wealthy' are subsets of 'breadline poor' and 'asset wealthy' respectively); see main report for estimates of variability around the exclusive wealth estimates.

** Housing wealth data were unavailable for 1970; since asset wealth could not be calculated, neither could the proportion of non-poor, non-wealthy at this time.

Table 10.2 The Index of Dissimilarity for each of the five measures.

	1970	1980	1990	2000
Core Poor	12.3%	15.6%	15.3%	14.1%
Breadline Poor	14.7%	16.7%	17.1%	18.3%
Non-poor, non-wealthy	*	15.4%	16.7%	19.8%
Asset Wealthy	*	34.9%	34.5%	40.1%
Exclusive Wealthy	*	43.6%	60.6%	59.7%

*Small-area estimates of asset and exclusive wealthy households were not available for 1970, meaning that non-poor, non-wealthy households could also not be estimated at this time.

income and low wealth – whether they think of themselves as poor or not. Most people are happy that someone with savings who does not think of themselves as poor is not poor, even if they have a low income – and so on. This two out of three criteria rule was originally proposed by Bradshaw and Finch.[20] We do not use it further here but it is well worth considering for future use – and for measuring much more than poverty. The same principle would apply to the definition of the rich, e.g. that they satisfy any two of the following: thinking they are rich, having a high income and/or having high wealth.

Having determined the national proportions of households that can be categorized as asset wealthy, exclusive wealthy, breadline poor and core poor, or none of the above, we next need to show the spatial distribution of poverty and wealth.

The Index of Dissimilarity is the minimum proportion of households that would have to move between areas if each area were to have an even proportion of households of a given type. Table 10.2 gives the result of applying this statistical test and shows that by the year 2000, a majority (59.7%) of the exclusive wealthy would have had to move out of their neighbourhood to somewhere less exclusive were they to no longer be so extremely clustered (as shown in Figure 10.4). That proportion is much as it was in 1990, but much higher than it was in 1980.

Of all the five groups shown in Table 10.2 only the core poor are slightly less spatially concentrated by the year 2000 as compared to 1990. Every other group has become more spatially concentrated. Using the breadline measure from the time it was first deployed, we can say that those living beneath the breadline have never been as physically separated from the rest of society by their geography as they presently are. Similarly those who are 'normal' were by the year 2000 less likely to be mixing with folk who were either poor or wealthy. Finally, the asset wealthy are now more spatially segregated in Britain than they were in either 1980 or 1990.

The extent of these spatial divides change slowly. However, those divides are deep and in general they are deepening in England. What then of the rest of the world?

Economic spatial divisions worldwide

So far in this chapter, we have considered the spatial distribution of poverty and wealth at the local and then the national scale, showing that there have been significant increases in social and spatial inequalities within and between areas at all these levels. In countries like Britain, both poor and wealthy households have become more and more geographically segregated from the rest of society over the last three decades.

Now we turn our attention to the spatial manifestation of poverty and wealth at the global scale and we critically discuss the ways in which global institutions such as the World Bank, meant to deal with global poverty, approach these issues.

Similar trends of geographical polarization to those described at the national and local level are observed at the global scale but it is important to remember that when discussing global poverty and wealth different societies have different concepts of wealth. What people want and what people need changes over time and the concept of poverty constantly evolves and therefore, as noted earlier, the subsistence approach to the definition of poverty is inadequate.

> By necessities, I understand not only the commodities which are indispens-ably necessary for the support of life, but whatever the customs of the coun-try renders it indecent for creditable people, even of the lower order, to be without. A creditable day labourer would be ashamed to appear in public without a linen shirt.[21]

As the commodities that countries use to define what a person to be creditable are constantly changing, it can be argued that it is respect that matters most in people's lives and that nations provide respect through the equitable access to resources we allow each other. Some truths appear harder to grasp than others. In Britain econo-mists have known for over two centuries that a shoe is not merely an aid for walking to work as they have known in social policy for over one hundred years that a post-age stamp is not just a necessity for paying bills.[22] Adam Smith in the eighteenth century and Seebohm Rowntree at the end of the nineteenth explained how a little luxury is also a necessity of life. However, in the pits of the more dismal side of the science of economics this has yet to be grasped.

We can see this in the World Bank myths that nearly everything that matters is improving.[23] We end this chapter questioning those myths. By defining 'nearly everything that matters' as what is taken absolutely for granted in the rich world (or 'donor countries' in World Bank speak), Charles Kenney suggests that living standards worldwide are converging[24] and societal inequalities are decreasing. There are many simple mistakes in this work and they stem from the error in Kenney's (and by implication the World Bank's) central tenet which is summarized as follows:[25] if people in the poorest countries of the world begin to receive a little more of what the richest came to expect to receive generations earlier, then the world is becoming fairer. Or, in other words – if more of the world's poor can now afford a cheap pair of shoes (rather than no shoes) and live on an amount closer to 2 dollars a day rather than 1 dollar – then the world has become a fairer place. This ignores the growing incomes of the rich in the richest countries or the number and types of shoes worn there, or the fact that people no longer need to walk miles to get water in the rich world.

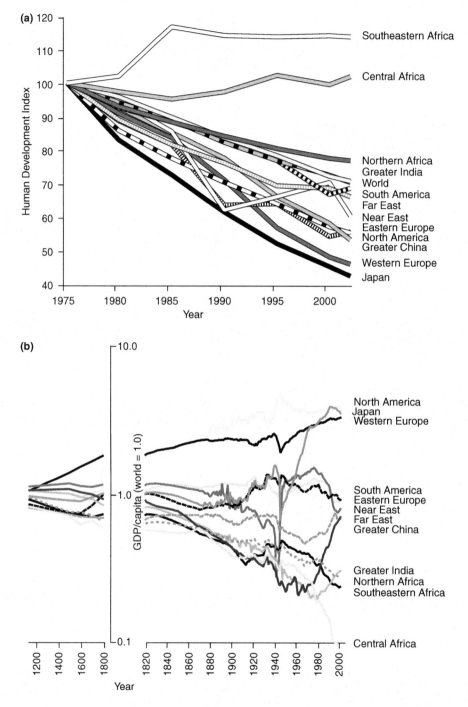

Figure 10.5 (a) Change in the Human Development Index 'to achieve', 1975–2005.
(b) Change in average incomes over time 1200–2000 compared to world average.

In his conclusion, Kenney implies that 'donor nations' should not be concerned that they may be impoverishing poor nations through debt repayments because the world is set to get fairer anyway.

Nevertheless, Figure 10.5a uses the same data as Kenney, and shows a somewhat different global trend. More specifically it shows the gap between full human development as defined by the United Nations Development Programme (UNDP) and the lack of progress since 1975. Figure 10.5a also shows how close to achieving a simple measure of the achievement of full human development is each of twelve regions of the world since 1975.

The extremes are defined by Japan and Africa. In Japan the majority of improvement towards UNDP 'utopia' has been achieved in the last 25 years. Utopia here is defined as living to the age of 85, being educated to tertiary level and having an average income of $40,000. Japan also has the most equitable income distribution of the twelve regions and it is often argued that it has a cohesive society.[26] In contrast most of Africa is further from that utopia than it was in 1975. On average central and south-eastern Africa's combined life expectancy, educational enrolment and incomes are worse now in absolute terms than they were in 1975.

In between these extremes the remainder of the world forms a diverging continuum. In general those who had most to begin with have gained most and those which had least have the furthest to go (and further now to go than they had in 1975).China has achieved a tiny fraction more since 1975 than North America but other than that not only has there been overall divergence worldwide (in everything that matters most: health, wealth and learning). The richer a set of countries was to begin with the better they have done.

Once countries are grouped as in Figure 10.5a there are no exceptions. In Figure 10.5a the twelve regions are comparable. In other words – even if you run things as well as China has done – or as badly as North America has done – you, as a world region, can hardly alter your end position that is determined by where you started in the 'development race'. The extent of such divergence is also mirrored in the global distribution of income as seen in Figure 10.5b that presents the estimated World Income by region, based on income estimates by Angus Maddison who developed a time series of historical statistics for the World Economy over the last 800 years.[27]

It is in the short-term interest of the bankers of the richest people in the richest (donor) nations to present a picture of world living standards converging, of a race where those who began miles behind the leaders are beginning to catch up. A fictional nanny gave good advice on the motivation of banking over four decades ago:

> They must feel the thrill of totting up a balanced book
> A thousand ciphers neatly in a row
> When gazing at a graph that shows the profits up
> Their little cup of joy should overflow![28]

Another way of demonstrating how unequal the world has become is to redraw the map of the world in proportion to the distribution of poverty and wealth. Figure 10.6a shows a world map where area is drawn in proportion to income of less than one

(a)

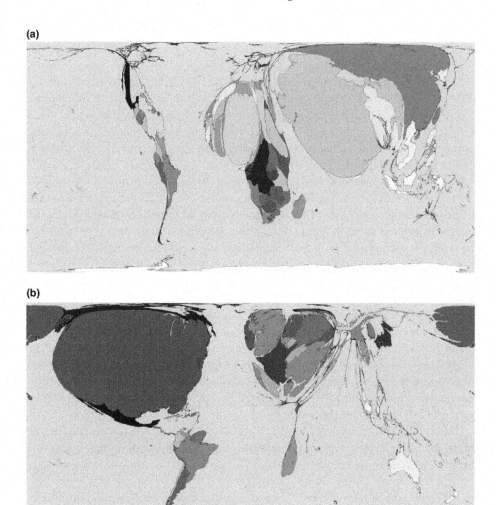

(b)

Figure 10.6 (a) The world drawn in proportion to those living on $1 a day or less. (b) The world drawn in proportion to those living on $200 a day or more.

US dollar a day. As can be seen, the areas of countries in Africa and Asia are by far the largest, whereas, it is very difficult to distinguish the shapes of countries in Europe and North America. Similarly, Figure 10.6b shows a world map where area is drawn in proportion to over $200 a day. In contrast to Figure 10.6a, European and North American countries dominate this map, whereas the areas of Asian and African countries have shrunk. It is interesting to note that the world has become so unequal that the rich folk of Macclesfield described earlier (see Figure 10.1), which a century ago was a remote rural settlement, are now part of the map of world wealth – and can be identified on a world map where area is drawn in proportion to who has an income of over $200 a day (see Figure 10.6b)!

Conclusion

There are leaps of imagination required to see the true extent of the spatial divisions of population and wealth in the world. Here we have tried to show how these can range from a journey across the city of Manchester to a journey across Britain on a map stretched and squeezed so that both poor and rich are equally visible to a map of the world as defined by average incomes received in each state.

Locally within Manchester, nationally across Britain and worldwide the spatial divisions of poverty and wealth are deepening. Locally, this is normally hardest to see and occurs more slowly. At times the trends are reversed. Nationally it is more obvious, especially in countries like Britain where a 'pear-shaped' picture of economic development is emerging,[29] where the bulk of the population were destined to live in an underperforming bulge of regions from which the 'productive' winners are moving further away. Worldwide the spatial divisions of poverty and wealth have never been as deep and inequalities across the planet are accelerating.

The geography of poverty that we illustrated in Figure 10.3 has continued to deepen and now there is absolute immiseration. Real incomes have fallen and for the first time since the 1930s. Modern-day soup kitchens have opened. Now they are called food banks and very large numbers of people in the poorest parts of the country are being fed for several days a year through such charity. At the very same time the geography of wealth that we showed in Figure 10.4 has also deepened. There has been a boom in housing prices in just those areas shown to have already been most wealthy in the year 2000. Those who own property in the South East are, and feel, much richer again. Those who have to rent often now spend the majority of their income on rent.

A comparable set of statistics to those shown in Table 10.1 has not yet been created, but when it is, it will show both core and breadline poverty and exclusive wealth to have risen. Preliminary results of more recent work were indicating this to be especially acute in London.[30]

On the other hand, some of the worldwide gaps illustrated in Figure 10.5 ('a' and 'b') may finally be narrowing. Since the 2008 economic crash economic growth has been slowest in some of the richest parts of the world (North America and Europe) and greatest in Africa and Asia – but from a very low base in Africa's case.

Nevertheless the richest 1 per cent of people in the world continue to become much richer and were expected to hold the majority of the wealth in the world by the end of the year 2016.[31] Locally, nationally and globally, for most people in the world, spatial divisions of poverty and wealth continue to widen. The US president, the Pope, the head of the IMF, and the president of China all lamented these developments very recently. However, it is not impossible that we are near a turning point. As Christmas 2016 approaches there are the beginnings of signs suggesting the wealthy might soon not be so wealthy, but as yet it is too early to tell.

Acknowledgements

This chapter is an abridged and updated version of D. Dorling and D. Ballas, chapter 6, 'Spatial Divisions of Poverty and Wealth', in T. Ridge and S. Wright (eds),

Understanding Poverty, Wealth and Inequality: Policies and Prospects, Bristol: Policy Press, 2008,103–34. We are grateful to our colleagues Jan Rigby, Ben Wheeler, Bethan Thomas, Eldin Fahmy, Dave Gordon and Ruth Lupton, Anna Barford, Mark Newman and John Pritchard who worked with us on projects upon which this chapter draws. We are also grateful to Ailsa Allen for redrawing and producing Figures 10.3 and 10.4 in a suitable format for this book.

Notes

1 D. Dorling, J. Rigby, B. Wheeler, D. Ballas, B. Thomas, E. Fahmy, D. Gordon and R. Lupton, *Poverty, Wealth and Place in Britain, 1968 to 2005*, Bristol: Policy Press, 2007 (free pdf copies available: www.jrf.org.uk/bookshop/eBooks/2019-poverty-wealth-place.pdf).

2 The Smiths, *Suffer Little Children*, 1984.

3 F. Engels, [online version], *Conditions of the Working Class in England*, Marx/Engels Internet Archive (www.marxists.org), 1845. Available from: www.marxists.org/archive/marx/works/1845/condition-working-class/index.htm.

4 S. Szreter and G. Mooney, 'Urbanization, Mortality, and the Standard of Living Debate: New Estimates of the Expectation of Life at Birth in Nineteenth-Century British Cities', *Economic History Review* 51(1), 1998, 84–112, 88.

5 Ibid. 90.

6 G. Newman, *Infant Mortality: A Social Problem*, London: Methuen & Co., 1906, 168–9.

7 D. Dorling, D. Ballas, B. Thomas and J. Pritchard, *Pilot Mapping of Local Social Polarisation in Three Areas of England, 1971–2001*, New Horizons Project Report to the Office for the Deputy Prime Minister, 2004. Available: www.sasi.group.shef.ac.uk/research/pilot_mapping.htm.

8 P. Rees, D. Martin and P. Williamson (eds), *The Census Data System*, Chichester: Wiley, 2002.

9 D. Ballas, 'What is Small Area Estimation?', Presentation given at the 6th ESRC Research Methods Festival, St Catherine's College, University of Oxford, 8–10 July 2014, UK National Centre for Research Methods (NCRM). Available: www.youtube.com/watch?v=g0I87SuRSWg.

10 B. Thomas and D. Dorling, *Know Your Place: Housing Wealth and Inequality in Great Britain 1980–2003 and Beyond*, Shelter Policy Library, 2004. Available: www.sheffield.ac.uk/sasi/publications/reports/knowyourplace.htm).

11 Dorling et al., *Poverty, Wealth and Place*. D. Dorling and B. Thomas, *Bankrupt Britain: An Atlas of Social Change*, Bristol: Policy Press, 2011.

12 D. Dorling, *A Human Geography of the UK*, London: Sage, 2005. B. Thomas and D. Dorling, *Identity in Britain: A Cradle-to-Grave Atlas*, Bristol: Policy Press, 2007. B. D. Hennig, *Rediscovering the World: Map Transformations of Human and Physical Space*, Heidelberg/New York/Dordrecht/London: Springer, 2013. D. Ballas, D. Dorling and B. Hennig, *The Social Atlas of Europe*, Bristol: Policy Press, 2014.

13 D. Dorling, J. Rigby, B. Wheeler, D. Ballas, B. Thomas, E. Fahmy, D. Gordon and D. R. Lupton, *Poverty, Wealth and Place in Britain, 1968 to 2005*, Bristol: Policy Press, 2007.

14 D. Gordon and C. Pantazis, 'Measuring Poverty: Breadline Britain in the 1990s', in D. Gordon and C. Pantazis (eds), *Breadline Britain in the 1990s*, Aldershot: Ashgate, 1997, pp. 1–47.

15 D. Dorling et al., *Poverty, Wealth and Place*.

16 P. Townsend, *Poverty in the United Kingdom*, London: Allen Lane and Penguin Books, 1979. Available free from: http://www.poverty.ac.uk/free-resources-books/poverty-united-kingdom (last accessed April 2016).

17 P. Toynbee, 'Downsizing Dreams', *Guardian*, 8 April 2006. Available from: http://books.guardian.co.uk/review/story/0,1749089,00.html, 23/08/2006.

18 D. Dorling et al., *Poverty, Wealth and Place*.

19 Ibid.

20 J. Bradshaw, N. Finch, 'Overlaps in Dimensions of Poverty', *Journal of Social Policy* 32(4), 2003, 513–25.

21 A. Smith, *The Theory of the Moral Sentiments*, reprint, Indianapolis, IN: Liberty Classics, 1759 (1952), 383.

22 Ibid. B. S. Rowntree, *Poverty: A Study of Town Life*, centenary edition, Bristol: Policy Press, 2000.

23 C. Kenney, 'Why are we Worried about Income? Nearly Everything that Matters is Converging', *World Development* 33(1), 2005, 1–19.

24 Ibid.

25 Ibid.

26 D. Ballas, D. Dorling, T. Nakaya, H. Tunstall, K. Hanaoka and T. Hanibuchi, 'Happiness, Social Cohesion and Income Inequalities in Britain and Japan', in T. Tachibanaki (ed.), *Advances in Happiness Research*, Springer, 2016, pp. 119–38.

27 A. Maddison, *The Contours of the World Economy 1–2030 AD*, Oxford: Oxford University Press, 2007.

28 M. Poppins, 1964 . . . can you quote a fictitious person?

29 D. Dorling, 'Inequalities in Britain 1997–2006: The Dream that Turned Pear-Shaped', *Local Economy* 21(4), 2006, 353–61.

30 D. Boffey, 'How 30 Years of a Polarized Economy Have Squeezed out the Middle Class', *Guardian*, 7 March 2015. Available from: www.theguardian.com/society/2015/mar/07/vanishing-middle-class-london-economy-divide-rich-poor-england.

31 D. Dorling, 'Inequalities in Britain 1997–2006'.

PART III

Urban spatial history

INTRODUCTION TO PART III

Don Lafreniere, Ian Gregory, and Don DeBats

Scholars have long had an interest in the study of urban environments and the residents who occupy them. Contributions to the study of the urban past are made by scholars across the social sciences, including geographers, historians, sociologists, economists, anthropologists, and political scientists and this is reflected in the scholarship found in this section and throughout the rest of this book. Mapping and analysis of urban social spaces arguably can be traced back to the work of Robert Park and the rest of the Chicago School of Urban Sociology in the 1920s. Park's work includes the now well-known concept of *human ecology*, the idea that the urban experiences of humans are divided along the lines of communities and society.[1] Park noted that in urban spaces, 'social relations are so frequently and so inevitably correlated with spacial [sic] relations'.[2] His concept inspired his colleague Ernest Burgess to develop the concentric ring model of urban development, a staple theory in urban geography, that illustrates how neighbourhoods of socially segregated peoples emerged in cities and would change through time.[3]

This interest in the spatial patterning and segregation of urban residents, especially of the industrial city, gained the further attention of scholars who embraced the 'new urban history' of the 1960–70s. Using quantitative methods and mapping techniques, scholarship emerged that aimed to understand the role of urban residents as agents in changing urban environments and social structures. The seminal work of the era included the examinations of nineteenth-century Philadelphia by Theodore Hershberg's Philadelphia Social History Project,[4] the work of Michael Katz on Hamilton Ontario,[5] Peter Goheen on Victorian Toronto,[6] Olivier Zunz on Detroit,[7] and Richard Dennis on the English industrial cities of Liverpool, Manchester, and Huddersfield.[8] These studies all include the mapping of samples of sources such as city directories, censuses, tax rolls, and employment records, to examine the nature and patterns of ethnic and socio-economic segregation, as well as other social indicators such as rate of home ownership, family organization, work, and demographic behaviour. Their results are summarized in indices, tables, graphs, and maps which highlight concentrations and fluctuations over time and space. What they lacked was the analytical and big data capabilities of the modern desktop GIS.

The use of GIS for the study of urban history first emerged in the late 1990s and early 2000s with studies such as those by Andrew Beveridge documenting the changing ethnic and racial distribution of New Yorkers through the twentieth century,[9] Etan Diamond and David Bodenhamer's examination of race and religion in Indianapolis,[10] and Amy Hillier's work on redlining in Philadelphia.[11] These studies utilized census tracts and similar aggregated geographies to spatially analyse urban historical social patterns. Jason Gilliland and Sherry Olson spearheaded a new approach to urban HGIS by applying what was learned from 'new urban history'; the need to focus on the historical record of individuals. Using Montreal as their case study, they developed the first HGIS that mapped individuals to their residential locations to study a range of topics from housing, residential mobility, segregation, and morphological changes to the urban environment.[12] Subsequent influential work followed that utilized this fine-scaled approach to the study of the urban past including the work by Don Debats on Alexandria, Virginia, and Newport, Kentucky,[13] John Lutz, Patrick Dunae, Don Lafreniere, Jason Gilliland, and Megan Harvey on Victoria, British Columbia,[14] Don Lafreniere and Jason Gilliland on London Ontario,[15] and S. Wright Kennedy, Andrew Curtis, and Jacqueline Curtis on Memphis, Tennessee.[16]

All of the five chapters in this section use the individual-level approach in historical GIS to either recreate past urban environments, or to map and analyse the social processes in the city such as segregation, settlement, or immigration, while many do both. This section begins with a study by sociologists John Logan and Weiwei Zhang who provide a detailed methodological approach to geocoding publicly available, individual-level census records from 1930 and 1940 to finer spatial scales such as enumeration districts, census blocks, and street segments. They provide guidance for how these datasets can be used to facilitate studies of residential patterning and segregation across urban America. Historian Jean-Luc Pinol also argues for the importance of geocoding individual level data and combines the population data with urban environmental data to present three case studies: the deportation of Jews from Paris during WWI, the transformation of Paris from an industrial to post-industrial city though following the growth of green space, and the use of geo-referenced aerial photography to discover urban change. Sociologist Kurt Schlichting uses the traditional mix of historical maps and census data, together with modern GIS data on Manhattan, to geocode German immigrants to the individual buildings they occupied. His study analyses the German immigration and settlement patterns in in New York's Lower East Side. Geographers Don Lafreniere and Jason Gilliland also use historical fire insurance plans and individual-level census and city directory data to geocode London Ontario's entire population to their individual residence and outline a detailed procedure for record linking individuals across the decade 1881–91. Using spatial analysis, they uncover the residential, occupational, and workplace mobilities of workers and their families. The final chapter by a collaborative team of historians and geographers, under the lead of John Lutz, uses the same combination of sources to identify where racialized populations in Victoria, British Columbia, lived and to show how three distinct racial spaces changed through the late nineteenth and early twentieth centuries. All of these chapters illustrate the range of sources, approaches, and analytical techniques used to study the spatial patterns and processes in our past urban environments at the scale of the individual.

Notes

1 R. Park, 'The Urban Community as a Spatial Pattern and a Moral Order', in E. Burgess (ed.), *The Urban Community: Selected Papers from the Proceedings of the American Sociological Society*, New York: Greenwood Press, 1925, 3–18.

2 Park, 'The Urban Community as a Spatial Pattern', 18.

3 E. Burgess, 'The Growth of the City', in R. Park, E. Burgess and R. McKenzie (eds), *The City*, Chicago, IL: University of Chicago Press, 1925, 47–62.

4 T. Hershberg (ed.), *Philadelphia: Work, Space, Family and Group Experience in the Nineteenth Century*, New York: Oxford University Press, 1981; T. Hershberg, 'The Philadelphia Social History Project: An Introduction', *Historical Methods Newsletter* 9, 1976, 43–58.

5 M. Katz, *The People of Hamilton, Canada West: Family and Class in a Mid-Nineteenth-Century City*, Cambridge, MA: Harvard University Press, 1975.

6 P. Goheen, *Victorian Toronto 1850–1900*, Chicago, IL: Department of Geography, University of Chicago, 1970.

7 O. Zunz, *The Changing Face in Inequality: Urbanization, Industrialization and Immigrants in Detroit, 1880–1920*, Chicago, IL: University of Chicago Press, 1982.

8 R. Dennis, 'Distance and Social Interaction in a Victorian City', *Journal of Historical Geography* 3, 1977, 237–50; R. Dennis, *English Industrial Cities of the Nineteenth Century*, Cambridge: Cambridge University Press, 1984.

9 A. Beveridge, 'Immigration, Ethnicity, and Race in Metropolitan New York, 1900–2000', in A. K. Knowles (ed.), *Past Time, Past Place: GIS for History*, Redlands, CA: ESRI Press, 2002, 65–78.

10 E. Diamond and D. Bodenhamer, 'Race and the Decline of Mainline Protestantism in American Cities: A GIS Analysis of Indianapolis in the 1950s', *History and Computing*, 13, 2001, 25–44.

11 A. Hillier, 'Redlining in Philadelphia', in A. K. Knowles (ed.), *Past Time, Past Place*, 79–92; A. Hillier, 'Spatial Analysis of Historical Redlining: A Methodological Exploration', *Journal of Housing Research* 14, 2003, 137–67.

12 J. Gilliland, 'Modeling Residential Mobility in Montreal, 1860–1900', *Historical Methods*, 31, 1998, 27–42; J. Gilliland and S. Olson, 'Claims on Housing Space in Nineteenth-Century Montreal', *Urban History Review/Revue d'histoire Urbaine*, 26, 1998, 3–16; J. Gilliland, 'The Creative Destruction of Montreal: Street Widenings and Urban (Re)development in the Nineteenth Century', *Urban History Review/Revue d'histoire Urbaine*, 31, 2002, 37–51; J. Gilliland, 'Muddy Shore to Modern Port: Redimensioning the Montreal Waterfront Time-Space', *Canadian Geographer*, 48, 2004, 448–72.

13 D. Debats, 'A Tale of Two Cities: Using Tax Records to Develop GIS Files for Mapping and Understanding Nineteenth-Century U.S Cities', *Historical Methods*, 41, 2008, 17–38; D. Debats, 'Using GIS and Individual-Level Data for Whole Communities: A Path toward the Reconciliation of Political and Social History', *Social Science Computer Review*, 27, 2009, 313–30.

14 P. Dunae, J. Lutz, D. Lafreniere, and J. Gilliland, 'Making the Inscrutable, Scrutable: Race and Space in Victoria's Chinatown, 1891', *B.C Studies*, 169, 2011, 51–80; P. Dunae, D. Lafreniere, J. Gilliland, and J. Lutz, 'Dwelling Places, Social Spaces: Revealing the Environments of Urban Workers in Victoria using Historical GIS', *Labour/Le Travail*, 72, 2013, 37–73; J. Lutz, P. Dunae, J. Gilliland, D. Lafreniere, and M. Harvey, 'Turning Space Inside Out: Spatial History and Race in Victorian Victoria', in J. Bonnell and M. Fortin (eds), *Historical GIS Research in Canada*, Calgary: University of Calgary Press, 2013, 1–24.

15 D. Lafreniere and J. Gilliland, '"All the World's a Stage": A GIS Framework for Recreating Personal Time-Space from Qualitative and Quantitative Sources', *Transactions in GIS*, 19, 2015, 225–46.

16 S. W. Kennedy, A. Curtis, and J. Curtis, 'Historic Disease Data as Epidemiological Resource: Searching for the Origin and Local Basic Reproduction Number of the 1878 Yellow Fever Epidemic in Memphis, Tennessee', *Annals of the Association of American Geographers*, 105, 2015, 1–16.

11

DEVELOPING GIS MAPS FOR US CITIES IN 1930 AND 1940

John R. Logan and Weiwei Zhang

Urban historians and historical geographers have a long tradition of mapping demographic data to study residential patterns, the assimilation or segregation of immigrants and minorities, and processes of neighborhood change, despite the difficulty of working from printed or microfilm copies of city directories and census manuscripts and drawing maps by hand. Dubois' study of Philadelphia was one of the earliest pieces of research of this type, including a detailed survey of the predominantly black Seventh Ward to depict the patchwork of poorer and more well to do blocks.[1] The early Chicago School sociologists used census data and data from many other sources to map the social characteristics of Chicago neighborhoods in the 1920s and 1930s. In 1976 Radford plotted locations of black and white residents in 1880 in Charleston, distinguishing between those residing on streets, in backyards, and on alleys.[2] In 1978 Rabinowitz mapped the streets block by block in four Southern cities to show the degree of racial segregation.[3] Groves and Muller similarly studied black residential concentrations in post-bellum Washington, DC.[4] Others have focused on white ethnic residential patterns in cities such as New York and Detroit.[5]

Historical GIS methods have combined with the digitization of census data from the late nineteenth and early twentieth centuries to unleash new possibilities for such research. This chapter focuses on methods that exploit digital databases and computerized mapping software to tackle similar issues. Such efforts have become widespread in recent years.[6] In the United States, census records for 100 percent samples of individuals are being made available in harmonized data files for several decades leading up to and including 1940 by the Minnesota Population Center (www.nappdata.org/napp/). This means that data can be aggregated easily into enumeration districts (areas smaller than contemporary census tracts) for any variables that were included in each census year. GIS maps are not readily available, but the materials required to create them (paper maps held by the National Archives, street maps for cities in various years, and written descriptions of enumeration district boundaries) are attainable.

In this chapter we begin by reviewing some recent analyses from the Urban Transition HGIS Project (www.s4.brown.edu/UTP) for the period 1880–1940 to illustrate the kinds of analysis that are now possible with mapped 100 percent samples of the census. We then deal with the concrete questions of how this kind of historical urban research is done – how to move from paper maps to GIS files that reflect a historically accurate street grid, how to determine the boundaries of census administrative areas, and how to transfer census data from computer files to the locations of specific addresses in a city. How is it possible to geocode the residences of virtually all the households in a city many decades ago? Some guidance is already available based on studies of 39 US cities in 1880 and thirteen cities in the period 1830–1930.[7] Here we describe in detail how we plan to develop a GIS database for 69 cities in 1930 and 1940.

Approaches to mapped data in the Urban Transition Project

We begin with a description of the Urban Transition Project. The initial step was to use the 100 percent samples from the 1880 census from the North Atlantic Population Project (NAPP) to map population characteristics in 39 US cities. Relying primarily on city directories to provide address ranges on city streets, all addresses were geocoded, making available spatial information at a very fine level of resolution. One analysis relied primarily on aggregating population data to enumeration districts in order to study variations in the degree of residential segregation of white ethnic groups in cities, and therefore it included all cities identified by the Census Bureau in 1880. The geocoded data were used to probe the relationship between an ethnic group's occupational pattern and residential location. A case that we gave special attention to is Buffalo, NY. Here as in many cities the most segregated ethnic group was German. But Germans were also highly over-represented in several occupations (sawmills, wood products, and furniture making), while being under-represented in others (paper, printing, and publishing). The question was this: to what extent did occupational segregation contribute to residential segregation? The conclusion was that this effect was modest. Regardless of occupational sector, most Germans were located in a dense enclave east of the city center, while native whites were more widely spread closer to the waterfront. One strong concentration of German sawmill workers in an area north of the city included almost no native whites in the same industry.

Another study exploited data from 1880 in conjunction with similar data from 1900 through 1940 for two cities, New York and Chicago.[8] Here we began with the question of when the black population first became highly residentially segregated. We also asked why blacks lived in residential clusters – was it mainly due to sorting by race, or did other factors such as occupational standing or migrant status (Southern vs. local birthplace) contribute to their separation? In this study more extensive use was made of the flexibility in spatial scale that was provided by having data geocoded to specific building locations in 1880. We compared segregation at the level of city wards (the scale at which census data have previously been easily available), census tracts, enumeration districts, and smaller areas such as specific street segments or even individual buildings. One conclusion was that already at this time, when less than

5 percent of city residents were black, they were highly segregated by building and street segment. Further, at no spatial scale was their residential concentration attributable to the fact that they were predominantly working class, and there were only small differences between Southern migrants and local blacks. These findings suggest that the origins of black ghettoization were already in place before the turn of the century, decades before the Great Migration that many scholars have considered to be the source of ghettoization in Northern cities. Maps of the location of the black population were used to chart their movement and the expansion of existing black clusters over time. These provided a useful supplement to summary measures of segregation that documented the trend of increasing separation.

A third study expanded this analysis to ten major Northeastern and Midwestern cities for the period 1880–1930.[9] The microdata were drawn from the online index of all residents created by Ancestry.com for the decades 1900–30 (these data will soon be in the public domain through the Minnesota Population Center). Maps were drawn for enumeration districts based on paper maps for each of these decades held by the National Archives. Segregation indices calculated from the aggregated microdata confirmed that in all but one of them the Index of Dissimilarity had reached the 'very high' threshold of .60 by 1900 and was above .80 in four of them by that time. Maps for every city are included in the online appendix to this chapter and they show that in most cases the location of the eventual large black ghetto was already evident in 1880 or 1900. In this instance the mapped data serve as a supplement to conclusions reached from a non-spatial analysis of small area statistics.

The Urban Transition Project: 1930–1940

The public release of census records from 1930 and 1940 has created new opportunities for spatial analysis of population data from this time. The United States had recently become a predominantly urban nation. The massive waves of international migrants had been interrupted by legislation in the early 1920s, and both the first and second generations of immigrants from Southern and Eastern Europe were establishing their place in cities. At the same time new migrant flows included African Americans' great migration from the South to Northern cities as well as Puerto Ricans heading in large numbers to cities like New York and Chicago. Data from the last two pre-World War II censuses provide rich new opportunities to study these groups' incorporation in urban America. The Urban Transition Historical GIS Project at Brown University seeks to add spatial information to the 100 percent sample of individual records that have been made available by the Minnesota Population Center's (MPC) ongoing Integrated Public Use Microdata (IPUMS) program. It will then be possible to aggregate data to neighborhoods at varying spatial scales in order to study processes of segregation, and neighborhood data can be combined with individual records to support multilevel analyses. In the longer term it appears that the methods used to create the 1880 and 1930–40 street maps and geocoding can be applied to additional intermediate census years. It may be possible to have a complete mapped dataset for many major cities that includes 1880 and every decade from 1900 through 1940.

Achieving this purpose requires an extensive mapping effort. Thanks to MPC's National Historical GIS Project (NHGIS) there already exists a 1940 tract map for those large cities where the Census Bureau had already defined census tracts. However these maps do not include the historical street grid, and they are of limited use for adding features at a finer spatial scale (enumeration districts, census blocks, and street segments). The Urban Transition HGIS aims to create an accurate 1940 street grid for the largest 69 cities in the country, create new layers to represent enumeration districts (EDs) and blocks in both 1930 and 1940, and geocode the addresses of all households in these cities in both years. Figure 11.1 maps the cities. Even without the city names it is clear that they are most concentrated in the Northeast. But the Midwest and South are well represented, and major cities in the more sparsely populated West (such as San Francisco, Los Angeles, Denver, Dallas, and Houston) are also included.

These are ambitious goals, but they are feasible through a series of steps that take advantage of several different sources of information. We treat the project as a complex puzzle. There is no single source that provides all the necessary information, but there are ways to piece together bits of data from different sources to complete the puzzle. This chapter describes these steps in some detail. The purpose is partly to document the procedures for future users of the data, pointing out potential sources of error. We also hope that they will prove useful to other HGIS projects with similar goals. Other projects will have different information sources and different challenges in combining them, but they are likely to proceed through many similar steps.

Figure 11.2 summarizes the approach as a 'recipe' for mapping and geocoding these cities. There were many useful sources of information from the Minnesota Population Center (MPC), its National Historical GIS Project (NHGIS), the Census Bureau, and search tools provided by a genealogy website (www.SteveMorse.org).

Figure 11.1   Location of cities in the 1930–40 mapping project (*n* = 69).

Ingredients:

2012 GIS maps with current address ranges (Census Tiger files)
1930 100% microdata with address, ED and block ID (Ancestry/MPC)
1940 100% microdata with address and ED (Ancestry/MPC)
1940 street map of cities showing census block IDs (Census)
1940 tract GIS map of tracted cities (NHGIS)
1940 ED and block definition documentation (Census)
Crosswalk linking 1930 and 1940 EDs (StevenMorse.org)
Digitized list of streets by ED (StevenMorse.org)

Prepare the ingredients

Digitize and edit block definition documents
Standardize street names across all sources
Edit 2012 shape files to match the 1940 street maps
Fill in missing street names and house numbers

Combine and stir

Combine sources to create 1940 ED and block polygons
Compare address ranges within blocks for 1930 and 2012 to label many 1930 blocks
Confirm/edit 1930 blocks and derive a full address range every block
Apply the 1930 address ranges to the 1940 street and block map

Construct an ESRI address locator for 1930 and 1940
Run 1930 and 1940 addresses of all city residents through the ESRI geocoder
Document and serve to public through a web-based mapping system

---

Figure 11.2   Recipe: 1930–40 GIS maps and geocoding of 69 cities.

We initially planned only to map cities in 1940. We had broken the problem down into quasi-independent components: 1) to create a 1940 street grid, 2) to develop a standardized list of street names, 3) to create polygons for physical blocks, census blocks, and EDs, 4) to organize and clean the geographic information in the census microdata, and 5) to array addresses along each street (geocoding). The last step could only be approximate: we could place residents on the right street and within the right ED, but we could only guess at the address range for each segment along that street within the ED. We didn't know which block they lived on.

We solved this problem by extending the project to 1930. The 1930 microdata include an extra piece of information that was not transcribed for 1940: the residents' block number. But there was less documentation for mapping in 1930, not even a paper map showing the location of blocks in any standardized form. So we knew people's block number but we didn't know the block's location. We describe below how we combined sources to overcome this obstacle. When we had mapped the 1930 blocks, we could geocode addresses with great accuracy. And having done this for 1930, we could then apply it to 1940.

Though we were led to 1930 for methodological reasons, having another decade of spatially referenced population data has important substantive consequences. First, it will be possible to ask how the composition of any given area, at any spatial scale,

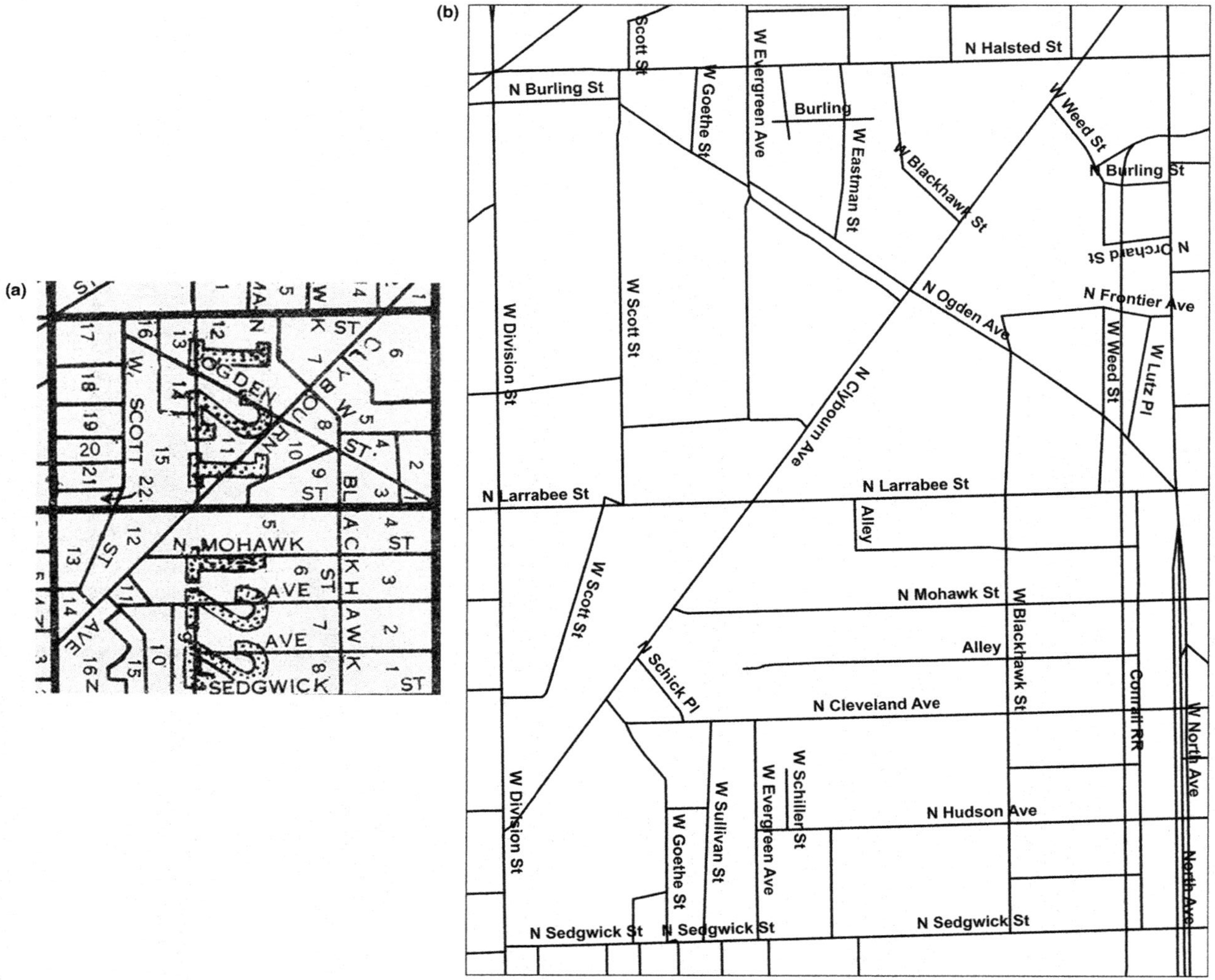

Figure 11.3 (a) A 1940 block map produced by the Census Bureau; (b) The 2012 GIS street grid for a portion of Chicago.

changed from 1930 to 1940 and what 1930 characteristics of the area might be considered to be predictors of change. Second, given the elapsed time of only one decade, it should be possible to link data for individuals from 1930, to ask who moved and where they moved, and to distinguish residents of the area in 1940 who already lived there in 1930 from those who moved there post-1930.

The following sections describe each of the components of the mapping effort, including details on the sources that are used in each one. We draw examples from the city of Chicago, the city that we used to develop these procedures. At the time of publication of this book, the mapping process will still be underway. Additionally most likely we will have uncovered new problems or developed more effective solutions. Hence this chapter is more a report of a project in progress than its final documentation.

The 1940 street grid

The Census Bureau published street maps of major cities in 1940 as part of a series of publications that reported block-level data for each city.[10] The map of a portion of Chicago is shown in the left panel of Figure 11.3. Note that it identifies boundaries of census tracts and block numbers of blocks within tracts, but it does not identify enumeration districts (EDs) – combinations of blocks that are typically smaller than a tract. In principle an accurate 1940 street grid with a tract and block layer could be created through manual editing of a contemporary GIS street map of a city (from TIGER line files as shown in the right-hand panel), using the 1940 map images as a reference.

The first step in linking these maps is to scan the 1940 map, add it as a layer on the 2012 map, and geo-reference it. Geo-referencing involves identifying some points (typically intersections of major streets) on the scanned map that are known to be the same on the GIS map. After geo-referencing the relationship between features in each layer is clear even when looking at them side by side, as in Figure 11.3. When available in color with one layer superimposed on the other, it is evident that most streets line up very well even though it is not possible to create an exact correspondence. Differences between the layers are also easy to see: 2012 streets that did not exist in 1940, 1940 streets that are missing in 2012, and the same street with a different name in the two years. In this section of Chicago, for example, West Lutz Place and West Weed Street are found in the upper left quadrant of the 2012 map but not in the 1940 map. West Blackhawk extends on both sides of Clybourne in 1940 but only on its west side in 2012.

Editing the contemporary map backwards to match the 1940 street grid was time-consuming. Fortunately it could be completed by undergraduate student research assistants with little training. The editing process preserved information about street segments, such as directionality and address ranges in 2012. The most frequent change was to remove a 2012 street (including highways and their associated on and off ramps) that did not exist in 1940. In cases of a name change, we adopted the name shown on the 1940 map. Where a name was missing on the 1940 map (e.g. several short north–south streets in the southwest quadrant of Figure 11.3), we initially applied the 2012 name, which had to be confirmed in a later step. But note that in some of these cases the street was also missing from the 2012 map and the name had to be found in another way. The 1930 and 1940 microdata (searching within EDs) provided candidate names, for example.

Though not shown in Figure 11.3, the edited 1940 street grid includes other features that are often used to define administrative boundaries, such as the city limits, railroads, and rivers. These were assigned the names that were found on the original 1940 census map and treated as though they were street segments.

The standardized street list

A key concern in creating the 1940 street grid was to maintain standardized street names. This is essential because we collate information from several data sources, and the street names (their spelling or misspelling and the abbreviations used) vary greatly across sources. Is it East 5 St, E Fifth St, or East 5th Street? Was there an S Boardway St in Chicago in 1940? If we change Boardway to Broadway should the full street name be written as S Broadway, S Broadway St, So Broadway Street, or some other variation? Different sources often follow different formats. Uniformity is essential. Achieving it requires procedures that are sometimes referred to as data mining – in cases where the name is nearly unrecognizable (e.g. Bdrwy), we must make an informed inference about the name based not only on the sequence of characters in the name, but also on its location in the city (by ED or tract), which limits the choice set.

We relied on three main sources in order to create a standardized street list. All three sources are available in digital form.

1   *Street names from 1930 and 1940 microdata*. The transcription of street names by Ancestry.com includes many potential spellings of the same name. However these are the streets that must be on the GIS map in order to geocode residents. The 1930 and 1940 files both identify the ED within which people living on a given street may be found, and we created lists of street names by ED. Because street names were transcribed with no use of naming protocols expected by a GIS (such as including directions, names, and street types in a standard order), these names required extensive cleaning prior to their use. Initial cleaning of street names, though partially automated (making many changes through what are called 'regular expressions' in STATA), was the most labor-intensive part of the project. Every city presented slightly different problems, and an average city could require 40 hours to do this initial cleaning even before comparing to other name lists.

2   *StevenMorse.org website*. Another valuable resource is a website that provides tools mainly to genealogists (www.StevenMorse.org). Among these tools is a listing of all streets found in every 1930 and 1940 ED in major cities. Our experience using this source is that it has a much higher degree of accuracy and consistency in spelling and completeness of names than do the microdata from Ancestry.com. We have been fortunate to obtain the full database that it draws upon (transcribed from original sources by well-trained volunteers).

We compared the microdata and SteveMorse lists within EDs, which greatly reduced the number of possible matches that needed to be evaluated.

3   *2012 GIS map.* The 2012 map includes many streets that did not exist in
    1930 or 1940. For streets that remained the same, however, it has the advan-
    tage that spelling is very uniform and the format of names has already been
    standardized, including a direction (such as East or South), a name, and a
    street type (such as Street or Avenue). Therefore the 2012 street list sup-
    ported many corrections in names. We created a master list of street names
    from these sources in a standard format including [direction] [street name]
    [type]. To this we added – where possible – the ED and tract that the street
    should be found in.

One purpose in standardizing names was to compare which streets were listed in
each source. We discovered that the 1940 map from the Census Bureau was
incomplete (some streets where people were listed as residing in 1930 or 1940 were
not included in SteveMorse.org or block description files). For example, the 1930
microdata included people on streets that did not exist on the 1940 map, but could
be found in 2012. It was important, therefore, to retain those streets when creating
the 1940 GIS street grid.

Many street names – especially from the microdata – could not be matched to a
street name in another source. This was usually because they were spelled too badly
to make a good match (or they included stray characters such as '??'). At this stage we
kept these unmatched names in our master list and corrected (imputed) them (often
manually) at a later point. We also used the master list to correct street names in
another kind of file: 1940 block definitions from the census bureau as discussed
below. These files list the boundary streets for 1940 blocks, and also provide the
1940 ED and tract where the block was located.

Mapping blocks and EDs

At this stage we are working with a 2012 GIS street grid that has been edited to
match the 1940 census map features, with a partially standardized list of street names
(and features such as rivers and railroads), and a layer identifying 1940 census tracts.
The next step is to add 1940 block and ED layers to the map.

We automatically drew physical blocks (polygons bounded by streets, rivers, or
railroads) using the 'features to polygon' tool in ArcGIS. Physical blocks based on the
street grid are not necessarily 'census blocks' and they do not have census ED or
block numbers. We learned these from block definition documentation provided by
the Census Bureau (www.archives.gov/research/census/1940/finding-aids.html#-
desc). This documentation lists all 1940 EDs in major cities and includes the block
number and the boundary streets (or other geographic features used as boundaries)
for every block in the ED. A portion of a page of block definitions is reproduced as
Figure 11.4.

In order to draw census blocks and EDs, we needed to convert these images into
accurate digital files. We used an OCR program (FineReader), yielding a transcription that requires further editing (shown in Figure 11.5). We extracted and manually
edited the lines that list the 1930 ED number (beginning with 16-) and 1940 ED
number (beginning with 103-) for a set of blocks, along with a ward and tract

ENUMERATION DISTRICTS—1940 CENSUS

State   Illinois   County   16 (103)   Cook   1940 S.D.

1930 E.D.	1940 E.D.	DESCRIPTION OF ENUMERATION DISTRICT	
16-1602 pt	103-2760	Chicago city - That part of Ward 43 (Tract 123-part) in Block 5 - W. North Ave., N. North Park Ave., W. Schiller, N. Orleans 6 - W. North Ave., N. Orleans, W. Schiller, N. Sedgwick	861
16-1605 pt	103-2761	Chicago city - That part of Ward 43 (Tract 122-part) in Block 1 - W. North Ave., N. Sedgwick, W. Blackhawk, N. Hudson Ave. 2 - W. North Ave., N. Hudson Ave., W. Blackhawk, N. Cleveland Ave. 3 - W. North Ave., N. Cleveland Ave., W. Blackhawk, N. Mohawk	965
16-1605 pt 16-1607 pt	103-2762	Chicago city - That part of Ward 43 (Tract 122-part) in Block 4 - W. North Ave., N. Mohawk, W. Blackhawk, N. Larrabee Show separately St.Juliana Day Nursery and Settlement House 5 - W. Blackhawk, N. Mohawk, N. Clybourn Ave., N. Larrabee	1023
16-1608 pt	103-2763	Chicago city - That part of Ward 43 (Tract 121-part) in Block 1 - N. Ogden Ave., N. Larrabee, W. Weed 2 - W. North Ave., N. Ogden Ave., W. Weed, N. Frontier Ave. 3 - W. Weed, N. Larrabee, W. Blackhawk, N. Ogden Ave. Show separately Y.M.C.A. Larrabee Branch, North Ave. 4 - W. Weed, N. Ogden Ave., W. Blackhawk, N. Frontier Ave. 5 - W. North Ave., N. Frontier Ave., W. Blackhawk, N. Clybourn Ave., N. Orchard 6 - W. North Ave., N. Orchard, N. Clybourn Ave., M. Halsted	1339

Figure 11.4   Block definitions for a portion of Chicago in 1940.

16-1602 pt 103-2760   Chicago city - Thit part of Ward 43 (Trsct 123-part) in xC /
5   - W. North Ave., N. North Park Ave., W. Schiller, N. Orleans
6   - W. North Ave., N. Orleans, W. Schiller, N. Sedgwick
16-1605 pt 103-2761   Chicago city - That part of Ward 43 (Tract 122-part) in
1   - W. North Ave., N. Sedgwick, W. Blackhawk, N. Hudson Ave.
2   - W. North Ave., N. Hudson Ave., W. Blackhawk, N. Cleveland Ave.
3   - W. North Ave., N. Cleveland Ave., W. Blackhawk, N. Mohawk
16-1605 pt 103-2762   Chicago city - That part of Ward 43 (Tract 122-part) in /o 2- 3
^ 4   W. North Ave., N. Mohawk, W. Blackhawk, N. Larrabee
Show separately St.Juliana Day Nursery and Settlement House
5   - W. Blackhawk, N. Mohawk, N. Clybourn Ave., N. Larrabee
16-1608 pt 103-2763   Chicago city - That part of Ward 43 (Tract 121-part) in J3 3^
ij 1   - N. Ogden Ave., N. Larrabee, W. Weed
| 2   - W. North Ave., N. Ogden Ave., W. Weed, N. Frontier Ave.
3   - W. Weed, N. Larrabee, W. Blackhawk, N. Ogden Ave.
Show separately Y.M.C.A. Larrabee Branch, North Ave.
4   - W. Weed, N. Ogden Ave., W. Blackhawk, N. Frontier Ave.
5   - W. North Ave., N. Frontier Avs., W. Blackhawk, N. Clybourn Ave.,
j 6   - W. North Ave., N. Orchard, N. Clybourn Ave., M. Halsted

Figure 11.5   FineReader product of the sample image in Figure 11.4.

number that those blocks are found in. These numbers were essential for geographic identification. We also corrected block numbers (such as ^4 changed to 4).

We created a python program to compare the street names in a given ED in the block definition file with corresponding names in the standard street list. The set of possible matches was greatly reduced by being able to limit the search to streets in a specific ED instead of having to consider all street names in the city. Like other standard data mining procedures, the matching program relied on calculating (for every name in one file in comparison with a potential matching names in the other file) the number of matching letters and the number of letters found in the same sequence. Some street names were unrecognizable, but a large share could be matched and corrected.

Another python code automated drawing polygons that are bounded by these listed streets with standardized names. In the majority of cases these polygons were identical to a physical block, and in these cases we assigned the ED and block number of the polygon to this block. In some cases more than one physical block was linked to a census block and we merged them.

Manual editing was required to confirm block numbers or (for unlabeled blocks) to discover them. Editing was facilitated by having multiple sources of information. Within the area of a 1940 ED we knew what 1930 block numbers should be found. We also knew which block numbers should be near one another because they were part of the same 1930 ED. There is also a pattern in the way block numbers were originally assigned by the Census Bureau, so that usually consecutive block numbers are found adjacent to each other, following a spatial sequence (often clockwise) within an ED. Consequently it was often a simple process of elimination to fill in a missing block number or a short series of block numbers. However it was sometimes necessary to refer back to the original block definition page image to read the boundary streets for a given block or to check the list of populated streets in the 1930 microdata. Finally the correct ED and block number were entered into the attribute table. Note that once blocks were correctly labeled, they could easily be aggregated into EDs and tracts because ED and tract ID numbers were assigned from the block description file or manual editing.

Adding addresses from the microdata

At this point we have constructed a historically accurate GIS street shapefile with layers for the 1940 labeled blocks, EDs, and tracts. The next step is to add information from the 100 percent microdata, and to place addresses on the map. The US 1940 full count census data include all individuals enumerated in the census with the person's name, age, gender, race, marital status, highest grade completed, place of birth, occupation, and income (https://usa.ipums.org/usa/voliii/items1940.shtml). Housing characteristics include whether the home is owned or rented and home value or monthly rental cost. Information on each person's relationship to the head of household is the basis for describing various aspects of household composition. Household identifiers also make it possible to determine the composition of the whole building in cases where there is more than one household at a given address. The address is provided as a street name and a house number. Other geographic identifiers include the state, county, city, ward, tract, and ED. The original census also includes a block number, but the block number has not been transcribed – a serious omission given our intention to geocode addresses.

There are many kinds of problems in the transcribed street addresses in the file provided by MPC. The street name may be completely missing (the field may be blank or coded as '???'), often because enumerators or transcribers omitted it or expected the user to assume that the street name previously listed would continue for subsequent households on the same page or next page. The house number is often missing. It may also have a value that is out of range for that part of the city. For example a Chicago address is transcribed as 3417 W Scott St in ED 2763; no other address on W Scott St in ED 2763 is larger than 400. Sometimes the information coded in the house number or street name field refers to some other geographic feature (e.g. the name of an apartment building, hotel, or boarding house) that may have an address embedded in it (e.g. *1250 South Broadway Apartments*).

Many such errors could be corrected by checking the original census manuscript, which is readily available online. However in a project dealing with millions of records, this is impractical. Instead, based on spot checking a non-random set of apparent problems, we have developed standard cleaning procedures.

1 *Extracting the street name.* The 'street name' field sometimes contains extra information. For example, it may include a word like 'Cont' (presumably short for 'continued'). In this case, we consider the record to have the same street name as the previous record. The street name field sometimes contains house numbers. This situation happens often for apartment complexes, where the numbers in the 'house number' field are actually apartment numbers and the real house number is found in the street name field. We used regular expressions in STATA to parse these variables, looking for specific words (e.g. 'apartment,' 'hotel') in the street name and then reassembling the information.

2 *Carrying forward a street name.* Some addresses have valid house numbers but no street names. Often the street name for the household on the previous line should be carried forward. We did this under two conditions. First, we borrowed street names only from the same enumeration page. Second, the adjacent cases should not have a large skip in the house number (after experimentation we set this skip at not greater than 6. We also took into account the distinction between odd and even house numbers, assuming that the enumerator generally stayed on the same side of the street when moving from building to building. Each time that a street name is carried forward this way, we update the file and move ahead to the next missing name. Sometimes the same name is carried forward several times on the same page.

3 *Cleaning house numbers.* There is considerable variation in the contents of the house number field, and these need to be standardized before we turn our attention to numbers that are entirely missing. The following invalid fields were all recoded to missing values that needed to be filled in by other means.

a A continuation of the previous house number indicated by 'continued', 'con', 'con't' etc. in the text.

b A location nearby the previous house indicated by '1/2', 'basement', 'front', 'back', 'rear', 'top', 'bottom', etc. in the text. These are recoded to missing numbers except when there is a new house number within the text. For example, 175rear is recoded as 175. We extract and store the extraneous text in a new variable and keep only house numbers.

c A different level in the same building indicated by 'floor', '[0-9] 1st', '1F [0-9]' etc.

d An apartment indicated by 'Apt' in the text.

e A miscellaneous group indicated by '[0-9][ ][a-zA-Z]', '[a-zA-Z][-][0-9]' etc. in the house number variable. The uniqueness of this category is that there is no other text or number except a single letter and a single number, sometimes with a space or a dash sign. This category is most likely the room in a hotel, like 9c, a5, 7-B.

4 *Dealing with missing house numbers.* Missing numbers will be dealt with in a similar way to missing street names, except that in addition to carrying forward we also interpolate numbers. Some house numbers are suspicious and need to be removed from consideration in this process. For example some house numbers are far outside of the logical possible range for a particular street segment and we wish to consider them as outliers (i.e. transcription errors). To identify these outliers, we compare all house numbers of the addresses on the same street in the same ED. The distribution of these numbers tells us the reasonable range for the segment of that street. This reasonable range can be predefined by us depending on prior knowledge about the size of an ED in a particular city. These 'suspicious' cases would otherwise mislead us in future steps.

The logic of interpolation is to borrow house number information from neighboring households on previous and subsequent lines. We treat renter households with a missing house number as living at the same address as the preceding household, so the house number can simply be carried forward. (For example in institutions like hotels and boarding houses, there may be many households listed, but only the first one carries a house number.)

We believe this is less likely if the household is identified as a home owner, because condominium ownership was rare in this period, and we expect at most one resident owner per building. In these cases we add a house number with the same parity (odd or even) based on interpolation (out of caution, we do this only among addresses that are listed on the same page and are on the same street). There are a few caveats. Sometimes there is no number between the previous and next neighbor addresses that can be used. For example, the previous address has a number 132 followed by an address that has no number and then an address 134. In this situation, we must assume the missing address has the same number as the previous one even if it means two 'owner' households are listed at the same address. When there are multiple households that have no numbers, we assign a separate number for each one.

Drawing the 1930 map in order to geocode 1940 addresses

The final step is to assign addresses to locations. One approach would be use a contemporary geocoding engine. That is likely to be effective for many addresses in many cities, but with an unknown reliability. We wish to have more certainty based on period information. If the 1940 block number had been transcribed by Ancestry. com it would have been a simple matter to place addresses on the proper street segment and side of the street to be on that block, and to array them in the correct order along the segment. But the smallest geographic unit that we have available to place addresses in 1940 is the ED.

Working at this scale has become our 'fallback' geocoding procedure. Let us define the length of a street that falls within a given ED as an 'ED segment.' It could be a single block long, or it could extend several blocks but typically not more than three blocks. The information that we have assembled up to this point allows us to place addresses on their ED segment in the correct order. The ambiguity in this procedure is that we don't know which block the address is on, so its position along the street is arbitrary. We divide addresses along a street equally among the street segments in a given ED and space them evenly within the street segment. When a street is a boundary between two EDs, we align addresses independently on either side of the street. This means, for example, that 2147 can fall between 2120 and 2140, because it is in a different ED.

For many purposes this placement is acceptable (and more useful than if data had to be aggregated to the ED level). It is approximately accurate at the scale of the ED segment, and we will apply it when we cannot improve it. However in most cases we can do better by taking advantage of the 1930 full-count microdata file that includes not only addresses, ED and tract numbers, but also block numbers. If we assume that an address that lies in a given block in 1930 can be found at the same location in 1940, this additional information should be able to inform our 1940 geocoding. Our approach is to draw the 1930 block map, geocode addresses in 1930, then apply the same address ranges to 1940. If the result does not contradict other known information (e.g. such as being placed in the wrong ED) we accept it as correct. We have no additional way to confirm it.

Although we could not locate an original census block map for 1930, we could exploit the progress that we had already made in mapping the historical street grid and ED layer for 1940 to create a 1930 block map. The procedure involves several steps and additional manual editing. It was facilitated by another datum from the 1940 block definitions: next to every 1940 ED number was a list of 1930 EDs that were wholly or partly within it (this crosswalk was collated by SteveMorse.org and made available for our use). This provided a means of locating the approximate location of 1930 EDs.

1930 block map: first draft and editing process

In 1930 Chicago contained more than 15,000 populated blocks. However if we could locate a single address on a block in 1930 (if we knew its location and which side of the street it was on) we could assign a block number to that location. The

1930 microdata file includes at least one address in 12,000 blocks, so most blocks in Chicago could be labeled this way. But how could we place these blocks on the map?

For the purpose of making a first draft of the 1930 block map we relied on contemporary 2012 address geocoding in the following way. We treated every street segment in 1930 and 2012 as two cases, an odd numbered and even numbered segment. We also knew in 2012 which side of the street was odd or even. If there were a street segment in 2012 whose address range coincided with the address range on that same street and on a single block in 1930, there was a good chance that these were actually the same block.

A question is how much the 1930 and 2012 address ranges should overlap in order to consider them the same. After some experimentation we decided that if the lowest house number and the highest house number on the street segment in 1930 were within 30 of the lowest and highest numbers in 2012, or if the range of addresses in either year could fit within the range in the other year, it would be a likely match. Of the 15,522 census blocks in Chicago in 1930, more than 13,000 blocks included at least one 'matching' street segment by this criterion. If there were a match, then we knew the coordinates of the 1930 street segment. We also knew whether the addresses were on the odd or even side of the street, and based on that we could assign them to a specific 1930 block. That 1930 block number could then be added to the corresponding 1940 census block polygon. A majority of blocks were given a tentative 1930 block number in this way.

The result of this procedure for a portion of Chicago is illustrated in Figure 11.6 (upper panel). The figure shows several blocks with no label. In some cases two or more blocks are assigned the same block number. And in some cases more than one number has been assigned to a block. Clearly this map needs further attention. However the map also displays a pattern that suggests that many blocks are correctly labeled: there is only one block with a given block number, and there is an apparent logical pattern of block numbering. Upon further inspection we noticed that every Chicago ward had its own series of block numbers (from 1 to as high as 700+). Successive block numbers were usually adjacent to one another. ED numbers showed much less pattern in numbering, but typically each ED contained a set of consecutive block numbers.

The editing process in reflected in the lower panel of Figure 11.6. This illustration merits close examination. Note first that different shades (and thick boundary lines) have been drawn on each panel to identify the boundaries of 1940 EDs. The 1940 block descriptions list which 1930 EDs (or parts of EDs) are within each 1940 ED. Therefore, for example, we know from the start that all the blocks in 1930 ED 1605 would be found in one of three 1940 EDs in the eastern section of this neighborhood and above N. Clybourne Avenue. One of these blocks (1605–14) was tentatively located north of W. Blackhawk Street and west of N. Mohawk, and we confirmed this location by discovering in the 1930 microdata that people on this block were listed as living on Blackhawk, Mohawk, North, and Larrabee – evidently the boundary streets of this block. In the course of checking block by block, we also found errors on the map. For example, note that W. Scott Street in the southwest corner turned out to be Vedder Street. We deduced this because block 1609–73 had no residents on Scott but many on Vedder (and Vedder had to be the southern boundary street

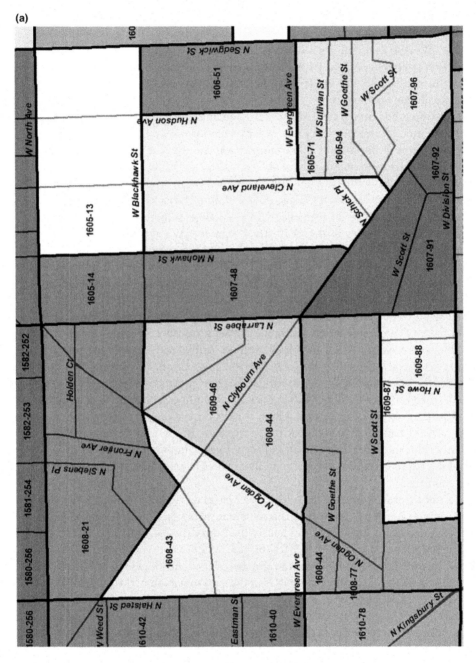

Figure 11.6 The physical blocks identified as polygons with automated census block labeling (a) and the final corrected map for 1930 (b).

(b)

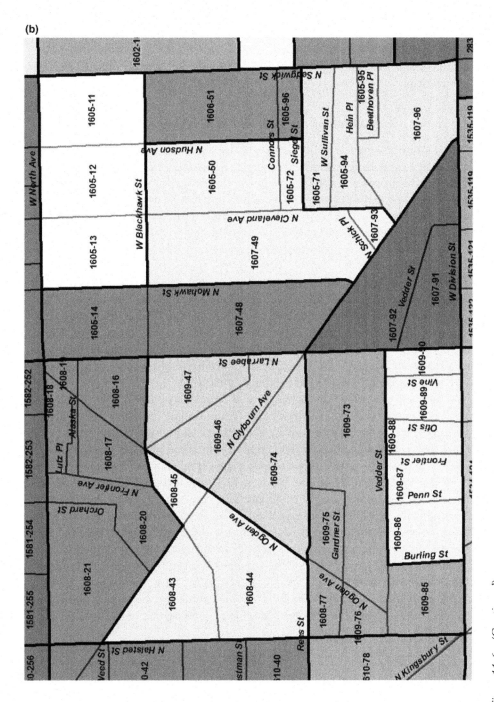

Figure 11.6 (Continued).

for the block because other boundary streets were properly named. Finally, we note missing street names in the initial map in the area below Scott/Vedder. Several north–south one-block street segments were on the Census Bureau's 1940 street map but without names. We followed an interactive process linking 1930 ED numbers and possible boundary streets for those EDs based on the 1930 microdata, correcting one name, adding others, and correcting the two tentative block labels on the initial map.

Geocoding the 1930 and 1940 addresses

Based on a nearly complete 1930 ED-block map and knowing from the microdata which addresses were found in which block, it is straightforward to place 1930 addresses in the proper order along a street segment on a single block. In cases where a single block number is unclear the geocoding can often be done by elimination – if there are four blocks along a street in the 1930 ED and three of them have identified block numbers, then any residual addresses are logically on the fourth block. If there is greater uncertainty, the division of residual addresses into blocks in that ED will have to be arbitrary.

Figure 11.7 illustrates the difference between the original geocoding of 1940 addresses (numbered points with markers on the streets) and the geocoding of 1930 addresses that takes advantage of 1930 block information (numbered points with markers offset from the streets). Note that the original address range for North Larrabee Street between Blackhawk and Holden was 1445–81. In the revision, the range is 1500–38. All of the 1400s have been moved to the block south of Blackhawk (which is in the same 1940 ED but a different 1930 ED).

We then use the 1930 address range to inform geocoding in 1940. As noted above, we assume that a given address range (again, dealing separately with odd and even numbers) on a given street will lie along the same physical block in 1940 as it did in 1930. The main ambiguity here comes about when there are 1940 addresses on that street that fall outside those address ranges. For example, suppose numbers 320–50 East Fifth Street are on one block in 1930, and 402–86 East Fifth Street are on another. Where would we place 380 East Fifth Street in 1940? We do not know for sure and any decision may introduce error. We hesitate to rely on placement in 2012, especially because in some cases the same street is not found in 2012 but also because we are uncertain whether there has been a change in the numbering scheme. Our approach is first to place 380 on the same block as the closest geocoded address, in this example on the 402–86 block. But since the skip between blocks in this case includes a number evenly divisible by 100, we assume that the actual theoretical range of the 320–50 block is 300–98, and we place 380 on that block.

Conclusion

Creating a historical GIS infrastructure of US cities will generate many new opportunities for historical analysis. The initial shapefiles with geocoded census data offer an extremely flexible basis for spatial analysis. It is vastly different from the data on city wards that was for so long the principal source for cross-city and over-time

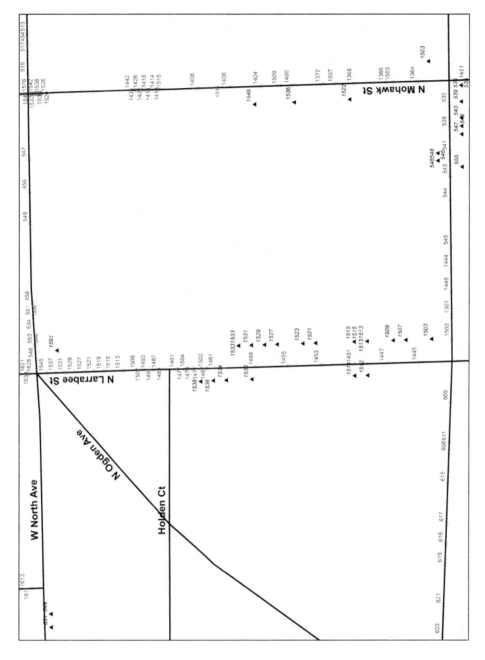

Figure 11.7 Area of Chicago showing original 1940 geocoded addresses and revised based on 1930 address ranges.

research. This also opens up new questions, especially what is the spatial scale at which analyses should be conducted? Our assumption has been that neighborhoods were an essential building block of social life in the period of urban transition that we are studying. But what is a neighborhood, and how do we place boundaries on it? Freed from what many researchers have described as the forced choice of treating census tracts as neighborhoods, what is the alternative? That is a problem that we have begun to focus on,[11] a task that relies on the sort of geocoded 100 percent data that we are developing in this project.

Another opportunity is to add information from other sources to these base maps. For this purpose the accurate historical street grid and address ranges are crucial, because any event or institution or photograph with a known address (or at least an approximate location) can easily be added to the GIS. While many questions can be directly answered with population data, for many other questions the population distribution is only a backdrop. A strength of GIS is its expandability.

This chapter has provided much more detail about how to construct a GIS than on how it can be used. Interested readers can consult the studies referenced here and other studies for that purpose. Our primary goal here is to lay out the methodology of a specific HGIS project, partly to document it but equally to reveal the complexity of the mapping process. Contemporary GIS research counts on shape files of all kinds that are often preprepared and validated. Historical studies regularly need to create the spatial data. In this case the innovation lies in how disparate sorts of information could be pieced together. This project nevertheless has much in common with others: the need for an accurately projected base map, the importance of consistent place names and ways to estimate their locations, a tolerance for simplifying assumptions combined with a constant concern for accuracy and replicability. In these respects every HGIS project builds on the experience of previous ones and helps pave the way for the next.

Acknowledgements

This research was supported by research grants from National Science Foundation (SES-1355693) and National Institutes of Health (1R01HD075785-01A1) and by the staff of the research initiative on Spatial Structures in the Social Sciences at Brown University. The Population Studies and Training Center at Brown University (R24HD041020) provided general support. The authors have full responsibility for the findings and interpretations reported here. John Logan is the corresponding author, Department of Sociology, Box 1916, Brown University, Providence RI 02912; phone 401-863-2267; email john_logan@brown.edu.

Notes

1 W. E. B. Du Bois and I. Eaton, *The Philadelphia Negro: A Social Study: Published for the University*, 1899.

2 J. P. Radford, 'Race, Residence and Ideology: Charleston, South Carolina in the Mid-Nineteenth Century', *Journal of Historical Geography* 4, 1976, 329–46.

3 H. N. Rabinowitz, *Race Relations in the Urban South, 1865–1890,* Athens, GA: University of Georgia Press, 1978.

4 P. A. Groves and E. K. Muller, 'The Evolution of Black Residential Areas in Late Nineteenth Century Cities', *Journal of Historical Geography* 1, 1975, 169–91.

5 T. Kessner, *The Golden Door: Italian and Jewish Immigrant Mobility in New York City,* New York: OUP, 1977. O. Zunz, *The Changing Face of Inequality: Urbanization, Industrial Development, and Immigrants in Detroit, 1880–1920,* Chicago, IL: University of Chicago, 1982.

6 I. N. Gregory and R. G. Healey, 'Historical GIS: Structuring, Mapping and Analysing Geographies of the Past', *Progress in Human Geography* 31, 2007, 638–53. A. K. Knowles and A. Hillier, *Placing History: How Maps, Spatial Data, and GIS are Changing Historical Scholarship,* Redlands, CA: ESRI, 2008. J. R. Logan and W. Zhang, 'White Ethnic Residential Segregation in Historical Perspective: US Cities in 1880', *Social Science Research* 41, 2012, 1292–1306. O. Zeller, 'Historical GIS: The Spatial Turn in Social Science History', *Social Science History* (Duke University Press) 24(3), 2000. C. Gaffield, 'Conceptualizing and Constructing the Canadian Century Research Infrastructure', *Historical Methods: A Journal of Quantitative and Interdisciplinary History* 40, 2007, 54–64. I. N. Gregory, C. Bennett, V. L. Gilham and H. R. Southall, 'The Great Britain Historical GIS Project: From Maps to Changing Human Geography', *The Cartographic Journal* 39, 2002, 37–49. M. De Moor and T. Wiedemann, 'Reconstructing Territorial Units and Hierarchies: A Belgian Example', *History and Computing* 13, 2001, 71–97. P. K. Bol, 'The China Historical Geographic Information System (CHGIS): Choices Faced, Lessons Learned', Conference on Historical Maps and GIS, Nagoya University, 2007.

7 J. R. Logan, J. Jindrich, H. Shin and W. Zhang, 'Mapping America in 1880: The Urban Transition Historical GIS Project', *Historical Methods* 44, 2011, 49–60. C. Villarreal, B. Bettenhausen, E. Hanss and J. Hersh, 'Historical Health Conditions in Major US Cities: The HUE Data Set', *Historical Methods: A Journal of Quantitative and Interdisciplinary History* 47, 2014, 67–80. See also D. Lafreniere and J. Gilliland, 'All the World's a Stage: A GIS Framework for Recreating Personal Time-Space from Qualitative and Quantitative Sources', *Transactions in GIS* 19, 2015, 225–46. J. Gilliland and S. Olson, 'Residential Segregation in the Industrializing City: A Closer Look', *Urban Geography* 31, 2010, 29–58.

8 J. R. Logan, W. Zhang and M. Chunyu, 'Emergent Ghettos: Black Neighborhoods in New York and Chicago, 1880–1940', *American Journal of Sociology* 120, 2015, 1055–94.

9 J. R. Logan, W. Zhang, R. Turner and A. Shertzer, 'Creating the Black Ghetto: Black Residential Patterns Before and During the Great Migration', *Annals of the American Academy of Political and Social Science* 660, 2015, 18–35.

10 US Bureau of the Census, *Sixteenth Census of the United States: 1940. Housing. Supplement to the First Series [Data for Small Areas] Block Statistics for Cities,* Washington, DC: Government Printing Office, 1941–2.

11 J. R. Logan, S. Spielman, H. Xu and P.N. Klein, 'Identifying and Bounding Ethnic Neighborhoods', *Urban Geography* 32, 2011, 334–59. S. E. Spielman and J. R. Logan, 'Using High-Resolution Population Data to Identify Neighborhoods and Establish their Boundaries', *Annals of the Association of American Geographers* 103, 2013, 67–84.

12

GEODETIC DATA AND SPATIAL PHOTOGRAPHY

New assets for urban history

Jean-Luc Pinol

Introduction

The spatial approach to urban history is not new. In the nineteenth century, for example, John Snow used maps to trace the presence of cholera in London. Today, however, urban historians can use GIS far more easily.[1] Although most scholars use big data for studies that concern the post-WWII period, town planning offices produced large data which could be used to spatialize information well before the war, thus offering material with the potential to challenge interpretations in urban history. And yet this perspective remains underdeveloped in many cases. Shane Ewen's recent synthesis *What is Urban History?* devotes many pages to the 'linguistic turn' or to the so-called 'cultural turn' but says nothing about the 'spatial turn'.[2] This contribution addresses this absence, showing how the spatial – and one of its main tools, the GIS – constitutes a powerful approach in urban history, allowing us to use and combine a variety of sources including some which are not necessarily familiar to urban historians.

In this chapter, I use examples of different studies using GIS to illustrate the ways the digital humanities change the writing of urban history, notably thanks to the ability to geocode street addresses. I used this method in the *Atlas des Parisiens* that I published with Maurice Garden, where we charted information about religion, consumption or housing, for example.[3] Then, with the same tools, I charted the arrests of Jewish children in Paris during WWII. The results illuminated a surprising number of questions about the transformation of an industrial city into a city characterized by deindustrialization, the disappearance of slums and the development of green spaces. In this chapter that illustrates a number of concrete cases, I will begin by explaining the technicalities in geocoding with contemporary reference tables and the necessity, for historians, to develop what might be termed a topographical scholarship.

The first case study involves visualizing the data concerning the deportation of Jewish children mentioned above. The analysis of the spatial distribution of arrests then leads me to analyse spatially a number of urban transformations, especially the disappearance of slums and the emergence of green spaces. The chapter concludes using the geo-referencing of aerial photographs taken at the time which provide precious source material to understand the persistence of shanty towns until after WWII and the development of green spaces alongside the ring boulevard of Paris. These developments occurred in zone qualified as *non aedificandi,* territories where it was forbidden for military reasons to erect permanent houses. The spatial approach adopted here seeks to illuminate different facets of urban history with respect to fields as varied as social, political, leisure, housing or economic history. More importantly, it highlights how aerial photography can now be used to trace urban transformations.

Spatial scholarship for efficient geocoding

Before proceeding further, it is necessary to provide some general information about the spatial history of Paris and the geographical terms used to describe the city. 'Old Paris' refers to the territory surrounded by the Farmers-General Wall, which was initially built to ensure the payment of a tax on goods, and especially wine, entering Paris. In the 1840s, the State erected fortifications around Paris for foreign policy reasons; in the process they included large sections of the suburbs. After 1860, the area between the Farmers-General Wall and the fortifications, and parts of communes such as Ivry, were annexed to Paris. Old Paris encompassed an area of 34 square kilometers; the annexed territories encompassed 44 square kilometers. Eleven *arrondissements* (wards) composed the old Paris, while the new Paris had nine. Figure 12.1 depicts these changes, their localization and their designations.

Geocoding offers a way to visualize a range of phenomenon that accompanied urban transformations. Thanks to an initiative of the town planning office of Paris,[4] the Atelier Parisien d'urbanisme (APUR), a reference table for geocoding exists. They have developed a database with 148,000 dots corresponding to the different current addresses. This database allows historians to manipulate big data for urban history,[5] but it requires to do so an excellent knowledge of administrative and urban history, what one might term topographical scholarship. It is essential, as a result, to use a publication of the municipal services that contains the official list and history of all Parisian streets.[6] An example of the complexity involved can be seen with the following example. After WWII the 'rue de la Chapelle', 1480m long, was split in two parts; the northern part of the street kept the name 'rue de la Chapelle', 990m long, while the southern part, 590m, was renamed 'rue Marx Dormoy', in honour of a former minister of Léon Blum's leftist government who was assassinated by French collaborationists. This division had consequences for the street numbers. The first 76 numbers were in the southern section while the authorities attributed new numbers to the northern section. When preparing the data for geocoding, it is necessary to transform the data to adapt old names (and numbers) to the information available for today.

In the *Atlas des Parisiens,* we used geocoding to study the evolution of the spatial distribution of petty commerce or different professions, such as midwives or physicians. We also used geocoding to map the bombing of the French capital in January 1871, in WWI and in WWII. Visualization of the deportation of Jewish children required more preparation in order to create a larger scale for remembrance

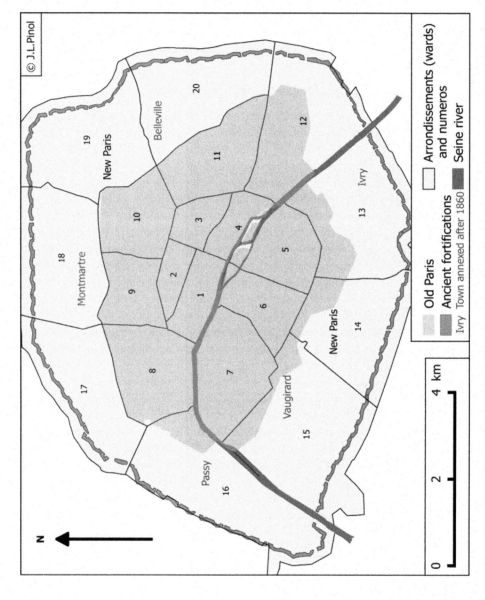

Figure 12.1 Paris: locations and names.

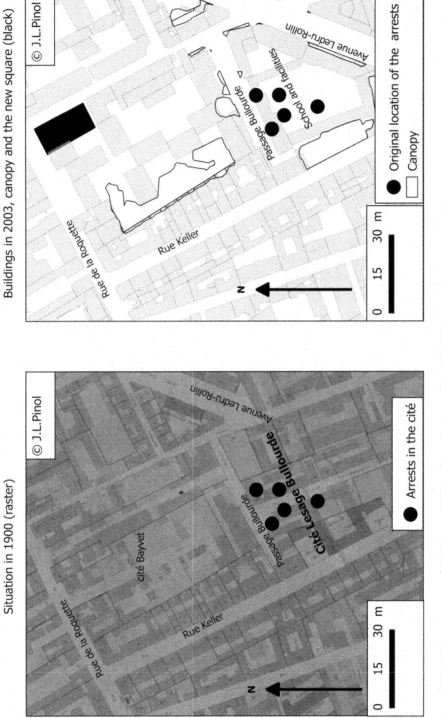

Figure 12.2 Disappearance of Cité Lesage Bullourde and arrests of Jewish children.

purposes, in particular, it was necessary to add new dots to complete the original reference table since these addresses disappeared with the urban transformations of the 1960s.

Over the last 50 years, deindustrialization and the expansion of the service sector has deeply transformed Parisian space. The demolition of workshops and factories, the disappearance of small alleys and dead-ends (known as *impasse, cité* or *passage* in French) generated profound transformations in urban working spaces. The situation of the 'cité Lesage-Bullourde', near the Bastille, offers a good example to understand this phenomenon. This 'cité' was destroyed at the beginning of the 1960s. As a result, it is not possible to geocode former addresses such as 3, 4, 5, 6 or 8 cité Lesage Bullourde – where 34 Jewish children were arrested – since they are not in the reference table of the APUR. To add them to the reference tables, old maps were used and georectified as shown on Figure 12.2.

The 'cité Lesage-Bullourde' is visible on a map at 1:500 that dates from the end of the nineteenth century.[7] On this map of 1900 the large avenue Ledru-Rollin is not yet completely finished. The completion of the Ledru-Rollin breakthrough in the 1930s shortened the cité's central alley. Censuses and directories show that the 'cité' was a mix of housing for the poor, workshops and small factories. The arrests of Jewish children took place in the northern part of the alley, close to the passage Bullourde which still exists today. On the other side of this passage was the 'cité Bayvet' which was also destroyed in the 1960s.

The second map depicts the situation in 2003. The contemporary buildings are very different from those existing before the 1960s; high quadrangular buildings have replaced the cité Bayvet and there is a garden with planted trees and small artificial ponds. The canopy's area has more than 2,000 square metres. The result today is that the area has become an upper-class gated block. A synagogue was built in the 1960s and in 2003 a municipal square replaced a house at the angle of the street La Roquette. Its area is a little bit more than 1,000 square metres, half of the private canopy in the block. Schools and recreational facilities for children replaced the 'cité Lesage Bullourde', although the passage Bullourde still exists. All these transformations are clearly visualized on the website of the Institut national de l'information géographique et forestière (the IGN) where it is possible to compare today's aerial photographs with those of the 1950s.[8]

Topographical scholarship requires in-depth knowledge of the history of streets since it is necessary to prepare the historic data by adapting street names, and sometimes numbers, to the current database. In addition, as we have seen, it is often necessary to add new dots to the reference table; this requires culling information from the archives in order to adapt the reference table used by the GIS for geocoding.

The deportation of Jews and the visualization of data

Serge Klarsfeld has written widely about the Shoah and has recently published a new version of his research about children: *Les 11400 enfants Juifs déportés de France*.[9] I began working with Serge Klarsfeld for an exhibition in the Camp des Milles, near Aix-en-Provence (department of the Bouches-du-Rhône). The camp is 'the only large internment and deportation camp in France that is still intact and open to the public'.[10]

For the opening of the exhibition on 10 September 2012, Gerald Foliot (CNRS) and myself prepared an interactive map of Paris with the addresses of where more than 6,000 Jewish children were arrested. For many people, including Serge Klarsfeld himself, the map was a 'revelation'.[11] Numerous users sent us remarks and material that improved the quality of the data thanks to communication with friends or relatives of the victims who were able to specify details concerning the conditions of arrest.[12]

The data we used for mapping included the first name, the family name, age and address where the children were arrested or lived before their arrest. Before geocoding data curation was necessary to check the quality of information and its coherence. The disappearance of many addresses, very often occupied by low-standard buildings and slums is an indication of the transformations of Paris that occurred between the 1960s and the 1990s. The end product of our work was the creation of a map of Jewish children arrested in Paris between 1942 and 1944 which we made available online,[13] thus attracting a large audience.[14]

The base map used for the web mapping of the deportation of Jewish children corresponds to Parisian *îlots* (or blocks) in 1954, since this represents a very good proxy for the situation in World War II. There were more than 5,000 blocks in Paris in 1954. To draw them, we modified the first vector base map of the blocks that was produced in 1982 by the APUR. We then modified or added blocks to match the block maps of 1954, which the Préfecture de la Seine published for the 80 wards (*quartiers*) of Paris following the 1954 census.[15] We added both the green spaces and cemeteries of today's Paris in order to help contemporary users read the map. One of the strengths of the map is its ability to change scale rapidly. For Paris the different scales range from 1/3,000 to 1/100,000. The first scale addresses remembrance needs (the names of victims are legible) and the second offers a more comprehensive approach to urban history showing the distribution of arrests across the city. One of the most striking results is the very high proportion of Jewish children who were arrested in unsanitary areas as shown in Figure 12.3.

Figure 12.3 presents the arrests by address (for the sake of visibility, the map only represents addresses with more than two arrests) and the location of the officially recognized unsanitary areas. The two distributions overlap clearly in eastern Paris. Before World War I, high mortality due to tuberculosis led the municipal administration to define eighteen locations as *îlots insalubres*. These 'official' unsanitary areas – constituted by blocks[16] – had significantly higher mortality rates due to tuberculosis than the rest of the city. In the post-war period, state or municipal authorities either destroyed or improved these blocks, which were very often practically slums, in order to raise the level of comfort and amenities.

As Claire Lévy-Vroelant noted, one of the most striking characteristics of these unsanitary areas was the overcrowding of apartments.[17] With the help of GIS it is possible to calculate the population density in these unsanitary areas in 1954. Not surprisingly, these areas have the highest density.[18] At that time the mean density in Paris was between 712 and 772 inhabitants per hectare used for housing; the same index value was at 919 for unsanitary areas, between 20 per cent and 28 per cent above the mean.[19] Although the tuberculosis death rate had diminished strikingly since World War I, it was still much higher in the unsanitary blocks than in Paris as a whole.[20] Working-class people, new immigrants and poor people were concentrated

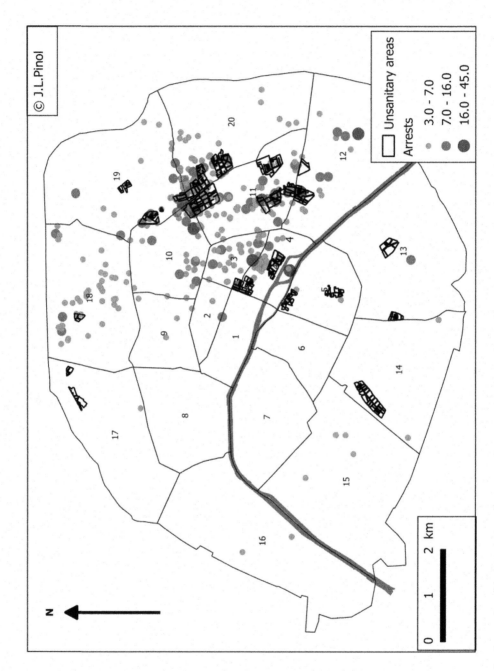

Figure 12.3   Arrests by address and unsanitary areas.

in these buildings, notably a large number of East European Jewish immigrants who arrived in Paris in the 1930s.[21]

Almost 24 per cent of the Jewish children deported from Paris were arrested in the unsanitary areas on the right bank of the Seine. If we define a buffer zone of 200m around these areas, the percentage of children arrested in these areas rises to 40 per cent. The urban areas most concerned by the arrests were in the 11th, 19th and 20th arrondissements; some were also located on the border of the 3rd and 4th arrondissement, within the unsanitary area no. 1, as well as area no. 16 (4th arr.), where a large Jewish population had settled since the nineteenth century.

Among all the Jewish children deported from France, 47 per cent were arrested in eight arrondissements in northeastern Paris and 7 per cent in the other remaining twelve arrondissements.[22] The 11th arrondissement – with many unsanitary areas – was the district with the most arrests: 1,217 children lived there before deportation. The 20th arrondissement followed, with 1,092 arrests, then the 18th with 674 and the 3rd with 577 children.[23]

As mentioned, many of the addresses where the arrested Jewish children were living in Paris – more than 10 per cent – have disappeared since the 1940s. This was the result of urban transformations, both within and outside unsanitary areas, where buildings were destroyed and green spaces developed to air the city. Until the end of the 1960s the construction of new buildings was rare. As very few buildings were destroyed by the bombings of WWII, the city was materially the same in the 1930s and in the 1960s. For example, a part of the unsanitary area no. 1 was destroyed in the 1930s and served as a parking lot for years, while the surrounding old buildings remained in the same dilapidated state. In 1971 the situation finally began to change with a new building project that was finished in 1977: the famous Pompidou Centre.[24] This was the decade of major changes for the French capital. Businesses and factories moved from the city: the wholesale food market (Les Halles) near the Pompidou Centre, La Villette slaughterhouses, the large car factory Citroën, for example. Many large facilities, infrastructures or factories moved away and were replaced by large green spaces.

Green spaces and the transformation of Paris

Green space policy does not develop separately from other facets of urban change; it is only one of the dimensions affecting the way a city is transformed. Once again a spatial approach to the distribution of vegetation in the different districts yields interesting results. In particular, an analysis of the chronology of municipal green spaces[25] reveals, contrary to received wisdom, that if we consider Paris strictly speaking – excluding the Bois de Boulogne and the Bois de Vincennes – the 'greening' of Parisian urban space really began in the 1970s not during the Second Empire (1852–70).[26]

My spatial approach to the study of green spaces in Paris requires the use of many datasets, beginning with a database of land use prepared by the APUR. This dataset has almost 11,190 lines corresponding to polygons representing elementary schools, high schools, churches, public offices, different kinds of public buildings, museums and . . . green spaces. For each polygon, some attributes indicate the perimeter, area, different names and other specifications; there is also a very important parameter for historians, which is termed 'creation'. Unfortunately, this chronological information is rarely documented. Green spaces represent 688 items, which are not all within Paris. After excluding the polygons which correspond to the outlying Bois de Boulogne (845 hectares) and the Bois de Vincennes (995 hectares), to the west and to the east of Paris, I created a usable file of 661 polygons representing 536 hectares. I completed it with an open data file coming from data. gouv.fr that specifies in particular the date of creation. This information, which is mandatory for a chronological approach, is not always indicated in the APUR database.[27]

Not all the vegetation of the capital city is included in the file described above. In particular, I added cemeteries, selecting them from the dataset of APUR, but also added non-municipal areas planted with trees, which are not in the dataset. I completed my own file with information from the interpretation of satellite images, with a precision of 5m which corresponds to canopy, produced by National Geographic Institute or IGN.[28] Attributes are limited to ID and area. In Paris, strictly speaking, there are 9,111 different polygons and the total area covers 1,310 hectares. Another file that shows the alignment of trees is also available for large-scale representations (cf. Figure 12.5).[29]

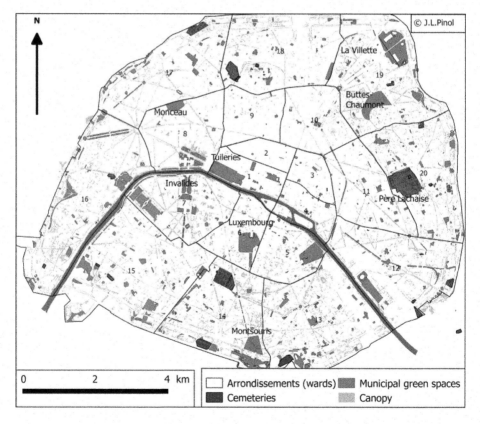

Figure 12.4 Municipal green spaces, cemeteries and canopy.

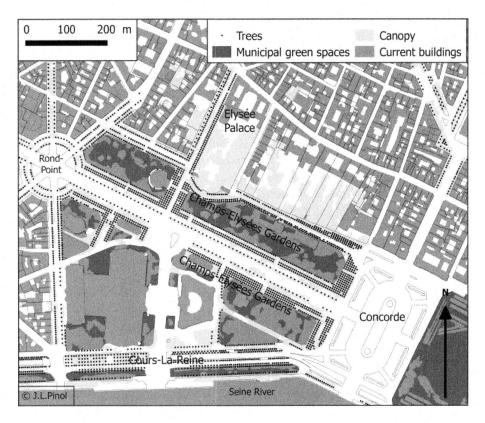

Figure 12.5   Champs-Elysées.

Figure 12.4 presents the results for cemeteries, municipal green spaces and canopy. Canopy covers 1,310 hectares, while municipal green spaces account for 536 hectares. These two sets of vegetation overlap over a total of 239 hectares. Cemeteries occupy 112 hectares, 47 hectares of which overlap with the canopy. This means that there are 1,024 hectares of canopy outside the official green spaces and cemeteries of the Parisian municipality. This includes the trees that line the streets, most of which are under the responsibility of the Direction des espaces verts et de l'environnement (DEVE) (the Direction of green spaces and environment), but other administrations or institutions also have green spaces. Finally one also finds private green spaces in urban plots. It is possible to estimate the area of these different categories but before doing so it is useful to consider a large-scale map of the area around the Champs-Elysées in order to understand a number of issues related to the study of vegetation in the capital.

This large-scale map (Figure 12.5) shows where the Champs-Elysées begins and represents the extent of the vegetation in this part of Paris. Municipal green spaces do not represent all the vegetation; on the contrary, the canopy covers more land. Some of the canopy is superposed on the municipal green spaces but not the totality. The case of the Elysée Palace is interesting, because a large canopy occupies the south of the plot but is not integrated into the municipal green spaces. The municipality pays the gardeners of the municipal green spaces but the gardeners of the Elysée Palace are civil servants dependent on the Presidency of the Republic. The map also shows the large number of aligned trees in this part of Paris.

Using the tools of GIS on the basis of our data it is possible to calculate, for the 80 districts (*quartiers*, four per arrondissement) of Paris, the vegetation available per inhabitant and identify the different types of vegetation along the streets,[30] within municipal spaces, in cemeteries as well the space corresponding to the canopy cover inside urban plots. Table 12.1 presents the absolute figures for each of the Parisian districts and Table 12.2 gives the area of greenery per inhabitant.

Figure 12.6 shows the square metres of vegetation per inhabitant in each district and it illustrates how the distribution varies depending on location, with the highest levels in the traditional wealthy districts in western Paris and in the southern and eastern districts where unsanitary areas were widespread before the 1960s. To understand the spatial logic of this distribution, it is necessary to analyse the chronology of the creation of green spaces. This information is only available for municipal green spaces, which are represented in Figure 12.7.

Figure 12.7 represents existing municipal green spaces and the date of their creation.[31] I selected only three periods: the Second Empire (1852–70), 1914–50 and 1970–99. The first period lasted 18 years and covers 55 hectares, the second one 36 years and 70 hectares and the last period spans 29 years and 167 hectares. When related to the length of time, that means 30,000 sq. m for the first period, 20,000 for the second and 60,000 for the last.

During the Second Empire, the city built the largest park, the Buttes-Chaumont, in the northeast of Paris; this section of the new Paris previously had no green spaces.

Table 12.1 Vegetation in Paris.

	Canopy along the streets	Canopy within plots	Municipal green spaces	Cemeteries	Total
Total Paris (hectares)	664	516	535	111	1827
Proportion in Paris	7.59	5.90	6.12	1.27	20.88
Standard deviation	3.34	3.15	6.99	3.78	10.40
Coefficient of variation	0.44	0.53	1.14	2.98	0.50

Table 12.2 Square metres of vegetation in Paris per inhabitant.

	Canopy cover along the streets	Canopy cover within plots	Municipal green spaces	Cemeteries	Total
Sq. m per inhabitant*	3.72	2.39	2.49	0.36	8.49
Standard Deviation	3.89	2.19	17.63	1.56	21.25
Coefficient of variation	1.05	0.92	3.37	4.28	1.85

* For the population, I used the numbers of the 1999 census.

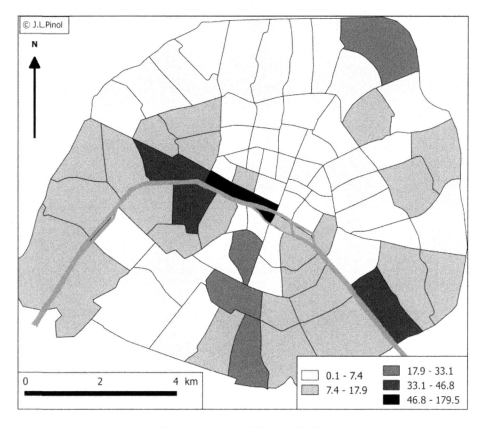

Figure 12.6   Square metres of vegetation per inhabitant, 2000s.

The park – a total of almost 25 hectares – was built to refurbish old gypsum quarries in a location that had a bad reputation due to the infectious emanations stemming from a sewage dump. The park was part of a wave of new green spaces build under the aegis of the Baron Haussmann, Prefect of the Seine whose ambitious program of urban transformations included beautification and sanitation. For the first time, a municipal service was in charge of green spaces.

From 1915 to 1950, the major works involved the destruction of the fortifications and their replacement by a large amount of low-cost housing. Major operations were conducted on the zone *non aedificandi*, notably the construction of the International University Campus, and a number of green spaces were opened in certain wards such as the 13th.

In the 1970s, the magnitude of green spaces increased tremendously thanks to the exodus from Paris of certain large enterprises, such as the La Villette slaughterhouses (19th) or those of Vaugirard (14th), but the municipality also initiated smaller planning operations too, such as the Parc de Belleville (20th). The building of this last park, opened in the 1980s, resulted in the disappearance of many of the alleys and dead-ends with slums where Jewish families had lived during WWII. This trend toward the greening of insalubrious areas continued at the beginning of the

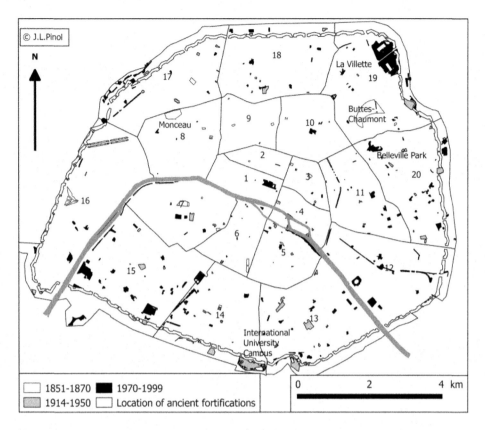

Figure 12.7   Periods of municipal green spaces.

twenty-first, as we have seen, with the transformation of the blocks around 'cité Lesage-Bullourde' and the creation of a very small square in 2003.

Many previous studies have analysed the zone *non aedificandi* using literary sources but a more spatial approach is rare.[32] Today, the existence of aerial photographs produced by the IGN, combined with GIS, offers new forms of knowledge about this specific urban space.

Aerial photos and the evolution of the zone *non aedificandi*

It is now possible to download aerial photos from the IGN website. After selecting a location, the different aerial missions concerning the location are indicated. For Paris the missions started in the 1920s. The spatial extent of each photograph is indicated and it is possible to download it. This kind of historical resource has only become easily available since July 2012.[33] Both landscape and rural historians could use these photographs and their methods are comparable, for example, when they drew upon historical maps (from 1817, 1875, 1960 and 2006) to document the evolution of land cover in the Sorrento peninsula.[34]

Here I will focus on how urban historians can use these new sources by focusing on a specific location of the zone *non aedificandi* where the International University

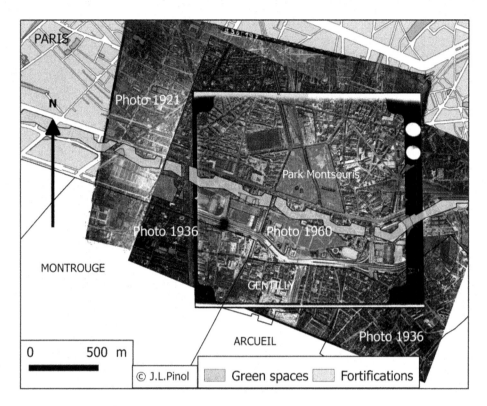

Figure 12.8   Parc de la Cité universitaire.

Campus of Paris was built in the 1920s. The area concerned is an area in southern Paris, where the destroyed fortifications were replaced by the Cité universitaire internationale (International University Campus). The authorities decided to build a new park on the area that lay 250m beyond the fortifications. Jean-Claude Nicolas Forestier was in charge of the project in the 1920s but the works lasted a long time given the presence of densely populated shanty towns in the zone. The park's official opening in 1935 occurred years after Forestier's death. Despite the onset of the building project, people continued to live in the grounds up until 1934, and the aerial photos show that some barracks still existed in that part of the zone until 1936.[35] I have selected for analysis three photos (some ten are available): the first one was taken in June 1921[36] at the scale 1:9841; the second is dated 15 May 1936 and the scale is 1:11082;[37] the last one was taken in April 1960 at a scale of 1:8738.[38]

   Figure 12.8 superposed the three pictures, after georectification of the photos. They do not cover an identical area since the initial scale is different: for the 1960s photo only 6 sq. km are in the shot compared to 9.5 sq. km for 1936 and 9 sq. km for 1921. Georectification allows us to work with information coming from documents of different scales and the comparison of layers sheds insight on the processes of transformations of a specific place. The location of fortifications is indicated by a vector layer as well as the Park Montsouris and the future location of the park of the

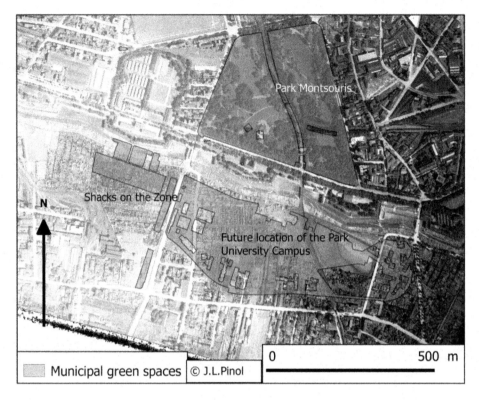

Figure 12.9 Parc de la Cité universitaire, aerial photo, 1921.

Cité universitaire internationale. For my analysis, I will focus on a larger scale reproduction of this location using the three different photos.

On the aerial photo of 1921 (Figure 12.9), the fortifications are not yet destroyed –
it is possible to see them under the transparent vector layer – and a lot of shanties and
shacks are visible on the zone exactly at the location where the park was then built.
Fifteen years later, in 1936 (Figure 12.10), the situation is different. There are no
longer shacks at the location of the park but on the west end some shacks still exist;
in addition between the park and the shanties some sport facilities are visible. The
park is visible but vegetation is still rare. It is noticeable that the park is larger than
the zone, which went only 250m beyond the fortifications. Under the destroyed
fortifications (transparent vector layer) the different buildings of the International
University Campus are clearly visible.

In the 1960s picture (Figure 12.11), the landscape is transformed. The park now
has vegetation and the ring boulevard of Paris is visible although not completely
finished. The black spot on the southwest corner of the park is the result of a technical problem on the film. Sporting facilities are well developed; at the location of
the ancient fortifications to the west there are signs of low-cost housing[39] and just
south of the Park Montsouris different buildings of the International University
Campus are present and clearly observable. In contrast, shanties and shacks are gone.
This kind of precarious housing that long defined the zone has now completely

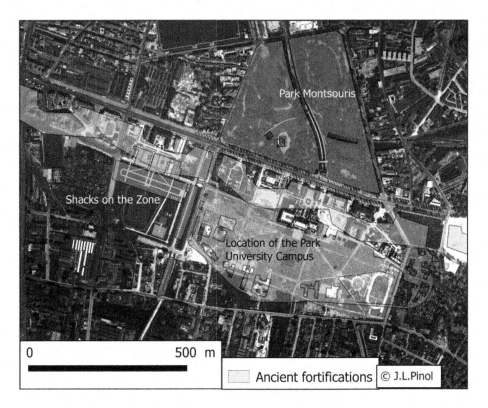

Figure 12.10   Parc de la Cité universitaire, aerial photo, 1936.

disappeared. Evidence from only three dates is sufficient to document the evolution of the zone, offering another perspective on this space than that which literary and sources transmit.

While I have focused here on a small sector of the zone, Anne Granier has developed a similar analysis for the totality of the 34 km no-building zone around the fortifications. Beginning in 2014 Anne Granier georectified a great number of aerial photos from 1921 to 1955[40] choosing time periods when the entire zone area was covered by aerial missions at the same date and at the same scale. She is building up a spatial database to study some 4,500 plots and to document all these plots with information coming from other sources, notably expropriation documents. The municipality generated these documents in its concern to control the entire area for the placement of different kinds of infrastructure. Expropriation documents include very large-scale 1:500 (or 1:2000) plans and maps – much larger than the scale of the aerial photos. Without rectifying the aerial photos, whose scale ranges from 1:5000 to 1:20000, it would be impossible to use these plans since no location pins exist today. These expropriation documents, which are legal documents, are linked with tables for each plot – each has a specific and unique ID – its size, its price and the date of expropriation. They also indicate the name of the owner and his or her address, the activities developed – for example, gardening, laundering, rag picking, buying and selling old stuff – the name of the tenant(s), the numbers of buildings.

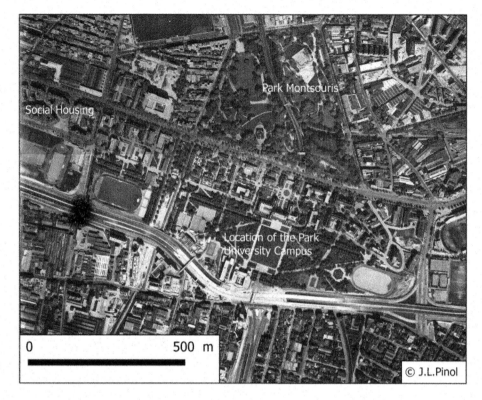

Figure 12.11   Parc de la Cité universitaire, aerial photo, 1960.

Anne Granier's research depends on the use of GIS given the scale of the area she is exploring.

This illustrates how the spatial approach of history, which GIS allows, can transform the way historians work and directs them to new sources. At the same time, spatial historians still need to know and document the political and administrative history of specific cities, to develop what can be called topographical scholarship.

Spatial urban history

In Kristen Nawrotzki's and Jack Dougherty's online book, *Writing History in the Digital Age* the fifth chapter, 'See what I Mean', is dedicated to Visual, Spatial and Game-based History.[41] Most of the examples evoked are linked with urban history. Stephen Robertson in *Putting Harlem on a Map*[42] highlights the fact that mapping events on the web changed his vision of Harlem. Now he pays attention to events whose significance he ignored before mapping – notably the concentration of traffic accidents on Seventh and Lenox 'offer another example of how *Digital Harlem* changed how I thought'. I share exactly the same sensation after working on the visualization of the deportation of Jewish children from Paris; the experience led me to explore new fields of urban history.

The concentration in slums of the Jewish children deported, the disappearance of addresses linked to the transformations of cities at the end of the twentieth century helped me to reconsider previous knowledge. The same process occurred with green spaces. I was struck by the distribution of disappeared addresses and their very frequent replacement by squares or even parks – which was the case with the Belleville Park opened in 1986. That led me to work more systematically on this relationship. As Karen Kemp states:

> What is important about assigning a geographic reference to data is that it then becomes possible to compare that characteristic, event, phenomenon, etc. with others that exist or have existed in the same geographic space. What were previously unrelated facts become integrated and correlated spatial analysis helps us understand what is going on in our geographic information.[43]

A spatial approach to urban history allows us to test hypotheses in the interpretation of urban evolution.[44] Using GIS introduces the historian to big data initially conceived by municipal services for purposes that are not those of historians. Using this data correctly requires historians' skills, which means an in-depth knowledge of the studied city. By combining base maps with information collected in other digital sources or in more traditional not digitalized sources – archives, books, statistics, etc. – it is possible to develop spatial databases, to check their internal coherence and to produce new knowledge using GIS tools. To achieve this, historians need to be explicit in explaining how they collect information and how they have worked so others can use layers and produce databases. An important step follows, the production of working maps: historians must critically examine the results and question their relevance. When a phenomenon appears inconsistent with our knowledge of a specific space, might this be the result of a change in the name of an address?[45]

Another example illustrates problems resulting from an error of date in the initial database. My working maps showed a garden created in 1877. When I examined the results I was surprised since the area was significantly transformed in the sort of 'above the street' urban planning that was common in French town planning in the 1960s and 1970s. The garden in question was in the middle of an area revamped in the 1970s. In reality, the garden was created in 1977 and not 1877 . . . It is important to keep in mind that historians have powerful tools and especially their critical skills to check the consistency between our scholarship and the new knowledge produced with the help of GIS tools. Before the digital age, critical analysis was one of the historian's best tools; this remains the case in the digital age.

As the authors of *Spatial Humanities* argue:

> The power of GIS for the humanities lies in its ability to integrate information from a common location, regardless of format, and to visualize the results in combination of transparent layers on a map of the geography shared by the data . . . Scholars now have the tools to link quantitative, qualitative, and image data and to view them simultaneously and in relationship with each other in space where they occur.[46]

Geodetic data and aerial photographs can now be used systematically and can help us to understand more traditional sources such as directories, censuses, police archives or juridical decisions. Undoubtedly, these possibilities constitute valuable new assets for urban history.

Notes

1 D.J. Boddenhamer, J. Corrigan and T.M. Harris (eds), *The Spatial Humanities, GIS and the Future of Humanities Scholarship,* Bloomington, IN: Indiana University Press, 2010.

2 S. Ewen, *What is Urban History?* Cambridge: Polity Press, 2016.

3 Maurice Garden and myself prepared several base maps of Paris for our Atlas. See M. Garden and J.-L. Pinol, *Atlas des Parisiens de la Révolution à nos jours*, Paris: Parigramme, 2009. In the *Atlas*, we showed how digital and spatial humanities could transform research in urban history. See also J.-L. Pinol, 'Les atouts des systèmes d'information géographique (SIG) pour «faire de l'histoire» urbaine, *Histoire urbaine*, 3, 2009, 139–58.

4 See www.apur.org./

5 The controlling reference table is very important for the quality of geocoding. Very often, geocoding online means no access to reference tables, and so no opportunity to rectify.

6 See Mairie de Paris, *Nomenclature officielle des voies publiques et privées*, 10th ed., 2004. In this publication of more than 700 pages, the history of each street of Paris, even those that have disappeared, is presented.

7 These maps were drawn for tax reasons at the very end of the nineteenth century or at the very beginning of the twentieth century. See J.-L. Pinol, 'Les atouts', 141–42. For the online map of the cité Lesage-Bullourde, https://tinyurl.com/ybjp3kt4.

8 See http://urlz.fr/3fQp.

9 S. Klarsfeld, *Les 11400 enfants Juifs déportés de France*, Paris: Association Les Filles and Fils des Déportés Juifs de France FFDJF and the Beate Klarsfeld Foundation, new ed., 2013, 362.

10 See www.campdesmilles.org./

11 Serge Klarsfeld uses this precise word in his oral presentation of the project. See http://tetrade.huma-num.fr/Fond/Films?ID=101; Serge Klarsfeld describes our work and the role of cartography as a remembrance tool in his recent memoires, See Beate and Serge Klarsfeld, *Mémoires*, Paris: Flammarion, 2015, see p. 657.

12 On these points, see J.-L. Pinol, 'Mapping the Deportation of Jewish Children from France, 1940–1944', in R. Tamborrino (ed.), *Digital Urban History: Telling the History of the City in the Age of the Ict Revolution*, Rome: CROMA, 2014.

13 The map can be seen at the following address: http://tetrade.huma-num.fr/Tetrademap_Enfant_Paris./

14 Many journals and newspapers mentioned it. See, for instance, *Le Monde*, 15 Feb. 2014, Denis Cosnard, 'Déportation: La carte et la mémoire'.

15 See Préfecture de la Seine and INSEE, *Données Statistiques sur la Population et la Ville de Paris: Répartition par Îlots* [1954], Paris: Imprimerie Municipale, 1957, 623.

16 In French, the same word *îlot* designates parcels of urban space without streets running through them but also an agglomeration of unsanitary blocks. To avoid misunderstanding, *îlots insalubres* is translated by unsanitary areas.

17 C. Lévy-Vroelant, 'Le diagnostic d'insalubrité et ses conséquences sur la ville, Paris 1894–1960', *Population* 54(4–5), 1999, 707–44.

18 On this point, see *Map of the Density in 1954*, in Garden and Pinol, *Atlas des Parisiens*, 52.

19 We could estimate the housing area in Paris at 3,700–4,000 ha in 1954 (the area of Paris is around 10,500 ha, but the area of streets, green spaces, public buildings, cemeteries and

railways spaces are here omitted). The unsanitary areas represent 180 ha. That means that the density in Paris, in relation to inhabited space, is between 712 and 772 persons per hectare. In 1901, the official density was 345 inhabitants per hectare but it reached 655 inhabitants per inhabited hectare; at this time the inhabited space was estimated at 4,100 ha.

20 See C. Lévy-Vroelant, "Le diagnostic d'insalubrité', figure 3, p. 725.

21 Regarding these unsanitary areas, see L. Sellier, *Rapport au nom de la 6ᵉ Commission, sur la Question des Ilots Insalubres*, Paris: Imprimerie Municipale, 1937, 474. See also Y. Fijalkow, *La Construction des Îlots Insalubres: Paris 1850–1945*, Paris: L'Harmattan, 1998.

22 46 per cent were arrested in Parisian suburbs and in the rest of France. For the map concerning the arrests from France, see http://tetrade.huma-num.fr/Tetrademap_Enfant_France./

23 The 18th arrondissement of Paris had almost as many arrests as all the communes of the department of Seine. The department of Seine was constituted by Paris and its 20 arrondissements and 80 communes (such as Saint-Denis, Aubervilliers, Nanterre, Neuilly and Boulogne-Billancourt) existed until 1968. The 3rd arrondissement had more arrests than the total arrests in three great cities: Nice, Marseille and Lyon.

24 See the comparison: http://urlz.fr/3fQE.

25 For a comparison with other large European cities (Stockholm, Helsinki and St Petersburg), see P. Clark (ed.), *The European City and Green Space*, Aldershot: Ashgate, 2006.

26 For greater detail, see J.-L. Pinol, 'Vegetation and Green Spaces in Paris: A Spatial Approach', in P. Clark, M. Niemi and C. Nolin (eds), *Green Landscapes in the European City*, Abingdon: Routledge, 2017. A new book about green spaces in Paris was published in 2015. It argues that the main period for green spaces is the Second Empire but a spatial approach is absent. See R.S. Hopkins, *Planning the Greenspaces of Nineteenth-Century Paris*, Baton Rouge, LA: Louisiana University Press, 2015.

27 See the link www.data.gouv.fr/fr/datasets/liste-des-parcs-et-jardins-donnees-geographiques-prs./

28 It is easy for a researcher to get an account on IGN and to upload files on topography, transports, population, administrative data. Most of the data are organized at the level of the department. For Paris, and for all departments, it is possible to get blocks, plots, addresses, topography, hydrology.

29 See the link www.data.gouv.fr/fr/datasets/arbres-d-alignement-donnees-geographiques-prs./

30 For the estimation of vegetation in the streets we used two different methods and privileged the highest estimation, which is coherent with the results of the Interatlas society. The latter calculates the vegetation of Paris with a laser system to 1m precision, the vegetation of Paris in 2008 was 1,824 ha. The distribution of what I calculate with a precision of 5m is the same but with a markdown of 8 per cent. See APUR, *Note de 4 pages*, 29, February 2008, 'La couverture végétale de Paris et des communes du centre de l'agglomération parisienne'.

31 The completed dataset of APUR gives dates for 556 polygons out of 661. The polygons for which I have no data are fairly small and represent less than 30 ha out of 536.

32 For an approach based on literary sources, see J. Cannon, *The Paris Zone: A Cultural History, 1840–1944*, Aldershot: Ashgate, 2015. For a town-planning perspective see the very good exhibition catalogue, C. Jean-Louis and L. André, *Des fortifs au périf: Paris, les seuils de la ville*, Paris: Ed. du Pavillon de l'Arsenal, 1991.

33 On the historical aerial photos, see www.geoportail.gouv.fr/actualite/181/telechargez-les-cartes-et-photographies-aeriennes-historiques.

34 See S. Pindozzi, E. Cervelli, A. Capolupo, C. Okello and L. Boccia, 'Using Historical Maps to Analyze Two Hundred Years of Land Cover Changes: Case Study of Sorrento

Peninsula (South Italy)', *Cartography and Geography Information Science*, 2015, http://dx.doi.org/10.1080/15230406.2015.1072736.

35 The 'question' of the zone and the inhabitants called *zoniers* lasted till WWII.

36 The mission is CCF00B-361_1921_CAF_B_-36 (11 June 1921) and the shot has the number 198.

37 Mission C3636_0561_1936_PARIS-ENT-CARLIER-DANGER (15 May 1936) and the shot has the number 25.

38 Mission C2314-1691_1960_CDP1570 (24 April 1960), shot number 1221.

39 There are different kinds of housing at the location of fortifications, in this sector is more often low-cost housing but the standing could be different from one block to another.

40 See the PhD of Anne Granier, *La Zone et les zoniers de Paris, approches spatiales d'une marge urbaine (1912–1946)*, Université de Lyon, Ecole Normale Supérieure Lyon, décembre 2017.

41 See http://writinghistory.trincoll.edu./

42 http://writinghistory.trincoll.edu/evidence/robertson-2012-spring./

43 K.K. Kemp, 'Geographic Information Science . . .', in Boddenhamer et al., *The Spatial Humanities*, 32.

44 For an example of urban historical GIS, see D. Lafreniere and J. Gilliland, '"All the World's a Stage": A GIS Framework for Recreating Personal Time-Space from Qualitative and Quantitative Sources', *Transactions in GIS*, 2015.

45 In a large city such as Paris with approximately 6,000 different street names, there are numerous pitfalls to be considered. For example, if street 1 was named A at date X, and then name B replaced A, name A would become available and it could be given again to street 2 at X + n. For geocoding with strings the name of street 1 would automatically, and mistakenly, be affected to the second location. It is only the critical analysis of the historian that reveals the incoherence.

46 Boddenhamer et al., *The Spatial Humanities*, p. ix.

13

'KLEINDEUTSCHLAND', THE LOWER EAST SIDE IN NEW YORK CITY AT TOMPKINS SQUARE IN THE 1880s

Exploring immigration at street and building level

Kurt Schlichting

Introduction

Advances in historic geography and especially the use of historic GIS (HGIS) have enabled historians, demographers, and social scientists to explore important urban research questions at a spatial scale not possible before. When combined with 'big data' resources, such as the 100 percent US 1880 Census, spatial patterns can be studied at the neighborhood, street, and building level.

This study examines the spatial distribution of the immigrant population in New York City, specifically the German immigrants in the Lower East Side around Tompkins Square that became 'Kleindeutschland', Little Germany. The ethnic composition of the wards forming the neighborhood was German, both immigrants and their first-generation children, and stood in contrast to other ethnic neighborhoods that were Irish. HGIS maps of the blocks adjacent to the square were created to allow for analysis at the spatial level of the New York 'block', the street segment between two cross streets, a salient feature of the 1811 Manhattan grid. With the historic GIS maps, 19,213 records from the 1880 Census were geocoded to block and building level. When aggregated to the block and the tenements on the block, the ethnic segregation intensifies. In addition, German immigrants from specific states and principalities are concentrated on certain blocks and in individual tenements, illustrating chain migration at a very small spatial scale.

By 1880 when immigration transformed American society, Manhattan became a 'city of immigrants' with distinctive spatial neighborhoods occupied by one immigrant group that brought its distinctive culture with them. Their children and their children's children would face the challenges of assimilation; many would acculturate, while others would retain a distinctive cultural identity for generations.

During the century of immigration, 1820 to 1920, two immigrant groups predominated in New York: the Irish and the Germans. The area around Tompkins Square in the Lower East Side became the center of the German immigrant community – 'Kleindeutschland' or 'Little Germany'. German immigrants followed a pattern of chain migration to the Lower East Side. Nadel argues that within Little Germany immigrants spatially clustered by the small states or areas in Germany they emigrated from, following relatives, neighbors, or earlier migrants to a specific location, a single street, or even a building on the Lower East Side.[1]

HGIS was used to reconstruct the street and streetscape pattern in a nine-block area adjoining Tompkins Square. German immigrant spatial patterns will be examined at the block and building level. Many residential buildings from the 1880s remain as do churches and cultural institutions. At the micro-spatial level, the residential buildings can be used as the unit of analysis. For over 150 years these buildings provided an entry point for thousands of people coming to America just as New York did at the macro level.

Kleindeutschland

Immigration shaped the history of the United States in the nineteenth century and nowhere more decisively than in New York City. Oscar Handlin, the preeminent historian of immigration, argued that contrary to Frederick Jackson Turner's famous 'frontier thesis', the driving force in the American experience has been immigration.[2] New York served as the main entry port for millions of European immigrants who came to the United States for economic opportunity or religious freedom or to flee political and religious persecution in their home country. As a result of immigration, New York's population increased more rapidly than any other place in the country. Numbering just over 50,000 in 1800, by 1880 the population exceeded 1.2 million people and certain neighborhoods became the most densely populated place on earth. Foreign-born immigrants comprised 47.4 percent of New York's population in 1860 and 44.5 percent of the total population in 1870. In 1860 German-born immigrants comprised almost 15 percent of Manhattan's population and over 17 percent in 1900.

Germany's history in the nineteenth century is complicated. Before 1871 the country consisted of 39 states, principalities, and free cities such as Berlin. When Prussia led the consolidation of Germany in 1871, 'cultural, religious, and linguistic boundaries cut across those of states, customs, unions, and empires dividing German Europe into a multitude of small cultural and linguistic regions'.[3] German immigrants to New York carried their regional identities with them to the Lower East Side. Before the consolidation of Germany, emigrants left for a variety of reasons: Burrows and Wallace point to the potato blight in the south, small land holders forced off the land by depressed agricultural prices, weavers put out of work by a flood of English textiles, and general economic stagnation.[4] Political unrest and an aborted revolution in 1848 led to the flight of craft workers, small shop owners, and radical intellectuals.

In 1855 New York State took a much more active role in overseeing immigration, establishing Castle Garden in Battery Park at the southern tip of Manhattan as the official entry location for all immigrants to pass through. At Castle Garden careful

Table 13.1 New York (Manhattan) population: 1790–1880.

	Population	Born Germany	% Germ
1790	20,661		
1800	54,133		
1810	86,550		
1820	112,820		
1830	188,613		
1840	296,352		
1845*	371,233	24,416	6.6%
1850	501,732	50,688	10.9
1860	801,088	119,964	14.9
1870	929,199	151,203	16.3
1880	1,222,237	163,482	13.4
1890	1,515,371	210,723	13.9
1900	1,850,093	324,224	17.5

Source: US Federal Census, 1790–1900, www.census.gov. New York State Census, 1845.
Note: US Census did not include place of birth until 1850.

Table 13.2 Immigrants arriving in port of New York and Castle Garden.

	1847–1869	%
Port of New York		
Total	4,297,980	
Ireland	1,664,009	38.7
Germany	1,636,254	38.1
England	539,668	12.6
Scotland	111,238	2.3
France	77,200	1.8
Other	269,611	6.3
	1855–1869	**%**
Castle Garden		
Total Arrivals	2,296,619	
Avowed Destination		
New York State	972,297	42.3

Source: Frederick Knapp, *Immigration and the Commissioners of Emigration* (New York: Nation Press, 1870), 232–5.

statistics were collected detailing the country of origin of immigrants arriving in New York. Between 1847 and 1870 over 4 million arrived in the city; two countries dominated: Ireland and Germany, each with over 1.6 million immigrants. Once Castle Garden opened in 1855, immigrants were asked their 'avowed destination' and over the next decade and a half, almost 1 million indicated New York State as their final destination; many simply left Castle Garden for one of the city's crowded immigrant neighborhoods. For the Irish, the journey ended about a mile north of the

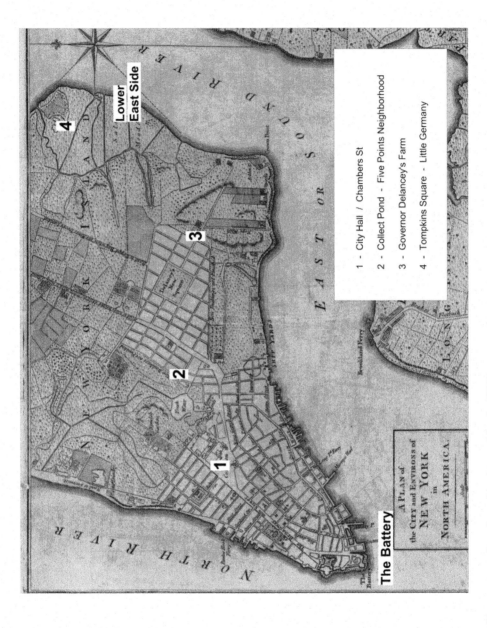

Figure 13.1 Ratzer map of southern Manhattan Island – 1776.

Battery in the Five Points and Bowery, while the Germans traveled a little farther north to the Lower East Side.

Lower East Side – Tompkins Square – Little Germany

The flood of immigrants to New York in the first half of the nineteenth century dramatically changed the social geography of the city. Both Dutch and British colonial New York remained concentrated at the southern tip of Manhattan Island, with few residents beyond modern City Hall and Chambers Street. A British military map of 1776 identifies the 'salt marshes' along the East River, which will become the Lower East Side, developed in the nineteenth century to provide housing for the city's exploding population (see Figure 13.1). Delancey's farm, owned by the last British governor of New York and confiscated at the end of the American Revolution, became the first part of the Lower East Side to be developed for immigrant housing (often referred to as the 'Lower' Lower East Side).

Peter Stuyvesant, the last Governor-General of Dutch New York, and his descendants owned the salt meadows along the East River, which had little value until the nineteenth century. In 1829, a Stuyvesant descendent gave land along East 8th Street to the City of New York for a park and the city filled in the marshland to create Tompkins Square. In the 1840s German immigrants, arriving in large numbers, settled around Tompkins Square in tenements on the streets to the south of the Square: East 6th, East 5th and East 4th. Avenue B became known as the German 'Broadway', a center of commercial activity. Over the next 60 years, Tompkins Square and the surrounding streets would remain the center of the German community in New York.

Methodology – Building an HGIS for Kleindeutschland

The base layer of the HGIS consists of an 1891 Robinson map of the area overlaid with the modern digital street map from the New York City Planning Department (Figure 13.2). New York City adopted its grid pattern of avenues and cross streets in 1811 based on the meticulous work of John Randall.[5] New York's grid, which forms the streetscape around Tompkins Square, begins south of the square at Houston Street, first named 'North' street because in the early 1800s it stood as the northern boundary of the developed part of New York City. As with many of the nineteenth-century cartographic maps of New York, the work of the surveyors and cartographers proved to be meticulous and the Robinson map aligns with the Planning Department's current digital street map.

With the base layers established, other contemporary digital maps were added including street centerline and pavement edge that defines the interior of the grid's blocks. The modern digital street maps are used to recreate historic administrative districts: wards, sanitary districts, and EDs, Census Enumeration Districts (Figure 13.3). EDs in densely populated areas often consist of a single block and the

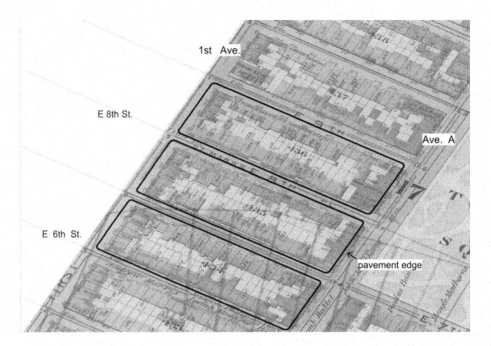

Figure 13.2 Tompkins Square – Lower East Side. Robinson map 1891.

Source: NYC digital street maps (Manhattan, Double Page Plate No. 12 Figure bounded by E. 14th St., East River, E. 3rd St., 1st Ave. From Atlas of the city of New York, Manhattan Island. From actual surveys and official plans (In 2 layers) Depicts: 1891 (New York Public Library, Figure Division)).

pavement edge digital map aligns with the historic blocks between 5th and 8th streets adjacent to Tompkins Square. Figure 13.2 includes the Robinson raster as the base map overlaid with the NYC digital street and pavement edge maps. For many areas of Manhattan, the street addresses have not changed over time and the digital street layer was used to geocode individual census records to the block and to the exact historical address.

The city's blocks are the interior of two avenues and two cross streets. Residents of Manhattan historically and today refer to the place of residence as the street segment between two cross streets, for example 8th Street between 1st Avenue and Avenue B. Residential buildings on both sides of 8th Street form the streetscape of memory. To create these 'imagined' blocks polygons were drawn around a single street segment to include the residential addresses on both sides of the street (Figure 13.8).

The Robinson maps include detailed information for each property on the city blocks including street addresses, width of lot, and each building's lot coverage. The 1811 grid plan created uniform city blocks between the north–south avenues with standard lot sizes, 25 × 100 feet; for example, 411 E 8th Street is a standard city lot 25 feet wide and 100 feet in depth (Figure 13.3). Where the lot size varies, the maps include the width facing the street (e.g. 414 E 9th Street – width 37.6 ft.). Buildings

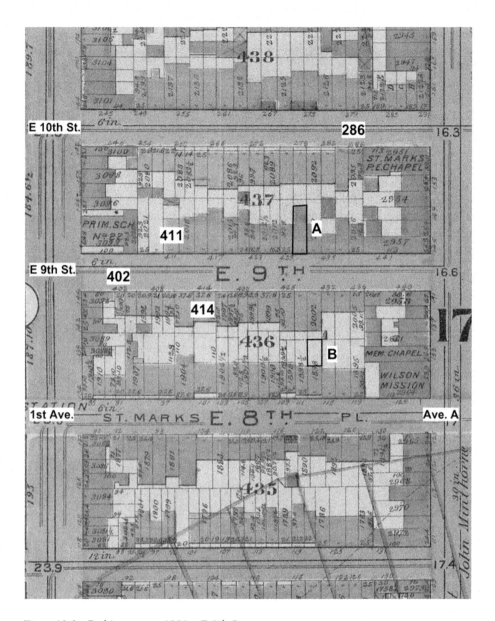

Figure 13.3 Robinson map 1891 – E 9th St.

Note: 411 E 9th is labeled; the two adjacent vacant properties would be 409 and 407.

are delineated by darker color (Figure 13.3A) and the rear yard, where the privies were located by white (Figure 13.4B). Individual properties are identified by block and property number, which can be used to locate historic valuation and tax information (e.g. 286 E 10th Street: block 437, property 2095). For each block, a number of properties are labeled with street address and these data are used to establish the address range of each street segment for geocoding. For example, the address range on the north side of East 9th Street is even from 402 to 440 and the south side, odd from 407 to 441.

New York City's grid provides a decided advantage for creating an HGIS. In many areas on Manhattan Island the 1811 grid remains intact. Even where major development occurred, most of the original grid remains. For example, Pennsylvania Station, now the site of Madison Square Garden, occupied two city blocks: W 31st St. to W 33rd St., between 7th and 8th Avenues. In 1901 the Pennsylvania Railroad bought all the buildings on the two blocks, tore down the existing tenements, removed W 32nd Street between 7th and 8th Avenues, and built a Beaux-Arts masterpiece station.[6] To restore the original 1811 street pattern, only W 32 St. between 7th and 8th Avenues would need to be edited back onto the current digital street map (Figure 13.4).

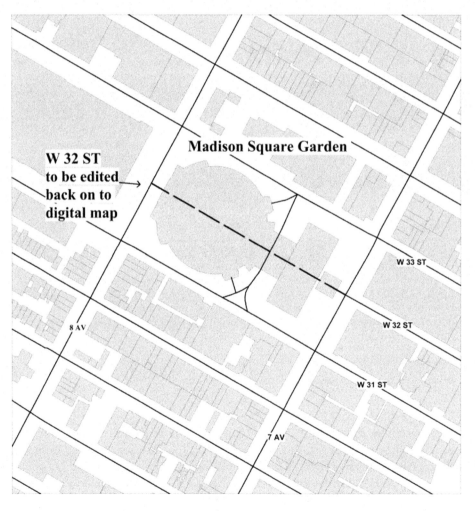

Figure 13.4 Madison Square Garden area: digital streets and building footprint maps.

HGIS – Spatial Scale

Building an HGIS at the block, street segment, and building level dramatically reduces the spatial scale as Gilliland and Olson do in their study of Montreal in 1881.[7] Before HGIS any analysis of immigrant neighborhoods in the American city was limited by the spatial units the census published statistics for, usually the political ward. In New York the wards were the city's primary voting districts: each elected an alderman and an assistant alderman to the City Council. For the New York State Senate and Assembly, the City's wards were subdivided into Senate and Assembly districts. Four wards defined Little Germany: the 10th, 11th, 13th and 17th, on the east side of lower Manhattan. While not large geographically, the four wards were among the most densely populated places, not just in New York City, but in the United States (Figure 13.5).

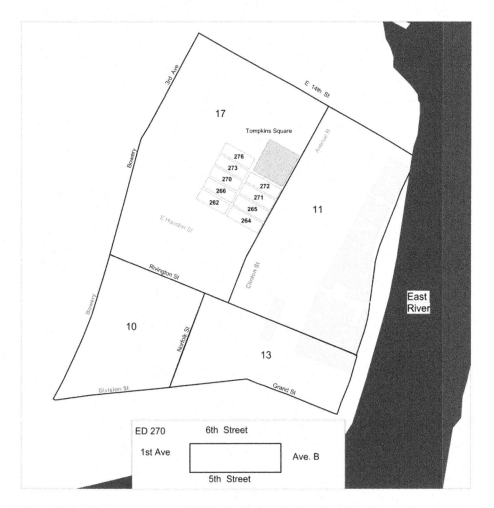

Figure 13.5 Kleindeutschland. 1880 Wards: 10, 11, 13, 17 – Tompkins Square Enumeration Districts.

Note: Gray along East River – public housing.

Between 1800 and 1840 the decennial census enumeration was organized by political ward boundaries and later by ward and election districts within from 1850 to 1870. The population of New York increased dramatically and residential density followed; the average population of the aggregate census data units also increased, reaching over 18,000 by 1850. For the 1860 and 1870 Census the number of spatial units was increased. Regardless of the area of each ward/district any aggregate data from the census before 1880 cannot be used to analyze population at the small neighborhood or street level. In 1880 the census used enumeration districts (ED) as the primary spatial units to collect individual level data. With almost 700 EDs in Manhattan, the average population enumerated in each dropped to under 2,000 and provides the necessary data for analysis at a much smaller spatial scale. Enumeration districts were used in all American cities from 1880 until the 1920 Census when census tracts were first used in New York, Chicago, and a few other major cities. The 1880 Census was also the first census to include street address for each household in all cities including New York. The nine EDs adjacent to Tompkins Square include all of the interior tenements on two avenues and two cross streets.

Table 13.3 New York City (Manhattan) – US Census 1800 to 1880: census spatial units.

	Population	*Census Spatial Units Districts*	*# of units Germ*	*Avg. Pop/Unit*
1800	54,133	Wards	7	7,733
1810	86,550	Wards	10	8,655
1820	112,820	Wards	10	11,282
1830	188,613	Wards	14	13,472
1840	296,352	Wards	17	17,432
1850	501,732	Wards/Districts	27	18,583
1860	801,088	Wards/Districts	96	8,345
1870	929,199	Wards/Districts	388	2,395
1880	1,222,237	Enumeration Districts	691	1,769

Table 13.4 Tompkins Square – EDs (1880 Census).

	Population
276	1,722
273	1,456
270	2,697
266	2,364
262	1,998
272	2,361
271	2,493
265	2,300
264	1,840

Official city blocks were used to define the 1880 enumeration districts (EDs) and, in the crowded immigrant neighborhoods, EDs consisted of one or two blocks with a single census taker assigned to each. Paper maps of the 1880 EDs are available at the New York Public Library. For this study of Little Germany, nine EDs to the west and south of Tompkins Square between 1st Avenue and Avenue B are analyzed.

While the Census used the New York City blocks as EDs, the interior space bounded by two avenues and two cross streets, in the collective imagination of millions of New Yorkers both past and present, the 'block' has another designation. The 'block' where one lives or works or visits is both sides of a city street between two cross streets. If one reads diaries or reminiscences, residents always refer to a street as a single segment, 'East 6th between A and B', and do not think of the street segment as one of New York's official blocks (401 or 402 – see Figure 13.6). Nadel identifies these street segments as 'the basic sociographic unit . . ., a one-block-long stretch of roadway with associated buildings'.[8]

1880 Census data

The North Atlantic Population Project (NAPP) at the Minnesota Population Center (MPC) constructed a database for the entire 1880 Census with the standardized variables and coding that the MPC uses for all of its historic census data.[9] The number of records for New York City, Manhattan Island, in 1880, totals 1,222,237.[10] The nine EDs for the Tompkins Square area include 19,213 records. The NAPP database does not include street address, but the NAPP file was constructed from the microfilmed 1880 Census manuscript records. Ancestry.com has created a webpage of every microfilm page of the 1880 Census. The NAPP files are in the same order as the Ancestry webpages, which simplified adding street name and address for each household to the 1880 database.[11]

Creating an HGIS for the area adjacent to Tompkins Square has a number of decided advantages. In Ward 17 (Figure 13.9) the 1880 streetscape remains intact and required editing back in only one street segment: East 4th Street, between 1st Avenue and Avenue B. The street numbering system has also not been changed; the spatial location of most street addresses from 1880 is exactly the same as the current street address. On many streets the buildings constructed to house the German immigrants are still standing.

Other areas in the Lower East Side, especially along the East River (Ward 11), have undergone significant redevelopment. A waterfront filled first with shipyards and later with tenements, warehouses, factories, and coal yards fell into decay and abandonment in the twentieth century. In the post-WWII era, the City, in partnership with the federal government, undertook massive 'urban renewal' projects, which included building thousands of units of public housing. Land along the East River could be condemned at a reasonable cost and used as the location for public housing (Figure 13.5). To construct an HGIS for Ward 11 along the East River would require extensive revision to the current digital street map to restore the historic streetscape.

Figure 13.6 Lower East Side – Tompkins Square – 1880 EDs.

Note: length of street between avenues: approx. 700 ft.

HGIS Geocoding

The 1891 Robinson map provided street address ranges for all of the EDs in the study area, which were used to modify, where necessary, the GIS street address files for geocoding.[12] The 19,213 1880 Census records were geocoded and with multiple passes; a 99.7 percent match rate was achieved. This result illustrates the advantages of an HGIS for areas in New York that have retained the historic streetscape and did not undergo urban renewal in the 1950s. The geocoding was also successful because of the population density in 1880. The nine EDs included a total of only 552 unique addresses with an average of 35 people at each street address.

For this analysis, sociographic street segments, the block between two cross streets and the tenements on both sides of the street, were created as polygons including the individual census records for the buildings on both sides of the street. These street segments reflect the 'imaginative blocks' people lived on; GIS enables us to create the street segments and then code each census record to the imaginative blocks (Figure 13.8).

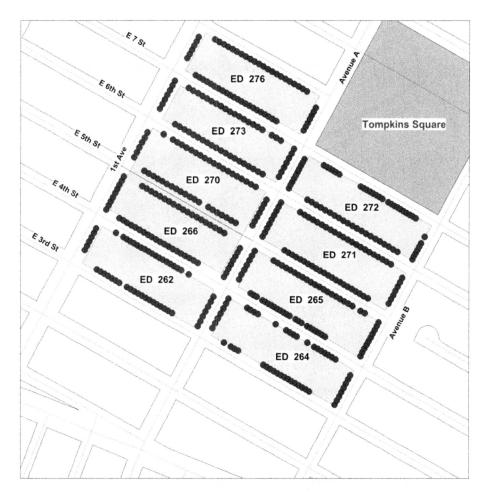

Figure 13.7   Geocoded 1880 Census records – 552 street addresses.

Figure 13.8 Tompkins Square – street segments. Geocoded 1880 Census records.

Spatial analysis – German immigration to Kleindeutschland

Nadel identifies chain migration as the primary determinant of the spatial concentration of the German immigrant community in New York on the Lower East Side. Social networks provided information and contacts that guided the choice of where the newly arrived decided to live.

People tended to settle in groups: national, regional and local. On these bases they choose one city over another, one neighborhood over another, one block over another, or street or house over another ... migrants choose to live among kin, fellow townsmen, fellow provincials or fellow nationals whenever possible. This preference in turn, influenced the nature and structure of the settlements of Germans [in New York] (as it did other immigrants).[13]

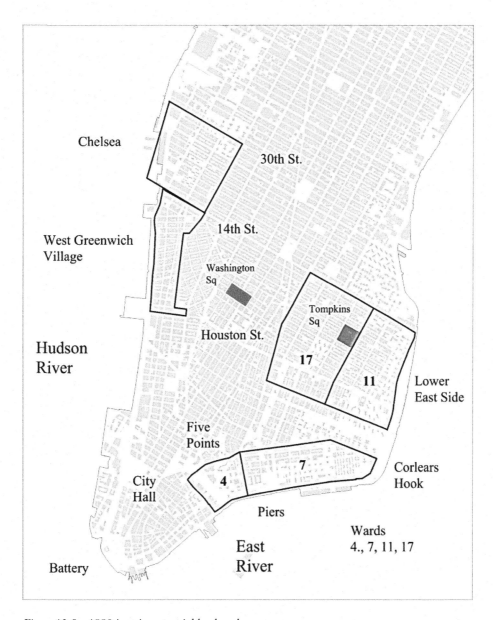

Figure 13.9 1880 immigrant neighborhoods.

While New York City was popularly described as a melting pot, in the second half of nineteenth century there were distinct neighborhoods in Manhattan where the Irish and the Germans lived. In addition to Little Germany in the Lower East Side, major Irish immigrant neighborhoods evolved: one along the East Side and two along the Hudson River in Greenwich Village and Chelsea (Figure 13.9). Both of the Irish neighborhoods were home to many longshoremen who worked the docks and warehouses that lined the Manhattan shore.

The 1880 Census included detailed nativity data: the place of birth of the individual and the place of birth of the father and mother by country of origin. Nativity variables were constructed for this study that include the foreign born and the first generation born in the United States whose parents were foreign born. Both are combined to identify the 'German' and 'Irish'. Combining the foreign born with the first generation provides a much richer analysis of ethnicity than focusing on the foreign-born immigrants alone. Nadel, Handlin, Moynihan and Glazer, and other scholars of American immigration have studied the complex relationship between the immigrant generation and their children born in America.[14] The first generation often was torn between the ethnic heritage surrounding them and the draw of assimilation into the mainstream of American life. A rich literature describes the tension between the immigrant generation and their children, a drama that played out in New York's German and Irish neighborhoods.

By 1880, immigration had transformed New York City; the native born, with parents born in the United States, had become a distinct minority overshadowed by the Irish and Germans. By 1880 just 18.2 percent of the residents of Manhattan Island were native born, with native born parents; over 80 percent of the population were either foreign born or the children of immigrants. New York was truly a city of immigrants. This tidal wave of people coming to America continued for 40 more years and eventually evoked bitter opposition and drastic limitations put upon immigration in 1924, ending the 'Century of Immigration'.[15]

The German and Irish neighborhoods were places apart. Overall German immigrants and their children accounted for 34.2 percent of New York's population, but 55.1 percent in Ward 11 and 58.1 percent in Ward 17, the two wards at the north end of Kleindeutschland. The ward-level data hide the intense residential segregation of the Germans living in the EDs adjacent to Tompkins Square. Among the population of 19,231 in the nine EDs, just 2.5 percent were native, a total of 476

Table 13.5 Home blocks (1880 Census).

Street	Between	# Geocoded
E 7th St	1st Ave and Ave A	1,108
E 6th St	1st Ave and Ave A	1,688
E 5th St	1st Ave and Ave A	2,205
E 4th St	1st Ave and Ave A	1,455
E 6th St	Ave A and Ave B	2,082
E 5th St	Ave A and Ave B	1,668
E 4th St	Ave A and Ave B	1,663

Table 13.6 1880 Census – immigrant neighborhoods.[16]

1880 Manhattan Immigrant Neighborhoods

Irish Waterfront Neighborhoods

Nativity	New York/ Manhattan	East River	West Greenwich Village
Native	18.2%	9.0%	30.5%
Born Ireland	16.5	24.1	18.5
1st Gen. Ireland	17.7	29.6	23.0
'Irish'	**34.2%**	**53.7%**	**41.5%**
Born Germany	13.3	7.6	5.1
1st Gen. Germany	15.0	8.7	6.1
'German'	**28.3%**	**16.3%**	**11.2%**
Other Foreign Born	10.0	9.9	6.9
1st Gen. Other Foreign Born	9.3	11.1	10.0

Kleindeutschland

Nativity	New York/ Manhattan	Ward 11	Ward 17	Tompkins Square EDs
Native	18.2%	6.9%	8.0%	2.5%
Born Ireland	16.5	6.8	8.8	1.3
1st Gen. Ireland	17.7	9.3	9.1	1.5
'Irish'	**34.2%**	**16.1%**	**17.9%**	**2.8%**
Born Germany	13.3	24.1	28.5	36.4
1st Gen. Germany	15.0	31.0	29.6	41.2
'German'	**28.3%**	**55.1%**	**58.1%**	**77.6%**
Other Foreign Born	10.0	12.6	8.7	10.0
1st Gen. Other Foreign Born	9.3	9.3	7.3	7.1

individuals, and fewer were Irish. In the Irish waterfront neighborhoods the reverse pattern prevailed.

Wards are comparatively large-scale spatial units and mask ethnic segregation – separation – at the block and street level. The streets just north of Tompkins Square comprise a transition area between Kleindeutschland and the Gas House District to the north of 14th Street, an Irish enclave. The block on the north side of Tompkins Square between Avenue A and B was 66.7 percent German and the next two blocks north were 67.9 and 66.2 percent German. One block farther to the north, the ethnic composition changes. Along 14th Street, the percentage of Germans declines dramatically, delineating a spatial boundary between Little Germany and the Gas House District that cannot be identified with the ward-level aggregate data.

Figure 13.10 Ward 17 northern part – % German.

Note: German = German born + first-generation German.

Walking south from 14th Street and passing Tompkins Square one arrives in Kleindeutschland; the streets are crowded with German immigrants and their children, few natives or Irish live on East 7th, 6th, or 5th Streets. The block immediately to the south of the square was 90 percent German; home to 2,231 residents: 38 born in the United States, 12 born in Ireland, and 11 with parents born in Ireland. At 190 East 7th Street facing the square lived ten families, including Andrew and Grace Kelly, both born in Ireland, and their four children all born in New York. In another apartment Thomas and Elizabeth Hart, also Irish immigrants, lived with their six children born in New York. Thomas' nephew James, who also emigrated from Ireland, lived with them, illustrating chain migration at the family level. Down the block at 172 East 7th Street lived five other Irish immigrants. The Kellys and Harts shared their building with eight other households, in seven of which both parents were born in Germany; one native couple George and Ann Dennis lived at 190. Among the other 48 residential buildings on the block only two also had Irish residents. The remaining buildings were completely German with only a small number of immigrants from other countries.

In 1880 the Germans and Irish, both immigrants and first-generation, comprised 62.5 percent of the city's population (Irish 34.2 percent, German 28.3 percent: Table 13.6). German immigrants living in the Tompkins Square EDs were intensely spatially isolated from the Irish, as were the Germans in the larger Kleindeutschland, but the geographical scale is important. Logan et al. in a recent analysis of racial segregation in northern American cities in the period 1880–1940 first use ward as the unit of analysis to measure black segregation and find 'black isolation was quite low through 1910' at the ward level.[17] When they use the ED as the unit of analysis, however, the analysis finds that segregation was high as early as 1880. Logan et al. use the Index of Dissimilarity (D) to measure black residential separation. Duncan and Duncan developed the index in 1955 that has been widely used.[18] A D of 60 or above indicates a very high level of separation between ethnic or racial groups; an index of 60 means that 60 percent of an ethnic/racial group would have to move from the ward/enumeration district/street/building to mirror the ethnic/racial composition of the total population. For Manhattan in 1880 each spatial unit would require a population of 34 percent Irish and 28 percent German to have a D of 0.

For the four wards that form Kleindeutschland, 10, 11, 13, and 17, the dissimilarity index for the Germans is 42, a moderately high level of ethnic separation. When the nine EDs adjacent to Tompkins Square are analyzed the index increases dramatically to 72, a very high level of ethnic separation. Once again spatial scale is crucial to understanding the intense ethnic separation/segregation in the heart of Little Germany. Logan characterizes this as a common pattern for European immigrants: 'It would be considered "normal" for immigrants in this period [beginning in 1880] to live in segregated ethnic neighborhoods.'[19] Ethnic spatial segregation does not have the connotation that African-American segregation does. Historically, second- and third-generation European immigrants, who assimilated and achieved upward mobility, could leave Kleindeutschland or the Irish waterfront neighborhoods and move to middle-class neighborhoods and eventually to the suburbs. African-Americans, regardless of their class status, could not move and remained 'entrapped' in segregated neighborhoods. The German exodus from the Lower East Side was underway by the early 1900s; many moved to another German neighborhood on the more affluent Upper East Side, Yorkville, centered around East 72nd Street.

Spatial scale – street and residential building

Individual-level, geocoded census data for the EDs in the Tompkins Square neighborhood enable the construction of street segments: both sides of a street between two avenues where people spent much of their lives, often not venturing too far away. The street remained the family's American place of origin for generations. These street segments reduce the spatial scale and recreate the small, intimate space

Table 13.7 HGIS research – neighborhood, street, building levels.

Author(s)	City	Year Publ.
Anbinder[a]	New York, NY	2002
Debats[b]	Alexandria, VA	2008, 2011
Gilliland & Olson[c]	Montreal, CAN	2011
Hillier[d]	Philadelphia, PA	2002
Dunae et al.[e]	Victoria, CAN	2013
Lafreniere & Gilliland[f]	London, CAN	2015
Schlichting & Tuckel[g]	Hartford, CT	2015, 2007

Notes

[a] T. Anbinder, *The Five Points: The 19th Century New York City Neighborhood that Invented Tap Dance, Stole Elections, and Became the World's Most Notorious Slum*, New York: Simon & Schuster, 2001.

[b] D. Debats, 'Political Consequences of Spatial Organization: Contrasting Patterns in Two Nineteenth-Century Small Cities', *Social Science History* 35(4), Winter 2011, 505–41; D. Debats, 'A Tale of Two Cities: Using Tax Records to Develop GIS Files for Mapping and Understanding Nineteenth-Century U.S. Cities', *Historical Methods: A Journal of Quantitative and Interdisciplinary History* 41(1), 2008.

[c] J. A. Gilliland, S. Olson and D. Gauvreau, 'Residential Segregation in an Industrializing City; A Closer Look', *Urban Geography* 31(1), 2010, 29–58.

[d] A. E. Hillier, 'Redlining in Philadelphia', in A. K. Knowles (ed.), *Past Time, Past Place: GIS for History*, Redlands, CA: ESRI Press, 2002, 79–93.

[e] P. Dunae, D. Lafreniere, J. Gilliland, and J. Lutz, 'Dwelling Places and Social Spaces: Revealing the Environments of Urban Workers in Victoria Using Historical GIS', *Labour-Le Travail* 72, 2013, 37–73.

[f] D. Lafreniere and J. Gilliland, '"All the World's a Stage": A GIS Framework for Recreating Personal Time-Space from Qualitative and Quantitative Sources', *Transactions in GIS* 19(2), 2015, 225–46.

[g] K. Schlicting, P. Tuckel, and R. Maisel, 'Great Migration of African-Americans to Hartford, Connecticut: 1910–1930: A GIS Analysis at the Neighborhood and Street Level', *Social Science History* 39(2), Summer 2015, 287–310; P. Tuckel, K. Schlichting, and R. Maisel, 'Social, Economic, and Residential Diversity within Hartford's African American Community at the Beginning of the Great Migration', *Journal of Black Studies* 37(5), 2007, 710–36.

shared in the collective memory. Seven street segments were created and the geo-coded census records assigned to each (Figure 13.8). The geocoded records at street level were aggregated to individual residential buildings, further reducing the spatial scale. A number of HGIS research projects have used street and residential building as the primary spatial scale (Table 13.7).

On E 6th Street between Avenue A and B were 49 tenement buildings, home to 2,028 people. As with the surrounding area, the street was ethnically segregated: 81.7 percent of the population was born in Germany or their parents were born in Germany. Only 2 percent of population, 41 individuals, were born in the United States to parents also born in America; even fewer Irish lived on the street (1.4 percent). Among residents 21 years and older, 67.1 percent were born in Germany; the first-generation Germans were almost all young children. Their parents arrived and then began to have their families once settled in Kleindeutschland. German would have been the language heard on the street.

Ten of the eighteen Irish residents on the street lived at one address, 538 E 6th Street. Thomas and Anne McCann were both born in Ireland. Thomas worked as a stone cutter, as did his son Peter. There were three other children in the family.

The widow Kate McCosker, born in Ireland, lived with her daughter Kate, born in New York, who worked as a furrier. Thomas and Mary Gough, both born in Ireland, had three children. Alexander Gibbs, a waiter, and his wife were born in Scotland. All of the parents of the other three families at 538 were born in Germany. What brought these Irish to 538 E 6th street remains lost in time, but they lived on a street where almost everyone else was German. On each of the six other streets, the few Irish residents lived clustered together in two or three tenements. They certainly knew one another, if they lived in the same building, and on the micro-scale chain migration may have brought them together to a tenement in Kleindeutschland.

Tyler Anbinder's ground-breaking study of the Irish Five Points neighborhood used 1855 New York State census data, aggregated to the building level, to analyze ethnic and racial segregation at the street and building level on Mulberry Street. Most of the tenements were filled with the Irish; the African-Americans lived in just two buildings and the other foreign born also clustered in a few locations.[20] Twenty-five years later the same pattern at the street level emerges in Little Germany around Tompkins Square.

Brief biographical profiles of residents on E 6th Street adds a personal dimension to the analysis of 1880 Census data and contributes to the recreation of the historic streetscape. A research question remains: Is it possible to imagine how people lived in a crowded tenement on 6th Street? Jacob Riis used the new science of photography to stun the conscience of New York when in 1890 he published *How the Other Half Lives,* with stark photographs of the poverty and squalor of life in the tenements.[21] Prodded by Riis and other reformers, the City of New York introduced legislation to force tenement owners to improve the appalling conditions in their buildings. In 1901 the State and City created a Tenement Department with direct responsibility to clean up the immigrant housing. As a first step, the Department undertook a survey of all tenements. The information gathered included floor plan diagrams on information cards, 'I' cards, which can be accessed through the NYC Department of Housing Preservation and Development.[22]

At 503 E 6th Street lived 35 people, 34 of whom were either born in Germany or first generation born in New York. The one other individual, August Bolt, was born in Bohemia and was a lodger, sharing an apartment with one of the German families. East 6th Street was not among the worst tenement districts in New York. The tenements Riis photographed were on the Lower East Side below Houston Street and in the notorious Five Points neighborhood, today part of Chinatown. A five-story walkup, 503 E 6th Street had two apartments on each floor, commercial space on the first floor, and two apartments in the basement. The 1880 Census enumerated nine households including a family of six, husband and wife and four children, a widower with three children and two boarders, a widow with two children and a boarder, and a single male living alone. Boarders, common in immigrant neighborhoods, provided additional income to cover expenses.

On East 6th the tenement at 503 still stands, 137 years after the 1880 Census, today a little down on its heels. East 6th Street is now part of the hip East Village neighborhood, home to thousands of young people and Hispanic residents. Over

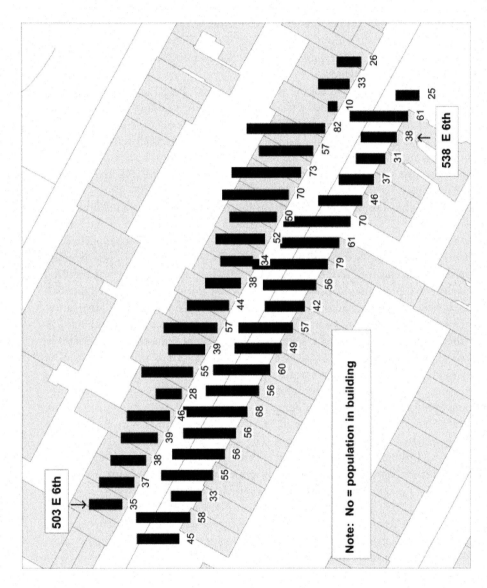

Figure 13.11 East 6th St – 1880 Census aggregated to building level.

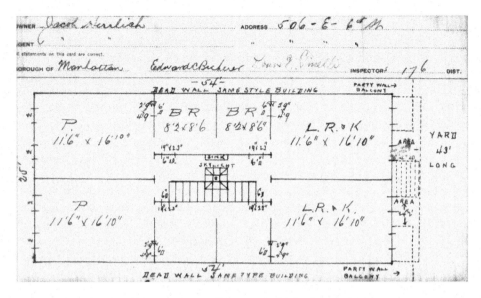

Figure 13.12   503 E 6th St. – Tenement Department 'I' Card – c.1901.

more than a century and a half, the buildings along 6th Street have been home to tens of thousands of immigrants coming to the promised land of New York.

The 'I' card data indicates that the tenement, constructed before 1879, was an 'Old Law' building without an air shaft; only the front and rear rooms had exterior windows. The interior bedroom windows opened onto the hall or to the front and back rooms in each apartment. A single sink in the hall on each floor provided city water; there were no toilets, only privies in the rear yard.

Each apartment was approximately 518 sq. ft. The six members of the Schneider family made do with just two bedrooms. So too did the widower Eugene Sass, his two daughters Paulina, 21, and Anna, 18, and two sons, Hugo and Alfred. In addition, the Sass family took in two boarders: Louis Henke, 20, who worked making cigars and 27-year-old Jacob Merkle, a painter. Throughout Kleindeutschland families took in boarders no matter how overcrowded conditions became. In all likelihood, the Sasses used one front or back room as a bedroom, but there was absolutely no privacy. In the Sass apartment, each of the seven people had an average of 74 sq. ft. of living space. All of the apartments on 6th Street were similar to the thousands of other tenements in Little Germany. Overcrowding was even worse in other immigrant neighborhoods as Riis documented, with people living in cellars. Beds were often shared: one person was at work while the other slept. The Jewish immigrants who followed the Germans to the Lower East Side used their apartments during the day as a workplace, sewing garments on a piecework basis.

Subgroups in Kleindeutschland

The flood of German immigrants in the nineteenth century came from the states and principalities that eventually formed the German nation in 1871. Nadel and other historians point out that the Germans who emigrated brought with them a strong sense of place of origin. Nadel characterizes this sense of subgroup identity as a 'nationality': 'the presence of strikingly different proportions from each major German state in each of the wards suggests that each "nationality" had separate [spatial] concentrations of settlement'. He adds that aggregate data hides this separateness of the subgroups defined by the part of Germany they emigrated from: Prussia, Bavaria, or Hessen, for example. Each block with hundreds of families can have 'small colonies of several dozen families from the same locality . . . hard to pick out from their neighbors – though they can be found in profusion if the effort is made'.[23] HGIS provides the analytical tool to identify the spatial location of the subgroups within Kleindeutschland.

Instructions given to the census takers in 1880 required them to list for the German immigrants the state, principality, or city they came from. Unfortunately, not all followed instructions. Among the total of 161,795 people born in Germany, 53,953 (33.3 percent) have their place of birth listed simply as 'Germany'. Among the remainder who do have a specific place of birth listed, the highest percentage are from Prussia, 35.2 percent, followed by Bavaria, 18.3 percent, Baden, 9.9 percent, Hessen, 9.7 percent, and Berlin, 7.2 percent. Among the four Kleindeutschland wards there are significant statistical differences by locality of origin (Table 13.8).

At the ward level it is impossible to identify geographical concentrations of subgroups from specific localities in Germany, which mirrors the pattern Logan et al. found.[24] At the much smaller spatial scale of the ED, there are significant statistical differences between blocks, evidence of ethnic segregation by place of origin. In two EDs in the Tompkins Square area, Bavarians were concentrated: ED 264 and ED 265 (Table 13.9). ED 272 had high percentages born in Hessen and Prussia. Chain migration brought many Bavarian, Prussian, and Hessen immigrants to specific blocks where they lived in close proximity to others from the same region: the Bavarians in ED 264 and 265 and the Hessens in ED 265 and 272. When the analysis moves to the street and building level, Nadel's 'small colonies' appear. There is a very strong relationship between place of birth in Germany among the residents in the 43 tenements on East 6th Street between Avenue A and B (p < .05 and the .000 level C = .651).

Table 13.8 Kleindeutschland wards – % born in Germany: place of origin.

	Wards				Total
	10	11	13	17	
Prussia	45.8	28.6	44.3	32.2	35.1
Bavaria	13.2	28.7	14.4	21.0	20.8
Baden	9.8	10.5	12.3	9.5	9.9
Hessen	7.6	12.5	8.3	11.4	10.6
Berlin	6.9	7.2	7.0	8.7	7.8
Other	15.8	12.5	15.7	17.4	15.8

P < .05 at the .0000 level Contingency coefficient - C = .192
Note: In three of the EDs adjacent to Tompkins Square very high numbers were listed as born in 'Germany' and are not included in the analysis in Table 13.8: ED 262 (58.1%), ED 266 (85.3%), ED 273 (98.8%).

Table 13.9 1880 Census: Germany: place of origin – Tompkins Square EDs.

	New York	Ward 17	Tomp. Sq. EDs	264	265	270	271	272	276
Prussia	35.2%	23.7%	22.2%	26.5%	11.5%	12.8%	23.8%	**33.7%**	18.8%
Bavaria	18.3	31.6	31.9	**41.4**	**41.7**	28.4	29.4	30.2	22.0
Baden	9.9	9.6	9.6	10.9	11.1	12.6	8.1	8.1	7.7
Hessen	9.7	9.7	15.4	7.1	11.0	**21.2**	14.0	**21.3**	14.6
Berlin	8.9	8.7	9.8	9.1	10.6	10.7	12.0	0.0	8.7
Other	18.0	15.8	11.1	5.0	14.1	14.6	2.0	6.7	28.9

P < .05 at the .000 level C = .361.

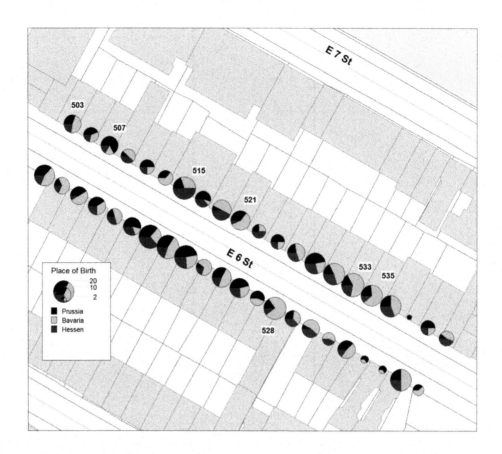

No. of records: **19,231**

No. of households: **4,627**

Figure 13.13 East 6th between Ave. A and B – place of birth in Germany.

Table 13.10 E 6th Street.

		N
Total		782
Prussia	27.2 %	167
Bavaria	31.3	222
Hessen	16.6	167
Other	24.6	193

There are a number of tenements with a very high proportion born in Bavaria: 521, 533, and 535 on the north side of the street and 528 on the south. Living at 515 E 6th Street was a concentration of people born in Hessen; 507 was home to many immigrants from Prussia. At the building level, ethnic residential separation is evident, especially for the Bavarians on E 6th Street. This result supports Nadel's argument that the Bavarians 'withdrew to the northern wards [East 6th Street is in the 17th Ward] . . . At all times, however, the most distinctive characteristic of their settlement pattern remained that they would be found wherever the Prussians were least.'[25] Prussians did live on East 6th Street but in only a few tenements. The six other streets show similar patterns of ethnic segregation by place of origin in Germany.

Observations

The fact that the grid, established in 1811, remains in many Manhattan neighborhoods facilitated the building of an HGIS. The historic insurance maps provided the street addresses used to update the GIS address range files and enabled the geocoding of census records to their exact historical location at the street level.

In cities that underwent urban renewal in the 1960s, which destroyed whole neighborhoods, the historic street patterns can be reconstructed. Using a georeferenced historic map as a base layer, streets that disappeared in the 1960s can be restored and address ranges provided for geocoding. New streets can be deleted. The reconstructed street segments can be employed to create polygons defining administrative districts from paper maps or written boundary descriptions.

Adding historic addresses to census files presents a challenge. The NAPP files are in the same order as the microfilmed manuscript records and this simplifies adding street name and number using Ancestry.com. In densely populated urban neighborhoods, the number of residential building addresses will not be overwhelming. The 19,213 people living adjacent to Tompkins Square in 1880 lived in 552 individual buildings and adding 552 addresses proved manageable. With the individual census records coded to street address, the records can be aggregated to the individual residential building level.

The HGIS for the Lower East Side of Manhattan, c.1880, addresses the 'problem of geographical scale' that masks the population dynamics at the street and building level in Kleindeutschland. The ethnic segregation by place of origin in Germany for the neighborhood around Tompkins Square is clear at the street and building level, but masked at a larger spatial scale. A parallel research project underway in the Irish neighborhoods finds similar patterns. The small numbers of Germans in those Irish wards and EDs live on a few streets and on those streets live in tenements with other Germans, as the Irish clustered in Kleindeutschland. In both the German and Irish neighborhoods, chain migration operated at the spatial level of the residential building level.

Notes

1 S. Nadel, *Little Germany: Ethnicity, Religion and Class in New York City, 1845–1880*, Urbana, IL: University of Illinois Press, 1990.
2 O. Handlin, *The Uprooted: The Epic Story of the Great Migrations that Made the American People*, Cambridge, MA: Harvard University Press, 1951, 2nd enl. ed. 1973.

3 Nadel, *Little Germany,* 14.

4 E. Burrows and M. Wallace, *Gotham, A History of New York City to 1898,* New York: Oxford University Press, 1999, 735.

5 See M. Holloway, *The Measure of Manhattan: The Tumultuous Career and Surprising Legacy of John Randall Jr. Cartographer, Surveyor, Inventor,* New York: W. W. Norton, 2013.

6 See Google Figure: www.google.com/maps/place/Madison+Square+Garden/@40.7505 045,-73.9934387,17z/data=!3m1!4b1!4m2!3m1!1s0x89c25a21fb011c85:0x33d-f10e49762f8e4

7 See J.A. Gilliland and S. Olson, 'Residential Segregation in an Industrializing City; A Closer Look', *Urban Geography* 31(1), 2010, 29–58.

8 Nadel, *Little Germany,* 3.

9 S. Ruggles and M. Sohek, *Integrated Public Use Microdata Series (Version 1.0).* Minneapolis, MN: University of Minnesota, Social History Research Laboratory, 1995.

10 See www.nappdata.org/napp/intro.shtml. The North Atlantic Population Project (NAPP) is a machine-readable database of the complete censuses of Canada (1881), Great Britain (1881), Norway (1801, 1865, 1900, 1910), Sweden (1890, 1900), the United States (1880) and Iceland (1801, 1901).

11 Special thanks to Prof. John Logan, Brown University, and Director of the S4 Spatial Structures in the Social Sciences center. Brown graduate students read the manuscript census records on Ancestry and added street addresses to the database.

12 See K. Schlichting, P. Tuckel, R. Maisel, 'Residential Segregation and the Beginning of the Great Migration of African Americans to Hartford, Connecticut: A GIS-Based Analysis', *Historical Methods* 39(3), Summer 2006, 132–43.

13 Nadel, *Little Germany,* 23.

14 D. Moynihan and N. Glazer, *Beyond the Melting Pot: The Negroes, Puerto Ricans, Jews, Italians and Irish of New York City,* Cambridge, MA: MIT Press, 1963.

15 See J. Hingham, *Strangers in the Land: Patterns of American Nativism 1860–1925,* New York: Antheneum, 1955.

16 The 'Irish' are defined as persons born in Ireland and persons born in the United States with both or one parent born in Ireland. The later are the first-generation Irish. The 'Germans' are defined as persons born in Germany and persons born in the United States with both or one parent born in Germany. The later are first-generation German.

17 J. Logan, W. Zhang, R. Turner and A. Shertzer, 'Creating the Black Ghetto: Black Residential Patterns Before and During the Great Migration', *Annals of the American Academy of Political and Social Science* 660, 2015, 20.

18 O.B. Duncan and B. Duncan, 'A Methodological Analysis of Segregation Indexes', *American Sociological Review* 20, 1955, 210–17; see for the use of D with data at a large spatial scale in Toronto in 1961: A. Gordon Darroch and G. Marston, 'The Social Class Basis of Ethnic Residential Segregation: The Canadian Case', *American Journal of Sociology* 77, 1971, 491–510.

19 Logan et al., 'Creating the Black Ghetto', 21.

20 Anbinder, *The Five Point.*

21 J. Riis, *How the Other Half Lives; Studies among the Tenements,* New York: Charles Scribner's Sons, 1890.

22 www1.nyc.gov/site/hpd/index.page.

23 Nadel, *Little Germany,* 37.

24 Logan et al., 'Creating the Black Ghetto', 19.

25 Nadel, *Little Germany,* 37.

14

FOLLOWING WORKERS OF THE INDUSTRIAL CITY ACROSS A DECADE

Residential, occupational, and workplace mobilities, 1881–1891

Don Lafreniere and Jason Gilliland

Introduction

When taking a new job, either across town or across the country, individuals and families face the difficult task of balancing their residential needs while minimizing their commute to work. We know that the decision where to live is based largely on where one is in the life course (Mulder and Hooimeijer, 1999). Moves are triggered primarily by changes in family composition (Clark and Huang, 2003; Mok, 2007; Mulder, 2007), job changes (Brown, 1975; Dieleman, 2001), economic hardship (Clark and Onaka, 1983; Crowley, 2003), the desire to reduce the daily journey to work (Prillwitz et al., 2007; Zax and Kain, 1991), or, often, a combination of these factors (Feijten et al., 2008; Gilliland and Olson, 1998; Kronenberg and Carree, 2012; Olson and Thornton, 2011; Sadler and Lafreniere, 2017). The decision or need to move affords individuals an opportunity to choose an environment that best meets their needs or desires. It may be living in a dense, walkable urban community, on an expanse of land in a rural setting, near specific amenities, or within easy access to the school of choice for their children. With voluntary moves, individuals attempt to improve their overall quality of life through increases in earned income, job satisfaction, social/familial ties, or improvements in their dwelling or neighbourhood quality. These decisions are weighed against the cost of housing and the distance or travel time to work.

Despite these understandings, little work has been done to examine this intertwined relationship between an individual's residential, workplace, and occupational situation changing over time. A wealth of research exists on the changes in home ownership, and a notable literature has reviewed changes in the residence itself, but few have concerned themselves with evaluating how residential mobility was associated with changes to the daily journey to work, despite the commute being recognized as an important factor in residential choice. This chapter presents a historical GIS approach to uncovering changes in individuals' and families' residences, occupations, and workplaces over the decade 1881–91. By harnessing the built and social environment stages created during the construction of the Imag(in)ing London HGIS (Lafreniere and Gilliland, 2014), we follow the same individuals, over time, and evaluate the changes in their residences, workplaces, and occupational or social mobility and critique the impact these mobilities have on the daily journey to work. This unique geospatial view of the interplay between residential, workplace, and social mobility provides a new perspective on daily life in Canada's early industrializing cities.

The chapter begins with the methods used to establish the longitudinal links needed to create the longitudinal study of the journey to work. It continues by evaluating the extent of residential, occupational, and workplace mobilities of the workers of London from 1881 to 1891 and concludes with a discussion of its impacts on the journey to work.

Establishing longitudinal links

To facilitate an analysis of the changing journey to work and residential and social mobility, we first need to establish longitudinal links across datasets to identify the same individuals over time. For several decades geographers, historians, and demographers have been labouring on projects that aim to link large samples of individuals from individual cities, regions, or countries across decennial censuses and other nominal datasets such as annual city directories and tax registers. First the domain of the quantitative scholars of the 'new urban history' of the early 1970s, today historical demographers push the level of sophistication and rigour in matching individuals across time. Some early examples include the parallel social history projects in Hamilton led by Katz (1975) and in Philadelphia led by Hershberg (1981). These early models used a combination of manual and automated record linkage procedures to link censuses over time and other enumerated sources, such as city directories, to the census. Steve Ruggles, the director of the Minnesota Population Center (MPC), one of the world's leading developers of linked demographic datasets, notes that these early studies generally lost between 60 and 80 per cent of the population each decade due to linkage failures (Ruggles, 2002). With the availability of national-scale datasets in the last few decades and the capabilities of computer-aided linkages, significant progress has been made to improve techniques, though there are still many issues to overcome.

Important issues must be considered when attempting to record link the census. When working with national datasets, Ruggles (2002) outlines the need to control for migration, emigration, and immigration to achieve the best results and Hautaniemi et al. (2000) argue that you must first determine deaths before controlling for various types of migrations. Steckel (1991) and later Dillon (2002) identify that infants, children, young adults, low-income individuals, manual labourers, black Americans, and single men are difficult to link. There are also issues of errors in enumeration (Curtis, 2001; Dunae, 1998; Hamilton and Inwood, 2011), name changes (Dillon, 2002), and transcription errors and bias (Antonie et al., 2010). Early attempts at record linkage were done exclusively by hand, but as computing became mainstream, so did procedures to automate record linkages. All semi-automated or fully automated linking procedures attempt to use as many variables as possible to establish a true link between datasets; combinations of name, age, birthplace, gender, and occupation are common. However, with each variable included in the automation attempt, the processing time is increased. Antonie et al. (2010) observed in their attempts to link the 3.5 million records of the 1871 Census to the over 4 million records in 1881 that it would take nearly two years to complete an automated analysis of all of the possible matches.

A number of models and procedures have been developed to overcome these issues while maintaining as high a match rate as possible. The first, addressing the issues identified by Antonie et al., is known as *blocking*. Blocking reduces the number of possible pairs by assigning an absolute clause to the match algorithm. For example, Antonie et al. used the first letter of the last name as well as birthplace. So thus, only someone with the same birthplace *and* first initial would be included in the subsequent analysis that looks for potential matches. There is no accepted standard for blocking, as the determination of good blocking is the careful balance between a high match rate and the accuracy of the matches, and this varies with the data sources being matched. For example, Ruggles (2002) used state of birth, race, and gender, while his colleagues from the Minnesota Population Center used only race and gender in their study (Goeken et al., 2011). In this study we are record linking a sample of workers, derived from a combination of the 1881 Census of Canada and local city directories, to their corresponding records in the 1891 Census and directory. Since we are interested in the changing journey to work and residential environments of workers, we blocked first on geography, limiting our matched sample only to those who persisted in London over the decade.

The most researched procedure in historical census linking is related to *name matching*. It is recognized that names are not unique; however, they are the most unique of any individual characteristic in the census. Some researchers, such as Dillon (2002), have struggled with the linguistic differences found in Canada's early censuses by separating French and English surnames into two groups prior to attempting to link across censuses. To facilitate name matching researchers have adopted the use of a range of phonetic algorithms such as Soundex, NYSIIS, and Double Metaphone. Each one uses a different set of rules to convert names into an alpha–numeric code based on the phonetic composition of the name (see Elmagarmid et al. (2007) for a review). This indexing of names allows for quicker processing and potentially greater matches across datasets. Most early attempts at automated record linkage used one of these phonetic algorithms to help with issues related to misspellings and poor transcription, which are an unfortunate reality of working with historical censuses. Later projects, including those of the MPC and Antonie et al. (2010) at the University of Guelph, have begun using Jaro-Winkler distance algorithms to improve name and birthplace matching. Rather than convert a string into a pre-set alpha–numeric code as phonetic algorithms do, Jaro-Winkler measures the similarity between two strings (number of like characters) as well as measuring the distance between characters in each potential link set. Additionally, rather than having a binary result of 'yes' or 'no' to a potential name match, Jaro-Winkler creates a probability score ranging from 1, a direct match, to 0, or highly unlikely.

Similar to the probability metrics used in Jaro-Winkler, the most sophisticated researchers have started using probabilistic record linkage rather than the deterministic methods used in the field's infancy. Unlike deterministic methods, where a set of rules are created to allow for a positive match, probabilistic methods use weights as well as support vector machines (algorithms that analyse data and recognize patterns) to teach the software what positive matches typically look like between the two datasets (Goeken et al., 2011). This allows for the creation of 'fuzzy' matches that can then be interpreted by the knowledgeable scholar for validity. To our knowledge, no literature exists to support which algorithm (deterministic or probabilistic) is best suited to particular historical sources. For our case study, we employ a probabilistic record linkage approach and complete several passes across the dataset, adjusting weights each time after manually reviewing possible linked pairs.

Preparing data for record linkage

To overcome some of the issues outlined above while maintaining as high a match rate as possible, it is necessary to first prepare data for use in a probabilistic record linkage software. Although it has not always been outlined in explicit detail in other studies, this procedure is critical when working with historical data, as it helps overcome both transcription error and short-hand notations that were widely used in non-digital census enumerations (Winchester, 2002, is a notable exception). As our interest in this study is the relationship between the journey to work and environmental change, we need to first isolate only those individuals for whom we have positive links between home and work in both 1881 and 1891. The procedure of creating these links is outlined in Lafreniere and Gilliland (2014). For 1881, this resulted in a sample of 5,081 workers; when the same procedures were run for 1891, the result was a sample of 7,956 individual workers. These two samples, when record linked, will represent our *worker sample* used in this study.

As is necessary with most large projects, transcription and digitalization of data was performed by different groups of researchers. The worker sample was extracted from the 1881 100 per cent count of the census provided by the 1881 Canadian Census Project, led by Lisa Dillon (University of Montreal) with researchers from the Church of Jesus Christ of Latter-day Saints and the Institute of Canadian Studies at the University of Ottawa (Dillon, 2000). The 1891 worker sample was extracted from a 100 per cent sample compiled by the Historical Data Research Unit at the University of Guelph with assistance from the Minnesota Population Center. City directories for London were transcribed and coded primarily by student researchers in the Human Environments Analysis Lab in the Department of Geography at Western University, numbering several dozen over the course of nearly ten years. With such diversity comes the need to clean and standardize data for record linkage. Simple transformations, such as spelling, punctuation, and the treatment of initials, need to be considered but are relatively easy to standardize. Nicknames or short forms for first names are more problematic, as is age. A lookup table was created due to the heavy use of short forms or nicknames used in the city directories for individuals' first names; examples include 'Wm' for William, 'Jn' for John, and 'Thos' for Thomas.

It is generally agreed that ages recorded in early censuses are unreliable, with rounding to the nearest 0 or 5 common (Knights, 1971; Mason and Cope, 1987; Steckel, 1991), yet there is no agreed-upon standard approach to dealing with the age variable. Hershberg et al. (1976) were the most generous in assigning weights, giving credit to links where individuals' reported age increased anywhere between two and eighteen years between decennial censuses. Katz (1975) was similarly generous, with a variance of ± 9 years still receiving consideration. Goeken et al. (2011) and Ruggles (2002) both accepted ± 7 years, while Antonie et al. (2010) and Olson and Thornton (2011) only accepted a tolerance of ± 2 years from the expected age. After several trial passes and observing how known matches were treated, we limited matches to ± 3 years, with significantly higher weights given to those within ± 1 year (Table 14.1).

To record link workers from 1881 to 1891, we employed a semi-automated approach to record linkage. A semi-automated approach allows the researcher, who has an intimate knowledge of the database, the population it represents, and its nuances, to review the matches and make necessary adjustments, all the while still benefiting from the techniques and algorithms provided by an automated approach. We began by harnessing the capabilities of a customized version of LinkageWiz, software that allows for probabilistic record linkage of large datasets (LinkageWiz, 2013). Figure 14.1 outlines the workflow used to record link these two datasets. As our concern was not to record link the entire population, but only our sample of workers, we started with the linked city directory-census database outlined in Lafreniere and Gilliland (2014). This sample had already been blocked to only include those who lived in London or the surrounding suburbs. We further blocked using a Jaro-Winkler variable weight on the individuals' last names. Weights were then assigned for each variable as outlined in Table 14.1. A minimum matched pairs retention threshold (MPRT) score of 10 (*s*-10) was needed for matches to be considered on a first pass. This first pass group only includes individuals with

Table 14.1 Match weights used to record link 1881 worker sample to 1891 worker sample record linkage results.

Variable	Match Weights
Last Name	Jaro–Winkler Variable Exact Match: 7.5 Phonetic Match: 6
First Name	Exact Match: 5 Phonetic Match: 3 Nickname Match: 3
Gender	Exact Match: 1 Disagree: -1
Age	± 1: 8 ± 3: 5
Occupation	Exact Match: 2
Birthplace	Exact Match: 5

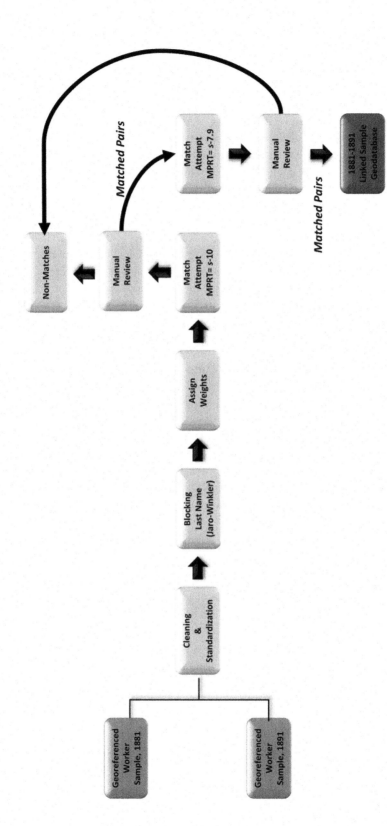

Figure 14.1 Record linkage procedure.

Jaro–Winkler scored similar last names and one additional variable other than gender (or two if occupation was matched). Accurate record linkage requires a reflexive approach, where researchers intimately familiar with not only the dataset, but the local geography, history, and economy, review each linkage run before discarding possible matches. After review, the dataset was run again with a minimum first name score of s-3 required, as this eliminated false matches that met the threshold of s-10 because of similarities in combinations such as last name and birthplace (s-12.5), last name and age (s-10.5-15.5), or last name, occupation, and gender (s-10.5). The second run MPRT was set at 7.9, with the last name weight not included and age reduced to 5 for a ± 1 year match and 2 for matches ± 3 years. This demanded that a minimum of two additional variables matched before the pair was considered for linking. The matched pairs were manually reviewed and the results joined in ArcGIS to each of their respective original 1881 or 1891 feature classes.

The result is a geographically referenced linked dataset of 1,209 workers from 1881 to 1891, each with absolute links between home and workplace. Caution must be taken when comparing match rates between studies, as each utilizes different source material and sampling strategies—or a 'different universe' (Dillon, 2002; Ruggles, 2002). There is a need to examine differing record linkage methods with like data samples – an aim outside of the scope of this research, but an area we hope to contribute to in the near future. For consideration, the match rate we captured is higher than that reported by Antonie et al. (2010), similar to that reported by Hershberg et al. (1976), but lower than the 39 per cent rates captured by Darroch (2002). This is largely due to differing universes; ours is restricted by geography and work status, a rather restrictive universe, whereas Darroch was working with a sample across a much larger region. Although robust, our 24 per cent link rate of the 1881 population does suffer from omissions. First, Ruggles (2002: 217) reminds us that forward-linked samples, such as our desire here, are more challenging than backwards-linked ones because of the effects of mortality and emigration. Our sample here suffers from these challenges, as well as losing individuals who left paid employment. We also miss young adults, who were under working age in 1881. For women, name changes due to marriage limit our ability to match across decades. Despite these omissions, this linked dataset will permit us to complete the first (to our knowledge) historical journey to work study that views the same population over time.

Residential, occupational, and workplace mobilities

The study of the journey to work is fundamentally about the spatial relation-ship between home and work. We are reminded that residential mobility in the nineteenth-century city was higher than it is today, with families and individuals constantly changing their residence due to changes in family composition, social status, or access to work (Gilliland, 1998; Gilliland and Olson, 1998; Pooley, 1979). Studies of job or workplace mobility are dwarfed by the ubiquitous interest among social historians in the extent of occupational mobility. Led by the pioneering work of Curti (1959) and Thernstrom (1964), occupational mobility, or the ability to move to an occupation with a higher wage, has been the primary indicator used to measure an individual's upward social mobility. Meanwhile economic historians have not exhibited much interest in workplace mobility, but instead have focused on the duration and drivers of individual job tenure, noting that industrial jobs during the late nineteenth century were brief, citing that high labour mobility was an indicator of the 'tenuousness of the employment relationship and fluidity of the labour market' (Jacoby, 1985: 36–7; Jacoby and Sharma, 1992) These separate but complementary areas of scholarship all agree that individuals were mobile, constantly changing the relationship between home and work. Despite this agreement, the study of the changing relationship over time has received little attention, other than anecdotal cases about individuals (Pooley and Turnbull, 1997; Ulrich, 1990) or studies limited to employees from one workplace (Green, 1988; Hoskins, 1989).

Residential mobility

To understand the changing relationship between home and work, we must first examine the rate and intensity of residential mobility. In London, we observe high residential mobility, similar to that reported for other Canadian cities during the same period. Of our sample, 74.4 per cent ($n = 900$) of workers were living in a different residence ten years later. The moves varied in intensity or spatial separation, from moves as close as across the street, to substantial moves of over 4 kilometres (Figure 14.2). Similar to the pattern found by Gilliland (1998) for Montreal, most moves were short, with a median Euclidean distance of 741m. The distances moved over the decade vary by the size of the household. We see a strong effect of the age of the household head on the distances of residential moves, with the distances decreasing as age increases (Figure 14.3). An increase in median distance moved is noted during the traditional years of retirement, likely indicating moves into residences of kin or to secure a residential environment more suitable to an individual with more limited personal mobility.

The effect of household size is less pronounced than the age-effect, but is still visible. The smallest and largest households moved greater distances as a response to socio-demographic changes (Figure 14.4). Small households were comprised primarily of young workers or widowed individuals who lived on their own. Over the course of a decade, both transitioned into midsized households, the younger adding children and the widows often taking residence with younger kin. These mid- to large-sized homes were located largely in the city's emerging neighbourhoods, further from the established neighbourhoods from which the families moved. Those in the largest households were generally young as well, living in boarding houses or residential hotels in the city's core. They were largely employed by the very hotels they lived in, as housekeepers, cooks, and barbers. The hotelkeepers themselves are found in this group, as well as individuals who worked at downtown factories such as Perrin's biscuit company or McClary's foundry. Ten years later, many of these individuals were living in small dwellings with families or had moved to smaller boarding houses in London East to take employment in one of the factories there. This pattern is consistent with that observed by Dunae et al. (2013) for a similar population of residential hotel dwellers in Victoria.

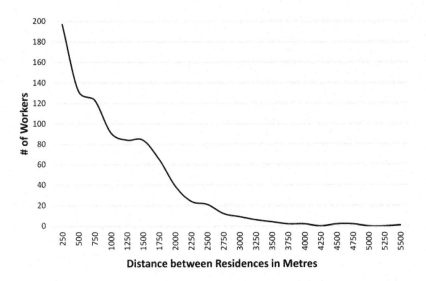

Figure 14.2   Distance of residential moves from 1881 to 1891.

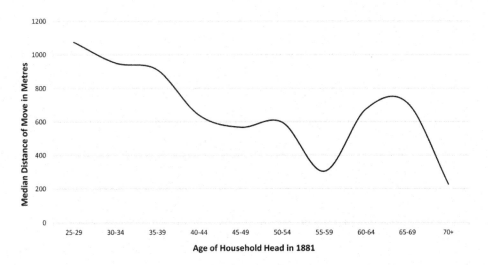

Figure 14.3   Distance of residential moves from 1881 to 1891 by age of household head.

We observe that moves vary based on occupational class. Significant differences are found between higher and lower class workers (Figure 14.5). Higher class occupations such as merchants, manufacturers, and professionals had the shortest distance moves on average (median). A sharp increase is noted for the middle classes. Labourers moved shorter distances than their middle-class counterparts, whereas servants had the longest moves, with a median distance of over 1,100m.

The directionality of the moves presents a clearer picture. Figure 14.6 outlines the linear directional mean of the moves by occupational class. The linear directional mean is calculated by first obtaining the average distance of moves, by measuring the

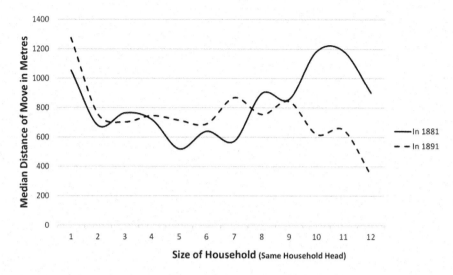

Figure 14.4 Distance of residential moves from 1881 to 1891 by household size.

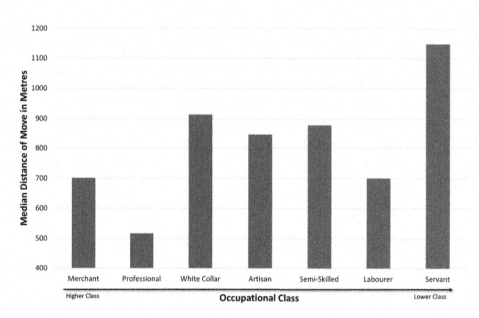

Figure 14.5 Distance of residential moves from 1881 to 1891 by 1881 occupational class.

Euclidean distance between origin and destination for each individual. The directional mean of the lines is then calculated by statistical comparison of X and Y coordinates of the origin and destination points and the trend presented on a street map. The length of the line represents the mean distance between origin and destination. From inspection of the map, we discover that many of the upper-class workers (merchants and manufacturers, professionals, and white collar) moved into the wealthy near

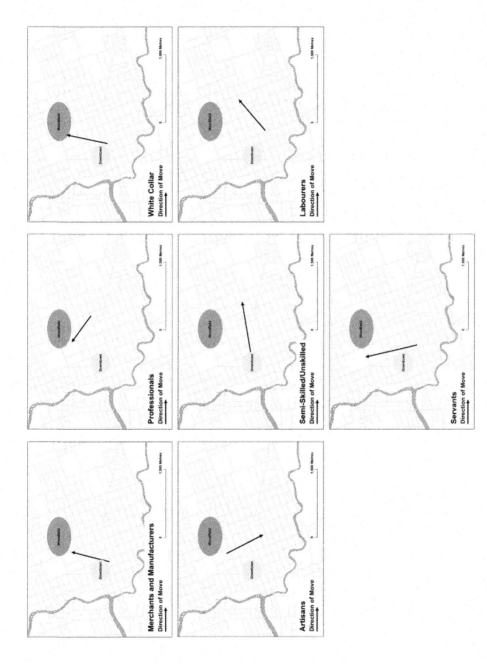

Figure 14.6 Linear mean direction and distance of moves by 1881 occupational class, occupational mobility, and job tenure.

north neighbourhood of Woodfield. Woodfield sits north-east of downtown and abuts Victoria Park, at the time the city's largest public space. Today, Woodfield is designated as two heritage conservation districts (West and East Woodfield) to help preserve the eclectic mix of Victorian architectures that adorn the neighbourhood. Many of the homes in what has been dubbed the 'Greatest Neighbourhood in Canada' were built by the individuals we are examining in this study (Canadian Institute of Planners, 2012). We also see that servants, the lowest occupational class from Figure 14.6, followed their employers. They took residence in small, scattered cottages at the edge of the city's northern development, north of the present-day CP Rail line on streets such as Pall Mall, Maitland, and Miles. The middle classes of artisans, semi-skilled, and labourers moved further eastward into the rapidly growing suburb of London East (which was amalgamated into the city in 1885). Carpenters, blacksmiths, painters, and rail-workers moved into the village to work at the oil refineries, rail yards, and car shops that were built in the southern portion of the community. They occupied modest, well-appointed homes, mostly Ontario cottages or homes built in the Queen Anne style, on streets north of Dundas, such as Dufferin, Lorne, and Princess. Known today as Old East Village, this thriving neighbourhood of past and present wage-workers has also been designated a heritage conservation district.

In studies of nineteenth-century populations, occupational mobility has been widely used as a proxy for understanding social mobility. This is largely due to the gulf of primary sources available that provide actual wages for large numbers of individuals. This study is limited by the same lack of material and so we employ a method similar to most other studies. We apply the modified Darroch and Ornstein (1980) occupational class scheme (see Table 14.2) to our sample workers' 1881 and 1891 occupations. The result is a snapshot of social mobility across the decade.

Tables 14.3 and 14.4 illustrate the results of our brief look at occupational mobility for those in our population sample who did and did not change residence between 1881 and 1891. For those who changed residence, we observe that nearly three-quarters (74.6 per cent) of the workers were not occupationally mobile, staying within the same occupational class. The remaining 25 per cent of the workers were not exclusively upwardly mobile: 11.3 per cent of the workers were downwardly

Table 14.2 Modified Darroch and Ornstein (1980) occupational class scheme.

Occupational Class	Description
1	Merchant/Agent/Manufacturer
2	Professional
3	White Collar
4	Artisan
5	Semi-Skilled and Unskilled
6	Labourer
7	Servant
8	Farmer
9	No Occupation or Ambiguous

*Note that this class includes students and gentlemen.

Table 14.3 Percentage of occupational mobility, 1881–91, by direction and occupational class.

Occupational Class	Upward Mobility	Not Mobile	Downward Mobility
Merchants and Manufacturers (1)	N/A	75.2%	24.8%
Professionals (2)	4.8%	80.2%	14.8%
White Collar (3)	22.4%	59.0%	18.7%
Artisan (4)	13.3%	81.4%	5.3%
Semi-Skilled/Unskilled (5)	30%	64.2%	5.7%
Labourer (7)	35%	50.0%	14.6%
Servant (8)	14%	86.5%	N/A

mobile, moving down the occupational ranks over the course of the period. A slightly higher number were upwardly mobile (14.1 per cent), moving into higher classes of occupations. Surprisingly, those individuals who were not residentially mobile (did not change homes over the decade) saw the same aggregate rate of occupational mobility as those who were residentially mobile. There was a slight trend (3 per cent) towards being more upwardly mobile for those who stayed at the same residence, but this variance is minor.

When we observe mobility across the occupational classes we note that, as a group, labourers were the most mobile, with 35 per cent showing upward mobility and nearly 15 per cent downward mobility into the servant class (Table 14.3). The servant class was the least mobile, a pattern that is similar to that noted in the social mobility literature. The two upper classes were generally not mobile either, maintaining their position at the top of the social hierarchy. It is interesting to note, however, that the amount of mobility between the merchant class and the artisan class is rather high, with 13.3 per cent of artisans moving upwards into the top class and nearly a quarter of merchants and manufacturers moving downwards. Upon further examination, we see that most of the individuals who moved down the occupational class scheme were owners of small- to mid-sized businesses who later went to work for one of the larger industrial operations in the city. For example, John Fleming, owner of an axe factory in 1881, was found ten years later widowed and working as an engine man for the large Forest City Machine Works. Another, John Murphy, a grocer in 1881, became a box maker at Fleischmann's paper company. We see the reverse experience in the group of workers who were upwardly mobile into the merchant class. Workers left industrial employment to start small shops within the same industry in which they were previously working, often in partnership with other artisans. We must remind readers that observing occupational mobility through the use of coded occupational titles (such as the North American Population Project HISCO codes used in this study) does present challenges, as the ability to calculate changes relies on the proper coding of occupation titles into the appropriate groups. The meaning and nature of work associated with any given occupational title changes over time, and some of the mobility we uncover may be an effect of these changes.

Table 14.4 Occupational mobility by occupational class, 1881–91, by residential mobility, percentage of individuals.

Residential Mobility is Present

	Occupational Class	1	2	3	1881 4	5	6	7
	1	11.1%	0.4%	2.4%	3.9%	0.3%	0.1%	0.0%
	2	0.8%	7.2%	0.9%	1.3%	0.1%	0.3%	0.2%
	3	0.8%	0.2%	8.8%	0.9%	0.4%	0.4%	0.2%
1891	4	2.1%	0.7%	1.7%	37.4%	0.9%	0.8%	0.1%
	5	0.0%	0.1%	0.4%	0.6%	3.8%	0.2%	0.0%
	6	0.0%	0.2%	0.2%	1.4%	0.1%	2.7%	0.0%
	7	0.0%	0.1%	0.4%	0.4%	0.2%	0.8%	3.6%
		Downward Mobility			No Mobility		Upwards Mobility	

Residential Mobility is Not Present

	Occupational Class	1	2	3	1881 4	5	6	7
	1	15.8%	0.0%	3.6%	3.9%	0.3%	0.0%	0.0%
	2	1.0%	6.6%	1.0%	0.0%	0.0%	0.3%	0.0%
	3	0.0%	0.0%	11.5%	2.3%	0.7%	0.3%	0.0%
1891	4	2.3%	0.0%	1.3%	32.6%	1.3%	2.3%	0.3%
	5	0.0%	0.0%	0.0%	2.0%	2.3%	0.3%	0.3%
	6	0.7%	0.0%	0.3%	0.7%	0.3%	3.6%	0.3%
	7	0.0%	0.0%	0.0%	0.0%	0.0%	0.0%	1.6%
		Downward Mobility			No Mobility		Upwards Mobility	

Job tenure in London was remarkably high. We estimate that 34.8 per cent of workers who were employed outside of the home were employed by the same firm ten years later. This is higher than the estimates of 26.9 per cent reported by Carter and Savoca (1990) for San Francisco. Whether someone had changed employers is not a simple determination. As the primary concern of this study is the changing relationship between home and work, we briefly examine job tenure along lines of residential and workplace mobility. We view job tenure as whether a worker is travelling to the same *worksite* in 1891 as they were ten years earlier in 1881. We employ this approach to overcome the issues of changing employers' names, which was common during this period. Many companies changed from surname-based monikers to less personalized descriptions; for example, John Elliott & Son's Foundry became Phoenix Foundry and E. Leonard and Sons became London Engine and Boiler Works. We are uncertain if these name changes were in everyday use or if city directory enumerators began to formalize the titles of the firms they recorded. To determine if an individual was working at the same worksite, we compared the latitude and longitude in both time periods, providing a modest buffer of 50m for geocoding differences in the two datasets. For a study of job tenure, this is imperfect, as it does not account for individuals who stayed with the same employer but either the employer changed location or they took up a position at a different worksite operated by their employer. For a study of the changing journey to work, however, it is essential. Reviewing our sample of job tenure, we observe an expected pattern: the sample of workers who did not move had a higher percentage of decennial job tenure than did those who did move over the period (Table 14.5). What is of interest is that the differences were not great, 32.8 per cent for those who were residentially mobile versus 40.8 per cent for those who were not. Home-based job tenure was expectedly higher for the non-residentially mobile group versus the residentially mobile group.

Changing home–work relationships

We have established how workers in London were residentially and occupationally mobile and considered the lengths of their job tenure. What we have yet to review is the extent of workplace mobility that was present over the period. Workplace mobility is the critical missing link to completing our understanding of the changing relationship between home and residence and its corresponding effect on the daily journey to work, an area that, to our knowledge, has never been studied before using the same population over time. Table 14.5 outlines the changing relationship between work and home for our sample of 1,209 workers in London. We observe that for those that were residentially mobile, nearly three out of five (60 per cent) changed their workplace. More than two out of five (43.8 per cent) worked outside

Table 14.5 Changing home–work relationships.

Same Residence		n = 309	
		n	*%*
Same Workplace			
	Home-Based	42	13.6
	Outside Home	126	40.8
	Total	168	54.4
Different Workplace			
	Outside Home	107	34.6
	Home-Based to Outside Home	20	6.5
	Outside Home to Home-Based	14	4.5
	Total	141	45.6
Different Residence		n = 900	
		n	*%*
Same Workplace			
	Home-Based	69	7.7
	Outside Home	295	32.8
	Total	364	40.4
Different Workplace			
	Outside Home	394	43.8
	Home-Based to Outside Home	90	10
	Outside Home to Home-Based	52	5.8
	Total	536	59.6

Table 14.6 Linked worker sample journey to work, 1881–91, by occupational class.

Occupational Class	Median 1881 (km)	Median 1891 (km)
Merchants/Agents/Manufacturer	.86	1.16
Professional	1.04	1.32
White Collar	1.07	1.15
Artisan	.98	1.05
Semi-Skilled and Unskilled	.89	.98
Labourer	.98	1.14
Servant	.19	.18

of the home in both periods, where another 15 per cent of workers had shifted their employment either into or out of their homes. For the remaining 40 per cent of residentially mobile workers, the vast majority (82 per cent) continued employment outside the home and a small cohort moved residences and maintained home-based employment. As we might expect, this cohort of home-based workers is smaller than the cohort of home-based workers who were not residentially mobile. We see a 14 per cent difference in workplace persistence between the residentially mobile and non-mobile groups. These patterns reinforce our notion that relationships between home and work are complex and appear in various configurations.

In the aggregate, the average commute for all workers in the city in 1891 was 1,305m (the median was 1,216m). This is 22 per cent longer than the average commute a decade before. The change can be largely attributed to the continued suburbaniza-tion of the city, especially to the north and east. The continued establishment of new factories in London East drew workers to commute longer distances in order to secure jobs, many of whom either elected not to move or did not have the means to do so. The average for our sample of 1,209 workers whom we have record linked across time is similar to, but slightly shorter than, the overall average (1,206m vs. 1,305m). When we view our sample across time, we see that journeys increase across every occupa-tional class except for servants, which stayed the same (Table 14.6).

The changing journey to work

As we outlined earlier, a near limitless combination of factors influences an individ-ual's decision to change either their residential or workplace situation. To illustrate this complexity and its effects on the journey to work, we look closer at two individuals who represent the two largest groups in our sample.

Ira Collins, a 27-year-old harness maker, represents the largest group, those individuals who were residentially mobile and changed their workplace location over the course of the decade. In 1881, Ira lived on York Street, near Rectory Street, in the Village of London East with his wife Mary Jane and his 3-year-old son Russell (Figure 14.7). He had a below-average commute of 858m to work each day at Globe Agricultural Works, where he was a saddle and harness maker. In 1891, at the age of 37, we find Ira and the rest of his family living across town on Clarence Street, near Horton Street. He is now employed as a yard man in the Grand Trunk Rail Grounds

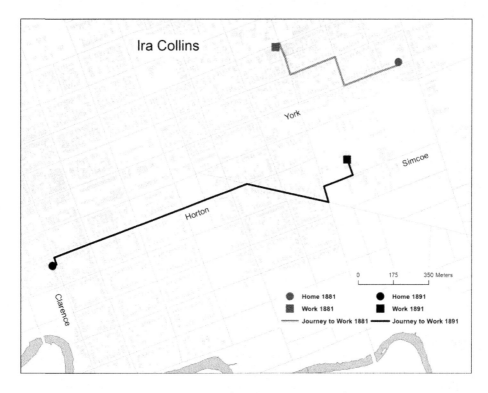

Figure 14.7 The changing journey to work and residence: Ira Collins.

in London East, making repairs on the wooden slats and doors on rail cars. His commute has increased 50 per cent to nearly 1,700m. This would have been an increase of over ten minutes if we assume that individuals walk an average of 5 kilometres per hour, though it must have been much longer at times in the winter, when having to trudge through heavy snow. What caused this significant increase in Ira's daily commute?

Amelia Miller, a 24-year-old elementary school teacher, represents the second largest group, which includes those individuals who were residentially mobile but did not change workplace location over the course of the decade. Amelia was of Irish descent, but born in Ontario in 1857. In 1881, Amelia lived on Waterloo Street, at the eastern edge of downtown, renting a room in a house owned by the widowed Mary Dempster (Figure 14.8). Mrs Dempster may have opened her home up to renters to help support herself after her husband Robert died. Also in the home with Amelia was her older sister Anna (26), and Isabella Quinn, a dressmaker. Amelia commuted just over 1,600m each day to teach grade 7 at the Talbot Street School and had an income of $350 a year (we established her income from a database built for another project on the changing journey to school: Board of Education for the City of London, 1891). In 1891, at the age of 34, we find Amelia still teaching grade 7 at the same school. However, instead of a long commute, we find Amelia living 71 per cent closer to work, residing in a boarding house on Kent Street only 463m

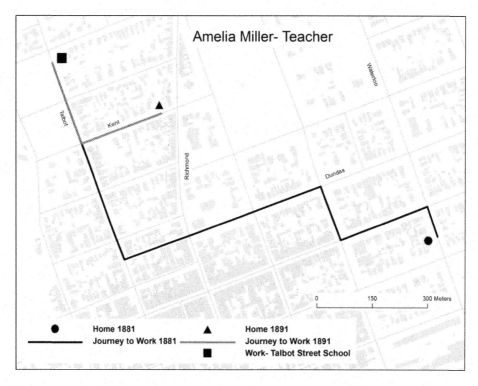

Figure 14.8 The changing journey to work and residence: Amelia Miller.

from the school. Her income is now $450 a year, but she is living with seven other individuals rather than the four she did a decade before. The boarding house is run by Grace Heron, the oldest of the four Heron siblings who live together in the home. Her brothers George (41, a travelling salesman) and James (34, cabinetmaker), as well as her sister Maggie (35, no occupation listed – she likely helped run the house) share the living space with 26-year-old Mary Austin, a housekeeper at the Grigg House, young William Geary (22, an assistant druggist), and Amelia.

Conclusion

This paper has aimed to complete a longitudinal study of a population and their changing residences, workplaces, and social mobility. First, we extended the historical record linkage literature by developing a protocol that record links geocoded samples of workers with high precision across time using public databases of decennial census records. These record linkages allowed us to follow the same workers as they changed residences and workplaces, permitting us to complete the first known study of the journey to work over an extended period of time with the same population. We established the extent of residential, occupational, and workplace mobilities for over 1,200 workers with a high degree of spatial precision.

It must be acknowledged that there are limitations to the methodologies and assumptions we present here. Baker (1991: 226) reminds us that all inferences made in historical geography 'whether drawn directly from empirical evidence or indirectly from theory, are probabilistic statements', a warning that surely applies to the work we present here. Our study is fundamentally based on two time slices that follow the decennial census, 1881 and 1891. We know that many individuals would have changed their residence and/or workplace more than once during the course of this decade. With the methodologies and environmental stages in place, we hope to revisit this study in the future to see it is possible to follow individuals every calendar year. This would provide a more fine-grained understanding of life histories and the frequency of change.

Regardless of these opportunities for further development, what we have shown in this study is that the relationship between home and work is complex. For example, Amelia may have moved to shorten her long journey to work. However, it is also possible that she wished to secure accommodation with similarly aged people, that the relationship with Mary Dempster went sour, or perhaps she sought a living situation that included both men and women. After moving, however, she shared a house with more people; was the consequence less living space and greater crowding? What about the environment outside the front door? Was the Kent Street location a more appealing residential environment than Waterloo Street? Did it better represent her social status as a white collar worker? Did it suggest that she was of an even higher class? As for Ira, did he choose to move to a different neighbourhood? Or was he forced to leave his home in London East because of fire or financial difficulties? Did he lose his job at Globe Agricultural Works, or did he seek a new job with the GTR? Was he seeking a better physical or social environment for his family? Some of these questions we cannot answer without detailed personal or business records, however what we have demonstrated here is that with the combination of record-linked big datasets, the high-resolution of an urban HGIS, and a spatial approach to history, we soon we will be able to examine Ira and Amelia's residential and neighbourhood environments over time to glean a different perspective on why individuals may have changed their residential and workplace environments in the industrial city.

References

L. Antonie, P. Baskerville, K. Inwood, and A. Ross, *An Automated Record Linkage System: Linking 1871 Canadian Census to 1881 Canadian Census*, s.l., s.n, 2010.

A. Baker, 'The Limits of Inference in Historical Geography', in D. B. Green (ed.), *Historical Geography: A Methodological Protrayal*, Savage, MD: Rowman & Littlefield Publishers, 1991, 219–30.

H. J. Brown, 'Changes in Workplace and Residential Location', *Journal of the American Institute of Planners* 41(1), 1975, 32–9.

Canadian Institute of Planners, *Great Places in Canada*, 2012. Available at: http://greatplacesin-canada.ca (Accessed July 2016).

S. Carter and E. Savoca, 'Labor Mobility and Lengthy Jobs in Nineteenth-Century America', *Journal of Economic History* 50(1), 1990, 1–16.

W. Clark and Y. Huang, 'The Life Course and Residential Mobility in British Housing Markets', *Environment and Planning A* 35(2), 2003, 323–39.

W. Clark and J. Onaka, 'Life Cycle and Housing Adjustment as Explanations of Residential Mobility', *Urban Studies* 20(1), 1983, 47–57.

S. Crowley, 'The Affordable Housing Crisis: Residential Mobility of Poor Families', *Journal of Negro Education* 72(1), 2003, 22–38.

M. Curti, *The Making of an American Community: A Case Study of Democracy in a Frontier County*, Redwood City, CA: Stanford University Press, 1959.

B. Curtis, *The Politics of Population: State Formation, Statistics, and the Census of Canada, 1840–1875*, Toronto: University of Toronto Press, 2001.

G. Darroch, 'Semi-Automated Record Linkage with Suname Samples: A Regional Study of "Case Law" Linkage, Ontario 1861–1871', *History and Computing* 14(1–2), 2002, 153–83.

G. Darroch and M. Ornstein, 'Ethnicity and Occupational Structure in Canada in 1871: The Vertical Mosaic in Historical Perspective', *Canadian Historical Review* 61(3), 1980, 305–33.

F. Dieleman, 'Modelling Residential Mobility: A Review of Recent Trends in Research', *Journal of Housing and the Built Environment* 16(3), 2001, 249–65.

L. Dillon, 'International Partners, Local Volunteers, and Lots of Data: The 1881 Canadian Census Project', *International Journal of Humanities and Arts Computing* 12(2), 2000, 163–76.

L. Dillon, 'Challenges and Opportunities for Census Record Linkage in the French and English Canadian Context', *History and Computing* 14(1–2), 2002, 185–212.

P. Dunae, 'Making the 1891 Census of British Columbia', *Histoire sociale/Social History*, 31(62), 1998, 223–39.

P. Dunae, D. Lafreniere, J. Gilliland, and J. Lutz, 'Dwelling Places, Social Spaces: Revealing the Environments of Urban Workers in Victoria using Historical GIS', *Labour/Le Travail* 72, 2013, 37–73.

A. Elmagarmid, P. Ipeirotis, and V. Verykios, 'Duplicate Record Detection: A Survey', *IEEE Transactions on Knowledge and Data Engineering* 19(1), 2007, 1–16.

P. Feijten, P. Hooimeijer, and C. Mulder, 'Residential Experience and Residential Environment Choice over the Life-Course', *Urban Studies* 45(1), 2008, 141–62.

J. Gilliland, 'Modeling Residential Mobility in Montreal, 1860–1900', *Historical Methods* 31(1), 1998, 27–42.

J. Gilliland and S. Olson, 'Claims on Housing Space in Nineteenth-Century Montreal', *Urban History Review/Revue d'histoire urbaine* 26(2), 1998, 3–16.

R. Goeken, L. Huynh, T. A. Lynch, and R. Vick, 'New Methods of Census Record Linking', *Historical Methods* 44(1), 2011, 7–14.

D. R. Green, 'Distance to Work in Victorian London: A Case Study of Henry Poole, Bespoke Tailors', *Business History* 30(2), 1988, 179–94.

M. Hamilton and K. Inwood, 'The Aboriginal Population and the 1891 Census of Canada', in P. Axelsson and P. Skold (eds), *Indigenous Peoples and Demography: The Complex Relation between Identity and Statistics*, New York: Berghahn, 2011, 95–115.

S. Hautaniemi, D. Anderton and A. Swedlund, 'Methods and Validity of a Panel Study Using Record Linkage', *Historical Methods* 33(1), 2000, 16–29.

T. Hershberg (ed.), *Philadelphia: Work, Space, Family and Group Experience in the Nineteenth Century*, New York: Oxford University Press, 1981.

T. Hershberg, A. Burnstein, and R. Dockhorn, 'Record Linkage', *Historical Methods Newsletter* 9(2–3), 1976, 137–63.

R. Hoskins, 'An Analysis of the Payrolls of the Point St.Charles Shops of the Grand Trunk Railway', *Cahiers de Géographie du Québec* 33(90), 1989, 323–44.

S. Jacoby, *Employing Bureaucracy: Managers, Unions, and the Transformation of Work in American Industry*, New York: Columbia University Press, 1985.

S. Jacoby and S. Sharma, 'Employment Duration and Industrial Labor Mobility in the United States 1880–1980', *Journal of Economic History* 52(1), 1992, 161–79.

M. Katz, *The People of Hamilton, Canada West: Family and Class in a Mid-Nineteenth-Century City*, Cambridge, MA: Harvard University Press, 1975.

P. Knights, 'Accuracy of Age Reporting in the Manuscript Federal Censuses of 1850 and 1860', *Historical Methods Newsletter* 4(3), 1971, 79–83.

K. Kronenberg and M. Carree, 'On the Move: Determinants of Job and Residential Mobility in Different Sectors', *Urban Studies* 49(16), 2012, 3679–98.

D. Lafreniere and J. Gilliland, '"All the World's a Stage": A GIS Framework for Recreating Personal Time-Space from Qualitative and Quantitative Sources', *Transactions in GIS*, 19(2), 2014, 225–48.

LinkageWiz, *LinkageWiz Data Matching Software*. [Online], 2013. Available at: www.linkage-wiz.net.

K. Mason and L. Cope, 'Sources of Age and Date-of-Birth Misreporting in the 1900 U.S. Census', *Demography* 24(4), 1987, 563–73.

D. Mok, 'Do Two-Earner Households Base their Choice of Residential Location on Both Incomes?' *Urban Studies* 44(4), 2007, 723–50.

C. Mulder, 'The Family Context and Residential Choice: A Challenge for New Research', *Population, Space and Place* 13(4), 2007, 265–78.

C. Mulder and P. Hooimeijer, 'Residential Relcations in the Life Course', in L. van Wissen and P. Dykstra (eds), New York: Kluwer Academic, 1999, 159–86.

S. Olson and P. Thornton, *Peopling the North American City: Montreal 1840–1900*, Montreal: McGill-Queens University Press, 2011.

C. Pooley, 'Residential Mobility in the Victorian City', *Transactions of the Institute of British Geographers* 4(2), 1979, 258–77.

C. G. Pooley and J. Turnbull, 'Changing Home and Workplace in Victorian London: The Life of Henry Jaques, Shirtmaker', *Urban History* 24(2), 1997, 148–78.

J. Prillwitz, S. Harms and M. Lanzendorf, 'Interactions between Residential Relocations, Life Course Events, and Daily Commute Distances', *Transportation Research Record: Journal of the Transportation Research Board* 2021, 2007, 64–9.

S. Ruggles, 'Linking Historical Censuses: A New Approach', *History and Computing* 14(1–2), 2002, 213–24.

R. Sadler and D. Lafreniere, 'Racist Housing Practices as a Precursor to Uneven Neighborhood Change in a Post-Industrial City', *Housing Studies* 32(2), 2017, 186–208.

R. Steckel, 'The Quality of Census Data for Historical Inquiry: A Research Agenda', *Social Science History* 15(4), 1991, 579–99.

S. Thernstrom, *Poverty and Progress: Social Mobility in a Nineteenth Century City*, Cambridge, MA: Harvard University Press, 1964.

L. Ulrich, *A Midwife's Tale: The Life of Martha Ballard, Based on her Diary, 1785–1812*, New York: Knopf, 1990.

J. Zax and J. Kain, 'Commutes, Quits and Moves', *Journal of Urban Economics* 29, 1991, 153–65.

15

'A CITY OF THE WHITE RACE OCCUPIES ITS PLACE'

Kanaka Row, Chinatown, and the Indian Quarter in Victorian Victoria

John Sutton Lutz, Don Lafreniere, Megan Harvey,
Patrick Dunae, and Jason Gilliland

In this chapter we use HGIS to step onto the rich avenue of inquiry opened up by Henri Lefebvre with his observation that 'space' is both 'producing and produced by social relations'.[1] In this one elegant phrase Lefebvre linked space and time, geography and history, and lived realities with political ideas. For Lefebvre, social relations were largely the relations of capitalism. We are interested in how another set of social relations – race – was produced by and was producing space in the British colonial city of Victoria, British Columbia. We use HGIS to map the racial contours of how people lived in Victoria while we overlay a textual analysis to map the changing social relations of race.

Lefebvre started his study of space with the body. A body occupies a physical space surrounded by social relations.[2] Which part of the house does the Chinese servant sleep in? In what hotels and restaurants are only Whites permitted? In which neighborhood will we find the 'Indian Dance Houses'? Race finds real existence, as Lefebvre said of social relations generally, 'in and through space'.[3]

Saying race is produced by and productive of space is one thing, but demonstrating it is no easier for social scientists than observing the Higgs Boson particle is for physical scientists. In both situations we need to see and to freeze, for analytical purposes, processes that are both invisible to the eye and always in motion. For our starting point we turned to the insight of Edward Said who observed, 'the main battle in imperialism is over land, of course; but when it came to who owned the land, who had the right to settle and work on it, who kept it going, who won it back and who now plans its future – these issues were reflected, contested, and even for a time, decided in narrative'.[4]

Narrative, the writing of observations, ideas, predictions, and warnings, is our stop-motion camera that has allowed us to 'freeze' and observe social relations. We have taken a series of 'snapshots' of racial discourse in the local newspapers between 1858 and 1911 and compared those to corresponding GIS analyses of racial space in Victoria at ten-year intervals. The comparisons permit us to see the different systems of racial space in different historical periods, and to discern relationships between the lived space of racialized bodies, and the discursive space of social relations.[5] Ultimately we would like to know if we can observe them producing each other.

Victoria, the capital of one of Britain's most remote colonies until 1871, and, after that, of Canada's most western province, was the commercial capital of the British and Canadian possessions on the Pacific Coast of North America until Vancouver superseded it in the late 1890s.[6] Victoria was more racially diverse than most North American cities in the late nineteenth century, so an excellent venue to search for Lefebvre's spatial dynamic. To do so, we have mapped racial space in Victoria utilizing the censuses and city directories of 1881, 1891, 1901, and 1911 when the city's population reached 32,000. To build the HGIS for this project, we scanned archival maps of Victoria, circa 1891, and geo-referenced them to a modern map of the city. Since legal descriptions have not changed over time, we used the modern cadastral layer as a reference point and redrew historic lots that had been amalgamated or disappeared in twentieth-century redevelopments. We then linked nominal census

Figure 15.1 Victoria area in 1842 with two Lekwungen villages in bays (top right and bottom left) and location for the proposed Fort Victoria, a square on the harbour (bottom middle).

records which provide detailed personal information on individuals, including information relating to age, origin, religion, civil condition and occupation, to each lot – a task that was challenging because Victoria had no street numbers until 1891 and the census did not include addresses until 1901. We linked individuals to their street address and lots using directories and addresses from an 1891 municipal check census, which was undertaken a few months after the official Dominion census. By using these sources in combination, we have been able to link 93 per cent of household heads to their home addresses in 1891 and over 85 per cent in the 1881, 1901 and 1911 censuses. This afford us the opportunity to chart the evolution of racial space at the individual level in Victoria over 30 years and, at a neighborhood level, using historic maps, over a period of 70 years, stretching back to 1842 when the settlement was founded.

A careful examination of a map of the Victoria area as it appeared in 1842 (Figure 15.1) shows two Indigenous villages in bays at either end of the territory and a proposed Hudson's Bay Company fort in the bottom middle. From negotiations that took place in 1850 we know that the entire space between them was owned, used and controlled by seven Indigenous families (Figure 15.2).

Compare this to our GIS-produced map of 1901 (see Figure 15.11 on p. 355) and the displacement of Indigenous space by settler space is starkly demonstrated. How did it happen? Not by war. This displacement can only be understood through the discourse of colonialism, the discourse of inequality, and a discourse of rights which accorded primacy to British settlers and very few rights to Indigenous People. It is

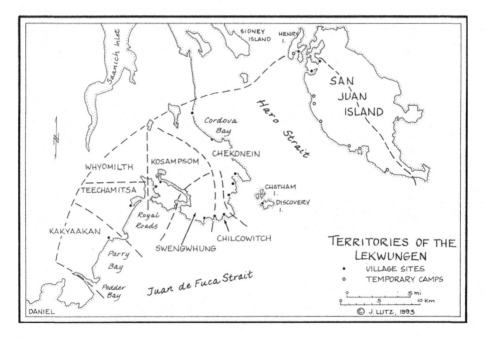

Figure 15.2 Territories of the Lekwungen families based on descriptions in the treaties of 1850.

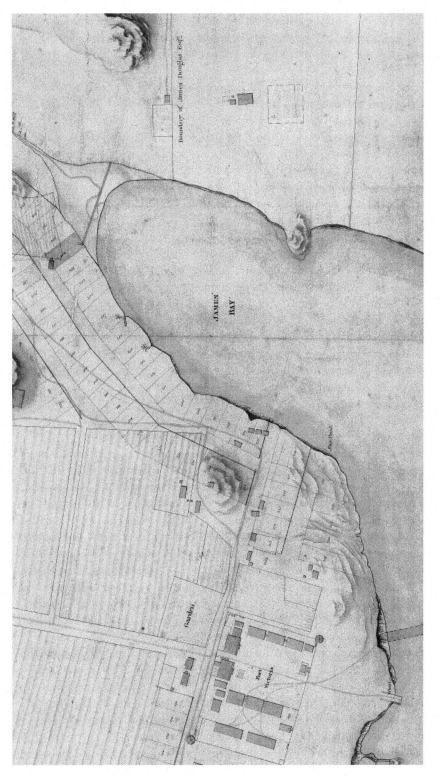

Figure 15.3 The cabins on the left side of James Bay are the beginnings of Kanaka Row from J. D. Pemberton's 1852 'A Plan of the Town of Victoria Shewing Proposed Improvements', BC Land Title and Survey Authority, 7 Locker 9.

language like 'the indolent, contented savage, must give place to the busteling [sic] sons of civilization and Toil' from James Bell[7] and reflected in the language of the main newspaper, called, appropriately, the *British Colonist*:

> Our race sweeps on, our civilisation knows no halt, and as fast as we cut down trees the red man disappears.[8]

This common narrative, embedded in both law and popular discourse, reflected settler ideas, supported the settlers, and affirmed to them their self-assumed right to unsettle Indigenous residents and resettle themselves. This was a peaceable subordination[9] that took place largely in narrative.

Founded in 1843 as an entrepôt for the Hudson's Bay Company's fur-trading interests west of the Rocky Mountains, Victoria became the capital of the British Colony of Vancouver Island founded in 1849. Victoria started as a mixed-race village with many of the new inhabitants, including the elite, of mixed European and Indigenous descent, and as new settlers arrived they often married into Indigenous or other mixed-race families. Among the immigrant population of the 1840s–1850s were Scots who held the positions of authority in the Hudson's Bay Company, and a workforce of French Canadians, Iroquois – Indigenous People from the other side of the continent – and many people of mixed heritage.[10] In the 1840s, except for the mixed-race space of Fort Victoria and the couple hundred acres of farmland and scattered houses that spread east and south of it (Figure 15.3), this was the territory of the Lekwungen (Songhees) People.

Kanaka Row

Among the 30 or so first settlers in Fort Victoria were Indigenous Hawaiians who had been hired by the Hudson's Bay Company when supply ships from England made regular stops in Hawaii. In 1850, Hawaiians, or 'Kanakas' as they were called, made up about a quarter of the male population of the fort and were among the first to marry into the local Indigenous communities.[11] Charles Bayley, in 1851, recalled that the whole settlement was contained within the fort 'except a few log shanties occupied by half-breed Iroquois, French Canadians and Kanack[a]s who risked their lives outside relying upon the women influence, most of them living with Native women'.[12] With a kin connection to the Lekwungen came security, so the Kanakas set up households outside the protection of the fort and created an area known as Kanaka Row (later Road or Street), a series of simple cottages that hugged the rocky shore of James Bay just south of the fort (Figures 15.3 and 15.4).[13]

The fur trade village erupted into a small city in 1858 when gold was discovered on the nearby mainland and Victoria became the access point to the new *Eldorado*. The HBC capitalized on the real estate boom and from the company a few Kanakas purchased several lots along Kanaka Row.[14] From the newspapers we learn that the occupants of gold rush era Kanaka Row expanded to include visiting Indigenous People, newly arrived Black Americans, and mixed-race households.

The name Kanaka Row derived from the birthplace of the original male residents of the area. Originally, the name carried an ethnic rather than a pejorative connotation.

Figure 15.4 James Bay, 1860, showing Kanaka Row in foreground and the government buildings across the Bay.

However, beginning in 1858, the local newspapers linked this Kanaka Row with undesirable people generally. The papers associated Kanaka Row with drunken fights, stabbings, illegal liquor sales, and break-ins.[15] Among the residents, a Kanaka named 'Nahor' (Nahoua) and his Indigenous spouse 'Catch-hus' were often in court, charged with operating a brothel, a dance house, and 'selling liquor to Indians'. Another Kanaka, 'Karahue Toimoro', also married to an Indigenous woman, 'Keteka', was also often in trouble for selling liquor and abetting prostitution. In October 1861, the *British Colonist* ran a lengthy article about Kanaka Row:

> **A Disorderly Neighborhood.** The state of moral degradation into which a number of habitués and resident so Kanaka Road have fallen, is a . . . standing disgrace to the town. Hardly a day passes but one or more fights between squaws or squaw men transpire in that vicinity, and a continual howling nightly is maintained by the drunken wretches who occupy or visit the miserable huts that have been erected along the bank of James Bay . . . The vicinity named is a perfect sink-hole of iniquity-a lazar house of vice and immorality . . . a neighborhood of [a] blackguard population.[16]

On Christmas Day, 1862, the paper recommended the area, sarcastically, 'to families who like a lively neighborhood' as it reported a two-day series of fights between 'about 15 drunken men – whites, kanakas and Indians.'[17]

Through the 1860s some commercial enterprises were established on Kanaka Road close to the busy Government Street, including a shipyard, a butcher, a buyer and seller of furs and a tannery which likely added unpleasant odours to the neighborhood. These businesses largely replaced earlier residences leaving a scattering of huts that became Victoria's 'skid row'. By the late 1870s Kanaka Row had ceased to exist as a place name. The last reference to the area as Kanaka Row in the city papers, the *Gazette* and the *British Colonist,* was in 1873 and thereafter the papers used the formal name, Humboldt Street, which had been first designated in 1859.[18]

Symbolic of the racial cleansing, the tannery had become a soap factory. The iniquity described by the paper as associated with the former Kanaka Row was, by the 1870s, more commonly linked to Chinatown or the Songhees Indian Reserve on the opposite side of the harbour where at least one of the Kanaka families had moved. In 1881, when we are first able to use a census to apply the GIS lens, the census takers only found one person in the city of Victoria who was of Hawaiian ancestry.[19]

Black space

The scathing *British Colonist* article in October 1861 about Kanaka Row suggests the name had more to do with the character of the street, than the ethnicity of most of the residents. The paper urged the authorities to send the Indigenous women to the Indian Reserve[20] and charge 'the white and black men who glory in keeping them' with vagrancy, alerting us to both the undesirable presence of racial mixing and the presence of a population of African Americans.

Before the gold rush to Victoria and British Columbia, African Americans in California had been looking at Vancouver Island as potential refuge where they could escape much of the racism and legal barriers that were part of American and Californian law. When the American Supreme Court ruled in the 1857 Dred Scot decision that people of African origin could not be American citizens and were not protected by the Constitution, and a proposed law in California, Bill 339, 'to restrict and prevent . . . the residence in the State of Negros' was about to make free Blacks vulnerable to slavery, a group exodus to Victoria was organized. The vanguard of the Black settlers booked passage on the ship the *Commodore* scheduled to depart in April 1858.[21] If they had been unaccompanied, this vanguard would have comprised a quarter of the population of Victoria at that time and since more had planned to follow, Victoria might have been at least half of African American origin with a few years. But, in the meantime, gold was discovered on the Fraser River and Victoria was the nearest access point. As it transpired, there were also 450 White gold seekers on the *Commodore*, and tens of thousands of Whites followed in the next few months, which left the Blacks as a small minority.

The narrative of Black racial space came and went quickly in Victoria and was concentrated, not in residential areas, but on two indoor spaces: Black seating in the theatres and the churches. Some White theatre goers objected to being seated with Blacks in a dispute that occupied the papers on and off from 1858 to 1861. A group of parishioners and one Congregationalist Minister insisted the Blacks sit in separate pews at the back of the church.[22] The Anglican Church made no such distinction. After much recrimination the segregationist minister left town, the churches and the theatres integrated, and the narrative of racial space faded leaving no discernable area in Victoria that could be considered 'Black Space'.

The estimates for the total Black immigration between 1858 and 1865 range as high as 600. While Blacks were sometimes associated with unsavory activities in Kanaka Row, aside from the debate about indoor spaces, in which the papers generally argued for equal treatment for Blacks, there was no sustained public negative racial narrative around Blacks. Without such a narrative there could be no racial space. Some Blacks bought property, including Mifflin Gibbs who served two terms on Victoria City Council and owned a fine house on the corner of Michigan and Menzies Street in the genteel neighborhood next to the Government Buildings on the shore of James Bay opposite Kanaka Row. Although treated as citizens, racist snubs were common. After the Civil War ended and Constitutional Amendments ended slavery and awarded African Americans legal rights, many of the Blacks returned to the United States.

A municipal census in 1871 only counted 196 'coloured' adults, about 5 per cent of the population. By 1901 when the census first asks about 'race' the Black population had fallen to 131 adults and children constituting a miniscule percentage of the 25,000 Victorians.[23] By 1911 only 36 people reported themselves 'Negro or African in Origin'. The numbers are small and from the GIS data in 1901 we can see there was no discernable residential segregation of the Blacks. The remaining single Black men lived in rooming houses downtown, sharing spaces predominantly occupied by Whites, and the few Black families lived in the predominantly White working-class neighbourhood of Fernwood (see Figure 15.5). Unlike the case of the equally small population of Kanakas who arrived before them or the more numerous Chinese, there was no sustained negative narrative of Blackness that isolated this very visible minority and therefore no social relations that would create a 'Black space'.

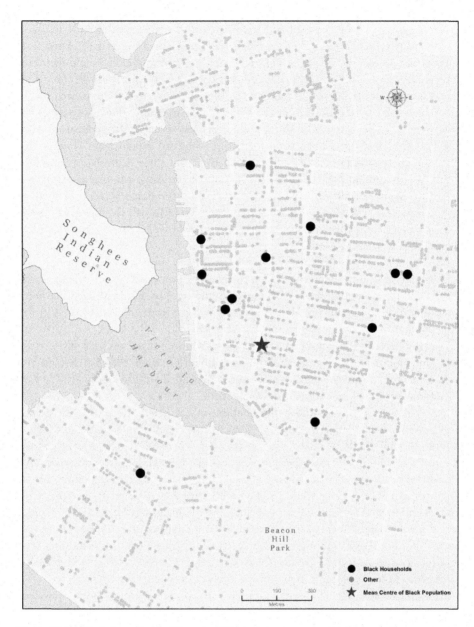

Figure 15.5 Black households, Victoria, 1901.

'Indian Quarter'

When James Douglas arrived in 1843 to build the HBC's fort, he chose a spot between the Lekwungen's *Pallatsis*, 'the Place of Cradles', and *Meeqan,* 'warmed by the sun'. The arrival of the newcomers did not drive the Lekwungen away – actually the reverse. The Lekwungen, or Songhees as they are also called, moved their main village from 7 km away at Cadboro Bay to be beside the fort.[24] In 1850, as agent of

Figure 15.6   Lekwungen (Songhees) village across the harbour from Victoria town, c.1860.

the HBC and the British Crown, James Douglas moved to formalize the relationship with the Lekwungen 'whose land we occupy' by a treaty.[25] Douglas wrote that he:

> summoned to a conference, the Chiefs and influential men of the Sangees [Lekwungen] tribe ... After considerable discussion it was arranged that the whole of their lands, forming ... the District of Victoria, should be sold to the Company, with the exception of Village sites and enclosed fields, for a certain remuneration ...[26]

From the point of view of the settlers, these treaties – two-paragraph narratives – along with 300 blankets, reracialized most of what had been Indigenous space into settler space. In making the treaty Douglas counted 700 men, women and children amongst the Lekwungen. One of the sites reserved by the treaty was the village that had grown up across the harbour.

By 1858 there were three Indigenous 'communities' in what is now Victoria: the Lekwungen (Songhees) Indian Reserve located across the harbour from the booming town, the shanty towns of 2,000–4,000 migrant Indigenous workers around Victoria's outskirts which ballooned in the summer and dwindled in the winter, and the Indigenous residents of the urban town itself (Figure 15.6, 15.7). A visitor to Victoria recorded in 1861 that 'Indians ... are seen everywhere throughout the town – in the morning carrying cut wood for sale; the women, baskets of oysters, clams etc.'[27]

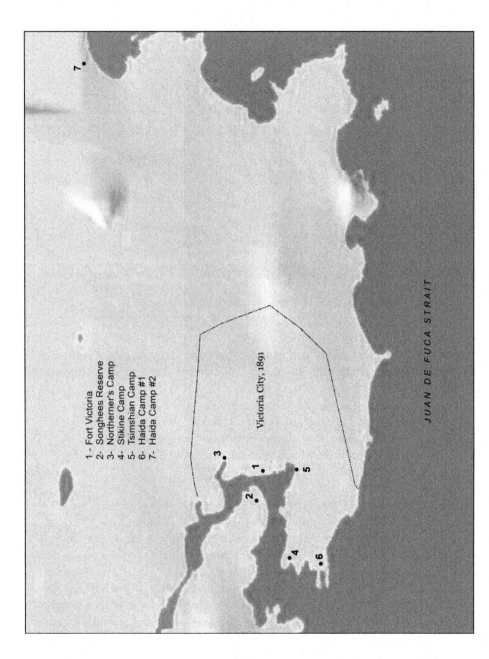

1 - Fort Victoria
2 - Songhees Reserve
3 - Northerner's Camp
4 - Stikine Camp
5 - Tsimshian Camp
6 - Haida Camp #1
7 - Haida Camp #2

Victoria City, 1891

JUAN DE FUCA STRAIT

Figure 15.7 Seasonal Indigenous villages around Victoria in 1862 showing 1891 city limits.

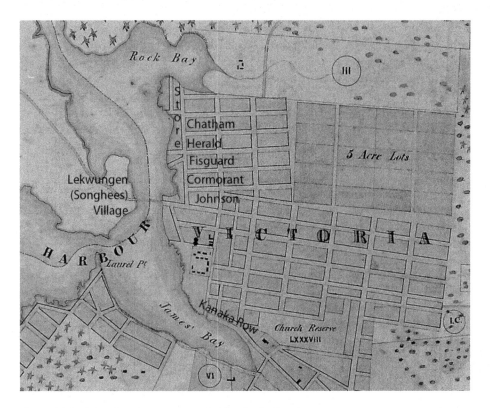

Figure 15.8 Map showing area occupied by the Indian Quarter.

As the city grew, the Lekwungen harbour-side village site came to be among the most commercially valuable property in the city. Starting with a letter to the editor in the *British Colonist* newspaper on 15 January 1859 and followed a few days later by a resolution in the Vancouver Island Legislature, White residents of Victoria regularly called for the removal of the Indian Reserve from the harbour.[28] James Douglas, by this time Governor of the Colony, declined such requests, referring to the treaties and stating that the government was 'bound by the faith of a solemn engagement'.[29]

In January 1863 the *British Colonist* newspaper reflected:

> A few years ago, the sight of a Hudson's Bay Company fort with its hand-ful of whites would be enough to account for the very prominent part filled by the Indians in its neighbourhood. The fort has disappeared; *a city of the white race occupies its place*. The refinements of civilization have been introduced, yet King Freezy [Lekwungen Chief] and his fishy, clam eating subjects are still located upon what ought to be part of the site of the city.[30]

In the 1850s and early 1860s the town was bounded by a ravine on the north side, opposite the narrowest part of the harbour and across from the Lekwungen Village. The town-side of ravine became Johnson Street where urban Indigenous residents made homes alongside the businesses which served them and the Indian Quarter crept into and across the ravine as far as Rock Bay (Figure 15.8).

After incorporation in 1862, Victoria's City Council became one of the loudest voices in this chorus to remove the Lekwungen.[31] Disease, drunkenness and prostitution, all exchanges with the immigrants, were the reasons offered by a faction of the Victoria community to justify ridding the city of Indigenous People (Figure 15.9).

The superintendent of police Philip Hankin wrote Governor Kennedy in February 1866 that:

> there are about 200 Indian prostitutes living in Cormorant, Fisgard, and Store Streets in a state of filth, and dirt beyond all description. In one place known as the 'Gully' between Johnson and Cormorant Streets some of these dens of infamy are two and three stories high, the rooms about eight feet square, and as many as 6 or 8 persons living in each room.[32]

We can get a picture of Indigenous urban residents in Victoria thanks to a municipal census in 1871, the year British Columbia joined Canada (Table 15.1).

The census was a limited one, just capturing the head of household by name, occasionally a street address, and the number of adults by race and gender in the household. We can see that adult urban Victoria was 10 per cent aboriginal, 5 per cent coloured, 7 per cent Chinese, and 78 per cent White. There were 45 per cent more native women than men, reflecting both the presence of sex trade workers in the city, and Indigenous wives or common-law wives of White settlers. Of the 1,083 households enumerated, 66 contained only Indigenous People, and another 36 contained White males living with Indigenous females. There were 36 Indigenous women living in households with no men. Where a street address was given, all the Indigenous People living without Whites were on Johnson Street and a third of those cohabiting with Whites were also living on Johnson Street.[33] Across the Harbour, on the Lekwungen Reserve, the population had fallen from 700 in 1850 to 182 in 1876, including 55 adult males and 62 adult females.

When renowned anthropologist Franz Boas visited Victoria in 1884 he recalled 'The Indians are at present in the habit of living part of the year in Victoria . . . working in various trades: in saw-mills and canneries, on wharves, as sailors, etc . . . They have their own quarter in every city.'

The 1891 Municipal Check Census recorded 377 Indigenous People in Victoria, accounting for 1.6 per cent of the population. From our GIS work we know the Indian Quarter was centred on Herald Street (Figure 15.10).

But when the next census was taken in 1901, only 53 people who identified their race as North American Indian resided in Victoria and of these 27 were living on

Table 15.1 Victoria Municipal Census, 1871.

White Males	White Females	Chinese Males	Chinese Females	Coloured Males	Coloured Females	Native Males	Native Females	Children
1716	1188	219	29	119	77	144	210	1231

Source: British Columbia Archives, GR 428.

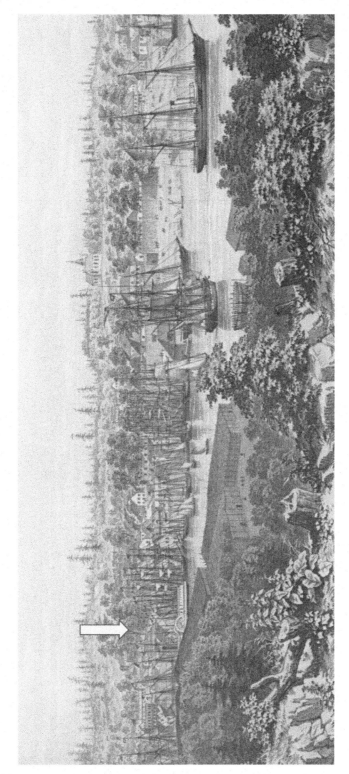

Figure 15.9 Victoria, 1860, with Songhees village in foreground and Indian Quarter in background indicated by arrow.

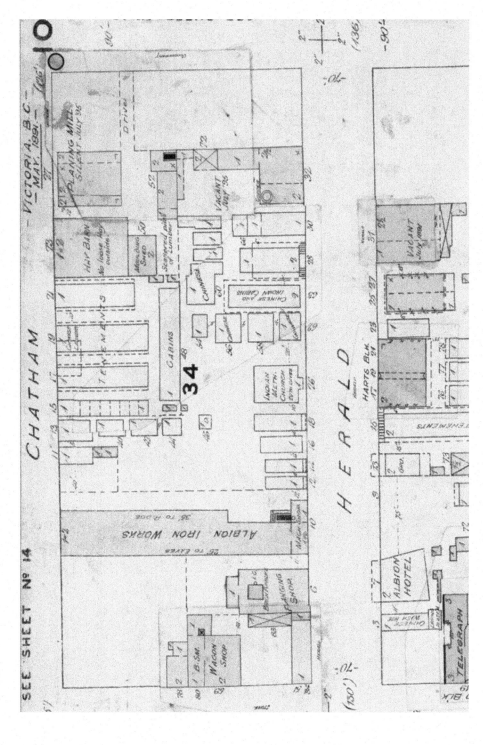

Figure 15.10 Victoria Fire Insurance Plan, 1891, showing north side of Herald Street with Indian Methodist Church and Indian and Chinese cabins.

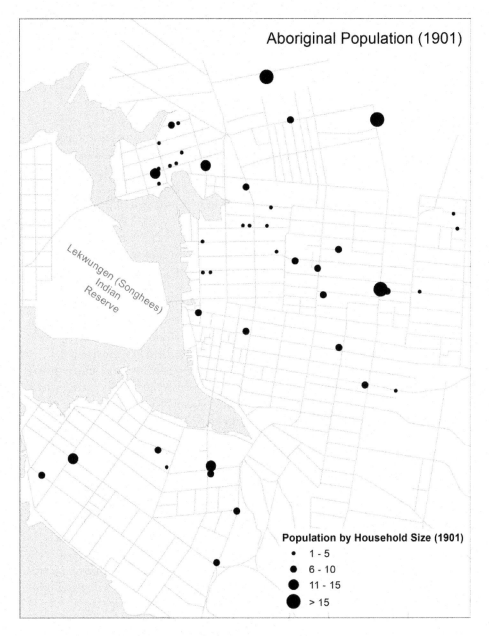

Figure 15.11 Indigenous population in Victoria, 1901 not including Lekwungen (Songhees) Indian Reserve.

sealing ships in the harbour. The Indigenous population had all but abandoned what had been the Indian Quarter, with a small concentration still discernable on the north side of Rock Bay. In total 'red people' were a mere half a per cent of the population of the city. By the time of the 1911 Census, the Lekwungen reserve had been dissolved, and only four families whose racial ancestry was indicated as North American Indian lived in the city itself out of the total population of Victoria of 28,500.[34] The Indians did not just vanish, they had been *vanished*.[35]

Chinese and the unforbidden city

While this history of Indigenous People in Victoria is one of steady population decline, the history of the Chinese in Victoria starts with the first arrival in 1858 and grows through the century. The change is captured by former newspaperman Edgar Fawcett, writing in 1912, about the early 1860s: 'I might say that Chinese were almost as rare in those days in Victoria as Turks. Indians performed all manual labour – in fact were to that day what John Chinaman is to this.'[36]

The Victoria *Gazette* reported on 30 June 1858 that a shop's sign had appeared with 'the euphonious and suggestive legend, Chang Tsoo' and wonders if the efforts of the new arrivals will 'be devoted to the washing of gold or of clothing?' The Chinese bought inexpensive lots in the Indian Quarter. They were cheap because they were *beyond the pale*, past the 'Indian Street' and the Johnson Street ravine which was the effective northern boundary of Victoria at the time. The area to the north was only accessible by three narrow footbridges which spanned the ravine at Store, Government, and Douglas Streets.[37] This area became known as Chinatown.

By 1862 the Victoria city directory estimated that there were 300 Chinese living in the city, about 6 per cent of the population, though the number fluctuated wildly as vessels arrived, with up to 600 arriving on one day in 1865 on a ship from Hong Kong, and seasonally, with miners spending their winters in Victoria away from the frozen conditions of the mining districts.[38]

The municipal census of 1871 showed 111 households with Chinese residents. In the few cases where street addresses are given, four lived on Johnson and one each on Government, Humboldt (Kanaka Row), Yates, and Fort Streets. Men outnumbered women 9:1 but there were three households with only Chinese women. There was little inter-racial mixing. Only three households contained Chinese male adults and Indigenous female adults. There were no cases of co-living between Chinese or Indigenous men and White women. Neither were any White or Indigenous men living with a Chinese woman. The GIS shows that the only cases of Chinese cohabiting with Whites were single Chinese males, presumably domestics, living in twelve prominent White households distributed through the residential district.

Ten years later, in 1881, the Chinese population had doubled, swollen by the importation of labourers to help build the Canadian Pacific Railway. The 1881 GIS shows 590 Chinese in the three Victoria wards, of which 65 were female, keeping the ratio of men to women at 9:1, the same as a decade earlier.[39] Of the 38 married Chinese women, all lived with Chinese men. There were only fourteen single Chinese women over 17, eight of which lived in three female-only houses. From our census analyses we know that in 1881 Chinese made up 10 per cent of the 5,922 people enumerated in Victoria's three wards and 464 or 79 per cent of the Chinese lived in the Johnson Street Ward where Chinatown was located.

In many colonial cities racial segmentation was largely effective. Cities were physically divided in 'quarters' with their borders clearly defined and highly segregated. Victoria's Chinatown has this reputation.[40] The histories of what is Canada's oldest Chinatown has been portrayed in popular and scholarly literature as a racially segregated ghetto, a 'Forbidden City', an inscrutable place closed to outsiders.[41] The use of historical GIS allows us to test some longstanding assumptions about Chinese space in Victoria and the interactions between Chinese and non-Chinese residents.

The historical GIS of Victorian Victoria's Chinatown in 1881 shows a neighbourhood with a quarter of its population not Chinese – still highly segregated but not at all a 'Forbidden City'.[42] Spatializing the census data allows us to see that several of the streets in the neighbourhood were heterogeneous, with White workers living beside Chinese shops, Indigenous women living with White men and between Chinese families. When we also map outside Chinatown, we see a city in which Chinese lived in every neighbourhood.[43] With a GIS perspective, the alleged gulf between East and West in Victoria was not nearly as pronounced as historians have claimed.

In 1891, at least five hundred Chinese people – about one quarter of Victoria's Chinese population – lived outside of Chinatown. Chinese were located near the lime kilns and pottery works across the harbour in Victoria West, at the brickyards at the northern end of the city, at Chinese laundries situated throughout the Yates Street ward, in the central part of Victoria, and James Bay ward. The largest vegetable market gardens were located near the south end of Cook Street, in an area known as Fairfield.[44] There were also Chinese cooks, servants, and gardeners who resided in at least 50 of the wealthiest homes in Victoria's most prestigious suburbs. Many less-affluent middle-class households employed Chinese domestics on daily or weekly basis, and in such cases workers would travel from their abodes in Chinatown to their place of employment in White neighbourhoods. Chinese peddlers sold their wares door to door in all parts of the city. Clearly, the Chinese shared much of the city with White settlers and the physical distance between them was not great (Figure 15.12).[45]

Michel Foucault asked historians to map 'discursive practices in so far as they give rise to a corpus of knowledge' about race, among other things. Drawing on Michel Foucault in part, but more substantively on the work of Teun Van Djik and Margaret Whetherell and Jonathan Potter, we wanted to see if a more concerted attempt at 'mapping the language of racism' would support the conclusions of our maps of racial space.[46] As a check on our conclusions drawn from the GIS, we sampled the major colonial/provincial paper, the British Colonist, in the decades 1858–1911, coinciding in the later period with census years. (See Figure 15.13.) In the census years we read every word in every paper from a two-week period in the spring and a two-week period in the fall, a sample of 8 per cent in the chosen years.

We found, as we expected, that the negative references to the Chinese outnumbered the positive, though positive references were not uncommon. What was unexpected was a major thread of neutral discourse: most of the time the discourse was not pushing an interpretation about the Chinese that was either negative or positive. As illustrated in our 1891 sample the majority of references to Chinese were

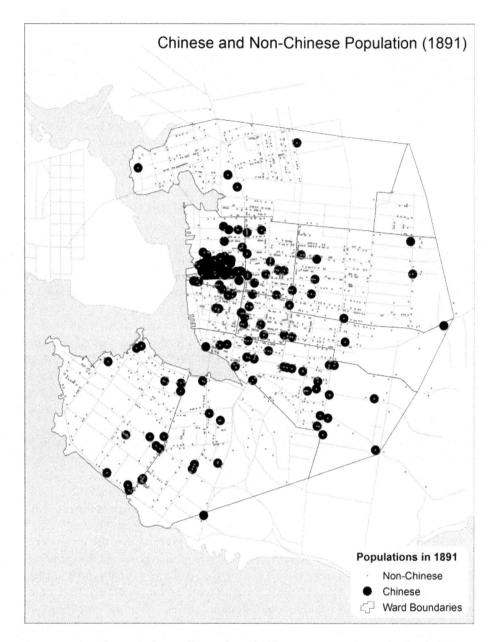

Figure 15.12   Chinese and non-Chinese households, 1891.

in advertisements (Figure 15.14). Most were Chinese merchants selling goods to other settlers, some were White merchants selling Chinese goods, and some were Chinese and White merchants offering to contract Chinese labourers. The large number of advertisements is consistent throughout the 60-year analyses of papers and suggests that the main interactions between Chinese and other immigrants were the buying and selling of goods and services.

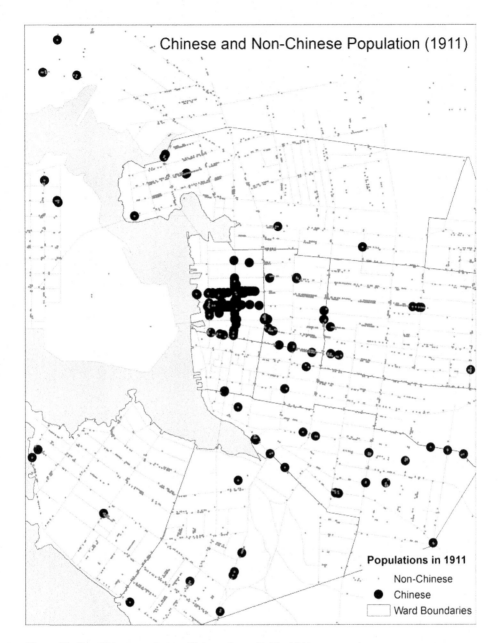

Figure 15.13 Chinese and non-Chinese households, 1911.

Even at this surface level, the mapping of racial narrative in the newspapers aligns with some of the conclusions suggested by our historical GIS research and offers a partial explanation for the openness of Chinatown. Where there was charged language, the preponderance of the negative supports the conclusions of earlier scholars that this was a society structured by race, in which the White immigrants worked to maintain a hierarchy that put them at the top.

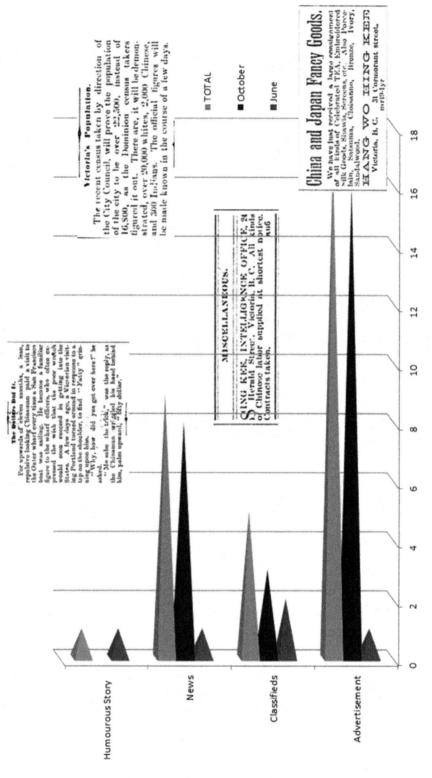

Figure 15.14 Kinds of articles referring to Chinese in *British Colonist* in sample weeks, 1891.

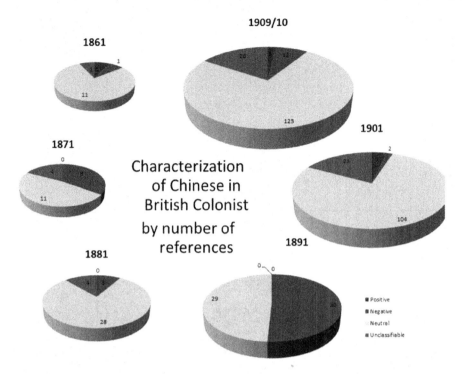

Figure 15.15   Positive, negative and neutral characterizations of Chinese in the *British Colonist*, sample weeks 1861–1910.

However, the relative lack of charged language compared to purely neutral, commercial references, and the apparent success of both Chinese and White merchants in selling Chinese goods to the colonial population, suggests a vibrant transactional space where Chinese and other Victorians frequently met and exchanged goods and services in a regime more structured by the impersonal relations of capitalism than the embodied and personal relationships of race. Moreover, the presence of both positive and negative references suggests competing ideas of Chineseness among the White settlers of the colony. The key point is, despite earlier scholarly analyses to the contrary, the narrative describes a racial and commercial regime which required an unforbidden city, in which Chinese and White, lived, worked, and shopped alongside each other, just as they bought and sold from each other.[47] In spite of the racist attitudes held by many, the social relations between the Chinese and other residents required unsegregated racial spaces (Figure 15.15).

The textual mapping aligns with the spatial analyses which show us that in Victoria there was no hermetically sealed 'Forbidden City' and that certain kinds of racial borders (commercial transactions, hiring labour) were very porous while others (like intermarriage) were very strict.

Conclusion

Victoria, from the mid-nineteenth century to 1911, had significant populations of Indigenous Hawaiians, Indigenous People, African Americans, Chinese, and a diverse

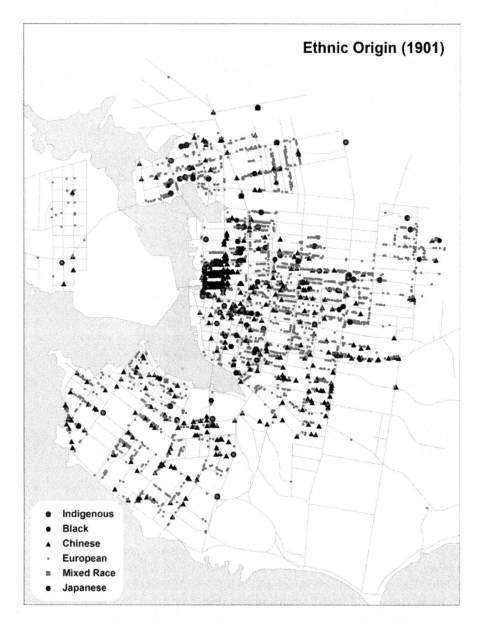

Figure 15.16   Racial identification of residents by census takers, Victoria, 1901.

settler population loosely constructed as 'White' (Figure 15.16). Thanks to the power of GIS we now see what earlier generations of scholars could not: the Forbidden City was not Forbidden, the ebb and ultimate vanishing of Kanaka Row and the Indian Quarter, and the distinctive lack of any Black neighbourhood.

In this chapter we have followed the invitation of Henri Lefebvre to 'read space' along with Michel Foucault's invitation to 'map language'. Bringing the language of Historical GIS into conversation with the changing narrative of race in Victoria demonstrates how space – take, for example, the undesirable ravine on the north side of Victoria – produced social relations of marginality that produced the Indian Quarter and Chinatown. We can also show how social relations – like those on Kanaka Row – created racialized spaces. The experience of the Black population, who were racially marked but not spatially distinguished, also demonstrates the power of social relations in creating, or not differentiating, racial spaces. The mutually reinforcing power of space and social relations is apparent in the narrative of 'Chinese' in the newspapers. When the full range of narrative characterizations are analysed they show a set of interwoven social relations that also appear in clear relief in the porosity of Chinese racial space. These 'spatializations' of social action suggest the immense analytical power of bringing space and social relations, GIS and textual analyses, together into one field of vision. We have in Victoria, the 'complicated, messy, intersubjective relations of colonialism in a particular spot',[48] but the patterns articulated by GIS and confirmed by narrative analyses offer a fresh understanding of how race was articulated spatially and socially, and how space both produced, and was produced by, social relations.

Notes

1 H. Lefebvre, 'Reflections on the Politics of Space', trans. Michael J. Enders, *Antipode* 8(2), 1976, 30–7.
2 Lefebvre started his analyses with the body but does not explore differentiated bodies; he was interested in class, not race.
3 S. Elden, *Understanding Henri Lefebvre: Theory and the Possible*, London: Continuum, 2004, 219.
4 E. Said, *Culture and Imperialism,* New York: Vintage, 1994, p. xiii.
5 Lefebvre distinguished between 'Concrete Space', the space of gestures and journeys, of the body and memory, of symbols and sense and 'Abstract Space', the space of the planner, the architect, the imagination. R. Shields, 'Henri Lefebvre', in A. Elliot and B. S. Turner (eds), *Profiles in Contemporary Social Theory*, London: Sage, 2001.
6 The economic development of Victoria is described in H. Gregson, *A History of Victoria, 1842–1970*, Victoria, BC: Victoria Observer Publishing Co., 1970; D. Pethick, *Summer of Promise: Victoria 1864–1914,* Victoria, BC: Sono Nis Press, 1980; C. N. Forward, 'The Evolution of Victoria's Functional Character', in A. F. J. Artibise (ed.), *Town and City: Aspects of Western Canadian Urban Development*, Regina: Canadian Plains Research Center, University of Regina Press, 1981; and P. A. Baskerville, *Beyond the Island: An Illustrated History of Victoria,* Burlington, ON: Windsor Publications, 1986.
7 BC Archives, J. Bell to J. Thompson, 27 February 1859, Add Mss 412, Box 8, file 5.
8 *British Colonist*, 22 August 1860, 2.
9 The concept of 'peaceable subordination' is more fully fleshed out in J. Lutz, *Makúk: A New History of Aboriginal White Relations*, Vancouver: UBC Press, 2008, 24–5.
10 J. Barman, *French Canadians, Furs and Indigenous Women in the Making of the Pacific Northwest*, Vancouver: UBC Press, 2014, 244–9; J. Barman and B. M. Watson, *Leaving Paradise: Indigenous Hawaiians in the Pacific Northwest, 1878–1898,* Honolulu: University of Hawaii Press, 2006, 171–3.
11 T. Koppel, *Kanaka: The Untold Story of Hawaiian Pioneers in British Columbia and the Pacific Northwest*, Vancouver: Whitecap, 1995, 66; The population estimate is based on references in the 'Fort Victoria Journal', Hudson's Bay Company Archives, B.226/ a/1, edited and transcribed by G. Brazier et al., Fort Victoria Journal www.fortvictoriajournal.ca.

12 C. A. Bayley, 'Early Life on Vancouver Island', MSS P-C 3, Bancroft Library, University of California at Berkeley.

13 Later, in the 1850s, Hawaiian farm workers squatted on 'Kanaka Ranch' which was on Constance Cove beside the Puget Sound Agricultural Company's Viewfield Farm on Esquimalt Harbor. The area was known as Kanaka Ranch into the 1890s and was a favorite summer camping site for Victorians until it was subdivided in 1903. Koppel, *Kanaka*, 67, and *British Colonist*, 27 December 1874; 29 December 1883; 2 August 1899, 8; 19 July 1911.

14 In 1862–4 the city assessment rolls listed two Hawaiians Thomas Keavē and Louis Keavē owning lots next door to each other valued at $1,200 and $1,500 respectively and Nahua owned a lot valued at $1,200 on Kanaka Row/Humboldt Street. Barman and Watson, *Leaving Paradise,* 172.

15 *Victoria Gazette*, 23 and 24 September 1859, 3; 15, 29 May 1860, 2; *British Colonist*, 26 May 1860; 31 July 1860; 19 September 1860; 15 January 1861; 16 September 1861; 24 October 1861; 4 April 1862; 3 July 1862; 28 May 1864; 28 October 1872; 3; 7 February 1873, 3.

16 *British Colonist,* 14 October 1861, 2.

17 *British Colonist,* 25 December 1862, 3.

18 Barman and Watson, *Leaving Paradise*, 271–3; T. Ross, 'Then and Now: The Pendray Family', *James Bay Beacon* (August 2014), http://jamesbaybeacon.ca/?q=node/1303. Although soap seems better smelling than tanning, in fact soap making used the tallow of animals scraped from their skins so there was not much difference. The soap factory 'contribut[ed]to the stench that sickened local residents and assailed the nostrils'. Danda Humphreys, *The Islander,* 1 November 1999. For skid row see P. A. Dunae, D. J. Lafreniere, J. A. Gilliland and J. S. Lutz, 'Dwelling Places and Social Spaces: Revealing the Environments of Urban Workers in Victoria Using Historical GIS', *Labour/Le Travail* 72, Fall 2013, 37–73. See esp. p. 52 and photograph; and p. 70.

19 It appears that many of the Kanakas sought agricultural land once they left the employ of the HBC and several families moved to nearby San Juan, Salt Spring, and Russell Islands. See Koppel, *Kanaka,* 67–8, 107–8.

20 After Fort Victoria was established in 1843 the local Indigenous People the Lekwungen (also known as Songhees) established a village immediately across the harbor. Approximately 90 acres including this village was reserved for them by treaties of 1850 and formed the basis of the Indian Reserve system where village, fishing, and agricultural areas were held for Indigenous people by the colonial, and later, federal governments.

21 C. Killian, *Go Do Some Great Thing: The Black Pioneers of British Columbia*, Burnaby: Commodore, 2008, 16–17, 21.

22 Killian, *Go Do Some Great Thing,* 43–8.

23 Identified by the attribution in the census 'Black Race'. Searching the categories of 'Negros' and 'Africans' yields only 79 in Victoria City and district.

24 There is evidence that one or more families of Songhees continued to live at Cadboro Bay through the 1880s and probably as late as 1911.

25 Douglas to the Governor and Committee, 6 November 1847 and Douglas to Archibald Barclay, 3 September 1849, in H. Bowsfield (ed.), *Fort Victoria Letters 1846–1851,* Winnipeg: Hudson's Bay Record Society, 1979, 16, 39.

26 Douglas to Barclay, 16 May 1850 in Bowsfield (ed.), *Fort Victoria Letters,* 95.

27 S. Cracroft, *Lady Franklin Visits the Pacific Northwest, February to April 1861 and April to July 1870,* D. B. Smith (ed.), *Victoria: Provincial Archives of British Columbia Memoir 11,* 1974, 79.

28 *British Colonist*, 15 January, 1859; James Yates moved motion, 18 January 1859 in the Vancouver Island Assembly Minutes, *Journals of the Colonial Legislatures* (JCL) J. Hendrickson (ed.), Victoria: BC Archives, 1981, vol. 2, 67; see also *British Colonist*, 2 and 26 February 1859.

29 25 January 1859 J. Hendrickson (ed.), *Journals of the Colonial Legislature*, Victoria: BC Archives, 1980, vol. 2, 72. In March 1859, J. S. Helmecken asks the Governor to move the reserve, *Journals of the Colonial Legislature*, vol. 2, 80–1.

30 *British Colonist*, 8 January 1863, 2. My italics indicate the source for the title of this paper.

31 W. A. G. Young to Mayor of Victoria, Colonial Secretary Correspondence Outward to Mayor and Council of Victoria, 9 Sept. 1862–25 April 1864, British Columbia Archives (BCA) CAA 30.1J 7. *British Colonist*, 22 November 1864; P. Dunae, 'Geographies of Sexual Commerce and the Production of Prostitutional Space: Victoria, British Columbia, 1860–1914', *Journal of the Canadian Historical Association*, 2008, 122–4.

32 P. Hankin to A. Kennedy, 8 February 1866, as enclosed in A. Kennedy to E. Cardwell, 13 February 1866, 3246 CO 305/28, p. 135, received 2 April.

33 Marital status was not given, only the race of household residents.

34 Online at P. Dunae (ed.), *ViHistory*, http://vihistory.ca.

35 G. Keddie, *Songhees Pictorial. A History of the Songhees People as seen by Outsiders, 1790–1912*, Victoria, BC: Royal British Columbia Museum, 2003, and R. Mawani, 'Legal Geographies of Aboriginal Segregation in British Columbia: The Making and Unmaking of the Songhees Reserve, 1850–1911', in C. Strange and A. Basher (eds), *Isolation, Places and Practices of Exclusion*, London: Routledge, 2003, 173–90.

36 Fawcett, *Some Reminiscences*, 84.

37 D. C. Lai, *Chinatowns: Towns within Cities in Canada*, Vancouver: UBC, 1988, 184–6.

38 Lai, *Chinatowns*, 184.

39 Though race was not asked for, the Chinese can be identified by questions on birthplace of father and Chinese surname.

40 In Victoria's case the British-European settlers displaced Indigenous People in the large sense but Chinatown moved into what had been the 'Indian Quarter' and so it was Chinese immigrants who physically replaced Indigenous People.

41 This interpretation is emphasized by geographer D. C. Lai in *Chinatowns* and *Forbidden City within Victoria: Myth, Symbol and Streetscape of Canada's Earliest Chinatown*, Victoria, BC: Orca Books, 1991. Historians have also represented Victoria's Chinatowns as a defensive ghetto, sealed off from the surrounding host community. See Patricia E. Roy, *A White Man's Province: British Columbia Politicians and Chinese and Japanese Immigrants, 1858–1914*, Vancouver: UBC Press, 1989, and W. P. Ward, *White Canada Forever: Popular Attitudes and Public Policy toward Orientals in British Columbia*, 3rd ed., Montreal and Kingston: McGill-Queen's University Press, 2002.

42 P. Dunae, J. Lutz, D. Lafreniere and J. Gilliland, 'Making the Inscrutable, Scrutable: Race and Space in Victoria's Chinatown', *BC Studies* 69, Spring 2011, 51–80.

43 The federal census was done on the *de jure* model, meaning that people were enumerated at their usual place of residence, rather than where they were found by census enumerators.

44 K. Roueche, *A Fairfield History*, Victoria, BC: Trafford Publishing, 2005, 51, 67.

45 Dunae et al., 'Making the Inscrutable, Scrutable'.

46 Wetherell and Potter, *Mapping the Language of Racism: Discourse and the Legitimation of Exploitation*. London and New York: Harvester Wheatsheaf and Columbia University Press, Teun Adrianus van Dijk, *News as Discourse*, Hillsdale, NJ: L. Erlbaum, 1988.

47 We explore this in more detail in Dunae et al., 'Making the Inscrutable, Scrutable'.

48 A. Lester, 'Colonial and Postcolonial Geographies', *Journal of Historical Geography*, 29(2), 2003, 277–88. He is drawing here on the work of Catherine Hall.

Bibliography

J. Barman, 'Aboriginal Women on the Streets of Victoria: Rethinking Transgressive Sexuality during the Colonial Encounter', in K. Pickles and M. Rutherdale (eds), *Contact Zones: Aboriginal and Settler Women in Canada's Colonial Past*, Vancouver: UBC Press, 2005, 205–13.

J. Barman, *French Canadians, Furs and Indigenous Women in the Making of the Pacific Northwest*, Vancouver: UBC Press, 2014.

J. Barman and B. M. Watson, *Leaving Paradise: Indigenous Hawaiians in the Pacific Northwest, 1878–1898*, Honolulu: University of Hawaii Press, 2006.

P. A. Baskerville, *Beyond the Island: An Illustrated History of Victoria*, Burlington, ON: Windsor Publications, 1986.

C. A. Bayley, 'Early life on Vancouver Island', Bancroft Library, University of California at Berkley MSS P-C 3.

J. Bell to J. Thompson, 27 February 1859, BC Archives, Add Mss 412, Box 8, file 5.

H. Bowsfield (ed.), *Fort Victoria Letters 1846–1851*, Winnipeg: Hudson's Bay Record Society, 1979.

G. Brazier et al. (eds), *Fort Victoria Journal*, Hudson's Bay Company Archives, B.226/ a/1 www.fortvictoriajournal.ca.

British Colonist, 1859–83.

British Columbia, *Papers Connected with the Indian Land Question*, Victoria: R. Wolfenden, 1875, reprinted 1987.

G. Caesar et al. 'Victoria's Secret: Dance Halls of Early Victoria, 1859–1866', http://web.uvic.ca/vv/student/dance_halls.

S. Cracroft, 'Lady Franklin Visits the Pacific Northwest, February to April 1861 and April to July 1870', in D. B. Smith (ed.), *Victoria: Provincial Archives of British Columbia Memoir* 11, 1974.

W. Duff, 'The Fort Victoria Treaties', *BC Studies*, 3, Fall 1969, 3–57.

P. Dunae (ed.), *ViHistory*, http://vihistory.ca./

P. Dunae, 'Geographies of Sexual Commerce and the Production of Prostitutional Space: Victoria, British Columbia, 1860–1914', *Journal of the Canadian Historical Association*, 2008.

P. Dunae, J. Lutz, D. Lafreniere, and J. Gilliland, 'Making the Inscrutable, Scrutable: Race and Space in Victoria's Chinatown', *BC Studies* 69, Spring 2011, 51–80.

P. Dunae, D. Lafreniere, J. Gilliland, and J. Lutz, 'Dwelling Places and Social Spaces: Revealing the Environments of Urban Workers in Victoria Using Historical GIS', *Labour/Le Travail* 72, Fall 2013, 37–73.

S. Elden, *Understanding Henri Lefebvre: Theory and the Possible*, London: Continuum, 2004.

E. Fawcett, *Some Reminiscences of Old Victoria*, Toronto: William Briggs, 1912.

C. N. Forward, 'The Evolution of Victoria's Functional Character', in A. F. J. Artibise (ed.), *Town and City: Aspects of Western Canadian Urban Development*, Regina: Canadian Plains Research Center, University of Regina Press, 1981.

H. Gregson, *A History of Victoria, 1842–1970*, Victoria, BC: Victoria Observer Publishing Co., 1970.

P. Hankin to A. Kennedy, 8 February 1866, as enclosed in A. Kennedy to E. Cardwell, 13 February 1866, National Archives of the United Kingdom, 3246 CO 305/28.

S. Hall and P. du Gay (eds), *Questions of Identity*, London: Sage, 1996.

J. Hendrickson (ed.), 'Vancouver Island, Assembly Minutes', *Journals of the Colonial Legislatures 2*, Victoria: BC Archives, 1981.

D. Humphreys, *The Islander*, 1 November 1999.

D. James to A. Barclay, June 15, 1854, BC Archives, A/C/20/Vi2A.

G. Keddie, *Songhees Pictorial: A History of the Songhees People as Seen by Outsiders, 1790–1912*, Victoria, BC: Royal British Columbia Museum, 2003.

C. Killian, *Go Do Some Great Thing: The Black Pioneers of British Columbia*, Burnaby: Commodore, 2008.

A. King, 'Colonial Cities: Global Pivots of Change', in R. Ross and G. Telkamp (eds), *Colonial Cities*, Leiden: University Press, 1985.

T. Koppel, *Kanaka: The Untold Story of Hawaiian Pioneers in British Columbia and the Pacific Northwest*, Vancouver: Whitecap, 1995.

D. C. Lai, *Chinatowns: Towns within Cities in Canada*, Vancouver: UBC, 1988.

D. C. Lai, *Forbidden City within Victoria: Myth, Symbol and Streetscape of Canada's Earliest Chinatown*, Victoria, BC: Orca Books, 1991.

H. Lefebvre, 'Reflections on the Politics of Space', trans. M. J. Enders, *Antipode* 8(2), 1976, 30–7.

C. E. Leonoff, 'Pioneer Jewish Merchants of Vancouver Island and British Columbia', *Canadian Jewish Historical Society Journal* 8(1), Spring 1984, 12–34.

A. Lester, 'Colonial and Postcolonial Geographies', *Journal of Historical Geography* 29(2), 2003, 277–88.

J. Lutz, '"Relating to the Country": The Lekwammen and the Extension of European Settlement, 1843–1911', in R. Sandwell (ed.), *Beyond the City Limits: Essays from British Columbia*, Vancouver: UBC Press, 1999, 17–32.

J. Lutz, 'Work, Sex, and Death on the Great Thoroughfare: Annual Migrations of "Canadian Indians" to the American Pacific Northwest', in J. M. Findlay and K. Coates (eds), *Parallel Destinies: Canadian–American Relations West of the Rockies*, Seattle: Center for the Study of the Pacific Northwest and University of Washington Press, 2002, 80–103.

J. Lutz, *Makúk: A New History of Aboriginal White Relations*, Vancouver: UBC Press, 2008.

R. Mawani, 'Legal Geographies of Aboriginal Segregation in British Columbia: The Making and Unmaking of the Songhees Reserve, 1850–1911', in C. Strange and A. Basher (eds), *Isolation, Places and Practices of Exclusion*, London: Routledge, 2003, 173–90.

D. Pethick, *Summer of Promise: Victoria 1864–1914*, Victoria, BC: Sono Nis Press, 1980.

T. Ross, 'Then and Now: the Pendray Family', *James Bay Beacon*, August 2014, http://jamesbay beacon.ca/?q=node/1303.

K. Roueche. *A Fairfield History*, Victoria, BC: Trafford Publishing, 2005.

P. E. Roy. *A White Man's Province: British Columbia Politicians and Chinese and Japanese Immigrants, 1858–1914*, Vancouver: UBC Press, 1989.

E. Said, *Orientalism*, New York: Vintage, 1978.

E. Said, *Culture and Imperialism*, New York: Vintage, 1994.

R. Shields, 'Henri Lefebvre', in A. Elliot and B. S. Turner (eds), *Profiles in Contemporary Social Theory*, London: Sage, 2001.

A. Smedley and Brian. *Race in North America: Origin and Evolution of a Worldview*, Boulder, CO: Westview, 2012.

T. A. van Dijk, *News as Discourse*, Hillsdale, NJ: L. Erlbaum, 1988.

Victoria Gazette, 1859–60.

Victoria Press, 1862.

W. P. Ward, *White Canada Forever: Popular Attitudes and Public Policy toward Orientals in British Columbia*, 3rd ed., Montreal and Kingston: McGill-Queen's University Press, 2002.

M. Wetherell and J. Potter, *Mapping the Language of Racism: Discourse and the Legitimation of Exploitation*, New York: Columbia University Press, 1992.

W. A. G. Young to Mayor of Victoria, Colonial Secretary Correspondence Outward to Mayor and Council of Victoria, 9 Sept. 1862–25 April 1864, British Columbia Archives, CAA 30.1J 7.

PART IV

Spatial rural and environmental history

INTRODUCTION TO PART IV

Ian Gregory, Don DeBats, and Don Lafreniere

Arguably Geographical Information Systems (GIS) originated in the 1960s with the Canadian Land Inventory (CLI) that was designed as a computer system to catalogue and study Canada's environment. Similarly ESRI, the dominant player in GIS software since the 1970s, started as a not-for-profit environmental consultancy that developed ArcInfo for internal purposes.[1] Environmental research has thus been fundamental to the development of GIS in the mainstream as well as in academic history. The reasons for this are two-fold: first, environmental phenomena are well-suited to a GIS-style data model that combines spatial data, representing where features are, with attribute data that represent what the features are. Second, many of the questions asked in environmental studies tend to be explicitly geographical – why are things happening in these places? Why are they not happening in other places? What else is happening in these places? How did these places change over time?

Given this, it is perhaps not surprising that rural and environmental studies are also among the areas where historical GIS (HGIS) has made the most progress. Two of the classics in the field are Brian Donahue's *The Great Meadow: Farmers and Land in Colonial Concord*[2] and Geoff Cunfer's *On the Great Plains: Agriculture and Environment*.[3] These two books cover very different times, places, and scales. *The Great Meadow* studies agricultural land use around a single town in colonial-era Massachusetts, while *On the Great Plains* takes a long-term perspective to explore environmental degradation on the Great Plains with a focus on the causes of the Dust Bowl in the 1930s. In both cases, they produce pieces of revisionist history that challenge well-established orthodoxies: namely that colonial farmers were inefficient and negligent, and that the Dust Bowl was caused by over-intensive agriculture and poor farming practices in the 1930s. In both cases, GIS is fundamental to the authors' research, but the implications of the studies go far beyond historical GIS to be relevant to a wide sweep of environmental historians. These are far from the only HGIS studies that focus on rural and environmental issues. Some very early work in this area includes A. W. Pearson and P. Collier's study of agriculture in mid-nineteenth-century Wales[4] and B. M. S. Campbell's studies of medieval England.[5] More recent work includes P. C. Brown's work on nineteenth-century Japan,[6] R. Hunter's study of sixteenth-century New Spain,[7] N. Levin et al.'s study of twentieth-century Israeli wetlands,[8] and M. G. Hatvany's study of salt marshes in the St Lawrence Estuary.[9]

This section contains four chapters. In the first Geoff Cunfer provides an overview of his work on the Great Plains and shows how a wide range of sources covering a large geographical area and a long period of time can be integrated to challenge existing orthodoxies. Gustavo Velasco uses an ingenious way of investigating the spread of population through western Canada in the late nineteenth century. Rather than using traditional sources such as census data, Velasco uses postal records as a proxy to model how population spread across Canada in this period. Moving over the Atlantic and to a much more localized scale, Nigel Walford reports on a wide range of work looking at agricultural change in a small area of south of England through the twentieth century. Finally, Robert Schwartz, moves from the quantitative to the qualitative, using text mining approaches to explore British responses to overfishing and French responses to American cereal imports in the nineteenth century. Between them, these papers illustrate the range of sources, approaches, and findings that GIS enables in the study of rural and environmental history.

Notes

1 I. N. Gregory and P. S. Ell, *Historical GIS: Technologies, Methodologies, Scholarship*, Cambridge: Cambridge University Press, 2007, 12–13.

2 B. Donahue, *The Great Meadow: Farmers and Land in Colonial Concord*, New Haven, CT: Yale University Press, 2004.

3 G. Cunfer, *On the Great Plains: Agriculture and Environment*, College Station, TX: Texas A&M University Press, 2005.

4 A. W. Pearson and P. Collier, 'The Integration and Analysis of Historical and Environmental Data Using a Geographical Information System: Land Ownership and Productivity in Pembrokeshire c.1850', *Agricultural History Review* 46, 1998, 162–76.

5 B. M. S. Campbell, *English Seigniorial Agriculture 1250–1450*, Cambridge: Cambridge University Press. See also K. Bartley and B. Campbell, '*Inquisitiones Post Mortem*, GIS, and the Creation of a Land-Use Map of Medieval England', *Transactions in GIS* 2, 1997, 333–46.

6 P. C. Brown, 'Corporate Land Tenure in Nineteenth Century Japan: A GIS Assessment', *Historical Geography* 33, 2005, 99–117.

7 R. Hunter, 'Methodologies for Reconstructing a Pastoral Landscape: Land Grants in Sixteenth-Century New Spain', *Historical Methods* 43, 2010, 1–13.

8 N. Levin, E. Elron, and A. Gasith, 'Decline of Wetland Ecosystems in the Coastal Plain of Israel during the 20th Century: Implications for Wetland Conservation and Management', *Landscape and Urban Planning* 92, 2009, 220–32.

9 M. G. Hatvany, 'Growth and Erosion: A Reflection on Salt Marsh Evolution in the St. Lawrence Estuary Using HGIS', in J. Bonnell and M. Fortin (eds), *Historical GIS Research in Canada*, Calgary: University of Calgary Press, 2014, pp. 181–95.

16

RE-EVALUATING AN ENVIRONMENTAL HISTORY ICON

The American Dust Bowl

Geoff Cunfer

The iconic Dust Bowl myth

In the nineteenth century American settlers invaded the Great Plains. Moving west into ever-drier lands, they occupied a fragile environment then proceeded over the next fifty years to create one of the worst environmental disasters in world history. Through a combination of ignorance, greed, and hubris they plowed soils that should have been left in grass. Having stolen the land from Indians and destroyed vast herds of buffalo, Americans now plowed up sod that held the earth intact, exposing the land to wind erosion and eventually to the devastating dust storms of the 1930s. Driven by capitalist avarice, powered by new machinery, and concerned only about short-term profits, homesteaders recklessly devastated a pristine wilderness. The ultimate consequence was environmental destruction, widespread impoverishment, and traumatic out-migration. The history of the Dust Bowl reminds us of the need for careful stewardship of the natural environment. It reveals the risks inherent in unregulated capitalism and self-interested exploitation of fragile environments. It is a cautionary tale to guide our future engagement with the natural world.

Federal bureaucrats in President Franklin Roosevelt's New Deal administration were the first to articulate the Dust Bowl Myth encapsulated above.[1] Building a political case for land use reform in the depths of the 1930s Depression, they proposed that the nation's frontier era of free access to seemingly unlimited natural resources had come to a close.[2] No longer could Americans simply move west to exploit new resources after exhausting those behind them. In the modern, industrial world, New Dealers argued, natural resources were in limited supply and only a national

Figure 16.1 Understanding that images can be more powerful than words, *The Future of the Great Plains* opened with 'A Pictorial Survey of the Great Plains,' a visual representation of the Dust Bowl Myth: 'The Great Plains of the Past. As the first white settlers drove their covered wagons slowly westward across the seemingly limitless expanses of the Great Plains they found the Red Man living in rude but productive harmony with Nature. The Winter snows and Spring rains clothed the land in grass; forests covered the foothills and lined the upper reaches of clear streams; the buffalo furnished food, clothing, shelter, and other simple necessities without diminishing in number. Living as he did, the Indian could laugh at the burning sun, the strong but dustless winds. He had made his truce with them, and with the land.'

Figure 16.2 The second image illustrated the region's environmental decline from pristine grassland to impoverished and eroded wasteland: 'The Great Plains of the Present. The White Man knew no truce. He came as a conqueror first of the Indian, then of Nature. Today we see foothills shorn of timber, deeply gullied, useless or rapidly losing their fertile soil under unwise cultivation; the fertile earth itself drifts with the wind in sand hills and in dust clouds; where once the grass was rank, cattle nibble it to the scorched roots; the water of streams and the ground waters too often irrigate poor land, leaving the richer thirsty; men struggle vainly for a living on too few acres; the plough ignores Nature's "Keep Off" signs; communities, for all the courage of the people, fall into decay, with poor schools, shabby houses, the sad cycle of tax sales, relief, aimless migrations.'

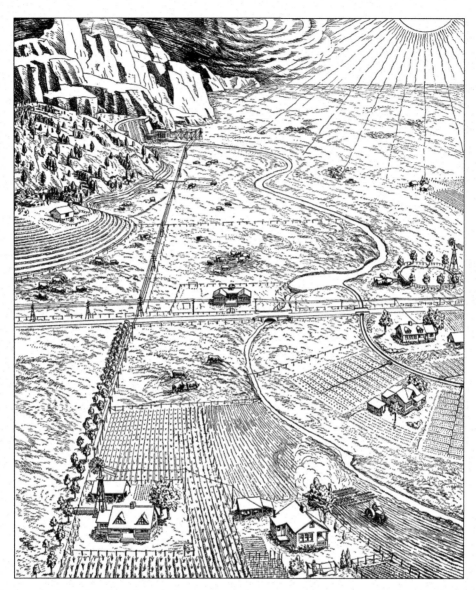

Figure 16.3   Finally, a rosy future built upon New Deal land use reforms: 'The Great Plains of the Future. The land may bloom again if man once more makes his peace with Nature. Careful planting will give him back the foothill trees; terracing will save lush foothill farms; a wise use of the land will restore grass for controlled grazing; fewer and larger farms on scientifically selected sites may yield under the plough a comfortable living; dams will hold back the waters from rains and melting snow, giving power and controlling the flow of the life-giving streams; springs may be developed, water pumped by windmills to water cattle, moisture held in the soil by scientific methods of tillage; by such means the life of man on the land may be made happier, more prosperous, more secure. The sun, the wind, the rain, the snow can be friends of man, not enemies. This is no Utopian dream. It is a promise, to be realized if we will.'

government operating in the public interest and guided by scientific expertise could manage the nation's patrimony for the good of all citizens and in trust for future generations (Figures 16.1–16.3). Under a previous President Roosevelt the federal government had, in the 1890s, begun to conserve forests and parks on public land; now the government aimed to extend its management of natural resources to include rivers and private property, especially farmland whose soil fed the nation.[3] Thus the literature and documents created by a multitude of New Deal agencies in the 1930s and 1940s presented the Dust Bowl Myth as an explanation and justification for a raft of proposed land use reform initiatives.

Donald Worster rehearsed and revitalized that basic New Deal story in his 1979 book, *Dust Bowl: The Southern Plains in the 1930s*.[4] Constructing his story around the traumatic experience of two counties in the heart of the Dust Bowl, he identified capitalism as the driving force behind farmers' misuse of land, a greedy exploitation of nature that caused disastrous dust storms. Evocatively written, the book became a foundational text of the new sub-discipline of environmental history, assigned to undergraduate students by the thousands. Although other histories of the Dust Bowl published around the same time presented contrasting interpretations, Worster's account became the standard version.[5] The Dust Bowl Myth persists through widespread repetition. It returned to public prominence in journalist Timothy Egan's 2006 bestseller, *The Worst Hard Time* and in filmmaker Ken Burns' 2012 PBS documentary, 'The Dust Bowl.'[6]

This chapter reviews my own scholarly journey reconsidering and then deconstructing the Dust Bowl Myth. Historical GIS methods provided access to a suite of new historical sources about the Dust Bowl that had been virtually unused by historians. It also presented an opportunity to re-analyze some well-known historical sources. Eventually I proposed a new environmental history narrative of wind erosion and dust storms on the southern plains, one that broadens the spatial scope and chronological extent of the story. GIS made it possible to integrate multiple historical documents based on their spatial location; the result is a narrative quite different from the iconic Dust Bowl Myth.

Traditional sources of Dust Bowl history

The narrative structure of the Dust Bowl Myth rests upon three foundations: 1) a vast body of publications created by New Deal agencies that aimed to solve the Great Depression and the devastating Dust Bowl; 2) an impressive collection of artwork created or supported by those same government agencies; and 3) the recollections of those who lived through it. During the first months of his administration, at the depth of the 1930s economic crisis, Roosevelt and the US Congress created dozens of new federal agencies, the famous 'alphabet soup' bureaus that brought the three-letter acronym to American government. The Agricultural Adjustment Administration (AAA), the Land Utilization Program (LUP), the Soil Conservation Service (SCS), the Farmers' Home Administration (FHA), and many others set out to reform American agriculture, to raise farm incomes and standards of living, and to solve the soil erosion crisis. Combining political propaganda and reformers' zeal with a sincere interest in improving citizens' lives, New Dealers went to work. They conducted

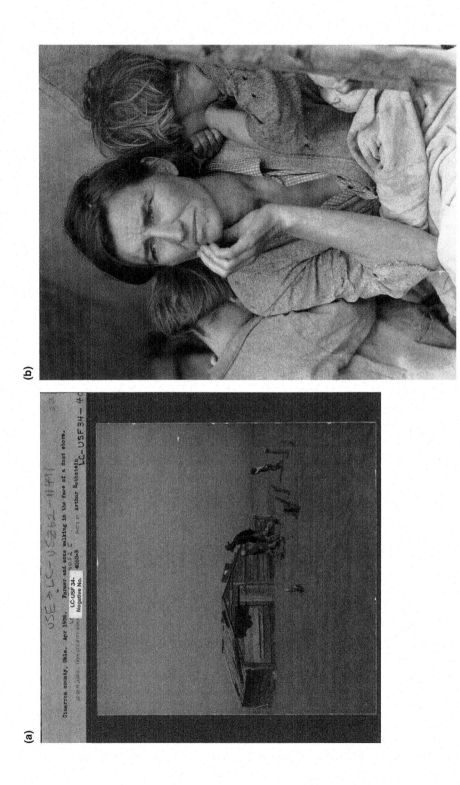

Figure 16.4 Iconic Farm Security Administration photographs from the Library of Congress Prints and Photographs Division's FSA-OWI Collection: (a) Arthur Rothstein, 'Farmer and sons walking in the face of a dust storm. Cimarron County, Oklahoma.' April 1936, LC-USZ62-11491; (b) Dorothea Lange, 'Destitute pea pickers in California. Mother of seven children. Age thirty-two. Nipomo, California.' February 1936, LC-USZ62-95653.

surveys and investigations, wrote a multitude of reports, designed action plans, and generated a vast historical record built around the assumption that misuse of land was the primary cause of the Dust Bowl.[7] These documents became the primary foundation for historians studying the period.

Roosevelt was also a master of political communication through new media. For example, he deftly exploited radio – a novel technology only recently installed in most American homes – to engage the public through weekly 'fireside chats'. In the Resettlement Administration (RA), later reconfigured as the Farm Security Administration (FSA), publicist Roy Stryker assembled world-class photographers and dispatched them throughout the nation to capture images of drought, dust storms, and economic devastation.[8] Virtually inventing the genre of modern documentary photography, such leading lights as Dorothea Lange and Arthur Rothstein produced hundreds of thousands of photos that reveal the extent of suffering during the Depression (Figure 16.4).[9] The same agency produced the now-classic 1936 Pare Lorentz documentary film, 'The Plow that Broke the Plains.'[10] Songwriter Woody Guthrie (an occasional employee of the New Deal's Bonneville Power Authority) crafted 'Dust Bowl ballads' describing the life and experience of poor farmers in the region.[11] Most prominently, after writing a seven-part story in the *San Francisco News* about the Resettlement Administration's migrant farm worker camps, author John Steinbeck penned *The Grapes of Wrath*, one of the greatest American novels.[12] The book opens with an Oklahoma dust storm and then follows the Joad family's exodus from a devastated southern plains. Taken as a whole, the New Deal created a wealth of artwork, much of it in the public domain, that structured Americans' perception of the Dust Bowl for generations to come. Historians have depended heavily on both the bureaucratic publications and the artistic representations created by New Deal agencies during the 1930s.

Another important source for historians has been oral history accounts. Worster interviewed numerous aged farmers who still remembered the Dust Bowl in the 1970s. Egan's *Worst Hard Time* is built around interviews, and Burns' film revolves around a handful of interviews with the last remaining elderly plains residents, people who had experienced the Dust Bowl as young children. Virtually all professional and popular histories of the Dust Bowl have depended on these three types of evidence: New Deal agency documents, New Deal artistic products, and oral history interviews. My exploration of the event began with these same sources, but Historical GIS methods provided an opportunity to reinterpret them and then to bring new sources to bear. The result was a different understanding of the causes and chronology of wind erosion and dust storms on the southern plains.

Rethinking the Dust Bowl

At first I accepted the Dust Bowl Myth as self-evident. I grew up listening to Woody Guthrie's Dust Bowl ballads. I read *The Grapes of Wrath* in high school and was familiar with some of Dorothea Lange's photographs of desperate migrants and Arthur Rothstein's scenes of drifted soils on bleak farms. In an undergraduate environmental history course I read Worster's *Dust Bowl*. By then an environmentalist, the book fit perfectly with my expectations of environmental mismanagement and capitalist exploitation. Only later, as I set out to conduct research for my Masters thesis, did I begin to question some of the assumptions behind the Dust Bowl Myth. The thesis was about land use history in eastern New Mexico, an area targeted by the Resettlement Administration during the 1930s.[13] I happily dug into documents created by that agency. The federal government had determined that farmers there were misusing the land, and offered to buy them out. The FSA eventually repurchased land that had been given free to homesteaders only a generation earlier, and created what later became a National Grassland.[14] An exploration of agency documents revealed graphic descriptions of severe wind erosion and damaging dust storms.[15] Dorothea Lange visited the place in 1935 to snap photographs of blowing dust and drifted soil. But the agricultural census returns revealed that there was very little cropland in this portion of the southern plains. Over 90 percent of Harding County, where the RA program was deployed, remained in native grassland through the 1920s and 1930s, grazed but not plowed for crops.[16] If unwise plowing of vulnerable grassland was the cause of the dust storms, what was the explanation for extensive wind erosion on Harding County's natural pastures? And why was the federal government so anxious to revegetate land that was already in native grass?

These questions led to an initial effort at mapping historical sources, and an emergent computer technology – Geographic Information Systems – provided the means to do so.[17] I first used GIS in the mid-1990s to make simple descriptive thematic maps of agricultural census data reporting the amount of cropland in southern plains counties during the 1920s and 1930s (Figure 16.5a). These maps answered a basic question: Where was the plowed land in the 1930s? If the Dust Bowl Myth was correct, the worst dust storms should more or less correlate with this map of cropland. But where, exactly, were the dust storms? Further research revealed a set of archival maps created by New Deal agencies that located the worst erosion areas at several time points (Figure 16.6). Finally, everyone agreed that dust storms were a result of misused land in combination with drought. Where was the drought worst? A map of weather data answered the question (Figure 16.5b). These descriptive GIS maps provided new information about the spatial relations of environmental conditions in the 1930s.

These primary sources were not new; other historians had consulted weather station data for specific locations or used census information about individual counties, and some of the dust storm maps appeared in Worster's book.[18] GIS, however, made it possible to broaden the spatial scope of analysis. Rather than a case study approach, the wider maps revealed the extent of plow-up over several hundred counties. Rather than citing weather statistics about one town, it became possible to assess drought across an entire region. Importing maps for multiple time points into a PowerPoint slide show created animated sequences of change over time. For example, census data revealed the progressive expansion of crop agriculture at ten time points through 65 years and an annual weather sequence illustrated the high fluctuation of rainfall through half a century after 1895.[19]

But the most powerful aspect of the GIS, previously unavailable to scholars, was the ability to combine multiple primary sources based on their spatial location (what GIS specialists call 'overlay analysis'). Overlay maps directly compared land use and

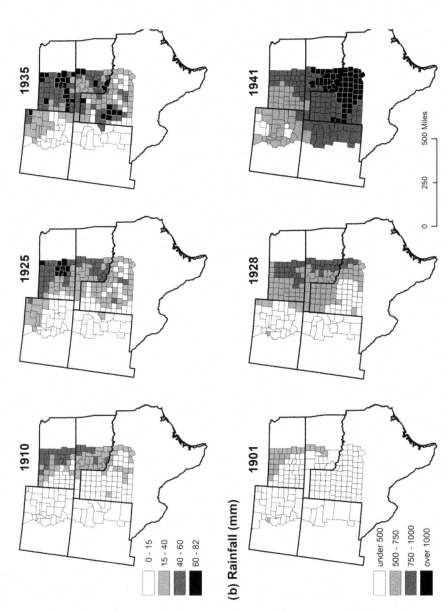

Figure 16.5 Descriptive thematic maps: (a) Percent of total county area devoted to cropland, southern Great Plains, 1900–45, from US Censuses of Agriculture; (b) Rainfall in southern Great Plains counties, examples of dry, moderate, and wet years, from T. R. Karl, C. N. Williams, Jr., F. T. Quinlan, and T. A. Boden, United States Historical Climatology Network (HCN) Serial Temperature and Precipitation Data, Environmental Science Division, pub. no. 3404, Carbon Dioxide Information and Analysis Center, Oak Ridge National Laboratory, Oak Ridge, Tennessee, National Climatic Data Center, Arizona State University, and Oak Ridge National Laboratory, Global Historical Climatology Network (GHCN).

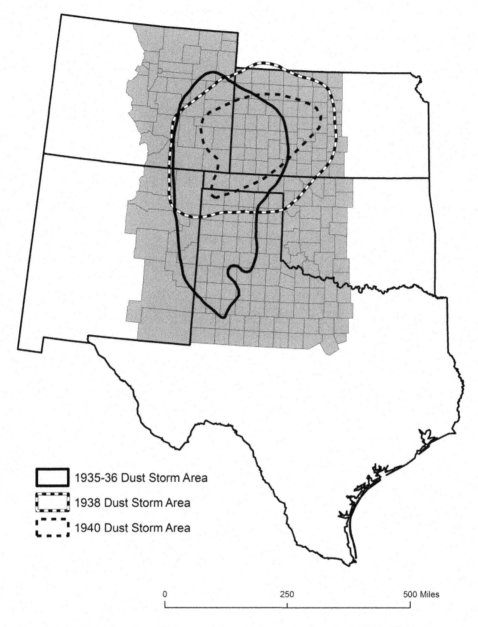

Figure 16.6 Southern Great Plains counties and dust storm locations, 1935–40.

Source: 'Great Plains Area' map, Soil Conservation Service, March, 1954, National Archives and Records Administration, College Park, MD, RG 114, Entry 5, 330/c/17/1–2; 'The Dust Bowl: Agricultural Problems and Solutions,' US Department of Agriculture Editorial Reference Series 7, 15 July 1940, NOAA Central Library.

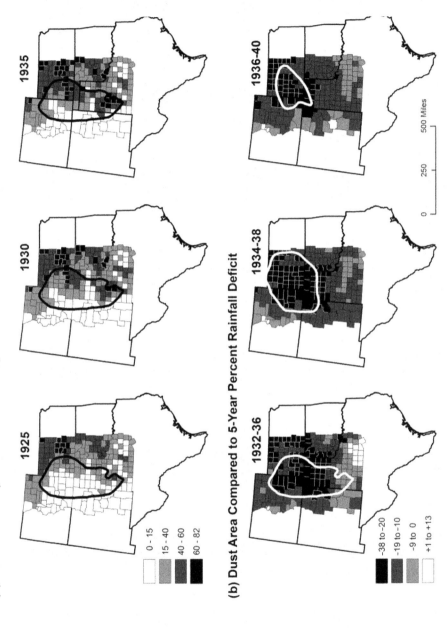

Figure 16.7 Examples of overlay analysis: (a) Percent of total county area devoted to crops compared to the 1935–6 dust storm area; (b) Percent difference from average rainfall for five-year periods preceding dust storm seasons, compared to the 1935–6, 1938, and 1940 dust storm areas.

dust storm locations (Figure 16.7a) or drought and dust storm locations (Figure 16.7b). The results – now analytical rather than only descriptive – created significant doubt about the Dust Bowl Myth. Some of the worst wind erosion happened in places with extensive plowing, but a lot of drifting soil also occurred where most land remained in native grass. And through time it appeared that the dust storms tracked shifting drought rather than plow-up. There appeared to be more to the environmental history of the Dust Bowl than expected, prompting a full re-evaluation of the topic.

Dust storms before the Dust Bowl

If drought could generate dust storms on land that had never been plowed, then there should have been dust storms in earlier years whenever rains failed. After all, drought was nothing new on the Great Plains. And yet the Dust Bowl Myth asserted that severe dust storms were a novelty in the 1930s. The purported progression went from rapid plow-up in the 1920s to severe dust storms in the 1930s, but no one suspected that dust storms might have existed before the plow-up, right? It turned out that at least one person had investigated earlier dust storms. Kansas historian James Malin, writing from the 1920s to the 1950s, undertook research about past wind erosion and documented scores of nineteenth-century dust storms. A political conservative, a vehement opponent of Roosevelt's New Deal, and an unlikable curmudgeon to boot, modern historians did not take Malin seriously. They considered his rants against Democrats as evidence of political bias.[20] But his documentation was meticulous. In 1946 Malin took advantage of his editorship of *Kansas Historical Quarterly* to publish a 71-page article spread across three consecutive issues. In it he essentially reprinted snippets of primary sources, most of them articles from small-town newspapers that reported dust storms that happened between 1850 and 1900.[21]

Malin's article is tedious to read, but it provides convincing evidence that dust storms were far from new in 1932. Malin did not have access to a computer, let alone GIS software, but I did. I took the opportunity to employ another important function of Historical GIS: re-analyzing previous scholars' research. Each of the nineteenth-century dust storms described in Malin's article could be placed on a map based on the location of the newspaper that reported it. Using the GIS to animate these maps showed the location of reported dust storms across Kansas, year-by-year, over five decades (Figure 16.8).[22]

Malin had concentrated his study in Kansas, but with a growing body of evidence that the Dust Bowl Myth needed revision, I launched a new research project seeking dust storms across the southern plains and as far back in time as possible.[23] The goal was to create a historical geography and chronology of dust storm activity in the century before the onset of the famous Dust Bowl. Traditional archival methods turned up farmer's diaries, explorer's journals, and government publications such as *Monthly Weather Review*, all of which contained occasional references to dust storms. Computer-based internet searches in recently digitized newspaper collections extended Malin's list to include hundreds of additional dust storm

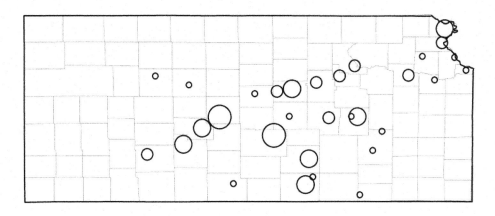

One dust storm

Several dust storms

A month of dust storms

A season of dust storms

Figure 16.8   Kansas dust storms in 1880. Proportional circles appear at each newspaper's city
of publication.

Source: James Malin, 'Dust Storms', *Kansas Historical Quarterly* 14 (1946).

references. Finally, the National Archives collection of frontier military fort weather
records and Smithsonian Institution volunteer weather reports added a couple hundred more dust storm observations from the nineteenth century. The result is an
HGIS database of more than 600 dust storm events on the southern plains between
1830 and 1930, each mapped to a specific location. It is now beyond doubt that
dust storms were regular and sometimes frequent occurrences on the southern
plains long before the first American plow bit into prairie sod. Traditional archival
research, computer-based primary research, and Historical GIS mapping reveal a
broader and lengthier history of wind erosion, one that places the 1930s Dust Bowl
in its proper context.

Exploiting New Deal surveillance

Drought, crop failure, dust storms, and farm abandonment were not new in the
1930s. All of them had happened more than once during the late nineteenth and
early twentieth centuries. But in those earlier events the nation paid little attention
to distress in the Great Plains, and the federal government none at all. Only in the
1930s did new media (radio, newspaper photography, news-reel journalism, and
film) combine with an activist federal bureaucracy to focus the nation's gaze on the
dilemma of southern plains farmers. And, with that attention came a new and
remarkably high level of surveillance. In order to solve the Dust Bowl crisis, bureaucrats had to understand it. Swarms of federal and university scientists implemented

social surveys and field studies to reveal soil and land-use dynamics, agricultural economics, and social inequality. The federal farm programs that subsidized farmers, raised their standards of living, and implemented land-use controls all required careful monitoring. For example, the commodity subsidy programs provided desperately needed cash payments if farmers agreed to reduce the acreage planted in certain crops, including wheat, cotton, and corn. Voluntary participation was nearly universal; now program managers needed a way to verify that farmers had actually reduced their cropland.[24] The result was a new aerial photography program that provides historians with an unprecedented record of actual land use and land cover change from 1938 to the present.[25] Three types of surveillance documents are particularly useful to environmental historians interested in understanding the Dust Bowl and agricultural land use in the twentieth century: 1) reconnaissance erosion maps, 2) aerial photos, and 3) soil surveys. Until GIS became available historians had not used these sources to any significant extent, despite the rich environmental information they contain.

In the National Archives I came across a remarkable cartographic collection: a set of 26 large-scale county maps created in the mid-1930s by Arthur Joel.[26] Part of a reconnaissance survey conducted by the Soil Conservation Service, they provide parcel-level information about the extent and severity of soil erosion in 1936 across 25,000 square miles (6.5 million hectares) of the southern plains.[27] The survey crew reported the amount of soil eroded away, the amount accumulated or drifted into dunes, the type of land use, and the slope and soil characteristics of each farm in the region. It is certainly our best source of information about the conditions of wind erosion in the midst of the Dust Bowl. Other historians had discovered these maps, but none made anything of them; no one had the tools necessary to extract and analyze such rich geographic information.[28] But this source was perfectly suited for GIS analysis. Fully exploiting the maps' detailed information required external research funding and a team approach to historical scholarship. With support from Canada's Social Sciences and Humanities Research Council and the help of several talented graduate students at the University of Saskatchewan, the Historical GIS Laboratory scanned, georectified, and then digitized the entire map series (Figure 16.9).[29] One of the core functions of Historical GIS has been to revive archival maps and bring to bear historical analysis never before possible.

A second source of environmental surveillance information originally created by the New Deal is the now 80-year record of land use and land cover contained in aerial photographs (Figure 16.10a). Beginning in 1936 the federal government flew routine and full-coverage aerial photography missions to ensure that farmers reduced crop acreage as required by subsidy programs. From that time to the present we have detailed aerial photos for the entire nation at multiple time points across nearly a century. Again, the aerial photos were known and relatively easy to access in the archives, but so voluminous and so detailed that historians were rarely able to exploit the information they contained. Historical GIS provided a method to access that valuable record of land-use change.[30] Another team-based historical research project, this one based at the University of Michigan and funded by the US National Institutes of Health, collected a sample of aerial photos from across the Great Plains at five

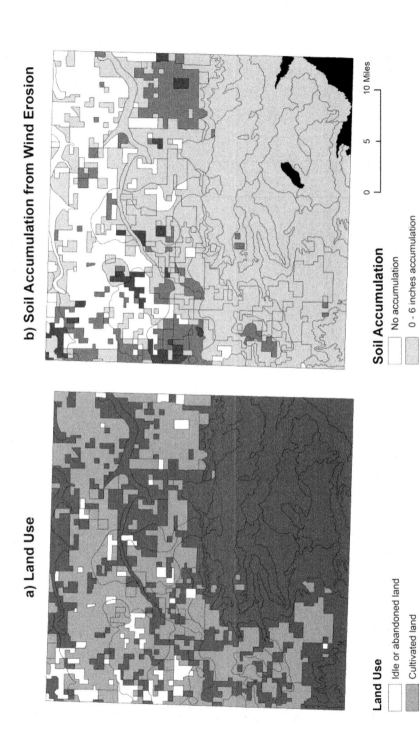

Figure 16.9 Digitized GIS version of land use and erosion information contained in the Moore County, Texas 1936 wind erosion map created by Arthur Joel.

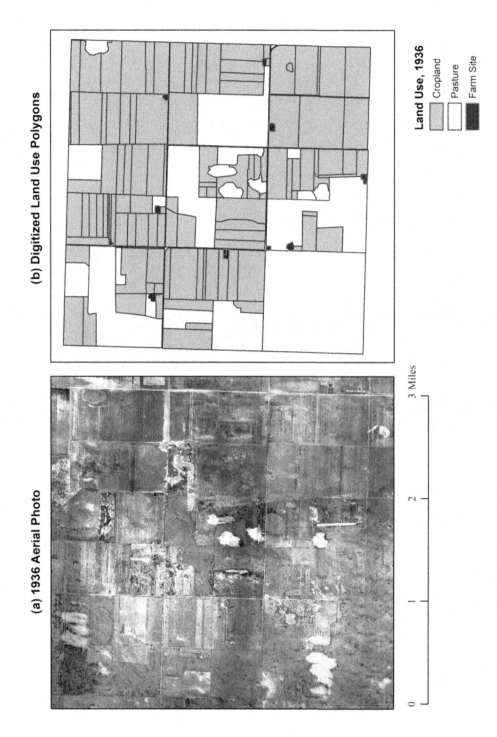

(a) 1936 Aerial Photo

(b) Digitized Land Use Polygons

Land Use, 1936

Cropland
Pasture
Farm Site

0   1   2   3 Miles

Figure 16.10 (a) A georectified aerial photo of nine sections of land in Stevens County, Kansas, 17 August, 1936; (b) The same image digitized in a GIS and classified according to land use.

time points between 1936 and 2006.[31] A team of students scanned, georectified, and digitized the photos into a GIS, then classified each parcel into one of a dozen land use categories (Figure 16.10b).[32] The Joel maps present land use and erosion conditions in the midst of the Dust Bowl; the aerial photos track evolving land use over the next 80 years.

The New Deal also spawned a comprehensive soil survey of the entire United States. Early efforts at systematic soil surveys had begun as early as 1899, but the 1930s crisis prompted a massive investment in scientific soil mapping across the nation, with an overarching aim to guide wise land-use choices by farmers in support of soil conservation.[33] Soil scientists walked the fields of every American county, drew soil map units onto aerial photos (further justifying their creation), and published comprehensive guides and maps of all soil types in each county. The effort took decades and most of the New Deal-era soil surveys were finally published in the 1960s.[34] Useful for farmers, engineers, planners, and a vast array of people, the soil survey is just one of the New Deal's important environmental science legacies. In recent years the US Department of Agriculture has published digital, GIS-ready versions of the nation's soil maps (Figure 16.11).[35] Environmental data are some of

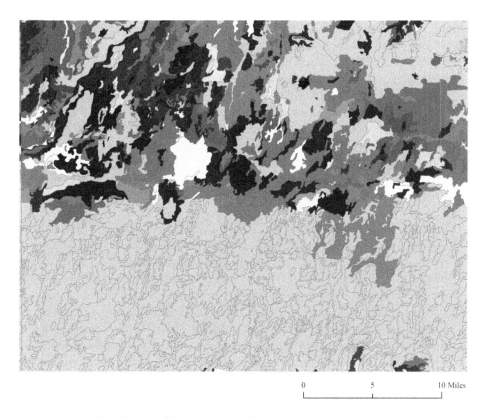

0   5   10 Miles

Figure 16.11   GIS soil map of Stevens County, Kansas.

the most widely available free GIS products. Thus it is relatively simple to bring soil conditions to bear on historical analysis of past wind erosion and land use in the Great Plains.

Conclusions: the integrative power of GIS

GIS technology provides a venue that can bring together a multitude of historical primary sources about the history of agriculture and wind erosion. The result is a 'deep map' of the southern Great Plains, including over 150 years of evolving land use.[36] The GIS organizes these materials spatially, based on the location of events and characteristics. Sources currently contained in the Great Plains Wind Erosion HGIS include explorer journals, military fort weather reports, Smithsonian volunteer weather reports, weather station data, farmer diaries, newspaper articles, archival maps, aerial photos, soil survey information, and agricultural census data. Integrated and overlain, the relationship between multiple types of information, time periods, and locations supports an entirely new line of research questions about the history of dust storms.

Which soils were most likely to erode in the 1930s? The Joel maps combined with soil survey data provide answers. How much pasture eroded compared to cropland? The Joel maps have this information. How accurate was the agricultural census? A comparison between the Joel maps of land use and county agricultural census data provides corroboration. Where were dust storms most common in the century before 1930? Animated maps of dust storms reported at military forts, in local newspapers, by Smithsonian volunteers, and by farm diarists reveal their frequency and spatial extent. What happened to severely eroded land after the 1930s – was it permanently destroyed or did farmers return it to crop production in later decades? The Joel maps combined with aerial photo sequences reveal later developments. These are just a handful of the myriad research questions that the Great Plains Wind Erosion HGIS can address.

This extensive reassessment of Dust Bowl history supports a new narrative of wind erosion and dust storms on the Great Plains:

> Geological conditions and a semi-arid climate created a landscape of shifting soils, many of which originated in wind-blown depositions over tens of thousands of years. In wetter periods, prairie sod covered the land and stabilized soils. Droughts – some of them deep, extensive, and long-lasting – reduced grass cover and exposed soils to periodic blowing. Over thousands of years plains soils alternated between periods of dust storms and wind erosion followed by eras of stabilization. When American farmers entered this landscape in the mid-nineteenth century they did not understand the region's climate, biology, or geomorphology. The soils were rich and grew bumper crops when enough rain fell. During droughts crops failed, cattle sought in vain for grass to graze, and soils blew. Through the first 75 years of agricultural colonization frontier farmers experienced frequent dust storms. Droughts plagued the plains in the 1860s, 1880s, 1890s, and 1910s; in each instance dust storms were widespread and many farmers abandoned

their land. The 1930s drought was worse than any so far experienced by American farmers. It was longer-lasting, dryer, and hotter. Plowed cropland eroded before strong plains winds and so did native grassland, where grasses died and soils, previously stabilized, moved once again. The 1930s decade of wind erosion and dust storms was worse than those experienced during the previous 75 years. For the first time the federal government became interested in the region's condition and sent an army of scientists and bureaucrats, plus massive amounts of money, to address the problem. The New Deal raised farm standards of living and implemented scientific land use management. Farmers are now better able to withstand droughts and dust storms whenever they return to the plains, as they always do in this semi-arid landscape.

Historical GIS has made possible a comprehensive revision of Dust Bowl history. It allows us to understand the 1930s event in a longer chronological context and a broader spatial scope. This story is more nuanced and more interesting than the old morality tale that simply blamed farmers for being too greedy. By now the strengths of Historical GIS methods are evident, but it is worth commenting on some of the challenges to employing GIS for historical research. Much of the information gathered in the Great Plains Wind Erosion HGIS was generated not by an individual but by whole teams of researchers working together in joint projects. While team-based research is common in the natural sciences, it is unusual in history, where individual scholars typically toil away quietly in the archives writing sole-authored books. Such collaborative efforts may be unfamiliar or even uncomfortable for traditionally trained historians. Interdisciplinary teams bring important conceptual benefits but can also create significant friction between scholars coming from different backgrounds. And team-based research almost inevitably requires significant external research funding. Historians who want to undertake this type of study need to apply for grants and organize a variety of resources that are often not necessary for solo historical research. Historical GIS allows the mobilization of new primary sources, the reanalysis of traditional primary sources, the recovery of previously ignored or unusable information, and a high level of integration that is possible with no other technology. It is not surprising that such reassessments of historical events can result in major revisions to our understanding of the past.

Notes

1 The outstanding example appears in *The Future of the Great Plains*, Report of the Great Plains Committee, Washington: GPO, 1936, but the basic narrative can be found repeated in hundreds of government publications from the 1930s and 1940s.

2 H. A. Wallace, *New Frontiers: A Study of the Mind of America and the Way that Lies Ahead*, New York: Reynal & Hitchcock, 1934.

3 For the beginnings of conservation ideology, see S. P. Hays, *Conservation and the Gospel of Efficiency: The Progressive Conservation Movement, 1890–1920*, Cambridge, MA: Harvard University Press, 1959; and R. F. Nash, *Wilderness and the American Mind*, 4th ed., New Haven: Yale University Press, 2001; 1st ed. 1967.

4 D. Worster, *The Dust Bowl: The Southern Plains in the 1930s*, New York: Oxford University Press, 1979.

5 P. Bonnifield, *The Dust Bowl: Men, Dirt, and Depression*, Albuquerque, NM: University of New Mexico Press, 1979; R. D. Hurt, *The Dust Bowl: An Agricultural and Social History*, Chicago, IL: Nelson-Hall, 1981.

6 T. Egan, *The Worst Hard Time: The Untold Story of Those Who Survived the Great American Dust Bowl*, New York: Houghton Mifflin, 2006; D. Duncan and K. Burns, *The Dust Bowl: An Illustrated History*, San Francisco, CA: Chronicle Books, 2012.

7 W. E. Leuchtenburg, *Franklin D. Roosevelt and the New Deal*, New York: Harper & Row, 1963; S. T. Phillips, *This Land, This Nation: Conservation, Rural America, and the New Deal*, New York: Cambridge University Press, 2007; N. M. Maher, *Nature's New Deal: The Civilian Conservation Corps and the Roots of the American Environmental Movement*, New York: Oxford University Press, 2008.

8 B. Ganzel, *Dust Bowl Descent*, Lincoln, NE: University of Nebraska Press, 1984; G. Cunfer, 'Creating the Dust Bowl: Making History, Making Art', digital supplement in A. K. Knowles (ed.), *Placing History: How Maps, Spatial Data, and GIS are Changing Historical Scholarship*, Redlands, CA: ESRI Press, 2008.

9 Most of these photographs are readily available through the Library of Congress's Prints and Photographs Online Catalog (www.loc.gov/pictures/collection/fsa/). Accessed January. 2017; F. Dunaway, *Natural Visions: The Power of Images in American Environmental Reform*, Chicago, IL: University of Chicago Press, 2005, 33–113.

10 Pare Lorentz's Resettlement Administration movies *The Plow that Broke the Plains* and *The River* were rereleased on DVD in 2007 with a soundtrack score by the Post-Classical Ensemble, conducted by Angel Gil-Ordonez (ASIN B000L42J5E).

11 W. Guthrie, 'Dust Bowl Ballads', RCA Victor Records, 1940; reissued by Smithsonian Folkway Records, 1964.

12 J. Steinbeck, 'The Harvest Gypsies', *San Francisco News*, 5–12 October 1936; J. Steinbeck, *The Grapes of Wrath*, New York: Viking Press, 1939.

13 G. Cunfer, 'An environmental history of the Canadian River Gorge', MA thesis, Department of History, Texas Tech University, 1993.

14 For details on the region-wide farm purchase and resettlement efforts, see G. Cunfer, 'The New Deal's Land Utilization Program in the Great Plains', *Great Plains Quarterly* 21, 1987, 193–210; R.D. Hurt, 'The Morton County Land Utilization Project in the Kansas Dust Bowl', *Kansas History* 19, 1996, 140–53; R. D. Hurt, 'Federal Land Reclamation in the Dust Bowl', *Great Plains Quarterly* 6, 1986, 94–106; E. G. Grest, 'The Range Story of the Land Utilization Projects', *Journal of Range Management* 6, 1953, 44–50; H. H. Wooten, *The Land Utilization Program, 1934–1964: Origin, Development, and Present Status*, Agricultural Economic Report no. 85, Washington, DC: GPO, 1965.

15 See e.g. 'Land Acquisition Plan (Part One) Mills Land Use Adjustment Project LA-NM-5-38', MS 11, 14 February 1938, in the Kiowa National Grassland office, Clayton, NM.

16 G. Cunfer, *On the Great Plains: Agriculture and Environment*, College Station, TX: Texas A&M University Press, 2005, 143–63.

17 This first Historical GIS analysis appeared in G. Cunfer, 'Causes of the Dust Bowl', in A. K. Knowles (ed.), *Past Time, Past Place: GIS for History*, Redlands, CA: ESRI Press, 2002, 93–104, and in a revised version in Cunfer, *On the Great Plains*, 150–63.

18 Worster, *Dust Bowl*, 30.

19 Animations in PowerPoint format are available in the digital supplement published with Knowles, *Placing History*.

20 Worster, *Dust Bowl*, 205–6.

21 J. C. Malin, 'Dust Storms, 1850–1900', *Kansas Historical Quarterly* 14, 1946, 129–44, 265–96, 391–413.

22 See the animated sequence in the digital supplement published with Knowles, *Placing History*.

23 This research was supported by Standard Research Grant no. 410-2006-1641 from the Canadian Social Sciences and Humanities Research Council.

24 Cunfer, *On the Great Plains*, 136–9.

25 M. Monmonier, 'Aerial Photography at the Agricultural Adjustment Administration: Acreage Controls, Conservation Benefits, and Overhead Surveillance in the 1930s', *Photogrammatic Engineering and Remote Sensing* 68, 2002, 1257–61; A. Dunlop, 'Progress, Crisis, and Stability: Making the Northwest Plains Agricultural Landscape', PhD dissertation, University of Saskatchewan, 2014.

26 Items 1–20 and Folder 'Erosion Maps of Counties in New Mexico', Shelf 1-5, Compartment 32, Row 17, Stack Area 330, Entry 155, RG 114, Cartographic Research Room, National Archives and Records Administration II, College Park, Maryland. See W. J. Heynen, *Preliminary Inventory of the Cartographic Records of the Soil Conservation Service: Record Group 114*, Washington, DC: National Archives & Records Service, General Service Administration, 1981, p. 39.

27 A. H. Joel, *Soil Conservation Reconnaissance Survey of the Southern Great Plains Wind-Erosion Area*, USDA Technical Bulletin no. 556, Washington, DC: UPO, 1937.

28 The leading historians of the Dust Bowl have all grappled with Joel's published report, but none made use of the maps; see Hurt, *Dust Bowl*, 17–19, 29; Worster, *Dust Bowl*, 216–17; and Bonnifield, *Dust Bowl*, 3, 162–65, 182. The maps are not mentioned or cited in those works, nor in B. Lookingbill, *Dust Bowl, USA: Depression America and the Ecological Imagination, 1929–1941*, Athens, OH: Ohio University Press, 2001; V. Johnson, *Heaven's Tableland: The Dust Bowl Story*, 1947, repr., New York: Da Capo Press, 1974; or J. R. Wunder et al. (eds), *Americans View their Dust Bowl Experience*, Niwot, CO: University Press of Colorado, 1999.

29 At the University of Saskatchewan's Historical GIS Laboratory (www.hgis.usask.ca) Andrew Dunlop, Alice Glaze, John Gow, Elise Pietroniro, Mike St. Louis, Matt Todd, and Gina Trapp all contributed to the project. A summary of the HGIS dataset appears in G. Cunfer, 'The Southern Great Plains Wind Erosion Maps of 1936–1937', *Agricultural History* 85, 2011, 540–59.

30 See e.g. K. M. Sylvester and E. S. A. Rupley, 'Revising the Dust Bowl: High Above the Kansas Grasslands', *Environmental History* 17, 2012, 603–33.

31 This research was supported by the Eunice Shriver National Institute of Child Health and Human Development grant no. R01HD044889. Myron Gutmann was Principle Investigator on the project and major collaborators included Susan Hautaniemi Leonard, Kenneth M. Sylvester, Daniel G. Brown, Geoff Cunfer, Glenn D. Deane, William Parton, and Fridolin Krausmann.

32 K. M. Sylvester, D. G. Brown, G. D. Deane, and R. N. Kornak, 'Land Transitions in the American Plains: Multilevel Modelling of Drivers of Grassland Conversion (1956–2006)', *Agriculture, Ecosystems and Environment* 168, 2013, 7–15.

33 D. Helms, A. B. W. Effland, and P. J. Durana (eds), *Profiles in the History of the U.S. Soil Survey*, Ames, IA: Iowa State University Press, 2002.

34 PDF versions of most of these county soil surveys can be downloaded for free from the US Natural Resources Conservation Service (formerly SCS) website at www.nrcs.usda.gov/wps/portal/nrcs/soilsurvey/soils/survey/state. Accessed January 2017.

35 Download GIS soil survey data from the Natural Resources Conservation Service at http://websoilsurvey.sc.egov.usda.gov/App/HomePage.htm. Accessed January 2017.

36 On the concept of 'deep mapping,' see D. J. Bodenhamer, J. Corrigan and T. M. Harris (eds), *The Spatial Humanities: GIS and the Future of Humanities Scholarship*, Bloomington, IN: Indiana University Press, 2010, 26–8, 97–100, 174–6; and D. J. Bodenhamer, J. Corrigan, and T. M. Harris (eds), *Deep Maps and Spatial Narratives*, Bloomington, IN: Indiana University Press, 2015.

17

THE POST, THE RAILROAD AND THE STATE

An HGIS approach to study Western Canada settlement, 1850–1900

Gustavo Velasco

From the 1850s to 1900, almost two million immigrants from Great Britain, the United States and continental Europe arrived in Canada. Early studies that analyse the frontier of settlement asked, as this chapter does: Where did settlers establish themselves? When did they settle? What was the role of railroads in promoting settlement? These questions have in common the importance of space in the evaluation of the particular area.

Previous analyses that dealt with quantitative or demographic aspects of Western Canada historical development used census records to estimate the region's settlement, modest growth and uneven development. Other studies that focused on more regional or local aspects relied on homesteads records to establish with more accuracy the evolution of settlement in particular areas.[1] While those early studies represent the 'classical view' in the analysis of Western Canada settlement, their approaches need a revision.

The Census of Manitoba of 1870 gives a sense of demographic variables; however, not much can be drawn from it, even if we consider those figures accurate.[2] The first national census in 1871 provided data mainly from the older provinces. Even though Manitoba existed as a province from 1870, the Census of 1871 provided little information about the region's development. Censuses taken every five years (for the Prairie provinces) or ten years (in the case of the federal censuses) describe an incomplete reality in a moment of great frontier dynamic. Settlers moved from place to place frequently. That changing presence of recent migrants and immigrants made census records of very limited use for understanding a society in its making. Similarly, the use of homestead records to understand a pattern of settlement carries a great challenge, as potential settlers were a very mobile population. Applying for a homestead entry in a particular area did not mean a certain possibility of settlement. Some immigrants applied for a homestead entry but, for different reasons, they abandoned the homestead shortly after or never took possession of their parcel at all.

In 1882 alone, for instance, out of 7,400 homestead entries, 3,500 were cancelled.[3] For these reasons, postal and railroad records provide a more detailed picture in time and space.

The increasing availability of new data, digitized maps and digital libraries puts in the hands of researchers new evidence that in some way facilitates the task and circumvents the tiresome endeavour of on-site archival investigation. This chapter takes advantage of the availability of Western Canada sources in digital format and incorporates them into new approaches and methodologies. The use of Geographic Information Systems (GIS) helps to put these new postal and railroad data in historical perspective.

The focus of this chapter will be on the timing and the movement of the frontier of settlement through the analysis of the expansion of the postal and railroad networks from the 1850s to 1900. If the location of post offices represents the presence of nearby settlements then it is possible to ask more questions: Was there a 'pattern' of settlement? If so, does that pattern tell anything about location and distance? Did the arrival of the railroad change the dynamic of settlement? The location of post offices gives in this case a more nuanced understanding of the evolution of the frontier of settlement. The presence of a railroad line or branch after 1878 also demonstrates the influence of means of communications as promoters of certain type of urbanization. From a macro-level analysis, it shows a pattern of occupied space year by year. From a micro-level analysis, it shows with certain precision the formation of communities, villages and towns that emerged during the period. In this way, almost 1,000 post offices have been mapped and geo-referenced in GIS alongside the reconstruction of the Canadian railroad network to 1900.[4]

In addition, postal revenues for individual post offices suggest urbanization and in some cases are an indication of economic activity. Spatial analyses that take into account the distance of post offices, first from rivers and then from the railroad network, allow one to evaluate the importance of means of communications in the evolution of the frontier of settlement. The production of space in Western Canada from the 1850s to 1900 shows the dynamic of capitalist expansion in a new territory. The location of post offices helps us to understand the uneven development of regions and the emergence of small communities that later became nodes of an important railroad network.

The next section describes sources, methodologies and the use of GIS in spatial historical analysis. The following one discusses the influence of the postal and rail-road systems in the building of the Canadian state, with emphasis on Western Canada expansion. Then I discuss empirical evidence and spatial analysis and the last section is the conclusion.

Sources and methodology

This study introduces data from the Annual Reports of the Postmaster General of Canada and incorporates them into GIS to map the dynamic transformation of Western Canada during the second half of the nineteenth century. The use of statistics and new data within a spatial analysis in GIS will allow one to understand the process of settlement in motion and precisely demonstrate the uneven development between regions. In this sense, the use of GIS in economic history analysis becomes an effective way to show spatial transformation and development over time.

Data were extracted from Library and Archives Canada, Postmasters and Post Offices Records. This database is important because the records show the name of the post office, census district, name of the postmasters and the dates they were in service, when it was opened, when it closed (if closed) and where it was located following the Dominion Lands Act notation to register homesteads, i.e. Section, Township, Range, Meridian. Another valuable piece of information was found in the Annual Report of the Postmaster General of Canada published within the Sessional Papers of the Dominion of Canada from 1867 to 1901.[5]

Post offices were geo-referenced by transforming their location from Lands Office notation into decimal coordinates.[6] For instance, Dundee Post Office, a rural post office, was located in section 16, township 11, range 6 east of the principal meridian in Manitoba.[7] The decimal notation once converted was 96.70 decimal degree of longitude west from Greenwich and 49.92 decimal degree of latitude north from the Equator (see Figure 17.1). This transformation of the post office location into a decimal coordinate system helped to situate post offices in a GIS map.

The use of GIS in economic historical analyses is enhancing the scope and broadening historical inquiries across disciplines.[8] The interconnection of space and data plotted on a world map following its geographical coordinates allow researchers to establish with certain precision local or regional economic activity. Historical GIS allows one to connect sparse dots of information into a comprehensive analysis of the region in question. Furthermore, spatial queries can separate different sets of data to provide a more precise information in the micro-level analysis; for instance, when and where an area was occupied by settlers, when it became economically important and so on. In sum, a historical database incorporated into a GIS produces a fine-grained analysis in time and space and as such it is able to create new explanations of historical transformations. This study used QGIS to perform almost all the spatial analysis and maps presentations except for the calculation of post offices' distances to rivers and railroads where ESRI ArcMap was used.

The incorporation of GIS to perform spatial analysis was valuable in embracing a cross-field study where history, geography, economics and politics combine their particular methodologies to bring about a more systematic and comprehensive understanding of the societies of the past. Different projects around the world contribute in a new way to position the fields of history, geography and economics together. For instance, Great Britain Historical GIS developed and extended the limits of the study of geography to include vital census data and poor laws records from the early nineteenth century until 1970.[9] Similarly, the National Historical Geographical Information System (NHGIS) has made available the United States census records from 1790 until 2011 compatible with GIS shapefiles.[10]

In Canada, Historical GIS, although in a developing stage, has recently expanded its studies.[11] The Canadian Century Research Infrastructure (CCRI), a collaborative project of seven Canadian universities with the support of Statistics Canada, completed Canadian censuses from 1911 until 1951.[12] A partial analysis based on a sample of industries and rural studies from the Census of 1871 that analyse county settlements in Ontario have produced, yet limited, a new approach to digitize

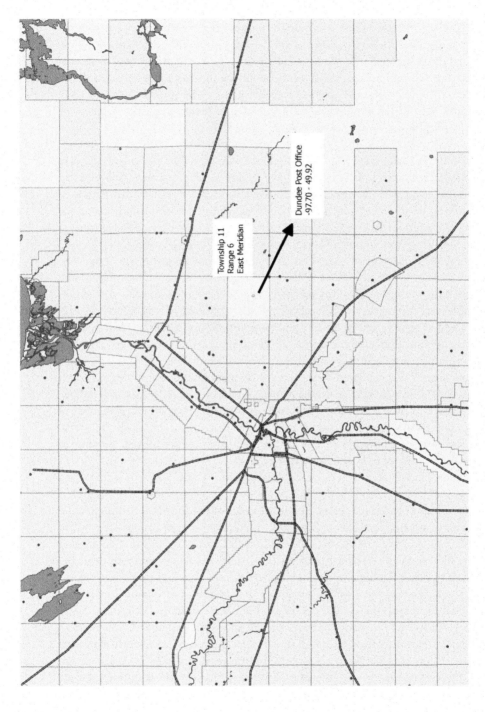

Township 11
Range 6
East Meridian

Dundee Post Office
-97.70 - 49.92

Figure 17.1 Map showing post offices and railroads in Southern Manitoba. Township notation and decimal degree transformation of Dundee Post Office, east of Winnipeg.

Source: Author's design.

census data.[13] GIS work on previous censuses and other geo-referenced historical statistics are yet to be completed.

This chapter contributes in a small part to provide more easily accessible historical spatial data of Manitoba and the North West Territories for future research. Its main feature is the reconstruction of the historical railroad and the expansion of the postal network in time and space. Data incorporated into GIS analysis were collected by this author from digital databases and textual records extracted from published documents, historical maps, government publications, almanacs and gazetteers. It is important to note, however, that maps and government contemporary publications need to be analysed with political history in mind. Published records vary according to the time they were published, the publisher or the political body in charge of the publication. This fact cannot be truer than in the case of railroad maps.

Working with maps published during the period encompasses certain risks in terms of precision and accuracy, not to mention bias. During this investigation this author found sets of maps published from different sources and, possibly, with different agendas in mind. The Department of Interior frequently published maps that highlighted the evolution of Western Canada. In these maps finished and projected railroad lines were frequently plotted alongside the location of schools, churches and post offices. Similarly, the Canadian Pacific Railway (CPR) published its own maps reflecting the extension of the rail network or the proposed extension. Land companies that worked in partnership with rail companies frequently distributed maps to potential settlers with information about the state of development in the region in which they had land interests. Other sources, mainly booklets and pamphlets aimed at promoting the 'West' to potential settlers, produced their own maps. While these records are of invaluable importance, they often reflected the 'booster' spirit of the times and the enthusiasm of a salesperson. Frequently, the extension of the railroad network plotted in different maps did not coincide in time and space when compared with similar maps from different sources or against textual records, for instance the reports of the Postmaster General of Canada (RPGC), who described in his Annual Reports the evolution of the railroad network year by year.

This study takes into account these disparities. The mapping on GIS of the evolution of the railroad network is based on the actual railroad network of North America extracted from Natural Resources Canada.[14] For the purpose of this investigation, I have only included those railroad lines that ran within the old political boundaries established in 1881, in the case of Manitoba, and 1882 when the North-West Territories were divided into the District of Saskatchewan, the District of Assiniboia and the District of Alberta. Similarly, topographic information displayed in maps and representations include only rivers and lakes within the old boundary. To represent the evolution of the network over time, I added a 'year' column to the GIS database to reflect the year this extension became operative according to the Report of the Postmaster General (RPGC), which usually was dated to 30 June of each year. Though highly detailed, the layout of maps on GIS confronts technological constraints, mainly coming from the transformation of a nineteenth-century paper map into a geo-referenced digital version. The plot of rail tracks on paper maps was represented with solid, thick lines and did not reflect any scale or proportion, so the comparison of the railroad lines from the paper maps and the digital version of the actual track suffers from certain imprecisions due to scale problems, geo-referencing stretching and coordinate systems (see Figure 17.2).[15] Taking into account these glitches and once compared with maps of the time, the railroad lines, overall, did not experience substantial changes. The maps on GIS reflect the evolution of the network year by year as it appeared in the RPGC with the incorporation of missed textual information extracted from digitized and geo-referenced maps.

Base GIS shapefiles of Canada and the provinces come from Natural Resources Canada and the dataset of Western Canada townships distribution come from CCRI and Atlas Canada.[16] Additional data incorporated into GIS tables were extracted from Historical Statistics of Canada and Canada Year Book.[17] Certainly, data collected for this study face some restrictions as they are based on a limited number of published records, mainly due to time constraints; nevertheless, the use is valid as no other source based on post offices development in Western Canada has been published at the present.

Post offices revenues were extracted from the Postmaster Annual Report published in the Sessional Papers from 1867 to 1901. The Reports register post offices' gross

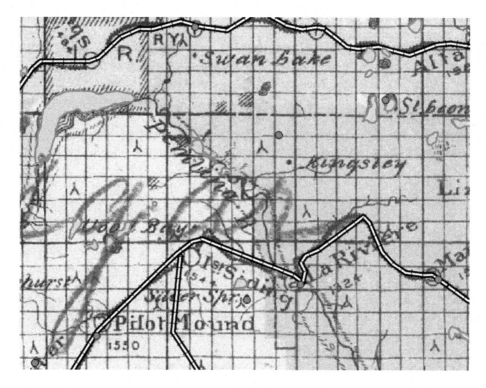

Figure 17.2 Extract of a digitized and geo-referenced map showing the overlapping of a digital rail track over the original railroad map. Author's design based on a Manitoba map of 1897 (excerpt from Bulman Bros. and Co, 'Map of Manitoba Published by Authority of the Provincial Government,' Winnipeg: Manitoba Department of Agriculture and Immigration, 1897, University of Manitoba: Archives and Special Collections).

revenues from the sale of stamps year by year for each post office in operation in Canada. In the case of Manitoba and the North West Territories, complete records began in 1872 until the year 1889. After this year, records show only the performance of those post offices that became 'accounting offices', that is, those offices that in addition to selling stamps acted as postal saving agencies and issued and received money orders and, after 1890, postal notes. The exceptions were the years 1892, 1899 and 1900 when the Annual Reports added an appendix with the revenues of all non-accounting offices in Canada. Taking into consideration those key years where data were complete for all post offices, accounting and non-accounting offices – 1889, 1892, 1899 and 1900 – I performed a simple interpolation between the years that the Report did not provide information from non-accounting offices. In this way, the database was completed with estimated and real revenues from 1872 to 1900.

The cost of spatial control

The formation of the Canadian modern state from the 1850s to Confederation in 1867 and from 1867 to 1900 marked a radical spatial transformation. In 1850, Canada comprised a small territory concentrated mainly in the east coast. The Provinces of Ontario, Quebec, Nova Scotia and New Brunswick in the east, the colony of Vancouver's Island in the Pacific and the Red River Settlement alongside the Red and Assiniboine rivers formed the British North America domains. The Hudson's Bay Company (HBC) maintained control in Rupert's Land and the North-West Territories through a series of posts disseminated across the territory (Figure 17.3). By 1900, the Canadian state exercised control over the whole territory. Land had been divided and large extension allocated to the CPR, HBC and different land companies. An important extension of land was also allocated to settlers. The economic enterprise of forming this extended state was costly indeed. This section analyses the economy of nation building through the expansion of the postal network.

The real dimension of the economic enterprise of building the nation can be seen from the expenditure of the postal system from 1857 to 1914, as Figure 17.4 shows. Except for an unusual surplus shortly after Confederation, the rest of the period the postal system produced deficit. This was normal business in a period of great territorial expansion as the Post Office Department had to provide the necessary funding for the salaries of postmasters and other officers involved in the everyday maintenance of the system. As more post offices opened, more postal routes were incorporated. This expansion demanded important expenditures as postal routes were under private contractors. According to government data, the portion of the Federal Budget destined to cover the cost of the operation of the postal network was very important. In 1867, 7 per cent of the budget was directed to the operation of the postal system reaching more than 10 per cent by the end of the nineteenth century.[18] It is important to note that new buildings destined to be post offices were in the sphere of the Department of Public Works, and, if we include those new and costly buildings, especially after the 1880s, the cost of maintaining the postal network increases substantially.

Canada had long established a postal service in Ontario and Quebec as well as in the other provinces before Confederation but the Post Office Act of 1867 sanctioned

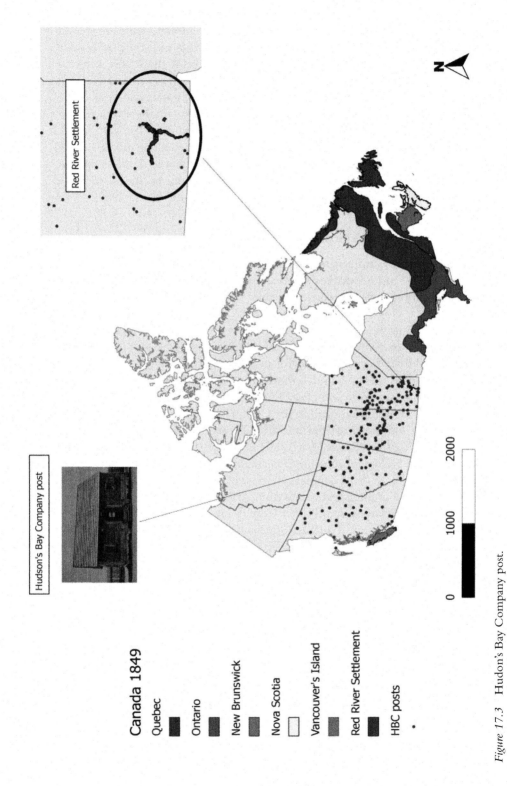

Figure 17.3 Hudon's Bay Company post.

Source: Own design based on HBC post maps and National Atlas Maps, Natural Resources Canada.

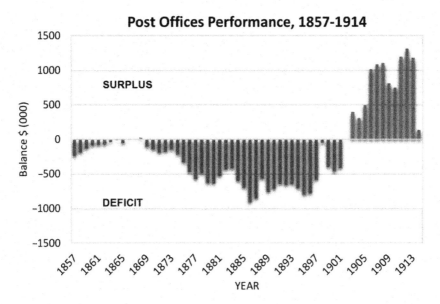

Figure 17.4 Surplus and deficit in the Canadian postal system.

Source: Sessional Papers 1926 and Yearbook of 1868.

in the First Parliament set the basis for the administration of the postal service in the new Dominion. Once Manitoba became a province in 1870 and the Dominion Lands Act of 1872 organized the administration of public land in the west, the expanding location of post offices increasingly connected scarce dots of settlements into the realm of state organization. The Postmaster General was the main figure in the administration of the postal service and had the power to organize the regional or provincial administration. The Postmaster General among other tasks had the authority to open or close post offices and to appoint postmasters. Postmasters received a government salary and a commission according to the operation of the post office. Mail routes were allocated to private contractors.[19]

The location of post offices was very sensitive to the location of settlers from the initial settlement of the Red River. An editorial published in 1860 in the *Nor'Wester* warned local authorities about the lack of communications. The report complained that '[t]he time seems to have come when our post Office system should be organized. The simple machinery that has hitherto preva[i]led is not sufficient to meet the conveniences or wants of the place.'[20] The complaints continued even after Manitoba became a province in 1870. An editorial published in the *Manitoba Free Press* in 1874 stated, '[I]n our intercourse with the new settlers, we found an almost common complaint on the want of post offices and postal facilities . . . It must be as apparent to Governments as to all others, that nothing has a more healthful influence in promoting settlement in a new country than good postal accommodation.'[21] If the press unveiled local concern, no less important was the perception of postal inspectors. As settlements expanded to the West, the federal government sought to organize its domains by establishing a network of post offices distributed according to settlers' necessities. In the Annual Report of 1879, the Postmaster General described the relationship between settlements and post offices:

> The impulse given last summer to the settlement of the unoccupied lands in Manitoba and the contiguous sections of the North-West Territories, rendered it necessary to send the Chief Post Office Inspector to that part of Canada, to ascertain by personal examination and enquiry what was required to give such postal accommodation as might be needed by the new settlements, and to organize accordingly the new Post Routes and Post Offices found to be necessary.[22]

What these fragments suggest is that post offices opened where settlers were already established. Thus, following the location of post offices it might be possible to estimate with more precision where and when immigrants homesteaded; which areas were populated; which others became urbanized over time or what was the role of railroads and post offices.

Figure 17.5 shows a map series illustration of post offices locations alongside the evolution of the extension of the railroad network in time and space. In 1853, only one post office administered the flow of information between the Red River Settlement and the rest of the world. By 1870 post offices were opened in the Red River, north of Winnipeg and to the west along the Assiniboine River. By 1875, post offices opened alongside the Assiniboine River following a predictable pattern as settlements had existed in the area for several years. The graphic also shows a spread into the southern part of the province following the course of the Red River but most importantly, old settlements north of Winnipeg continued growing and, as such, the number of post offices in the area increased.

In 1878, the first railroad line connected the town of Selkirk with Winnipeg. The line extended to Pembina on the American border in 1879. The establishment of the first railroad line in the new territory changed the speed of the flow of information between the Red River and Ottawa as a daily postal route accelerated the connection with the federal government. In terms of business activity, merchants no longer relied on cart transportation or steamers exclusively to receive their supplies; the railroad increased business between the wholesalers in the East and Winnipeg.[23]

By 1880, the expansion of post offices through southern Manitoba and west of the province suggests that the frontier of settlement was moving toward the projected railroad network. Maps that publicized the railroad projected lines appeared to influence the settlement of new farmers. The movement of the frontier of settlement was sensitive to the publicized advance of the railroad network as it appeared in maps included in pamphlets and other pieces of information aimed at luring potential settlers to move westward. As the graphic shows, the opening of new post offices into the actual province of Saskatchewan followed the projected railroad line.

In 1883, the railroad reached Calgary and by 1885, the transcontinental railway was a reality connecting the East with Vancouver. The following fifteen years show a slow railroad development in Saskatchewan and Alberta; yet the track laid the foundation for future development and a number of branch lines connected promissory towns with the Canadian Pacific Railway (CPR) main line. A branch line

Figure 17.5 Time series map of post offices and railroads. GIS author's design based on collected data.

connected Saskatoon and Prince Albert with the CPR main line that passed through Regina. Alberta's southern area increased its economic importance by connecting a branch line with the American railroad. Branch lines in Southern Manitoba gave the impulse and dynamism to new agricultural areas recently settled. By 1900, post offices in Manitoba had spread through the southern and western part of the province, while in Saskatchewan the location of post offices followed the railroad line that boosted urban locations such as Regina in the middle of the province, Saskatoon, and Prince Albert in the north. In the case of Alberta, post offices mushroomed in the old stagecoach corridor that ran from Calgary to Edmonton, which eventually became connected by train in 1892.

It is interesting to note that locations where the railroad line finished its tracks experienced an important increase in the number of post offices; noticeable were the cases of Edmonton, Prince Albert, north of Saskatoon and Yorkton in the northeast part of the District of Assiniboia, close to the Manitoba border. We see the dynamic passage from a fur trade society where the importance of old trader trails and rivers mattered into a settler society embedded with embryonic signs of modernization and urbanization.

Spatial analysis and discussion

The first question that emerges from the evaluation of the transformation experienced by Western Canada in the period may possibly be: Did railroads follow post offices or the other way around? How important was the arrival of the railroad to the development of the region? Did post offices reflect the importance of the transportation network in the development of new regions?

One way to determine the importance of railroads in the opening of post office can be explained through Figure 17.6. For this exercise, we used the location of post offices, the railroad lines and the location of the principal rivers to determine the importance of means of transportations in the selection of settlement. First, we made a buffer zone of 10 kilometres each side of rivers and the railroad lines on a GIS map and then performed a spatial query to determine how many post offices were inside of the 10 kilometres buffer zone. Figure 17.6 clearly shows the importance of, first rivers and then railroads, in the opening of post offices. If we agree that the location of post offices was a clear indication of settlement, then it is safe to suggest where settlers established. As Figure 17.5 showed, the first post offices opened close to rivers, principally the Assiniboine and Red Rivers. Figure 17.6 shows that the graph line that represents the evolution of post offices alongside rivers slowly increases from 1853 when the first post office was opened until 1878. Its growth is more important after that; however, this is not as important as the sheer increase in the total opening of post offices in Western Canada in general. In 1878 the first railroad branch opened in Manitoba and the railroad trend continues to increase and overtakes the number of post offices opened alongside rivers. By 1885 post offices that opened alongside the railroad line increased its importance. What this trend shows is the importance of different means of transportation over time. Until 1885 the number of post offices located along rivers where old settlers were established earlier suggests the importance of a community that still relied on old means of transportation. Rivers were

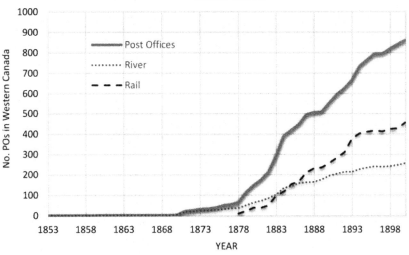

Post Offices within 10 km from rivers and railroads, 1853-1900

Figure 17.6   Spatial query using GIS that shows the expansion of post offices.

used from spring to early autumn to move goods from point to point while old trade routes marked the path to carts and sled dog transportation in winter.

Once the railroad system started its expansion, rivers became less important and it seems that railroad lines displaced the means of transportation traditionally used by the old fur traders. In 1878 more than 50 per cent of post offices were located alongside rivers whilst those near the newly established railroad line were only 15 per cent. In 1885, the expansion of the railroad network gave an important impulse to the establishment of new post offices; 35 per cent were located alongside rivers and 36 per cent were located within 10 km of the railroad. By 1900, these figures experienced a substantial change; 29 per cent of post offices, an important decline, were located within 10 km of rivers while those located within 10 km of the rail network comprised 53 per cent.

As Figure 17.5 showed, the distribution of post offices across the region was very unbalanced. While in southwestern Manitoba post offices cluttered over the whole area, farther west the situation was different. The concentration of post offices in Saskatchewan and Alberta shows a territory in the making, even after the arrival of the railroad. Except for a few locations, the North-West Territories were mainly a rather unconnected space despite the economic and political effort the government put into bringing European immigrants.

Figure 17.7 shows the average distance between post offices over time in Western Canada (7A) and in Manitoba (7B). For this exercise, we performed a GIS distance matrix analysis to obtain a basic descriptive statistic and estimate the relationship between post offices. In this case, we chose the distance between the five nearest post offices as it would not be of any value to estimate the distance between post offices in Manitoba and Alberta, for instance, as there was no close and immediate

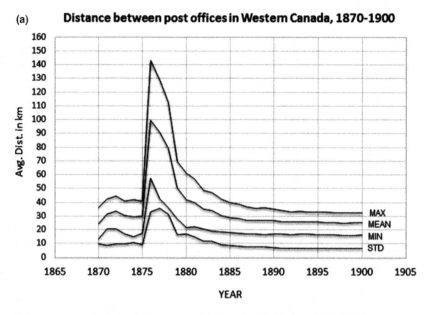

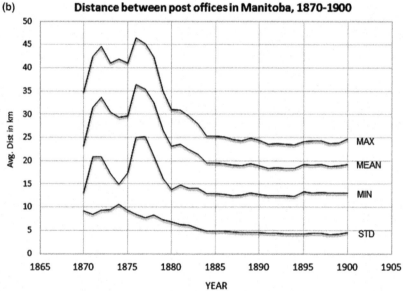

Figure 17.7   Descriptive statistics from GIS distance matrix analysis.

communication between them. A distance matrix analysis uses the centroids of each post office and measures the Euclidean distance between each of them. The descriptive statistics takes the average distance of the selected group of post offices year-by-year. The distance matrix analysis suggests in this way the agglomeration or isolation between communities in the making. In Figure 17.7 (A), the period 1870 to 1875 represents only Manitoba, as no post offices were present in the NWT at that time. The period 1875 to 1880, on the other hand, shows the dynamism of the region.

As the number of post offices increased and extended over a large space, the distance between them increases; the maximum distance in 1876 was 142 km and the minimum 57 km. After 1876, the distance between post offices in Western Canada decreased and by 1885, it stabilized; the average distance until 1900 was about 25 km. In Manitoba, a sense of agglomeration was present earlier. As Figure 17.7 (B) shows, the period 1870–80 was one of great expansion. Post offices opened in isolated areas and, later on, once settlers established and petitioned the government for more postal services, the distance between them decreased. From a maximum distance of 47 km in 1876, the concentration of post offices and settlers in a smaller area determined an average distance of 19 km between post offices by 1900.

Distance between post offices and distance from post offices to the railroad decreased once the frontier of settlement moved westward. The concentration of post offices in determined regions and shorter distances from the post office to the railroad are clear indicators of new urban spaces in the making. This section analyses how influential was the distance of post offices to the railroad to post office revenues. The analysis we aim to perform in this section is to determine how the presence of the rail station and post office provided a clear sign of settlement, economic activity and urban dynamic. Postal revenues were good indicators of the importance of key urban places alongside the railroad. Higher or lower revenues marked the development (or lack of it) of places that eventually became important towns and cities.

This analysis goes from 1878, when the first railroad connection established between Selkirk and Winnipeg, to 1900. As we did before, data were loaded into GIS and then a spatial analysis of distance in ArcMap was performed. Once the

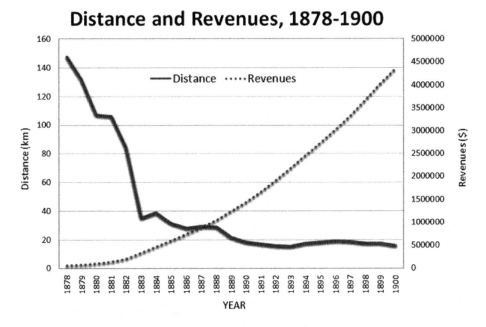

Figure 17.8 Mean distance post offices/railroads and revenues.

Source: Author's GIS spatial analysis.

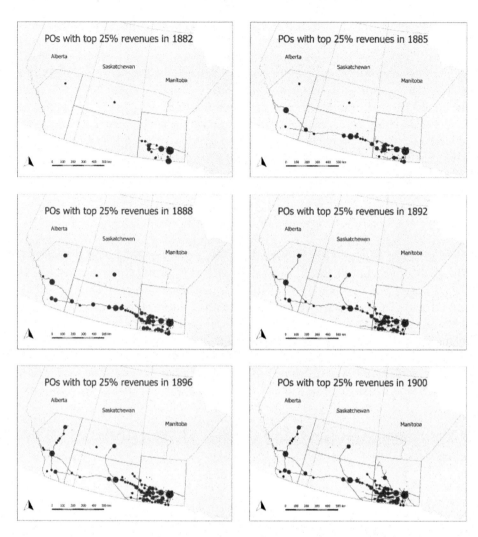

Figure 17.9 Top 25 per cent post offices by total revenues, 1885–1900. GIS author's design.

results were obtained, we performed a descriptive statistics analysis to obtain the mean, maximum and minimum distance. Mean distance and revenues were then computed together (see Figure 17.8).

As Figure 17.8 shows there was a sudden decrease in the mean distance once the railroad reached Calgary in 1883; coincidentally, postal revenues started to experience a big jump, noticeable after 1888 when the mean distance remained at 20km until the end of the period. Figure 17.9 shows a summary of the results on GIS that highlight the importance of the top 25 per cent post offices according to their revenues. We see here a clear indication of the importance of the railroad not only connecting communities but also as the engine of development. During the period 1860–1900 almost 1,000 post offices established in the new areas of settlement; of

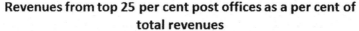

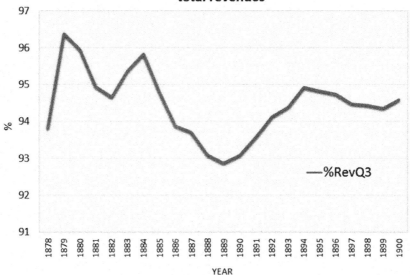

Figure 17.10 Revenues of top 25 per cent post offices compared with total revenues.

Sources: GIS spatial analysis and Postmaster Annual Reports.

those, the ones close to the railroad produced the highest revenues. As Figure 17.10 shows, the top 25 per cent post offices according to their revenues generated more than 90 per cent of revenues for the whole area. The distance of those post offices to the railroad varied over time as new post offices established in the region and railroads expanded their lines or new branches opened, but the mean distance to the railroad was 170 km in 1879, decreasing to 10 km in 1890 and 4.8 km in 1900.

Conclusion

During the second half of the nineteenth century, the expansion of capitalism in vast areas of the world required the spatial transformation of rather unpopulated areas. The settlement of European immigrants alongside the extension of communication networks aimed at creating the conditions for the consolidation of the state and building the nation. The spatial organization of Western Canada after 1870 provides the elements that validate our understanding of the production of space: the incorporation of Prairie lands into the realm of a new capitalist endeavor – first, the appropriation of indigenous communal land, then the transformation of that land into public domain and later the transfer of the land to private property for capitalist exploitation. In so doing, a new produced landscape emerged with the creation of settler communities and the establishment of a state bureaucracy unevenly distributed across regions. A time/space framework shows more clearly a society in the making. In Western Canada, Alberta and Saskatchewan started its development late in the nineteenth century, while Southern Manitoba emerged in this period as the main center of business operations marking the importance of the city of Winnipeg as Western Canada's economic hub.

Post offices locations and the layout of the railroad system help to understand with another empirical evidence the movement of the frontier of settlement year by year. If the opening of post offices in new areas marked the presence of the state ex-post-facto of the presence of settlers, the arrival of the railroad changed that dynamic. As the evidence demonstrated, post offices close to the rail line generated the higher revenues during the period. This latter observation is a clear indication of the presence of a community in its making and the evidence of an important economic activity. Data extracted from different census records produced gaps of meaningful information and did not provide a detailed impression of the dynamic period under scrutiny. Putting together data that were not used before to fill the gap years between censuses provide a more nuanced understanding of historical development.

The use of GIS enriches the understanding of the geography of the past by providing a graphical and empirical evidence of a changing period. Certainly, for an individual researcher, the use of GIS becomes more effective within the limits of small projects like the one represented in this chapter. The construction of bigger databases needs the collaborative effort of different agents as time constraints, accessibility and expenses could jeopardize good intentions and quality investigations. Nevertheless, taking into account those restrictions, the use of GIS enhances the experience of historical research, put on the agenda the study of space by using new data and resources and set the basis for further research and new enquiries.

Notes

1 Among the most important works, see: K. G. Grant, 'The Rate of Settlement of the Canadian Prairies, 1870–1911: A Comment', *Journal of Economic History* 38(2), 1978, 471–3; F. D. Lewis, 'Farm Settlement on the Canadian Prairies, 1898 to 1911', *Journal of Economic History* 41, 1981, 517–35; W. Marr and M. Percy, 'The Government and the Rate of Canadian Prairie Settlement', *Canadian Journal of Economics/Revue Canadienne d'Economique* 11, 1978, 757–67; J. Tyman, 'Patterns of Western Land Settlement', *MHS Transactions Series* 3, 1971, www.mhs.mb.ca/docs/transactions/3/landsettlement.shtml. In addition, perhaps the most influential historical geographical account of Western Canada settlement, W. A. Mackintosh, *Prairie Settlement: The Geographical Setting*, Toronto: Macmillan Company of Canada, 1934.

2 Archives of Manitoba. Manitoba Census of 1870. MG 9 E3, vol. 3, 1870.

3 Canada. Parliament. Sessional Papers, *Annual Report of the Department of the Interior for the Year 1899*, vol. 10, Ottawa: S. E. Dawson, 1900, p. vii.

4 The evolution of the railroad network has been reported in several works and in contemporary maps; however, there is no GIS format of the historical network. This chapter is the first to use a digital version of the Canadian railroad network.

5 A very few post offices did not provide geographical location. I used Historic Sites of Manitoba from Manitoba Historical Society, www.mhs.mb.ca/docs/sites/index.shtml and Geographical Names from Natural Resources Canada, www.nrcan.gc.ca/earth-sciences/geography-boundary/geographical-name/11680 to obtain the coordinates for the different missing places.

6 I used an online service to transform the location into decimal coordinates, www. prairielocator.com.

7 See www.bac-lac.gc.ca/eng/discover/postal-heritage-philately/post-offices-postmasters/ Pages/item.aspx?IdNumber=7340&

8 Among other scholars, this work incorporates GIS to map railroads in the United States. J. Atack et al., 'Did Railroads Induce or Follow Economic Growth? Urbanization and Population Growth in the American Midwest, 1850–1860', *Social Science History* 34, 2010, 171–97.

9 I. Gregory and R. Healey, 'Historical GIS: Structuring, Mapping and Analysing Geographies of the Past', *Progress in Human Geography* 31, 2007, 640.

10 See NHGIS online resources at www.nhgis.org/.

11 Recently an edited volume by Canadian scholars across the disciplines put together a welcoming initial work that dealt with space or historical space from different point of views. See M. Fortin and J. Bonnell (eds), *Historical GIS Research in Canada (Canadian History and Environment)*, vol. 2, Canadian History and Environment, Calgary: University of Calgary Press, 2014.

12 C. Gaffield, 'Conceptualizing and Constructing the Canadian Century Research Infrastructure', *Historical Methods: A Journal of Quantitative and Interdisciplinary History* 40, 2007, 54–64.

13 An interesting project of Canadian industries are mapped in 'Canadian Census of Industrial Establishments 1871', 2008-1982, www.canind71.uoguelph.ca/index.shtml and 'Rural History | University of Guelph', 2004, www.uoguelph.ca/ruralhistory/resources/ GIScaseStudy.html.

14 Canada. Natural Resources Canada, 'GeoBase – List of Available Datasets', www.geobase. ca/geobase/en/search.do?produit=nrwn&language=en.

15 This is a common problem for every researcher. See for instance J. Atack, 'On the Use of Geographic Information Systems in Economic History: The American Transportation Revolution Revisited', *Journal of Economic History* 73, 2013, 313–38. A similar issue was raised in W. G. Thomas, 'Map Inaccuracies in Railroad Sources', *Railroads and the Making of Modern America*, 2011, http://railroads.unl.edu/views/item/mapping?p=4.

16 Canada, 'GeoBase – List of Available Datasets.'

17 Statistics Canada, 'Historical Statistics of Canada: Sections', accessed 10 March 2014, www.statcan.gc.ca/pub/11-516-x/3000140-eng.htm; Statistics Canada, 'Canada Year Book (CYB) Historical Collection', 31 March 2008, www65.statcan.gc.ca/acyb_r000-eng.htm.

18 Federal Budget from Historical Statistics of Canada, Series H1-18. Federal government, budgetary revenue, by major source, 1867 to 1975, www.statcan.gc.ca/pub/11-516-x/ sectionh/H1_18-eng.csv. Postal expenditure from Sessional Papers 1926 and Yearbook of 1868.

19 See Canada, Parliament, *The Post Office Act, 1867, and the General Regulations Founded Thereon*, Ottawa: G. E. Desbarats, 1868.

20 'Branch Post Offices', *Nor'Wester*, 14 March 1860, 2.

21 'Deficient Postal Facilities', *Manitoba Free Press*, 30 November 1872, 4.

22 Canada. Sessional Papers, *Annual Report of the Postmaster General for the Year Ending 30th June, 1879*, vol. 5, Ottawa: McLean, Rogers & Co., 1880, p. 9.

23 H. C. Klassen, 'The Red River Settlement and the St. Paul Route, 1859–1870', MA thesis, University of Manitoba, 1963.

18

USING GIS TO TRANSITION FROM CONTEMPORARY TO HISTORICAL GEOGRAPHICAL RESEARCH

Exploring rural land use change in southern England in the twentieth century

Nigel Walford

Restructuring of the agricultural industry of Britain during the twentieth century has arguably had as great an impact on rural landscapes and land use as in any period since the eighteenth century Agricultural Revolution.[1] World War II stimulated post-war changes that have been divided into two main phases labelled the 'productivist' and 'post-productivist' periods.[2] The drive towards a more efficient, productive and scientific mode of operation after World War II is reflected in a change from viewing farming as a 'way of life' to regarding it as managing an 'agricultural business'. Much has been written about this change of orientation and detailed examination is beyond the scope of this chapter.[3] The turning point in the advance of the post-World War II modernizing agenda came in the early 1980s after Britain's accession to the European Economic Community in 1973, with the attendant modification and realignment of national agricultural policy to fit with the production support measures of the EEC's Common Agricultural Policy. At this time 'structural surpluses' (i.e. surplus production arising from expansionist policies) led to popular epithets such as wine and olive oil 'lakes', butter and grain 'mountains' being applied.

The farming and policy communities responded to the imperative for a change of approach in different but also complementary ways. Some farmers diversified into various types of alternative agricultural or non-agricultural enterprise, often continuing to receive financial support for producing traditional agricultural outputs. Others adopted a 'business as usual' approach and developed their businesses along a trajectory that expanded production and increased the size of their farms. The policy community was initially reluctant to initiate a reduction in agricultural output, apart from introducing quotas on dairy products in 1984, which were only rescinded in 2015. It favoured providing financial incentives encouraging farmers to 'set aside' some land under various forms of agri-environmental measure, such as planting trees and creating corridors for wildlife migration.[4] Initially these measures focused on redressing the effects of modern, intensive farming operations and assuaging popular concern about its impact by creating enclaves of biodiversity.

Morris and Evans consider use of the terms 'productivism' and 'post-productivism' to describe these phases of agricultural restructuring as somewhat misleading.[5] Chief among the criticisms is that they imply a linear progression from one phase to the other, fostering the impression that farmers universally adopted 'productivist' characteristics and traits up to the mid-1980s before switching wholeheartedly to a 'post-productivist' ethos thereafter. Looking at the British agricultural industry as a whole over the second half of the twentieth century, there is nothing more certain than the fact that all farmers were neither 'productivist' nor 'non-productivist' at the same time or in the same place. In other words, there was geographical and historical differentiation in the extent of and depth to which the industry restructured itself. In the vanguard of the assault on this terminology, Wilson[6] argued that the term 'multi-functional' agriculture offered a more realistic interpretation of the spatial and temporal diversity. He indicated that farmers could 'serve different masters' or achieve different objectives simultaneously. According to this scenario agriculture could concurrently yield products to eat, wear or otherwise consume, and create environments and landscapes capable of being consumed and enjoyed as public goods.

We join this timeline of agricultural restructuring in the late 1970s with the author's doctoral research[7] focusing on the almost iconic large-scale arable farms with their increasing levels of mechanization and decreasing use of human labour producing an environmentally distinctive, but ecologically depleted landscape. By the close of the 1990s subsequent research combined retrospective and contemporary approaches by drawing on data from the then recently available National Farm Survey and from a new enlarged survey of farmers in south-east England.[8] The third phase of the author's research into this region's agricultural and rural land use change has involved the integration of these survey data sources with other geospatial and geocoded administrative data into a geographical database covering the farms, land and physical landscape of parishes stretching some 83 km across the South Downs, a sub-region within the larger area in which the original research was carried out.[9] Following a brief review of the survey-based investigations carried out during the early phases of this research, this chapter considers two central questions: first, how has GIS been implemented as an organizing framework for harnessing, analysing and visualizing a collection of data sources; and second, what new knowledge was generated as a result of building an historical-geographical database of farms, farmers and farming for a defined area spanning the twentieth century. Finally, the 'value added' arising as a result of developing this database in a GIS-based framework considers both the strengths and weaknesses of this approach.

From contemporary survey to historical record

Research in agricultural geography during the 1950s and 1960s focused on regional, geographical patterns of agricultural production, reflecting the traditions and methods dominating the discipline as a whole. Coppock's *Agricultural Atlas of England and Wales* was preeminent in assembling a set of over 200 choropleth maps showing the patterns produced by a range of crops and livestock, which were generated using an early form of computer mapping, not to say GIS, program.[10] From the 1970s onwards geographers concerned with farming and the countryside changed their focus from 'agricultural' to 'rural' geography and shifted their methodological framework from an examination of patterns to an understanding of processes using the quantitative and qualitative methods of the social sciences. Social scientific research challenged accepted norms and critiqued established orthodoxies in different disciplines. The author's doctoral research spanning the late 1970s and early 1980s was carried out at a time when questions were being asked about the primacy of farmers as benevolent custodians of the countryside and patriarchs of rural communities.[11] A face-to-face interview survey of 65 large-scale farms (>300 ha) in four counties of South East England (Kent, Surrey, East and West Sussex) was carried out in 1978/9. The initial survey sought to explore the operation and management of these agricultural businesses, especially in respect of their development of a 'productivist' mode of operation in their deployment of labour and machinery resources, although the research predates use of such terminology.

Some 20 years after the original sample survey of large-scale farms a second survey was undertaken with the twin aims of exploring continuity and succession and farmers' responses to the changing policy agenda. The 1998/9 survey drew on two populations of farms and farmers: first, the 65 included in the original survey and the population from which these had been sampled where directory lists indicated they remained agriculturally active businesses; and second the population of farms that could be identified as large-scale some 60 years earlier according the 1941 Agricultural Census records, which had been released as part of the National Farm Survey (see below). The threshold for defining a large farm in the 1978/9 survey (>300 ha, equivalent to 2 per cent of farms in the four counties) provided the starting for determining the area threshold that would yield the same percentage of NFS farms. In 1941 there were 453 farms in the top 2 per cent (>182 ha) and in 1978 there were 262 (>300 ha), and the 295 from these groups that were still actively farmed in 1998 constituted the sampled population for the late 1990s survey. A 52 per cent response rate was achieved with 154 farmer interviews completed, including 41 farms that had been in the 1978/9 survey. Thus, the survey data obtained in the original research was transformed into an historical record alongside the archived NFS records and both were combined with contemporary 1998/9 survey data. Together these surveys yielded a set of farms operated for over 60 years, in some cases by farmers sharing the same family name as those in the 1978/9 survey and/or the 1941/3 NFS:

41 farms in 1941/3 NFS, 1978/9 and 1998/9 surveys
65 farms in 1941/3 NFS and 1978/9 survey
48 farms in 1941/3 NFS and 1998/9 survey

Figure 18.1a shows the distributions of the populations of large farms in 1941 and 1978 together with the 295 still actively farm in 1998. Large farms, as defined in 1941, were a little more widespread at that time in comparison with the late 1970s,

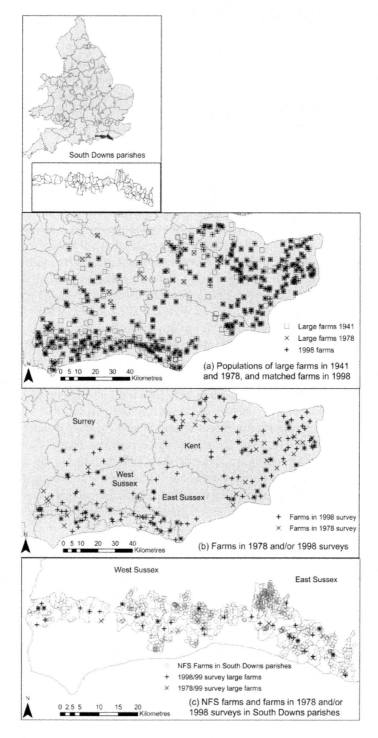

Figure 18.1 Location of large farms in the 1941/3 National Farm Survey and the author's 1978/9 and 1998/9 surveys in Kent, Surrey and East and West Sussex, and South Downs parishes, south-east England.

Note: Nine 1941 large farms (2 per cent) lacking grid references are not shown. Overlapping symbols denote occurrence in multiple surveys.

when there were fewer in the central Wealden area and Surrey. This undoubtedly reflects a traditional emphasis on livestock farming in this area, somewhat heavier soils and expansion of large-scale arable farming on the relatively free-draining soils of the North and South Downs. The population of farms used as the sampling frame for the 1998/9 survey (i.e. farms identified as large in 1941 and/or 1978, and that were still being actively farmed) were also distributed widely across the four counties. Farms in the 1978/9 and 1998/9 surveys reflected these distributions.

Historical GIS

The development of Historical Geographical Information Systems over the last fifteen years suggested that building a database combining the farm-based survey data with geospatial data and geocoded administrative records would allow exploration of contemporary and historical change amongst the constituent farms and farmers and enable examination of their contribution towards reshaping the rural and more specifically agricultural landscape. This geodatabase concentrates on 67 parishes lying wholly or partly on the South Downs in East and West Sussex. The South Downs constitute a recognizable landscape unit recently designated as a national park, which covers a smaller area previously comprising an Area of Outstanding Natural Beauty. Figure 18.1c focuses on the South Downs study area, showing the location of the NFS farms with addresses in these parishes including those in the author's 1978/9 and/or 1998/9 surveys used in building the Historical GIS. Figure 18.2 provides a visual representation of the timeline of key events and periods of development in British agriculture during the twentieth century and the principal sources included in the South Downs HGIS. The following section provides details of a selection of the data sources lying at the heart of the database collected during the mid-century decades around World War II. A review of how GIS helped with linking these datasets together and sample analyses showing how the technology enabled a spatial perspective of some of the issues to be addressed preface a concluding section summarizing the implementation and added value arising from using GIS.

Data sources

The records for farms with addresses in the South Downs parishes obtained from the National Farm Survey (NFS) arguably lie at the centre of the HGIS and we start our examination of data sources at this point. The NFS was administered by the County War Agricultural Executive Committees (CWAEC) on a county by county[12] basis mainly between 1941 and 1943.[13] The aim was to assess 'the condition of agriculture in England and Wales' and identify 'where inefficiencies and mismanagement were seen to exist, [so that] agricultural resources could be husbanded to make a more effective contribution to the war effort'.[14] The NFS records became available from The National Archives (TNA) in Kew in the mid-1990s and the paper records comprise the 4 June 1941 Agricultural Census (AC) return including the Horticultural and Occupation returns and the Primary Record (PR). The Agricultural Census returns were completed for each holding by the farmer (occupier). The PR was completed by surveyors appointed by the CWAEC, who visited all farms of 5 acres

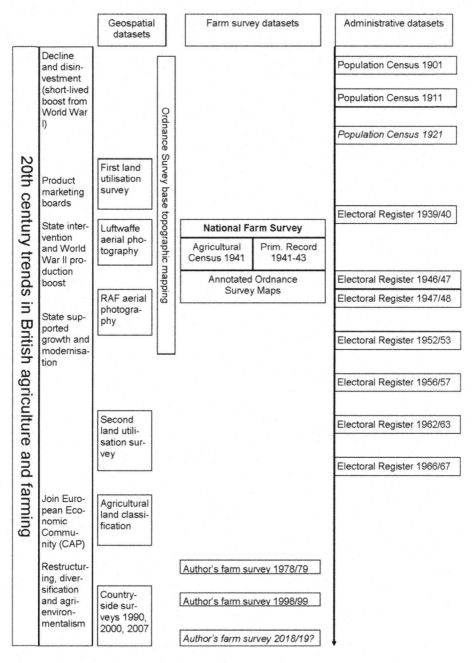

Figure 18.2 Timeline of data sources and summary of twentieth-century British agricultural change.

(2 ha) or more. The PR is effectively an administrative record relating to the condition of the farm, the occupier's managerial ability, the utility services supplied, the use of manures and fertilizers and the allocation of fields to the plough-up campaigns. Some farmers ran a number of holdings (possibly geographically dispersed) for which one combined PR was usually completed and sometimes a joint AC return as well. The NFS documents are held at TNA reference MAF 32/ followed by county and parish numbers. The document folder for each parish contains the AC and PR records with complete county/parish/holding (CPH) numbers. Gaps in the sequence of holding numbers within a parish document folder normally signify 'the NFS record was lost or damaged, never collected because of small size or the holding had ceased to exist as a separate unit'.[15]

The AC and PR records locate the farms geographically by means of their address within a parish and the PR also includes Ordnance Survey (OS) map sheet reference numbers and a grid reference to the farm's address. However more importantly for the HGIS is the accompanying set of published OS topographic maps normally at the 1:10,560 (6 inches to a mile) scale annotated with the boundaries of individual holdings and their CPH identifier. These maps are held separately from the parish document folders in TNA under the reference MAF 73/ followed by a county number (41 and 42 for East and West Sussex respectively). The amount of annotation varies between counties: in some cases farms are distinguished by a different colour wash around their boundaries, farmer names may have been written in the map margins and fields or land parcels that are part of one holding but divided by a physical barrier (e.g. a road) may be annotated with a linking symbol. Information from the AC and PR NFS documents can be connected with the maps by means of farm and field identification numbers.

The records of the NFS represent an unequalled source of information about the statistical population of farms during the early years of World War II and are potentially a valuable data source for researchers, provided that certain cautionary warnings are heeded. Some of these relate to the usual issues associated with using historical records, such as missing and damaged records, inconsistency, illegibility and inaccuracy; others concern avoiding double counting in cases where combined and individual records exist for multiple holding farms and distinguishing between the related terms 'farm', 'farmer', 'occupier' and 'farm business'. This issue becomes especially important when attempting to investigate change over time because the legal, economic, social and geographical constitution of the entity is likely to change: for example, when farms divide or combine because of intergenerational inheritance or when land acquired or disposed of is held under the same or different tenure to that which is retained. This research defined a farm as a single business entity when it first entered the database and when building the HGIS. No attempt was made to track land given up by farms over the period, although land acquired would be included. Three further issues should be heeded when using the NFS records for research purposes: some farms were under the administration of executors, although the deceased owner's name could normally be determined; and a few farms had already been brought under the management of the CWAEC on account of managerial failings by the owner/occupier. Finally, because the NFS was designed as an administrative procedure aimed at increasing agricultural output as distinct from an academic survey of farms, the data collection period ran from 1941 to 1943, with some farms visited on more than one occasion, potentially resulting in variability in the time to which any given set of NFS records relate. This applies not only in respect of the set of holdings within a county or study area, but also to an individual farm. The span of dates on the NFS PRs for farms in the South Downs parishes is from January 1941 to March 1945, although 91 per cent were dated between July 1941 and December 1942 and over 80 per cent of these were carried out in 1942.

Electoral registers include persons entitled to vote in parliamentary and/or local government elections and referenda have been collected annually by local authorities since 1832 except during both world wars. The information obtained is relatively basic, including name, address, postcode, parish or community of residence, ward, local authority and parliamentary constituency in which there is entitlement to vote. Electoral registers (ERs) are public documents available for consultation enabling people to confirm their inclusion. Historically these registers were produced from an annual electoral canvass of persons aged 21 years and over (now 18) or who would attain this age during the period when the annual May to April ER would be 'live'. ERs have been used in demographic, genealogical and local taxation research[16] and as a reasonably robust sampling frame for political and socio-economic surveying purposes.[17] A proportion of people elect to exclude themselves from this aspect of the democratic process through non-registration, nevertheless for the majority of the twentieth century and given the focus on farmers as a social group, it is reasonable to argue that most of the farming community would be included in the annual ERs.

Electoral registers were used to trace farms and farm families over a period of time in order to determine occupation of the NFS farms. Registered electors at the farm address in the ERs were determined and provided the opportunity to infer information about family composition and intergenerational succession, including relocation to a nearby address. However, the ERs are unable to yield information relating to agricultural activity itself. Rather than searching the paper records of the annual registers held in the East and West Sussex Record Offices for each year, the approach adopted involved starting with the last before World War II and the NFS in 1939/40 with a reference date in October 1938; and then moving to the first after World War II referenced to October 1945 (1946/7 ER). The next was for 1947/8 and thereafter they were examined quinquennially up to 1967/8. The statistical population of farms in the 67 parishes obtained from the NFS acted as the starting point for exploring occupational change and continuity. Searches in the 1939/40 and 1946/7 ERs served as checks against the NFS records themselves and as a way of populating the farm address with other household members of voting age. Examination of subsequent ERs focused on capturing occupational change on the farms in the area during the post-war decades. Searches for relocation to addresses outside of the study area parishes was not undertaken as this would have made the process even more time-consuming, irrespective of whether such a move was to a nearby external parish or to somewhere more distant. Despite these issues the searches have revealed the persistence of males and females at some NFS farm addresses with the same surnames and forenames. The appearance of new surnames potentially indicates the arrival of a new farm family and the disappearance of the farm address possibly denotes incorporation of the associated farm land into another holding.

Population censuses of Britain in the 'modern' era are generally accepted to date back to 1801, although the 1841 census is regarded as the first to have been completed with the rigour required to rely on this source as anything more than a head count. Enumerators' returns archived in TNA are released 100 years after a census took place. At present the twentieth-century censuses available via this means are for 1901 and 1911. The records from these and earlier censuses have been scanned and transcribed by organizations seeking to satisfy the growing demand for historical records as members of the public undertake genealogical research. One of the earliest cases of academic research digitally capturing and using historical census records is the work of Anderson[18] with the 1851 census.

The role of the 1901 and 1911 census records in the HGIS of the South Downs farms is similar to that of the electoral registers in that they provide a means of populating the NFS farms with other household members. The AC Occupation Return in the NFS documents gives dates when the 1941 owner/occupier arrived on the holding and acquired other agricultural land holdings. The early twentieth-century population censuses also allow other farms (and their household members) that disappeared by the time of the 1941/3 NFS to be identified, thus shedding further light on the period of declining fortunes in the agricultural sector. Occupational information in the historical census records also enables farm workers in the study area parishes to be identified, although these people cannot be definitively associated with specific NFS farms other than by inference in respect of the proximity of their residential addresses. There is the potential to continue this process as the 1921 and 1931 census records are released, thereby helping to consolidate and corroborate the information from other sources.

Geospatial data sources are here defined as datasets with an inherent geographical and spatial component, unlike those sources to which a geospatial element can be added by linkage with other information. The geographical component of the surveys outlined previously derives from them having been carried out within defined geographical regions, the NFS in England and Wales, and the author's 1978/9 and 1998/9 surveys in four counties of south-east England. However, each surveyed farm possessed other geographical characteristics, such as an address, a physical extent and layout of fields, which some farmers revealed during the interview, although these had not been solicited. The geospatial data sources used in building the HGIS include OS topographic mapping, Luftwaffe and Royal Air Force aerial photography, land utilization and agricultural land classification data, geological and soils data, and digital elevation data.

The Landmark Information Group scanned all the historical OS topographic maps during the 1990s and these were subsequently incorporated into the Digimap collection at Edina. The historic OS map collection includes maps in three series, although it is those from the second and third revisions of the first County Series at 1:10,560 respectively covering the periods 1900–49 and 1922–69 that were the most up-to-date ones available at the time the NFS surveyors were annotating farm boundaries. Digitizing from scanned images of published maps involves tracing the mouse cursor over features and creating vectorized digital representations. The process takes one form of cartographic representation (the source map) to generate another (the vector image) and has some advantages over other methods, such as automated recognition of features built from pixels on scanned rasterized images.[19]

The development of aerial photography as a means of capturing images of the land during the first half of the twentieth century was associated with the military actions of both World Wars. The Luftwaffe had been covertly undertaking such photo-reconnaissance of British towns and cities during the years before World War II and these were supplemented once hostilities commenced. Relatively few of these aerial photographs were taken of rural areas, but some are available covering part of the South Downs area. The RAF undertook comprehensive aerial photographic surveys after the war and these images provide a starting point for investigating land use change during these decades.[20] The aerial photographs were scanned at a high resolution and then geocorrected and orthorectified to adjust for variations in scale. Although the Luftwaffe aerial photographs cover a relatively small proportion of the 67 South Downs parishes, mainly around Brighton and Lewes in East Sussex, they were captured at a similar time to the start of the NFS. These together with the post-war RAF imagery were added into the HGIS, enabling each polygon to be classified on a field-by-field basis.

These aerial photographs predate the era of remotely sensed imagery obtained by orbiting satellites, although some modern information about landform (e.g. aspect, elevation and slope) may still be relevant in historical research in cases where changes can be regarded as insignificant. There has been considerable interest in the use of LIDAR (Light Imaging Detection and Ranging) in recent years and these data can be used to create a three-dimensional surface of the South Downs over which to drape the polygon data for farms and fields. Such data has been incorporated into the South Downs HGIS, for example, a digital elevation model (DEM) which provides a three-dimensional surface on which to visualize the boundaries of the NFS farms, their fields and those areas entered in the plough-up campaigns.

The OS had published large-scale maps of Britain (1:2500 County Series) by the end of World War I,[21] but these yielded only limited details about land use and failed to satisfy the growing need for this type of information. After some preliminary work supported by the Geographical Association during the 1920s, Sir Dudley Stamp noted its limited geographical coverage and inconsistent data quality.[22] In response he set about organizing the first National Land Utilization Survey, with data collection carried out on a county-by-county basis during the 1930s. Land use was recorded by volunteers on six inch scale maps and checked by a County Organizer, who edited this information down onto fourth edition OS one inch scale maps, checking for consistency across adjoining map sheets. Funding limitations delayed publication of these maps, although two generalized maps at 1:625,000 scale covering the whole of Britain were published in 1943. A national set of one inch scale maps was eventually published, maps showing a seven-fold classification of land, although their use for research purposes is not without its difficulties.[23]

A Classification of Agricultural Land was produced in 1972 by the Agricultural Development and Advisory Service with help from the Soil Survey of England and Wales.[24] This dataset is available from the Multi Agency Geographic Information for the Countryside (MAGIC) website (http://magic.defa.gov.uk). Agricultural land was graded into five classes with a further category representing land that was predominantly 'urban' or otherwise 'non-agricultural'. Land was assigned to classes 1 to 5 on the basis of a combination of variables concerning climate, location, soil and topography.

One of the main aims of the classification was to distinguish areas of agricultural land in respect of inherent differences in productivity, thus adding a qualitative assessment when it came to such matters as determining applications for development. The classification was published some 30 years after the NFS, nevertheless integrating these datasets provides a basis for exploring a number of issues, such as whether plough-up fields were over-represented on some of the agricultural land classes in comparison with their presence across the whole study area and whether longevity of occupation on farms by the same family was related to land quality.

Data linkage and analysis

The farm name and farmer surnames and initials together with the address were the basis for matching the NFS documents with subsequent farm survey data, the ERs and census records. Records matched between one or more of the sources indicate residence at an address and occupation of a farm by members of the same family but are unlikely to imply continuity of the extent of land managed for agriculture or type of farming practiced. Continuity of occupation between generations may be indicated by the combination of a person's surname and forename(s) and/or initials. Linkages between the NFS records and preceding and succeeding data sources resulted in six types of case:

- Person with identical name and farm address as NFS record
- Person with surname in common with NFS farmer and farm address as NFS record (includes married daughters)
- Person with identical name but a different address as NFS record
- Person with a different surname at NFS farm address
- No record of NFS farm address
- Person linked to multiple NFS records

Spatial matching of these data using grid references for farm addresses as well as farm and field polygons digitized from the NFS maps enabled these agricultural data sources to be connected with other geospatial data. There are 544 farms with PRs and 672 holdings with completed AC schedules in the NFS records held in TNA for the 67 South Downs parishes. Figure 18.3 shows TNA document references for these parishes in East and West Sussex. In addition to capturing the agricultural data from the NFS records the boundaries of the farm that had been annotated onto the OS base maps were digitized into a GIS using the same scanned and geo-referenced historical OS topographic mapping available from Digimap (http://Digimap.edina.ac.uk) as a consistent background for the whole area. The procedure for digitizing the farm boundaries and plough-up fields (referring to OS field numbers from section F of the PR) also used digitally photographed and georeferenced images of the NFS maps, which were viewed on-screen superimposed over those obtained from Digimap. This enabled any inconsistencies in geo-referencing between these sources to be overcome by standardizing to the Digimap images. In summary, farm boundary polygons were digitized for a total of 514 farms (including one that lacked AC data). This number took account of six farms whose boundaries could not be found on the

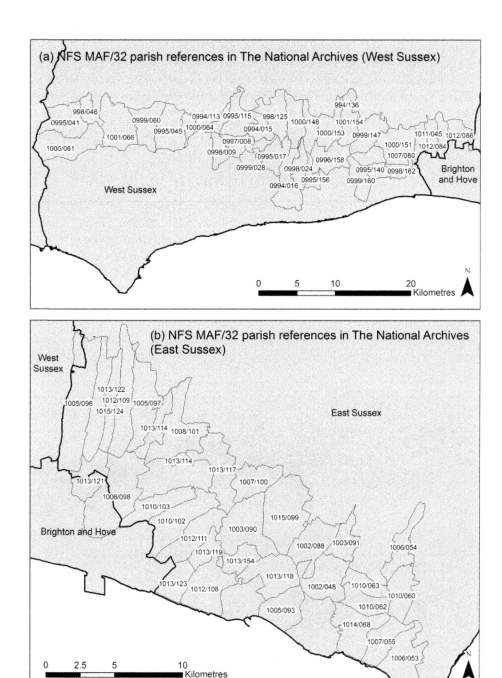

Figure 18.3 The National Archives' National Farm Survey document reference for parishes included in South Downs study area.

NFS maps, 102 farms composed of more than one holding which therefore had combined ACs and/or PRs or were joined as one record by the author, 12 farms already brought under the management of the CWAEC and 55 small NFS farms lacking address point grid references and farm boundaries on the OS maps, The 514 farms form the geographical basis of the following illustrative analyses of the data held in the HGIS. Finally, some agricultural land had been taken over for military training, mainly on the South Downs between Brighton and Eastbourne, and in both counties there were substantial areas not identified as belonging to agricultural holdings that were woodland, forestry, open space or otherwise non-agricultural.

Indicative analyses

Farms visited by the NFS surveyors were classified as A, B or C, with + or − signs sometimes added to indicate a relative position in each nominal category. Farms classified as C were deemed to have managerial failings that resulted in their productive potential not being fully realized. These failings included such things as an historical lack of investment, reluctance to use fertilizers or pesticides, insufficient attention paid to farming as a result of other business interests or personal character-istics, such an elderly farmer lacking motivation in the absence of a successor. The surveyors made repeated visits to class C farmers to determine if their advice on how to increase productivity was adopted and in extreme cases the CWAEC could take over the management of a farm. Figure 18.4 shows the distribution of this managerial

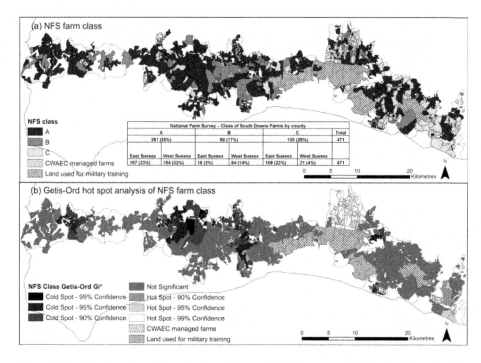

Figure 18.4 Visual and spatial statistics analyses of NFS managerial class for farms in the South Downs parishes where the primary record is available (471 farms).

classification of the NFS farms in the South Downs parishes HGIS and in the interests of clarity separately identifies areas taken over by the military and the CWAEC managed farms. Part (a) simply presents the raw spatial pattern, in other words each farm is shaded to represent its class (A, B or C) irrespective of size or proximity to farms of the same or a different class together with a cross-tabulation of the variables. This reveals that A, B and C class farms were distributed across the South Downs parishes in East and West Sussex, although the cross-tabulation reveals higher percentages of A and B farms in West compared with East Sussex. Part (b) illustrates how the application of a spatial statistics technique can illuminate concentrations of the three classes and reveal whether the overall pattern tends towards randomness or regularity. The technique applied in this case (Getis-Ord Gi★) focuses on spatial autocorrelation, which quantifies the tendency of high and low data values (i.e. farm classes expressed as numerical values 1, 2 and 3) to cluster spatially.[25] The technique works by examining the value for each feature (farm) in the context of the values possessed by its neighbours. A statistically significant hot spot occurs when the local sum of values is proportionately higher (or lower in the case of cold spots) than the expected local sum and is more than might have occurred through randomness, converting the difference to a z-score, the cluster is regarded as statistically significant. Figure 18.4b maps the confidence interval of these results and indicates a hot spot of class C farms in parishes on the northern side of the South Downs in East Sussex and a hot spot of class A farms towards the east of the same county. In contrast there is a statistically significant cool spot of class A farms in the centre of West Sussex.

One of the main drivers behind undertaking the NFS was to increase food production and ameliorate the effects of food rationing. The Agriculture Development Act[26] passed in April 1939 provided for the payment of £2 per acre (0.405 ha) to farmers who agreed to plough-up land and reseed or replant it with barley, oats, rye, wheat or potatoes. Each CWAEC was given a plough-up quota (approximately 10 per cent of the area of permanent grass[27] and nationally the scheme added some 2.8 million hectares of cultivated land.[28] The NFS surveyors' visits and the classification system were used to identify especially unproductive land, for example, weed-invested poor-quality permanent grass that could be ploughed-up and resown with 'approved crops'. Section F of the PR records the OS field numbers of those fields or parts of fields that the surveyor in discussion with the farmer felt should be ploughed-up and resown. Usually resowing was to one of the approved crops, although the NFS records reveal considerable variety and some fields resown to combinations of up to five different crops. There were plough-up campaigns in 1939, 1940 and 1941 for harvest one year later and all of the plough-up activity on the farms in this subset was only in the 1939/40 and 1940/1 campaigns. Given that the basis of the plough-up campaign was to improve land and increase its productivity, it is reasonable to hypothesize that those fields thus converted from poor pasture or similar to productive arable would impact on the agricultural landscape of the South Downs and contribute towards enduring profitability and occupational longevity. Details of the areas of plough-up land are incomplete on the East Sussex PR records and the analysis shown in Figure 18.5 focuses on West Sussex. Figure 18.5a examines the percentage of the area of NFS farms that was entered into the 1939/40 or 1940/1 campaigns and whether there was continuity of occupation by the same farm family up to 1967/8.

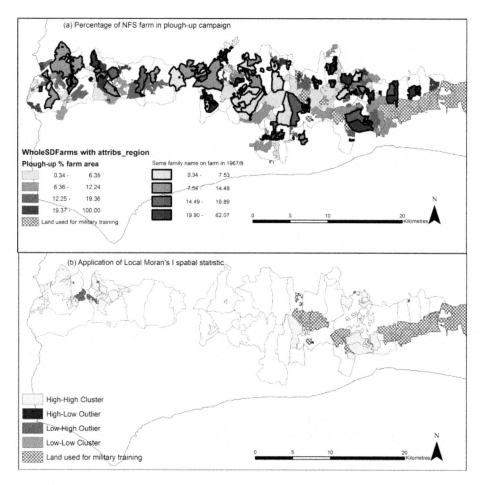

Figure 18.5 Visual and spatial statistics analyses of percentage of total land area entered into 1940 and 1941 plough-up campaigns by NFS farms in the West Sussex South Downs (425 farms).

It reveals a fairly scattered pattern of high and low percentage values, with little difference between those farms where the NFS occupier's family remained at the address in 1967/8 and those where a change had occurred or they could not be identified in the ER. However, application of the Local Moran's I spatial statistic[29] reveals three sizeable clusters of High-High similar percentage values close together. Two of these are separated by an outlier of Low-High values, where a small group of farms with low values is surrounded by others with high ones.

Farms and farm families are dynamic entities, changing their structure and composition over time. Each of the individual data sources provides a cross-sectional, qualitatively rich or poor insight into a set of farms moving forwards and backwards from the early years of World War II. Linkage of information between some of the sources provides a glimpse of transitional changes, but these discrete datasets cannot reveal what was occurring in between these data collection events. Figure 18.6

1901 Population Census						
Person	Relationship	Age	Gender (1-male, 2-female)	Marital Status (1-married, 2-single, 3 widowed)	Occupation	Place of Birth
1	Head	51	1	1	Farmer	Fletching
2	Wife	57	2	1	-	Framfield
3	Daughter	22	2	2	-	Fletching
4	Daughter	20	2	2	-	Fletching
5	Daughter	17	2	2	-	Fletching
6	Mother-in-law	71	2	3	Independent Means	Cuckfield
7	Servant		2	2	Domestic Servant	Hamsey
1911 Population Census						
1	Head	61	1	1	Farmer	Fletching
2	Wife	67	2	1	-	Framfield
5	Daughter	27	2	2	-	Fletching
6	Mother-in-Law	81	2	3	-	Cuckfield
8	Ladies Help	23	2	2	-	Depden
9	Servant	17	2	2	Independent Means	Fletching
10	Servant	17	2	2	Domestic Servant	Fletching
1939/40 Electoral Register (new surname)						
11	Head					
12	Wife					
13	Son					

1941/43 National Farm Survey					
Person	Relationship	Year on farm	Area	Motive power	NFS Class and summary
11	Head	1927	119.6 ha	2 wheeled tractors	A—A well managed farm. Dairy holding, bullocks being fattened on the brookland. About 30 acres of these have been ploughed and re-seeded and more will be seeded next year.

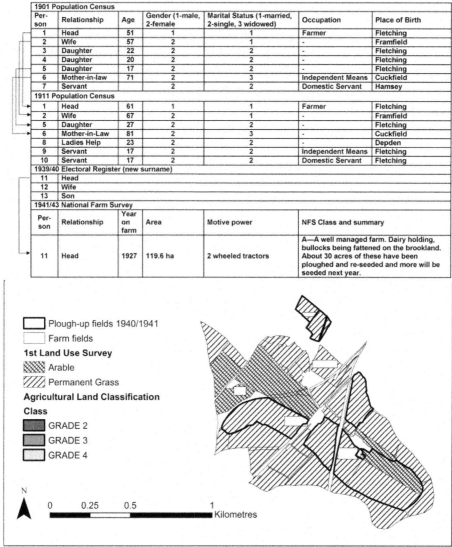

Plough-up fields 1940/1941

Farm fields

1st Land Use Survey

Arable

Permanent Grass

Agricultural Land Classification

Class

GRADE 2

GRADE 3

GRADE 4

N

0   0.25   0.5   1 Kilometres

1947/48 Electoral register		1952/53 Electoral register		1956/57 Electoral register		1962/63 Electoral register		1966/77 Electoral register	
Person	Relationship	Person	Relationship	Person	Relationship	Person	Relationship	Person	Relationship
11	Head	11	Head	11	Head	11	Head	11	Head
12	Wife	12	Wife	12	Wife	12	Wife	12	Wife
13	Son								
		14	Daughter						
				15	Son				
						16	Son	16	Son
								17	Daughter

Figure 18.6 Integration of survey, administrative and geospatial data sources in the South Downs HGIS for an NFS farm in East Sussex with fields in the 1940 and 1941 plough-up campaigns. Note: Names on the OS maps have been redacted and individuals in the 1901 and 1911 census records have been labelled with unique identifier numbers to limit the opportunity for identifying the farm. Greyscale shading of the agricultural land classes appears more muted than in the legend because of the semi-transparent overlain OS topographic maps.

offers some insights into the changes on one farm in East Sussex, whose identify has been obscured for reasons of confidentiality. The upper and lower parts reproduce coded anonymized information about the members of households living at the farmhouse in 1901 and 1911, and then in selected pre- and post-World War II ERs together with selected variables from the AC and PR; the central part maps some of the geospatial data and shows the physical extent of the farm as shown on the NFS maps. The farm was below the 'large' farm size (182 ha) at the time of the NFS, when it comprised two sizeable land parcels separated by a road and a smaller detached area close by, and it had not become 'large' by 1978 or 1998 and so was not sampled for inclusion in either survey. The map shows the farm's boundaries superimposed over the OS topographic map. These images have been made semi-transparent in order to 'see through' the different layers in the visualization. Four fields were entered in the 1939/40 and 1940/1 plough-up campaigns when these were resown to beans, oats and wheat. The farm at the time of the NFS included land that would subsequently be classified as Grade 2 (21.5 per cent), Grade 3 (58.1 per cent) and Grade 4 (20.4 per cent). Most of the farm's land in the plough-up campaign was Grade 3 (78.2 per cent), although 11.1 per cent and 10.7 per cent was respectively Grades 2 and 4). Across the study area farms as a whole 2.5 per cent, 63.6 per cent and 26.7 per cent of plough-up land was graded 2, 3 and 4 respect-ively.[30] Two agricultural land use types on the First Land Utilization Survey occurred on the farm, arable and permanent pasture (see Figure 18.6) and not surprisingly all but 12.9 per cent of the plough-up land on the farm was permanent pasture. The NFS surveyor assigned the farm to class A and described it as well managed. The farm already had two wheeled tractors and the NFS occupier had added land to the holding that he acquired in 1920s.

The population census and electoral register data relate to the farm household rather than the farm itself. These reveal that the same farmer was present in 1901 and 1911 with a wife and three daughters in 1901 and one daughter in 1911. His widowed mother-in-law was living in the household at the time of both censuses and had attained 81 years in 1911. There was only one servant present in 1901, when the farmer's unmarried daughters were presumably assisting with household tasks. By 1911, with only one daughter remaining, the number of domestic servants had risen to three including a 'Ladies Help'. All household members according to both sets of census records were born in East Sussex (Fletching, Cuckfield, Framfield and Hamsey), apart from one of the domestic servants in 1911 who hailed from Depden (Suffolk). Until records from the 1921 and 1931 censuses are released, we are unable to determine changes that occurred between 1911 and the 1939/40 ER and the 1941/3 NFS. The later data sources show that a different farmer took over in the late 1920s and was living with his wife and son of voting age in 1939/40. But how old were the members of this farm family, was this the couple's only child or had older children left home by that time, did the new household include domestic servants and where were the household members born? The post-war ER records reveal that the husband and wife of new farm family remained on the farm and additional children were entered on and withdrew from the electoral register at this address up to 1962/3.

Conclusions

This chapter has sought to demonstrate how GIS has been implemented in respect of examining the historical development of farms, farming and the agricultural landscape of part of south-east England, focusing especially on a swathe of parishes stretching across the South Downs in East and West Sussex. It is difficult to conceive how the integration of the different data sources could have been achieved without doing so within a GIS framework. This framework has allowed survey and administrative types of data collected by the author and by government to be connected through time and by using a common geo-referencing system to be combined with geospatial data sources. Three illustrative analyses have shown how the GIS framework enables exploration of quantitative data to go beyond aspatial cross-tabulation to examine geographical pattern using both visualization and spatial statistics. The third analysis goes some way towards showing how qualitative data and analyses are possible within a GIS framework, enabling researchers to mine a variety of data sources to generate new knowledge and relationships.

Use of GIS for contemporary or historical research or other purposes is not something to be undertaken lightly and some perseverance is necessary to derive the value-added benefits. This chapter has touched on some of the issues associated with turning historical records into meaningful and useable information within a GIS. Further development and extension of the South Downs HGIS outlined here has been hinted at in a number of places (for example, see Figure 18.2) in relation to the extension of the timeline further backwards and forwards, the incorporation of additional data and potentially a further contemporary survey in 2018/19 to continue the 20-year interval between the author's work.

Acknowledgements

Initial doctoral research funded by Ministry of Agriculture, Fisheries and Food studentship, followed by ESRC award Ref. R000222512 Agricultural Policy Adjustment: Responses by Large Scale Farm Businesses, and by the British Academy Ref. SG-31506 An assessment of archival sources for monitoring the occupancy of agricultural land in South-East England. The work is based on an Ordnance Survey/Edina supplied service, © Crown Copyright/database right 2001. The paper includes information © Natural England copyright (1972). Contains Ordnance Survey data © Crown copyright and database right 1972.

Notes

1 J. Martin, *The Development of Modern Agriculture: British Farming since 1931*, New York: St Martin's Press, 2000.

2 D. Symes, 'Changing Gender-Roles in Productionist and Post-Productionist Capitalist Agriculture', *Journal of Rural Studies* 7, 1991, 85–90; B. Ilbery and I. Bowler, 'From Agricultural Productivism to Post-Productivism', in B. Ilbery (ed.), *The Geography of Rural Change*, Harlow: Longman, 1998, 57–84.

3 N. Evans, C. Morris and M. Winter, 'Conceptualizing Agriculture: A Critique of Post-Productivism as the New Orthodoxy', *Progress in Human Geography* 23, 2002, 313–32.

4 N. Walford, 'Agricultural Adjustment: Adoption of and Adaptation to Policy Reform Measures by Large-Scale, Commercial Farmers', *Land Use Policy* 19, 2002, 243–57.

5 C. Morris and N. Evans, 'Research on the Geography of Agricultural Change: Redundant or Revitalized?', *Area* 31, 1999, 349–58.

6 G. Wilson, 'From Productivism to Post-Productivism . . . and Back Again? Exploring the (Un)Changed Natural and Mental Landscapes of European Agriculture', *Transactions Institute of British Geographers* 26, 2001, 77–102.

7 N. Walford, 'The Future Size of Farms: Modelling the Effect of Change in Labor and Machinery', *Journal of Agricultural Economics* 34, 1983, 407–16.

8 N. Walford, 'Productivism is Dead: Long Live Productivism', *Journal of Rural Studies* 19, 2003, 491–502; R. Burton and N. Walford, 'Multiple Succession and Land Division on Family Farms in the South East of England: A Counterbalance to Agricultural Concentration?', *Journal of Rural Studies* 21, 2005, 335–47.

9 N. Walford, 'The National Farm Survey and the Tracing of Post-War Farmers', in B. Short, C. Watkins and J. Martin (eds), *Front Line of Freedom: British Farming in the Second World War*, Exeter: British Agricultural History Society, 2000, 217–29; K. Taylor, N. Walford, B. Short and R. Armitage, 'Cautionary Notes on Using the National Farm Survey Records in Conjunction with Other Sources for Investigating the Agrarian History of Second World War Britain', *Agricultural History Review* 60, 2012, 77–96.

10 J. Coppock, *An Agricultural Atlas of England and Wales*, London: Faber & Faber, 1964.

11 H. Newby, *The Deferential Worker*, London: Allen Lane, 1977; H. Newby, D. Bell, D. Saunders and D. Rose, *Property Paternalism and Power*, London: Hutchinson, 1978.

12 British counties are the top level of administrative unit, similar to US states rather than US counties.

13 B. Short and C. Watkins, 'Prelude to Modernity: An Evaluation of the National Farm Survey of England and Wales, 1941–43', in N. Walford, J. Everitt and D. Napton (eds), *Reshaping the Countryside: Perceptions and Processes of Rural Change*, Wallingford: CABI, 1999.

14 Walford, 'National Farm Survey', in Short et al., *Front Line of Freedom*, 220.

15 Walford, 'National Farm Survey' in Short et al., *Front Line of Freedom*, 220.

16 A. McCulloch, 'Turnover on the Electoral Register: Implications for the Administration of the Community Charge', *Local Government Studies* 14, 1988, 1–4; P. Longley, D. Martin and G. Higgs, 'The Geographical Implications of Changing Local Taxation Regimes', *Transactions of the Institute of British Geographers* 18, 1993, 86–101.

17 C. Smith, 'How Complete is the Electoral Register?', *Political Studies* 29, 1981, 275–8.

18 M. Anderson, 'Households, Families and Individuals: Some Preliminary Results from the National Sample from the 1851 Census of Great Britain', *Continuity and Change* 3, 1988, 421–38.

19 B. Davis, *GIS: A Visual Approach*, 2nd ed., Albany, NY: OneWord Press, 2001.

20 Hunting Surveys and Consultants, Ltd., *Monitoring Landscape Change*, vol. 10, Borehamwood: Hunting Surveys and Consultants, 1986.

21 J. Sheail, *Rural Conservation in Inter-War Britain*, Oxford: Clarendon Press, 1981.

22 L. D. Stamp, *The Land of Britain: Its Use and Misuse*, 3rd ed., Harlow: Longman, 1964.

23 Taylor et al., 'Cautionary Notes'.

24 Ministry of Agriculture, Fisheries and Food, *Agricultural Land Classification of England and Wales*, London: HMSO, 1988.

25 J. Ord and A. Getis, 'Local Spatial Autocorrelation Statistics: Distributional Issues and an Application', *Geographical Analysis* 27, 1995, 286–306.

26 Ministry of Agriculture, *Agriculture Development Act*, London: HMSO, 1939.

27 C. Rawding, 'Changing Land Use in North East Lancashire During the Second World War', *North West Geography* 8, 2008, 1–13.

28 B. Short, C. Watkins, W. Foot and P. Kinsman, *The National Farm Survey 1941–43: State Surveillance and the Countryside in England and Wales in the Second World War*, Wallingford: CABI, 2000.

29 L. Anselin, 'Local Indicators of Spatial Association—LISA', *Geographical Analysis* 27, 1995, 93–115.

30 N. Walford, 'The Extent and Impact of the 1940 and 1941 'Plough-up' Campaigns on Farming Across the South Downs, England', *Journal of Rural Studies* 32, 2013, 38–49.

19

FOOD, FARMS, AND FISH IN GREAT BRITAIN AND FRANCE, 1860–1914

A mixed-methods spatial history

Robert M. Schwartz

> They [trawlers] would go out on the Monday morning and be back again on the Thursday with 50, 60, and sometimes 70 and 80 boxes of large live plaice, take them out of the wells, put them into my boxes and send them to London. Now all these fish banks [in the North Sea] are absolutely fished out.
>
> Mr Joseph Mubbell of Grimsby, 11 May 1893

> Today American and Russian grain inundate our markets; without tariff protection it is impossible for French products to sustain themselves; in the near future it will be the same for our pastoral production. The current legislation [authorizing free trade] is the ruin of our agricultural in the south.
>
> M. de Plagniol, Chomeric in the Ardèche, 12 May 1879

For spatial history the digital partnership of text mining with GIS can lead to new insights and discoveries. This is particularly true in the examination of bulky documents of 500 pages and more. In 500 pages, significant details and patterns can hide in plain sight and escape our attention.[1] Two examples from my research in British and French history can serve to make the point. The first concerns sea fisheries in Britain in 1890s; the second, the situation of agriculture in France near the beginning of a long agrarian crisis from 1876 to 1896. In both cases the documents studied are lengthy published reports of the informed opinions of the respondents to national inquires. These are sources that usually invite mere selective attention rather than the systematic analysis undertaken for this article and its use of a mixed-methods approach to blend analysis and narrative.

The common context for the two inquiries was the transport revolution – steam ships, railways, and telegraphy – hand in hand with the globalization of foodstuffs during the second half of the nineteenth century. Whereas European countries in the seventeenth, eighteenth and early nineteenth centuries faced periodic and often severe food shortages, the food problem facing British and French farmers after 1860 was adjusting to *too much food,* coming, in particular, from the growing surplus of wheat and livestock in North American, Argentina, Australasia that arrived in their home markets, driving cereal and meat prices lower and putting many farmers in distress.[2]

Great Britain: railways, industrial sea fishing, and the discovery of ecological limits

In Britain, where free trade prevailed after the 1850, unimpeded American agricultural imports meant that cheaper food was now available for England's growing urban populations. Fresh meat, however, remained relatively expensive for workers' families but inexpensive varieties of fresh fish provided an abundant and cheaper source of protein in working-class diets.

In a country increasingly dependent on food imports, the government gave new and sustained attention to the fisheries of the United Kingdom. In 1863 Parliament established the first of what would be a series of investigations – 1879, 1893, 1900, and 1908 – into the state of sea fishing. The conclusion of 1863–6 investigation sounded a note of great confidence for the food supplies of the UK. There were no known limits to the sea fishing: 'The total supply of fish obtained upon the coasts of the United Kingdom has not diminished of late years, but has increased; and it admits of further augmentation to an extent the limits of which are not indicated by any evidence we have been able to obtain.'[3]

Twenty years later in 1883, at the first international congress on sea fishing, the commission head, scientist Thomas Huxley, defended that finding in sweeping terms:

> I believe, then, that the cod fishery, the herring fishery, the pilchard fishery, the mackerel fishery, and probably all the great sea fisheries, are inexhaustible; that is to say, that nothing we do seriously affects the number of the fish. And any attempt to regulate these fisheries seems consequently, from the nature of the case, to be useless.[4]

Even before the rise of steam trawling in the 1870s and 1880s, the great harvesting of fish by British vessels owed much to the expansion of rapid rail transport. In the 1840s rail transport to the cities of London, Birmingham, and Manchester was in place (see Figure 19.1), and the continued increase of fish sent by rail to privileged markets in London, Hull, Liverpool, Plymouth, and elsewhere was described by witnesses examined by the Royal Commission of 1863. Samuel Decent of Hull, with 20 years of experience, described how the greater demand for fresh fish was being met thanks to the rail service. The catch in recent years, he said, was about the same as 20 years ago, but now 'we bring ashore all we catch', instead of throwing some of it away at sea because 'we had no markets for it inland'. On the western coast of England in Liverpool, Robert Isaac, a fish merchant, explained important changes in marketing. In contrast to the situation 10 to 20 years before when fish in the city markets were in short supply during the winter and 'off seasons', the Liverpool markets were now well stocked all year round because large quantities from the

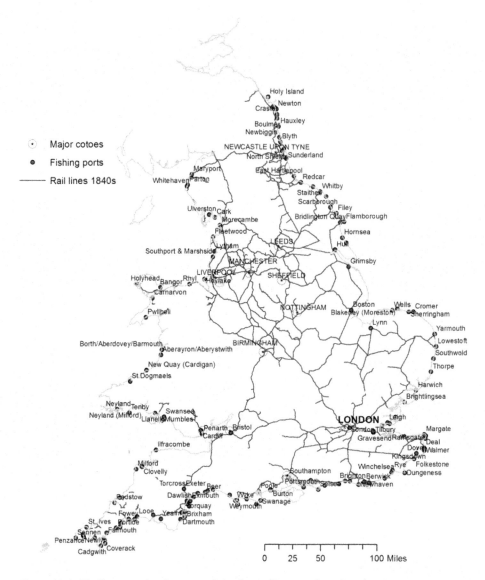

Figure 19.1 Rail connection between Grimsby and Yarmouth and major cities.

eastern fisheries (Hull, Grimsby, etc.) arrived by rail. The expansion of rail transport made it possible to ship growing stocks of landed fish to inland markets at considerable distance. Another example comes from the fishery at Fleetwood to north of Liverpool. When asked why trawlers had moved from Southport to Fleetwood, John Gibson, shipbuilder and ship's surveyor for the Board of Trade, explained that the relocation occurred in order to get direct access to rail service. Earlier many fish spoiled when delivered by horse cart from Southport to Manchester, and now with rail service they were being sent to more markets – Liverpool, Manchester, Birmingham, London, and Edinburgh. With business expanding, he was at work building more and bigger boats.[5]

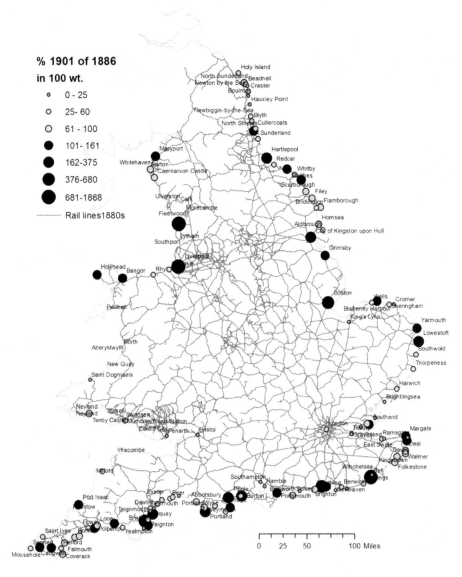

Figure 19.2   Fish landed by port, 1886 and 1901.

In the decades that followed the extension of rail service continued, reaching ports and inland markets throughout the country by the 1880s. (See Figure 19.2.) Correspondingly, the tons of fish landed in English and Welsh ports rose from 200,000 in 1879 to 800,000 in 1912, a four-fold increase, the majority of which was shipped by rail. (See Figure 19.3.) A GIS produced map adds the important geographic perspective. Not surprisingly, some ports did better than others. From 1886 to 1901, eastern ports devoted to fishing in North Sea waters, such as Sunderland, Yarmouth, Hartlepool, Whitby, Kingston upon Hull, Boston, and Lowestoft, saw increases in fish landed of more than 100 tons, placing them closer in rank to Great

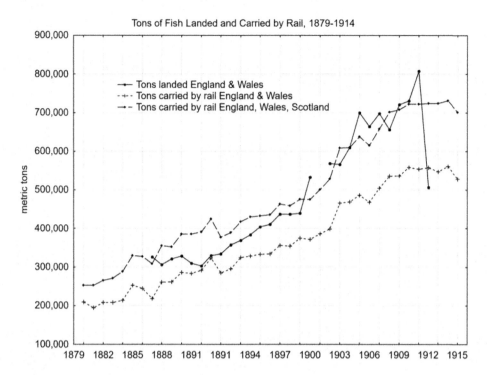

Tons of Fish Landed and Carried by Rail, 1879-1914

Figure 19.3 Tons of fish carried by rail.

Grimsby, the leading fishery in the British Isles by far. In the southern and western ports, large increases occurred in smaller fisheries, too: on the south coast, Dungeness, Brixham, Polpero, Plymouth, and Saint Ives; on the west coast, Cardiff, Swansea, Neyal, Pwllheli, Liverpool, and Fleetwood. In short, the English and Welsh supplies for fish 'n' chips were more abundant than ever.

As the catch grew enormous, fishermen, marine scientists, and governing officials began to understand that industrialized sea fishing could lead to overfishing. In the hearings of the first royal commission fishermen had already voiced concerns about declining fish stocks, concerns ignored in the final report of 1866.[6] The Royal Commission of 1893, however, took such disquiet into account. Indeed, the conclusions it drew marked a turning point in the discussions and policy regarding sea fishing, as we shall see.

My investigation into this change in government thinking and informed opinion combines text mining and GIS spatial analysis. The Select Commission on Sea Fisheries of 1893 heard testimony from 60 witnesses and published its report and the testimony in the same year. As in my examination of the 1863 commission, the 373 dense pages of testimony comprise a corpus of detailed evidence. New in this inquiry was the commission's interest in collecting evidence on the fish stocks at specific fishing grounds. Systematic analysis using Computer-Assisted Qualitative Data Analysis (CAQDA) enables the identification and retrieval of key terms in context and patterns of fact and opinion. Coding (or tagging) important words and phrases begins the process.[7]

Consider the following response from John T. Exton on 22 June 1893 (numbers identify each question and response in the document; key terms and phrases are in bold; significant additional information in italics):

Chairman.

5073. You and two other gentlemen from **Grimsby** have been chosen by the **National Federation of Fishermen** to represent their views to this Committee, I believe? Yes.

5079. As to yourself personally, what is your experience of fishing? I have had 20 years' experience out of Grimsby.

5080. In what form of fishing? Five years in the line fishing, as an apprentice. I was apprenticed for seven years, and served five years in the line fishery, when my master failed; then the other two years I served in the trawl fishery; I have been three years in oyster fishing, and *10 years master of a trawler.*

5081. Are you *master of a trawler now? No. I have been ashore two years and six months.*

5082. You have **retired**, have you? *Yes; but I get my living amongst the fishermen. I, am **a representative of their society**, and they keep me to look after their interests.*

5084. Do you consider that there has been a considerable falling off in the number of fish in the **North Sea? Yes, during the last ten years**.

5085. Have you noticed that falling off especially, amongst any particular class of fish? Yes, in **soles and plaice chiefly**.

5086. You do not think there has been a **falling off in the round fish, do you? No.**

5087. Then, may we put the question of round fish on one side? Yes.

5088. To what do you attribute the falling off in the flat fish? **The catching power. There is too much catching power.**

5089. From **over fishing**, in other words? **Yes.**

5090. Is that because you think the number of vessels fishing has increased too much or that the individual vessels have developed their own engines to too great an extent? *I think the introduction of steam and having double fishing gear is the great cause of the evil. You see one **steam fishing vessel** has two trawls to a sailing vessels' one. They work one at a time, but if a steam fishing vessel gets one net damaged, he has another ready to put down immediately, while a sailing vessel has to lose that time in getting the net ready to put down again.*

To illustrate the range of fact and opinion, a second example is a fish salesman and boat owner from an English Channel fishery, Mr W. J. Saunders, who explained that fish stocks there were abundant and sometime increasing.

9 May 1893
W. J. Saunders, called in; and Examined.
Mr. Mallock.

1457. You are a fish salesman, are you not? **Fish salesman and smack** [sail powered vessel] owner at **Brixham**.

1498. Do you remember if it was not generally admitted that small soles from the western coasts were much more valuable than soles of the same size from the east coast? That theory has always been accepted when I have heard the question asked.

1499. Therefore, do you think that if there is any hardship in limiting the sale, it would press much more seriously on the fishermen on the south coast than it would on other coasts? – I think so, yes.

1500. With regard to the **lemon soles and plaice**, are there as many of them now on the south coast as there were formerly, do you think? **I should say we catch 50 to 1 to what we did three years ago.** That is, lemon soles principally; but we have had a **similar increase in plaice**...

1520. Is there any other point you would like to refer to? –No.

1521. You are at any rate of opinion that, so far as the **west and south coasts of England** are concerned, the **fisheries have not fallen off**-? **Decidedly**.

1522. And that, therefore, there is no reason for legislation in order to maintain them in their satisfactory condition? – That is quite so.

The way that essential information from these extracts can be represented is shown in Table 19.1.

Good for purposes of illustration, the two selections and the table are not meant to convey the full complexity of the testimony. Witnesses sometimes describe grounds that were abundant in fish and others that were in decline or even 'fished out'; that the decline of one kind of fish, such as sole, was accompanied by an increase in mackerel; that line fisherman closer to shore were capturing fewer fish than before while steam trawlers with their deep nets and power to fish at great distance in several different fishing grounds continued to bring in larger catches. At the Dogger Bank in the North Sea, for example, trawlers (sail and steam powered) had mixed success, with varied reports of stocks on the *increase, no falling off,* or in *decline.*

These three categories are used to classify the fish-stock estimates. This simplification is the reasonable compromise needed to map comprehensible patterns and describe them with due qualification. Based on the accounts of 60 witnesses, Figure 19.4

Table 19.1 Coding of essential information from the Commission.

Witness	Occupation	Residence	Fishing ground worked	Estimate of fish stocks in that area
J. T. Exton	fishery representative; retired fisherman	Grimsby	North Sea	falling off
W. J. Saunders	fish salesman and boat owner	Brixton	English Channel Bristol Channel	Increase and abundance

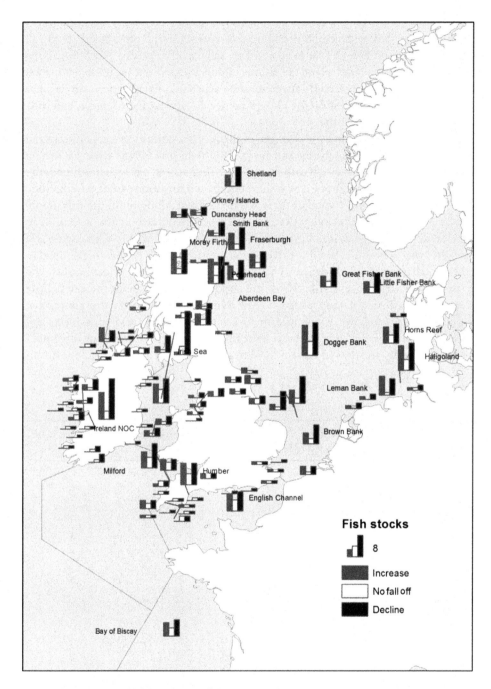

Figure 19.4 Estimated fish stocks by fishing ground, 1893.

shows the geography of estimated stocks recorded in the commission's minutes of evidence.

The term overfishing was not used without reason. Nearly every fishing area identified provided evidence on declining fish stocks. On the other hand, nearly all reported either some degree of increase or no falling off in stocks. Not surprisingly members and representatives of the fishing industry expressed more concern than witnesses who were less directly affected, often repeating their opinions on declines and overfishing in their testimony. Government officials, marine scientists, and professors nonetheless shared the same opinion, as Table 19.2 shows.

With these patterns at hand we can evaluate the committee's conclusion and recommendations more reliably and more fully than a reading of the *final report only* would allow. Because weather and fish migrations partly determined the relative success of any fishery it was difficult, the commission stated, to conclude from conflicting reports 'whether there has been a real falling off in the fish supply of a particular district'. Under that rather broad qualification, the commission concluded that there was no immediate threat to the supplies of cod, haddock, and mackerel that served the needs of mass consumption. With regard to the herring fisheries, there was no evidence of falling off, except for one exception on the Scottish west coast. In the fisheries of the south coast of England, there was little of no falling off of sole and plaice. In the North Sea, however, the committee concluded that evidence from fishermen, scientific experts, and statisticians left little doubt that sole and other flat fish were much depleted, a diminution attributed to overfishing by trawlers in certain localities as well as the taking of an enormous

Table 19.2 Opinions on the conditions of fish stocks by occupational group, 1893.

Occupational Group	Increase	Abundant	No falling off	Decline	Overfishing	Total mentions	No. (Docs)
Fishing trade							
fish association	8	5	1	6	5	29	6
fish merchant	2	3	3	6	11	36	11
vessel owner	5	4	7	8	17	48	13
fisherman	6	1	2	7	14	34	18
oyster merchant	0	0	0	0	2	7	2
government official	0	0	2	12	5	27	6
marine scientist	3	1	2	4	9	22	4
professor	2	1	3	0	6	13	3
lawyer	0	0	0	1	0	1	2
gentleman	0	0	0	2	1	5	1
Total	26	15	20	46	70	224	0
							66

Source: BPP, Report from the Select Committee on Sea Fisheries; Together with the Proceedings of the Committee, Minutes of Evidence, Appendix and Index, 1893.

number of smaller fish on the east side of the North Sea, off the Dutch and German coasts.[8]

Had the testimony indicated that only one or two fishing sites were depleted, the conclusions would likely have been less guarded and more optimistic, echoing the confidence in fishing without limits that the 1863 commission had conveyed. In 1893, however, a new, realistic consensus emerged. What was needed in future, the reported continued, was more research, improved data, better administration and policing of fishing, and the closing of certain fishing sites during parts of the year to protect spawning and the maturation of small offspring. Cautiously, the committee acknowledged that there were, in fact, limits to the number of fish that could be taken. Steam trawling had increased the catching power of vessels so greatly that the grounds the trawlers worked – more extensive than before – were being seriously depleted. The seas were not, after all, inexhaustible sources of food.

Meanwhile English farmers were struggling to adjust to increasing levels of imported cereals by turning arable land into grass for livestock in response to the collapse of wheat prices. And just as railways enabled the rise of industrial sea fishing, they made dairy farming and the fresh milk trade a profitable mainstay of English and Welsh agricultural business in this era of globalizing trade in food. French farmers faced the same pressures from foreign competition and American imports. Turning now to that situation takes us across the Channel and deeper into the world of agriculture, cereals, and meat.

France: too much food from America

'France is a country of cereals.' So began the report of the French Government's decennial inquiry on agriculture. More than a quarter of the national territory, the report continued, is under cereal cultivation.[9] This year's harvest was excellent and substantially exceeded the output of the average year. Wheat, the most important cereal cultivated in the country, supplies a great amount of food for the nation. Indeed, outside of the United States, France is the largest producer of wheat in the world.[10] Despite the decline of prices the production of grain during the past ten years has grown in value over the levels of 1856–65.[11] These are the signs of progress and even more promise that 'inspires full confidence in [the nation's] strength to cross over victoriously the crisis that it has suffered for some time and reach a new era of prosperity'.[12]

Reassuring and optimistic about the future, the 1882 report, published in 1887, was at pains to emphasize progress and ignore the matter of the agrarian crisis. Indeed, the word 'crisis' appeared only twice in the 400 pages of text. Had they read the report, land owners and farmers would have been puzzled or dissatisfied. There were only brief discussions in the report of foreign competition, only a few remarks about the importance of improved transportation, and no attention to the problems with open agricultural markets and the need for tariff protection.

When the inquiry was undertaken in 1882, the agrarian crisis in France was in its fifth or sixth year, and it was still serious when the Minister of Agriculture published the results in 1887. The report's silence on the issues of great concern to rural elites, large farmers, and the rural population concealed the mounting political pressure on the Third Republic to relieve the causes of the continuing crisis. In the unpublished evidence and opinion that local and departmental officials had submitted, however, there was no shortage of complaints and warnings about continuing distress and the widespread belief in protection as remedy. In response and with reluctance, tariffs were introduced, first on live animals, meat, and wine in 1881; then on cereals and wine in 1885, the rates of which were increased in 1887 and 1894 in an effort to raise the continuing depressed prices of cereals.[13] That tariffs were in place by the time the report was published perhaps suggests the conscious omission of that politically charged issue.

Something new about the political pressure and the conversion of rural elites to the cause of protection can be learned by examining the previous inquiry of 1879. An inquiry largely overlooked by historians, it was not, strictly speaking, a government inquiry but one that the Minister of Agriculture and Commerce, M. Charles Tirard, requested the National Society of Agriculture to carry out. Founded in 1761, it was the oldest and most prestigious academy of rural elites with members in every region of the country. The Minister's request for the Society's help was urgent. Recently, his letter began, unrest among farmers 'forcefully awakened' the Government's attention. Given the need to search for the causes of the complaints, it was crucial to discover whether they arose from temporary difficulties or enduring problems. With its 'learned men and correspondents owing property in all parts of France', the Society is ideally suited to clarifying the grave issues in question.[14]

Taking account of the Minister's specific concerns, the permanent secretary of the society sent a letter with eleven questions to which the designated local correspondents were to respond.[15]

> What differences in the state of agricultural exist in your locality between the period preceding 1861 and the last ten years? Specifically, changes in these matters:
>
> 1 The division of property;
> 2 The production of cereals;
> 3 Stock raising, fattening of cattle, and the different products of farm animals;
> 4 The production of industrial plants (Vineyards, Beets, Hops, Tobacco, Rape seed, Mulberry trees, etc.);
> 5 The production of woodlands;
> 6 The agricultural industries (distilleries, sugar processing, cheese making, oil mills, silk worm production, starch processing, etc.)
> 7 The agricultural equipment, field drainage, irrigation and other land improvements;
> 8 The use of commercial fertilizers and manure;
> 9 The number of workers employed in agriculture and their wage rates;
> 10 The taxes on land and other levies that overburden property;
> 11 The serviceability of roads, transportation, and markets.

In addition, the letter continued, your informed thoughts on the causes of change, on the legislation authorizing free exchange in grain and the meat trade (commercial treaties of 1869) would be welcome as would suggestions for improvements for advancing prosperity.

Responses to the questions were in the hands of the secretary by the end of June, two months after they had been sent out. Promptly returned, the 88 responses varied in detail and subject matter. A few were short and cursory, others were lengthy and substantial. Although all the information desired was rarely supplied, the responses provide a valuable sample of elite opinion in all major regions of France. (See list of respondents and their home departments in the Appendix.)

Asking the society to view the present situation in comparison to 30 years ago would, it was thought, put current dissatisfactions in a more positive light. Looking back two or three decades, the society's correspondents typically mentioned signs of progress in one or more categories. Improved communications through better roads and rail service had expanded access to markets. The application to poor soil of lime and artificial fertilizers shipped in by rail helped expand cultivation and larger amounts of manure resulting from increased livestock improved yields. Better agricultural implements and, in high farming areas in the north and northeast, the increased use of steam-powered threshing machines were mentioned, too. The developing of railway access to markets was another bright spot in the current situation, although the call for the lowering of rail transport fees was loud and clear. The need for railway expansion was frequently voiced, too.

According to the correspondents, there were fewer bright spots in the fortunes of cereal farming. Among the 55 departments surveyed, evaluations of production varied across the country. (See Figure 19.5.) Expanded or improved production were reported in some six departments: in east in Côte d'Or, and, in the centre west, in the Vendee, Charente-Inférieure, Indre, Haute Vienne, Creuse, and Dordogne. Stable conditions prevailed in six other departments scattered from northwest in the Eure and Seine-Inférieure, to the upland areas of Savoie and the Haute Alpes in the south, Cantal in the south, and the Gers in the southwest. Elsewhere, in the majority of the reporting departments, low prices and declining production went hand in hand. These were the areas where the crisis was judged intense.

The foundation for these varied conditions lay in part in the growth of wheat farming since mid-century. Government statistics for 1852 and 1882 show that the expansion and intensification of wheat production was widespread, notably in the north, northwest, and west. Declines were few and scattered. Figure 19.6 shows the geography of the change. The spread of wheat cultivation after 1852 reflected a shift in response to the increased price of wheat from 1855 to 1873, together with a growing preference in breadstuffs of wheat over rye and other grains.[16] But as prices fell after 1874–6, first because of bad weather and poor harvests and then more sharply due to surging American wheat imports, wheat farmers suffered more or less depending upon the amount of land they devoted to growing wheat. Under new market conditions, the exposure to depressed prices and financial loss was bound to be greater in areas where expansion and intensification had taken place. With the exception of the Vendée, Charente, Haute Vienne, and Creuse, Figure 19.7 overlays the correspondent evaluations of cereal production on the hectares of wheat cultivation in 1882. It shows a high degree of geographic coincidence between the two. By and large, areas of increased wheat growing were in greater difficulty than areas in which wheat was a smaller part of the agricultural economy.

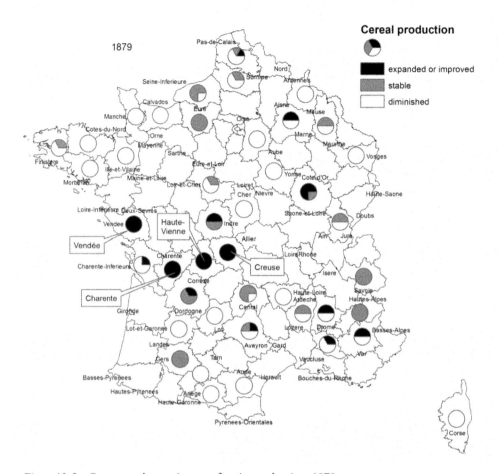

Figure 19.5 Correspondent estimates of grain production, 1879.

The spread of livestock farming was another, brighter story. According to the returns, expansion and relative prosperity prevailed in stock raising throughout the country, as Figure 19.8 indicates. With the decline of cereals prices, more land was converted from cultivation to grassland to make way for larger heads of cattle. The relative profitability of poultry – another alternative to wheat farming – was turning the *basse cour* (farmyard) and henhouse into a hedge against financial loss. Pig farming was another alternative enjoying expansion.

Prosperity in many southern departments depended upon the production of vineyards and the price of wine. Whereas land under the plough in central and northern France was frequently being converted to grassland, the parallel in the south was the conversion of land to vineyard and the growth of the wine trade. As frequently reported, however, the scourge of phylloxera was taking a toll, despite concerted effort to check the disease and its spread. The price of wine and profits declined because imports of wine from Italy and other countries flooded the market. The gradual replanting of vines with American rootstock was a long and expensive process. Marginal vineyards in the north would eventually cease production.[17]

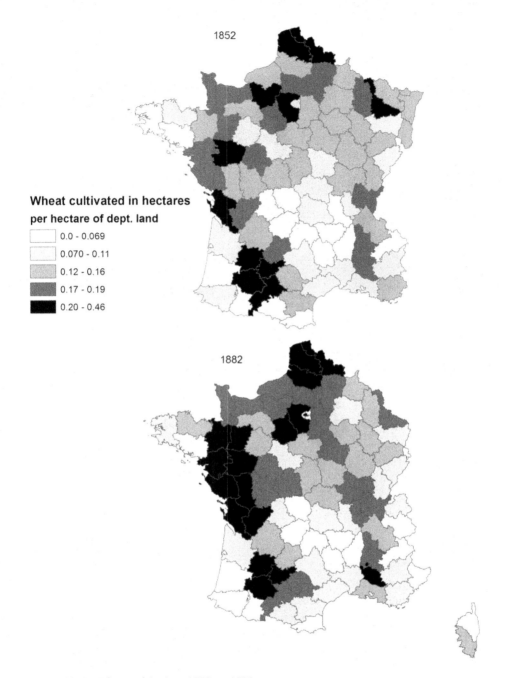

Figure 19.6   Wheat cultivation, 1852 vs. 1882.

When the correspondents turned to causes and remedies for agrarian distress, they were quick to note that a shortage of agricultural workers and the higher wages available workers demanded formed a major obstacle to recovery. Depressed prices and the rising cost of labour brought a series of changes. Land owners having

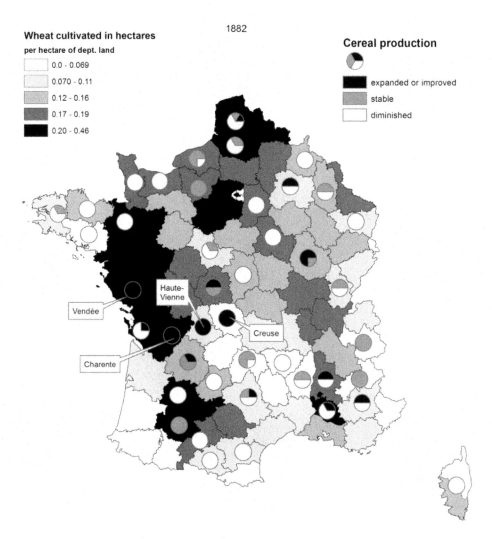

Figure 19.7 Correspondent estimates of cereal production (1879) and hectares of wheat cultivated in 1882.

difficulties leasing large farmsteads reduced rents; large tenants had trouble paying even reduced rents; capital for agricultural improvements was scarce; large leaseholds were broken up into smaller properties; land-owning cultivators gave up large tenancies and worked their own lands with little or no hired labour; as land prices declined, particularly in cereal-growing areas, agricultural workers were able to acquire small holdings, further reducing the supply of hired hands.

Just as frequently as labour shortage, correspondents cited the bad effects of foreign competition, imports from America, and the need for tariff protection. In sheep farming areas in the Aisne, the Ardèche, the Aveyron, Eure, Eure-et Loir, the Manche, the Oise, Seine-Inférieure, the Somme, and the Var, the sharp fall in wool and mutton prices was attributed to foreign imports. In the last two years, pig farming also suffered by the sudden increase in imports of American hams and

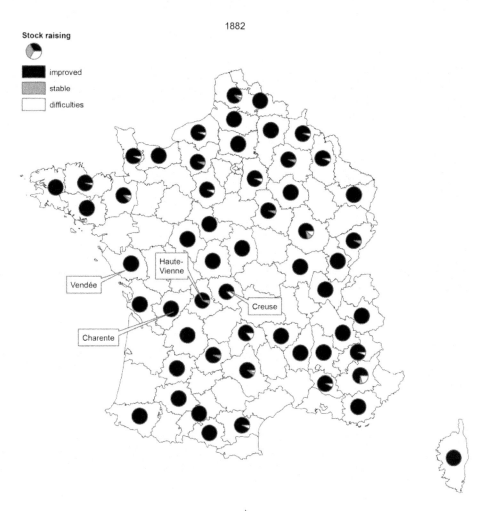

Figure 19.8 Correspondent estimates of livestock raising, 1879.

bacon. As with sheep, the depression of pork prices struck departments in the north and south – in the Ariège, the Basses-Alpes, and the Hautes-Alpes in the south; in the Ardennes, Côte-d'Or, Côtes-du-Nord, Ille-et-Vilaine, and Seine-Inférieure in the north.

In the 88 returns of the inquiry, there were three main causes cited. The need for tariff protection was mentioned 63 times; opposition to it, nine times; related complaints about the negative effects of imports and about foreign competition, 73 and 43 times respectively. Combining the complaints into one category (sum CPI) yields the results displayed in Figure 19.9. Only a few of the returns were silent on the issue. As for complaints, those from the Pas-de-Calais (north), Seine-Inférieure, Ille-et-Vilaine, Cotes-du-Nord and Finistère (northwest) were especially numerous, as were those in a line from the Loir-et-Cher in central France to the Aveyron. Three north-eastern departments – Seine-et-Marne, Marne, and Meuse – and the Charente-Inférieure in the centre west followed closely behind in expressing reasons for protection.

1882

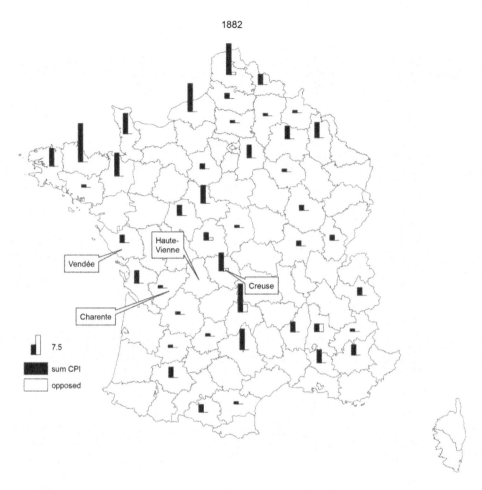

Figure 19.9 Correspondent mentions of causes related to foreign competition, imports, and need for tariff protection.

Some statements were blunt denunciations of the commercial treaties of 1869 that had authorized free trade in agricultural products. 'The current legislation', wrote M. de Plagniol in the Archdèch, 'is the ruin of our agriculture in the south.'[18] In the northwest department of the Eure, the marquis d'Argent attributed the destruction of sheep farming to American woollen imports and imports of German sheep: 'Free trade is the cause of the decline of prices in all our agricultural products. The wool industry, the former source of wealth in the Beauce, destroyed by the competition of American woollens, has reduced sheep farming to the production of mutton only, which is now threatened by an invasion of German sheep.'[19] According to Edmond de Roquefeuil of the Côtes-du-Nord in Brittany, the remedy for agricultural distress was the swift suppression of the commercial treaties, and the return to protection through duties at least equivalent to the tax burdens on agriculture.[20]

Other returns offered more balanced assessments. In the Pas-de-Calais, where prosperity from highly developed wheat production was disappearing, the comte de Marne argued the need to protect the profitability of a diversifying agrarian economy. 'I do not want excessive import duties', but duties sufficient to permit us to profit from 'our varied cultivations' of sugar beets, linens, vegetable oils, and stock raising.[21] Other comments invoked the need for equal treatment with manufacturing industries enjoying tariff protection. One such balanced approach came from M. Vandercolm in the very same department of Pas-de-Calais. The key principle to follow, based on his more than 60 years of experience, is equality, 'equal import duties for all industries – agriculture, commerce, and manufacturing – and reciprocity in the commercial accords with foreign countries'. Level the playing field of commerce.

Fewer returns voiced support for the continuation of free trade. M. Roche in the Drome seemed to draw on Adam Smith in arguing that competition would eventually bring renewed confidence and economic prowess. Import duties in the current world of rapid communications and advancing technologies would serve to isolate a country behind a wall of 'false protection', weakening its productive forces accordingly. Free trade for all – industry *and* agriculture – is 'the sole means to restore future confidence and energy to our agricultural population now so deeply in distress'.[22]

In the end, passionate calls for protection from cereal regions in the north and northwest, failed to carry the day. At meetings of society members in January, February, and March 1880, there was vigorous debate over the utility of raising tariffs on imported grain. Of the 88 members present when the issue come to a vote, five abstained. Of the 83 who voted, a slight majority (44) prevailed over the proponents of protection (33). The recommendation sent to the Minister was twofold: to continue the status quo in the grain trade and to aid cereal farmers not by increasing duties but by lowering the tax burden weighing on arable agriculture. That policy, a majority of Society believed, would go some way toward restoring profitability to cereal farmers without artificially raising the cost of essential food for the population.

A second vote, with little or no opposition, recommended tariff relief for livestock farming. A modest duty, equivalent to the small duty on imported wheat introduced in 1861, should be levied on foreign imports of animals and meat.

The Minister of Agriculture and the Chamber of Deputies evidently took these two recommendations seriously. While the grain trade remained an open international market until 1885, entry duties were placed on imports of live animals and meat as well as wine in 1881.

In light of the divided opinion on protection for domestic cereal production, a huge parliamentary inquiry was launched in 1884, under the initiative and direction of the republican deputy, Eugene Spuller. A vast body of opinion from farmers, tenants, sharecroppers, agricultural wage-workers, and Parisian artisans and workers was collected, and the returns, never published, live on in the National Archives. From a sample of the documents, Jonathan Liebowitz found that farmers – about 73 per cent of the responses – were uniformly agreed that agriculture was in crisis. Because about half of respondents attributed the crisis to foreign competition or low prices, the survey returns, Liebowitz concludes, suggest a widespread and growing belief among the rural population in the need for protection.[23]

However little Spuller and other republican deputies cared to study the survey returns, building pressure from agricultural associations and the republican desire to win the loyalties of the rural population led to the vote for protection of French cereal production in 1885. The rate was raised in 1887 and again 1894 in an attempt to increase the price of cereals during the continuing crisis.[24]

The value of analysing the 1879 enquiry is restoring an early moment in the shift from free trade to protection in French agricultural thinking and policy. A moment usually ignored, its study is revealing of elite opinion, outside of government circles, on the varied situation of agriculture under the new, challenging conditions of globalizing trade in food. Members of the National Society of Agricultural in France were divided on a central question of the time: whether agrarian distress from increasing foreign competition should be relieved through tariff duties or whether that very competition would keep food prices low and, as some believed, stimulate positive change, innovation, and profitable adjustments in French agricultural practice.

Using text mining greatly facilitates the analysis of some 500 pages of elite opinion in 1879 inquiry. Combining some of the results with a GIS of agricultural data makes it possible to discover overlapping geographic patterns of correspondent opinion and the differing agricultural systems across the country. Despite the claim to the contrary in the Minister's report of 1882 (published 1887) France was becoming less of a 'cereal country' and regional specialization was taking place. In the north, northeast, parts of the west, and centre west were the intense cereal producing areas; in the central south were the vineyard and wine regions; in Normandy, Brittany, in the west, and in upland areas of the Jura, the centre, the south, the Pyrenees, and Savoie were expanding pastoral areas with increasing numbers of beef cattle and dairy cows. With notable exceptions the geography of complaints concerning foreign competition, low prices, and the need for protective tariffs corresponds with that of cereal production and of those pastoral areas suffering from imports of sheep, woollens, and American pork products.

The same methods applied to historical documents on British sea fishing expand our understanding of the nature, timing, and geographical extent of concerns about declining fish stocks and overfishing. Spatial data on British railways adds further to that understanding by highlighting the essential role of rapid rail transport in the development of the industrialized trade in fresh fish. In that process fresh fish became a commodity – abundant, inexpensive, high protein food for mass consumption. The addition of steam-powered trawlers with greatly increased catching power and expanding geographical range multiplied the fish returned from sea and sent by train to markets. That multiplication and its effects on fish supplies worried rival fishermen, fishery associations, government officials, and marine scientists. The rise in English fish 'n' chips for all was thus accompanied by a growing ecological awareness of overfishing and 'fished out' banks in the North Sea.

Mixed methods in spatial history

The partnership of text mining and GIS, one could say, increased the historical catching power of our study of food from farms and from the sea. More broadly, the chapter shows the value of integrating systematic study of large document collections and historical geography with economic, agricultural, and environmental history. Such integration will hopefully interest students and scholars in France and the United States especially, for in these countries geographically thinking in studies of the past has nearly disappeared in favour of studying contemporary issues and cultural history. Although this situation is changing as interest in historical GIS grows, the advent of spatial histories that provide new understandings of change and persistence over time and space in readable articles and books is just beginning. This chapter combines geographical thinking and historical stories of place, space, perceptions, and actions at local, regional, national, and international scales. It illustrates a defining component of spatial history: identifying and interpreting spatial and temporal interconnections. With the transport revolution, the wheat harvest in Nebraska and pig production in Iowa came to affect market prices in Britain and France, showing how spatial relations evolve over time, and how a change in one part of a spatial system will likely affect others. It also shows that spatial histories have to move beyond the earlier concentration on database construction and the identification primarily of quantitative patterns across space and time. Typically, such patterns, however new and interesting, are by themselves open to limited interpretations, and they ignore the ideas and meanings in the minds of the historical actors. This is where the historian's eye for recovering information and meaning from historical sources matters. With the help of text mining this kind of recovery in combination with spatial analysis brings to the fore greater historical complexity and understanding.

Appendix: list of correspondents and their department

Region 1. Northwest

M. C. de Witt, Calvados
M. Le Sénéchal, Calvados
M. Besnard, Eure
M. le marquis d'Argent, Eure-et-Loir
M. le comte de Pontgibaud, Manche
M. Boudy, Manche
M. Marchand, Seine-Inférieure
M. Fauchet, Seine-Inférieure
M. Verrier, Seine-Inférieure

Region 2. West

M. E. de Roquefeuil, Côtes-du-Nord
M. Kersanté, Côtes-du-Nord
M. Briot de Mallerie, Finistère
M. le vicomte de Champagny, Finistère
M. le comte du Pontavice, Ille-et-Vilaine
M. Bodin, Ille-et-Vilaine
M. de Lorgeril, Ille-et-Vilaine
M. de Bouetiez de Kerorguen, Morbihan

Region 3. North

M. Vallerand, Aisne
M. Vandercolme, Nord
M. Alfred Dupont, Nord
M. Alexandre Adam, Pas-de-Calais
M. le comte de Marne, Pas-de-Calais
M. le marquis d'Havrincourt, Pas-de-Calais
M. Decauville, Seine-et-Marne
M. Garnot, Seine-et-Marne
M. Hecquet d'Orval, Somme

Region 4. Center

M. Gallicher. Cher
M. Le Corbeiller, Indre
M. Briaune, Indre
M. Goussard de Mayolle, Indre-et-Loire
M. Goffart, Loir-et-Cher

Region 5. Northeast

M. G. de Melcy, Ardennes
M. Charles Gossin, Ardennes
M. le baron Walckenaër, Aube
M. Duguet, Marne
M. Ségalas, Marne
M. Arnould, Marne
M. le baron de Benoist, Meuse
M. Millon, Meuse
M. Louis Gossin, Oise
M. Aymé, Vosges

Region 6. East

M. de Monicault, Ain
M. Detourbet, Côte-d'Or
M. Baudouin, Côte-d'Or
M. de Vergnette-Lamotte, Côte-d'Or
M. Paul Laurens, Doubs
M. Emmanuel Gréa, Jura
M. le Dr Bousson, Jura
M. le comte d'Esterno, Saône-et-Loire
M. Lacour, Yonne
M. Bazin, Yonne

Region 7. West Central

M. Clément Prieur, Charente
M. Menudier, Charente-Inférieure
M. Sauvé, Charente-Inférieure
M. Dièrers-Monplaisir, Charente-Inférieure
M. le comie de Saint-Marsault, Charente-Inférieure
M. de Larègle, Charente-Inférieure
M. Durand de Corbiac, Dordogne
M. A. Le Cler, Vendée
M. de Longuemar, Vienne
M. de Vanteaux, Haute-Vienne

Region 8. Southwest

M. Laurens, Ariége
M. Lavocat, Haute-Garonne
M. Seillan, Gers
M. le comte de la Roque-Ordan, Gers
M. de Lalyman, Lot-et-Garonne
M. de Marignan, Basses-Pyrénées

Region 9. South Central

M. Rodat, Aveyron
M. C. Roques, Aveyron
M. Monseignat, Aveyron
M. Sarrauste de Menthière, Cantal
M. Rames, Cantal
M. du Mirai, Creuse
M. Célarié, Lot

Region 10. East Central

M. de Plagniol, Ardèche
M. Hedde, Haute-Loire

Region 11. South

M. Louis de Martin, Aude
M. Cunéo d'Ornano, Corse

Notes

1 Parts of the section on fisheries draws upon my article: R. M. Schwartz, 'Digital Partnership: Combining Text Mining and GIS in a Spatial History of Sea Fishing in the United Kingdom, 1860 to 1900', *International Journal of Humanities and Arts Computing* 9, 2015, 36–56.

2 Further details and bibliography on the agrarian crisis in Britain and France can be found in several of my previous articles: R. M. Schwartz, 'Agricultural Change and Politics in Late Nineteenth Century Britain: The Enquiries of Two Royal Commissions, 1879–1897', in N. Vivier (ed.), *The Golden Age of Agricultural Enquiries*, Brussels: Brepols, 2014, 129–56; R. Schwartz, I. Gregory and T. Thevenin, 'Spatial History: Railways, Uneven Development, and Population Change in France and Great Britain, 1850–1914', *Journal of Interdisciplinary History* 62, 2011, 53–88; R. Schwartz, 'Rail Transport, Agrarian Crisis, and the Restructuring of Agriculture: France and Great Britain Confront Globalization, 1860–1900', *Social Science History* 34, 2010, 229–55.

3 House of Commons Parliamentary Papers [BPP], *Report of the Commissioners Appointed to Inquire into the Sea Fisheries of the United Kingdom*, vol. 1, The Report and Appendix, 1866, 173.

4 T. Huxley, 'Inaugural Address, Fisheries Exhibition, London (1883)'. Accessed June 2013. http://mathcs.clarku.edu/huxley/SM5/fish.html.Inaugural

5 *Report of the Commissioners Appointed to Inquire into the Sea Fisheries of the United Kingdom*, vol. 2, Minutes of Evidence and Index, 1866; testimony of 3 October 1863, 3 October 1864, and 1 October 1864.

6 Schwartz, 'Digital Partnership', 43–8.

7 The software program I use is MaxQDA from the German company Verbi; it is well suited to mining large corpuses of documents in pdf format.

8 BPP *Report from the Select Committee on Sea Fisheries; Together with the Proceedings of the Committee, Minutes of Evidence, Appendix and Index*, pp. iv–v.

9 *Statistique agricole de la France, publié par Le Ministre de l'Agriculture, Résultats Généraux de l'Enquête Décennale de 1882* (Nancy, 1887), 6.

10 *Statistique agricole de la France*, 19.

11 *Statistique agricole de la France*, 14.

12 *Statistique agricole de la France*, 404.

13 R. Price, *The Modernization of Rural France: Communications Networks and Agricultural Market Structures in Nineteenth-Century France*, London: Palgrave, 1983, 339.

14 Académie d'agriculture de France, *Enquête sur la situation de l'agriculture en France en 1879*, faite à la demande de M. Le Ministre de l'agriculture et du commerce (Paris, 1879), 1–2.

15 Académie d'agriculture de France, *Enquête sur la situation de l'agriculture*, 7–8.

16 France, *Statistique agricole de la France (Algerie et Colonies) Publiée par le Ministre de l'agriculture. Résultats Généraux de l'enquête décennale de 1882* (Nancy, 1887), 62, 'Prix de l'hectolitre de froment de 1756 à 1885'.

17 Price, *Modernization*, 317–18, 373–4.

18 Académie d'agriculture de France, *Enquête sur la situation de l'agriculture*, 475.

19 Académie d'agriculture de France, *Enquête sur la situation de l'agriculture*, 15.

20 Académie d'agriculture de France, *Enquête sur la situation de l'agriculture*, 70.

21 Académie d'agriculture de France, *Enquête sur la situation de l'agriculture*, 143.

22 Académie d'agriculture de France, *Enquête sur la situation de l'agriculture*, 534.

23 J. Liebowitz, 'Rural Support for Protection: Evidence from the Parliamentary Inquiry of 1884', *French History* 7, 1993, and 'The French Parliamentary Inquiry of 1884: A Response to Multiple Crises', in N. Vivier (ed.), *The Golden Age of Agricultural Enquiries*, Brussels: Brepols, 2014, 175–90.

24 Price, *Modernization*, 339.

PART V

Spatial political history

INTRODUCTION TO PART V

Don DeBats, Ian Gregory, and Don Lafreniere

Political history and spatial analysis are a long noted duality. A century ago (in 1914), in the United States, Frederick Jackson Turner proclaimed 'a geography of public opinion' and called for a mapping of election results by towns and counties, and, best of all, election precincts to show 'geographical influence'. While the work had been as yet 'insufficiently carried out', it had already revealed, Turner wrote, 'a most significant geographical influence in American political history'. Conceding that there was no absolute 'geographical control', Turner called particular attention to the 'areas influenced or controlled by geological factors wherein capitalistic considerations are strongest', and their affiliation with Whig and Republican parties.[1]

Inspired, an early generation of American political historians (and sociologists) led by legendary figures such as Orin Libby, Charles Beard, and Albion Small set forth to map and explain the political behavior of 'areas'.[2] They published in leading journals such as the *American Historical Review* and newly created journals such as *Political Science Quarterly*.

The pattern on the other side of the Atlantic was not so different, with path-breaking studies of the geographical influences on French and English elections appearing in 1913 and 1916.[3] The French tradition perhaps endured more rigorously than the English but the convergence of interests and methodologies in studying the role of geography in political history, and especially voting behavior, is striking.[4] The explanatory model placed the spatial unit at its core and sought to demonstrate the influence of the area's characteristics on its inhabitants.[5]

From this powerful base we might have expected the arrival of GIS methodologies and technologies to have re-energized the study of political history. Yes, to a degree that has happened, perhaps for two reasons. In part GIS's success reflects a lesson learned: for HGIS to succeed and flourish it must avoid the pathway of an earlier 'new political history' which in the 1970s drove toward ever more esoteric techniques and methodologies – the end result of which was to exclude many political historians from the movement.[6] By contrast, HGIS remains stridently inclusive, most clearly based in the Social Science History Association and the European Social

Science History Association networks, consciously reaching out to other disciplines, interests, questions, and data. Moreover, increasing numbers of historians attracted by the power of visualization that it presents have grasped the GIS nettle, not necessarily encumbered by the need to delve into the complexities of spatial measures that are also part of GIS packages.

The result is an expanding field of spatial political history, but in many more areas than those early enthusiasts for a more prominent role for geographic factors in historical political analysis might have anticipated. As two of the chapters in this section show, GIS has assisted in demonstrating the spatial influences that Turner, Libby, and Beard and Small anticipated in situations where individual level voting data survives and in others where it can be obtained for small units. When combined with these levels of past political information, GIS makes possible insights into the past electorate more precise than those available from most of our contemporary political analysis. A wide variety of political histories deploy GIS to generate new displays of spatial information that can, as visualization, generate new knowledge. That is the pattern of the chapters in this section.

Don DeBats shows how GIS's central attribute, locating an array of data at a point, can be used to repopulate a nineteenth-century land ownership map that originally excluded African-Americans, creating a more representative display of the actual residential population. Using rare individual-level political information and spatial statistics, this new knowledge makes possible fresh insights into the extent and circumstances of persisting African-American political engagement during the highly contested Reconstruction era. Using GIS to confront the challenge of visualizing change over space and time, Ruth Mostern combines gazetteer information with GIS to visualize Chinese political landscapes. A modified regional systems approach provides an opportunity to understand in new ways Chinese political authority over time and space, first in the Song dynasty and then, using an approach that incorporates events and narratives, along the Yellow River watershed. In the third chapter, George Vascik uses census data at the village level to examine landscape and soil patterns that were associated with different levels of social stratification during the volatile period following WWI. Having reconstructed electoral data in three German provinces in the period, he uses GIS to understand the spatial arrangement associated with rising levels of anti-Semitism and Nazi support. 'Redlining' is the theme of the final chapter written by Nathan Connolly, LaDale Winling, Robert Nelson, and Richard Marciano. They revisit the Federal government's Home Owners' Loan Corporation which gathered the four color risk maps (A–D, green–red) produced by local realators in every major American city for the information of all investors, re-enforcing the segregation of real estate in American cities and furthering the decline of those identified with the scarlet letter.

In all these ways, GIS is giving political history a welcome boost.

Notes

1   F.J. Turner, 'Geographical Influences in American Political History', *Bulletin of the American Geographical Society* 46, 1914, 591–5.
2   O. Libby, 'The Geographical Distribution of the Vote of the Thirteen States on the Federal Constitution, 1787–8', *Bulletin of the University of Wisconsin: Economics, Political Science, and*

History 1, 1894, 1–116; C. Beard, *An Economic Interpretation of the Constitution of the United States*, New York: Macmillan, 1913; A. Small, *General Sociology: An Exposition of the Main Development in Sociological Theory From Spencer to Ratzenhofer*, Chicago, IL: University of Chicago Press, 1905.

3 A. Siegfried, *Tableau Politique de la France de L'ouest Sous la Troisieme Republique*, Paris: A. Colin, 1913; E. Kareil, 'Geographical Influences in British Elections', *Geographical Review* 6, 1916, 429–32.

4 P. J. Taylor and R. Johnson, *Geography of Elections*, Harmondsworth: Penguin Books, 1979, 21.

5 R. Jensen, 'Six Sciences of American Politics', *Historical Methods* 17, Summer 1984, 110. See also Taylor and Johnson, *Geography of Elections*, 24–7.

6 For a critique at the time see S.P. Hays, 'Historical Social Research: Concept, Method, and Technique', *Journal of Interdisciplinary History* 4, 1974, 475–82.

20

WHITE MAPS AND BLACK VOTES

GIS and the electoral dynamics of white and African-American voters in the late nineteenth century

Don DeBats

GIS and political analysis

Technological advances in lithography in the mid nineteenth century presented commercial opportunities for American mapmaking companies to create and then supply a market for county landownership maps. As historical documents these maps preserve in exquisite detail the landscape and topography of the counties for which they were produced, locating and naming individual landowners in that colourful tapestry. But the business plan behind these enterprises was to restrict the names inscribed on the map to those landowners most likely to purchase the mapmakers' fine product. And fine they were. The inevitable result, however, was a map with a particularized presentation of a county's inhabitants. This chapter shows how Geographic Information Systems (GIS) technologies and methodologies can transform these suspect commercial products into rich historical resources. It demonstrates the utility of a transformed map of Garrard County, Kentucky to discover the spatial patterning and the socio-economic circumstances associated with the exercise of the suffrage by the newly enfranchised African-Americans along with their white allies and opponents in the dark and threatening days during and after the end of Reconstruction.

Deploying the power of the map to visualize and explain American history is as old as the profession itself, with Orin Libby's study of the geography of the votes on the ratification of the US Constitution a remarkable early effort.[1] Today GIS combined with individual-level political information brings new promise of a reinvigorated political history.

This chapter deploys GIS in two different ways. It first uses GIS to correct the deliberate omission of poor farmers, white and especially black, from the 1879 landownership map of Garrard County. GIS makes it possible to reinsert into that map those intentionally excluded from it, transforming a highly skewed historical document created for a privileged elite to an inclusive spatial database of the county's entire resident population. GIS does this by collecting and then locating at a point on the map all of the individual-level data (including in this case individual political behavior) associated with the residents of each dwelling. The chapter then uses GIS methodologies to specify the spatial characteristics of the fierce political and racial struggle then taking place over how the nation's social order would be reconstructed following the Civil War.[2]

GIS is best conceived of as a tool to create new information from existing data. Just as it can reconstruct Civil War battles to show us how the war looked from the vantage of soldiers and their generals, it can allow us to visualize the political battle-field of Reconstruction, shedding new light on how the struggle for political rights and power was won or lost.[3]

Viva voce voting: unique data from a persisting electoral form

Kentucky was Lincoln's birthplace and the largest slave-owning state that remained loyal to the Union: in 1860 23 percent of Kentucky's white families owned a total of 225,483 slaves, a commitment to slavery exceeding that of Tennessee, its Confederate neighbor. After the war, Kentucky alone among all states brought its large and newly freed African-American population into the electorate under oral or *viva voce* electoral laws.[4]

In elections conducted *viva voce*, each voter was required to announce (or had read aloud) his political choices. *Viva voce* elections, like all eighteenth- and nineteenth-century elections, were conducted out-of-doors, before interested observers.[5] There was no secrecy, whether votes were made orally or by party-produced ticket (the only two modes of voting until the adoption of the secret ballot in the 1890s). Under either system voting was public, at polling stations created on the steps or nearby the local courthouse or city hall, outside a private house, or even a tavern. In an election conducted *viva voce* voters ascended a platform where election officials administered oaths and clerks inscribed in a "poll book," the official record of the election, the name of each voter as he came forward, preserving the sequence in which votes were cast as well as the choice of all voters for all positions being filled, from president to alderman. Poll books, where they survive, are an unsurpassed trove of political infor-mation and the envy of political scientists studying modern political behavior.

In Washington, radical Republicans controlled the US Senate and, anticipating the Fifteenth Amendment which would enfranchise African-American males, feared that the newly freed slaves voting by voice would be subject to undue influence from their former owners, current employers, or the white population.[6] During debates over the Supplementary Reconstruction Bills in March, 1867, Senator Oliver Morton (Republican of Indiana) stated the case against allowing *viva voce* to continue in states where large numbers of newly freed slaves would vote:

They are dependent. Let me suppose a case where there are fifty colored voters on one plantation; their little homes are on that plantation; they are dependent upon the owner of it for their employment and their daily food. If he is a candidate and stands by the polls, and these poor men come up to vote and understand full well that if they vote against him they will be ejected from their homes and lose their employment, I say that they are not independent voters. It is, therefore, necessary to secure the independence of such voters that they be allowed to vote by ballot and to vote secretly.[7]

Morton confused, as have many political historians, a vote by ticket with a secret vote: the deliberate colors and distinctive designs of party-produced tickets ensured that an interested observer almost anywhere in eighteenth- or nineteenth-century America could determine the content of each individual's vote.[8] Nevertheless, Morton's fear that the autonomy and independence of African-Americans would be compromised carried the day, and states of the Confederacy like Virginia and Arkansas that had long conducted elections under *viva voce* law relinquished that tradition as a condition of re-entry into the Union.[9] But Kentucky, a Union state, was not subject to the demands of Reconstruction and it retained, with no scrutiny, its oral voting tradition even as it reluctantly freed and then enfranchised a large black population.[10]

Most of Kentucky's poll books, which existed at one time for all elections from its colonial experience as part of Virginia to the adoption of the secret ballot in 1891, have been lost, by fire, by flood, but mostly by indifference to their value as remarkable sources of past political information: the most accurate record of voter choice in American political history.[11] Where they survive, however, as they do for Garrard County, they provide the ultimate level of insight into past electoral behavior.

Black voters are recorded in the County poll books from enfranchisement in 1870 through the long period of intimidation and terror which ensued after the Republicans' pursuit of racial equality ended in 1877. African-American voting, and poor white voting too, was all but eliminated by 1896 following the adoption of the Australian written ballot in 1892 (which functioned as a literacy test) and other legislative means of disenfranchisement, including a more formal literacy test and the imposition of a poll tax.[12]

Nineteenth-century commercial mapmaking

The 1879 map of Garrard County and Lincoln Counties (Figure 20.1) was produced by the D. G. Beers and J. Lanagan Lithography Company of Philadelphia. Over 5,000 county-level maps showing individual landowners were produced in the US, mostly between 1850 and 1880.[13] They were powerful cultural documents, produced as part of public enthusiasm to prove individual participation in a tangible record of societal progress.

The maps were "a mass-market novelty item purveying personalized symbols of pioneer pride in agrarian progress and individual achievement… and a sense of personal participation in the epic of American westward colonization."[14] They were most popular in the north-east and the mid-west and far less common in the South, but when created, they reflected all of the additional social mores of that region.

The three most prominent companies producing landownership maps were the Philadelphia firms of D. Jackson Lake, Daniel G. Beers, and J. Lanagan. Often in partnership, as in the Garrard production, they created and marketed exquisite maps using the newest lithographic technologies, which were far cheaper than the traditional craft of laboriously engraving steel or copper plates. This technological revolution made possible at an affordable price a visualization of the spatial relationships of county residents to their neighbors, of roads and railroads, and of topographical

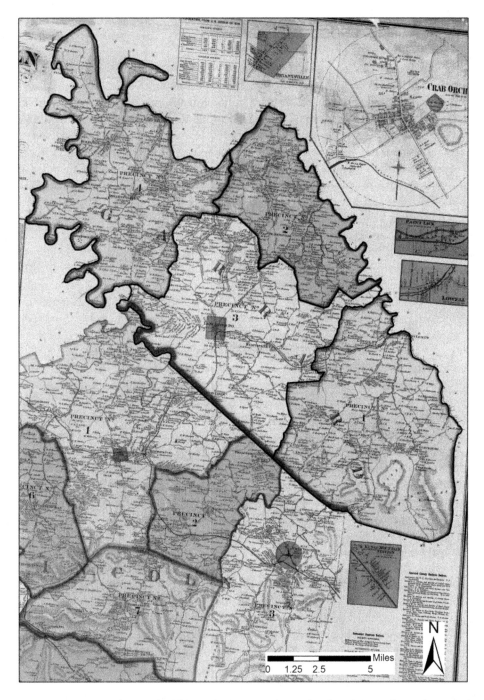

Figure 20.1 Map of Garrard and Lincoln counties, Kentucky, from 'new and actual surveys,'
D. G. Beers and J. Lanagan, Philadelphia, 1879.

features, large and small. They were the first views from above, a perspective the named individuals on the map had never before seen.

The commercial incentive dictating the production of these maps determined the companies' approach to the people and counties they were mapping. The business plan was as clear as it was ruthless: to produce a product that would sell to those able to buy and would place the buyers in a distinctive category. The possession of such a map was a dramatic novelty in the hard business of farming; they named the chosen landowners, attached them to a plot of land for all to see, offering proof of success, societal and individual. The maps were heavily advertised and offered in various sizes and configurations.[15] Prices ranged from about $6 to $60, depending on the size and coloration of the map and the number of additional property sketches included in the package. Bates Harrington, in his devastating critique of the county-map business, estimated that a map company could make a profit of nearly 100 percent with a run of about 1,200 prints.[16]

The Beers and Lanagan map of Garrard also included neighboring Lincoln County, an oft used technique that preserved detail while increasing the likelihood of a profit from the map by decreasing the number of necessary buyers in each county. The existing 1870 population figures showed Garrard and Lincoln as almost exactly the same size (10,376 vs 10,947), with 1,741 households in Garrard and 1,555 in Lincoln. On Harrington's calculations, the sales agents who toured the counties, selling the maps in advance of their creation, could achieve their targets if they were successful in making 600 sales (about 36 percent of all households) in each county to families who would pay to see their name on the map.

The resulting map, like all those produced by the Philadelphia firms, excels in fine detail and high production values, capturing geomorphic features at a scale of 1.25 miles to the inch (Figure 20.2). The map shows elevation contours and escarpments; it names rivers and creeks, ponds, bridges, railroad lines, and depots; and it presents five grades of road: pikes (named), major roads (solid double lines), secondary roads (dotted double lines), traces (single dotted lines), and lanes (faint solid lines). Also included are distances between all major junctions. And, best of all, there were the names of the proud landowners who were so instrumental to this physical and social landscape.

The map's inscription states that it was produced from "new and actual surveys," and there is every reason to believe the veracity of this claim: the maps were accomplished by waves of visitors, led by the sales agents, followed by a team of surveyors traversing the counties' roads and trails with an odometer, "an apparatus resembling a wheelbarrow, upon which is perched a clock-like mechanism." The surveyor, a tripod slung over his shoulder, wheeled his "clock on a wheelbarrow" among pathways, attracting attention (vital for sales) and creating local excitement. Each surveyor could map about 12 square miles a day: Garrard County's 234 square miles could be mapped in a month. "Sketchers" then visited selected properties and prepared, following the instructions of owners, images of real (or imagined) property development. Then came the "closers," the canvassers – map peddlers – who signed up subscribers, who paid in advance for their map. The whole process, from initial mapping to mailing the final version of the map to subscribers, might take six months.

The most important feature of the map was the individual names of landowners. The psychology of the mapmakers' salesmanship, Harrington explained, hinged on

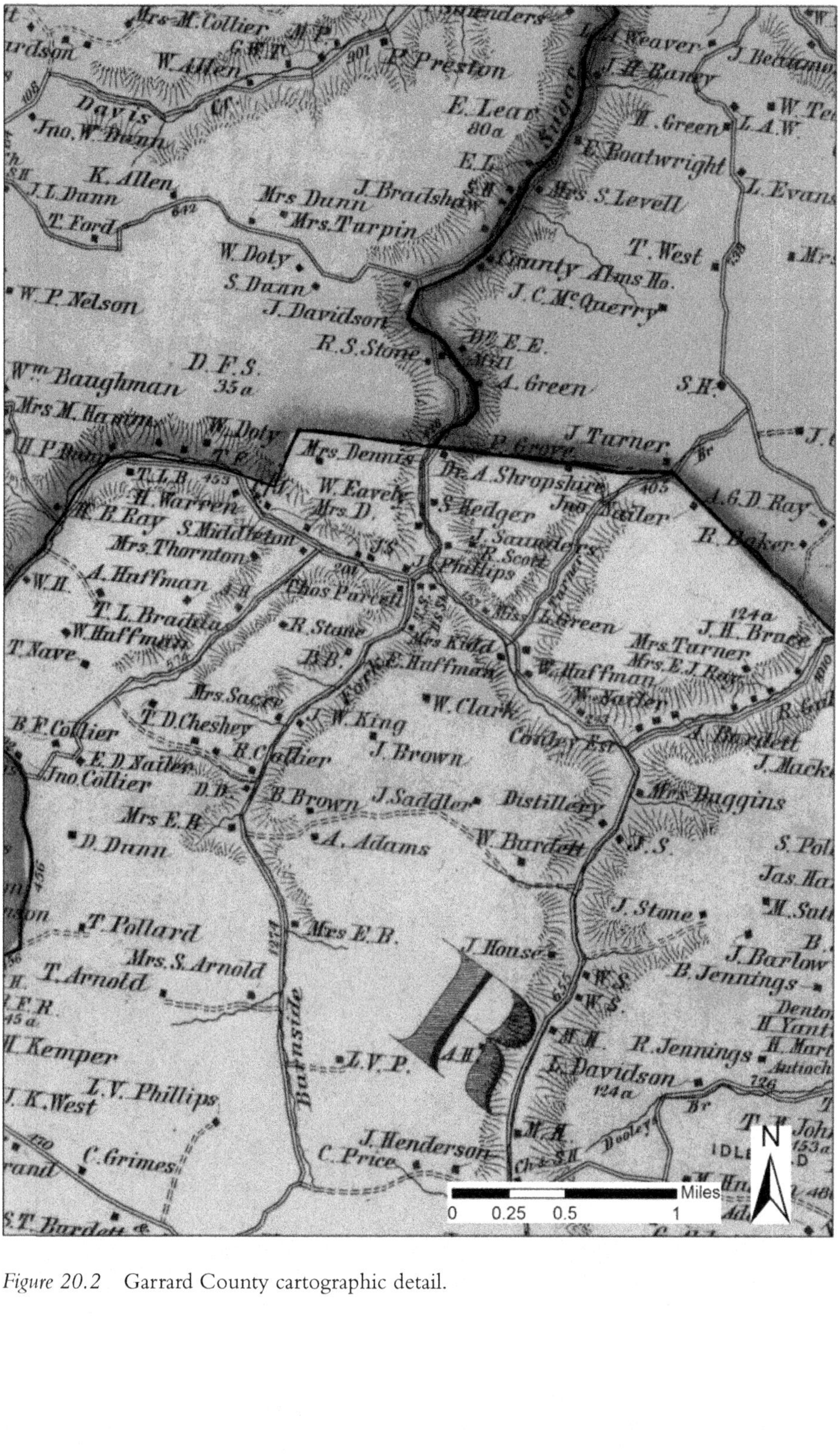

Figure 20.2 Garrard County cartographic detail.

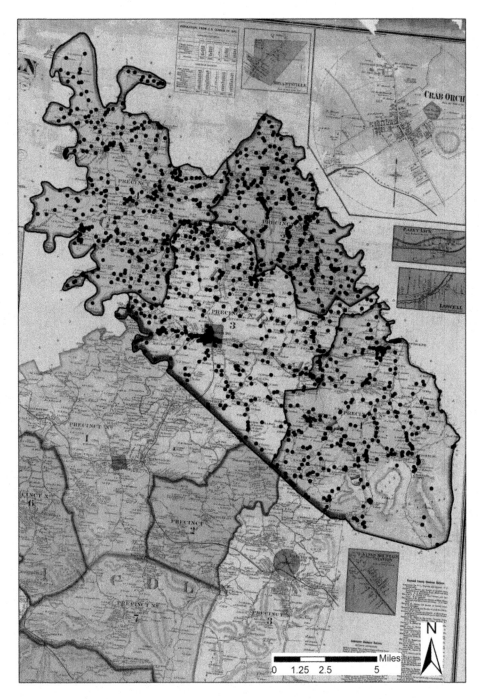

Figure 20.3   Garrard County landowners included on 1879 map.

the name that would appear on the published map: seeing "[h]is name in type was the bait that caught him."[17]

And in precisely that way the landownership mapmaking phenomenon allows us to use these objects, "to read and interpret [these] cultural landscapes for what they might tell us… about the social worlds of the past."[18] As Gary Lock puts it, "maps are not objective representations but rather the produce of a specific culturally positioned point of view and set of power relationships."[19] Indeed Garrard's map, in the selection of names it preserves, reveals much about economic and racial hierarchies in this place in the late nineteenth century. It is a representation of "power in the landscape."[20] The top of the hierarchy was visible for all to see in the names of the owners of the largest properties together with the names and acreage of their plantations: R.W. Givens' 600-acre "Fair View," Dr. G. W. Givens' adjoining 515-acre "Wood Lawn," G. R. and J. H. Bright's 500-acre plantations (Pine Grove and Sugar Grove), and J. L. Adams' 450-acre "Cliff Home."

We need not be too churlish or judgemental: this map was the first and only landownership map produced for Garrard County. It allowed all viewers, owners or not, named or not, to "see," for the first time, his or her relationship to neighbors, familiar landmarks, elevations and distances, roads, rivers, streams, and even pathways. It is by far the best historical map of the county and it had value for all residents. Figure 20.3 shows the location of the 653 rural property owners in Garrard identified on the 1879 map.[21]

Nevertheless, the hard-headed business strategy that produced this map and thousands of others like it did not allow for the creation of accurate historical documents.

The missing many in a nineteenth-century commercial landownership map

Inevitably, the published maps displayed the names of only a fraction of the heads of household, and they drastically misrepresented the class and racial structures of the areas presented. By 1880, a year after the map went on sale, the census reported Garrard's population as 11,704 (8,009 white, 3,695 black) living in 2,113 households of which 1,821 were in the countryside, the primary sales market for the map. There were 600 households headed by African-Americans, 458 in the rural sections of the county.

But the Beers and Lanagan map presented the names of only 56 African-American rural households, 12 percent of the number reported by the 1880 census and just 9 percent of the households identified by name on the map.

GIS allows us to correct this "racialized" landscape by discovering and adding those excluded from the initial map and placing them in it; we can do the same for many excluded poor whites. This use of GIS transforms a suspect document into a meaningful historical document; when individual votes are added, the augmented map becomes an opportunity to visualize the spatial dynamics of black and white voting as never before.

How to use GIS to correct a racialized landownership map

Correcting and augmenting the 138-year-old Beers and Lanagan map is complicated by the biases that determined the selection of names to be inscribed on it.

The company's business plan called for mapping landowners rather than residents and for portraying most fully and handsomely the properties of owners most likely to purchase the map. There was a corresponding disinclination to present the names of poor people and especially poor black people, who in many cases were residents but not landowners. The social hierarchy behind the map was brutally clear: the full names of the largest landowners as well as boundaries, acreages, and even the names given to their plantations; middle-order residents recorded by first initial and last name; lesser folk designated only by initials, while others even less esteemed were marked with a dot but no name. This representational hierarchy faithfully reflected the company's business plan and the need to identify the likely pool of buyers for the map, but it ensured that many residents and some landowners were excluded from the map.[22]

We initiated the corrective process by digitizing and geo-referencing the original 1879 Beers and Lanagan map, and we then used surviving records to place on the map people we know were present. The most useful records were the manuscript census returns of 1880, the 1875 and 1893 tax lists, and the poll books from eight elections chosen from the county's surviving poll books. The 1880 census returns and the 1875 county tax-assessment list helped us deduce the full names of owners identified on the map only by their initials.[23] The mapping protocol using census records to place additional people on the map began with the census entries of pairs of landowners (A and B) who appear on the Beers and Lanagan map as residents along the same road.[24] Heads of households listed consecutively in the census as being visited between A and B could then with some confidence be placed on the map along that road between the residences of A and B.[25] Using the information on "Name of Nearest Resident," which appeared for some residents on the 1875 tax list, began with finding on the map the nearest neighbor of an unmapped individual.[26] Working carefully with the data, we placed an unmapped person along the same road as the identified neighbor and closer to that neighbor than to any other mapped landowner.[27] The poll books were arranged by precinct; in this discussion we use the precinct-level information for the election closest to the implementation of the Fifteenth Amendment in Kentucky (April, 1870) and the election closest to Kentucky's implementation of the Australian secret ballot (August 3, 1891).[28] Those elections on average were 12 years apart, spanning the most controversial and violent period of the "First Enfranchisement."[29] Like the poll books, the 1893 tax list helped confirmed continued residence.

Aiding this work was the fact that the four precincts of Garrard County were strong administrative units. Those in charge of taking social inventories, whether the US census takers, the local tax collector, or the Beers and Lanagan mapmakers, hewed to those boundaries. This division of a large space into smaller units facilitated the efforts to correct the representational imbalances of the original map.[30]

Once we had located a head of household on the original map using one of our three techniques, we used GIS to consolidate all information on the entire household at that location. In these ways we added to the Beers and Lanagan map hundreds of people deliberately excluded from it when it was created 138 years ago. GIS allowed us to make these additions while preserving the original map's elegance and its detailed rendering of the topography of the landscape that made the map such a pleasing and aesthetic object. This successful combination of GIS technologies with a cautious use of census and tax information to improve the representativeness of the

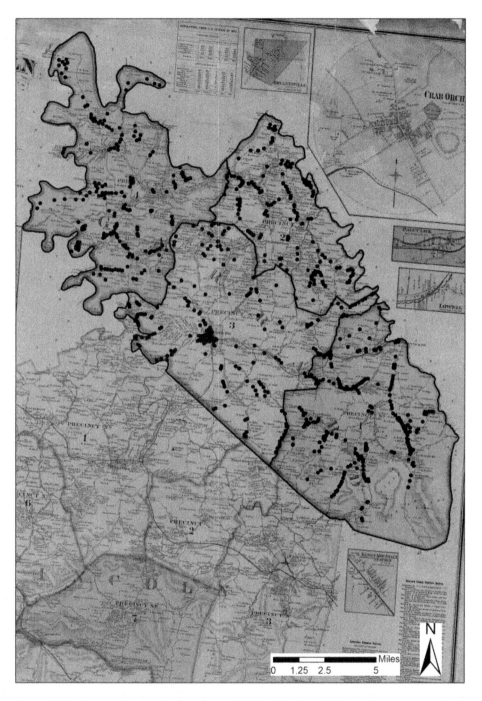

Figure 20.4 Garrard County heads of household included on 1879 map from census and tax records.

Table 20.1 Black and white headed households in rural sections of the original map and revised Beers and Lanagan map: Garrard County, Kentucky.

Precinct	Number of Black Head of Household			Number of White Head of Household			Total Number of Heads of Households			% of Census Households on Augmented Map
	on original map	added to map	total	on original map	added to map	total	original	augmented	1880 census	
Bryantsville	16	81	97	161	139	300	177	397	518	77
Buckeye	7	44	51	132	115	247	139	298	348	86
Lancaster (rural)	7	45	52	80	85	165	87	217	251	86
Brandy Springs	26	140	166	224	217	441	250	607	707	86
Total	56	310	366	597	556	1153	653	1519	1824	83

Table 20.2 Percent black heads of household by rural precinct: original map, revised map, and 1880 Census: Garrard County, Kentucky.

Precinct	Original Map		Revised Map		1880 Census
	number	% of 1880 census household heads on original map	number	% of 1880 census household heads on revised map	number
Bryantsville	16	**10**	97	**62**	157
Buckeye	7	**11**	51	**84**	61
Lancaster (rural)	7	**11**	52	**83**	63
Brandy Springs	26	**13**	166	**83**	201
Total	56	**11**	366	**76**	482

Table 20.3 Socio-economic-political profile of rural heads of household on original map, on augmented map, and in the 1880 Census.

		Original Map		Augmented Map		1880 Census	
		Black	*White*	*Black*	*White*	*Black*	*White*
Head of Household % Male		93	90	90	89	87	89
Median Age		41	48	39	43	40	44
Number of Acres	Mean	7	78	4	90	3	80
Taxed 1875	Median	0	14	0	44	0	27
Value of Acres	Mean	$119	$1,883	$57	$1,633	$39	$1,475
Taxed 1875	Median	$0	$597	$0	$600	0	$400
% Farmer		20	85	17	73	15	65
% Farm Laborer		72	4	66	13	56	15
N		56	597	366	1153	626	1542

1879 Beers and Lanagan map of Garrard County suggests these techniques might enhance the research utility of others of the more than 5,000 landownership maps created in the late nineteenth century.

The gains are threefold.

As Table 20.1 indicates, deploying these techniques more than doubled the number of heads of household placed in the rural precincts of the Beers and Lanagan map, giving us 1,519 households on the map rather than the original 653 and raising the coverage rate of the map from 36 percent to 83 percent of the 1824 rural households enumerated by the 1880 census (Figure 20.4).[31] The gain in knowledge of the location of black households creates the opportunity for a meaningful spatial analysis of racial dynamics in the county. The published map presented African-American households as 9 percent of all households identified; in the augmented map African-American-headed households constitute 24 percent of the households presented, mirroring the 1880 census which found black-headed households constituting 25 percent of households in the rural precincts.[32]

Moreover, as Table 20.2 shows, these gains in African-American representativeness are spread across Garrard's four rural precincts. The least well represented precinct is Bryantsville, in the far north of the county, but the gap between map presentation and census representation has narrowed considerably.

Finally, in demographic terms, Table 20.3 shows that the augmented population now contained in the 1879 map is far more representative of the black and white populations on the ground at that time than was the original map in terms of male-headed households, mean number and value of acres taxed, and percent farmers and farm laborers.[33] The white population too is better represented on the augmented map in terms of gender of heads of households, median age, value of acres taxed, and percent of farmers and farm laborers.[34]

Again the result is not perfect: the augmented map contains distinctively higher results than the value of acreages taxed: we still have on the map a wealthier population than that recorded in the census. In all, however, the augmented map is closer to the census profile in 14 of 16 categories of analysis: it is a far more demographically and culturally representative map than its original formulation.

Using GIS to study the effects of clustering on political behavior of African-American voters

The central defining feature of GIS is its capacity to consolidate all data associated with a point to that point. In this way, as Ian Gregory noted, GIS can be usefully thought of as "a spatially enabled database."[35] With this particular revised and spatially structured database in place we can deploy the two other defining features of GIS and

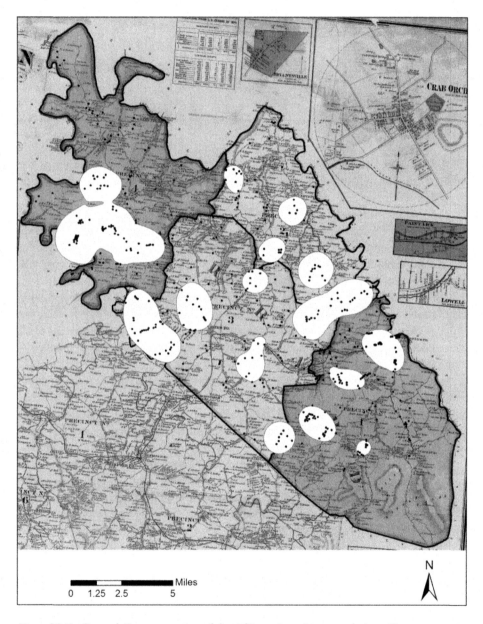

Figure 20.5   Garrard County, centers of the African-American population, 60 percent cores by precinct.

its attendant software to visualize distributions of the population on that original map and, with associated GIS technologies, to analyze aspects of that mapped distribution.

GIS technologies allow us to locate concentrations of population at any level sought; this project uses a non-parametric Kernel-density estimator with smoothing parameters to create contour lines for each gradient of the population.[36] In this project we use 60 percent as the threshold of concentration, meaning that the enclosed space contains that percentage of the total defined population. Figure 20.5 shows the spatial contours that encompass the most concentrated 60 percent of the total black population (men, women, and children; relatives, boarders, and tenants) in each of Garrard County's four precincts. This demarcation allows us to explore the effect of black-population concentrations on African-American political participation, testing a null hypothesis that strength is in numbers and that black voting was most likely to persist in areas containing the most intense concentration of fellow African-Americans.

Our measure of voting persistence is based on the earliest and latest *vive voce* election available: the election closest to enfranchisement in 1870 and the latest election before the adoption of the secret ballot in 1892. Perfect data for this analysis would consist of the same elections across all precincts for all intervening years. Unfortunately, the poll books discovered to date for Garrard County are far more irregular.

Nevertheless, we can utilize the fact that precincts were important demarcations to examine pairs of elections in each precinct. In three precincts (Bryantsville, Buckeye, and Lancaster) a presidential election is paired with a state election; in Brandy Springs the contests are both at the state level.[37] These necessary arrangements have the virtue of creating pairings that are randomized, partially controlling for the effects of peculiarities and dynamics associated with any specific election.

Table 20.4 presents data on African-American political participation in these pairs of elections in each precinct. The data include the percent of initial voters who cease to vote (Drop Out), the percent of voters in the second election who did not vote in the first election (Drop In), and the percent of initial voters who continued to vote in the second election (Continue Voting). On average the pairs of elections are 12 years apart.

We would expect turnover of the black population to be high in a period as tumultuous as Reconstruction in a former slave state, and yet there is no clear association between the length of time between elections and changes in black voting participation, whether dropping out, dropping in, or continuing to vote. Indeed, the

Table 20.4 Black voting continuity and concentration of black voters.

Precinct	*Drop Out: % Voters Cease to Participate Between Pairs of Elections*		*Continue Voting: % of Voters in First Election Who Vote in Second Election*	
	In Core	*Out of Core*	*In Core*	*Out of Core*
Bryantsville	55	**35**	45	**65**
Buckeye	83	**70**	17	**30**
Lancaster (rural)	94	**80**	6	**20**
Brandy Springs	43	**38**	57	**62**
Total	**61**	**53**	**39**	**47**
n	66	36	43	32

highest rates of change in all three dimensions occur in Buckeye precinct where the interval between elections is the lowest: 9 years.

Table 20.4 points to four important features of black voting during Reconstruction:

- In Garrard County black voting continued across the First Enfranchisement. Too often the story of Reconstruction is told only in terms of black voters being harassed, threatened, and denied the vote. That certainly happened in Garrard County. But Garrard County also tells us the beginning of another story: of black men who stood their ground and continued to vote, regardless of the pressure and threats exerted on and against their continued voting. The rates of continuity varied greatly, but continuity of voting there was.

- Second, there was an association between consistency of participation and the offices being contested. The Brandy Springs pair of elections linked state contests and, unlike the other three cases, involved no presidental election. Brandy Springs shows the lowest rates of existing voters leaving (Drop Out) and the highest rate of continuity of participation (Continue Voting). The data suggests that presidential elections with their intense partisanship and their national rather than local focus may have introduced a different dynamic into black voting participation. Indeed, rates of black participation were lowest in elections involving presidential contests. This is not the nationalization of politics, as some recent historians have suggested, but the localization of politics: perhaps all politics was local then because, to these African-American voters, local politics with its emphasis on schools and law enforcement mattered most.[38]

- Third, there was enormous movement of black voters in and out of the electorate during Reconstruction. The attrition rates between the first and last elections for which we have polls books are high in all precincts, ranging from 43 percent to 94 percent of initial voters. This is perhaps not surprising given the upheaval in the lives of these men, almost all of whom had emerged from slavery. One large part of those leaving the electorate would be black men and their families moving out of the Garrard County before the second election. We have not yet tracked those voters to their new residences.

- The most consistent finding is that black political participation was affected by the nature of the political community within which black voters resided. Reconstruction literature focuses on depredations visited upon isolated rural back families to intimidate their behavior and especially their voting behavior. The accounts of Ku Klux Klan raids are almost always of this nature. The evidence that GIS allows us to present for Garrard County suggests almost the opposite: that the black vote persisted more consistently in areas where the black population was more dispersed. In all four precincts there was a clear effect: continuity of black voting was greatest where African-Americans were most dispersed, not where they were most concentrated. Living in an area with a concentrated black population was more a detriment than a benefit to continued political participation.

Conclusion

This chapter demonstrates the utility of two different features of GIS: its inherent capacity to aggregate ranges of information at a point in space and the utility of methodologies associated with GIS in analyzing the spatial distributions of populations. GIS and its associated tools thus allowed us to augment the Beers and Lanagan map, to overcome its inherent racial and class limitations, and to transform a suspect historical document into a powerful and unique resource for historical research.

Rendering historically accurate a racialized presentation of nineteenth-century populations produced in 1879 by the Beers and Lanagan map company is not to argue that the individuals who did the field work on the ground in Garrard County in 1878 and the draftsmen in Philadelphia who prepared what is a beautiful map of population and topography were racists. Beers and Lanagan was a commercial firm aiming to produce a map that a thousand households in Garrard County would want to purchase; only their purchase would make the production of the map profitable and allow the firm to map additional counties. The households that were most likely to buy the map of Garrard County, presumably to both study and display it, were those that had money to outlay on an item of conspicuous consumption that was an interesting, and perhaps vainglorious, presentation of their lives.

GIS allows us to overcome the distortion that attended the commercialized mapping bonanza created by the combination of marketing prowess and technological advances in lithography. These changes made profitable the first mass production of maps in the United States, which showed many people their relationship to a milieu that they had never before seen. The maps were woefully inaccurate demographically if wonderfully precise topographically. GIS allows us to correct the deficiencies of these historical maps and to preserve the best of their characteristics. The virtue of the commercial nature of the map's production was the requirement for accurate information for those considered its potential purchasers. GIS allows us to reselect those families deselected for presentation in the Beers and Lanagan commercial approach to mapping of populations. It allows us to produce a map that comes very close to the records of the US census, which, while far from complete or even-handed in its own capture of resident populations, operated under a public mandate that resulted in far more inclusive data. The techniques used in the correction of the Garrard County map could be applied to any of the thousands of landownership maps produced in the county-mapping craze of the late nineteenth century.

The second utility of GIS is the capacity of software associated with digitized spatial distributions to study secondary characteristics of selected populations. The behavior of members of groups in concentrated and dispersed populations has long attracted the attention of political historians.[39] In this chapter we have seen evidence that black voting too has a "group effect," but it is almost the opposite of that implied by the prevailing historical literature. The data shows that continuity of African-American political participation was higher in areas where the black population was most dispersed, in areas that contained the least-concentrated 40 percent of black residents. So far from there being political "safety in numbers," it was the relative dispersal, and with that presumably an intermixture of the black and white populations, that was most associated with continued participation of African-Americans in the utilization of the suffrage right that the sacrifices of the Civil War had delivered.

GIS as applied to this study of Reconstruction political history has the capacity not only to correct old data (nineteenth-century county landownership maps) and make it available for a new use, but also to make new discoveries that challenge some

fundamental assumptions about the American political past. Perhaps most importantly, the work on Garrard County, using GIS, invites a new interpretation of black
history and the conditions that facilitated the continuation of black political participation in the dark and bloody years of the First Enfranchisement in the American
South. It is a worthy theme, showing why, as we approach Reconstruction's sesqui-
centennial, a celebration, not a dirge, may be in order.

Notes

1 O. G. Libby, 'The Geographical Distribution of the Vote of the Thirteen States on the
  Federal Constitution, 1787–8,' *Bulletin of the University of Wisconsin Economics, Political
  Science, and History* Series 1, 1894, 1–116.
2 D. A. DeBats, 'A Republic of Maps: Presenting a View of the Citizenry,' *Australasian
  Journal of American Studies* 31, 2012, 1–26.
3 A. Knowles et. al., 'A Cutting Edge Second Look at the Battle of Gettysburg,' *Smithsonian
  Magazine,* June 27, 2013, available online at www.smithsonianmag.com/history-
  archaeology/A-Cutting-Edge-Second-Look-at-the-Battle-of-Gettysburg.html.
4 See P. F. Bourke and D. A. DeBats, 'Identifiable Voting in Nineteenth Century America:
  Toward a Comparison of Britain and the United States before the Secret Ballot,' *Perspectives
  in American History* 9, 1977–8, 259–88. In the mid nineteenth century *viva voce* was the
  mode of voting used in Great Britain, Canada, Australia, South Africa, New Zealand, the
  provinces that would become Germany, most Scandinavian nations, and seven American
  states: Virginia, Kentucky, Illinois, Arkansas, Missouri, Texas, and Oregon.
5 Prior to the passage of the Fifteenth and Nineteenth Amendments, only adult white males
  could vote.
6 P. F. Bourke and D. A. DeBats, 'Charles Sumner, The London Ballot Society and the
  Senate Debate of March, 1867,' *Perspectives in American History* 1 New Series, 1984, 343–57.
7 Congressional Globe, 'Supplemental Reconstruction Bill, Debate on Amendments,' 40th
  Congress, 1st Session, March 14, 1867, 103.
8 The most conspicuous exceptions were Massachusetts' short experiment with a requirement that party tickets be placed in envelopes before being deposited and California's
  much later stipulations that party tickets be uniform in color, size, order of offices, and
  paper.
9 Oral voting was abolished in Virginia and Arkansas while under military rule. See Public
  Acts of the 40th Congress, Public Act 6, March 23, 1867: Sections 3 and 6, "An Act Supplementary to an Act Entitled 'An Act to Provide for the More Efficient Government of the
  Rebel States' . . . and to facilitate restoration": "all elections in the States mentioned . . . shall
  be by ballot." The Virginia Constitutional Convention of 1864, composed of delegates from
  that portion of Virginia "within the Union lines," initially approved voting "by ballot, and
  not viva voce," but this was reversed by amendment. See A. R. Long, *The Constitution of
  Virginia: An Annotated Edition,* Lynchburg: J.P. Bell Company, 1901, p. 185. Among the
  other Confederate states Texas had experimented briefly with oral voting but abolished it in
  1848; Missouri did so in 1863. See Bourke and DeBats, "Identifiable Voting," 270.
10 Those states conducted their elections using the alternative party-supplied ticket system. See
  sociallogic.iath.virginia.edu for a discussion of ticket voting and oral voting as the only two electoral systems in nineteenth-century America. Both systems made individual votes knowable
  to participants and observers, whether by sound (*viva voce*) and recorded in poll books or by
  sight (the brightly colored and distinctly marked tickets) which were deposited in public, in
  order to make visible "the color of the ticket." Poll books were official and public documents.

11 In 1872 Congress precluded the use of *viva voce* electoral law in Congressional elections; other elections in Kentucky continued to be conducted by public voting until 1892 and the adoption of the secret ballot.

12 See A. Keyssar, *The Right to Vote: The Contested History of Democracy in the United States,* New York: Basic Books, 2000, pp. 105–16.

13 M. P. Conzen, 'The County Landownership Map in the Americas: Its Commercial Development and Social Transformation,' *Imago Mundi: The Journal of the International Society for the History of Cartography* 36, 1984, 10.

14 Conzen, 'The County Landownership Map in America,' 20.

15 B. Harrington, *How 'Tis Done: A Thorough Ventilation of the Numerous Schemes Conducted by Wandering Canvassers Together with the Various Advertising Dodges for Swindling the Public,* Chicago: Fidelity Publishing Company, 1879.

16 Harrington, *How 'Tis Done*, p. 49. Michael Conzen came to a similar figure, calculating that a run of about 1,000 maps would ensure a profit. See M. P. Conzen, 'Landownership Maps and County Atlases,' *Agricultural History* 58, 1984, 119.

17 Harrington, *How 'Tis Done,* pp. 27–8.

18 R. H. Schein, 'The Place of Landscape: A Conceptual Framework for Interpreting an American Scene,' *Annals of the Association of American Geographers* 87, 1997, 5.

19 G. Lock, 'Representations of Space and Place in the Humanities,' in D. Bodenhamer, J. Corrigan, T. M. Harris (eds), *The Spatial Humanities: GIS and the Future of Humanities Scholarship,* Bloomington: Indiana University Press, 2010, p. 91.

20 R. H. Schein, 'Race and Landscape in the United States,' in R. H. Schein (ed.), *Landscape and Race in the United States,* New York: Routledge, 2006, p. 3.

21 The 653 rural landowners identified by full first and last names or by initials and last name resided in Brandy Springs (250), Buckeye (139), Lancaster (87), and Bryantsville (177); 180 village landowners were also named: Lancaster (150), Paint Lick (13), Bryantsville (12), and Lowell (5). Garrard was divided into these four precincts in the 1870 census; by 1880 a fifth district had been created, very largely from Brandy Springs. To maintain continuity with the Beers and Lanagan map, residents in new district have been placed in the Brandy Springs precinct.

22 In the case of multiple properties owned by the same individuals, we assumed the owner's place of residence was the property associated with the individual's full name. Multiple property ownerships in close proximity to a principal holding were shown by fine lines connecting the name of the owner of the principal holding to the ancillary holdings. Initials were used to associate the owner with more dispersed holdings.

23 The census was also organized by the four precincts; the available versions of tax lists are alphabetic, also organized by precinct, and divided into white and "colored" taxpayers. We were left with a number of as yet unmatched initials in each rural precinct: Brandy Springs 39, Buckeye 19, Lancaster 57, and Bryantsville 46.

24 While census takers were instructed "to visit personally each dwelling house," close study of the census returns shows that census takers could be quite elastic in following that instruction. See Conzen, 'The County Landownership Map in America.'

25 We used this same technique in mapping the cities of Alexandria, Virginia and Newport, Kentucky. See D. A. DeBats, 'A Tale of Two Cities: The Utility of Tax Records in Mapping and Understanding the Nineteenth Century American City,' *Historical Methods* 41, 2008, 17–38.

26 This assumes that the nearest neighbor will be on the same road as the named individual in the tax list; "nearest resident" information was differentially collected, especially in the "colored" section of the tax list.

27 We recognize of course that "nearest neighbor" may have been interpreted by the respondent as the nearest neighbor with whom he or she had a cordial relationship.

28 The Fifteenth Amendment passed the US House and Senate on February 25 and 26, 1869 and was adopted on March 30, 1870. All Confederate states were forced to adopt the Fifteenth Amendment as a condition for reentry to the Union. Kentucky adopted the Fifteenth Amendment a century later, on March, 18, 1976. On the other hand, in early 1870 Attorney General Amos Akerman made it clear that Kentucky's own Enforcement Act of May 31 would be fully enforced and that black franchise would be exercised. See R. A. Webb, *Kentucky in the Reconstruction Era,* Lexington: University Press of Kentucky, 1979, pp. 70–1. Kentucky was the last state to adopt the secret ballot and was the only state to move directly from *viva voce* voting to the secret ballot.

29 The matched elections for the four precincts are: Brandy Springs (August, 1875 State election and August, 1886 State election; Byrantsville (August 1875, State election and November, 1888 Presidential election); Buckeye (August, 1879 State election and November, 1888 Presidential election); Lancaster (November, 1876 Presidential election and August, 1891 State election).

30 See note 20.

31 Nineteenth-century census enumerations at mid century missed up to 15 percent of the population with the least well off being the most likely to be missed. The miss rate was likely higher among a poor and highly mobile newly freed slave population. See D. A. DeBats, 'Who Votes? Who Voted? The 2008 American Elections: Contexts for Judging Participation and Partisanship,' *Australasian Journal of American Studies* 27, 2008, 16–36.

32 The Beers and Lanagan mapmakers also located 72 percent of the population of Lancaster town, the County seat and the largest non-rural population center in Garrard, identifying by name the head of 164 of the 228 households in Lancaster in 1880 as well as presenting the footprint of most structures.

33 There is no difference for African-Americans between the original and augmented map in terms of median age, median acres, or median value of acres taxed.

34 There is no difference for whites between the original and augmented map in terms of median acres taxed.

35 I. Gregory and P. Ell, *Historical GIS: Technologies, Methodologies and Scholarship*, New York: Cambridge University Press, 2007, p. 11; see also I. Gregory, *A Place in History: A Guide to Using GIS in Historical Research,* Oxford, Oxbow Books, 2003, pp. 2–3.

36 See D. A. DeBats and M. Lethbridge, 'GIS and the City: Nineteenth Century Residential Patterns,' *Historical Geography* 33, 2005, 78–98.

37 See note 29.

38 For a recent statement of the nationalizing school, see E. J. Engstrom and S. Kernell, *Party Ballots, Reform, and the Transformation of America's Electoral System,* New York: Cambridge University Press, 2014.

39 For a summary, see J. M. Kousser, 'Ecological Inference from Goodman to King,' *Historical Methods* 34, 2001, 101–26.

References

Bourke. P. F. and D. A. DeBats, 'Identifiable Voting in Nineteenth Century America: Toward a Comparison of Britain and the United States before the Secret Ballot,' *Perspectives in American History* 11, 1977–8, 259–88.

—— 'Charles Sumner, The London Ballot Society and the Senate Debate of March, 1867,' *Perspectives in American History* 1 New Series, 1984, 343–57.

Congressional Globe, 'Supplemental Reconstruction Bill, Debate on Amendments,' 40th Congress, 1st Session, March 14, 1867, 103.

Conzen, M. P., 'Landownership Maps and County Atlases,' *Agricultural History* 58, 1984a, 118–22.

Conzen, M. P., 'The County Landownership Map in America: Its Commercial Development and Social Transformation, 1814–1939,' *Imago Mundi* 36, 1984b, 17–23.

DeBats, D.A., 'A Republic of Maps, Presenting a View of the Citizenry,' *Australasian Journal of American Studies* 31, 2012, 1–26.

DeBats, D.A., 'Who Votes? Who Voted? The 2008 American Elections: Contexts for Judging Participation and Partisanship,' *Australasian Journal of American Studies* 27(1), 2008, 16–36.

DeBats, D.A., 'A Tale of Two Cities: The Utility of Tax Records in Mapping and Understanding the Nineteenth Century American City,' *Historical Methods* 41(1), 2008, 17–38.

DeBats, D.A. and M. Lethbridge, 'GIS and the City: Nineteenth Century Residential Patterns,' *Historical Geography* 33, 2005, 78–98.

Engstrom, E. J. and S. Kernell, *Party Ballots, Reform, and the Transformation of America's Electoral System*, New York: Cambridge University Press, 2014.

Gregory, I. and Paul Ell, *Historical GIS: Technologies, Methodologies and Scholarship*, Cambridge: Cambridge University Press, 2007.

Gregory, I., *A Place in History: A Guide to Using GIS in Historical Research*, Oxford: Oxbow Books, 2003.

Harrington, B., *How 'Tis Done: A Thorough Ventilation of the Numerous Schemes Conducted by Wandering Canvassers Together with the Various Advertising Dodges for Swindling the Public*, Chicago: Fidelity Publishing Company, 1879.

Keyssar, A., *The Right to Vote: The Contested History of Democracy in the United States*, New York: Basic Books, 2000.

Knowles, A., et. al., 'A Cutting edge Second Look at the Battle of Gettysburg,' *Smithsonian Magazine*, June 27, 2013, available online at www.smithsonianmag.com/history-archaeology/A-Cutting-Edge-Second-Look-at-the-Battle-of-Gettysburg.html.

Kousser, J. M., 'Ecological Inference from Goodman to King,' *Historical Methods* 34(3), 2001, 101–26.

Libby, O. G., 'The Geographical Distribution of the Vote of the Thirteen States on the Federal Constitution, 1787–8,' *Bulletin of the University of Wisconsin Economics, Political Science, and History*, Series 1, 1894, 1–116.

Lock, G., 'Representations of Space and Place in the Humanities,' in D. J. Bodenhamer, J. Corrigan, T. M. Harris (eds), *The Spatial Humanities: GIS and the Future of Humanities Scholarship*, Bloomington: Indiana University Press, 2010, pp. 89–108.

Long, A. R., *The Constitution of Virginia: An Annotated Edition*, Lynchburg: J.P. Bell Company, 1901.

Schein, R. H., 'Race and Landscape in the United States,' R. H. Schein (ed.), *Landscape and Race in the United States*, New York: Routledge, 2006, pp. 1–22.

Schein, R. H., 'The Place of Landscape: A Conceptual Framework for Interpreting an American Scene,' *Annals of the Association of American Geographers* 87, 1997, 660–80.

US Congress, Public Acts of the 40th Congress, Public Act 6, March 23, 1867, Sections 3 and 6, 'An Act Supplementary to an Act Entitled "An Act to Provide for the More Efficient Government of the Rebel States and to Facilitate Restoration."'

Webb, R.A., *Kentucky in the Reconstruction Era*, Lexington: University Press of Kentucky, 1979.

21

THE SPATIAL HISTORY OF STATE POWER

A view from imperial China

Ruth Mostern

Introduction

Spatial history, a field that is still coming into clear focus, combines the geographer's focus on landscape variation with the historian's analysis of past social structures and their transformation. Yet early on, Richard White noted the challenge of representing movement and change over time and through space simultaneously. As he points out, GIS 'often ends up emphasizing not the constructed-ness of space, but rather its given-ness'.[1] Nevertheless, White simply proposes more compelling visualization. He does not introduce a theoretical or analytical agenda that would allow the field to integrate complex spatial and temporal processes in a single interpretive model, nor does he suggest a methodological alternative to GIS.

I have suggested elsewhere that spatial history engage four interrelated premises: 1) that landscape is constructed through human activity; 2) that multiple places and landscapes are related to one another in complex and contingent ways; 3) that places, landscapes, and their relationships emerge, collapse, and change; and 4) that it is possible to identify and describe multiple and intersecting temporal and spatial scales at which landscapes and places of varying size and duration emerge and endure.[2]

Historical GIS has increasingly become the primary method by which spatial historians have addressed these questions, but it is not the only approach. GIS is poorly suited to projects for which it is impossible to achieve geospatial accuracy. It also offers no advantages to projects for which careful modeling and analysis of change over time is more significant than spatial visualization. For many spatial history projects, especially those with a focus on change over time, effort is better expended identifying place names and spatially located events, formally articulating their attributes (for instance their relationships, the duration of their existence, and the sources in which they are attested) and analyzing them in a database environment. GIS is essential only for projects with a strongly visual character or those that require topological and other analyses that rely upon the standard GIS toolkit. It is not indispensable to spatial history nor indivisible from it.

Political landscapes are well suited to study using the methods and propositions that I have just laid out.[3] I am not using the term political landscape in the vernacular sense of an overall picture of the political situation in a given region. Rather, it refers to geographical arrangements of varying scales that permit regimes or other political actors to organize themselves spatially. Political landscapes permit people to exercise authority over some part of the earth's surface during some period of time. These landscapes may take any number of forms, from international borders and local government units, to school districts, military bases, or refugee camps. What they have in common is that they are tangible geographical manifestations of political authority that exist in absolute space. As spatial manifestations of power relations, political landscapes may be artifacts of government policy. Alternatively they may arise from a political culture that indirectly spatializes the relations of political power. Political landscapes of this sort, like segregated neighborhoods or irrigated orchards, are the spatial results of differential access to limited resources such as affordable mortgages or abundant water.

This chapter argues for devising a spatial history approach for the study of political landscapes, one that foregrounds temporally and spatially referenced knowledge organization systems (KOS) such as gazetteers and historical event databases.[4] Fundamentally, a gazetteer uses place names as a spatial referent. A historical event database uses named events in the same way. It may be preferable to start with a KOS rather than a GIS when a set of names or events is the best reference point for organizing complex and heterogeneous items of information about places. For instance, a KOS can model the changes that places undergo, the people or things associated with places, the multiple names attributed to places, or the spatial hierarchies with which places are associated. If a KOS includes spatial references, it can readily be imported into a GIS as needed.

This chapter also argues for using regional systems theory as the basis for spatial analysis at the scale of the state. It is organized into two sections. The first, 'Structure and process', uses regional systems theory and gazetteer data to explain why the spatial organization of state power changed as it did in China during the Song 宋 dynasty (960–1276 CE). The second section, 'Toward an eventful spatial history', proposes a framework for incorporating historical narrative, change in scale, and historical contingency into spatial analysis and visualization. Using a historical event KOS about the Yellow River, I pinpoint when and where this human-managed river fell into disequilibrium and disasterousness. Historians have no methodological consensus about how to move between multiple temporal and spatial scales. There are not yet any digital spatial history models to follow, and it is not clear that GIS alone will help. This chapter suggests a way forward.

Structure and process

Spatial political history focuses on the processes that cause a given political landscape to emerge or grow, and to contract or collapse. It is not simply about reconstructing territorial units, borders, and administrative subdivisions as they existed at some point in the past, or even as they changed over time. It also explains practices that maintained such landscapes. At the scale of the state, spatial history can describe the geography of interstate relations, highlight the spatial differentiation of particular policies within the territory of the state, and illuminate how states demarcate the physical limits of their power, with diminishing precision at earlier points in history, and often under conditions of contestation.[5] Spatial history reveals the process of creating and maintaining territory by combining spatial analysis and visualization from GIS with modeling and analysis of complex spatial arrangements in databases, in particular databases of named places known as gazetteers.[6]

Since the capacity to govern people and control resources is a consequence of the ability to delimit territory, internal and external boundaries are not just lines on a map. They are the ideological basis of state power. The spatial political history of state power is tractable to formal modeling, analysis, and visualization because, historically, governments themselves have aspired to maintain increasingly precise data about spatial dynamics. That is one of the reasons why gazetteers are such an important part of the political spatial history toolkit. Gazetteers, not maps, were the tools that governments used for most of history to keep track of their territories, and their formal jurisdictions in particular.[7]

The global consolidation of state power thus reflects a state's ability to gather information about people, places, and resources with increasing consistency and efficiency. States have historically put resources into creating maps, censuses, tax rolls, and surveys, which have allowed them to surveil their territory, their citizens and their resources with ever closer scrutiny. Collecting information about the spatial distribution of people and resources, recording it in a state bureaucracy, and using it to govern a population: these are the essential tools of governance. As many theorists have explained in recent decades, this process requires governments to simplify the complex variations of social, environmental, and geographical reality into relatively fewer and more comparable categories and thereby make large-scale structures legible to rulers and tractable to policy. It is the spatial historian's task to reveal the day-to-day activities by which states create, refine, and maintain a political landscape. It is a paradoxical agenda, since, like the state itself, maps and databases rationalize and standardize heterogeneous kinds of spatial experience. Spatial historians who gather and model information about the political landscape at the scale of the state should design systems that preserve and restore complexity and do not simply recapitulate the technologies and ideologies of modern governance.

G. William Skinner's work on regional systems theory is one good path from theory to spatial history practice. Skinner, active from the late 1950s to the early 2000s, worked primarily on China, and secondarily on Japan, France, and Southeast Asia. Among his many research interests, the one that best helps to set an agenda for the study of the political landscape at the scale of the state is his work on physiographic macroregions and hierarchical regional space. He was an inveterate collector of data and producer of maps and schematic spatial visualizations, although his career began before the development of desktop GIS.

Skinner recognized that imperial China's provincial boundaries rarely corresponded with either natural or socioeconomic systems. He therefore defined nine physiographic macroregions in late imperial China on the basis of watershed boundaries, taking rivers as the natural transportation corridors for people and resources until the modern era. He used the macroregions to empirically identify regional systems which internally self-organized into urban centers and their hinterlands, cores and peripheries, on the basis of marketing networks and political activity. Over the course of his career, he also defined regional systems below the level of the macroregion, and discovered that the macroregions were only tenuously connected to one another.[8] Skinner described the geography of Chinese social structure in a way that integrated spatial scale from the village to the empire and explained the way that spatial location differentiated peoples' access to resources. His work is still continues to offer fundamental and practical insights for spatial history.

Skinner rarely investigated how Chinese hierarchical regional space emerged or persisted. He was more interested in describing the dynamics of a stable and mature system. Nevertheless, his limited and speculative insights about the processes of political landscape formation suggest an agenda for studying the development and maintenance of a political landscape. In particular, Skinner recognized that during the two thousand year arc of imperial Chinese state power, local government units – counties – remained relatively stable in number even as population increased tenfold during that time span. That was possible because counties were founded and abolished in accordance with the expectations of hierarchical regional space. Regimes founded new counties when they established effective state power at the edges of macroregions or the periphery of the empire itself, and simultaneously they merged small counties in core regions where robust transportation networks and stable governance made it possible for larger units to govern effectively.[9] Skinner's explanation of this phenomenon occupies only a few pages, but it offers a hypothesis for empirical spatial history research, not only in China, but anywhere in the world with a form of rule that includes local administrative units managed by a bureaucratic government. With some variation, the same hypothesis could apply to feudal, colonial, or other forms of state power that are spatially demarcated within their domain of authority. Effectively, Skinner's hypothesis suggests a core agenda for spatial political history. Tracing the evolution of local government geography can yield significant insights into the political landscape as it changes during very long timeframes and over very large distances.

Sociologist Charles Tilly elaborated Skinner's model, observing that as state power solidified in early modern Europe, the struggle to fund and wage war created the central organizational structure of states. Over the course of this process, states became territorially defined, centralized, and came to possess a monopoly on coercive power within their boundaries. This contrasted with earlier periods, when a plethora of individuals and organizations claimed power over territory. Expanding governments had to develop institutions that allowed them to wage war and to extract the tax revenue needed to pay for it.

Each of these tasks called for the development of a spatial landscape, but the type of landscape that was ideal for each purpose was different. Indeed, they were generally at cross-purposes with one another. Military forces had to be located between likely sites of battle and major sources of supply, often in remote spots near international frontiers. However, civilian officials who collected taxes had to be geographically distributed in correspondence with the geography of trade, wealth, and income. The two activities generally map to the cores and peripheries of regional systems, since lucrative and efficient tax collection was a feature of central regions, while invasion and rebellion generally occurred around frontiers. Thus spatial organization was often unstable, as fiscal and military imperatives vied for precedence. At the same time, short-term political considerations often prevented the emergence of landscapes that were ideal in either fiscal or military terms. The actual arrangements that emerged reflected the agendas of politically successful parties and the 'organizational residues' of past landscapes as well as the tension between fiscal and military spatial organization.[10]

Tilly's work was based on significant historical research, but not formal spatial analysis. In order to test and extend Skinner and Tilly's work, I created the Digital Gazetteer of the Song Dynasty (DGSD) (songgis.ucmerced.edu) to track all of the counties and prefectures that ever existed during China's Song dynasty, which ruled from 960 to 1276 CE. The Chinese case generally is a good fit for the European cases that inspired Tilly's work. Like early modern European states, China during the Song was surrounded by militarily coequal rivals. It was also a state intent upon increasing revenue by fostering and taxing a growing economy, extending the power of the state into previously under-exploited internal hinterlands, and identifying and rectifying administrative inefficiencies. Tilly's work offers a rubric for pinpointing locations where the state was likely to take certain kinds of actions in support of war-making or revenue extraction. The DGSD tracks the founding and abolition of local government units in order to test, describe, and visualize a regional systems perspective.

The Song records are such that it is feasible to precisely track the distribution of such units over time. The DGSD is structured around two tables. One lists the names and coordinates of all of the local government units that ever existed at any time during the Song regime along with additional attributes such as population. The other lists all place-making events (merges, splits, changes in unit rank, and so on), their dates, and the units affected by them.[11]

The entire analytical framework of my project relied on query of the gazetteer database. None of the questions that emerged from regional systems theory required GIS functionality. It was trivial to create shapefiles based on the database when I needed to make maps for publication (Figure 21.1). GIS is an exceptional methodology for revealing spatial variation, but a historical gazetteer like the DGSD, designed with spatial change event tracking in mind, is more valuable than a standard GIS for designing queries to explore and explain temporal variation in spatial transformation. Query of a gazetteer database is an essential aspect of spatial history method. The DGSD is a database optimized for spatial history, for exploring when and where a landscape was adjusted and when and where it remained stable, and is better suited to a project about early modern governmentality, inspired by Skinner and Tilly, than a GIS would be. The discussion that follows summarizes the argument of my book, *Dividing the Realm in Order to Govern: The Spatial Organization of the Song State, 960–1276 CE*, a work that is based on gazetteer analysis integrated with readings of historical documents.[12]

The Song state maintained a three-tier spatial landscape, consisting of quasi-provinces, prefectures, and counties. Tax revenue was assessed and collected at the county, while military officers and troops were distributed by prefecture, and Song fiscal policy required each prefecture in the realm to be financially self-sufficient.

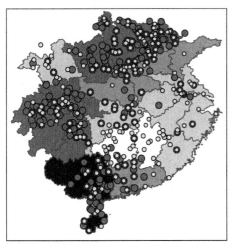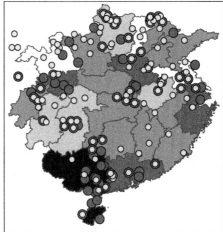

Figure 21.1   Counties (left) and prefectures (right). These maps depict the relative change in the density of state presence over the course of the Song dynasty. Circuits (quasi-provinces) where the number of jurisdictions contracted the most are black, and those where they contracted less are diminishing shades of grey. Circuits where the number of jurisdictions expanded are white. Light grey icons are established jurisdictions, dark grey icons are abolished jurisdictions.

As the Tilly-Skinner model would predict, in the imperial core both counties and prefectures tended to be large. By contrast, colonial and military outposts on fractious imperial peripheries required a dense imperial field presence relative to their size and population. In those regions, prefectures tended to be small while counties were large. The ratio of counties to prefectures varied from over ten to one in the imperial core, to barely over one to one on the far periphery. It was impossible for small frontier prefectures to be fiscally solvent. The ideal of the bureaucratic state thus contradicted the reality of local financial autonomy and the logic of warfare. In many regions of the empire, prefectures were frequently in deficit. The problem was particularly pronounced among the newest and smallest ones on the military frontiers, with many troops to support.[13] For these reasons, the Chinese political landscape was spatially unstable. When financial crisis became unsustainable, prefects had no viable alternative but to petition the court to revise the spatial organization of their districts. These could be expanded to create a larger tax base, or contracted to reduce defense and administrative costs.[14] A great many territory-making decisions rested explicitly on revenue considerations (Figure 21.2).

The spatial landscape was also shaped by the imperative to constrain local power bases of frontier officers, whose potential to rebel was a vivid memory from the recent past. Indeed, for this reason, civil prefects directed military affairs.[15] In the year 1066, prominent statesman Ouyang Xiu 歐陽修 (1007–1072) attributed the Song defeat in the war against the Tangut Xi Xia 西夏 regime to their northwest to the fact that Song armies were stationed in nearly 200 small and decentralized forts and

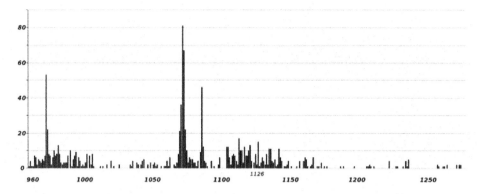

Figure 21.2 A timeline of Song spatial renovation. Each vertical bar represents the number of changes to the spatial landscape completed in a given year.

garrisons, governed by 24 prefectures in five provinces, and coordinated military movements were almost impossible.[16]

As this timeline depicts, the rate of formation and maintenance in the Song political landscape varied temporally as well as spatially. Most Song spatial change clustered in three distinct eras. The tenth-century Song founders made hundreds of adjustments to the spatial landscape of their tax-farming warlord predecessors in order to create a unified spatial organization appropriate to a single imperial entity. One-third of all spatial changes during this era transpired on the southern frontiers, where the Song court consolidated remote, miasmic, and impoverished jurisdictions where civil officials sometimes refused to serve. The year 1005, when the Song court signed a peace treaty with their Khitan Liao 遼 neighbors to the north, marks the end of the founding generation. Spatial change essentially ceased the same year.

The second era roughly spanned the eleventh century. It was marked by mounting hostility on the northern border and intensive colonization on the southern periphery. In order to invest in a wartime landscape of new prefectures in the north and a colonial landscape of new counties in the south, the regime consolidated numerous low-revenue counties and prefectures elsewhere. The century closed with a political landscape that had shifted toward a new center of gravity on the northern and southern frontiers. As regional systems theory would predict, the political landscape of the economic core in the Yangzi delta barely changed in spite of massive growth in population, commerce, and urbanization.

The third era began suddenly in 1127, when the Song regime lost the northern half of its territory to invaders from the north. A long and destructive war devastated farms and cities in the Song heartland, and at the end, a new international border cut through the middle of lands once controlled by the Song. In retreat, the Song army breached the Yellow River's levees to slow the advance of the invading horsemen, unleashing massive devastation but securing little military benefit.[17] The regime established an arc of new prefectures that protected the new border, while an innovative policy allowed for jurisdictions to be temporarily demoted in the parts of the empire where flooding or fighting led to demographic collapse. As refugees moved into the far south, many jurisdictions that had been abolished there two centuries before were restored. However, once a peace treaty was signed in 1142, the spatial landscape became almost completely stable for the last century of the Song reign.

In summary, spatial politics involves sustaining structures of long duration, but these structures are regularly transformed by sudden and contingent events, with consequences that are unpredictable and that transpire at many different spatial and temporal scales. The same failed fortification drive that portended Song stalemate with the Tanguts also increased erosion on the frontier grasslands where the forts were being built, destabilizing the course of the Yellow River and rapidly transforming China's spatial landscape.[18] Skinner does not have a way to accommodate this insight, and Tilly (as I have quoted above) dismisses such events as 'organizational residues'. That is not methodologically satisfactory. The next section of this chapter therefore proposes a way forward to incorporate contingency and narrative into spatial history.

Toward an eventful political geography

Thus far this chapter has introduced a framework for describing the spatial structure of state power over a long timeframe in an existing, mature, and relatively stable large-scale regime. However, this approach subsumes all but the most significant upheavals in order to explore gradual processes by which existing spatial landscapes evolve. Spatial history has not yet devised an approach for adding narrative or contingency to such analysis of slowly changing spatial structures. Fernand Braudel's 1949 masterwork of large-scale history famously does this, focusing on the sixteenth and seventeenth history to discuss eventful political history (*histoire événementielle*) while ranging through millennia of environmental and cultural time (the *longue durée*) to make sense of it.[19] But because Braudel necessarily presented his research in book format and without much attention to spatial change, the temporal scales remain essentially distinct from one another.

Geographer Doreen Massey offers a theoretical starting point for eventful spatial history, especially with her aphorism that 'geography is the meeting up of histories in space'.[20] Eventful spatial history can start by identifying the moments in time and space when histories collide. Massey's quintessential example of this is the meeting of Hernan Cortez and King Moctezuma at Tenochtitlan in 1519: the occasion when one empire ended, and another, with a totally different spatial and historical logic, took its place.

Often, the multiple histories that meet up in space are of different temporal scales. The environmental ethicist Thom Van Dooren has recently written of 'dense webs of overlapping temporalities and inheritances'[21] His study of species extinction examines how individual lifespans and the place-making activities of specific migrating, mating, and nesting birds relates to a longer arc of environmental collapse and an even longer timeline of species evolution. As Van Dooren puts it, 'encountering the world through an attentiveness to divergent and overlapping temporal frames is not always easy or straightforward, but doing so enriches our understanding of these troubling times'.[22]

What kit of spatial history tools can support analytical and empirical scholarship that accords with these concepts? Eventful spatial history is difficult because landscapes usually evolve slowly and exist at a large spatial scale, while politics moves quickly, and momentous action often occurs in particular locations. The fact that Braudel's work is so cumbersome and poorly integrated suggests that spatial visualization and database analysis is potentially a more promising approach to the challenge than text. Unlike digital ecosystems that allow users to move easily between scales, books that engage multiple temporal scales within the same text tend to be long, usually organized such that each chapter takes up one temporal scale in particular. The relationship between David Christian's Big History classic *Maps of Time* and the same work presented using the ChronoZoom timeline platform is a salutary example. In the book, readers move chapter-by-chapter from the history of the universe to the history of modernity; on the timeline, visitors move seamlessly between temporal scales.[23] However, Chrono-Zoom is a teaching tool and a proof of concept, not a platform for generating or communicating new knowledge. Spatial history has not as yet provided compelling exemplars for eventful history, only relatively unsatisfactory web platforms that include both maps and timelines but are not informed by a theory either of scale and causality.

Spatial history now has the problem of integrating eventfulness and multiple temporal scales in an analytically fundamental way, rather than as a data visualization problem. I suggest, following Massey, that the key to the approach is to identify the specific moments when multiple geographies and multiple temporalities converge. William Sewell offers the useful concept of social *structures* that evolve slowly through *processes* but are occasionally turned into something new by sudden and transformative *events*. However, he focuses on social abstractions, not landscapes. A Sewellian approach to spatial historical eventfulness would necessarily concern the transformation of spatial structures *per se*. For instance, a catastrophic flood may simultaneously transform a political landscape at the scale of state power and a hydrologic system at a planetary scale. The event conjoins the two frameworks and makes it possible to examine the logic of their convergence. These kinds of temporality, too, can be examined through place-name gazetteers. Gazetteers can be rich in information about historical events, and they can be integrated with other kinds of KOS.[24] Karl Grossner, Kryzjof Janowicz, and Carsten Keßler have recently explained how to formally model place, event, and spatiotemporal setting in an integrated way. Methods for creating and integrating complex knowledge systems that meet the demands of spatial history research are rapidly coming into focus.[25]

The multiple scales of human and natural history on China's Yellow River generally converged in ways that were uneventful and invisible, though environmental stability and human wellbeing gradually declined over the last millennium. However, periodically, sudden and momentous events such as course changes or major engineering works initiated long-lasting systemic changes. These events can be located with precision in space and time (Figure 21.3). From the mid-eleventh century to the mid-twelfth century, the Song regime transformed the political landscape by transforming the natural landscape. A fortification campaign on the fragile grasslands of the loess plateau set in motion an era of mounting erosion that lasted through the twentieth century. On the floodplain, the 1128 levee breaches initiated an era of course instability and declining agricultural productivity from which it never recovered.[26]

In an environmental framework, the temporal scale is set by the natural background rate of erosion on the loess plateau over the course of the Holocene era, beginning about 12,000 years ago at the end of the last ice age. The associated spatial scale is the whole Yellow River watershed, and indeed the entire East Asian

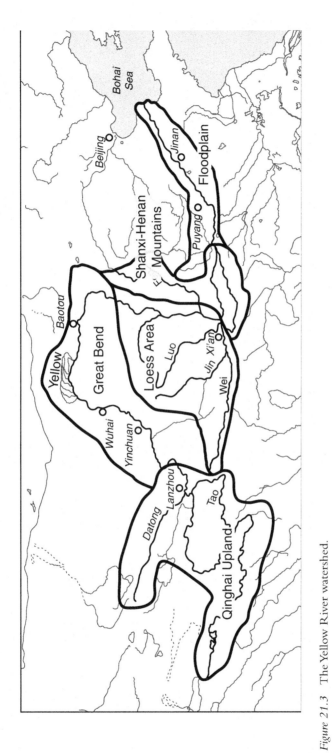

Figure 21.3 The Yellow River watershed.

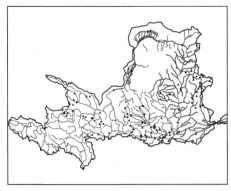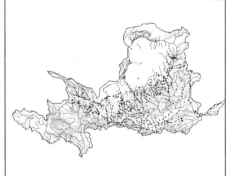

Figure 21.4 Fortification on the Yellow River watershed before and after the eleventh century.

monsoon system. From a human perspective, and one of spatial politics, the actual rate of erosion increased when farming began approximately 7,000 years ago, intensified during the iron age approximately 2,000 years ago under a regime of intensive state colonization, and intensified again with the rise of mass military fortification approximately 1,000 years ago (Figure 21.4).

By contrast, human spatial activity occurs at the scales of fortified military frontiers, agricultural intensification, earthwork constructions, and canal transportation. Finally, temperature and precipitation fluctuated over long cycles, but climate only really mattered during the catastrophic downpours that washed accumulated sand and silt into the river. Thus the shortest timeframe of all is the duration of particular storms that precipitated course changes and major floods: approximately 1,500 events that can be located in time and space. For instance, the 1128 course change was an event in which the environmental history of the river collided with the political history of the Song–Jurchen war during one particular month when a certain individual, Kaifeng 開封 Governor Du Chong杜充 (?–1141), opened breaches in the dikes 80 miles north of the city at specific locations in Huazhou 滑州, Shanzhou 澶州, and Puzhou 濮州. This event can be mapped, as can the longterm structural effects of Du Chong's endeavor on hydrology, soil quality, the international border, and administrative geography. All of these structural changes were set in motion by the dike breaches.

A historian can narrate the eventfulness of Du Chong's decision using traditional methods, but these tools do not explain or visualize its impact on the structure of imperial or environmental geography. The standard toolkit of historical GIS also captures only some of this history. A Yellow River Historical GIS can include settlement geography, hydrology, soil and slope, and levees and canals as they change over time. A GIS can certainly map events and course changes. This is a useful way to depict large-scale spatial and temporal structures and to perform standard kinds of spatial analysis, for instance to determine the likely erosion impacts of building forts in locations with steep slopes, heavy runoff, and loose soil. However, traditional HGIS does a poor job of capturing eventfulness as the basis for analysis. It is more productive to begin with a spatially and temporally referenced database of events.

This can be integrated with a historical GIS, but it can also be used outside of it. For instance, it can be analyzed together with annual and decadal environmental science information about erosion, temperature, and precipitation in order to explain how coupled human and natural systems interacted spatially and temporally. It can be used to track the rate of events over time and the temporal relationships of different events. The most compelling visualizations of the insights gained thereby may not be maps at all.

With these insights, I have embarked on a Yellow River database design project with the assistance of my graduate student Kaiqi Hua. We identified and collected all secondary sources that listed river event information in the form of lists or tables from 33 relevant publications, including articles, books, and book series, creating approximately 8,711 unique entries, of which we determined that 3,407 were within the scope of the project. After we parsed, split, merged, and de-duplicated these events, we ended up with an event database of 3,949. We also analyzed the events semantically to develop a list of event types, ten of them recording various natural events such as droughts and floods, and ten of them distinguishing human activities like canal building and funding requisitions. The database is now almost complete, save for geo-referencing all of the locations mentioned in it. At that point, I will embark on a project of spatial political history analysis.

Although neither the database nor the GIS is complete, I have drawn some preliminary conclusions about Chinese spatial environmental and political history. The most significant finding is that the precariousness of the river system and the political reaction to it both increased over time, both distasterousness and the response to it varied by regime, and that a sudden increase in disasterousness coincided with two political events: the Song–Tangut war in 1040–4 with its loess plateau fortification drive, and the Song–Jurchen war that precipitated the intentional levee breaches in 1128 (see Table 21.1). This is eventful spatial history coupled with *longue durée* environmental and political spatial history.

In order to tell and to map the story of long-term environmental decline and sudden change in Yellow River history, it is essential to move seamlessly and analytically among numerous temporal and spatial scales. There must also be a way to describe

Table 21.1 Yellow River events per dynasty. Note the dramatic increase in eventfulness immediately before and during the Song dynasty.

Era	Dates	Events	Events/Year
Xia–Zhou	c.207–0221 BCE	105	n/a
Qin–Han	221 BCE–220 CE	165	0.4
Six Dynasties	220–589	49	0.1
Sui–Tang	581–906	137	0.4
Five Dynasties	906–960	105	2
Northern Song	960–1127	608	3.6
Jin	1127–1234	235	2.2
Yuan	1234–1368	243	1.8
Ming	1368–1644	712	2.6
Qing	1644–1911	1578	5.9

stable and slowly evolving spatial structures, and also the unanticipated and sudden events that transformed them. A Yellow River KOS organized around spatially and temporally referenced and type-coded events is yielding insights about the times and places when human and natural histories of various scales 'met up' in significant ways and created an environment that was decreasingly conducive to the wellbeing of the imperial Chinese regime and its people.

Conclusion

The two Chinese spatial political history cases that I have presented in this chapter are related to one other. Both concern spatial political arrangements during the same era of the same empire. However, one is a structural approach focusing on a single timeframe and spatial scale, while the other uses the concept of eventfulness to integrate multiple temporal and spatial scales across a much longer timeframe. These cases underscore the value of a regional systems approach, revisiting Skinner's assumption about the relationship between hydrology and socio-political geography; but also reveal the limits of Skinner's model. As my first case demonstrates, the regional systems of Song dynasty political geography were less physiographic and more political, functional, and historical than those that Skinner propounded. In the Yellow River case, regional systems are more explicitly hydrological and environmental than Skinner's, since the river itself is central to the analysis and is not a proxy for other kinds of human behavior. Both of these cases focus upon transformative events and actions, a topic that has not been much discussed in spatial history but which should be critical to it going forward. This still-new field needs ways to accommodate events and narratives. Otherwise, spatial history is just a new name for historical geography, offering snapshots of human landscapes in the past.

From the point of view of spatial history method, I offer two suggestions. First, GIS is a significant component of the spatial history toolkit, but it is at least as important to develop and analyze spatially and temporally referenced gazetteers and other related kinds of KOS that are able to handle rich attribution and temporal information with as much sophistication as spatial information. Second, the challenge of spatial history is to do history and geography better using these new methods. I have written this chapter with the conviction that the field needs a more firm theoretical foundation, and I hope that this work will help to provide one.

Notes

1 R. White, 'What is Spatial History?' Spatial History Lab Working Paper, 2010. Online. Available HTTP: <http://web.stanford.edu/group/spatialhistory/cgi-bin/site/pub.php?id=29> (accessed March 2016). H. Lefebvre, *The Production of Space*, Oxford: Blackwell, 1991.

2 R. Mostern and E. Gainor, 'Traveling the Silk Road on a Virtual Globe: Pedagogy, Technology and Evaluation for Spatial History', *Digital Humanities Quarterly* 7(2), 2013.

3 I use this term in my book: R. Mostern, *Dividing the Realm in Order to Govern: The Spatial Organization of the Song State, 960–1276, CE*, Cambridge, MA: Harvard Asia Center, 2011.

4 For a recent discussion of the Knowledge Organization System as an information genre, see R. Shaw, 'Gazetteers Enriched: A Conceptual Basis for Linking Gazetteers with Other

Kinds of Information', in M.L. Berman, R. Mostern and H. Southall (eds), *Placing Names: Enriching and Integrating Gazetteers*, Bloomington, IN: Indiana University Press, 2016.

5 M. Jones, R. Jones and M. Woods, *An Introduction to Political Geography: Space, Place and Politics*, London: Routledge, 2004, 20.

6 M.L. Berman, R. Mostern and H. Southall (eds), *Placing Names: Enriching and Integrating Gazetteers*, Bloomington, IN: Indiana University Press, 2016.

7 R. Mostern and H. Southall, 'Gazetteers Past', in M. L. Berman, R. Mostern and H. Southall (eds), *Placing Names: Enriching and Integrating Gazetteers*, Bloomington, IN: Indiana University Press, 2016. M. Curry, 'Toward a Geography of a World Without Maps: Lessons from Ptolemy and Postal Codes', *Annals of the Association of American Geographers* 95(3), 2005, 680–91.

8 For a summary and extension of Skinner's macroregion concept, see M. Henderson, 'Macroregions', in *Oxford Bibliographies*, Oxford: Oxford University Press, 2013. Online. Available HTTP: <http://www.oxfordbibliographies.com/view/document/obo-9780199920082/obo-9780199920082-0055.xml> (accessed March 2016).

9 G. W. Skinner, 'Cities and the Hierarchy of Local Systems', in G. W. Skinner (ed.), *The City in Late Imperial China*, Stanford, CA: Stanford University Press, 1977, 275–352.

10 C. Tilly, *Coercion, Capital and European States, 990–1992*, vol. 1, Cambridge: Blackwell, 1992.

11 R. Mostern and E. Meeks, 'The Politics of Territory in Song Dynasty China', in I. Gregory and A. Geddes (eds), *Rethinking Space and Place: New Directions with Historical GIS*, Bloomington, IN: Indiana University Press, 2014, 118–42 and R. Mostern and I. Johnson, 'From Named Place to Naming Event: Creating Gazetteers for History', *International Journal of Geographic Information Science* 22(10), 2008, 1091–1108.

12 Mostern, *Dividing the Realm*.

13 S. Wang 汪聖鐸, *Liang Song caizheng shi* 兩宋財政史, Beijing: Zhonghua shuju, 1995, 529–34.

14 W. Bao 包偉民, *Songdai difang caizheng shi yanjiu* 宋代地方財政史研究, Shanghai: Shanghai guji chubanshe, 2001, 71–2.

15 Z. Wang 王曾瑜, *Songdai bingzhi chutan* 宋朝兵制初探, Beijing: Zhonghua shuju, 1983. This discussion is also indebted to C. Hucker, *A Dictionary of Official Titles in Imperial China*, Stanford, CA: Stanford University Press, 1985, 46.

16 T. Li, 李燾 *Xu zizhi tongjian changbian* 續資治通鑑長編, vol. 5, Shanghai: Xinhua shudian, 1986, p. 1183, 204.4a–b.

17 C. Lamouroux, 'From the Yellow River to the Huai: New Representations of a River Network and the Hydraulic Crisis of 1128', in M. Elvin and T. Liu (eds), *Sediments of Time: Environment and Society in Chinese History*, Cambridge University Press, 1998, 545–84.

18 C. Lamouroux, 'From the Yellow River to the Huai'.

19 F. Braudel, *The Mediterranean and the Mediterranean World in the Age of Philip II*, New York: Harper & Row, 1972.

20 D. Massey, *For Space*, London: Sage, 2005.

21 T. Ingold, 'The Temporality of the Landscape', *World Archaeology* 25(2), 1993, 152–74.

22 T. Van Dooren, *Flight Ways: Life and Loss at the Edge of Extinction*, New York: Columbia UP, 2014, 34.

23 D. Christian, *Maps of Time: An Introduction to Big History*, Berkeley, CA: University of California Press, 2004. R. Saekow and W. Alvaraz, *ChronoZoom*, 2009–12. Online. Available HTTP: <http://eps.berkeley.edu/~saekow/chronozoom/news/index.html> (accessed March 2016).

24 R. Mostern and I. Johnson, 'From Named Place to Naming Event'. R. Shaw, 'Gazetteers Enriched'.

25 K. Grossner, K. Janowicz and C. Kessler, 'Place, Period and Setting for Linked Data Gazetteers', and R. Simon, L. Isaksen, E. Barker and P. de Soto Canamares, 'The Pleiades Gazetteer and the Pelagios Project', both in M. Berman, R. Mostern and H. Southall (eds), *Placing Names: Enriching and Integrating Gazetteers*, Bloomington, IN: Indiana University Press, 2016.

26 R. Mostern, 'Sediment and State in Imperial China: The Yellow River Watershed as an Earth System and a World System', *Nature and Culture* 11(2), 2016.

Bibliography

W. Bao, 包偉民, *Songdai difang caizheng shi yanjiu* 宋代地方財政史研究, Shanghai: Shanghai guji chubanshe, 2001.

M. L. Berman, R. Mostern and H. Southall (eds), *Placing Names: Enriching and Integrating Gazetteers*, Bloomington, IN: Indiana University Press, 2016.

F. Braudel, *The Mediterranean and the Mediterranean World in the Age of Philip II*, New York: Harper & Row, 1972.

D. Christian, *Maps of Time: An Introduction to Big History*, Berkeley, CA: University of California Press, 2004.

M. Curry, 'Toward a Geography of a World Without Maps: Lessons from Ptolemy and Postal Codes', *Annals of the Association of American Geographers* 95(3), 2005, 680–91.

M. Elvin and T. Liu (eds), *Sediments of Time: Environment and Society in Chinese History*, Cambridge: Cambridge University Press, 1998.

K. Grossner, K. Janowicz and C. Kessler, 'Place, Period and Setting for Linked Data Gazetteers', in M. Berman, R. Mostern and H. Southall (eds), *Placing Names: Enriching and Integrating Gazetteers*, Bloomington, IN: Indiana University Press, 2016.

M. Henderson, 'Macroregions', in *Oxford Bibliographies*, Oxford: Oxford University Press, 2013. Online. Available HTTP: <www.oxfordbibliographies.com/view/document/obo-9780199920082/obo-9780199920082-0055.xml> (accessed March 2016).

C. Hucker, *A Dictionary of Official Titles in Imperial China*, Stanford, CA: Stanford University Press, 1985.

T. Ingold, 'The Temporality of the Landscape', *World Archaeology* 25(2), 1993, 152–74.

M. Jones, R. Jones and M. Woods, *An Introduction to Political Geography: Space, Place and Politics*, London: Routledge, 2004.

C. Lamouroux, 'From the Yellow River to the Huai: New Representations of a River Network and the Hydraulic Crisis of 1128', in M. Elvin and T. Liu (eds), *Sediments of Time: Environment and Society in Chinese History*, Cambridge: Cambridge University Press, 1998, 545–84.

H. Lefebvre, *The Production of Space*, Oxford: Blackwell, 1991.

T. Li, 李燾, *Xu zizhi tongjian changbian* 續資治通鑑長編, vol. 5, Shanghai: Xinhua shudian, 1986, 1183.

D.Massey, *For Space*, London: Sage, 2005.

R. Mostern, *Dividing the Realm in Order to Govern: The Spatial Organization of the Song State, 960–1276, CE*, Cambridge, MA: Harvard Asia Center, 2011.

R. Mostern, 'Sediment and State in Imperial China: The Yellow River Watershed as an Earth System and a World System', *Nature and Culture* 11(2), 2016, 121–47.

R. Mostern and E. Gainor, 'Traveling the Silk Road on a Virtual Globe: Pedagogy, Technology and Evaluation for Spatial History', *Digital Humanities Quarterly* 7(2), 2013.

R. Mostern and I. Johnson, 'From Named Place to Naming Event: Creating Gazetteers for History', *International Journal of Geographic Information Science* 22(10), 2008, 1091–1108.

R. Mostern and E. Meeks, 'The Politics of Territory in Song Dynasty China', in I. Gregory and A. Geddes (eds), *Rethinking Space and Place: New Directions with Historical GIS*, Bloomington, IN: Indiana University Press, 2014, 118–42.

R. Mostern and H. Southall, 'Gazetteers Past', in M. Berman, R. Mostern and H. Southall (eds), *Placing Names: Enriching and Integrating Gazetteers*, Bloomington, IN: Indiana University Press, 2016.

R. Saekow and W. Alvaraz, *ChronoZoom*, 2009–12. Online. Available HTTP: <http://eps. berkeley.edu/~saekow/chronozoom/news/index.html> (accessed March 2016).

W. Sewell, *Logics of History: Social Theory and Social Transformation*, Chicago, IL: University of Chicago Press, 2005.

R. Shaw, 'Gazetteers Enriched: A Conceptual Basis for Linking Gazetteers with Other Kinds of Information', in M. L. Berman, R. Mostern and H. Southall (eds), *Placing Names: Enriching and Integrating Gazetteers*, Bloomington, IN: Indiana University Press, 2016.

R. Simon, L. Isaksen, E. Barker and P. de Soto Canamares, 'The Pleiades Gazetteer and the Pelagios Project', in M. Berman, R. Mostern and H. Southall, *Placing Names: Enriching and Integrating Gazetteers*, Bloomington, IN: Indiana University Press, 2016.

G. W. Skinner, 'Cities and the Hierarchy of Local Systems', in G. W. Skinner (ed.), *The City in Late Imperial China*, Stanford, CA: Stanford University Press, 1977, 275–352.

C. Tilly, *Coercion, Capital and European States, 990–1992*, vol. 1, Cambridge: Blackwell, 1992.

T. Van Dooren, *Flight Ways: Life and Loss at the Edge of Extinction*, New York: Columbia University Press, 2014.

S. Wang, 汪聖鐸, *Liang Song caizheng shi* 兩宋財政史, Beijing: Zhonghua shuju, 1995.

Z. Wang, 王曾瑜, *Songdai bingzhi chutan* 宋朝兵制初探, Beijing: Zhonghua shuju, 1983.

R. White, 'What is Spatial History?' Spatial History Lab Working Paper, 2010. Online. Available HTTP: <http://web.stanford.edu/group/spatialhistory/cgi-bin/site/pub.php?id=29> (accessed March 2016).

22

PEASANTS AND POLITICS

How GIS offers new insights into the German countryside

George Vascik

Politics in the German countryside was intensely local, framed by deep social, economic and historical causality.[1] It was driven by a complex dialectic of actors and events working across a historically differentiated and physically diverse landscape. GIS enables us to understand this landscape in all its nuance and complexity by using space (in the form of polygons, lines and points) as a tool for collating and correlating this mass of complex, interacting data in ways not possible in earlier statistical studies. Harnessing the power of a GIS based on village census data and election returns, I have been able to analyze variables in a way impossible at a higher level of spatial abstraction – the county – than has been the norm for German election studies.[2] In my work on rural politics and anti-Semitism, to be published in 2018 by Bloomsbury Press, I have attempted to disentangle the complex, intersecting variables that governed political behavior in the German countryside, asking how differently situated people responded politically to events, change and crisis and how their reaction to macro events was refracted in different ways through the prism of past local political experience.

Rural studies have experienced a renaissance in the second decade of the twenty-first century. Historical GIS has played an important role in this renaissance. Unfortunately the manifold aspects of political society have been poorly represented in the rebirth of rural studies. Why is this the case? A major impediment to a comprehensive GIS of German rural politics has been coordinating the vast amount of existing quantitative and qualitative data on the countryside (increasing amounts of which are available online in digitized form). It requires the disaggregation of contemporary political entities to reveal deeper, meaningful historical units – such as *Ämter*, *Kirschpielen* and *Bauernschaften* – and demands a degree of spatial specificity not usually possible with quantitative data.

The region that I study is 753,451 hectares or 3,673 square miles in size. It includes the Grand Duchy (later Free State) of Oldenburg and the Prussian administrative districts of Aurich (East Friesland) and Stadxe (the Elbe-Weser *Dreieck*). For electoral purposes, in the imperial period that preceded the First World War, each district was divided into six parliamentary constituencies. These were single member seats

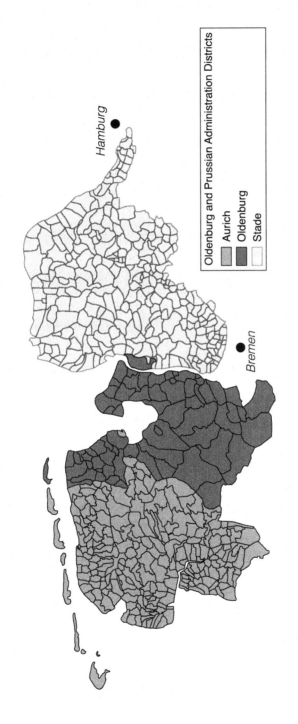

Figure 22.1 Polling places.

filled by a majority + 1 vote. Under the constitution that created the Weimar Republic, East Friesland and the western portions of Oldenburg became part of the new Reichstagswahlkreis of Weser-Ems while the *Dreieck* and the eastern portions of Oldenburg became part of Hannover-Ost. Under this new system, multiple members drawn from party lists were chosen to represent the constituencies. (See Figure 22.1.)

The three mostly rural, thinly populated districts served as an agricultural hinterland for Hamburg and Bremen, providing those cities with meat, dairy, fish and peat. They boasted a surprising diversity: three significant landscape types, three core ethnicities (including long-standing communities of *Dorfjuden*), differing social hierarchies, varying inheritance customs, multiple village structures, farming/crop differentiation and an incredibly active and contentious political press.[3] This rich diversity provides a social scientist with a vast array of variables by which to measure the electoral behavior central to my main research question: how did a region that was one of the most liberal and least anti-Semitic in the Empire before 1918, after the revolutionary upheaval and economic dislocations that followed the First World War, become a bastion of support for National Socialism?

In this chapter, after briefly describing the creation of the GIS and the collection of data pertinent to rural politics, I will reference four areas – landscape and soil, settlement types and village location, distance and deep history – as they impact my research. I will then summarize a few specific conclusions that I have been able to draw from my data and conclude with a recapitulation of what GIS has to offer those studying the countryside and future directions for research.

Data sources for the study of rural politics

We possess plentiful data on German rural life and politics: qualitative and quantitative, official and non-governmental, broad brush and fine grained. The imperial and state governments (in my case, Prussia and Oldenburg) conducted numerous censes, population, industrial and agricultural, and government ministries conducted regular surveys of farm units, crop production, livestock holding and land values and occasional studies on topics such as rural indebtedness. While these data were collected at the village level, with the exception of the decennial censes, they were published only at the county level.[4] The district administrator (*Regierungspräsident*) of each Prussian administrative district, using monthly data provided by the county administrators (*Landräter*) in their jurisdiction, made quarterly reports via the minister of the interior directly to the king which discussed both crop conditions and political unrest.[5] Local chambers of commerce and agricultural associations published data measuring various aspects of the rural economy (such as the level of production, product prices and amounts of goods shipped by boat or rail). Weekly and monthly datasets were regularly reported in the newspapers of the government-sponsored agricultural associations.

On the electoral side, collecting polling place level results is a difficult and time-consuming task. When the date for an election was set, it was the responsibility of the county administrator to publish a list of polling places, along with a list of eligible voters in that jurisdiction (the former were listed in county newspapers; the later no

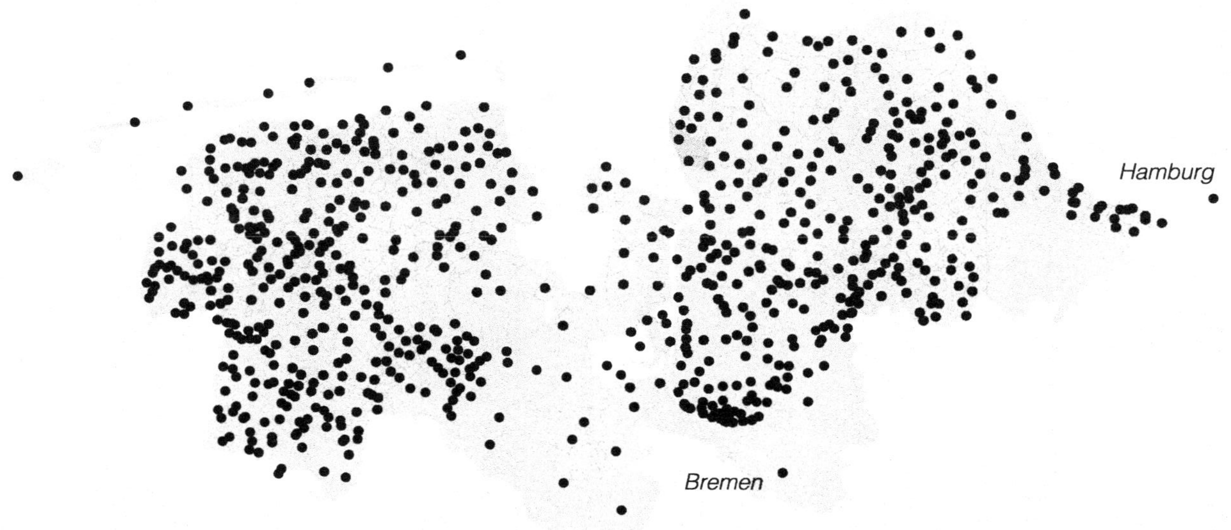

Figure 22.2   Census places.

longer exist). On election day, a three-member 'electoral commission' (composed of prominent and trusted notables) sat at a table in an open public room (usually in a pub). As each voter stepped forward, they handed in their ballot and their name was ticked off the list.[6] After the polls closed and the ballots were counted, the commission chair telegraphed the results to the county administrator, who sent the collated results up the administrative chain of command. The county administrator's report always included the number of eligible voters, the number of ballots cast for each candidate or party list, and how many ballots were spoiled or inadmissible in some way. With extremely rare exceptions, all of these records were destroyed in the Second World War. Fortunately, we are able to recreate *some* of the lost data. When the local commission chair telegraphed the results to the county administrator, he also sent the results to one or more county newspapers and (in most cases) the leading regional newspapers.

Using 52 newspapers found at 36 libraries and archives, I have reconstructed results from the region's 582 polling places (made up of 761 census units).[7] This dataset comprises 8148 polling place results. When the votes cast for the competing parties is taken into consideration, the result is over 200,000 dependent variables. Building the polling place polygon map was also an act of historical reconstruction. The shapefile of contemporary community (*Gemeinde*) boundaries is readily available for download from the Bundesamt für Kartographie und Geodäsie.

Unfortunately, it is organized by current communal boundaries. While these stayed remarkably stable for 100 years after German unification, a major communal reform in 1972 consolidated many historically distinct villages into 'consolidated communities'. To reconstruct the old boundaries, I digitized a 1957 communal boundary map for the state of Lower Saxony. Using the resultant map, I was then able to reconstruct with a high degree of accuracy the original census unit and polling place boundaries, adjusting the map boundaries to take proper account of watercourses and field boundaries to ensure the precision needed for more fine-grained spatial analysis (Figure 22.2). As a last step, in specific instances I referenced cadastral office maps online. The result was a set of polygon boundaries accurate at 1:10,000 scale.

Place and space

How does GIS help us to assess variables in our data that non-spatial statistical analysis does not? Let me offer four instances. GIS gives us the tools to accurately map and analyze the impact of two of the most salient determinants of political interaction and behavior in Northwest Germany – the first being the nexus of landscape/landscape subtype/soil and the second crop regime/village type/social structure (the later changing over time). GIS also facilitates the measure of distance and connectivity – politically, socially and economically. Lastly, it enables us to explore deep history and temporality, allowing us to display change over time. Through the use of digitized historical maps we are able to discern changing coastlines, the draining of wetlands and the creation of new fields and villages. GIS is particularly suited to tracking the development of transportation (rail, road, water) and market linkages, a process that scholars universally recognize as having a profound impact on all aspects of rural life.

Landscape and soil

Geographers frequently refer to the '*social* construction of space.' Northwest Germany is a sterling example of the *physical* construction of space, which GIS can fruitfully explore through soil and landscape maps. There are three major landscape types in Northwest Germany: *Geest*, *Marsch* and *Moor*, each of which can be divided into sub-types (Figure 22.3). While *Geest* and *Moor* existed from the first settlement of the region (although their settlement structure and density changed over time), the *Marsch* were the creation of human endeavor. Each landscape sub-type exhibited different soil horizons, which determined whether or which crops could most profitably be grown.[8] My analysis has shown that there is a correlation between the landscape where a census or polling place is located and voting pattern, which intensifies when one correlates subtype.

When the glaciers retreated at the end of the last Ice Age, they left behind a sandy, habitable series of moraine ridges (*Geest*) interspersed with *Moor* that cut diagonally west to east across the landscape, providing habitable space for the region's earliest settlement.[9] These sand and *Moor* areas (constituting roughly 60 per cent of the region's surface) were surrounded to the east, north and west with wetlands subject to tidal flooding along a constantly changing coastline. (See Figure 22.4.) Within these wetlands were outcroppings of sand (known as *Geest* islands) large enough to hold a household or village and surrounding fields. A notable example is the *Harlingerland* the 30 km² island surrounding Esens. Many *Geest* area farms, with their poorer, drier soil, tended to be more subsistence-based and the farmers there practiced rye monoculture.[10] (See Figure 22.5.) In the period before the First World War, most *Geest* voters supported the importation of cheap fodder from overseas and opposed those parties and candidates who supported higher tariffs. In the period following the War, the most forward-looking of these *Geest* farmers embraced 'modernization' with exuberance, upgrading their production facilities and buying fodder to fatten large herds of swine. These activities left them dependent on easy credit for both expanding their plant and financing the next year's crop.[11]

The coastal and riverine wetlands (known as *Marsch*) were systematically drained by a network of improved natural waterways (*Tiefe*) and field drainage ditches (*Wieken*), protected by a complex, ever expanding system of sea and field dikes. The earliest settlements on the *Marsch* were small raised areas known as *warfen* or *wurten*, some barely large enough to hold a family farmstead, others (such as Emden) were large enough to hold a church and small village. With time, new *wurten* were created or enlarged by piling up material above the tidal flow. The process of drainage began in earnest during the early medieval period (creating the so-called Old *Marsch*) and continued into the modern era (New *Marsch*). There were pronounced differences in field formation and settlement type between the two. (See Figure 22.6.) Dutch settlers and engineers – particularly Mennonites after the Reformation – played an important role in the creation of the New *Marsch*. Reclaimed *Marsch* soil was predominately heavy, highly fertile clay, with various admixtures of sand, stone and the remains of marine organisms. Up until 1900, farmers in the New *Marsch* grew wheat, leaving the lower laying parts of their fields to pasture. In the 1920s, in response to market conditions and the increasing cost of farm labor, they began to concentrate

Figure 22.3   Landscape types.

Figure 22.4 Soil types.

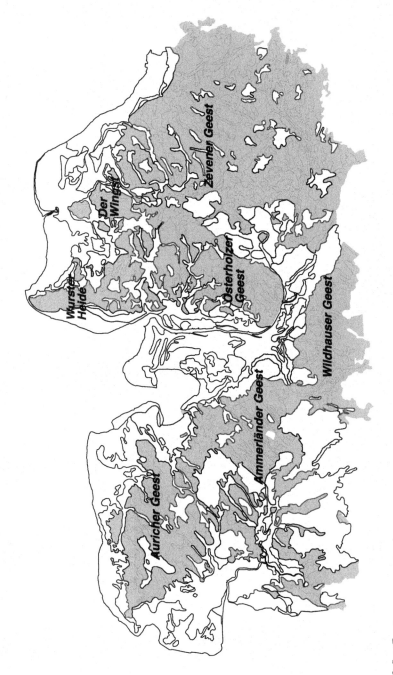

Figure 22.5 Geest.

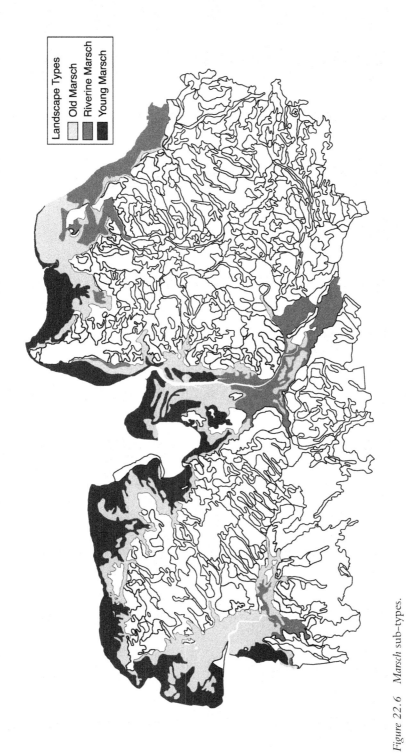

Figure 22.6 *Marsch* sub-types.

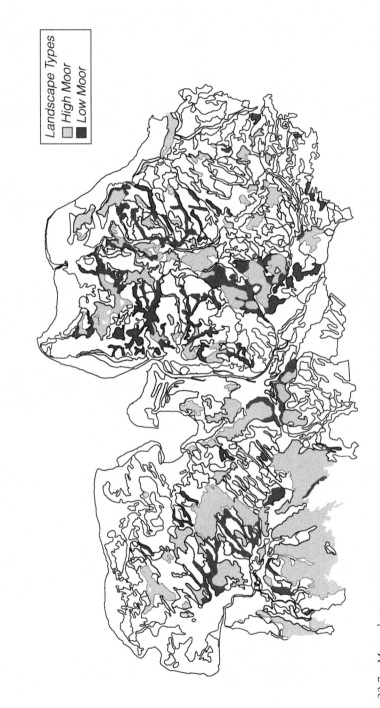

Figure 22.7   Moor sub-types.

more heavily on meat and dairy production. Their economic and political associations advocated lower taxes, higher tariffs and policies geared towards better controlling their resident labor force.

Within each village's boundaries there was a bewildering patchwork of soil gradations suitable to different forms of exploitation: dryer or damper, sandy or pebbled, plots suitable only for meadow or pasture, those requiring deeper plowing and those easily furrowed. Known as *Meed-*, *Knick*, *Esch-*, or *Siet-* lands, the proportion present in each village determined the average land tax that was assessed and the relative wealth of a place's farmers. Changing market conditions resulted in these places being used differently across the period that I study. GIS allows me to identify these soil pockets and correlate property ownership, land use changes and political affiliations over time.

The third landscape type in the region was the *Moor* (Figure 22.7). During the pre-modern period, *Moor* were rarely inhabited and formed a barrier to communication and transport of people and goods. They also helped to isolate northeast Germany from predation of the states to the south. In the late eighteenth century, state authorities, stock companies and individuals tried to make these traversable and bring them under the plough through the creation of *Fehnsiedlung*. The entity creating the settlement would dig a canal (or *Fehn*) through the *Moor*. Houses and allotments for colonists would build a house along the canal, with their property stretching in narrow strips back out into the *Moor*. The earliest *Fehn* colonists would burn the surface vegetation off their land and plant buckwheat. They typically would prosper for two to three years until the new soil lost it fertility. Unable to farm, the settlers would cut peat or raise livestock with purchased fodder. Some settlements also provided laborers for neighboring *Marsch* or *Geest* villages. Desperately poor, *Moor* dwellers time and again were political outliers, supporting radical movements of both Right and Left. I have also found that individual *Fehn* voters were stubbornly independent and *Moor* villages displayed a broader range of party affiliations than either *Marsch* or *Geest* places.[12] As part of this study, I have been mapped over 250 of these *Fehne* and analyzed the extent to which their political behavior differed both from *Geest* and *Marsch* places and among themselves.

Village types and settlement patterns

Different lived environments sustained varied village political cultures reflecting social and economic power relations within the *Dorf*. Identifying and plotting these allow us to create 'norms' for different types of village political interactions. German scholars disagree over how to classify villages; some using settlement form ('open' and 'nucleated' villages) and others field structure. My preference is to identify first settlement form and then differentiate these by field patterns. The 'open' villages were known as *Hufendörfer* or *Streuseidlungen* (scattered villages). In these, each farmer tilled a *Hufe* (field) adjacent to his home. As a map of settlement forms in East Friesland indicates (Figure 22.8), this settlement form predominated in the northernmost part of the region and on the *Geest* ridges that ran in parallel lines through the *Moor* north of the Jümme River.

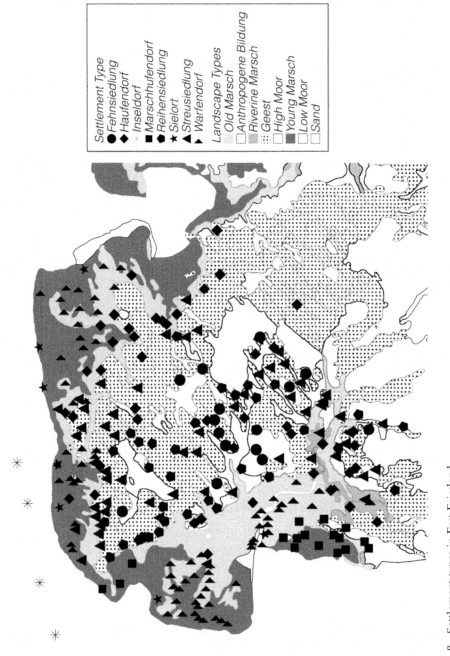

Figure 22.8 Settlement types in East Friesland.

The two primary types of 'nucleated' villages were the *Haufendorf* – built around a central place (usually a church) and characterized by irregular field patterns – and *Reihendorf* (row settlement). *Haufendörfer* (including the subset of *Warfendörfer* built on raised mounds) were primarily a *Marsch* phenomenon. *Geest* villages are exclusively *Reihensiedlung* or *Streusiedlung*, the later usually in close proximity to *Moor* areas. There are two types of *Reihensiedlungen* that are not on the *Geest*: *Fehnsiedlungen* on the *Moor* (described above) and *Poldersiedlungen* in *Marsch* areas reclaimed since the late early modern era (from the Leyebuch near Norden and the Dollert between the Ems and the Dutch border).

Each of these landscape and settlement types possessed distinct social hierarchies. The *Marsch* areas were distinguished by pronounced social stratification. Social and economic stratification was less pronounced, although still extent, in *Geest* villages and nearly non-existent in *Moor* colonies, where the inhabitants shared a crushing poverty. On the *Marsch*, a handful of well-to-do peasant families – the *Buuren* – living in free-standing houses complete with in-living dependent men and women dominated economic and ecclesiastical life. A larger population of poor agricultural workers – the *Arbeider* – lived in small cottages and depended upon the *Buuren* for employment. The people who lived in the towns, known as *Boergers*, operated small businesses or provided services to the farming sector. Although they were invested in the well-being of the farm economy, they were socially and politically distinct from the farmers. It is impossible to separate out *Buuren*, *Arbeider* and *Boerger* votes in national parliamentary elections, but qualitative evidence suggests that while *Buuren* voted Agrarian and conservative before 1919 (as did their dependent workers) the *Boergers* tended to favor Liberal and Progressive candidates. The small communities of Jews living in these rural towns were completely integrated into village social and economic life. My evidence suggests that the greater the number of Jews, Mennonites or Catholics in a village, the higher the percentage of votes cast 1893–1912 went to left of center parties.[13]

Distance

My work indicates that distance (to church, school, or rail station) was an important element in rural political behavior. Parishes in the long-settled Prussian territories (as opposed to the newer *Moor* colonies) were relatively compact, while in Oldenburg they were much larger, as were the polling places. The Oldenburg *Amt* of Westerstede, on the *Ammerländer Geest* and the Prussian *Kreis*, of Osterholz, north of Bremen east of the Weser, were of analogous size. Both were predominantly podsol areas with similar crop regimes and field patterns. There were, however, only four polling places in *Amt* Westerstede, while *Kreis* Osterholz had 26 polling places. (On the Prussian model, *Amt* Westerstede could hold up to ten polling places.[14]) The polling place of Westerstede had, in addition to its eponymous center, 21 hamlets (*Bauernschaften*) ranging in size from 191 to 543 inhabitants (1925). The straight-line distance from its northern and southern most hamlets to the church at the center of Westerstede was circa 9 km; from its east and west 7 km. The result was lower church attendance and less clerical supervision and influence than was the case in smaller parishes in Osterholz. By contrast, in the tiny villages of *Kreis* Selsingen on the *Zevener Geest*, a walk to church was usually less than 1 km. Parish councils dominated by nobles sympathetic to the anti-Prussian German-Hanoverian Party appointed the pastors of these churches. They enjoyed far greater moral and political influence on the lives of their parishioners. These pastors were closely observed by the local gendarmerie (and their sermons recorded) lest they express anti-government views. Because village and hamlet schools were thicker on the ground in Oldenburg than parish churches village schoolteachers had a greater impact on village politics than elsewhere. Before the First World War many of these were outspokenly progressive but the War and its aftermath transformed many of them, especially the large cohort of returning veterans, into extreme nationalists and anti-Semites.[15]

Distance also served as an important variable in the immediate post-1918 period. Using the GIS, it is possible to calculate the distance each village was from the centers of revolutionary upheaval, whether the naval base at Wilhelmshaven or the urban centers of Hamburg, Bremen, Emden and Leer. In the course of the revolution, bands of armed marines plundered the countryside in search of food and valuables and villagers responded by creating Home Guard units. I have plotted the location of these *Einwohnerwehr* units, their distance from the nearest center of unrest and correlated later support for the right-wing parties. Not surprisingly, perhaps, there was a high correlation between individual organizers of these Home Guard units and Nazi party membership.

Deep history

GIS reminds us of the importance of deep historical place. Social scientific logic tells us that to varying degrees the variables that I have collected *must* have an impact on people's political behavior. And indeed, my initial statistical analysis of voting results for East Friesland showed the population, population density, per capita income, land value per hectare, transportation connectivity and religious diversity all played role in predicting electoral support for agrarian conservatives, National Liberals and Progressives in the district's villages. When I expanded my analysis to the entirety of the northwest, despite the clear spatial ordering clearly present in voting behavior, these independent variables lost all of their impact. In instance after instance, the only significant dependent variable determining the extent of support for the Nazi party in the Weimar era was the degree to which a place had voted for liberal candidates in the imperial era.

Why was this? Working on a paper looking at the transformation of the *Kreis* of Wittmund from a reliably liberal area during the imperial period into an anti-Semitic stronghold in the era immediately following the Great War, I found that the radical anti-Republican vote was concentrated in the sub-county (*Amt*) of Friedeburg – a historically distinct area separated from the other two *Ämter* in the county – that had been traumatized by the revolutionary events at the nearby naval base of Wilhelmshaven in 1918. Using this insight, I broke the entire northwest region down into a variety of subunits and found that votes from Oldenburg skewed my results. Before the War, political competition in the section of Oldenburg that I study had been between two competing liberal parties. As the Oldenburg electorate moved earlier and more heavily towards National Socialism than either of the other two regions, 'historic liberality' reduced all other dependent variables to insignificance.[16] Once I broke my results down into the three main areas (East Friesland, Oldenburg and the *Dreieck*), then into counties and sub-counties, the dependent variables become significant again, proving that variables have to be placed into appropriate historical boxes.

Examples

Documenting the many insights that I have gained through the use of GIS would require more time than this chapter allows, as each of necessity must be placed within both its specific local context and the broader political narrative. I will limit myself to a few examples, with the admonition that the reader should consult my website, <http://peasantsandjews.org>.

It is a stereotype of rural life is that it is unchanging or at best changes very slowly. The volatility of rural politics was particularly evident after the revolution of 1918, when people cycled through political parties and agenda at a frightening pace as if they were constantly grabbing for a new life preserver and then discarding it when it did not serve. As a rule, in the election of January 1919, the Deutsche Demokratische Partei carried villages that did not offer plurality support to the Mehrheits-Sozialdemokraten or Deutsch-Hannoversche Partei. Sixteen months later, many of these same places had been won over to Gustav Stresemann's Deutsche Volkspartei, only to abandon the liberals four years later for either the German National Peoples' Party or the anti-Semitic Völkisch-Sozial Bloc. GIS lets us trace these local responses and shifts with exacting specificity. One can witness this spatially as parties ascended from nowhere and then crashed. An excellent example of this is the ill-fated Christian Nationalist Peasants and Rural Peoples' Party. Founded in the spring of 1928 in response to the economic downturn in the rural economy, it was extremely successful in the Elbe-Weser *Dreieck*, only to disappear by 1932.[17] Another locally concentrated new party was the Christlich-Soziale Volksdienst. Looking at county-level support the party looks insignificant but when charted in the GIS it is clear that it had enormous appeal in Reformed villages of the *Krummhörn* region and the city of Emden in 1930 where it was allied with the Konservative Volkspartei created by Nationalist dissidents unhappy with Alfred Hugenburg's leadership of the Deutschnationale Volkspartei.[18]

A recurring theme in the historiography of German politics is the persistence of local notables. Notables had positions of influence not only because of their importance as employers but also because of their prominent place in the rural world. They sat on parish boards and selected the local pastor. They held important offices such as dike warden. They were village election supervisors and sat on village and county councils. They were active in the agricultural associations and had access to funds and prestige. Without GIS, it is impossible to effectively place these elites and their interconnectedness. A major set of evidence for reconstructing these local elites was the custom begun in the 1890s of candidates collecting the names of supporters at their rallies and then publishing them in the county papers. Frequently, the signatories would list their occupation beside their name. We are able to ascertain that larger landowners frequently brought their dependent workers along with them, these signing immediately after the *Gutsbesitzer*. It is even possible, using address books and land records, to place these landowners on the GIS, see how they are distributed across the terrain and identify areas that supported opposing candidates. In this way I have been able to trace continuities between old Bund der Landwirte and post-1920 Reichs-Landbund, Stephanie Merkenich has shown how these organizations differed at the national level and most recently Rainer Pomp has delineated the connectedness between the Landbund and the DNVP in Brandenburg; my work is able to measure the allegiance of specific individuals and community interests that constituted the very different Kreislandbünde of northwest Germany.[19] This spatial prosopographic study demonstrates that the new Landbund was more politically open than its legal predecessor (including not only Liberals but also German-Hanoverians, who were excluded from the old BdL) and more locally varied. While pre-War leaders of the BdL headed the Hadeln and Emden Landbünde, the German-Hanoverians shared power in the Bremervörde Landbund and a former National Liberal-turned anti-Semite Georg Weidenhofer chaired the Stade Kreislandbund.

My own work has shown that the region's Bund der Landwirte was less uni-partisan than in other parts of the Kaiserreich, drawing support from farmers and voters who were otherwise oriented towards the Reichspartei or the National Liberals. In its political aspects – as distinct from its economic aspects – maintaining the non-partisan Agrarian coalition required careful negotiations over candidate selection and the drawing up of candidate manifestos. As my data show, when anti-Semitic elements within the Agrarian coalition were able to dictate candidate selection, the Bund der Landwirte lost on average 20 per cent of the votes that it normally received in national elections. I have termed this the 'anti-Semitic penalty' and have been able to map individual villages where the choice of an anti-Semitic candidate hurt the coalition's vote total and conversely, where the population was more open to anti-Semitic utterances. Interestingly enough, my GIS demonstrates that voters in *Amt* Friedeburg, who in May 1924 voted overwhelmingly for the Völkisch-Sozial Bloc in 1900 were steadfast in rejecting an anti-Semitic candidate.

GIS is uniquely qualified to help us identify political trends. We can deduce 'hot spots' of support for political parties using simple polygon maps, geographically weighted regressions, ordinary least squares or non-parametric core density. I can, for instance, create a map that displays the average percentage of votes cast that candidates supported by the Bund der Landwirte received when they were put forward in the five Reichstag elections between 1893 and 1912. The next step is to focus in on where the Agrarians were most and least successful and try to determine what independent variables might be salient in determining pro-Agrarian voting behavior (Figure 22.9).

In a similar fashion, I can display which of the two competing anti-Semitic parties – the Völkisch-National Bloc or the NSDAP – received the largest number of votes in each polling place.[20] Similar maps could show percentages won by each party in each village and overall percentages of the combined anti-Semitic vote. (I have created comparable maps exploring completion within the Socialist milieu after 1912.[21]) As otherwise significant independent variables were not determining voter choice, the spatial representation of anti-Semitic votes directs us into a microhistorical analysis of polling places to suggest what other factors (campaigns, local actors, press

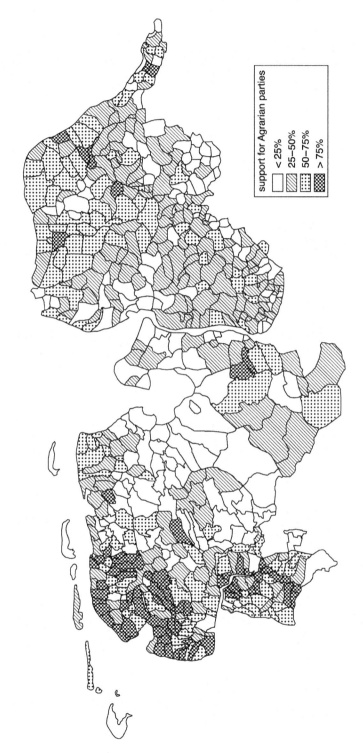

support for Agrarian parties

☐ < 25%
▨ 25–50%
▦ 50–75%
▩ > 75%

Figure 22.9 Percentage of votes cast for Agrarian candidates.

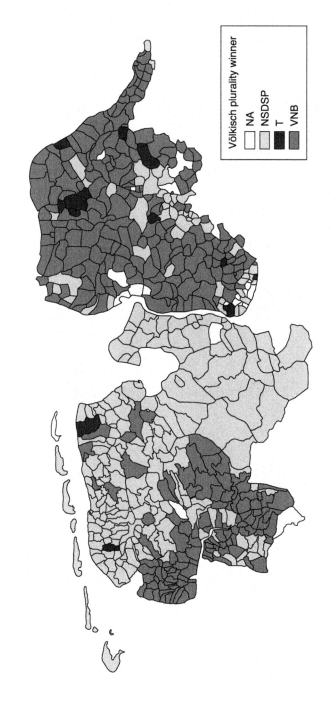

Figure 22.10 VNB/NSDAP competition, 1928.

environment, etc.) might have been important. Ethnographic studies and travel literature has been particularly useful in this regard.[22] Something more was at work with rise of NSDAP than variables can suggest. In a field that too frequently sees the triumph of National Socialism in 1933 as the *telos* of German history, GIS gives us the tools to see the contingency of German history and measure the impact of exogenous events on rural society.

In addition to looking at individual parties, GIS helps us identify areas of support for different parties or factions within specific movements and recreate regional voter milieu. It is possible, for instance, to create a 'bloc analysis' of liberal, conservative and socialist support. Throughout the imperial and Weimar periods, electors could always choose between at least two liberal parties. After 1918, socialists could choose between at least two (and once as many as five) socialist parties. In the two national elections held in 1924, anti-Republicans could vote for either the more traditional German Nationals or the anti-Semitic Racist (*völkisch*) Bloc, while in 1928, there were two competing *völkisch* parties. (See Figure 22.10.)

Along with changes in the party landscape, there were changes in campaign intensity and style that can be mapped to good effect. Campaigns before 1890 were conducted on a 'Grand Tour' model; the candidate would travel to each county seat in the constituency, make a standard speech and leave the distribution of ballot papers to local party activists. When Agrarians challenged the regionally hegemonic National Liberals in the Prussian areas in 1893, the model changed as candidates held scores of rallies, many outside the county towns, and published lists of supporters. With each election cycle, one can map the increased length and intensity of campaigning and hypothesize the strategies involved. By 1912, all parties held rallies throughout all the villages of the constituency. In some cases, the candidates would travel from rally to rally by automobile, sometimes speaking as many as four times a day. In 1924, the young Nazi, Jan Blankemeyer, used a motorcycle to drive himself to quick impromptu talks in the hamlets on the *Ammerländer Geest* that he conducted *auf Platt*. This level of retail politics was completely new to these most isolated *Bauernschaften* and proved highly effective.

Mapping the changes in political style and discourse has allowed the development of what I would term an epidemiological model of radical political activity.[23] One example is in the growth of anti-Semitism after 1918. We have next to no local records on the most important anti-Semitic pressure group to emerge from the First World War – the Deutschvölkisch Schutz- und Trutzbund – that was very active in the cities along the North Sea coast.[24] While we have pretty extensive records in some areas of the growth and membership of the German National Peoples' Party after its creation in 1918 for one or two administrative districts, we have no membership figures or local chapter records of the German Racist Freedom Party, created in 1922 when the most virulent anti-Semites were expelled from the DNVP.[25]

If we adopt an epidemiological model to explain the growth of Jew hatred, one way to gauge the spread of anti-Semitism is to examine the growth of antibodies, in this case chapters of the Central Association of German Citizens of the Jewish Faith. Using surviving records of the Central-Verein held at the Wiener Library in London, I have been able to map a growth in the size and number of such local chapters in the period 1922–4, followed by a decline until 1931, when activity resumed at a fevered pace. From this statistical and spatial evidence, one can posit that anti-Semitism seemed well contained after 1924 (a view supported with qualitative evidence from the archive), only to revive again after the economic collapse.[26]

It would be useful to map anti-Semitic incidents and violence, such as those recorded by Michael Wildt, but in my area such events were a rarity. My evidence very much confirms what Stefanie Fischer has found in her work on *Mittelfranken*, that the livestock trading business – and the main economic interaction between peasants and Jews in the northwest was the buying and selling of livestock – was a confidence-based relationship. Relationships were nurtured over years, business was conducted by verbal agreement and a handshake, there were sufficient *Viehhändler* that if one developed a bad reputation, another could take his place.[27] While Hannah Ahlheim has done an excellent job recording boycotts of Jewish merchants, they were rare in my region and the subject of vigorous prosecution.[28]

The impact of significant events can be followed through GIS as well. 1921 saw a wave of agricultural worker strikes as Social Democrats and Communists competed to unionize farm laborers, with the tacit support from the government. In the districts were the strikes were most intense – the *Marsch* counties of Kehdingen, Hadeln and Emden – the *Buuren* relied on the Kreislandbünde and the semi-official agricultural associations to protect their interests and put down the strikes. These areas later proved most likely to support the German National Peoples' Party against their National Socialist opponents well into 1932, that is long after the Nazis had emerged as the dominant party in the northwest German countryside. Conversely, Nazi calls for a 'peoples' community' was more successful in the relatively egalitarian *Geest* districts where there were no strikes.

Conclusion

How does GIS create new knowledge useful in understanding political processes? GIS has proven to be extremely useful for my own work. I can test hypotheses of electoral behavior. The spatial dimension brings unexpected insight. Its ultimate utility is as an organizing tool for resources, putting quantitative data into boxes and thinking through the spatial representation of qualitative data.

Among the many thematic questions not addressed in this chapter, rural political GIS allows us to study change over time, political modernization (mass mobilization, campaign style, lingering impact of *Honoratiorenpolitik*) and the impact of economic modernization. We can chart the changing forms and goals of agricultural representation (semi-governmental associations, economic and political interest groups) and economic cooperation (the buying and insurance co-ops run by the agricultural associations and the Raiffeissen). We can demonstrate the impact of a little discussed phenomenon, anti-anti-Semitism and the various forms of religious and ethnic cooperation and antagonism. Lastly, it allows us to test explanations of electoral behavior, such as milieu voting, put forward by other scholars.

Fully realized, GIS allows for the possibility of an integrated study of the country-side that will spatially contextualize data in a way that supports fine-grained analysis of complex, interlocking variables. A GIS of rural politics requires deep local study and enormous amounts of digitization and cartographic work. To be fully successful, as in so much of GIS, it must be collaborative, multi-disciplinary and locally grounded. In a perfect world, the result would be a deep map, where vast amounts of information could be stored in a spatial context. At some point perhaps the gains will diminish, but at this point in my own research each new question asked offers new and exciting insights into political behavior in the northwest German countryside.

Notes

1 Thanks to Anne Vascik, who assisted in the creation of the GIS and produced the maps, and to my colleagues in the Miami University Hamilton Research Seminar who commented on an early version of this chapter. Thanks as well for the many insightful suggestions offered by the participants of the colloquium of the Seminar für Neuere Geschichte at the Eberhard Karls Universität Tübingen under the direction of Prof. Dr. Ewald Frie.

2 For a complete bibliography of work on German elections see <www.peasantsandjews. org/bibliography/html>.

3 Characteristic of the kind of interesting comparative work that can be done here is H. Denker and B. Mütter, 'Landwirtschaftspolitik in der Epoche des Kaiserreichs 1871–1914/18: Ein interregionaler Vergleich mit dem preußischen Regierungsbezirk Stade (Provinz Hannover – Handelspielräume eines kleinen Bundesstaat', *Niedersächsisches Jahrbuch für Landesgeschichte* 87, 2015, 163–201.

4 Previous electoral studies by Anglo-American and German scholars have relied on county-level analysis using data published by the Imperial Statistical Office. The data used in my GIS are derived from *Gemeindelexikon für die Provinz Hannover. Auf Grund der Materialien der Volkszahlung vom 2. Dezember 1895*, Berlin: Königlichen Statistischen Bureau, 1897; *Gemeindelexikon für die Provinz Hannover: Auf Grund der Materialien der Volkszahlung vom 1. Dezember 1905*, Berlin: Königlichen Statistischen Landesamts, 1908; and *Gemeindelexikon für den Freistaat Preußen. Band X, Provinz Hannover*, Berlin: Preußischen Statistischen Landesamts, 1933.

5 The Prussian portion of the study area contained two administrative districts divided into twelve counties (*Kreise*), which were in turn divided into twenty-four sub-counties (*Ämter*).

6 Little work has been done on the actual process of voting with the exception of R. Arschenschek, *Der Kampf um die Wahlfreiheit im Kaiserreich: Zur politischen Realität der Reichstagswahlen 1871–1914*, Düsseldorf: Droste, 2003. Most recently, see I. Mares, *From Open Secrets to Secret Voting: Democratic Electoral Reforms and Voter Autonomy*, Cambridge: Cambridge University Press, 2015, is a good step in addressing this deficit. The form of the ballot changed over time. Before the December 1924 election, the voters brought their own ballot to the polling station. These ballots were of a regulation size, upon which was written or printed the name of the candidate (or after 1919 the party list) for which the individual voted. In 1903, envelopes were introduced to increase confidentiality. Urns that ensured that voter preference could not be determined were only universally required in May 1924. The national election in December of that year was also the first to feature the Australian ballot where all potential party choices were listed and the individual ticked off their preference.

7 387 of these census units (66.5 per cent) were congruent with single polling places across the full timespan of the study. 70 were part of continuously pared units, where the polling place might sometimes shift from village A to village B; 38 consisted of more than two census places. The remaining 87 places (15 per cent of the sample) were at some point consolidated into larger units and disappeared as reported entities.

8 There were 65 different soil types in the German Soil Survey. The German system (as opposed to the FAO and the USG) differentiates seven different *March* soils and recognizes different clay and podsol horizons.

9 The term *Geest* is thought to have derived from Low German *gest* or *gust*, both of which mean 'dry' and 'infertile'.

10 This form of rye monoculture, known as *ewige Roggenbau*, was extremely hard on the soil, and required constant field work as the arable had to be annually replenished with manure, faeces and legumes.

11 Important elements in their calculation were the credit market and commodity prices that existed during the great hyperinflation. The stabilization of the German currency after January 1924 left many of them in difficult straits.

12 I came to this conclusion by modifying the GINI formula to determine income equality/inequality to show the range of votes cast for different parties in individual villages. My data show that *Geest* villages deserved their reputation for political homogeneity, while *Marsch* villages displayed a pattern of large landowner domination prior to the First World War with sharp upper/lower class division after 1918.

13 I hypothesize that familiarity with Jews as neighbors and useful members of the community made these locales less open to anti-Semitic propaganda.

14 The median size of the Westerstede polling places was 9,854 hectare, median population 5,186 inhabitants, with a density of 0.49 people/hectare. *Kreis* Osterholz, in contrast, had 26 polling places, with a median size of 1,309 hectares and 429 inhabitants, with a median density of 0.40 people/hectare.

15 G.-A. Hilke, *Volkschullehrer und Nationalsozialismus: Oldenburgischer Landeslehrerverein und Nationalsozialistischer Lehrerbund in den Jahren der politischen und wirtschaftlichen Krise 1930–1933*, Oldenburg: H. Holzberg, 1983.

16 In the national election of 1930, the Nazis were plurality winners in many Oldenburg villages. This was two years before their 'breakthrough' in the Prussian parts of Northwest Germany.

17 M. Müller, *Die Christlich-Nationale Bauern- und Landvolkpartei 1928–1933*, Düsseldorf: Droste Verlag, 2001.

18 G. Opitz, *Der Christlich-soziale Volksdienst*, Düsseldorf: Droste, 1969.

19 S. Merkenich, *Grüne Front gegen Weimar: Reichs-Landbund und agrarischer Lobbyismus 1918–1933*, Düsseldorf: Droste Verlag, 1998; R. Pomp, *Bauern und Grossgrundbesitzer auf ihrem Weg ins Dritte Reich: der Brandenburgische Landbund, 1919–1933*, Berlin: Akademie Verlag, 2011.

20 This later map, I think, points to the importance of personal agency, a topic I discussed in the paper, '"Is Hitler Racist Enough?" Competition among the *völkisch* Parties in North-west Germany', presented in April 2012 at the European Social Science History Association conference in Glasgow, UK. <www.peasantsandjews.org/Competition.html>

21 See 'Party Politics and State Power: The Rise and Fall of Social Democracy in the North-west German Countryside, 1890–1933', paper presented in September 2010 at the Social Science History Association conference in Chicago, IL. <www.peasantsandjews.org/Socialists.html>

22 J. Kleinpaul, *Wanderungen in Ostfriesland*, Berlin: F. Fontana, 1909, and H. Allmers, *Marschenbuch*, Gotha: Hugo Schenke, 1858.

23 See H.-G. Aschoff, 'Die Deutsch-Hannoversche Partei zwischen Revolution und Machtergreifung (1918–1933)', *Stader Jahrbuch* 78, 1988, 71. More recently, T. Riotte, 'Seiner Magistät allergetreueste Opposition: Welfische Bewegung und politische Sprache in Kaiserreich und Weimare Republik', *Jahrbuch für Niedersächsische Landesgeschichte* 82, 2010, 412–38.

24 U. Lohalm, *Völkischer Radikalismus; die Geschichte des Deutschvölkischen Schutz- und Trutz-Bundes, 1919–1923*, Hamburg: Leibnitz, 1970, and S. Breuer, *Die Völkischen in Deutschland*, Darmstadt: Wissenschaftliche Buchgesellschaft, 2008.

25 On the German Racists see R. Wulff, *Die Deutschvölkische Freiheitspartei 1922–1928*, Marburg: E. Mauersberger, 1968. We are more fortunate regarding the growth of the Nazi party, see D. Stegmann, *Politische Radikalisierung in der Provinz. Lageberichte und Stärkemeldungen der Politischen Polizei und der Regierungspräsidenten für Osthannover 1922–1933*, Hanover: Verlag Hahnsche Buchhandlung, 1999.

26 Following up on what the spatial evidence seemed to suggest, I visited the Kreisarchiv Wittmund and worked through the remembrances collected by Edzard Eichenbaum from members of Wittmund's Jewish community and met with Gerd Rokahr at the August-Gottschlk-Haus memorial site in Esens.

27 M. Wildt, *Volksgeminschaft als Selbstermächtigung: Gewalt gegen Juden in der deutschen Provinzen 1919–bis 1939*, Hamburg, 2007; S. Fischer, *Ökonomisches Vertrauen und antisemitische Gewalt: Jüdische Viehhändler in Mittelfranken, 1919–1939*, Göttingen: Wallstein, 2014.

28 H. Ahlheim, *'Deutsche, kauft nicht bei Juden!': Antisemitismus und politischer Boykott in Deutschland 1924 bis 1935*, Göttingen: Wallstein, 2011.

Bibliography

M. Anderson, *Practicing Democracy: Elections and Political Culture in Imperial Germany*, Princeton, NJ: Princeton University Press, 2000.

B. Ault and W. Brustein, 'Joining the Nazi Party. Explaining the Political Geography of NSDAP Membership, 1925–1933', *American Behavioral Scientist* 41, 1998, 1304–23.

B. Fairbairn, *Democracy in the Undemocratic State: The German Reichstag Elections of 1898 and 1903*, Toronto: University of Toronto Press, 1987.

J. Falter, *Hitlers Wähler*, Munich: Beck, 1991.

C. Flint, 'Forming Electorates, Forging Spaces: The Nazi Party and the Social Construction of Space', *American Behavioral Scientist* 41, 1998, 1282–1303.

R. Hamilton, *Who Voted for Hitler?* Princeton, NJ: Princeton University Press, 1982.

G. King, O. Rosen, M. Tanner and A. Wagner, 'Ordinary Economic Voting Behavior in the Extraordinary Election of Adolf Hitler', *Journal of Economic History* 68(4), 2008, 951–96.

J. O'Loughlin, 'The Electoral Geography of Weimar Germany: Exploratory Spatial Data Analyses (ESDA) of Protestant Support for the Nazi Party', *Political Analysis* 10(3), 2002, 217–43.

W. Pyta, *Dorfgemeinschaft und Parteipolitik 1918–1933: Die Verschränkung von Milieu und Parteien in den protestantischen Landgebieten Deutschlands in der Weimarer Republik*, Düsseldorf: Droste, 1996.

J. Sperber, *The Kaiser's Voters: Electors and Elections in Imperial German*, Cambridge: Cambridge University Press, 1997.

23

MAPPING INEQUALITY

'Big data' meets social history in the story of redlining

N. D. B. Connolly, LaDale Winling, Robert K. Nelson, and Richard Marciano

Urban historians love redlining maps, the real estate appraisal documents created during the 1930s and early 1940s by the Home Owners' Loan Corporation, or HOLC (pronounced 'holk'). Used to visually represent home-loan risk in American cities, these 'security maps' offer a powerful and almost self-evident look at one of the central contradictions of New Deal America, namely the effort to bring about *national* economic recovery on a *racially segregated* basis. With redlining maps, HOLC, and later the Federal Housing Administration (FHA), assessed mortgage risk as part of broader deliberations about who deserved rescuing from mortgage default during the Great Depression and which neighborhoods seemed most creditworthy and safe for debt financing. HOLC and their maps were supposed to help all of America return to economic stability, but, according to federal and local housing officials, that recovery could only be secured if lenders, realtors, developers, and home-sellers controlled, on a racial basis, who could live where.[1] The term 'redlining' comes from the red colors used on HOLC maps some 80 years ago to mark communities that were considered high investment risk. Today, we know 'redlining' as a general term for any form of institutional housing discrimination. In spite of having updated our language, though, security maps themselves have largely been frozen in time, used mostly as mere illustration for what many consider a largely unchanged, if important, argument about past segregation.

The *Mapping Inequality* project updates our use of HOLC redlining maps and, by extension, the ways in which we interpret the history of redlining. This initiative offers a layered digital rendering of redlining maps. It takes security maps backward and forward in time through a single visualization.[2] Examining the 'concentric circles' model of urban space that was popular among sociologists during the Progressive Era, *Mapping Inequality* shows how redlining maps echoed earlier efforts to organize American cities based on the principles of social and natural science. By looking at what preceded redlining, we can appreciate how HOLC maps both reflected and made real earlier ideas about the mixing of different racial groups and different uses of the city. *Mapping Inequality* also overlays the maps on present-day cityscapes to create juxtaposition of past and present urban conditions. Through an interface that allows viewers to fade HOLC maps to the point of transparency, visitors can see how communities today bear the mark of risk designations that were institutionalized almost a century ago.

The study of redlining needs this kind of update for the digital age because of the ongoing, vigorous debate about the economic and social impact of federally sponsored housing segregation. For years, scholarly and popular engagement with the maps differed little from what Kenneth Jackson advanced some 30 years ago, first in a *Journal of Urban History* article, and then his book, *Crabgrass Frontier: The Suburbanization of the United States.*[3] Jackson detailed how the federal government steered white Americans into single-family homes and black Americans into public housing (Figure 23.1). This story has been corroborated and, in important ways, expanded through a variety of case studies, as scholars today continue to deploy security maps

Figure 23.1 Hand-drawn representation of the Essex County, NJ, HOLC security map, published as part of Kenneth Jackson's article on the Home Owners' Loan Corporation maps in the *Journal of Urban History* in 1980.

Source: Journal of Urban History.

to explain a range of historical problems in political economy, real estate economics, liberalism, or racial formation (Figure 23.2).[4]

Since the early 2000s, scholars have challenged the racial impact and racist inspirations of federal redlining. In popular and scholarly venues, observers question

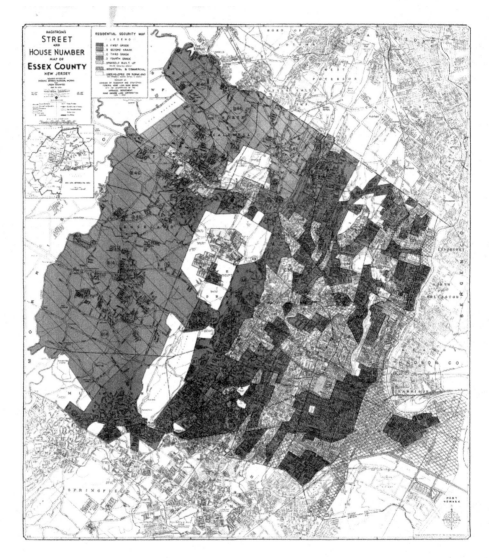

Figure 23.2   HOLC 'redlining' or security map for Essex County, NJ, among approximately 200 stored in the National Archives and Records Administration II site. The graded and color-coded map serves as a visual assessment of investment risk, drawing on extensive demographic and economic data, that prioritized stasis and segregation, especially benefiting professional class residents. In the original, the darkest areas are red and the lightest yellow.

Source: RG 39, NARA II, College Park, MD.

whether New Deal mapping practices caused white flight, or whether white flight was caused by earlier, more individuated concerns originating in the urban ethnic enclaves of the Progressive Era.[5] Through her study of HOLC actions in Philadelphia, Amy Hillier contended that security maps were not widely distributed enough to prompt realtors or lenders to impose a national, segregationist home-financing policy and lenders often made loans in red, 'D' areas.[6] James Greer argued that, of all the empirical determinants that went into HOLC maps, the *age* of the housing was a 'stronger, negative correlate of HOLC risk assessment grade' than the perceived race of that housing's occupant.[7] 'While race certainly informed the development of these maps', he writes, 'the presence of non-whites and foreign born ethnics are rather modest (albeit clearly negative) correlates of the final HOLC mortgage risk grade.'[8]

In this chapter, we explore some critical questions still left unanswered by the racial history of redlining, and contend that the future of studying redlining – its history and its effects – demands bringing 'big data' mapping techniques together with established approaches to social and urban history. Geographical Information Systems (GIS) technology can be applied to real estate history, and especially the history of the Home Owners' Loan Corporation, to give a greater understanding of HOLC's creation, operation, and administrative aims. Historians can and should use archival methods in tandem with contemporary mapping techniques to capture the dynamism of what may best be called the mapping state. In order to appreciate redlining as a process of defining and, indeed, of creating risk, one must combine New Deal America's security maps with period real estate data, with government archives detailing the logics of redlining, and with present-day images of, data regarding, and narratives about neighborhoods forever changed by state-underwritten racial discrimination.

Security maps are more than pictures. They served as instruments of political and social conflicts happening before, during, and after the time of their production. And when rigorously considered *as sources*, not just as illustrations, HOLC security maps provide evidence of a feedback loop that existed between citizens and their state. How did the New Deal state, as a mapping state, exercise its role as protector against risk for American citizens and financial markets? More pertinently, how might historians and researchers marry evolving uses of GIS with approaches to social history to assess how New Dealers themselves used security maps to balance and govern both white racism and American capitalism?

An examination of the process of assessment and a big data rendering of redlining leave little doubt that, following the Great Depression, racism stood at the heart of America's rebuilt real estate economy. Racially restrictive covenants, racial self-interest among real estate investors, racist theories of home value, and even discriminatory office politics within the federal bureaucracy all provided the raw materials for New Deal mapmaking. Through a cocktail of formal and informal means, HOLC used decidedly *white* notions of risk as the foundation for its cartographic renderings of America.

By bringing GIS capabilities to bear on social and policy history questions, *Mapping Inequality* can open new debates more poignantly than settling old ones. It uses HOLC maps in tandem with the corporation's broader archive to invite scholars to consider racism as a social force that drew on social processes. Scholars still know very little about HOLC's relationship to social science thinking of the day and to the wider cultural landscape of white expectation and aspiration. New research must still be done exploring how white folk notions of community and efficiency, codified by the New Deal state, helped standardize lending practices, construction quality, and long-term economic growth for the entire country.

Neither an objective assessor of reality nor an impartial arbiter of potential social conflict, the New Deal state amplified and laundered white power through its mapping process, effectively projecting into the present the whims and wishes of white communities from 80 years ago. The ostensible 'science' of mortgage economics happened, in practice, as a dialectic between white supremacist understandings of 'risk' and opposing or countervailing commitments to racial equality among African Americans and their allies. Many historians have come to appreciate this dynamic on a local level. Our current 'big data' moment gives us yet another opportunity to consider the redlining story nationally and to reconsider a source – the HOLC security map – that many historians thought they knew.

The incredible HOLC

Residential finance and home construction were key contributors to the Depression – in 1933, as many as half of American mortgages were in default.[9] Housing was also a major component of the employment crisis. National construction spending had plummeted from $11 billion to $3 billion, and three-quarters of the nation's construction workers remained out of work.[10] A cornerstone of the country's housing recovery was the 1933 Congressional Act creating the Home Owners' Loan Corporation. Established in the same flurry of legislation that birthed the National Recovery Administration and the Federal Deposit Insurance Corporation, HOLC featured two phases of activity. In the first phase, from its inception through 1936, the agency refinanced mortgages that had gone into default and worked to improve credit markets and the overall borrowing climate for those everyday Americans who had taken on real estate related debt. The agency institutionalized the long-term, fully amortized mortgage and allocated money based on apparently objective metrics like income and credit rating.[11] During HOLC's active lending program, the agency made nearly three billion dollars in loans, allowing borrowers to refinance mortgages, pay delinquent taxes, and make home repairs and improvements.[12] Eventually the agency acquired approximately one sixth of all urban home mortgages in America.[13] In the second phase, HOLC shifted from rescue to setting new structures for the home finance sector, establishing financial terms and outlining standards of risk and appraisal that materially changed the real estate market. In ways that reverberated out into the real estate industry at large, HOLC practices became national standards.[14] It helped private lenders by refinancing homes deemed a threat to their bottom line, only to foreclose on many of those homes and resell them to developers and landlords.

All of this was done with federal funds and capital borrowed in the private market with federally guaranteed bonds. Like corporations generally, the Home Owners' Loan Corporation used collective leadership and shared capital to manage risk.[15] And as a government body, it debt-financed its projects with taxpayer money, thereby keeping capital moving through the economy on a scale that few private entities could muster. The sum total of these actions allowed HOLC to structure an entirely new lending market.[16] As the historian David Freund contends, 'More than simply "embrac[ing] the discriminatory attitudes of the marketplace," the HOLC initiated the creation of a new kind of discriminatory marketplace, one that functioned very differently and that achieved and justified discrimination in a wholly new manner.'[17]

HOLC maps drew on emerging social science research that, in turn, imposed and reinforced a model of racial and ethnic succession and segregation in cities across the country. Thus, *Mapping Inequality* provides with each Security Map a diagram of concentric circles illustrating the preponderance of A through D areas in relation to the center of a given city (Figure 23.3).

Our interface borrows from and modifies the 1920s-era concentric zones theory of Ernest W. Burgess, which was itself drawn from earlier models. These diagrams offer a view of how redlining concentrated populations, and did so along a generally consistent pattern. Our concentric rendering enables observers to assess redlining's consequences on a metropolitan scale, while also inviting viewers to compare segregation patterns across cities. Lastly, by harkening to Burgess, our diagram binds the history of redlining to widely held ideas in the fields of sociology and urban economics in the early twentieth century. The apparent common sense of residential segregation did not emerge whole cloth in the 1930s, nor did it materialize out of thin air. Redlining in the New Deal era represented but the latest power play of a growing collection of real estate lobbies, and served as an extension of eugenicist thinking about racial segregation as a necessary feature of the healthy city.

The sector theory of Homer Hoyt eventually replaced Burgess' theory. Hoyt, trained at the University of Chicago, became the principal housing economist at the Federal Housing Administration and shaped decades of real estate policy. Thus, our appropriation of the Burgess model is not meant to resuscitate his discredited theory. Rather, we aim to show just how profoundly segregationist practices of redlining actually shaped American cities to resemble this dominant social theory. Segregation was not natural. On the contrary, redlining greatly impeded the natural flows of people and capital. Through federal action and local manipulation, life was made to imitate art.

HOLC's efforts rebuilt the notion of what constituted 'risk' in America by disseminating ideas and industry standards through city survey work and security maps.[18] Between 1935 and 1940, the agency recruited mortgage lenders, developers, and real estate appraisers in nearly 250 cities to create maps that color-coded credit worthiness and risk on neighborhood and metropolitan levels. Security maps used four colors tied to four letter grades. Green, blue, yellow, and red corresponded respectively to letters A through D. 'Safe' neighborhoods for home mortgages received 'A' and 'B' grades, with a respective green or blue color designation on the map. 'Risky' communities were graded 'C,' with a yellow coloring, and 'D' neighborhoods were colored red, the lowest possible grade. These were places where demographic or economic transitions had already occurred and where investors' fears of the riskiest investments already seemed realized. The maps, in the words of one real estate trade publication, 'graphically reflect[ed] the trend of desirability of neighborhoods from a residential viewpoint'.[19]

Logistically, security maps helped streamline what would have otherwise been an impossible project. Prior to HOLC, only the largest lenders or realty boards could get a sense of metropolitan real estate markets, and then usually only on a regional

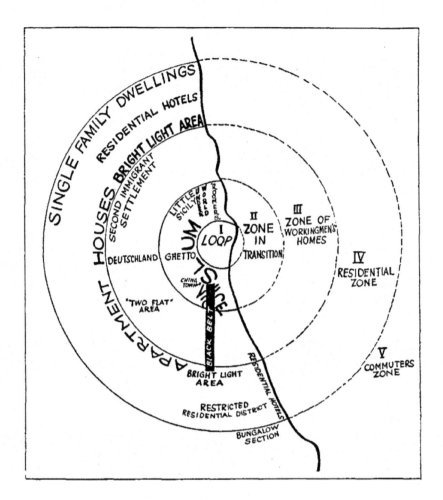

CHART II. Urban Areas

Figure 23.3 Diagram of urban organization from the book *The City*, by Robert Park and Ernest Burgess. The pair drew upon notions of urban development and their social science research on Chicago to institutionalize a model of city space that emphasized segregation along racial, social, and economic lines. Their 'Chicago School' of thought at the University of Chicago proved influential, to the point that the concentric circle framework can be seen in security maps of the Home Owners' Loan Corporation.

Source: Robert E. Park, Ernest W. Burgess, Roderick Duncan McKenzie, *The City*, University of Chicago Press, 1925.

scale at best. In a handful of cities, such as Baltimore and Chicago, dense information and publication networks could offer some synopses of market trends and the qualitative opinions of trendsetters. Demographic and transaction data, however, proved difficult to manage, and the analog nature of documenting the market meant that real estate interests could generate voluminous information but would often have

AREA DESCRIPTION

(For Instructions see Reverse Side)

1. NAME OF CITY ___Richmond, Virginia___ SECURITY GRADE ___C___ AREA NO. ___4___

2. DESCRIPTION OF TERRAIN.
   Rolling

3. FAVORABLE INFLUENCES.

4. DETRIMENTAL INFLUENCES. **Apartments along the park front. Home for Incurables east of the park down at Powaton Street. 4-family flats on Rosewood street. On Maplewood there are cheap frame bungalows near Meadow Street. Balance of this street going west fairly good single-family bricks.**

5. INHABITANTS:
   a. Type ___Working people___ ; b. Estimated annual family income $ ___1,500-2,500___

   c. Foreign-born ___ ; ___0___ %; d. Negro ___ ; ___0___ %;
   (Nationality)   (Yes or No)

   e. Infiltration of ___0___ ; f. Relief families ___Few, if any___ ;

   g. Population is increasing ___No___ ; decreasing ___No___ ; static. ___Yes___

6. BUILDINGS:
   a. Type or types **All types of single-family homes; brick pre- dominates** ; b. Type of construction ___ ;

   c. Average age ___10 to 30 years___ ; d. Repair ___Only fair___

7. HISTORY:

YEAR	SALE VALUES			RENTAL VALUES		
	RANGE	PREDOM-INATING	%	RANGE	PREDOM-INATING	%
1929 level	$2,500 to $8,00	$8,000	100%	$25 to $45		100%
1933 low		5,000		20 to 35		
1937 current		5,000		25 to 45		

Peak sale values occurred in ___ and were ___ % of the 1929 level.

Peak rental values occurred in ___ and were ___ % of the 1929 level.

8. OCCUPANCY: a. Land ___%; b. Dwelling units ___%; c. Home owners ___%

9. SALES DEMAND: a. ___ ; b. ___ ; c. Activity is ___

10. RENTAL DEMAND: a. ___ ; b. ___ ; c. Activity is ___

11. NEW CONSTRUCTION: a. Types ___ ; b. Amount last year ___

12. AVAILABILITY OF MORTGAGE FUNDS: a. Home purchase ___ ; b. Home building ___

13. TREND OF DESIRABILITY NEXT 10-15 YEARS ___

14. CLARIFYING REMARKS: **This area is yellow, largely because the school for white children is in the negro area, D-8, and because the negroes of D-8 pass back and forth for access to the William Byrd Park which lies to the west. For this reason losses on properties are being taken.**

    Southeasternmost cheap bungalows.

15. Information for this form was obtained from ___Mr. Arnold - Pollard and Bogby___

Date _____ 193__

(Over)

Figure 23.4 This area description for a C-rated neighborhood in Richmond, VA, illustrates the variety of data HOLC officials collected from local lenders and realtors about American cities. The clarifying remarks section poses the effect of African Americans walking through the neighborhood as detrimental. HOLC institutionalized racial animosity in the process of assessing and defining market forces and trends.

Source: RG 39, NARA II, College Park, MD.

difficulty retrieving it, much less analyzing it systematically. County recorders dutifully entered every transaction in their deed books, but no one could spend the time paging through book after book of ledgers and deed transfers to proffer anything approaching reasonable market analysis. Studies like real estate economist Homer Hoyt's *One Hundred Years of Land Values in Chicago* stood as unprecedented achievements requiring data tabulation over several years.[20] Such studies were the exception that proved the broader rule.

Realtors and lenders needed to be able to act on simple models and key principles in order to keep pace with the speed and scale of everyday buying, selling, renting, and moving. HOLC's survey and mapping activities thus promised an easily transferable template for real estate activity independent of certain local variables on the ground (including, for instance, the creditworthiness of wealthy African Americans). Maps, in particular, could be easily understood and quickly processed by the real estate interests. They could be recognized at a glance by realtors and lenders who specialized in assessing, pricing, and selling property. They also reflected institutionalized ideas that regional business leaders already held about their cities, making them great instruments of real estate speculation.

HOLC staffers bundled the maps with considerable supporting documentation, including tables about lending activity and 'Area Descriptions'. The descriptions catalogued an entire city's housing quality, its racial and ethnic make-up, and more – neighborhood by neighborhood. Area descriptions allowed appraisers to forecast an area's prospects for development and to explain why certain areas received certain grades (Figure 23.4). HOLC also paired its maps with detailed appendices and tables outlining the real estate infrastructure for a given city – insurance companies, real estate brokers, lenders, as well as employment, demographic, and population trends. HOLC created surveys of every major city in America, as battalions of appraisers and their numerous informants compiled everything an investor would need to know before entering a given city's real estate market.[21] It was a Herculean effort.

Redlining revisited

If historians and other observers know anything about HOLC, it is usually that lenders used the agency's security maps to advance racial segregation. The story about redlining is one about benign government neglect, about African Americans being prevented access to single-family homes, and about the generations of wealth inequality that followed when one group of Americans were excluded in blanket fashion from the right to benefit from compounded home equity and the wealth it generated.

When we take a closer look at the HOLC and the purpose of its security maps, however, we realize that the real story about redlining is likely *worse* than we know. 'D' areas were entire communities of buyers that the government would *intentionally allow to fail*. To be clear, living in 'D' communities generally brought considerable difficulties, regardless of the color of the occupants. These neighborhoods tended to have older housing stocks, outdated or non-existent infrastructure, and very few prospects for financing even basic repairs. Banks in San Francisco, for instance, offered residents in 'D' grade areas smaller sums and worse loan terms than residents of 'A' and 'B' areas with equivalent homes and equal appraisals.[22]

Security maps depicted notions of risk incorporating pre-existing racial politics and local interests on the part of realtors, developers, and landlords. In city after city, HOLC's appraisers were realtors, insurance men, and other entrepreneurs who were already invested in their respective local markets. And in those cities with large black populations, security maps served, in effect, as menus that enabled landlords and speculative buyers to choose the most appealing and most confined neighborhoods in which to satisfy profit-seeking appetites.

Residential Jim Crowism thrust black Americans into a private mortgage market with exorbitant interest rates, dangerous balloon payments, and/or 'rent-to-own' arrangements that meant the loss of one's home after missing a single payment.[23] Other consequences included being forced to rent from landlords who overcharged for rundown apartments, being subject to sexual assaults or other violence at the hands of rent collectors, and suffering under any number of environmental hazards. HOLC and FHA's redlining practices also weakened the network of lending institutions upon which black communities depended.[24] Black banks and insurance companies tended to have portfolios heavy in real estate or weighed down with other illiquid land assets gained through already-defaulted loans.[25] HOLC's discrimination against black neighborhoods thus created a domino effect. Falling property owners hastened the collapse of banks and insurance companies holding those mortgages. Those closures, in turn, ruined the fortunes of any bank depositor or policyholder invested in those institutions. As each domino fell, neighbor-by-neighbor, entire communities of businesspeople, consumers, and families experienced heavy personal losses.

Segregation by way of security maps had adverse effects on white property owners as well. In 'A', B', and 'C' communities, the relative availability of HOLC funds made it easier for lenders to press distressed white homebuyers. Why negotiate down the principal on a defaulted loan if the government was paying the bank or lender full price?[26] In fact, lenders often pressured white families to seek out federal assistance knowing that their borrowers – based solely on the neighborhoods in which they lived – would be more eligible for government support. Under the mapping state, working white Americans suffered predations of an altogether different kind. According to Charles Abrams, 'companies with hundreds of millions in resources and needing no federal help whatever pressed [owners] to compel them to apply for HOLC's aid'.[27] Some white neighborhoods could still be denied access to government help, as well, as illustrated by HOLC assessments of one Florida community in 1938. As described in HOLC records by Greater Miami's real estate establishment, the residents of Hialeah 'belong to the low grade white population'.[28] Their community therefore suffered a 'D' grade.

Getting behind the logic of mapping requires understanding the broader culture of real estate assessment and risk assessment. The documentation accompanying security maps offers a great place to start. Through *Mapping Inequality*, we pair area descriptions with the colored maps of every available American city as a way to introduce viewers to the world of informal transactions and alliances that lay beneath and beyond the colors and grades. However, there are countless other sources that allow one to access the cultural assumptions that white economists, government officials, and real estate appraisers brought to the mapping process. Societies of real estate appraisers, government correspondence, developer records, and supplemental HOLC reports offer compelling windows into the clear and at times conflicted ideas about race, place, and real estate markets. 'To avoid . . . setting up . . . two grades of residential trends (one for whites and one for negroes)', explained one HOLC staffer in 1938, 'it was decided to approach the city-wide picture [of Greater Miami] from the trend of the desirability of white residential property.'[29] Drawing exactly converse conclusions in 1940, a white appraiser from Chicago condemned one of his colleagues for 'failing to keep his own personal preferences in the background', when assessing the value of a black South Side neighborhood.[30] In that instance, believing in 'two grades of residential trends' was the only option. This example alone suggests that a Miami security map and one from Chicago could exhibit drastically different bureaucratic approaches, even if they evidenced the same real estate trends.

Mapping Inequality treats the map itself as a text *among* texts. In so doing it considers the professional habits and rich pre-history of federal redlining. Developers, life insurance, and mortgage companies attempted to standardize practices of discrimination among themselves decades before the Home Owners Loan Corporation was even established. Members of groups like the National Association of Real Estate Boards and Metropolitan Life Insurance Company of New York swapped notes at conventions on how best to implement deed restrictions and 'prospect cards' that racially and class-profiled potential sales leads. At these same conventions, America's emergent class of housing experts took in blackface minstrel shows together and shared other forms of 'darky' humor.[31]

The early intellectual advocates of what became New Deal mapping remained steeped in the assumptions and logic of eugenics as well. Richard Ely, one of the most important advocates of 'land economics', helped birth the methods HOLC officials used to justify their assessments of real estate risk and home value. Apart from serving as faculty member at several elite institutions and helping establish several professional organizations over the course of his career, including the American Economics Association and the Institute for Research in Land Economics and Public Utilities, Ely belonged to a class of professionals who looked to control environmental factors as part of a more general effort to further white proliferation and advancement.[32]

White Progressives like Ely used their civic work to 'improve' the white race. In Ely's case, he turned the pseudoscience of eugenics into the much more acceptable social science of land economics. The difficulty of handling the tremendous amounts of information in large urban residential real estate markets prompted the federal government to search for a solution to the problem of value and uncertainty. The HOLC Department of Research and Statistics numbered more than 60 employees and included economists such as FHA staff Ernest Fisher and Frederick Babcock within its organizational penumbra. They corresponded with local informants, tabulated neighborhood and regional data, and made final decisions on the boundaries of neighborhoods across the country. Thus, instances of individual white racism were focused into an institutional process, then refracted through the lenses of Burgess' and Ely's social, economic, and scientific theories into a diffuse light of the marketplace that illuminated new forms of economic value across the country. Racism was a hatred the nation could bank on, giving consistency and legibility to a key economic sector.

The development of the New Deal state fused together professional practice and personal bias, in other words. After Congress established HOLC, agency heads encouraged federal employees to subscribe to the professional journals and supplemental publications of the country's whitest and most well organized groups of real estate speculators. Real estate associations enjoyed an 'influence [that] went far beyond direct collaboration; [their] literature formed the cornerstone of HOLC institutional culture'.[33] By the same turn, professional appraiser organizations made sure all their members received copies of the government's residential risk preferences.[34] This proved important because the federal government was the appraisal industry's largest and wealthiest client. HOLC paid for appraisals on hundreds of thousands of homes, providing essential support for a fledgling industry seeking legitimacy. As the central buyer of appraisal services in the Depression, HOLC set the standards for appraising that, along with the FHA, shaped practice for the rest of the century. Finally, HOLC subsidized professional development sessions at private real estate conventions. These conventions proved key, for they offered meeting places where members of the National Association of Real Estate Board and other trade organizations further developed the patronage networks that later allowed them to assume positions within the federal housing bureaucracy.[35] Thus, HOLC established a professional cycle that first rescued realtors and the real estate market from economic crisis, granted real estate appraisers professional recognition and an economic lifeline, allowed well-placed local realtors to exercise heavy influence over an entire region's real estate market, and then provided venues and training for the dissemination and growth of these practices, institutionalizing the new mortgage regime for decades (Figure 23.5).

Big data deepens what other research has revealed about the relationship between race and real estate more broadly. As Arnold Hirsch and others have detailed, influential white real estate interests usually forced minorities and poor immigrants into communities that suffered from the oldest housing stock.[36] Just as often, the presence of non-whites and black people, in particular, went a long way to ensuring that new housing would not be built in a given neighborhood. Race and the age of real estate, in other words, often lined up. Regarding the circulation of the security maps themselves, Louis Woods argues that the maps did not have to travel widely for lenders and realtors to learn their contents by way of professional networks and trade organizations.[37] Not infrequently 'best practices' for discrimination traveled in anticipation of new markets and preceded the creation of new maps and area descriptions. Indeed, in most metropolitan areas, the people who actually made HOLC maps were developers, realtors, and planners who had local knowledge, a vested interest in steering populations into emerging home and rental markets, and an awareness of an increasingly national practice of discrimination through publications such as *Federal Home Loan Bank Review* (one of many trade publications).[38] In sum, exploring area descriptions and looking at the country as a whole illustrates that HOLC's security maps were intensifications of pre-existing discriminatory thinking and practice as much as an inspiration for fresh acts of racial discrimination.

Mapping Inequality interrogates this data with GIS tools that only now, 80 years after the creation of the agency, can do justice to this body of big data. Thirty-five years after the maps' rediscovery by historians, scholars can visually represent the

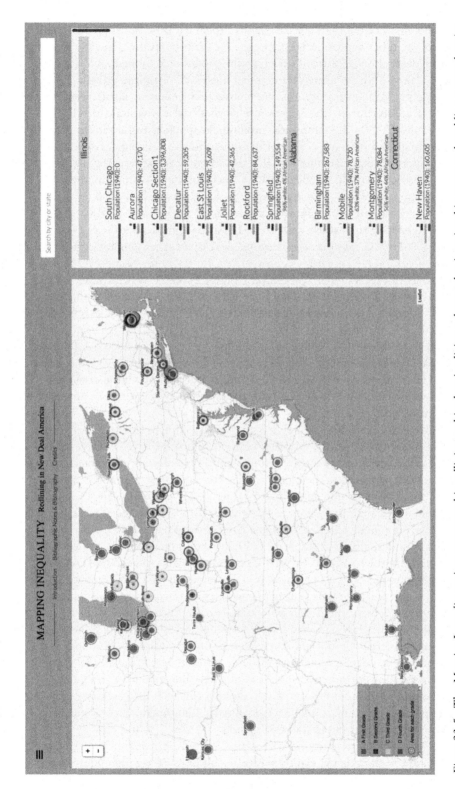

Figure 23.5 The *Mapping Inequality* project excavates this redlining archive by visualizing a dataset that is national in scope and enabling comprehensive and comparative analysis.

Source: Mapping Inequality, Digital Scholarship Lab, University of Richmond.

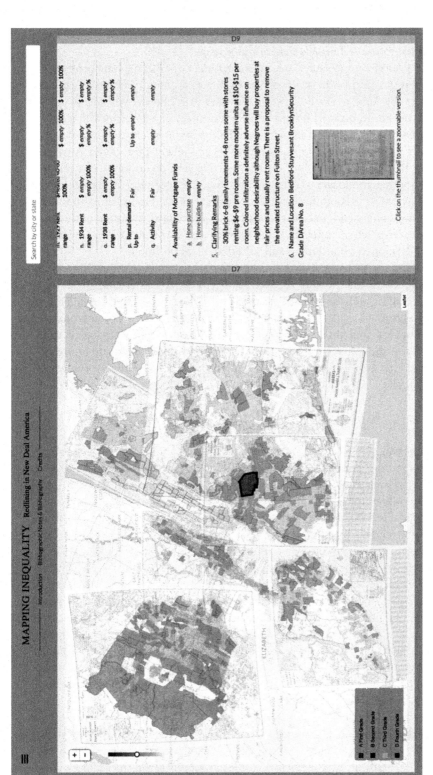

Figure 23.6 Users have access to all security maps at launch and soon will be able to access all the area descriptions digitally. These resources recreate the data-driven process that HOLC agents and local lenders used to assess neighborhoods and direct financial capital at mid-century, and will allow present-day researchers to investigate redlining at the national, regional, or neighborhood level, as with this area description of the Bedford-Stuyvesant area of Brooklyn, New York City.

Source: Mapping Inequality, Digital Scholarship Lab, University of Richmond.

maps, aggregate the data, and synthesize the variety of HOLC sources to make them comprehensible to researchers at a generalizable scale.

HOLC city surveys represented one of the nation's original big data projects, far surpassing even the neighborhood-level data of the US Census.[39] Historians can now take a big data approach to the New Deal and American housing without abandoning the analytic innovations in cultural and political history developed during the 1980s and 1990s. Mapping software now enables historians to expand their range of inquiry to ask programmatic data questions at several levels. First, about American cities during the Great Depression – querying the area descriptions can provide insight into housing and local real estate that it took the decennial census decades to match in many cities. Second, how real estate professionals responded to and translated raw demographic trends into market analysis and economic valuation in this era – the area grades are based on input from and illustrate the consensus of leading lenders, realtors, and developers about urban and suburban neighborhoods.

Perhaps most importantly, GIS continues the spatial turn in urban history by enabling today's scholars, by way of data management, to understand more thoroughly the creation and use of HOLC maps in the 1930s (Figure 23.6). Federal bureaucrats envisioned paper maps as tools, spatial indices to represent builders' choices and buyers' preferences geographically. Through digital layering of maps, area descriptions, and other documentation, we can both reconstruct and reinterpret the shorthand that investors and regulators developed in their highly subjective, paper-based system.

Enter social history

Apart from showing the racial roots and legacies of federal redlining, *Mapping Inequality* provides a starting point for asking fresh questions. Not the least of these being how exactly did appraisers and mapmakers know where one community or grade began and the other ended.

The first variable to consider is the racially restrictive covenant. Documents in the HOLC archive suggest that the agency incorporated racially restrictive covenants into their neighborhood grading system. Restrictive covenants were legal agreements through which property owners agreed to establish shared exclusions pertaining to their properties and what owners could do with them. Frequently mentioned in HOLC area descriptions, covenants served as the spatial template of security maps. They detailed neighborhood boundaries. They promised to hold property values. And they could still be enforced after racial zoning was deemed unconstitutional in 1917. HOLC staffers had their work cut out for them, however, if they hoped to make effective use of the covenants. As a federal agency representing the whole American population, HOLC could not explicitly use deed restrictions to deny black people access to property.[40] The staff had to find other ways.

Through their maps, HOLC could use restrictive covenants as a proxy for 'the market'. In the absence of large-scale market research, the existence of restrictive covenants on a given community served as facile evidence of what buyers and owners wanted. By the 1930s, in fact, restrictive covenants served as the chief lubricant in a policy feedback loop between white buyers and their government. Realtors and homeowner associations initiated covenants locally. HOLC assessors, in turn, used the prevalence of the covenants to set a neighborhood's grade. Back at street level, local realtors and lenders in search of government subsidies remained aware of mandates for community 'stability' at the federal level, thus they demanded and created new covenants to make their neighborhoods eligible for further federal financing. And so the cycle went.

HOLC and FHA strongly encouraged restrictive covenants in order to maintain racial stasis. The *Underwriting Manual*, the federal government's published standards for home finance, phrased it thus: 'Where . . . deed restrictions relate to types of structures, use to which improvements may be put, and racial occupancy, a favorable condition is apt to exist.'[41] Further, the manual outlined, 'Where adjacent lots or blocks possess altogether different restrictions, especially for type and use of structures and racial occupancy, the effect of such restrictions is minimized and adequate protection cannot be considered to be present.'[42] Areas without 'adequate protection' could not expect federal aid, and, through the professional connections between the federal government and the industry, one could safely expect that realtors, developers and planner knew it.[43] One Detroit-area HOLC official explained, 'the infiltration of inharmonious racial or nationalistic groups speed the once desirable residential neighborhood toward the end of its life span'.[44]

The racial intent of federal mapping was most clear at the local level. Some neighborhoods, immediately upon the establishment of the federal safety net in housing, responded by creating clear racial restrictions where, before, there had been none. Less than a year after the formation of HOLC, for instance, lenders, developers, and homeowners in the Washington Heights section of southwest Chicago moved to establish a large, multi-neighborhood covenant explicitly denying ownership to African Americans (Figure 23.7). 'No part of said premises shall in any manner be used or occupied directly or indirectly by any negro or negroes,' the restriction read. 'No part of said premises shall be sold given conveyed or leased to any negro or negroes,' it went on. However, it included the typical servant's exception, mandating that 'no permission or license to use or occupy any part thereof shall be given to any negro except house servants or janitors or chauffeurs employed thereon'.[45]

Another important variable in the advancing of segregationist federal housing policy had to do with the general absence of government oversight. There was no civil rights regulatory state at this time – no US Commission of Civil Rights (established in 1948), and the Racial Relations Service, developed in 1938, was supposed only to address 'minority interests' insofar as they did not conflicts with the interests of the housing agencies and the federal government itself.[46] The mapping state regulated itself on matters of racial justice. And its default position, when not relying upon free market rhetoric, was to deny that state sponsored discrimination even existed. In regard to one New York case about racial steering, 'The Regional Office [of the Federal Home Loan Bank Board] reports that, after careful investigation, it has found no evidence of racial discrimination.' As the representative of the FHLBB chairman responded to inquiries from Eleanor Roosevelt on the matter, 'Reassurances on this point are hardly necessary, but it might be stated that discrimination, whether racial or otherwise, is of course, directly contrary to the [Home Owners'

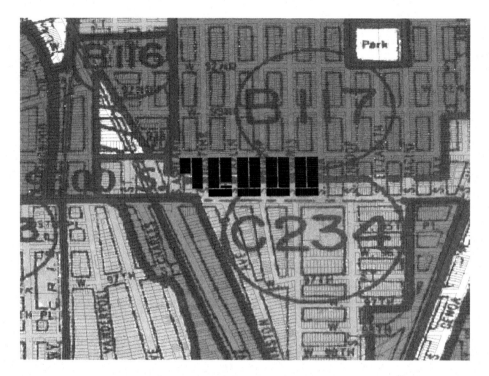

Figure 23.7 In the Washington Heights neighborhood in Southwest Chicago, white professional-class residents established a restrictive covenant to exclude African Americans at the edge of their neighborhood north of 95th Street. This came shortly after the creation of the Home Owners' Loan Corporation and Federal Housing Administration, which emphasized the utility of restrictive covenants to prevent racial and environmental change. The signatories, who lived in the parcels colored black, numbered in the dozens and sought to insulate the neighborhood from African Americans who might move from neighborhoods to the south to buy or rent properties in this more upscale area. This parcel map has been overlayed upon the Chicago security map, where B is blue and C is yellow, to illustrate how HOLC subsequently institutionalized this segregation.

Source: Cook County Recorder of Deeds, LaDale Winling, Virginia Tech.

Loan] Corporation's policies and regulations.' [47] HOLC only reflected the whims of the market, staffers argued. That market was measured in white desires for racial restrictions.

HOLC agents also used the racial designation of 'risk' and insecurity, by way of their maps, to allocate or deny financing. Yet HOLC agents also manipulated prices of properties the agency owned. One fair housing case in Washington, DC, in 1943 revealed that HOLC had sold property to white buyers for less than black buyers had offered, just so the agency would not be party to racial 'infiltration'. [48] HOLC was willing to sell a property to a white man in the disputed zone in NW DC for $2,000 less than the price offered a black clergyman, a bishop. It was long understood that black families paid a premium to move into all-white communities, sometimes 20 to

25 percent more.[49] HOLC's congressional mandate bound it to find the best possible prices for its properties in order to keep the corporation solvent. Under a racial notion of risk, however, $2,000 lost on one property could, in theory, save thousands of dollars more in neighborhood property values lost if whites responded by selling in a panic.

Thus, HOLC preserved a 'whites only' market, and sometimes even created one where one did not already exist. A case in St Albans, New York, included HOLC using covenants as a placeholder for 'the market'. White HOLC supervisors barred their black staffers from showing houses in the white community, even when whites declined to sign restrictive covenants.[50] HOLC had black brokers, in part, to help African Americans access the program, but only on a strictly segregated basis, and only to fulfill established notions of what the public wanted.[51]

Conclusion: mapping the state

Considering maps not merely as objective reflections of social or political conflicts – but as *products* and *instruments* of such conflicts – requires revisiting HOLC redlining maps more holistically, as *images*, as *data*, and as *texts* that stand in conversation with other texts both within and outside of government agencies. Historians will continue to debate the degree to which New Deal-era mortgage programs actually contributed to the ongoing racial wealth gap, the continued transformation of American cities, and the deeper structural ties between capitalism, racism, and the state. Thus, as we go forward with *Mapping Inequality* and other new imaging tools, historians must remain attentive to traditional social and political history methodology. Few can deny that understanding *how* the state mapped will remain at least as important as knowing *what* it mapped and how those maps looked.

People with access to state power advanced their respective agendas through data collection and mapping. Security maps thus represented an idealized means among the powerful for outlining the future of the city. Still it was a future that had to reckon with and recruit the economic and political power of lenders, builders, realtors, and activists. For this reason and more, security maps should not be taken simply as the raw information for historians to glean data and statistics, or on which to base their own maps. The maps themselves are the product of historical processes that we must interrogate. The representation of space and risk on a map could seem objective, an economic fact of the marketplace, but space served as a site of profound political conflict and action.

As it concerns the mid-twentieth century, in particular, state real estate maps reflect two core New Deal priorities – indeed, state priorities generally: the power to reform social problems and to promote future development.[52] The maps also reflect a truism about the Roosevelt administration: that navigating white urban machines, old Progressive reformers, and winning black Democratic support required a government that was both nimble on matters of racial liberalism *and* considered dependable by its core constituents, white voters. In the housing arena, that meant cultivating happy white homeowners and hopeful black liberals, all while ensuring that cities continued to grow and pull the country further from depression. The mapping state's ability to take stock of real estate power (through appraisal networks), to recruit informants and partners (through political appointment and finance), and to build functional models of urban growth (albeit on the principles of eugenics and apartheid) all serve to illustrate why something as simple as a colored map was no simple matter at all.

Through digitizing, geo-referencing, and rendering the agency's records in an interactive format, *Mapping Inequality* updates the study of the federal government, housing, and inequality for a twenty-first-century audience. It brings audiences rich real estate data and hundreds of maps, while also offering valuable evidence about the private sector's role in shaping the culture of both the American citizenry and the federal bureaucracy.

Notes

1 See e.g. Douglas S. Massey and Nancy A. Denton, *American Apartheid: Segregation and the Making of the Underclass*, Cambridge, MA: Harvard University Press, 1993, 50–5; Dalton Conley, *Being Black, Living in the Red: Race, Wealth, and Social Policy in America*, Berkeley and Los Angeles, CA: University of California Press, 1999, 37; Thomas M. Shapiro, *The Hidden Cost of Being African American: How Wealth Perpetuates Inequality*, Oxford: Oxford University Press, 2004, esp. ch. 5, the 'Home Ownership Crossroad'.

2 'Mapping Inequality: Redlining in New Deal America', www.mappinginequality.us; 'American Panorama', http://dsl.richmond.edu/panorama./

3 Kenneth T. Jackson, 'Race Ethnicity, and Real Estate Appraisal: The Home Owners Loan Corporation and the Federal Housing Administration', *Journal of Urban History* 6(4), 1980, 419–52; Kenneth T. Jackson, *Crabgrass Frontier: The Suburbanization of the United States*, Oxford: Oxford University Press, 1985, esp. ch. 11.

4 Andrew Weise, *Places of their Own: African American Suburbanization in the Twentieth Century*, Chicago, IL: University of Chicago Press, 2004, Matthew Lassiter, *The Silent Majority: Suburban Politics in the Sunbelt South*, Princeton, NJ: Princeton University Press, 2006. Robert Self, *American Babylon: Race and the Struggle for Postwar Oakland*, Princeton, NJ: Princeton University Press, 2003.

5 Allison Shertzer and Randall P. Walsh, *Racial Sorting and the Emergence of Segregation in American Cities*, National Bureau of Economic Research, NBER Working Paper No. 22077, March 2016; see also, Emily Badger, 'White Flight Began a Lot Earlier than We Think', *Washington Post*, March 17, 2016, www.washingtonpost.com/news/wonk/wp/2016/03/17/white-flight-began-a-lot-earlier-than-we-think/?tid=a_inl; David M. P. Freund, 'We Can't Forget How Racist Institutions Shaped Homeownership in America', *Washington Post*, April 28, 2016, www.washingtonpost.com/news/wonk/wp/2016/04/28/we-cant-forget-how-racist-institutions-shaped-homeownership-in-america.

6 Amy E. Hillier, 'Redlining and the Home Owners' Loan Corporation', *Journal of Urban History* 29(4), 2003), 394–420; see also Amy E. Hillier, 'Residential Security Maps and Neighborhood Appraisals. The Homeowners' Loan Corporation and the Case of Philadelphia', *Social Science History* 29(2), 2005, 207–33.

7 Greer, 'Home Owners' Loan Corporation and the Development of the Residential Security Maps', *Journal of Urban History* 39, 2013, 284.

8 Greer, 'The Home Owners' Loan Corporation', 277.

9 Jackson, *Crabgrass Frontier*, 93.

10 Unemployment among construction workers was 73.9 percent. Robert A. Margo, 'The Microeconomics of Depression Unemployment', *Journal of Economic History* 51(2), 1991, 333–41. Construction funds Table A, Peter Stone, *Construction Expenditures and*

Employment, Washington, DC: Works Progress Administration, 1937, 14. $150.5 billion and 54 billion in 2013 dollars, respectively.

11 Milton P. Semer, Julian H. Zimmerman, Ashley Foard, and John M. Frantz, 'Evolution of Federal Legislative Policy in Housing: Housing Credits', in J. Paul Mitchell (ed), *Federal Housing Policy and Programs: Past and Present*, New Brunswick, NJ: Center for Urban Policy Research, 1985, 73.

12 Semer et al. 'Evolution', 73.

13 Charles Abrams, *The Future of Housing*, New York and London: Harper & Brothers, 1946, 246.

14 Price V. Fishback, Alfonso Flores-Lagunes, William C. Horrace, Shawn Kantor and Jaret Treber, 'The Influence of the Home Owners' Loan Corporation on Housing Markets During the 1930s', *Review of Financial Studies* 24(6), 2011, 1783.

15 On the safety generated by the formation of corporations in the nineteenth century, see Jonathan Levy, *Freaks of Fortune: The Emerging World of Capitalism and Risk in America*, Cambridge, MA: Harvard University Press, 2012, 4.

16 David M. P. Freund, 'Marketing the Free Market: State Intervention and the Politics of Prosperity in Metropolitan America', in Kevin M. Kruse and Thomas J. Sugrue (eds.) *The New Suburban History*, Chicago, IL: University of Chicago Press, 2006, 15.

17 David M. P. Freund, *Colored Property: State Policy and White Racial Politics in Suburban America*, Chicago, IL: University of Chicago Press, 2007, 115.

18 Semer et al, 'Evolution', 73.

19 Federal Home Loan Bank Board, 'Appraisal Methods and Policies', *Federal Home Loan Bank Board Review* 4 (January), 110; cited in Hillier, 'Residential Security Maps and Neighborhood Appraisals', 207.

20 Homer Hoyt, *One Hundred Years of Land Values in Chicago*, Chicago, IL: University of Chicago Press, 1933.

21 'Appendix: Report of Survey: Miami, Florida: For the Division of Research and Statistics', 1–26, RG 195, Records of the Federal Home Loan Bank Board, Home Owners Loan Corporation, Records Relating to the City Survey File, 1935–40, entry 39, 'Florida Miami' folder, box 81, National Archives and Records Administration II, College Park, MD (hereafter NARA II).

22 'INTERVIEW WITH MR. WILLIAM A. MARCUS,' San Francisco, California. T-RACES, Testbed for the Redlining Archives of California's Exclusionary Spaces. (http://salt.umd.edu/T-RACES/demo/demo.html) app0028. (Last accessed August 2015.)

23 St. Clair Drake and Horace Cayton, *Black Metropolis*, Chicago, IL: University of Chicago, 1945; Robert Clifton Weaver, *The Negro Ghetto*, New York: Russell & Russell, 1948; Beryl Satter, *Family Properties: How the Struggle Over Race and Real Estate Transformed Chicago and Urban America*, New York: Picador, 2010.

24 Charles Abrams, *The Future of Housing*, New York and London: Harper & Brothers, 1946, 240.

25 Abram Harris, *The Negro as Capitalist*, 167–68.

26 Abrams, *Future of Housing*, 246.

27 Abrams, *Future of Housing*, 246.

28 'Area Description – Hialeah Race Track Area', RG 195, Records of the Federal Home Loan Bank Board, Home Owners Loan Corporation, Records Relating to the City Survey File, 1935–40, entry 39, 'Florida Miami' folder, box 81, NARA II.

29 Alec C. Morgan, 'Report of Survey: Miami, Florida', 25. RG 195.39, 'Florida Miami' folder, box 81, NARA II.

30 Ayers J. du Bois, 'Pitfalls in Residential Appraising', *Review of the Society of Residential Real Estate Appraisers*, March 1940.

31 Paige Glotzer, 'Exclusion in Arcadia: How Suburban Developers Circulated Ideas about Discrimination, 1890–1950', *Journal of Urban History* 41(3), 2015, 479–94.

32 Madison Grant, for instance, served as chairman of the Committee on the New York State Plan, Alexandra Stern, *Eugenic Nation: Faults and Frontier of Better Breeding in Modern America*, Berkeley, CA: University of California Press, 2005.

33 Glotzer, 'Exclusion in Arcadia', 489.

34 'Members of Society to Receive F.H.A. Manual', *Residential Appraisers' Review*, June 1935, 15.

35 Several of Ely's protégés moved between the private, non-profit, and public sector, including Ernest Fisher, who eventually served as the director of research for the FHA, and Frederick Babcock, author of the FHA *Underwriting Manual* and another influential text, *The Valuation of Real Estate*; Glotzer, 'Exclusion in Arcadia', 479–94.

36 Arnold R. Hirsch, *The Making of the Second Ghetto: Race and Housing in Chicago, 1940–1960*, Chicago, IL: University of Chicago Press, 1998 [1983], 18–22.

37 Woods, 'The Federal Home Loan Bank Board, Redlining, and the National Proliferation of Racial Lending Discrimination, 1921–1950', *Journal of Urban History* 38, 2012, 1038–9.

38 N. D. B. Connolly, *A World More Concrete: Real Estate and the Remaking of Jim Crow Florida*, Chicago, IL: University of Chicago Press, 2014, 96–8.

39 HOLC's 200+ maps, each containing dozens of neighborhood-based area descriptions, surpassed the United States Census Bureau in comprehensive data aggregation. The census created neighborhood census tracts for only 18 cities in the 1930 census and 60 in 1940; 'Census History: Tracts and Block Numbering Areas', www.census.gov/history/www/programs/geography/tracts_and_block_numbering_areas.html.

40 'D.C. Court Upholds Housing Restriction; Appeal Planned', *Baltimore Afro-American*, November 22, 1941, 1.

41 Copy of FHA Underwriting Manual, Part II – Risk Rating Instructions, Section 2, Rating of Location (1938), Papers of the NAACP, file on the Federal Housing Administration, Part 5, Campaign Against Residential Segregation, Group II, Series L, Proquest History Vault (hereafter FHA file, NAACP History Vault).

42 Ibid.

43 Correspondence from John W. Childress, Assistant to the Chairman of the HOLC, to Sen. Robert Wagner, November 30, 1940, St. Albans New York, Home Owners' Loan Corporation file, FHA file, NAACP History Vault.

44 Arthur May, *The Valuation of Residential Real Estate*, New York: Prentice Hall, 1942, 107.

45 Book 31471 Page 1, Document 11469420 Cook County Recorder of Deeds, Chicago, IL.

46 Arnold R. Hirsch, 'Searching for a "Sound Negro Policy": A Racial Agenda for the Housing Acts of 1949 and 1954', *Housing Policy Debate* 11(2), 2000, 396.

47 Correspondence from John M. Hager, Executive Assistant to the Chairman of the Federal Home Loan Bank Board, John H. Fahey, to Malvina C. Thompson, Secretary to First Lady Eleanor Roosevelt, February 27 1941, St Albans New York, Home Owners' Loan Corporation file, FHA file, NAACP History Vault.

48 'Court Decision Shows HOLC Aided Prejudice', *The Chicago Defender*, March 13, 1943, 9.

49 'Detroiters Expose HOLC Discrimination', *Atlanta Daily World*, December 15, 1939, 1.

50 Goldstein and Goldstein, *Dury v. Neely* 'Defendants Brief', 2 (1941) St Albans New York, Home Owners' Loan Corporation file, FHA file, NAACP History Vault.

51 Freund, 'Marketing the Free Market', 15.

52 Colin Gordon, *New Deals: Business, Labor, and Politics in America, 1920–1935*, New York: Cambridge University Press, 1994.

Bibliography

Charles Abrams, *The Future of Housing*, New York: Harper & Brothers, 1946.

Dalton Conley, *Being Black, Living in the Red: Race, Wealth, and Social Policy in America*, Berkeley, CA: University of California Press, 1999.

N. D. B. Connolly, *A World More Concrete: Real Estate and the Remaking of Jim Crow Florida*, Chicago, IL: University of Chicago Press, 2014.

St. Clair Drake and Horace Cayton, *Black Metropolis*, Chicago, IL: University of Chicago, 1945.

Ayers J. du Bois, 'Pitfalls in Residential Appraising', *Review of the Society of Residential Real Estate Appraisers*, March 1940.

Price V. Fishback, Alfonso Flores-Lagunes, William C. Horrace, Shawn Kantor, and Jaret Treber, 'The Influence of the Home Owners' Loan Corporation on Housing Markets during the 1930s', *The Review of Financial Studies* 24(6), 2011, 1782–1813.

David M. P. Freund, 'Marketing the Free Market: State Intervention and the Politics of Prosperity in Metropolitan America', in Kevin M. Kruse and Thomas J. Sugrue (eds), *The New Suburban History*, Chicago, IL: University of Chicago Press, 2006.

David M. P. Freund, *Colored Property: State Policy and White Racial Politics in Suburban America*, Chicago, IL: University of Chicago Press, 2007.

Paige Glotzer, 'Exclusion in Arcadia: How Suburban Developers Circulated Ideas about Discrimination, 1890–1950', *Journal of Urban History* 41(3), 2015, 479–94.

Colin Gordon, *New Deals: Business, Labor, and Politics in America, 1920–1935*, New York: Cambridge University Press, 1994.

James Greer, 'Home Owners' Loan Corporation and the Development of the Residential Security Maps', *Journal of Urban History* 39(2), 2013, 275–96.

Amy E. Hillier, 'Redlining and the Home Owners' Loan Corporation', *Journal of Urban History* 29(4), 2003, 394–420.

Amy E. Hillier, 'Residential Security Maps and Neighborhood Appraisals: The Homeowners' Loan Corporation and the Case of Philadelphia', *Social Science History* 29(2), 2005, 207–33.

Arnold R. Hirsch, *The Making of the Second Ghetto: Race and Housing in Chicago, 1940–1960*, Chicago, IL: University of Chicago Press, 1998 [1983].

Arnold R. Hirsch, 'Searching for a 'Sound Negro Policy': A Racial Agenda for the Housing Acts of 1949 and 1954', *Housing Policy Debate* 11(2), 2000, 393–441.

Homer Hoyt, *One Hundred Years of Land Values in Chicago*, Chicago, IL: University of Chicago Press, 1933.

Kenneth T. Jackson, 'Race Ethnicity, and Real Estate Appraisal: The Home Owners Loan Corporation and the Federal Housing Administration', *Journal of Urban History* 6(4), 1980, 419–52.

Kenneth T. Jackson, *Crabgrass Frontier: The Suburbanization of the United States*, Oxford: Oxford University Press, 1985.

Matthew Lassiter, *The Silent Majority: Suburban Politics in the Sunbelt South*, Princeton, NJ: Princeton University Press, 2006.

Jonathan Levy, *Freaks of Fortune: The Emerging World of Capitalism and Risk in America*, Cambridge, MA: Harvard University Press, 2012.

Robert A. Margo, 'The Microeconomics of Depression Unemployment', *Journal of Economic History* 51(2), 1991: 333–41.

Douglas S. Massey and Nancy A. Denton, *American Apartheid: Segregation and the Making of the Underclass*, Cambridge, MA: Harvard University Press, 1993.

Arthur May, *The Valuation of Residential Real Estate*, New York: Prentice Hall, 1942.

Beryl Satter, *Family Properties: How the Struggle Over Race and Real Estate Transformed Chicago and Urban America*, New York: Picador, 2010.

Robert Self, *American Babylon: Race and the Struggle for Postwar Oakland*, Princeton, NJ: Princeton University Press, 2003.

Milton P. Semer, Julian H. Zimmerman, Ashley Foard, and John M. Frantz, 'Evolution of Federal Legislative Policy in Housing: Housing Credits', in J. Paul Mitchell (ed), *Federal Housing Policy and Programs: Past and Present*, New Brunswick, NJ: Center for Urban Policy Research, 1985.

Thomas M. Shapiro, *The Hidden Cost of Being African American: How Wealth Perpetuates Inequality*, Oxford: Oxford University Press, 2004.

Allison Shertzer and Randall P. Walsh, *Racial Sorting and the Emergence of Segregation in American Cities*, National Bureau of Economic Research, NBER Working Paper No. 22077, March 2016.

Robert Clifton Weaver, *The Negro Ghetto*, New York: Russell & Russell, 1948.

Andrew Weise, *Places of their Own: African American Suburbanization in the Twentieth Century*, Chicago, IL: University of Chicago Press, 2004.

Louis Lee Woods II, 'The Federal Home Loan Bank Board, Redlining, and the National Proliferation of Racial Lending Discrimination, 1921–1950', *Journal of Urban History* 38(6), 2012, 1036–59.

Web Sources

Emily Badger, 'White Flight Began a Lot Earlier than We Think', *Washington Post*, March 17, 2016, www.washingtonpost.com/news/wonk/wp/2016/03/17/white-flight-began-a-lot-earlier-than-we-think/?tid=a_inl.

David M. P. Freund, 'We Can't Forget How Racist Institutions Shaped Homeownership in America', *Washington Post*, April 28, 2016, www.washingtonpost.com/news/wonk/wp/2016/04/28/we-cant-forget-how-racist-institutions-shaped-homeownership-in-america/.

US Census Bureau, 'Census History: Tracts and Block Numbering Areas', www.census.gov/history/www/programs/geography/tracts_and_block_numbering_areas.html.

PART VI

Spatial humanities

INTRODUCTION TO PART VI

Ian Gregory, Don DeBats, and Don Lafreniere

The previous parts have shown the use of historical GIS in a range of subjects where the use of GIS has reached maturity leading to scholarship that has delivered new understandings. This has occurred in a range of subjects: population and demographic history, economic history, urban history, rural and environmental history, and political history. These fields are all well-suited to GIS because they all make extensive use of quantitative or cartographic sources that can be effectively modelled and analysed within a GIS environment. This has led to a situation where GIS has become an established approach in fields where quantitative sources can be used, but has left the field as largely irrelevant to much of mainstream history which does not use these types of source or approach There has been much resulting critiquing of the limitations of historical GIS and currently conceived.[1]

A recent development has been the call for the field to evolve from historical GIS to spatial history and on to spatial humanities.[2] For this to happen, the field needs to develop in three complementary ways: first, it needs to be able to draw on a much wider range of sources, particularly textual sources which, after all, are the bread and butter of most historical research. Second, the field must also draw on a wider range of techniques than those available within the traditional GIS toolkit. These new approaches need to range from social network analysis to mobile apps and many others that make use of geographical data or concepts but apply them in different ways than traditionally used by GIS. Finally, research must be able to look at the richness of individual lives and agency rather than as aggregate quantitative data. If GIS is able to do some or all of these then not only will it be able to penetrate further into mainstream history, it will also be able to spread across the humanities into other disciplines within the humanities. It may also cross the divide between history and archaeology, two subjects that have made extensive use of GIS but in such different ways that the two fields rarely overlap.[3] Some progress has already been made in these areas, in particular, there has been methodological work exploring how GIS can be used with textual sources,[4] and studies in a range of subjects including history,[5] literary studies[6] and classics.[7]

The chapters in this part explore these developments in more detail. In the first, D. Bodenhamer outlines a vision of how geographical technologies can be used across the humanities to explore space and time. Z. Frank then presents a chapter based on the urban history of Rio de Janeiro, particularly looking at renters and rentiers. It is based on broadly traditional types of sources but uses them to explore individual lives, relationships and social networks. I. Gregory and C. Peniston-Bird present another historical study that also explores how individual lives are affected by larger events. They focus on the experiences of soldiers from a single English town in one largely forgotten battle in the First World War using a digital textual record that they convert into a range of GIS layers. In the fourth chapter, J. Hayes et al. use a variety of sources, including archaeological, historical and ethnographical, to explore how GIS can contribute to land use planning in Alaska. Finally, J. Loxley et al. draw on an example from literary studies to explore how geographical technologies can be used to enrich and explore a large corpus of literature from the city of Edinburgh.

Notes

1 See D. J. Bodenhamer, J. Corrigan and T. M. Harris, *The Spatial Humanities: GIS and the Future of Humanities Scholarship*, Bloomington, IN: Indiana University Press, 2010, and; D.J. Bodenhamer, J. Corrigan and T.M. Harris, *Deep Maps and Spatial Narratives*, Bloomington: Indiana University Press, 2015.

2 I. N. Gregory and A. Geddes, 'From Historical GIS to Spatial Humanities: Deeping Scholarship and Broadening Technology', in I. N. Gregory and A. Geddes (eds), *Toward Spatial Humanities: Historical GIS and Spatial History*, Bloomington, IN: Indiana University Press, pp. ix–xix

3 P. Murrieta-Flores and I. Gregory, 'Further Frontiers in GIS: Extending Spatial Analysis to Textual Sources in Archaeology', *Open Archaeology* 1, 2015, 166–75.

4 See e.g. C. Grover, R. Tobin, K. Byrne, M. Woollard, J. Reid, S. Dunn and J. Ball, 'Use of the Edinburgh Geoparser for Georeferencing Digitized Historical Collections', *Philosophical Transactions of the Royal Society A* 368, 2010, 3875–89; I. Gregory, P. Atkinson, A, Hardie, A. Joulain-Jay, D. Kershaw, C. Porter, P. Rayson and C. J. Rupp, 'From Digital Resources to Historical Scholarship with the British Library 19th Century Newspaper Collection', *Journal of Siberian Federal University: Humanities and Social Sciences* 9, 994–1006; I. Gregory and C. Donaldson, 'Geographical Text Analysis: Digital Cartographies of Lake District Literature', in D. Cooper, C. D. Donaldson and P. Murrieta-Flores (eds), *Literary Mapping in the Digital Age,* Abingdon: Routledge, 67–87.

5 See e.g. R. Schwartz's chapter in this volume; U. Hinrichs, B. Alex, J. Clifford, A. Watson, A. Quigley, E. Klein and C. M. Coates, 'Trading Consequences: A Case Study of Combining Text Mining and Visualization to Facilitate Document Exploration', *Digital Scholarship in the Humanities* 30, 2015, 50–75; P. Murrieta-Flores, A. Baron, I. Gregory, A. Hardie and P. Rayson, 'Automatically Analysing Large Texts in a GIS Environment: The Registrar General's Reports and Cholera in the Nineteenth Century', *Transactions in GIS* 19, 2015, 296–320; C. Porter, P. Atkinson and I. Gregory, 'Geographical Text Analysis: A New Key to Nineteenth-Century Mortality', *Health and Place* 36, 2015, 25–34.

6 B. Alex, C. Grover, J. Oberlander, T. Thomson, M. Anderson, J. Loxley, U. Hinrichs and K. Zhou, 'Palimpsest: Improving Assisted Curation of Loco-Specific Literature',

Digital Scholarship in the Humanities 2016, 1–13; D. Cooper and I. N. Gregory, 'Mapping the English Lake District: A Literary GIS', *Transactions of the Institute of British Geographers* 36, 2011, 89–108.

7   E. Barker, S. Bouzarovski, C. Pelling and L. Isaksen, *New Worlds from Old Texts: Revisiting Ancient Space and Place*, Oxford: Oxford University Press, 2015.

24

CHASING BAKHTIN'S GHOST

From Historical GIS to deep mapping

David J. Bodenhamer

The 1970s and 1980s the humanities and social sciences witnessed numerous challenges to interpretations and methods that had dominated their disciplines for decades. Commonly called turns, signifying departures, the list included the cultural turn, linguistic turn, contingency turn, and a host of others.[1] Prominent among them was the spatial turn, with concepts of space and spatiality suddenly in vogue among scholars. It promised new perspectives to our study of society and culture, but what was this spatial turn? When did it begin – and why? What relationship did it have to Geographic Information Systems (GIS), a powerful technology with increasing presence in our daily lives? And what has been its impact in the humanities?

The phrase 'spatial turn' has a murky lineage, but it reflected the influence of a new critical geography that posed a more complex definition of space than most humanists employed. 'Rather than being seen only as a physical backdrop, container, or stage to human life,' Edward Soja, a leading theorist argued, 'space is more insightfully viewed as a complex social formation, part of a dynamic process.'[2] The sense of space as social process owed much to postmodernism, which rejected the notion of an objectively superior culture and refuted claims of a central hierarchy or organizing principle in society. The world, postmodernists noted, did not divide neatly into free or not free, western and eastern, familiar and foreign, superior and inferior; instead, it embodied complexity, contradiction, ambiguity, uncertainty, and diversity.[3]

A more complex and nuanced understanding of space revealed itself in the way historians thought about the larger categories that framed their work. Subject matter once organized largely by periods of time increasingly embraced spatial rubrics, such as region, diaspora, border, and boundary. Increasingly, research in the humanities focused on movement and encounter, on what happens in the spaces between cultures, on processes of transculturation, and on how differently separate cultures perceive the worlds they inhabit. Historians also turned attention to other conceptions of space, from gendered and racialized spaces to interior and intimate spaces.[4] As a result, our sense of space and place became more complex and problematic, and in the process it assumed a more interesting and active role in how we understand history and culture.[5]

But for all its explanatory power the spatial constructs employed by historians and other humanists frequently were metaphorical, not geographical. Far less often have we grappled with how the physical world has shaped us or how in turn we have shaped perceptions of it.

GIS and the epistemological divide

GIS facilitated a (re)discovery of geographical space in history and the humanities. Its power stems from an ability to correlate different types of data – quantitative, textual, image, audio, and the like – based on their shared location, regardless of format, as well as to manage vast quantities of these data within their spatial context. Equally important, it visualizes these relationships on a map of the geography in which they all occur, allowing users to see the information separately or together and to see it at different scales.

Even though GIS revealed the power of the map in a new form, its use in studying society raised serious questions about the view of the world it presents, namely, it manages and visualizes data in a culturally uninformed way. GIS allows us to know where something occurs and to see what else is happening in the same space, but it tells us nothing about the meaning of what we see. As with many technologies, GIS promises to reinvigorate our description of the world through its manipulation and visualization of vast quantities of data by means previously beyond the reach of most scholars. We have been swayed by its magical power but have little knowledge of how it developed or why. Yet it is this history that makes us aware of both the limits and potential of GIS for the humanities.

GIS emerged independently in the early 1960s from both the Harvard Laboratory for Computer Graphics, which aimed to produce automated cartography, and the Canadian GIS, which developed computerized methods to map the land capability of Canada.[6] Its intellectual and methodological lineage is much longer than this recent past; the concept of overlays, for instance, can be traced to the eleventh century. What was new were powerful computers and a demand from users who prized its ability to overlay data on a map of the earth's surface. With the creation of ArcInfo in the 1980s, GIS quickly moved into the mainstream of computing applications and spawned a wide array of location-based services.[7] Today, it enjoys such widespread use that we take it for granted.

Within the academy, GIS became the focus of quantitative geographers who saw its potential to detect spatial patterns that remained hidden in statistical analyses. Human geographers, on the other hand, were unconvinced. As late as 1988 the president of the American Association of Geographers labeled GIS as 'a mere technique', automated cartography without intellectual substance.[8] The divide ran along a fault line increasingly known as Geographic Information Science, a critique that GIS, although well equipped to manage quantitative spatial data, rested on a positivist and naïve empiricism.

Representing this view was *Ground Truth* (1995), a collection of essays edited by John Pickles, a prominent critic of GIS. Its authors expressed several concerns reminiscent of postmodern thought: the technological design of GIS inevitably favored certain conceptualizations of the world; it addressed corporate problems, such as route logistics or market analysis, and employed a limited linear logic inadequate for understanding societal complexity; as a consequence, it represented and perpetuated a particular view of political, economic, and social power.[9] It delineated space as a set of coordinates with characteristics or attributes attached to an identified location, a cartographic concept, rather than as relational space that maps interdependencies linked to the location, a social concept. It also favored institutional or official databases as the primary source of information about the world. These tendencies excluded non-Western conceptions of the world. American Indians, for example, defined the world as a set of interlinked phenomena, only some of which can be defined as geographic space.[10] Ancient Chinese dynasties identified its administrative units as networks of places and actors rather than as prescribed jurisdictions with formal boundaries.[11] GIS had difficulty managing these different meanings of space.

At its heart, the debate between advocates and opponents of GIS exposed epistemological and ontological differences that had implications for the construction of a humanities-based GIS.

At play was a conflict about spatial representation that stemmed from the early twentieth century. The demands of a modern industrial and technological society required 'scientific practices such as classification, quantification, and instrumentation to secure the truth of its visual records and representations'.[12] This literal representation of the world commodified cartography, often to the benefit of a range of location-based services from Google Maps to Yelp. But such statistical mapping was at odds with the shift elsewhere from traditional conceptions of fixed space to an Einsteinian view of relative space-time, or as Henri Lefebvre observed, we 'live in a world of Euclidian and Newtonian space while knowledge moved in the space of relativity'.[13] Computer cartography portrayed the world as geo-coded, whereas both geographic science and the humanities increasingly viewed the map not as a fixed container but as an active representation that had to be interpreted. GIS did not allow scholars to see this dynamic world easily, if at all.

Historical/humanities GIS

These problems did not stop humanists from experimenting with geospatial technologies. Archeologists came early to GIS because it provided a handy toolkit for managing their research in familiar but more efficient ways. Human habitats were easier to chart with the survey-based techniques of GIS, and with a 3-D extension it provided a new way to recreate past landscapes and cityscapes. Architects joined with archaeologists to create virtual worlds of ancient Rome, Jamestown in 1607, or medieval Welsh villages, for example, to test our understanding of form and function. Seeing a lost landscape, reconstructing historical view sheds, and traversing a highly detailed built environment provided an experiential understanding previously unavailable as scholarship.[14]

Historians also drifted toward GIS, but without the intense visualization employed by archaeologists. Early efforts centered on the development of large quantitative datasets, especially national censuses, for use within a GIS. An example was the Great American History Machine, which allowed students to explore county-level census and election data. Soon a variety of national historical GIS projects emerged, first in

Great Britain with the Great Britain Historical GIS and later a companion website that allowed a spatial exploration of a variety of information about British places.[15] By the early twenty-first century the United States, Germany, Netherlands, Belgium, Russia, South Korea, and China (one from the People's Republic and one from Taiwan), among others, boasted a national historical GIS.[16] Elsewhere, variants of this genre emerged, usually based on particular themes, e.g. The Cultural Atlas of Australia or the Literary Atlas of Europe, or on cities, with Sydney, London, and Tokyo among the best examples.[17] These projects made significant progress in how to manage changing boundaries, thus solving a major problem in the effective use of GIS for historical analysis – and the German Historical GIS linked dynastic information to the rapidly changing geopolitical landscape of nineteenth-century Germany.[18] But more often the analytical toolkit for these projects came straight from GIS software. An exception was the Digital Atlas of American Religion, which used Flash and Google tools to permit a spatially based comparative view of the data alongside a traditional GIS.[19]

The movement toward a humanities-based geospatial infrastructure also led to an early international effort, the Electronic Cultural Atlas Initiative, to spur the development of GIS-based, linked cultural atlases.[20] Its view of networked spatial data found expression elsewhere, as in the Greater Philadelphia Geohistory Network, which touted spatially referenced archival resources to enhance the study of local history.[21] By 2011 Harvard University launched its ambitious WorldMap as an open source platform to allow easy access to historical and cultural data.[22] Impressive work occurred as well in making historical maps available for use within a GIS, with a private map collector, David Rumsey, funding software development that facilitated access to his extensive collection through an eponymous website.[23] Significantly, these efforts, although essential for a robust approach to spatial history, focused more on creating framework data for other scholars than on addressing research problems.

Humanities researchers who embraced GIS saw its potential for creating a new form of interdisciplinary scholarship identified more by its characteristics than any theoretical approach or body of scholarship. Anne Knowles, a US pioneer, defined historical GIS, which increasing was called spatial history or spatial humanities, as having the 'elements of *geohistoire*, historical geography, and spatial and digital history'. Its characteristics included the dominance of geographical questions and geographical information in framing inquiries and the use of maps to present results.[24]

Although historical GIS (or spatial history) was a young sub-discipline, it grew rapidly as a distinct field of inquiry, with an impressive body of literature and applications. As late as 1997 a survey of historical geography made no mention of historical GIS;[25] few historians in the mid-1990s had even heard of GIS, much less its application to their discipline. Early efforts took advantage of GIS to relate data of different formats based on their common location, at times using the internet to bring spatial and archival evidence together and allow readers to explore the evidence afresh. Historians Ed Ayers and Will Thomas fashioned a cultural geography of two counties, one Northern and one Southern, during the American Civil War with spatial data drawn from the Valley of the Shadow Project and its much-visited website.[26] Their University of Virginia colleague, Ben Ray, brought a spatial approach to the Salem witchcraft craze of the 1690s (Salem Witchcraft Project).[27] In both of these expressions, however, GIS was part of what might otherwise be called digital history rather than spatial history because the approach was only in part about space.

The turn of the twenty-first century witnessed a sharp uptick in activity. *Social Science History* dedicated a special issue to historical GIS in 2000, and the next decade saw a minor flood of works, including two special journal issues – *History and Computing* (2001) and *Historical Geography* (2005) – a practice guide (2003), two collections of essays (*Past Time, Past Place,*2002; *Placing History*, 2008), and, in 2007, Ian Gregory and Paul Ell's *Historical GIS*, the first book by a major university press on historical GIS as a distinct approach to scholarship.[28] Major conferences on the use of GIS in the humanities began to appear; a gathering at the University of Essex in 2008 had presentations on such topics as GIS and biblical research, the spread of disease in nineteenth-century Kyoto, and the financial geography of the US oil industry during the American Civil War, among dozens of other equally diverse subjects. Scholarly networks dedicated to historical GIS appeared in Europe and the United States, and funding agencies across the world financed important GIS projects in heritage and culture.[29] Stanford University created a multifaceted project on spatial history that stemmed from a large Mellon Foundation grant to explore the usefulness of the technology for history.[30] Researchers from three US universities, representing the disciplines of history and geography, formed the Virtual Center for Spatial Humanities in 2008, with spatial history as an emphasis area. By decade's end, Indiana University Press had launched a first-ever series on spatial humanities with an inaugural title by the same name, *The Spatial Humanities: GIS and the Future of Humanities Scholarship*; within five years the list had grown to ten titles representing a number of humanities disciplines.[31] Interest has continued with new titles claiming a place on the rapidly growing bookshelf of relevant works, for example, Alexander von Lunen and Charles Travis, *History and GIS* (2014) and Charles Travis, *Abstract Machine: Humanities GIS* (2015).[32]

This GIS-based history has produced work that challenged existing interpretations or raised new questions. Geoff Cunfer, an environmental historian, used spatial tools and methods to challenge the standard interpretation that over-farming caused the American Dust Bowl of the 1920s and 1930s.[33] Richard White's prize-winning book, *Railroaded* (2012), used GIS as a spine for his argument that the rapid development of American railroads in the late nineteenth century was more the result of crony capitalism than the spatial elixir that boosted the national economy.[34] Scholars have engaged in GIS-facilitated efforts to understand the geographic roots of Irish religious strife,[35] to track the racial segregation of housing in Philadelphia,[36] to understand the spatial relationship among Enlightenment correspondents in the so-called Republic of Letters,[37] and to probe the link between agriculture, railroad expansion, and urban development in nineteenth-century Britain and France.[38] Elsewhere, scholars have used GIS to map the location of Holocaust sites across Europe, making it clear that the Nazi efforts at extermination were omnipresent on the landscape.[39]

Even though it is gaining adherents, most historians – indeed, most humanists – have not adopted GIS or, more fundamentally, found it helpful. What remains puzzling to its practitioners is why the technology is not finding its way into the toolkit of these scholars. After all, human activity is about time and space, and GIS provides a way to manage, relate, and query events, as well as to visualize them, that should be attractive to researchers.

The problems with GIS as a platform for humanities research are well recognized. Spatial technologies in general, and especially GIS, are expensive, complex, and cumbersome, despite recent advances that have driven down costs and simplified the user experience. They require significant investments of time to learn the toolsets they employ. GIS and its cousins are literal technologies: they favor precise data that can be managed and parsed within a highly structured tabular database. Yet ambiguity, uncertainty, nuance, and uniqueness are the characteristics of historical and other humanities evidence. GIS also has difficulty managing time, which it treats as an attribute of location within a GIS, although it is a much more complicated concept for humanists, who view it at multiple scales – days, centuries, and epochs – and often inexactly.

More important, GIS uses methods and approaches that are not part of the historians' professional culture. Historians find words, with their halos of meaning, better suited for describing the complexity we see in our subjects, yet GIS relies heavily on visualization to display its results. It demands the use of spatial questions, whereas most historians think rarely about geographical space and often do not understand how to frame a spatial query.[40] It requires collaboration between technical and domain experts, thereby putting humanists, who work in isolation and often are inept in the lingo, at a two-fold disadvantage. Finally, GIS appears reductionist in its epistemology. It forces data into categories; it defines space in limited and literal ways instead of the metaphorical frames that are equally reflective of human experience; and, while managing complexity within its data structures, it too often simplifies its mapped results in ways that obscure rather than illuminate.[41]

Yet the promise of GIS is so seductive that perhaps we have been asking the wrong question. Would it be more fruitful to bend geospatial technologies toward representing the world as culture and not simply mapped locations rather than to ask historians to adopt GIS? Achieving this goal requires us to reconceptualize historical GIS as the spatial humanities, a term that captures a potentially rich interplay between Critical GIS, spatial science, spatial systems, and the panoply of highly nuanced humanist traditions, including history. The focus, in other words, must not be on accommodating our questions to a tool that does not fit our needs, but rather on how we can bend the tools to explore space, time, and place creatively and constructively.

Towards deep mapping and the spatial humanities

Although epistemologically branded, geo-spatial technologies still offer potential for history and the humanities.[42] The challenge is bridge humanistic critical discourses and the theoretical perspectives of spatial science. The reward will be a historical scholarship that integrates insights gleaned from spatial theory into multifaceted and scaled narratives about human lives and culture. We can see the potential payoff in Mei-Po Kwan's and Guoxiang Ding's 'geo-narratives' drawn from the oral histories and mapped experiences of Muslim women in Columbus Ohio after 9/11.[43]

The question is how to design and frame narratives about individual and collective human experience that are spatially contextualized. At one level, the task involves reciprocal transformations from text to map and map to text, a practice that also can exploit the rich resources of the Geospatial Web.[44] Work already is well underway in this area. An interdisciplinary team at Lancaster University is using text mining and computational linguistics in two projects, one to understand the spatial dimensions of Lake District literature and the other to enhance the spatial context of nineteenth-century infant mortality data.[45] Another effort at University of Western Ontario places qualitative sources, such as narratives, within a stage-based GIS as a way of allowing researchers to tell spatial stories about lived experiences.[46] These projects also extend the significant work on narrative topographies and novel mappings in literary and cultural studies.[47]

Time poses another problem. There is an urgent need for the development of spatio-temporal tools that will enable humanities scholars, social scientists, geographers, and others to incorporate time into analyses that are spatially contextualized. Within GIS specifically and spatial technologies more generally, the fit is awkward because the technology treats time as categorical and discontinuous and defaults to a model that strings together spatio-temporal snapshots that approximate story-as-collage.[48] But time, as sociologist Andrew Abbott reminds us, is in fact a 'series of overlapping presents of various sizes, each organized around a particular location, and overlapping across the whole social process'.[49] The importance of narrative within history and the other humanities can stimulate the development of better spatial tools that incorporate time as well, just as spatial thinking and tools can encourage richer considerations of spatial relationships in narrative time.

Central to the emergence of spatial history and the spatial humanities is a trust that the contingent, unpredictable, and ironic in history and culture can be embodied within a narrative context that incorporates space alongside of time. Place is constructed out of the imagination as much as through what is visible and tangible in experience, and it is the thick weave of events, locations, behaviors, and motivations that make space into place. It also is the product of deep contingencies and emergent realities where we see the imprint of choices made or foregone.[50] A rich spatial history, then, embraces Franco Moretti's call for maps that are more than the sum of their parts but 'possess 'emerging' qualities, which were not visible at the lower level . . . [that] offer a model of the narrative universe which . . . may bring some hidden patterns to the surface'.[51] GIS at present cannot deliver on this promise, so how do we build increasingly more complex maps of the personalities, emotions, values, and poetics – the visible and invisible aspects of a place – that capture the matters that engage humanists?

Here is where the concept of a deep map becomes important. An avant-garde technique first urged by the Situationists International in 1950s France and popularized by William Least Heat-Moon's stratigraphic history of Chase County, Kansas,[52] the approach 'attempts to record and represent the grain and patina of place through juxtapositions and interpenetrations of the historical and the contemporary, the political and the poetic, the discursive and the sensual'.[53] Its best form results in a subtle and multilayered view of a small area of the earth. As a new creative space, deep maps have several qualities well-suited to a fresh, humanities-based conceptualization of GIS and other spatial technologies. They are meant to be visual, time-based, and structurally open. They are genuinely multi-media and multilayered. They do not seek authority or objectivity but involve negotiation between insiders and outsiders, experts and contributors, over what is represented and how. Framed as a conversation and not a statement, deep maps are inherently unstable, continually unfolding and changing in response to new data, new perspectives, and new insights.

Although much of the work around deep mapping to date has been conceptual, certain design principles have emerged to shape its expression, which in fact will take numerous forms. A multidisciplinary team of scholars at a 2012 NEH Advanced Institute on Spatial Narratives and Deep Maps identified five core principles: they are *flexible*, inviting exploration; *user-centric*, supporting differing views; *path-traceable*, supporting narration; *open*, admitting new material; and *immersive*, evoking experience. A deep map, in addition to taking multiple forms, can be any one of three things – a platform, a process, and a product – or all three at once. As platform, it is an environment embedded with tools to bring data into an explicit and direct relationship with space and time. As a process, it is a way to engage evidence within its spatio-temporal context and to trace paths of discovery that lead to a spatial narrative and ultimately a spatial argument. As product, it is the way we make visual the results of our enquiry and share the spatially contingent argument enabled by the deep map. Within this environment, we can develop the event streams that permit us to see the confluence of actions and evidence; we can use path markers or version trackers to allow us (and others) to trace our explorations; and we can contribute new information that strengthens or subverts our argument, which is the goal of any exploration.[54] A deep map, in short, is a new curated and creative space that is visual, structurally open, genuinely multi-media, and multi-layered. It seeks to provoke negotiation between insiders and outsiders, experts and contributors, over what is represented and how.[55]

The analogue between a deep map and advanced spatial technologies seems evident. Geographic information systems operate as a series of layers, each representing a different theme and tied to a specific location on planet earth. These layers are transparent, although the user can make any layer or combination of layers opaque while leaving others visible. A deep map of heritage and culture, centered on memory and place, ideally would work in a similar fashion. The layers of a deep map need not be restricted to a known or discoverable documentary record but could be opened to anyone with a memory or artifact to contribute. However structured, these layers would operate as do other layers within a GIS, viewed individually or collectively as a whole or within groups, but all tied to time and space that provide perspectives on the places that interest us. The deep map is one in which both horizontal and vertical movement is possible, with the horizontal providing the linear progression we associate with rational argument and vertical movement providing the depth, texture, tension, and resonance of experience.[56]

The coalescence of digital technologies over the past decade makes it possible to envision how geospatial technologies might contribute to the formation of a deep map.[57] Archaeologists have used GIS and computer animations to reconstruct the Roman Forum, for example, creating a 3-D world that allows users to walk through buildings that no longer exist, except as ruins. We can experience these structures and spaces at various times of day and gain an immediate, intuitive feel for proximity and power that informs our sense of possibilities and enriches our understanding of lost worlds.[58] Another innovative effort, *HyperCities*, a GIS-based website, allows scholars to explore cities across time, using period maps overlaid on contemporary landscapes, viewing virtual buildings within their real-world context, and linking images and text to the locations they describe.[59] A West Virginia University project aims to go even further by combining a projection-based virtual reality system with GIS and Google tools to recreate a sense of nineteenth-century Morgantown. By adding sounds, smells, and touch, all within the capability of existing technology, this virtual reconstruction seeks to engage four primary senses, making the experience even more real.[60] Once expensive, the costs of immersive environments are dropping rapidly, but, in fact, a CAVE is not essential for making an immersive environment open to humanists. Serious gaming engines already allow us to explore virtual worlds with a high degree both of verisimilitude and agency.

As these examples suggest, GIS is merging with other Web technologies – for example, mash-ups, virtual research environments, augmented reality, among others – to move us beyond a map of geographical space into a richer, more evocative world of imagery. Over the past few years, GIScientists and informaticians have made advances in spatial multi-media, GIS-enabled web services, geo-visualization, cyber geography, and virtual reality that provide capabilities far exceeding the abilities of GIS on its own. Elsewhere, the commercial market is rapidly developing tools that can be appropriated for deep mapping. IBM's Watson Supercomputer, for example, employs a multi-variant visualization tool, Watson Paths, to comb research literature and visualize the junctures where its algorithms have chosen one diagnostic path over another to address patient symptoms.[61] Here perhaps is how deep map can create a path-traceable narrative that reveals the contingencies faced by the researcher. Or consider Oculus Rift, the virtual reality technology owned by Facebook, that permit users to have a distortion-free, immersive view of an environment enhanced by information and images harvested from the Web.[62] This convergence of technologies has the potential to revolutionize the role of space and place in the humanities by allowing us to move far beyond the static map, to shift from two dimensions to multidimensional representations, to develop interactive systems, and to explore space and place dynamically – in effect, to create virtual worlds embodying what we know about space and place.

What would a deep map look like, and how would it function? Consider the following example: A military battle is a discrete event bounded by space and time but with clear antecedents and discernible aftereffects. It exists not simply as a physical event but also as memory, in imagination, through artefacts and records, in images, and often as myth. We can understand the battle in all of these ways, but only as discrete elements. How do we understand it as all things at once, and how do we experience it? How can we recognize the contingencies facing participants and with this knowledge gauge the counterfactual? How can we move fluidly across spatial and temporal scales when considering the decisions made or not made, because surely that is how the participants judged their choices. As humans we cannot understand the battle in any general way than other than through analogy, metaphor, emotion, and cause and consequence, all the ways that we have invented over time to aid our understanding and our ability to communicate but which separate us from the experience of the event itself, even though we acknowledge that individual and collective experiences shape our understanding of it. But if we could recreate the battle, populating it with all we can discover about it, and if we could view this evidence simultaneously and from its own unique perspective, as well as from the perspectives we bring to it – if we could *see* what participants reported within its geographical, temporal, and cultural context – would not the battle appear more chaotic, more contingent, more fluid, more uncertain, more ambiguous, more immediate – in other words, more fully human?

Chasing Bakhtin's ghost: experiential spatial history

Deep maps also would address the problem noted almost a century ago by Mikhail Bakhtin, Martin Heidegger, Edmund Husserl, and other theorists who recognized the disjuncture between the Enlightenment world of logical-rational empiricism and the nascent world of Einsteinian relativity and phenomenology. Writing in the 1920s and 1930s but not rediscovered until the mid-1970s, Bakhtin, a Russian semiotician and literary theorist, captured the problem neatly in his notion of the chronotope, the inextricable linkage of time and space that defines both reality and our perception of it. As Bakhtin describes it, the chronotope is an experiential form: 'time, as it were, thickens, takes on flesh, becomes artistically visible; likewise, space becomes charged and responsive to the movements of time, plot and history . . . [It] . . . is the place where the knots of narrative are tied and untied . . . Time becomes, in effect, palpable and visible; the chronotope makes narrative events concrete, makes them take on flesh, causes blood to flow in their veins.'[63]

For Bakhtin, the world could not be understood without considering both when and where an event or action occurred, as well as when and where observers stood as they became aware of or considered an event. By its very nature, the time-space link within the chronotope emphasizes particularity; it reminds us of the distinction between the observed and the observer; and it reflects the dynamic, interdependent, and relative context of all knowledge. If all of these things seem commonplace today, it is because we have adopted these insights in the way we interpret reality. But this view is missing from typical applications of GIS to the humanities, which in turn makes the technology less appealing to scholars who might profit from it. If we are ever to develop a robust and meaningful spatial humanities that blends technology with the humanities, we must chase – and corral – Bakhtin's ghost.

The use of appropriately cast spatial technologies within history and the humanities – in sum, the spatial humanities – promises to develop a unique postmodern scholarship, one that accommodates the contingent, fluid, and ambiguous nature of human beliefs and actions. The goal is not to sacrifice the rational, logical, and empirical approach to knowledge that has been the hallmark of the humanities since the Enlightenment, but rather to complement it with different ways of discovery. For centuries we have defined history, in theory and practice, as the story of experience. Now we have an opportunity to experience the story: we can (re)live time-space in ways not possible before.[64]

The notion of a richer, dynamic, and experiential GIS resonates with the evocative and thick descriptions of place and time that humanists have long favored in their scholarship. The objective is not to model or replicate the past but to complicate it. Questions drive historical scholarship, not hypotheses, and the questions that matter most address causation: why matters more than whom, what, or when, even though these latter questions are neither trivial nor easy to answer. The approach is recursive, not linear: the aim is not so much to eliminate answers as to admit new perspectives. The challenge, then, for the spatial humanities is to use technology to probe, explore, challenge, and complicate, in sum, to allow us to see, experience, and understand human behavior in all its complexity.

We will satisfy this goal in ways that shift our ways of knowing from reason and logic alone to a more experiential understanding of the human condition as it differs from place to place. This perspective will be aided technically not through the use of GIS alone, which is a weak reed on which to base this shift, but rather on the continuing rapid convergence of technologies, operating in such a fashion as to blend space and time. In this view, space becomes an equal partner with time – and time with space – in providing the conceptual framework for the spatial humanities. It is a necessary alliance, not because it will replace narrative history but because it will allow us to complement our traditional practice with a more robust experience of our past.

Notes

1 S. Susen, *The Postmodern Turn in the Social Sciences*, London: Palgrave Macmillan, 2015.

2 E. Soja, 'In Different Spaces: Interpreting the Spatial Organization of Societies,' *Proceedings*, 3rd International Space Syntax Symposium, Atlanta, GA, 2001.

3 For a brief critical overview, see C. Butler, *Postmodernism: A Very Short Introduction*, New York: Oxford University Press, 2003.

4 Y. Tuan, *Space and Place: The Perspective of Experience*, Minneapolis, MN: University of Minnesota Press, 1977; D. Massey, *Space, Place, and Gender*, Minneapolis, MN: University of Minnesota Press, 1994, 1–24.

5 D. Cosgrove, 'Landscape and Landschaft', *GHI Bulletin* 35, 2004, 57–71; K. Olwig, *Landscape, Nature and the Body Politic: From Britain's Renaissance to America's New World*, Madison, WI: University of Wisconsin Press, 2002.

6 J. Coppock and D. Rhind, 'The History of GIS', in D. Maguire, M. Goodchild, and D. Rhind (eds), *Geographical Information Systems: Principles and Applications,* vol. 1, *Principles,* London: Longman Scientific and Technical, 1991, 21–43.

7 T. Foresman, 'GIS Early Years and the Threads of Evolution', in T. W. Foresman (ed.), *The History of Geographic Information Systems: Perspectives from the Pioneers*, Upper Saddle River, NJ: Prentice Hall PTR, 1998, 3–17.

8 N. Schuurman, 'Trouble in the Heartland: GIS and its Critics in the 1990s', *Progress in Human Geography* 24, 2000, 569–90.

9 N. Schuurman, *GIS: A Short Introduction*, Malden, MA: Blackwell Publishing, 2004, 21–52; E. Sheppard, 'Knowledge Production through Critical GIS: Genealogy and Prospects', *Cartographica* 40, 2005, 5–21.

10 R. Rundstrom, 'GIS, Indigenous Peoples, and Epistemological Diversity', *Cartography and Geographic Information Systems* 22, 1995, 45–57.

11 M. Berman, 'Boundaries or Networks in Historical GIS: Concepts of Measuring Space and Administrative Boundaries in Chinese History', *Historical Geography* 33, 2005, 118–33.

12 D. Cosgrove, 'Maps, Mapping, Modernity: Art and Cartography in the Twentieth Century', *Imago Mundi* 57, 2005, 37.

13 H. Lefebvre, *Critique of Everyday Life*, vol. 3, *From Modernity to Modernism (towards a Metaphilosophy of Daily Life)*, London: Verso, 2005, 46.

14 J. Conolly and M. Lake, *Geographical Information Systems in Archaeology*, New York: Cambridge University Press, 2006; M. Breunig and S. Zlatanova, '3-D Geo-Database Research: Retrospective and Future Directions', *Computers and Geosciences* 37, 2011, 791–803.

15 Vision of Britain. <www.visionofbritain.org> (last accessed 3 March 2016).

16 The most comprehensive listing of historical GIS projects can be found at The Historical GIS Research Network <www.hgis.org.uk/resources.htm> (last accessed 7 February 2017).

17 <http://australian-cultural-atlas.info> (last accessed 7 February 2017); <www.literaturat-las.eu> (last accessed 7 February 2017).

18 <www.hgis-germany.de> (last accessed 7 February 2017)

19 <http://religionatlas.org> (last accessed 7 February 2017).

20 <www.ecai.org> (last accessed 7 February 2017).

21 <www.philageohistory.org/geohistory/> (last accessed 7 February 2017).

22 <www.worldmap.harvard.edu> (last accessed 7 February 2017).

23 <www.davidrumsey.org> (last accessed 7 February 2017).

24 A. K. Knowles, 'GIS and history', in A. K. Knowles (ed.), *Mapping the Past: How Maps, Spatial Data, and GIS are Changing Historical Scholarship*, Redlands, CA: ESRI Press, 2008, 7–8.

25 I. Gregory and R. Healy, 'Historical GIS: Structuring, Mapping and Analysing Geographies of the Past', *Progress in Human Geography* 31, 2007, 638–53 at p. 638.

26 W. Thomas III and E. Ayers, 'The Differences Slavery Made: A Close Analysis of Two American Communities', <www2.vcdh.virginia.edu/AHR/> (last accessed 7 February 2017).

27 *The Salem Witch Trials Documentary Archive and Transcription Project*, <http://salem.lib.virginia.edu/home.html> (last accessed 7 February 2017).

28 I. Gregory and P. Ell, *Historical GIS: Technologies, Methodologies and Scholarship*, Cambridge: Cambridge University Press, 2007, 15–18.

29 I. N. Gregory, A. Kunz, and D. J. Bodenhamer, 'A Place in Europe: Enhancing European Collaboration in Historical GIS', *International Journal of Humanities and Arts Computing* 5, 2011, 23–40.

30 <www.stanford.edu/group/spatialhistory/cgi-bin/site/index.php> (last accessed 7 February 2017).

31 D. Bodenhamer, J. Corrigan, and T. Harris (eds), *The Spatial Humanities: GIS and the Future of Humanities Scholarship,* Series on the Spatial Humanities, Bloomington, IN: Indiana University Press, 2010; Indiana University Press Series on Spatial Humanities <http://bit.ly/1So7SJt> (last accessed 7 February 2017).

32 A. von Lünen and C. Travis, (eds), *History and GIS: Epistemologies, Considerations and Reflections,* Dordrecht: Springer, 2014; C. Travis, *Abstract Machine: Humanities GIS*, Redlands, CA: ESRI Press, 2015.

33 G. Cunfer, *On the Great Plains: Agriculture and Environment*, College Station, TX: Texas A&M University Press, 2005.

34 R. White, *Railroaded: The Transcontinentals and the Making of Modern America*, New York: W. W. Norton, 2012.

35 I. Gregory, N. Cunningham, C. Lloyd, I. Shuttleworth, and P. Ell, *Troubled Geographies: A Spatial History of Religion and Society in Ireland*, Series on the Spatial Humanities, Bloomington, IN: Indiana University Press, 2013.

36 A. Hillier, 'Redlining in Philadelphia', in Knowles (ed.), *Past Time, Past Place*, 79–92.

37 <https://republicofletters.stanford.edu/> (last accessed 7 February 2017).

38 R. Schwartz and T. Thevenin, 'Railways and Agriculture in France and Great Britain, 1850–1914', in I. Gregory and A. Geddes (eds), *Toward Spatial Humanities: Historical GIS*

and Spatial History, Series on the Spatial Humanities, Bloomington, IN: Indiana University Press, 2014, 4–34.

39 A. Knowles, T. Cole, and A. Giordano (eds), *Geographies of the Holocaust*, Series on the Spatial Humanities, Bloomington, IN: Indiana University Press, 2014.

40 D. Bodenhamer and I. N. Gregory, 'Teaching Spatial Literacy and Spatial Technologies in the Digital Humanities', in D. Unwin, K. Foote, N. Tate, and D. DiBiase (eds), *Teaching Geographic Information Science and Technology in Higher Education,* London: Wiley-Blackwell, 2011, 231–46.

41 D. Bodenhamer, 'History and GIS: Implications for the Discipline', in Knowles (ed.), *Mapping the Past*, 220–33.

42 P. Ethington, 'Placing the Past: Groundwork for a Spatial Theory of History', *Rethinking History* 11, 2007, 465–93.

43 M. Kwan and G. Ding, 'Geo-Narrative: Extending Geographic Information Systems for Narrative Analysis in Qualitative and Mixed-Method Research', *The Professional Geographer* 40, 2008, 60, 443–65.

44 M. Yuan, 'Mapping Text', in D. Bodenhamer et al, *The Spatial Humanities*, 109–23; T. Harris, L. Rouse, and S. Bergeron, 'The Geospatial Semantic Web, Pareto GIS, and the Humanities', in D. Bodenhamer et al., *The Spatial Humanities*, 124–42. Also, A. Scharl and K. Tochtermann (eds), *The Geospatial Web: How Geobrowsers, Social Software and the Web 2.0 are Shaping the Network Society*, London: Springer, 2007, 153–8.

45 D. Cooper and I. Gregory, 'Mapping the English Lake District: A Literary GIS', *Transactions of the Institute of British Geographers* 36, 2011, 89–108.

46 D. Lafreniere and J. Gilliland, '"All the World's a Stage": A GIS Framework for Recreating Personal Time-Space from Qualitative and Quantitative Sources', *Transactions in GIS*, 19, 2015, 225–46.

47 P. Valiaho, *Mapping the Moving Image: Gesture, Thought and Cinema circa 1900*, Amsterdam: Amsterdam University Press, 2010; F. Moretti, *Atlas of the European Novel, 18001900*, London: Verso, 1998; B. Piatti, H. Bär, A. Reuschel, L. Hurni, and W. Cartwright, 'Mapping Literature: Towards a Geography of Fiction', in W. Cartwright, G. Gardner, and A. Lehn (eds), *Cartography and Art: Lecture Notes in Geoinformation and Cartography*, Verlag: Springer, 2009, 177–91.

48 D. Peuquet, *Representations of Space and Time*, New York: Guilford Press, 2002, 12–15; D. Massey, 'Space-Time, "Science," and the Relationship between Physical and Human Geography', *Transactions of the Royal Geographical Society*, 24, 1999, 261–76; I. Gregory, 'Exploiting Time and Space: A Challenge for GIS in the Digital Humanities,' in D. Bodenhamer et al., *The Spatial Humanities*, 58–75.

49 A. Abbott, *Time Matters: On Theory and Method*, Chicago, IL: University of Chicago Press, 2001, 296. E. Ayers, 'Mapping Time', in M. Dear, J. Ketchum, S. Luria, and D. Richardson (eds), *Geo-Humanities: Art, History, Text at the Edge of Place,* London: Routledge, 215–25.

50 E. Ayers, 'Turning Toward Place, Space, and Time', in Bodenhamer et al., *The Spatial Humanities*, 1–13.

51 F. Moretti, *Graphs, Maps, Trees: Abstract Models for Literary History*, London: Verso, 2007, 53.

52 W. Heat-Moon, *PrairyErth (A Deep Map)*, New York: Houghton Mifflin, 1991.

53 M. Pearson and M. Shanks, *Theatre/Archaeology*, London: Routledge, 2001, 64–5.

54 'Spatial Narratives and Deep Maps: A Special Report', *International Journal of Humanities and Arts Computing* 7, 2013, 170–227.

55 D. Bodenhamer, J. Corrigan, and T. Harris (eds), *Deep Maps and Spatial Narratives*, Series on the Spatial Humanities, Bloomington, IN: Indiana University Press, 2015.

56 D. Bodenhamer, 'Creating a Landscape of Memory', *International Journal of Humanities and Arts Computing* 1, 2008, 97–110.

57 C. Leadbetter, *We-Think: Mass Innovation, Not Mass Production*, London: Profile Books, 2009.

58 *The Digital Roman Forum Project* <http://dlib.etc.ucla.edu/projects/Forum/> (last accessed 7 February 2017).

59 <http://hypercities.ats.ucla.edu> (last accessed 7 February 2017).

60 T. Harris, S. Bergeron, and L. Rouse, 'Humanities GIS: Place, Spatial Storytelling and Immersive Visualization in the Humanities', in M. Dear et al., *GeoHumanities*, 226–40.

61 <http://ibm.co/1JAPya6> (last accessed 7 February 2017).

62 <https://en.wikipedia.org/wiki/Oculus_VR> (last accessed 7 February 2017).

63 M. Bakhtin, *The Dialogic Imagination: Four Essays*, ed. M. Holquist, Austin, TX: University of Texas Press, 1981, 250.

64 D. Carr, *Experience and History: Phenomenological Perspectives on the Historical World*, New York: Oxford University Press, 2014, 173–98.

25

URBAN PROPERTY IN NINETEENTH-CENTURY RIO DE JANEIRO

Rent, neighborhoods, and networks

Zephyr Frank

This chapter explores the use of historical GIS in the service of a spatial history of property in the city of Rio de Janeiro. Exploration, as a way of conducting spatial history, emphasizes passages through space and time that are partial and probabilistic rather than complete and fixed.[1] Although the analysis avails itself of the seemingly exact tools of GI science, and it produces synoptic and distant views from above and far away, it cuts against these same tools and tropes of representation by purposeful selection of spatially distinctive categories and units of analysis including idiosyncratic individual case studies. It also improvises and uses tools and methods in novel ways, allowing for the intersection of network analysis with GIS methods.

But before theory and method, first some history. To begin with the obvious, the two basic constituents of the urban property scene in Rio de Janeiro during the 1800s were rentiers and renters. For property owners, the accumulation of urban real estate provided an important source of income and a marker of social and economic status in nineteenth-century Rio de Janeiro. A small, but important group of owners held many urban properties, living off ample rents and watching as their real estate portfolios grew in value. As for renters, a much larger group lacked the means to purchase property or chose not to do so for other reasons. Many renters struggled to pay for the roof over their heads; yet there were also prosperous renters who declined to purchase property.

Renters and rentiers alike faced a changing urban world during the second half of the nineteenth century. Over this period, the city more than doubled in population from under a quarter of a million inhabitants in 1850 to over half a million by century's end.[2] It grew outward, into new suburbs; it also grew upward, with the construction of multistory buildings, particularly in the old city center. Urban growth was accompanied by significant change in every sphere of life. The economy became more sophisticated, as banks, business partnerships, and joint-stock companies increased the scale of activity.[3] Slavery was gradually attenuated and finally abolished in 1888, thereby removing one of the central pillars of the old regime and its property relations.[4] Abolition and other issues contributed to the collapse of the empire and the advent of the first Brazilian republic in 1889.

In this historical context, this chapter examines the history of property in Rio de Janeiro with the aim to illuminate the experiences of renters and rentiers alike. For many among the rich, the property market made up a major part of their fortunes and provided a significant portion of their income.[5] For middling groups, owning property provided stability and status; and for the working poor and destitute, the struggle for shelter extended from comfortable rental housing to desperate and insalubrious boarding houses and shanties in the city.

The study of property ownership provides one of the foundational building blocks with which a social and spatial history of Rio de Janeiro can be constructed. Such a study can measure degrees and patterns of concentration in property; it can also evaluate the ebb and flow of property ownership over time, in specific neighborhoods, with regard to the individual tenants and owners. In paying attention to neighborhoods and individuals, it is hoped that the texture of urban life will emerge and offer insight into the quotidian social and economic networks (explicit and implicit) associated with property and its occupation, whether by ownership or renting.

At the mezzo and micro scales, the aim is to present neighborhoods and individuals in sufficient detail so as to recreate sketch 'biographies' of properties, property ownership, and surrounding neighborhoods. These studies will be used to introduce puzzles – both of the historical and methodological kind. For example, the story of an individual can shed light on the historical problem of the division of property through Brazil's system of inheritance. The study of an individual, in his or her neighborhood, also highlights the challenges of tracking properties in an environment of changing owners and tenants and sometimes shifting street numbering rubrics.

Sources and methods

The foundation of this essay rests on the urban property tax rolls housed in the City Archive of Rio de Janeiro. These records were transcribed into a database by my research assistant, Tereza Cristina Alves, over the course of a year in 2003–4. Given the number of records, the transcription effort concentrated on three years' worth of property records: 1849, 1870, and 1888.[6] These years were selected with the aim to correspond more or less closely to major historical events. In the end, a total of 54,436 property records associated with individuals or institutions were transcribed into spreadsheets. Each record contains the address of the property, a code designating the kind of construction (whether one or more stories), the name of the property owner, and an indication of the imputed rental value of the property for the purpose of levying the tax, which was known as the *décima urbana*.

The property tax records are organized logically by street. Property owners, when multiple properties were in question, rarely owned all of their property in the same block. When sorted according to owner rather than street, the clean organization of the records is shattered. Where in the world are we? What is the relationship between any two properties owned by the same man or woman? This is where spatial history enters. The answer is provided, at least in part, through the construction of a historical GIS model of the space of the city. In order to fill in gaps and enrich the story of property, many other sources were collected and similarly geocoded with the same historical GIS model. Most important, among these, were the city directories, referred to as the *Almanak Laemmert*, which were digitized for the years 1849, 1870, and 1889.[7]

Building the model required two basic steps. First, a reconstruction of the historical street grid in Rio de Janeiro eliminated anachronisms that would otherwise impinge upon the map. Second, the names of streets and address ranges for each block had to be reconstituted with respect to the years 1849, 1870, and 1888.[8] Given the changes in the fabric of the city and the shifting names of streets and street numbering systems, these steps were required in order to render a reliable geocoding process. Once complete, the model allowed for locating addresses and tracking changes over time at different scales – from the synoptic view of the whole city to the detailed investigation of a specific neighborhood or parcel.

General trends, values, and inequality in property ownership over time

The mean property owner (with two or more names) held 1:088$065 worth of urban property circa 1849.[9] Roughly four decades later, in 1888, the equivalent figure was 2:392$302. Rendered in terms of a more stable world currency, at current exchange rates, the values are 117 and 252 pounds sterling respectively. Mean values held by individual property owners more than doubled by this measure.

In 1849, there were 5,925 individual property owners with two or more names – I was forced to drop the observations based on individuals listed with a single name because it was impossible to determine whether, in fact, these records attached to a single specific individual. By 1888, this number had grown to 8,162 individuals in roughly the same area of the city. In the simplest terms, the ratio of owners to total population was approximately 3 percent in 1849 and 2 percent in 1888. The clear implication, even at this level of abstraction, is that most residents in the city were renters and not property owners.

At the most general level, inequality among owners of urban property changed very little over the period 1849 to 1888. Among individual property owners, the Gini coefficient (measured 0 to 1, with higher values indicating greater inequality) rose from 0.627 in 1849 to 0.646 in 1888. These values, it should be noted, are approximations, given that some double counting of common individual names is inevitable, even when single names, like José, were excluded. The increase in overall inequality of property ownership by value, among those listed as owners, was just 3 percent by this measure.

Assuming for the moment that the underlying demographic situation was roughly stable in terms of age structure and family size, the decline in the ratio of property owners to the total population in the city implies that many more potential property owners were without urban real property in 1888. In order to approximate the full distribution, including those who did not own property, the ratio of owners to households was calculated for both years and zero cases were entered into the calculation of an adjusted Gini coefficient. There were about 20,000 households in the central parishes according to the 1849 census. In 1890, about 39,000 households were enumerated in the central parishes. Thus, the property-owning households comprised 30 percent of the universe in 1849 and 21 percent in 1888. Insertion of zero cases for the 'missing' 70 and 79 percent of households not owning property results in adjusted Gini coefficients of 0.889 and 0.926 in 1849 and 1888 respectively. Making this rough adjustment does not lead to a much higher rate of increase in overall inequality – just 4.2 percent – but it does put property inequality at a very high level when the entire universe of potential owners is taken into consideration.

Thus far, the focus of analysis has been at the level of average values for property holders. One of the advantages of historical GIS is that it allows for relatively easy calculations of change over time according to spatial location. In this regard, we can measure the rate of change in overall value and assess its spatial distribution. Because the geocoding process is based on street centerlines rather than individual parcels, the calculations presented here will be at the block level. Parcel-level calculations are possible, but the changing street numbering scheme and the merging of some parcels over time makes this a process best approached at a smaller scale, as much hand work and fine tuning is required for accurate results.

The question at the block level is: where did property values rise the fastest and what were the overall patterns in rates of change? The analysis filters out blocks with fewer than five observations.

Measured in current mil-réis, the rental value of properties rose at an annual compound rate of 3.35 percent over the period 1849 to 1888 (Table 25.1). The rate of increase was faster in the first two decades, which can be explained by the relatively low starting values in 1849. In that period, slavery was still the predominant force in the economy and a competing target for urban investors. By the 1870s, slavery was waning and investors placed a much greater proportion of their assets in urban property. From this point on, there was relatively less scope for rapid growth, holding other variables constant. In any case, the annual rate of return in implicit property values implies a doubling of invested capital every 20 years or so. Property ownership was a good investment both in terms of short- and long-term returns. Every year, the property generated rents. Over time, the underlying value of the property also increased. If the relationship between rents and underlying values remained relatively constant, and there is evidence to support this supposition, then the combined rental and capital returns to a piece of property, depending on the neighborhood, would have ranged according to the following estimates pegged to five blocks representing,

Table 25.1 Change in rental values at block level, 1849–88.

	1849	1870	1888
AVERAGE BLOCK RENT BY STARTING YEAR (nominal mil-réis)	641$	1:395$	2:279$
ANNUAL %	3.85	2.79	3.35

N OBS: 227 Blocks.

Source: Décima Urbana, Rio de Janeiro, 1849, 1870, 1888, AGCRJ. Blocks selected where N obs was >5 for each of the three study years.

Table 25.2 Quintile rates of growth in rental values with representative blocks and their locations, 1849–88.

Quintile	Q rate	Block #	Block rate	Block Street
1	4.95	572	4.25	Saco do Alferes
2	3.66	472	3.57	S Pedro
3	3.22	527	3.22	R Ciganos
4	2.81	77	2.81	R Ouvidor
5	2.15	707	2.04	R Vala

Source: Décima Urbana, Rio de Janeiro, 1849, 1870, 1888, AGCRJ.

Table 25.3 Nominal returns on capital invested in real property in the city of Rio de Janeiro, 1849–88.

Quintile	Q rate	Upper-bound Rent	Lower-bound Rent	Tax & Upkeep	Upper-bound Return	Lower-bound Return
1	4.95	15	5	−2	17.95	7.95
2	3.66	15	5	−2	16.66	6.66
3	3.22	15	5	−2	16.22	6.22
4	2.81	15	5	−2	15.81	5.81
5	2.15	15	5	−2	15.15	5.15

Note: Real returns require a deflator. A reasonable inflation rate for this whole period would be no more than 2 percent per annum, on average. At the upper bound, the real returns would have been quite substantial.

Source: Décima Urbana, Rio de Janeiro, 1849, 1870, 1888, AGCRJ.

in rough terms, the dataset divided into quintiles based on rates of increase over the period 1849–1888 (Table 25.2).

In order to model total returns to capital invested in real estate, one can add these estimates of the range of compound increase in property values, with the tax assessment as a proxy, to a range of estimates of annual rents. In order to capture some of the costs of property ownership, the model includes an estimate of the annual tax rate and also a factor for depreciation of physical structures and the implicit costs of repairs (Table 25.3).

At the upper-bound, property ownership was a very good investment, generating returns in capital gains, with rising property values, and in a regular stream of rental income. By reinvesting these returns in the purchase of additional properties, landlords were able to expand their real estate empires over time. Viewed from the point of view of renters, the rapid rise in property values, particularly between 1849 and 1870, must have posed significant economic challenges. Most families would have seen their rents rise by more than double during this period, and it was on the poorer periphery of the city where rents rose the fastest, implying that the greatest hardship associated with the rise in property values was likely shouldered by those who could least afford it. This rise in rents, particularly on the periphery, gave impulse to the sub-standard housing market based on subdivided properties and tenements.

Rentiers in spatial historical perspective

Rather than attempt a complete history of every kind of property ownership in Rio de Janeiro, a task that would be difficult if not impossible in a short essay, my intention here is to explore a critical category of owner – the wealthy landlord. For this purpose, I have selected Caetano José Ribeiro Lousada, a man who occupied an important position in the downtown real estate market as of 1849.[10] Owner of 29 properties, his total annual rent assessment, the basis of his property taxes, was 13:032$. Multiplied by the ratio of rents to actual property values, this implies a real estate fortune of around 130:000$.[11] In 1849, this amounted to a very large sum, given that the mean property owner in the same year held properties with a mean annual rental assessment of 1:088$ (in terms of property values, about $10:000). In subsequent years, it is possible to track the history of these properties and thereby illustrate important aspects of the urban property system, including the role of inheritance in determining long-term patterns in property holding.

Properties owned by Caetano José clustered around the intersection of Rua do Fogo and Rua Senhor dos Passos, to the west of the central business district and north of the bohemian theater district (Figure 25.1). His most valuable property, number 25, Rua da Ajuda, was assessed at 1:608$. A two-story structure with the lower level rented out to a commercial establishment, this may also have served as Caetano José's home for a time.

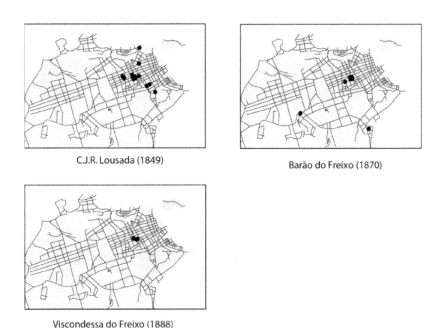

C.J.R. Lousada (1849)

Barão do Freixo (1870)

Viscondessa do Freixo (1888)

Figure 25.1 Properties of Caetano José Ribeiro Lousada and descendants, 1849–88.

Note: Closely located properties may overlap.

Source: Décima Urbana, 1849, 1870, 1888. Arquivo Geral da Cidade, Rio de Janeiro (AGCRJ).

Caetano José was the owner of a candle and soap factory located in the Rua do Fogo, number 37 (Figure 25.2).[12] Along with the candle works, he also owned a 184-ton ship, the *Sympathia*, indicating that he was engaged in seaborne commerce as well as manufacturing.[13] A successful entrepreneur, he probably expanded his property holdings all around his candle and soap factory. The annual rental assessment of the factory building itself was just 288$000. One avenue to property wealth, then, was entrepreneurial success in the growing urban marketplace. Rather than build an ever-larger candle factory, Caetano José likely channeled some his investments into the more prestigious and safer urban property market. As such, he will serve our purpose well as a representative of intensely localized property accumulation by resident entrepreneurs in the city in the decade of the 1840s.

Although Caetano José owned property in other parts of the city, the corner of the Rua do Fogo and Senhor dos Passos was the unquestioned center of his activities as a landlord. In terms of spatial scale, the neighborhood mattered a great deal. It is likely that Caetano José knew the area like the back of his hand and that he was attuned to opportunities to purchase neighboring properties, of which he would have a clear idea as to value. Moreover, as he purchased property in the neighborhood, he would have become a known entity to other prospective sellers. His activities in acquiring this small real estate empire in the neighborhood would prove decisive in subsequent years, long after he left the scene. Properties accumulated in groups were often either inherited by heirs or sold in groups, thereby constituting an ongoing pattern of concentration in the ownership of urban real estate.

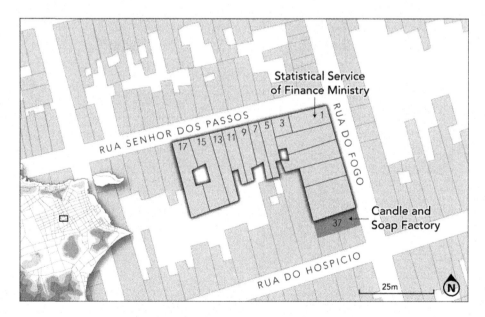

Figure 25.2   Detail and context of Caetano José Ribeiro Lousada's properties.

Source: Décima Urbana, 1849, AGCRJ; Almanak Laemmert, 1849. Map designed by Erik Steiner, Center for Spatial and Textual Analysis, Stanford University.

This pattern of localized accumulation meant that many neighborhoods contained pockets of stability in the sea of flux that typified the overall property market. Over two generations, most property would change hands in this little stretch of the Rua Senhor dos Passos, but over shorter spans, there was much more stability (Table 25.4). From 1870 to 1888, if we count the Viscondessa do Freixo as a continuous owner via her common property with the Barão, and we add the two properties owned continuously by Castão, then five of fourteen properties were still in the same hands.

Who were these property owners? As has been noted, Lousada was the owner of a candle and soap factory, along with a vast real estate portfolio circa 1849. He was rich, but the foundation of his fortune was as base as they come: rendered fat. The story of his properties is made especially interesting because he transferred them, probably in the early 1850s, to Antonio Affonso Vellado, the future Barão do Freixo, a title he held in Portugal, not Brazil.[14] The Baron, still known as Vellado at the time, first appears in the 1852 *Almanak* tied to just one address: number 37, Rua do Fogo, the candle and soap works previously owned by Lousada. Before becoming a Baron, Vellado is only listed as owning two modest properties in Rio de Janeiro circa 1849. His fortunes evidently improved quite dramatically shortly thereafter. Since Lousada does not appear in the 1851 *Almanak* or indeed in any subsequent database, it seems quite likely that he passed away around that time, leaving the candle and soap works to his son-in-law Vellado.[15]

By 1855, Vellado had moved his candle and soap works to the emerging center of production of these items in the area around Gamboa.[16] This migration out of the city center was typical of industries associated with odors and public nuisances.[17] In the new location, it can be reasonably assumed that he expanded his operations and built an even larger fortune than he had inherited from Lousada, paving the way to his eventual ennoblement in Portugal. This process was doubtless abetted by his moving from Brazil and residence in Portugal as of 1857.[18] At this stage, he made the full transition from odiferous candle and soapmaking entrepreneur to Europe-based absentee landlord.

Numbers 7 and 9 were owned, in 1888, by Pedro José da Costa Paiva, owner of a pawnshop and money lending business located, during the 1870s, in the same street. By 1888, the pawnshop had moved to the nearby address of number 6, Praça da Constituição. Neither Sá nor Castão, each owners of multiple properties, appear in the *Almanak* database. Likewise, Quintanilha and Joaquim Claro dos Santos do not appear. Antonio Manoel Ferreira Guimarães, owner of numbers 3 and 27 as of 1888, was also the proprietor of a cabinetmaking business and a furniture warehouse. In addition to this, he is listed as a capitalist and property owner. His cabinetmaking enterprise is listed at number 10, Rua Senhor dos Passos. Guimarães owned other properties along the street, including numbers 12, and 14 on the same side as his business. Another businessman, José Antonio Martins de Freitas, owned number 27 as of the assessment of 1870. Owner of a dry goods warehouse in numbers 25/27 since the late 1850s, José Antonio disappears from the property assessment rolls and the city directory after 1880 – most likely he died. His property was then purchased by Guimarães, another businessman and property owner. Anselmo da Luz Alvez Ribeiro, a businessman headquartered with an office in number 192 Rua do Hospício, owned number 19 Rua Senhor dos Passos in 1849. Anselmo owned quite a lot of

Table 25.4 A neighborhood history of ownership, Rua Senhor dos Passos, 1840s–80s.

Number	Owner 1849	Rent 1849	Owner 1870	Rent 1870	Owner 1888	Rent 1888
1	CJR Louzada	1:368$	Barão Freixo	2:688$	JAS Veloso	2:700$
3	CJR Louzada	384$	Barão Freixo	720$	AMF Guimarães	720$
5	CJR Louzada	396$	Barão Freixo	792$	JC Machado	840$
7	CJR Louzada	348$	Barão Freixo	696$	PJC Paiva	780$
9	CJR Louzada	408$	Barão Freixo	684$	PJC Paiva	780$
11	CJR Louzada	240$	Barão Freixo	1:044$	MF Sa	1:560$
13	CJR Louzada	144$	Barão Freixo	1:260$	Viscondessa Freixo	1:500$
15	CJR Louzada	144$	Barão Freixo	comb. with 17	Viscondessa Freixo	comb. with 17
17/15	CJR Louzada	120$	Barão Freixo	1:260$	Viscondessa Freixo	1:620$
19/17new	ALA Ribeiro	480$	JR Quintanilha	1:200$	MF Sa	1:800$
21/19	JJS Castão	300$	JC Santos	1:260$	JC Santos	1:200$
23/21	JJS Castão	216$	JJS Castão	540$	JJS Castão	600$
25/23	JJS Castão	192$	JJS Castão	540$	JJS Castão	540$
27/25	JJS Castão	288$	JAM Freitas	480$	AMF Guimarães	1080$

Source: Décima Urbana, Rio de Janeiro, 1849, 1870, 1888, AGCRJ.

property, placing him on par with Caetano José Ribeiro Lousada. The difference between them was the fact that Anselmo's main property interests were in other streets. Insofar as we can tell, then, the owners of properties along this little stretch of the Rua Senhor dos Passos were entirely drawn from the business class. Virtually all of the identified property owners also held property in other parts of the city.

Another useful example of the narrow group of big property holders is provided by the case of Maria Bibiana Araújo, owner of properties assessed at a total annual rent of 9:152$ in 1849. Gender and property holding were inextricably connected in Rio de Janeiro. Inheritance law and the vagaries of life ensured that a substantial proportion of all property was perpetually in the hands of women. Men were as likely to come into property through marriage (see the Barão do Freixo) as they were to collect it through their hard work and investment. Women also held property and were listed as owners even when they were married, although the law did give husbands a degree of control over their wives' economic activities. Maria Bibiana is unusual only inasmuch as she is much richer than the average woman property holder in the city.

As with Caetano José Ribeiro Lousada, there is a clear pattern of clustering in the properties of Maria Bibiana. She is listed in the *Alamank Laemmert*, of 1859, as a capitalist and property owner. Her business address, and most likely her home address as well, is listed at number 287, Rua do Hospício (Figure 25.3). Zooming in on this

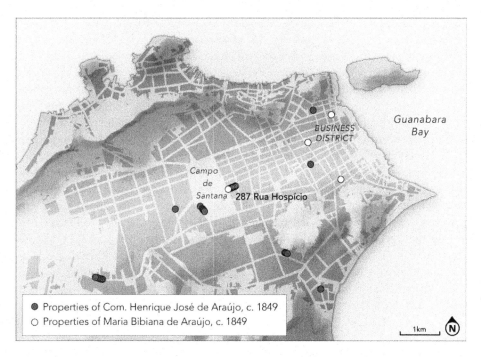

Figure 25.3 The properties of Maria Bibiana Araújo and Henrique José de Araújo, c. 1849.

Source: Décima Urbana, 1849, AGCRJ. Map designed by Erik Steiner, Center for Spatial and Textual Analysis, Stanford University.

Note: Closely located properties may overlap.

neighborhood, we see that her main property, number 287, stands at the intersection of the Rua do Hospício and the Rua dos Inválidos, bordering on the expanses of the Campo de Sant'Anna, Rio de Janeiro's largest public space. Along with this large property, she owned practically the entire south side of the block running from the Campo down Rua do Hospício to the Rua do Nuncio. Married to an equally wealthy man, Comendador Henrique José de Araújo, a relation of the Barão de Pirassinunga, together this socially prominent couple owned property with assessed annual rents approaching 30 contos. Consider that the income of a common laborer in 1849 averaged no more than 150 mil-réis – just 1/200th of the annual rents due this couple. Henrique's home base was on the other side of the square, in the Praca da Acclamação, very near the senate building.

In keeping with her designation as a 'capitalist and property owner', Maria Bibiana's real estate empire, when combined with her husband's, spanned the whole of the old city, with offshoots into some outlying districts. Several clusters of properties appear, suggesting that the properties in the couple's portfolio were purchased (or inherited) in bunches.

The property owners used in these examples show a pattern of clustered real estate holdings with offshoots sprinkled around the city, suggesting that the mode of accumulation and concentration of real property was both one of gradual conquest of neighboring properties and, to a lesser degree, a citywide strategy of purchase and administration. Although the city was still small in 1849, it made sense for property owners to concentrate their holdings in small areas where they could monitor and administer their property continually and with relative ease. In addition to this, the clustering of properties suggests that the real estate market was not entirely developed or competitive. Even so, all three individuals (if we include both members of the Araújo marriage) in our two case-study examples also branched out into properties at some distance from their core holdings. The pattern, in the 1840s, was thus one of clusters and small offshoots – outposts of property in other neighborhoods.

By the 1880s, the city was bursting at the seams, having more than doubled in population. Suburbs sprang up and filled in to the south, west, and northwest of the old city center. Patterns of real estate accumulation shifted with the transformation of the city, as neighborhoods were linked by better transportation, street lighting expanded the zones of commerce and the hours of street activity, and the cost and quality of real estate changed according to these and other neighborhood factors.

The most prominent urban property owners, by the late 1888s, held far more property than their counterparts four decades earlier. Bras Antonio Carneiro, one of the richest men in Rio de Janeiro, held no fewer than 173 urban properties as of 1888. Rather than clustering in one particular neighborhood, his holdings formed smaller clusters in diverse parts of the city. The total rental assessment for this empire of real estate came to 127:008$, a truly staggering sum that implied total holdings worth perhaps 1,127:000$ in 1888 values.[19]

Neighborhoods and networks

At this point, we can operationalize one of the concepts I have developed for the purpose of neighborhood-level spatial history. If blocks are construed as neighborhoods,

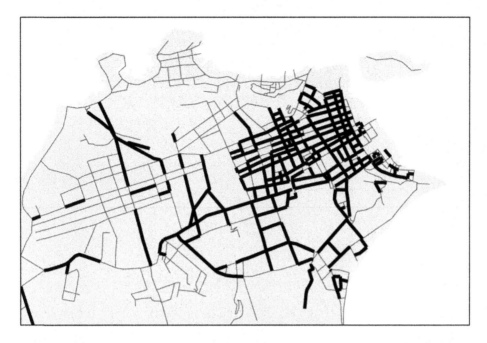

Figure 25.4 The City of Rio de Janeiro in the nineteenth century with blocks for analysis highlighted.

Source: Décima Urbana, 1849, 1870, 1888, AGCRJ.

then the intersection of these two streets can represent two adjoining neighborhoods. How far afield were Caetano José's other properties and in what kinds of neighborhoods?

Caetano José owned property that could be geocoded accurately in 29 locations distributed in seven blocks around the city. Because I am interested in comparing neighborhoods over time and the coverage from the property tax registers is not perfectly continuous, I have selected a subset of blocks for which good information is available for all three years in the database (Figure 25.4). The selection is broadly representative of the fabric of the city, but there are gaps. In the spirit of exploration rather than definitive representation, I have elected to use these blocks as the source for constructing a network model of neighborhoods. In each of the three years for which I have data, every block was coded as to the names of property owners and the values and numbers of their properties therein. With this information, one can generate network diagrams of property ownership wherein the blocks serve as the primary nodes and individual property owners provide the connections.

Returning to the story of Caetano José Ribeiro Lousada, our landlord based in and around the intersection of the Rua do Fogo and the Rua Senhor dos Passos, it is possible to measure his centrality within a network of blocks joined by people. Owing to his many properties in multiple neighborhoods, it comes as no surprise that Caetano José is located near the center of the force-directed graph (Figures 25.5 and 25.6). His network 'degree', measured in terms of the number of edges

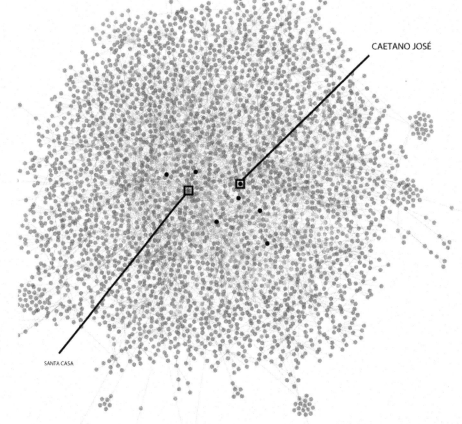

Figure 25.5 Property owners and networks of neighborhoods, 1849.

Note: Network generated by links between blocks forged by property owners in common. Black dots indicate network location of Caetano José's blocks. The largest property owner, the Santa Casa da Misericordia, is also indicated with respect to its network position.

Source: Décima Urbana, Rio de Janeiro, 1849.

connecting his node to various blocks is seven. This is by no means the highest value seen for an individual property owner. That honor goes to João da Costa Lima, with twelve edges. Nevertheless, Caetano José is highly ranked by this and other measures of centrality and connectivity. He is one of the small subset of property owners with extensive holdings spread across the city. His centrality is enhanced, likewise, by his ownership of property in central blocks that were popular with other major property holders.

Viewed in this respect, taking just the blocks he owned property in and connecting those to other property owners, we see that he shared ownership in several blocks with the most important institutional property holder in the city, the charity hospital known as the Santa Casa da Misericordia.

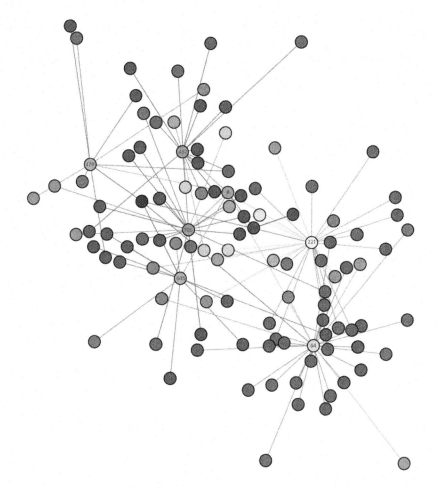

Figure 25.6 Caetano José's properties and related blocks in focus.

Note: Caetano José is indicated by the letter A in the node near the center of the graph and his blocks are indicated by their numbers. Other nodes refer to property owners associated with the designated blocks.

Source: Décima Urbana, 1849, 1870, 1888. Arquivo Geral da Cidade, Rio de Janeiro (AGCRJ).

One advantage of this approach to modeling the network of property ownership is that it allows for the analysis of the centrality of blocks themselves. Which blocks were central to the network of ownership and did the rank order of top blocks change in any significant way over time?

By constructing a historical GIS model of property ownership in the city, and by tying owners to blocks and blocks to other blocks through owners, a network of relations is generated. This network allows for the testing of critical hypotheses regarding the functioning of the property market. For instance, one hypothesis is that blocks that are central to the owner-linked network will exhibit different tendencies owing to the *greater concentration of information* about rents more generally. It is as if these blocks 'knew' more about what went on in other blocks, owing to the way that the owners connected them across the city. If this claim has any purchase in reality, several predictions can be made and tested. If blocks were 'central' to the network of information and home to many well-connected owners, this better information should lead to less variation in rents and there should be a convergence in the rate of growth in rents toward the city-wide mean.[20] Properties would be priced 'right' because of access to comparative information across many blocks. Because the market was competitive, no one owner would have access to significantly better information. The best-connected blocks in this network framework should, therefore, show relatively less variation in the values of properties and rates of growth over time. Conversely, the least connected blocks should show the greatest variance, as information regarding prices in other places would be far less evenly distributed and the 'consensus' on the right price would be partial at best.

At low levels of eigenvector centrality, between 0 and 0.01, the variance in observed rates of change in rents on the y-axis is enormous. For the small number of very central blocks with eigenvector values above 0.15, the variance is much less. Above a centrality value of 0.02, the variance practically vanishes.[21]

A related prediction, also derived from the information network hypothesis, is that reasonably well-networked blocks should generally exhibit a tendency to match or exceed the citywide mean in terms of rates of change. In other words, just as highly networked blocks will converge strongly toward the mean, all reasonably networked blocks should reside within a relatively close range of the mean and the greatest concentration of poor performers should be located in the lower left quadrant of a scatterplot.

Further statistical analysis offers support for the hypothesis that blocks more tightly networked through ownership exhibited a distinctive pattern with respect to the rate of growth in mean rental values. The closeness centrality statistic measures the distance from a given node to all other nodes in a connected network. The more central the node in question, the shorter those cumulative paths will be. In terms of information, this can be taken to represent a situation wherein knowledge about rental rates across the city is particularly concentrated in the more central nodes (blocks) because owners in that block will have the least network distance to travel in order to flesh out their information on the state of the rental market. Owing to

Table 25.5 Coefficient of variation regressed on degree and closeness centrality by block, Rio de Janeiro.

N obs	226				
F (2, 223)	10.7				
Prob > F	0.00				
R-squared	0.087				
	Coefficient	Std. Err.	t	P>|t|	Beta
Degree	−0.0001525	0.0000625	−2.44	0.02	−0.183
Closeness	−0.05193	0.025108	−2.07	0.04	−0.155
Constant	0.0223	0.004701	4.76	0.00	.

Note: Covar calculated on absolute values of difference in means.
Source: Decima Urbana, 1849, AGCRJ.

the fact that centrality measures are partially correlated with the number of owners in a given block (degree), I ran an OLS regression with degree as a control variable along with closeness centrality. Even after controlling for degree, the results of the regression show a negative and significant coefficient when the absolute mean variance from the average rate of increase is entered as the dependent variable (Table 25.5). The higher the closeness centrality, the lower the variance from the average rent increase.

Finally, the historical GIS approach bears upon the interpretation of these results, as the distribution of blocks according to rates of increase in value can be seen to be broadly distributed in such a way that the result is not merely an artifact of tendencies in localized zones of the city. Rates of increase cannot be boiled down, in the 1849–70 period, to specific areas of the city. The abstract network of blocks, therefore, may better represent the distribution of knowledge about rental conditions than a simple proximity model would imply.

More broadly, two processes were at work between 1849 and 1888, both of which added to the degree of inequality in property ownership in the city. First, there was the growth of great fortunes, which concentrated property in the hands of Carneiro and his ilk. Second, there was the continual subdivision of property in the city center among the many heirs and business partners of decedents from the earlier, more egalitarian period of the 1840s. By the 1880s, it was not uncommon for a single building to be assessed with several rents attributable to shared owners (brothers, sisters, cousins, and the like). While this had the effect of distributing property among a larger number of people than otherwise would have been the case, it also meant the proliferation of smallholdings, which translates into greater measures of inequality vis-à-vis the wealthy few. Along similar lines, the process of fragmentation also took hold of the interior of the buildings and urban lots in questions. The numbers of buildings divided up into single residential rooms (quartos) increased dramatically. In some cases, these collective housing operations spilled over to take account of neighboring buildings, resulting in tenement houses and vast tenement slums known as *cortiços*.

The neighborhood through the eyes of renters

Returning to the Rua Senhor dos Passos, who were the renters in this neighborhood? It is important to maintain the distinction between those renters whom we can identify, via the city directory, and other renters who no doubt occupied some of the buildings (or rooms) along this stretch of the street. The former, because they appear in the city directory, cannot generally be viewed as poor. They might be modest of means, but poor they are not.

Noteworthy changes are discernible in the mix of tenants along this little stretch of the Rua Senhor dos Passos. The dominant businesses were carriage works and blacksmith outfits during the 1850s. By the 1870s, the area was almost completely dominated by furniture warehouses. Finally, in a shift that may have resulted in a return to an older pattern of tenancy, a lawyer and a barber appear by 1880.

Keeping strictly to the side of the street numbered 1–27, we find the following tenants or owners, the latter highlighted with asterisks.

Occupants in the Rua Senhor dos Passos according to the *Almanak Laemmert* (1840s–1880s):

<u>1845</u>
#19 Francisco de Paula Santos Gomes, medical doctor

<u>1849</u>
No addresses listed in the *Almanak Laemmert* for this stretch of the street

<u>1854</u>
#19 Antonio José de Albuquerque, businessman, cabinetmaking operation
#21 Caetano Miguel da Luz, loja de corrieiros e forradores de carros
#23–25 Jacob Boebunke, blacksmith shop

<u>1859</u>
#1 Antonio Joaquim Teixeira Bastos, businessman, drygoods
#15 Antonio Curvelo Avila, blacksmith, sawsmith
#21 Caetano Miguel da Luz, loja de corrieiros e forradores de carros
#23–25, Jacob Boebunke, blacksmith, sawsmith
#23, manufacture of carriages and carts

<u>1870</u>
#1 Antonio J. Freitas, carpentry and furniture warehouse
#13 Albino Dias Pacheco, furniture warehouse
#15 Antonio Curvelo Avila, furniture warehouse (note the change)
#19 Antonio Fernandes Almeida, furniture warehouse
#21 Firmino Fernandes Castro, furniture warehouse
#23 Albino Pacheco Seabra, furniture warehouse
#25 Pascoal João Santos, furniture warehouse
#27 *José Antonio Martins de Freitas, drygoods

<u>1880</u>
#9 Feliciano Pinheiro Bittencourt, medical doctor
#13 Antonio Manoel Ferreira Guimarães, furniture warehouse
#15 Albino Santos Pereira, lawyer
#25/old #27 *José Antonio Martins de Freitas, capitalist
#25/old #27 Antonio Ferreira dos Santos, barber

Numbers 3 through 7 are never listed in the *Almanak*, nor is number 11. Otherwise, all of the numbers in this group were occupied at some point in time by a commercial establishment, an artisan, or a professional such as a doctor or lawyer. It seems likely that 3–7 and 11 were residential properties. They are among the smaller buildings on the block, of just one story as late as 1888, and assessed rents were correspondingly low. Number 5, for instance, occupied just under 700 square feet, with a small garden (open air) space of another 120 square feet. In 1849, a family renting this house would have paid a shade under 500 reis per square foot in rent. Translated into other values of the time, the annual rent of 396$ was roughly equal to the price of a prime age male slave in the city of Rio de Janeiro, or about three times the annual unskilled wage.[22] The residential quarters in this stretch, then, were not likely home to the very poor, unless two or more families shared the same small space.

If occupied by a single family in the 1840s, these households were headed indi-viduals earning something more than 1:000$ per annum and probably less than 3:000$ or 4:000$, which would have sufficed to pay for more comfortable lodgings away from the smoke of the blacksmiths and the bustle of the furniture shops. By the 1880s, however, prices had risen significantly throughout the city, even after accounting for inflation, and the type of renter in number 5, or Doctor Bittencourt in number 9 for that matter, had probably changed as well with the migration of many 'nuisance' establishments to lower-rent districts on the city periphery.

Voter qualification records provide critical evidence regarding the approximate incomes of renters as well as their occupations and other details. Although inherently limited as a source to the native born and naturalized, these records illustrate the range of people and financial circumstances associated with renters in the vicinity of Caetano José's cluster of properties. This is the other side of the rentier–renter equation. By con-necting voters to parcels through addresses, the spatial history of rent takes shape.

First, very few voters owned the residences they occupied according to the qual-ification rolls. An examination of 318 voters listed in the neighborhood in and around the Rua do Hospício yields just seven matches (2 percent) for the names or family names of voters in the corresponding list of property owners.[23] This result is frankly surprising. Qualified voters were only enrolled if they could prove a certain income level. Although the income level was not set particularly high, this group, if any, might have been expected to display a moderately high degree of property ownership with respect to their domicile.[24]

The average income-to-rent ratio in this neighborhood of the city was 1.62. It is unlikely that a person, even a single male worker, would pay this proportion of income on rent alone. Many voters must have shared accommodations with other renters. Having noted this, it is also evident that voters at different life stages and with different kinds of family background would find themselves more or less capable of making the rent and living without sharing space with other renters. Among married voters, the ratio of income to rent averaged 2.04 – perhaps just entering the realm of the possible. Families would be far less keen to share space with other renters than would single men; it took money to get married and married men generally earned higher incomes. Similarly, with respect to filiation, those voters for whom a father's name was entered in the rolls earned incomes with a ratio of 1.76 to the rents asso-ciated with their addresses. On the other hand, ratios for single voters and for those without named fathers were 1.29 and 1.22 respectively.

Ratios for high-status occupations were, as would be expected, higher: 4.33 for lawyers and 5.41 for medical men. These professionals could afford the rents in the area without great difficulty. Artisans and public employees fared far worse, with ratios of 0.71 and 1.09 respectively.

By the 1870s, rising rents and population pressures culminated in the growth of col-lective housing on the periphery of the city center. Where rents remained relatively low and use-value was largely associated with residential purposes, rooming houses, tene-ments, and larger conglomerations known as *cortiços* provided roofs over the heads of a growing number of poorer residents. The urban property tax rolls contain precious information on the size and location of these collective residences, indicating the number of rooms into which a given property had been divided for rental purposes (Figure 25.7).

Tenement Housing in Rio de Janiero, 1870

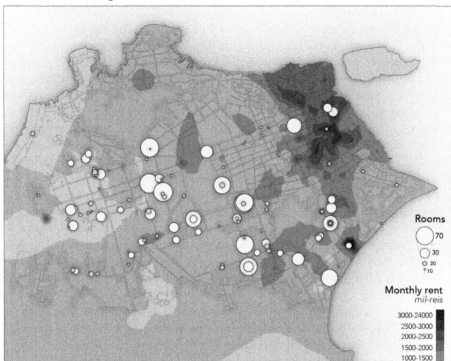

*Figure 25.*7   Tenements and cortiços in Rio de Janeiro, 1870.

Source: Décima Urbana, 1870, AGCRJ. Map designed by Erik Steiner, Center for Spatial and Textual Analysis, Stanford University.

In the two decades after 1870, the population of the city surged toward half a million residents. Collective housing also expanded and began to encroach more expressively in the old city center, especially to the east of the Campo de Santana, where in earlier times only a few such tenements were to be found. This process of growth and encroachment can be seen graphically in Figure 25.8, bearing in mind the distinction between the existence of a few outlier properties in the 1870s and the much greater number of tenements in the 1880s. This pattern can be further explored in an online visualization published on the Spatial History website.[25] Throughout this era of growth in tenement housing, renters and rentiers conducted a dance of unbalanced but reciprocal exchange. Renters needed cheap housing. This was especially the case for the many single male workers drawn to the growing metropolitan economy.

On the other side of the ledger, counting their rental receipts, owners of these properties cashed in on the hunger for shelter among the poor workers of the city. Properties that would otherwise have been relatively low in value suddenly became

Tenement Housing in Rio de Janiero, 1888

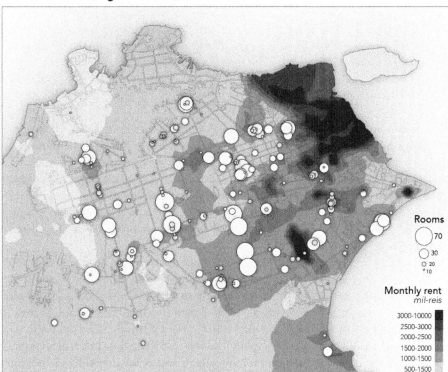

Figure 25.8 Tenements and cortiços in Rio de Janeiro, 1888.

Source: Décima Urbana, 1888, AGCRJ. Map designed by Erik Steiner, Center for Spatial and Textual Analysis, Stanford University.

some of the most remunerative addresses in the neighborhood and, indeed, in the city as a whole. Poverty was thereby hitched to prosperity for the lucky few.

Conditions of living, meanwhile, were far from salubrious. Using a government survey of *cortiços* and rooming houses, it is possible to estimate the living space in cubic feet given over to the average renter of a tenement room. Measured in this way, the poorest renters can be seen to have paid some of the highest rents per unit of living space in the city. The average area for living, according to this report, was a mere 7.1 meters per resident. Some individuals made do with just 2 square meters of living space – implying, perhaps, a pattern of sleeping in shifts or otherwise sharing space.[26]

Government officials took aim at cortiços as a primary source of disease in the city. Yellow fever, in particular, was associated with these dark and tight living spaces filled with poor workers. In a representative report from 1884, Francisco Antunes Maciel summarizes the predominant stance of health officials. He suggests that all cortiços 'infesting' the old city neighborhoods be condemned. What is more, any new collective housing built in the periphery should provide, according to this plan, a minimum area of 9 square meters of living space, with 4 meters of air space.[27] Although it would take decades to fully implement this plan, over time the *cortiços* were gradually removed from the core of the city. Poverty moved out into the suburbs and up into the hills where present-day communities (popularly known as favelas) cling to steep slopes above the formal space of the city.

Conclusion

This chapter attempts to move across several spatial and temporal scales.[28] It draws inspiration from the idea of a spatial history that explores and probes the outlines of the past rather than attempt an impossible complete accounting. All the tools and concepts are fair game in this exploratory research. Flashes of the past can appear as dots on a series of maps or the coefficient in a regression model. Stories about individual people can be sketched out, placed in a spatial context, and leveraged to imagine the challenges and opportunities associated with urban property in nineteenth-century Rio de Janeiro.

This approach suggests that the range of methods in historical GIS can be expanded in fruitful ways to include dimensions of human experience within and beyond the map. The intersection of distinct datasets and movement across scales of space and time responds to criticism of GIS as a top-down and distant view for historical research. Spatial relations can be recoded as networked relations. Data can begin in a coordinate space and end in a scatterplot. Outliers and difference can emerge as relevant categories alongside the general tendency to search for patterns and coherent geographical units.

Notes

1 See Paul Carter, *The Road to Botany Bay*, London: Faber & Faber, 1987. GI science might seem antithetical to Carter's notion of spatial history. It need not be so. ESRI's ArcMap can skim the waves along the coast rather than invade and settle the land.

2 The census of 1849 counted 205,906 inhabitants in the eight core parishes of the city, of whom 78,855 were slaves; the 1890 census enumerated 522,651 residents. 1849 census cited in Karash, *Slave Life*, Princeton, NJ: Princeton University Press, 1987, 66. 1890 figures published in *Recenseamento Geral 1890*, Rio de Janeiro: Typ. Leuzinger, 1895, 401.

3 For information on the growth of the financial sector, see William Summerhill, 'Sovereign Credibility', esp. table 5. For more on partnerships, see Ran Abramitzky, Zephyr Frank, and Aprajit Mahajan. 'Risk, Incentives, and Contracts: Partnerships in Rio de Janeiro, 1870–1891', *Journal of Economic History* 70(3), 2010, 686–715.

4 For the process of abolition, see Leslie Bethell, *The Abolition of the Brazilian Slave Trade: Britain, Brazil and the Slave Trade Question,* Cambridge: Cambridge University Press, 1970; and Robert Brent Toplin, *The Abolition of Slavery in Brazil*, New York: Atheneum, 1975.

5 Real urban property as a portion of wealth in Rio de Janeiro is discussed in Zephyr Frank, *Dutra's World: Wealth and Family in Nineteenth-Century Rio de Janeiro*, Albuquerque, NM: University of New Mexico Press, 2004, 78, 90.

6 Lançamento da décima urbana, Rio de Janeiro, Arquivo Geral da Cidade.

7 The *Almanak Laemmert*, for which the complete title during the era in question was *Almanak administrativo, mercantile e industrial do Rio de Janeiro*, contained lists of residents according to occupation and other social categories.

8 The key source is J. Cruvello Cavalcanti, *Nova Numeraçao dos Prédios da Cidade do Rio de Janeiro,* Rio de Janeiro: Typ. Gazeta das Notícias, 1878. This book lists property owners and corresponding new and old street numbers. The address ranges for each block could be inserted on the basis of the Gotto map digitized by the Cecult team at UNICAMP with assistance from the Spatial History Project at Stanford. The Gotto map can be explored online at: www.ifch.unicamp.br/cecult/mapas/mapasgotto1905/gotto1905.

9 Nineteenth-century Brazilian currency was denoted in mil-réis. 1:000$000 represented one thousand mil-réis, or one conto. This was worth roughly $500 dollars.

10 Caetano José's surname is sometimes spelled Louzada. In the text of this chapter, I use the spelling most common in the printed sources.

11 For data on the market prices for properties in 1849, see 'Recebedoria das sizas dos bens de raiz do ano financeiro de 1849/50', Arquivo Nacional, Rio de Janeiro, livro 19. In a sample of 55 transactions, the average value was 5:716$. This should be taken as an upper-bound for the ratio of rent to market value (0.19), as the small size of the sample does not capture less frequently occurring high-value properties, suppressing the mean. Further research in estate inventories suggests that the ratio was most likely closer to 0.10.

12 *Almanak*, 1848, 451.

13 *Almanak*, 1848, 411.

14 Vellado was ennobled as a Baron in 1865 and a Viscount in 1870. Augusto Soares d'Azevedo Barbosa de Pinho Leal, *Portugal antigo e moderno; diccionario . . . de todas as cidades, villas e freguezias de Portugal e de grande numero de aldeias,* vol. 7, Lisbon: Editora Mattos Moreira & Cia, 1876, 493.

15 Vellado was married to Laurinda Ribeiro Lousada. Note that the spelling of the last name varies across the documents. Esteves Pereira, *Portugal; diccionario historico, biographico, bibliographico,* vol. 3, Lisbon: João Romano Torres, 1907, 508.

16 *Almanak*, 1855, 595.

17 See Frank, 'Layers, Flows and Intersections: Jeronymo José de Mello and Artisan Life in Rio de Janeiro, 1840s–1880s', *Journal of Social History* 41(2), 2007, 307–28.

18 *Almanak*, 1857, 498. The circumstances of Vellado's departure from Brazil are murky. In 1856, an associate of Vellado's was apprehended in Rio de Janeiro on the charge of possessing counterfeit money. The details of this case are summarized in a consular report republished in the *Almanak*, 1865, supplement, p. 70.

19 Décima urbana, Arquivo Geral da Cidade, Rio de Janeiro, 1888.

20 For a classic statement, see Sanford J. Grossman and Joseph E. Stiglitz, 'Information and Competitive Price Systems', *American Economic Review* 66(2), 1976, 246–53. To be clear, my analysis is not an attempt to apply the questionable assumptions of efficient markets theory. Rather, it is to insist that the greater the information regarding the value and relative availability of property, the greater the tendency toward price convergence.

21 The coefficient of variation for the blocks with very low closeness scores (<.009) is 0.51; for those blocks with high closeness scores (>.15) the corresponding coefficient of variation is 0.001. Closeness scores reflect the centrality of a given node (in this case, a block) in a network by measuring how close it is to all other blocks. In simple terms, a block that can trace short paths to other blocks will have a higher score.

22 For the unskilled manual wage, see Frank, *Dutra's World*, 100, table 8.

23 Qualificação dos eleitores, Sacramento, 1880.

24 *Constituições do Brasil*, São Paulo: Ed. Saraiva, 1967, 20–1. The 1824 constitution set the income requirements at 100$ for lesser offices and 200$ for voting in higher political offices.

25 Please see: http://web.stanford.edu/group/spatialhistory/cgi-bin/site/viz.php?id=45& project_id=0.

26 For the interior space of tenements, see: IS4–32, Ministério do Império, Junta de Higiene, s.d. Note: the author is grateful to the Cecult research center at the Universidade Estadual de Campinas (UNICAMP) for access to the underlying data required to calculate these figures.

27 Francisco Antunes Maciel, *Relatorio apresentado assemblea geral legislativa quarta sessao decima oitava legislatura pelo ministro e secretario de estado dos negocios do imperio*, Rio de Janeiro: Typ. Nacional, 1884, annexos, 'Projecto dos novos alojamentos para a classe pobre da ciaded do Rio de Janeiro'.

28 A fine example of spatial history conducted across temporal and spatial scales and moving from pattern to idiosyncratic individual stories is found in Brian Donahue, 'Husbandry in Colonial Concord: GIS as a Tool for Environmental History', in A. K. Knowles (ed.), *Placing History: How Maps, Spatial Data, and GIS are Changing the Practice of History*, Redlands, CA: ESRI, 2008.

26

THE SECOND BATTLE OF YPRES AND A NORTHERN ENGLISH TOWN

Digital humanities and the First World War

Ian Gregory and Corinna Peniston-Bird

The First World War holds a unique position in British history and memory. The war killed over 700,000 people out of a total British population of 33.5 million; overwhelmingly the casualties were men between their late teens and late thirties. In demographic terms alone, the War was an unrivalled catastrophe.[1]

Certain elements of the war have come to dominate its memory: the Western Front over all other fronts; trench warfare over all other types of warfare; the British Army being made up of 'lions led by donkeys' and a narrative arc tracing a journey from naïve patriotism to disillusionment, fed by the futile loss of life.[2] The epitome of futile slaughter has become the Battle of the Somme in the summer and autumn of 1916. The first day of the Somme, 1 July 1916, saw the worst casualties in the history of the British Army, usually put at 50,000. An orthodoxy has emerged of the Somme campaign that represents the battle as a series of large-scale attacks against a well-prepared enemy achieving little but high casualties. This narrative is also applied to the other battles that loom large in the popular British memory of the war, particularly Gallipoli in the spring of 1915 and Passchendaele, the Third Battle of Ypres, in the summer of 1917. Recent years have seen a backlash against this 'Blackadder history', a reference to the popular television comedy that portrayed the war very much in these terms.[3] However, despite historians' challenges, these emphases have proved resilient in the popular imagination. This project explores how the digital humanities and historical GIS can nuance or challenge the dominant versions of the war, with a case study of the impact of Second Battle of Ypres on the town of Lancaster.

In Lancaster, a town of 41,000 people in 1911,[4] on the fringes of what was then industrial Lancashire, the main war memorial lists just over 1,000 names in alphabetical order.[5] Unusually, it also brackets brothers together. The paper draws on a digital record of the town's casualties created by Lancaster Military Heritage Group (LMHG), a group dedicated to enhancing public understanding of the links between the military and the local community in Lancaster.[6] Research by LMHG created the Reveille website which records, among other things, details of all of the First World War casualties from Lancaster drawn from a number of official sources and contemporary local newspapers.[7] This information was presented to the public as a conventional HTML-based website in which casualties are listed alphabetically by surname.[8] This is effective for genealogical purposes or casual browsing but does not permit discernment of any patterns, nor the impact of the losses on the town. By converting the HTML into a database and adding additional information such as locations, we are able enhance it significantly to produce a more flexible resource. This chapter focuses on how digital technologies, especially geographical information systems (GIS), can be used better to understand the way this one English town was affected during its worst period of the War, April and May 1915. It reveals how each town has its own chronology of war dependent on where local men saw action and it shows how digital technologies can underpin the leap of imagination required to begin to comprehend the impact of the War on the British communities waging it. It enables us to see that the 'futile attack' story of the war, whatever its merits or critiques, is far from the only one that led to mass casualties.

Building the *Reveille* database

Figure 26.1 shows a screenshot of a typical record from the Reveille website, showing the details of one George Cathcart. As with the rest of the site, this record brings together information from a range of different sources including the Borough of Lancaster Civic Reception HM Forces Report Form, a set of documents produced after the War in part to help prepare the war memorial, Soldiers Died in the Great War 1914–1919, information from the Commonwealth War Graves Commission, and summaries of obituaries from two local newspapers: the *Lancaster Guardian* and the *Lancaster Observer*. From these sources we are able to determine what regiment George was in, his age and date of death, who his parents were and where they lived, where he is buried or in this case – because he has no known grave – where he is memorialized, a photograph of him in uniform, and some other brief information about his life, military service and death. There is also a note at the top that his brother J. Cathcart also died. A surprising amount of this information is geographical. Two residential addresses are given: '97 Dale Street, Lancaster' (twice) and 'Cable Street, Skerton' (Skerton is part of Lancaster), as well as the address of his father's employer 'the Probate Office, Cable Street, Lancaster'. He is memorialized on the Menin Gate at Ypres, Belgium, and can thus be assumed to have died nearby.[9] This is confirmed by the *Lancaster Guardian* which states he was killed at St Jean, Ypres. Records for other casualties often also include information on his former school and on his employer's address, other sources of potential geographical information that are not present here. There is also temporal information such as dates of death and length of service, and much thematic information about, for example, rank, battalion and regiment or marital status.

The challenge was to take this HTML-encoded alphabetical list and convert it into a database and then to one or more GIS layers that enable us to understand more about the history in which George Cathcart and his contemporaries from the town died.

G F CATHCART

+ BROTHER J BELOW

GEORGE CATHCART

Private 2093 1st/5th Bn., King's Own (Royal Lancaster Regt.)
who died on Friday, 23/04/1915 . Age 19 .
Son of John and Mary Cathcart, of 97, Dale St., Lancaster. Enlisted 4th Sept.1914

YPRES (MENIN GATE) MEMORIAL, Ref:Panel 12, Ieper, West-Vlaanderen, Belgium

Borough of Lancaster Civic Reception H M Forces Report Form shows:

George Frederick Cathcart. Resided at 97 Dale Street, Lancaster. A single man. Private 2093. 1/5 King's Own Royal Lancaster Reg He served for 6 months at home, and 2 months abroad. Volunteered 6 September 1914. Killed.

George Cathcart. Private. 2093.King's Own[Royal Lancaster Regt.] 1/5th Bn.
Born, and enlisted in Lancaster
Died 27/04/15. Killed in Action. France & Flanders.

Source: Soldiers Died in the Great War 1914-1919

Cathcart G Private 2093 5th Battalion Kings Own Royal Lancaster Regiment killed in action 27 April, 1916 at St Jean Ypres, father Mr J Cathcart of the Probate Office, Cable Street, Lancaster.

Source Lancaster Guardian date 27 April, 1916 page 8, photo Code 447, 448 .

Cathcart George F Private 5th Battalion Kings Own Royal Lancaster Regiment Missing on 23 April, 1915 (presumed killed in action), age 20, address Cable Street, Skerton (now in Lancaster),. A member of Bailrigg Cricket club, Mr Aldous' Choir, the Male Voice choir and St Peter's Church choir. Parents, Mr John and Mrs Cathcart. Informant, his brother Private James Cathcart (446, 449) who was advancing with him, when he was lost.

Source Lancaster Observer date 7 May,1915 page 8, also 21 May 1915, page 10, photo 18 June 1915 page 5, 12 November 1915 page 8 Code 447, 448

Figure 26.1   A typical record from the Reveille website: George Cathcart.

Source: www.lancasterwarmemorials.org.uk/memorials/lancaster-c.htm#170.

This is not as difficult as it might appear as the HTML data are presented in a fairly structured manner. A program was written to read the HTML text in and then identify, for example, which part of the text referred to name, rank, service number and so on. Additional information also helped with this: text following the words 'died on' or just 'died' is likely to be the date of death; the text between 'Resided at' and either 'Lancaster' or 'Skerton' is likely to be a home address; and so on. In this way we were able to convert the HTML into a tabular database with fields including name, flags for brothers killed, was an officer or had won a medal, rank, the day of the week and date of death, age, addresses, school, employer, and grave or memorial site. Clearly this required a little tidying but was a manageable task. A screenshot of the database, highlighting George Cathcart's record, is shown in Figure 26.2.

	A	B	C	D	E	F	G	H	I	J	K	L	M	N	O	P	Q	R	S	T	U	V	W	X
1	ID	LMHG_ID	Name1	Name2	Brother	Officer	Awards	Nationalit	Service	Rank	Regiment	Bn KORL	Rank_Etc	DoW_Dea	Day_Deat	Month_D	Year_Dea	Month_T	MonthYe	Full_Date	Age_Deat	Address1_	Address1_	Address1_
167	166	166	F CARTMELL	FRED CARTMELL					Army	Private	KORL	8th	Private 32	Wednesd	26	9	1917	Sep	Sep-1917	1917-09-26	27	80	Dorrington Rd.	
168	167	167	G CARTWRIGHT	GEORGE CARTWRIGHT					Army	Private	KORL	2nd/5th	Private 24	Thursday	29	8	1918	Aug	Aug-1918	1918-08-29	N/A			
169	168	168	R CASSON	RICHARD CASSON					Army	Private	KORL	1st/5th	Private 24	Friday	30	11	1917	Nov	Nov-1917	1917-11-30	28	97	Main St.	
170	169	169	R E CASSON	RICHARD ERNEST CASSON					Army	Private	KORL	2nd/5th	Private 24	Thursday	29	8	1918	Aug	Aug-1918	1918-08-29	28			
171	170	170	G F CATHCART	GEORGE CATHCART	Y				Army	Private	KORL	1st/5th	Private 20	Friday	23	4	1915	Apr	Apr-1915	1915-04-23	19	97	Dale St.	
172	171	171	J CATHCART	JAMES CATHCART	Y				Army	Private	KORL	1st/5th	Private 20	Tuesday	4	5	1915	May	May-1915	1915-05-04	17	97	Dale St.	
173	172	172	J CATON	JOSEPH CATON					Army	Private	KORL	2nd/5th	Private 24	Friday	26	10	1917	Oct	Oct-1917	1917-10-26	26	17	Charnley !	Marsh
174	173	173	A CAVE	ALFRED CAVE					Army	Private	KORL	1st/5th	Private 18	Friday	4	8	1916	Aug	Aug-1916	1916-08-04	24			
175	174	174	J CHAMBERLAIN	JOHN CHAMBERLAIN					Royal Flyi	Airman 3r	Royal Flying Corps		Airman 3r	Friday	30	11	1917	Nov	Nov-1917	1917-11-30	37			
176	175	175	W T CHAMBERLAIN	WILLIAM THOMAS CHAMBERLAIN					Army	Private	King's Own Yorkshir		Private 30	Monday	20	11	1916	Nov	Nov-1916	1916-11-20	26			
177	176	176	J CHAPMAN	JOHN CHAPMAN	Y				Army	Lance Cor	Royal Warwickshire		Lance Cor	Tuesday	9	10	1917	Oct	Oct-1917	1917-10-09	24	7	River St.	Quay
178	177	179	A S CHRISTIAN	ALBERT STANLEY CHRISTIAN					Army	Gunner	Royal Garrison Artill		Gunner 1C	Saturday	28	4	1917	Apr	Apr-1917	1917-04-28	N/A			
179	178	180	JAMES CHURCHOUSE	JAMES CHURCHOUSE					Army	Lance Cor	KORL	1st/5th	Lance Cor	Tuesday	31	7	1917	Jul	Jul-1917	1917-07-31	24	14	Marton St.	
180	179	181	JOHN CHURCHOUSE	JOHN CHURCHHOUSE					Army	Private	KORL	1st/5th	Private 10	Wednesd	14	4	1915	Apr	Apr-1915	1915-04-14	19	6	Marton St.	
181	180	182	E CLANCY	EDWARD CLANCY					Army	Private	Lancashire Fusiliers		Private 96	Friday	26	4	1918	Apr	Apr-1918	1918-04-26	N/A			
182	181	183	W CLAPHAM	WILLIAM CLAPHAM					Army	Corporal	KORL	1st/5th	Corporal 2	Tuesday	31	7	1917	Jul	Jul-1917	1917-07-31	N/A			

Figure 26.2 The database version of the Reveille website. George Cathcart's record is highlighted.

The next stage was to convert this into geographical information. The main geographies of interest are addresses associated with the casualty, mainly his address or the address of close relatives, and the addresses of schools or employers. The second geography is that associated with where the casualty died, given by the grave or memorial site. There are two possible strategies for geo-referencing addresses within Lancaster. One is to locate the casualties to the street the address is found on but not the actual house. This was done starting with Open Street Map, a crowd-sourced geo-referenced dataset originally created to provide data for GPS-based navigation systems free from national mapping agency or commercial copyright.[10] The modern streets for the area around Lancaster were downloaded and converted to a shapefile.[11] The street names were then matched to those in the Reveille database allowing each casualty to be linked to a street and the number of casualties in each street to be calculated. There have been some limited changes to street names over time, 'Germany Street' being renamed 'Caton Road' being one of the more poignant, and some minor changes to the street layout as a result of traffic improvements, but nonetheless over 80 per cent of casualties could be allocated to at least one home street. An alternative approach is to upload the full street address to online geo-referencing sites such as *FindLatitudeandLongitude*.[12] These claim to give the coordinates of individual house addresses based on the full address including number. Obviously, this depends on the assumption that house numbers (along with street names) have not changed over time, and the accuracy of the coordinates is not always clear. It did, however, appear to give good results that enable individual properties to be geo-referenced.

Other sources of geographical information were also geo-referenced. The locations of schools and employers were located from historical maps and trade directories and the coordinates for grave and memorial sites are available from the Commonwealth War Grave Commission website[13] and Google Maps.[14] Over 90 per cent of casualties could be allocated to a grave or memorial site.

Once the database and its associate GIS layers had been created, some initial exploration could be done. Of the 1,055 casualties listed on the Reveille site[15] 967 were in the army and 425 of these were in the King's Own Royal Lancaster Regiment (KORL), a regiment based in barracks in the town. 647 of the deaths were among private soldiers and only 42, less than 5 per cent of those where ranks were known, were officers, which perhaps points to Lancaster being a working-class town at the time. The mean age of death among Lancastrians was 26.6, but 19 was the most common age of death.[16] The youngest casualties were two 16 year olds, while seven men aged over 50 also died, although most of the older casualties died from illness or accidents in the UK while acting as trainers, headquarters' staff or medical personnel.

April and May 1915 were the worst two months of the War, with 54 and 67 deaths respectively, well over the 44 killed in August 1916 during the Somme Offensive, and the 41 each in April and September 1918 during the German Spring Offensive and the subsequent Allied counter-offensive. Three of Lancaster's worst six days for casualties were in the spring of 1915: 8 May with 19 (equal highest with 25 September 1915 during the Battle of Loos), 27 April with 16, and 23 April with 12.

This simple exploration shows that in a little under two months in 1915, 121 'Men of Lancaster', to use the language on the war memorial, were killed and three days had a dozen or more casualties each. Exploring this further shows that 103 have grave/memorial sites in Belgium, 93 on the Menin Gate alone, and a further 13 are in France; 89 of the casualties were from one battalion, the 1st/5th Battalion of the King's Own Royal Lancaster Regiment. From this, and a little exploration of regimental histories, it becomes clear that the most destructive battle of the war for Lancaster was not the Somme, Gallipoli or Passchendaele, but the Second Battle of Ypres, a battle that Sir John French – then the Commander-in-Chief of the British Expeditionary Force – claimed at the time would 'rank among the most desperate and hardest fights of the war'.[17]

The Second Battle of Ypres

The town of Ypres in southern Belgium was strategically important, especially for the British, because of its role in protecting the Channel ports. The First Battle of Ypres took place in the autumn of 1914 and ensured that the town was in Allied hands when the War settled down to trench warfare at the end of 1914. The Second Battle of Ypres started on 22 April 1915 and lasted until 25 May. The battle was a German offensive against the town, remembered primarily for the first use of poison gas on the Western Front, initially against French colonial troops. Canadians also remember it because it is seen as the first time a Canadian army defeated a European one on the battlefield and because the battle inspired John McCrae's poem *In Flanders Fields*. British academic histories largely ignore the battle, John Keegan's *The First World War* is typical, devoting two of its 456 pages to the battle, focusing primarily on the use of gas.[18] Gary Sheffield, in a revisionist book that did much to challenge the 'Blackadder' approach, says even less, merely stating

> On 22 April, the Second Battle of Ypres began with the Germans launching a surprise attack heralded by a cloud of poisonous gas – the first major use of this weapon in history. While the 33-day struggle forced the allies back, the Germans seemed to have been surprised by the extent of their initial success and failed to exploit it.[19]

In this forgotten struggle the British Expeditionary Force (BEF) suffered 59,000 casualties (killed, wounded and missing) and there were also 10,000 French and 35,000 German casualties.[20] The effects on Lancaster must have been devastating.

What was the Second Battle of Ypres, why was Lancaster so badly affected, and how can GIS help us to understand this? At the start of the War, the KORL consisted of two regular battalions, the 1st and 2nd stationed in Dover and India respectively, two Territorial battalions, the 4th and 5th based in Ulverston and Lancaster respectively, and the 3rd (Special Reserve) Battalion.[21] Territorial battalions were part-time, reserve soldiers who, at the start of the war, were liable only for home defence. Early in the war they were asked to volunteer for overseas service and both KORL battalions agreed.[22] This explains how the 5th Battalion became embroiled at Ypres. The surge in recruitment at the start of the War meant that large numbers of volunteers were joining these battalions, resulting in the original 5th Battalion becoming the 1st/5th with the 2nd/5th being formed on 15 August 1914.[23] The 1st/5th moved to France in February 1915 with 31 officers and 1,026 men.[24]

It initially went into trenches near Wulverghem and Neuve Eglise. During this period eight soldiers were killed and one died from disease.[25] Cross-referencing these numbers, taken from regimental histories, with the Reveille database reveals that four of the deaths were Lancastrians. In mid-March the battalion was reallocated to the 83rd Brigade which also included the 2nd Battalion KORL, now back from India, and was part of the 21st Division. On 9 April the entire brigade marched to Ypres.[26] The composition of the brigade compounded the town's shock at their fate, as the *Lancaster Guardian* suggested:

> Much has been said – if not actually in the way of complaint, still in the shape of criticism – about the 5th King's Own and other Territorial units being there early on placed in the forefront of the battle. It is pointed out that they were enrolled for home defence, and that, in very many cases, it was never anticipated that they would be sent to the Front. This, of course, is true enough; but it should be remembered that, with a patriotism which does them the highest credit, they volunteered for active service at the Front or anywhere else where their services might be required.[27]

Lancastrians killed in April and May 1915

Figure 26.3 shows the deaths of Lancastrians in the period through April and May 1915 as derived from the Reveille database. After a quiet start, 121 Lancastrians were killed in the approximately six weeks from 12 April, just after the 83rd Brigade arrived in Ypres, until the end of May. Of these, 89 (74 per cent) were from the

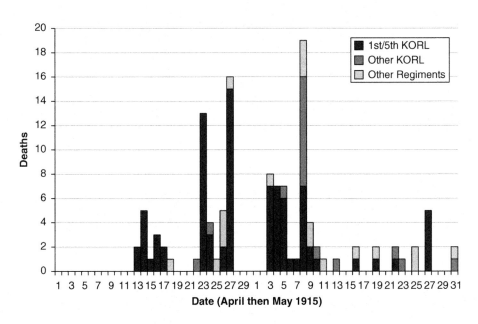

Figure 26.3 Deaths in April and May 1915. KORL refers to King's Own Royal Lancaster Regiment.

Table 26.1 The five periods of deaths in April and May 1915.

	Dates	No. of days	No. of deaths	Notes
1	13–18 April	6	14	
2	22–27 April	6	40	12 deaths on the 23rd and 16 on the 27th
3	3–7 May	5	24	
4	8–11 May	4	25	19 deaths on the 8th
5	13–31 May	19	17	

Source: Reveille database.

1st/5th KORL and a further 9 were in the 2nd KORL. Only 18 (15 per cent) were not in the KORL. The deaths break down into five periods as shown in Table 26.1.

A combination of GIS and traditional historical research can help us to understand the circumstances in which most of these men died. Three sources in particular tell the story of the 1st/5th at that time. The first is the Regimental War Diary which has been digitized.[28] The other two are heavily based on this: *The King's Own, 1/5th Battalion, TF in the European War, 1914–1918* compiled by Capt. Albert Hodgkinson[29] and J. M. Cowper's *The King's Own: The Story of a Royal Regiment*, volume 3, *1914–1950*.[30] One challenge is that the regimental sources give total numbers of casualties from the battalion but rarely give names, while the Reveille database only gives details of casualties from Lancaster. When a regimental history says that a certain number of men were killed on a certain day or in a particular incident, we have to deduce which Lancastrians this refers to based on dates of death and battalion information from the Reveille website.

A second problem is that while the regimental sources are detailed, they can be difficult to understand largely because of the lack of geographical information. They contain many place names, but these usually refer to small places like St Jean or Frezenberg with which the reader is unlikely to be familiar, or to military place names such as Polygon Wood. Hodgkinson includes some poor-quality sketch maps, the other two do not even go this far. To assist in understanding the events, a simple GIS of the battlefield was created drawing on Hodgkinson's sketch maps and a range of internet sources. This was used to locate the major incidents in which Lancastrians were involved. Figure 26.4 summarizes this using an image derived from modern aerial photography as a backcloth. The advantage of the modern image is that the field system gives a much better impression of distance and scale than traditional maps.

The first cluster of deaths from Figure 26.3 and Table 26.1 took place before the outbreak of the Second Battle of Ypres, when the 1st/5th took over trenches near Polygon Wood in the south-east of the Ypres salient. These trenches had been occupied by the French and the sources complain about their condition and a lack of sandbags to strengthen them. At most, the distance from German trenches was only 200 yards and there was extensive shelling which caused most of the casualties. Quoting the battalion's colonel's diary from 17 April, the day they were relieved, Hodgkinson states 'Returned to billets – Lunatic Asylum, Ypres. Our total casualties for the four days were 14 killed or died of wounds and 44 wounded. Three men's

Figure 26.4 Major actions involving Lancastrians around Ypres, April/May 1915.

nerves went and George (Medical Officer) fears that two may be permanently mad. The men are very cheerful . . .'[31] The Reveille database shows that 13 Lancastrians from the 1st/5th were killed in this period, giving some indication of how strongly the battalion recruited from the town.

After a few days' rest in Ypres, the battalion was moved to fields just north of St Jean, a few houses a mile or so east of Ypres. This is when the battle, and the second period of casualties, started. The first indication of this came on 22 April when the colonel's diary notes 'We then realized something serious had happened as one or two French soldiers and Zouvaves [sic – usually 'Zouaves', North African troops serving in the French Army] came straggling back, obviously panic stricken, not wounded, but suffering terribly and quite incoherent. We could make nothing out of them and do nothing for them.'[32] What had happened was the German gas attack on the northern part of the salient near Langemark which broke through the unprepared troops in that area. On 23 April the 1st/5th was involved, initially in a support capacity, in a major counter-attack on the Germans. This involved them advancing around a mile in view of the Germans under first shell and then rifle fire. Three officers and 23 men were killed and four officers and 99 men wounded.

> I was pleased with the way our fellows went ahead, continually meeting a stream of wounded going to the rear and the ground littered with dead. . . . There was one field with heaps of manure in rows. A lot of fellows thought that they could take shelter behind them. They are, of course not bullet-proof, and there was hardly a heap without a dead or wounded man beside it.[33]

The attack failed to get within 600 yards of German positions and most of the survivors returned to their start line. Twelve of the dead were Lancastrians. It is interesting to note the different attitudes to this counter-attack. Cowper says 'the 5th Battalion attacked the hordes of Germans pouring through the gap in the French line'[34] and all three sources stress the importance of this attack in preventing the Germans from exploiting their breakthrough. By contrast, the memoirs of a general in charge of another division in the salient refers to 'a lamentable counter-attack . . . The losses were very heavy and it never had any chance of success. No one knew the situation and there was practically no artillery support worthy of the name.'[35]

The next few days saw the 1st/5th digging in near their original positions and coming under heavy shellfire. The battalion was then pulled back to Potijze, still under shellfire. On 27 April they moved up to support another counter-attack. This attack was cancelled but 'We were just taking up our positions when one of the large shells exploded bang in the middle of a platoon of "B" Company, killing eight, two of whom were blown to atoms.'[36] The following day, five further bodies were found.[37] This cannot have been the only fatal incident of that day as a total of 16 Lancastrians were killed, all but one of whom were from the 1st/5th. On 29 April the battalion was finally pulled back two and a half miles west of Ypres for a rest. In this way 33 Lancastrians were killed with the 1st/5th. Of the other seven Lancastrians killed in these few days, two were with the 2nd Battalion fighting in the same brigade, and all but one of the others was also near Ypres. The final one, Frank Parkinson, was killed at Gallipoli, serving with the King's Own Scottish Borderers.[38]

The third phase began on 2 May when the 1st/5th moved back into the Ypres salient, taking up positions in a reserve trench near Frezenberg in the eastern part of the salient. A tactical withdrawal resulted in these positions becoming the front line on 3 May. They were then heavily shelled again to the extent that on 5 May the diary states 'We had rather a damnable day yesterday, being shelled continuously for about 16 hours. Our trenches were blown to bits and we had many casualties . . . It was the longest day, I think, I have ever spent.'[39] They were relieved by the 2nd Battalion on 6 May but the Reveille database reveals that this period saw 24 more Lancastrians killed, all but two from the 1st/5th.

The reason for the heavy shelling became apparent on 8 May when

> We then learnt that the Germans were making a big attack on the trenches at Frezenberg (where we had been three days before) . . . About 12 Major Clough and about 40 men of the 2nd Battalion came in and told us that the Germans had attacked that morning in overwhelming strength and had taken the trenches, and that they were the only survivors of the Battalion.[40]

While Major Clough may have overstated the losses, over 300 men from the 2nd Battalion were killed that day.[41] The 1st/5th was part of a counter-attack from the reserve trenches that they were occupying around a mile behind the front line. This again failed with heavy casualties. That day saw nineteen Lancastrians killed, including seven from the 1st/5th and nine from the 2nd Battalion. In total the four days until the 1st/5th were relieved back to billets west of Ypres saw 25 Lancastrians killed.

The Frezenberg attack marked one of the final phases of the Second Battle of Ypres. Despite the end of the battle, phase 5 still saw deaths of Lancastrians continuing at an average rate of almost one a day until the end of the month. Initially this was caused by a combination of injured men dying of wounds and occasional casualties among other regiments. As soon as the depleted battalion moved back up to occupy new positions in the southern part of the salient on 22 May, casualties began again. An officer, Captain Bingham, who had just returned from leave, was killed by a sniper while reconnoitring the new trenches. A former doctor, a tablet in his honour in the Royal Infirmary is believed to be the first war memorial unveiled in Lancaster.

In some ways the town was lucky. Over the period roughly 60 per cent of the 1st/5th's casualties were Lancastrians. Had the 1st/5th been in the frontline at Frezenberg rather than the 2nd Battalion who had just relieved them, and had they had experienced a similar number to the 300 casualties suffered by the 2nd Battalion, it is fair to estimate that around 200 Lancastrians would have been killed in one day attack. As it was, the *Lancaster Guardian* reported that

> The extreme severity of the fighting will never probably be thoroughly understood by people at home, but some idea may be formed from the fact that in our own Battalion over 200 were struck down in 'less than two hours'. Facts like these bring home to everyone in a way nothing else can do, the terrible realities of the most awful war in history.[42]

The impact on the town

The Second Battle of Ypres did not mark the start of Lancaster's experience of casualties during the war – from the outbreak of war in August 1914 until the end of March 1915, 59 men had already been killed. Nevertheless, in April and May 1915 the town lost twice that number in a mere six weeks. As the *Lancaster Guardian* pointed out, 'as a garrison town Lancaster has been in close touch with the war from its commencement'; but now every edition brought home with 'greater intensity the terrible nature of the hostilities and appalling sacrifice of life involved'.[43] The paper had started to speculate where the 5th King's Own might be on 10 April, when it was reported that 'Several letters received from the men of the 5th King's Own Royal Lancaster Regiment refer to the fact that they have this week arrived at a famous town, which has loomed largely in the fighting of the western front.' A local bookseller received a batch of picture postcards of Ypres from his son caught up in the fighting there. By 25 April 1915, the newspaper was filled with images and descriptions of the casualties, and many inches of column space were dedicated to letters from the Front and analysis of the battle.

> As the death toll mounted, the shock of Ypres resonates on every page:
> Further sad news from the Front confirms the fears entertained that Lancaster is likely to pay a heavy penalty for the patriotism and self-sacrificing spirit which sent many of its most promising sons to participation in the world's war. The 5th King's Own have been in the thick of the fighting during the last fortnight and though townspeople generally must have a feeling of pride in the way the Terriers are upholding the honour of the town and the prestige of the country, the feeling is mingled with one of sadness that so many gallant young fellows should be stricken down, some bereft of life, and others more or less severely wounded. . . . the families are few, indeed, who have not some direct representative or intimate friend either at the Front or in training for service in this terrible conflict.[44]

No subsequent battle would be covered in quite this detail.

As with the battlefield, GIS mapping can also help to convey this level of loss at home. The Reveille database provides addresses for 110 of the 121 casualties. These addresses need interpreting with a little care as they are not necessarily the address that the casualty himself lived at. In 27 cases, including George Cathcart from Figure 26.1, a casualty has more than one address. It is reasonable to suggest that each address indicates a loss either of someone who had previously resided there or a relative, often a wife or parent, who was currently living at that address. In total this gives 138 addresses in Lancaster. These have been converted into point locations using FindLatitudeandLongitude[45] and shown in Figure 26.5 where they have been superimposed over a contemporary map of the town. The map also includes a 100m buffer around each point that shows all areas with 100m of a casualty. The buffer brings home just how big the impact of these two months would have been – almost the entire built-up area of the town is within 100m of an address for someone who died. Estimates of the extent of bereavement in the First World War is part of the

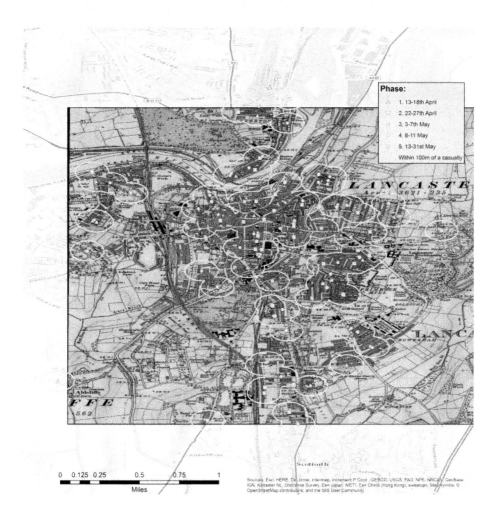

Figure 26.5 Addresses of Lancaster casualties in April and May 1915.

narrative of the tragic impact of the war on Britain. Adrian Gregory has convincingly revised downwards the statistics that suggest that every family 'lost someone' in the war by recalculating the highest conceivable number of those who lost an immediate family member.[46] However, mapping the deaths on to the cramped streets of industrial Lancaster suggests the significance of community relationships alongside blood relationships. The acknowledgement of brothers on the memorial draws attention to sibling and multiple bereavements, an under-researched dimension of the War. Many family members seem to have lived in close proximity even when no longer residing at the same address. Christopher Butterworth was killed with the 2nd Battalion when it was over-run on 8 May, becoming the second Butterworth brother to die after his brother William who had been killed in October 1914 also near Ypres. A third Butterworth brother, Hugh, was killed in August 1915 with the 1st/5th, and a fourth, John, in June 1917 with the 2nd/5th. The year before John was killed, their father James died. The *Lancaster Guardian* stated that he had 'died from debility, caused by having three sons killed and two severely wounded in the war, in the opinion of Dr Aitken'.[47] Apart from Christopher who lived just across the river in Skerton, the Butterworths and their families lived in three adjacent streets (Albion, Hinde and Green Street) in the Bulk area. Much of Lancaster's housing was terraced, with water and toilets located outside. As the interviews in the Elizabeth Roberts archive testify, neighbors were therefore involved in each other's lives in manifold ways. Mrs H.2.L remembered, '[The War] hadn't been going so long when Tom went and then young Ben. It broke half of George Street when he got killed.'[48]

As the mapping reveals, the worst affected street in Lancaster after Ypres was Marton Street from which six men died, followed by St Leonardsgate with five and Edward Street and Lune Street with four each. Marton Street is particularly shocking as the highest house number was 37, albeit that this is slightly misleading because one of the casualties was at number 6 Back Marton Street.[49] Figure 26.6 shows a map of the houses as they existed around the time of the War: Back Marton Street is the alley to the north of Marton Street. Perhaps unsurprisingly, given that much of Marton St would have been poor-quality housing near the town center, the street has been extensively redeveloped with the north of the street now largely being under the

Figure 26.6   Marton Street around the time of the First World War. Back Marton Street is the alley with the right-angle bend just to the north of Marton Street.

Source: Crown Copyright and Landmark Information Group Limited (2016). All rights reserved.

Figure 26.7 Marton Street today. (a) Number 6 where John Churchouse lived with his mother until his death on 14 April. The photo is taken from approximately where number 25 would have been home to R. Mansfield, killed on 5 May. (b) The square outside the court where numbers 29 and 37 would have stood, homes to John Lawrence and John Pye respectively who were probably killed by the same shell on 27 April.

main police station and the Magistrates Court. The only remaining house from which someone was killed is number 6, shown in Figure 26.7a, where John Churchouse lived with his mother. One of the first casualties of the period, he was probably killed in the shelling when the 1st/5th were in their trenches at Polygon Wood. He was 19. The next death was William Theobald, another 19 year old, who lived with his parents at 6 Back Marton Street. He was probably killed in the failed counter-attack north of St. Jean on 23 April. Three days later, 22-year-old Frank Parkinson, who lived at number 16 with his parents, was killed at Gallipoli. The following day, 22-year-old John Lawrence from number 29 and John Pye from number 37 were killed. Figure 26.7 shows these two were near neighbours. There is a good chance that they were killed by the single shell that killed thirteen members of the 1st/5th that day. At 43 years old, John Pye was one of the oldest Lancastrians killed in action in the entire war. He had previously been a regular soldier serving in India and South Africa and it is likely he re-enlisted as a territorial when war broke out. The street's final casualty was Richard Mansfield, who lived with his wife at number 25, across the street from John Churchouse. At 38, he was another veteran who had re-enlisted in the 1st/5th. He was killed on 5 May in the shelling leading up to the Frezenberg offensive. Research on the impact of mass bereavement has tended to focus on the fate of Pals' Battalions at the Somme: Lancaster's story suggests that some communities had to negotiate that form of loss far sooner in the war.[50]

Conclusions

The project described here started as a traditional piece of archival history, carried out by Lancaster Military Heritage Group, that brought together a number of sources to give details about each and every Lancastrian killed in the First World War. Its major output was the Reveille website which, while digital, was in many ways structured in an analogue way in that it could only be explored using an alphabetical list. The fact that the data were in digital form, however, allowed us to re-engineer it to convert it first into a database table and then into a range of GIS layers. The GIS layers were based on street addresses or on grave sites. Digital technology also allowed us to bring in other sources. Both the 1st/5th Battalion's War Diary and Albert Hodgkinson's record of the 1st/5th have been digitized and were available to us as a result. These allowed us to build up a picture of the actions in which the man died by providing the locations of obscure places such as Polygon Wood and Frezenburg and to present them in an understandable way.

The key abilities that enabled this research were, first, the capability to query the casualty database, using both attribute queries for elements such as date and regiment along with locational queries, and to integrate the results of these queries with close reading of regimental histories and other sources. Secondly, we were able to use mapping, in particular, to present a complex and confused battlefield to other researchers and the general public in a reasonably straightforward manner. Mapping also helps to disseminate and explore the enormity of the impact of the events on the town.

As stated in the introduction, the overwhelming narrative of Britain's experience in the First World War is concerned with large attacks that resulted in large loss of life for little territorial gain. Battles such as Second Ypres, that do not fit this narrative, receive far less attention. Simple querying by date allows us to see that the largely successful defensive Second Battle of Ypres was the most important battle of the First World War for Lancaster. The other major events for the town are very diverse. Loos was the British Army's first attempt at a major offensive on the Western Front, albeit on a much more limited scale than the Somme. It ended in bloody failure. The Somme was also clearly important, however, its impact was not much larger than the two major campaigns of 1918, which were both much more mobile than the conventional narrative of a First World War battle. The use of digital technology allows us to conduct our analysis at several scales: first concentrating on the pattern of casualties as a whole and then focusing on the event, in this case the Second Battle of Ypres, in which there were the most casualties rather than selecting more well-known battles. This approach reveals a more diverse and complex story than conventional histories would lead us to expect. It also powerfully reveals the local cost of the events.

As well as the academic side, this project has also had a strong emphasis on public engagement. We have used our findings in a range of public exhibitions and talks where combining the use of maps and graphs to summarize broad patterns with detailed stories of the regiment and the individuals provides a powerful way of understanding the experience of the war on the battlefield and at home. The fact that we also have the street addresses of the people killed means that we are able to present this to the public in a way that allows them to ask 'who from my street or my neighborhood was killed?' This has proved very popular and helps to create a community understanding of the War's local impact as well as raising a significant amount of attention in local and regional media. We have also developed a mobile app that provides a walking tour of Lancaster in the First World War.[51] This includes details of some casualties combined with other major sites such as the war memorial and the barracks with content such as contemporary photos and movie images. It has been developed to be both an enhancement of an existing guided walk, led by the curator of the King's Own Royal Regiment museum, and a self-guided tour.[52]

In short, the original Reveille research captured the fate of individuals: the application of digital technologies, particularly GIS, has allowed us to explore the collective narrative of a town at war.

Acknowledgements

Our sincerest thanks are due to Lancaster Military Heritage Group for making the material from the Reveille website to us and particularly to Brigadier Jim Dennis whose work created the site. We are also grateful to Joe Buglass and Lindsey King from the Engagement Team, Faculty of Arts and Social Sciences, Lancaster University, whose work with Campus in the City gave us access to a public audience for this work which revealed the depth of interest in it. This work has also benefited from support from the Heritage Lottery Fund under *Streets of Mourning and Community Memory in Lancaster* (FW-14-03372) and from the European Research Council (ERC) under the European Union's Seventh Framework Programme (FP7/2007-2013) / ERC grant *Spatial Humanities: Texts, GIS, Places* (agreement number 283850).

Notes

1 Jay Winter estimates the number of total deaths of British servicemen in the First World War at between 610,000 and 722,785; men aged 17–36 had between two and eight times the hypothetical mortality rate; men aged between 36 and 42 a 'modest' increase in mortality. J. M. Winter, 'Some Aspects of the Demographic Consequence of the First World War in Britain', *Population Studies* 30, 1976, 539–52; here 541, 545. See also his monograph, *The Great War and the British People,* Basingstoke: Palgrave Macmillan, 2003. Winter's findings were broadly confirmed by D. Jdanov, E. Andreev, D. Jasilionis, and V. M. Shkolnikov, 'Estimates of Mortality and Population Changes in England and Wales over the Two World Wars', *Demographic Research* 13, 2005, 389–414.

2 See e.g. A. Clark, *The Donkeys,* London: Hutchinson, 1961; B. Bond and N. Cave (eds), *Haig: A Reappraisal 70 Years On,* London: Pen and Sword, 1999.

3 *Blackadder goes Forth* (Richard Curtis and Ben Elton), 28 September–2 November 1989, BBC One sitcom.

4 Source: 1911 Census.

5 Lancaster Town Hall Memorial Garden, dedicated 1924. According to the UK War Memorials, it lists 1,012 names for the First World War. WM reference 3307.

6 Lancaster Military Heritage Group <www.lmhg.org.uk> (accessed 6 February 2017).

7 LMHG *Reveille* <www.lancasterwarmemorials.org.uk/memorials/lancaster-a.htm#1> (accessed 7 February 2017) provides examples.

8 HTML, Hypertext Markup Language, is the computer format used to encode most web pages. It allows text to be formatted, images to be embedded and hyperlinks to be included but only provides limited functionality beyond this.

9 The Menin Gate is one of four memorials to the missing in Belgian Flanders which cover the area known as the Ypres Salient. In the case of casualties of the United Kingdom, only those prior to 16 August 1917 are named: casualties after that date are named on the memorial at Tyne Cot. See www.cwgc.org/find-a-cemetery/cemetery/91800/YPRES%20 (MENiN%20GATE)%20MEMORIAL (accessed 7 February 2017).

10 OpenStreetMap (n.d.), <www.openstreetmap.org> (accessed 7 February 2017).

11 Shapefiles are the native format used by ESRI's ArcGIS software and are widely used to store GIS layers within the GIS community.

12 FindLatitudeandLongitude (n.d.) *Batch Geocoding,* <www.findlatitudeandlongitude.com/batch-geocode> (accessed 7 February 2017).

13 Commonwealth War Grave Commission (n.d.) 'Cemetery search' *Commonwealth War Graves Commission* <www.cwgc.org/find-a-cemetery.aspx> (accessed 7 February 2017).

14 Google Maps (n.d.) *Google Maps.* <www.google.com/maps> (www.cwgc.org/find-a-cemetery.aspx).

15 The Reveille website includes more people than the main war memorial due to different definitions of who exactly should be included.

16 On the national averages, Jdanov et al. note that 'the most striking excess male mortality in the total population has affected the ages 18–24, with the maximum peak being age at 23 in 1918. Between 1913 and 1918, the latter age shows a 15-16 fold increase in the probability of dying.' Jdanov et al., 'Estimates of Mortality and Population Changes', 407.

17 His speech to the men of the brigades of the 27th and 28th Divisons (which included the 2nd and 5th King's Own Royal Lancasters) on May 21/22 was reported in the *Lancaster Guardian.*

18 J. Keegan, *The First World War,* London: Bodley Head, 2014, 214–15.

19 G. Sheffield, *Forgotten Victory: The First World War: Myths and Realities,* London: Review, 2002, 124.

20 Commonwealth War Grave Commission (n.d.) 'The Ypres Salient: Second Ypres: Postscript', <www.cwgc.org/ypres/content.asp?menuid=35&submenuid=36&id=19& menuname=Postcript&menu=subsub> (accessed 7 February 2017).

21 A regiment was made up of a number of battalions who contained about 1,000 men each and acted independently from the regiment's other battalions. In active service a battalion would be allocated to a brigade, which consisted of four battalions, and brigades to a division. While a battalion would recruit locally, not all of the men it contained would necessarily have been from the local area. Although Lancaster was home to the KORL, Lancastrians also served in a wide variety of other regiments.

22 J. M. Cowper, *The King's Own: The Story of a Royal Regiment,* vol. 3, *1914–1950,* Aldershot: Gale & Polden, 1957, 5.

23 Kings Own Royal Regiment Museum (n.d.) 'First World War: 2nd/5th Battalion, King's Own Royal Lancaster Regiment', <www.kingsownmuseum.com/ww1-2-5korlr.htm> (accessed 7 February 2017).

24 A. Hodgkinson, *The King's Own, 1/5th Battalion, TF in the European War, 1914–1918* 2nd ed., Lancaster: King's Own Regiment Museum, 2005, 7.

25 Hodgkinson, *The King's Own,* 10.

26 Ibid.

27 'The Gallant Fifth', *Lancaster Guardian,* 15 May 1915.

28 *Digital Copy of the War Diary of the 1st/5th Battalion, King's Own Royal Lancaster Regiment,* Lancaster: King's Own Royal Regiment Museum, n.d.

29 Hodgkinson, *The King's Own,* 11–22.

30 Cowper, *The King's Own,* 51–68.

31 Hodgkinson, *The King's Own,* 11.

32 Ibid. 13.

33 Ibid. 15.

34 Cowper, *The King's Own,* 68.

35 D. Snow and M. Pottle, (eds), *The Confusion of Command: The War Memoirs of Lieutenant General Sir Thomas D'Oyly Snow, 1914–1915,* Barnsley: Frontline, 2011, 98–9.

36 Hodgkinson, *The King's Own,* 18.

37 Ibid.

38 LMHG *Reveille* <www.lancasterwarmemorials.org.uk/memorials/lancaster-p.htm#663> (accessed 7 February 2017).

39 Hodgkinson, *The King's Own,* 19.

40 Ibid., 20.

41 Figures from the Commonwealth War Graves Commission <www.cwgc.org> (accessed 7 February 2017).

42 'Splendid Heroism', *Lancaster Guardian,* 8 May 1915.

43 'The Gallant Fifth', *Lancaster Guardian,* 15 May 1915.

44 'Lancaster and the War', *Lancaster Guardian,* 1 May 1915.

45 FindLatitudeandLongitude, *Batch Geocoding.*

46 A. Gregory, *The Last Great War: British Society and the First World War,* Cambridge: Cambridge University Press, 2008, 253.

47 *Lancaster Guardian,* 12 August 1916.<www.lancasterwarmemorials.org.uk/memorials/ lancaster-b.htm#143B> (accessed 7 February 2017).

48 Mrs H.2.L, interviewed by Elizabeth Roberts, November 1974, Elizabeth Roberts Archive, Regional Heritage Centre, Lancaster University.

49 The north of England had a tradition of back-to-back houses where two rows of terraces would back onto each other so that the houses only had one external wall.

50 See e.g. M. Brosnan, 'The Pals Battalions of the First World War', <www.iwm.org.uk/history/the-pals-battalions-of-the-first-world-war> (accessed 19 April 2016).

51 T. V. Do, K. Cheverst and I. Gregory, 'LoMAK: A Framework for Generating Locative Media Apps from KML Files', *Engineering Interactive Computer Systems* 14, 2015, 211–16.

52 *Lancaster in the Great War: Community Memories* <http://wp.lancs.ac.uk/greatwar> (accessed 7 February 2017).

27

GIS FOR CULTURAL RESOURCES MANAGEMENT IN ALASKA

The Susitna-Watana Dam Project

Justin M. Hays, Carol Gelvin-Reymiller, James Kari,
Charles M. Mobley, and William E. Simeone

The state of GIS in Alaskan cultural resources management

There has been an increasing demand from clients for predictive location models in cultural resource management (CRM). Resource developers regularly require a geographical information systems-based (GIS) model that will optimize time in the field, thereby minimizing expense and unanticipated discoveries during the construction phase. GIS-modeled locational surfaces of landscapes that incorporate numerous environmental and cultural variables are categorized by cumulative numerical values. Higher values are areas of higher site potential, and lower values of lower site potential. The importance of defining and testing areas of *both* lower and higher site potential is fundamental for guiding survey efforts, i.e. confirming areas with higher values as holding most cultural resources, and confirming areas with lower values as having fewer cultural resources via empirical observation.[1]

This chapter presents a case study from the field of CRM that provides a recent example of how GIS is being used in the remote and undeveloped State of Alaska, United States. GIS is necessary to manage all of the project data from field collection forms to global positioning system (GPS) menus to data management and quality control. Additionally, numerous text documents and scanned paper maps from earlier times are also housed in the project geodatabase. As Alaska develops more and more of its resources, State and Federal laws must be adhered to before any development takes place. In the United States both natural and cultural resources are protected from potential harm. Below is an example of how archaeologists protect and preserve cultural resources in a state that is constantly developing. Cultural resources are usually sites where human activity once took place and material culture such as prehistoric stone tools, historic metal implements, or hunting camps and cabins once existed. GIS provides a powerful tool for archaeologists that manage the thousands of prehistoric and historic sites across the state. It has led to more informed approaches for investigating, documenting, and reporting of existing and newly discovered archaeological sites.

The purpose of the archaeological and ethno-geographical programs of the study was to determine if correlations exist between prehistoric, protohistoric, historic, and ethno-historic site locations and various ecological datasets in order to facilitate archaeological search strategies and inform spatial behaviors among site groups. Seeking out what affects human site placement across the landscape is not new to the Interior Alaskan archaeology.[2] These pioneering efforts identified patterns of site preservation along south-facing slopes, glaciated uplands, well-drained soils, and proximity to major food resources. These approaches, while informative, have become increasingly course-grained as more refined techniques have become available.

The Alaska State Historic Preservation Office (SHPO) within the Office of History and Archaeology (OHA) requires location models to be devised for large, multi-year projects. Today, almost all CRM survey methodologies are based on GIS landscape models including subsurface geology and, where available, protohistoric and historic resource harvests. The project report contains the most comprehensive assemblage of Native Alaskan place names. The names associated with the study area were first translated, then mapped on paper (United States Geologic Survey (USGS) map sheets), and finally, geo-referenced into a digital GIS geodatabase. The linguistic data have been incorporated to the locational model and are used as another variable to inform where cultural resources are likely to be located.

Case study: the Susitna-Watana Dam Project[3]

The proposed Susitna-Watana Dam Project would be located on the Susitna River roughly 90 river miles north of Talkeetna, Alaska. As currently envisioned, the project would include a roughly 700-foot tall dam with a 20,000 acre, 39-mile long reservoir. The dam has a nominal crest elevation at 2,050 feet mean sea level. As regulations go, the area of potential effect (APE) was significant to a large scale in the state of Alaska. The Alaska Energy Authority (AEA) attempted to obtain a Federal Energy Regulatory Commission (FERC) license application for the project. Their application required studies that would support FERC's National Environmental Policy Act (NEPA) analysis of the project license.

One of these analyses investigated the archaeological sites and land status information within the region. This was managed with GIS software. Within the dam location lie 73 known cultural resource sites (one paleontological, 58 prehistoric, four protohistoric, six historic, and four multicomponent). Additionally, 158 known cultural resource sites (two paleontological, 142 prehistoric, eleven historic, and three multicomponent) lie adjacent to or are associated with the project area. The proposed access corridors have a combined total of 53 previously documented sites (one paleontological, 47 prehistoric, four historic, and one multicomponent). Additional sites could exist in unsurveyed areas within the project area. Of these sites, 100 are located on State of Alaska lands, 40 lie on Native Corporation Lands, two on Alaska Railroad Corporation land, two are on privately held lands, and 139 on federally owned land.

The known sites were inventoried and recorded with survey-grade, handheld GPS. All site data were recorded and the site conditions verified. Phase I (Identification) surveys were conducted in areas of the study area not previously surveyed, or in areas that the locational model identifies as high potential for the occurrence of cultural resources. GIS was then used to prioritize areas of high potential that prehistoric peoples with subsistence-based economies and seasonal rounds may have used. The model does not predict or prioritize where historic sites related to mineral extraction may be located. Historic occupants included indigenous people, as well as foreign miners, traders, merchants, guides, and trappers.

Settlement patterns, as reflected by currently known Alaska Heritage Resource Survey (AHRS) site locations, were mapped by separating prehistoric sites, Native historic sites, and Euro-American site locations, based primarily on descriptions in the AHRS database. Because prehistoric resource locations are presumed to be similar but not exactly the same as modern resource locations, mapped resources were generalized by buffering in GIS. Caribou migration patterns and ranges appear to be closely associated with prehistoric settlement patterns. Ethnographic information was also assessed for identifying protohistoric and Native historic land use, which is characterized by a general use of the area. Euro-American historic land use represented by early exploration for routes for development of the railroad were mapped to assist in understanding spatially localized connections to area history. Several historic mining and trapping locations as well as historic trails were mapped, and additional trails were recorded in 2012 and 2013.

Research methods included a background study which examined satellite imagery, aerial photographs, maps, and literature relating to the history and archaeology of the region and the project area. Published and unpublished sources formed the primary source of information. These included previous technical archaeological survey reports as well as general references on the prehistory and history of the region. The AHRS files, maintained at the OHA, were consulted. The AHRS files, a database of recorded archaeological and historic site locations within Alaska, provide information about reported sites in the project vicinity. The review identified the potential to encounter cultural resources and anticipate the cultural resource site types that may be present in the project area.

We reviewed the project scope of works, available literature, and satellite/aerial photography to identify locations where archaeological materials are located within and surrounding the project area. The pre-fieldwork planning also involved examination of digital USGS topographic maps, historic maps, and historic photographs to document the nature of the terrain and vegetation types, and how it has changed over time. This also included the development of a prehistoric site location sensitivity model. The aim of this model was to determine a high- and low-sensitivity survey approach that allowed the project team to maximize the labor and field resources by targeting particular areas of the corridor for more intensive investigation, rather than conducting a 100 percent ground survey of the entire proposed survey area. Typically, high-sensitive zones are identified based on a host of information coinciding with key geomorphic and ecological features. This includes exposed ground, proximity to streams or ponds, good vista points of local features (such as natural animal corridors), and landform features such as kames, eskers, alluvial terraces, dune fields, ice patches, barrier falls, or rock outcrops. In contrast, low-sensitive zones are usually defined based on areas with steep slopes, low topographic relief, long distances to water, and restricted vistas.

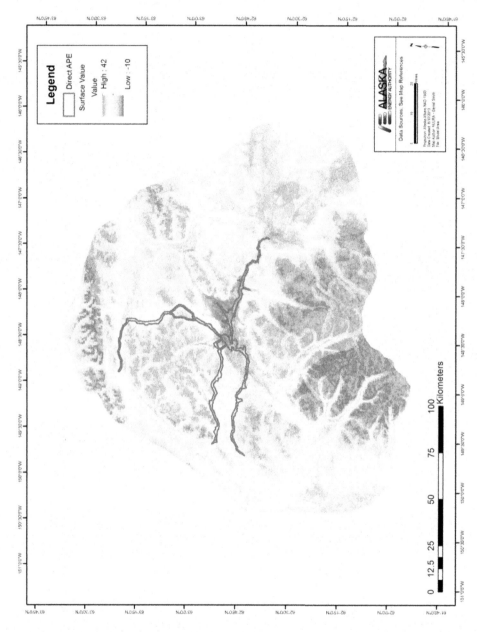

Figure 27.1   Map of the predictive model with the archaeological study area in dark bold outline. High potential areas for cultural resources are illustrated in medium to light values while lower potential areas are modeled in darker values. Map created by: Carol Gelvin-Reymiller; Permission to use by the author.

Inventory surveys and limited testing were conducted in areas of the APE not previously surveyed and in areas within the APE that modeled high potential for the occurrence of cultural resources (see Figure 27.1). Culturally sensitive surfaces of the APE (derived from the GIS model) were categorized by cumulative numerical values. Higher numeric values in the model correspond with an increased potential for cultural remains, and lower values with lower cultural potential. The importance of defining and testing areas of both lower and higher site potential is fundamental for guiding survey efforts, i.e. confirming areas with higher values as holding most cultural resources, and confirming areas with lower values as having fewer cultural resources via empirical observation.

The spatial extent for the Susitna-Watana model primarily was determined by assessing the range of topographic diversity within the region surrounding the study area. The model extent is 17,518 square miles or almost 7 million acres, and includes variation in ecosystems (see Figure 27.2). This breadth of area allows for the most inclusive dataset of prehistoric site types already discovered, which theoretically gives the model the ability to reflect a more realistic land use pattern within the region. The major ecozones within the model area are the high mountains and glaciers of the Alaska Range to the north of the proposed dam area, the highlands of the Talkeetna Mountain Range which surround the dam area, the valleys and lakes of the Susitna River and its tributaries, and lower terrain such as Lake Louise and Susitna Lake with associated wetlands to the east of the project area. Ethnographic research in the area indicates that several Na-Dene speaking groups of people, including the Ahtna, Den'aina, and Lower Tanana, inhabited this area, utilizing a wide range of flora, fauna, and geomorphic resources. Linguistic data which attest to their inhabitation may be incorporated into future models. According to Kari, 15 percent of toponyms in the Ahtna language, for example, refer to human activities on the landscape, such as subsistence locations, trails, or material culture.[4] Prehistoric archaeological sites, including individual loci ($n=510$), within all ecosystems were the basis of the dependent dataset for the model. Random points ($n=2000$) generated in ArcGIS software were used as a comparative dependent dataset.

The ethnogeographic portion of the 2013 study included direct consultation with Ahtna elders in order to integrate Alaska Native perspectives on historical land use and cultural values into the ongoing cultural resource investigation. Through a partnership with Ahtna, Inc., the regional corporation for the Ahtna people, the ethnogeographic component of the study documented Ahtna perspectives and ethnographic context for significance of the cultural resources sites potentially affected by the project. Included are traditional Ahtna land use and settlement patterns, seasonal migrations, religious and sacred sites, and traditional foot trail systems. Ahtna language place name records on file[5] were consulted, and linguistic analysis of Ahtna place names, including archival taped sources and confirmation interviews with Ahtna Elders, provided insight into the geographic information (notably hydrology) encoded in the Ahtna terms and narratives for important places.

The ethnographic data collected in 2013 was also added into the GIS locational model to also aid in the identifying of potential archaeological sites during the 2014 study season. For example, ethnographic data documenting annual or seasonal activity (including the type of resource used, where harvested, method of harvest, and season

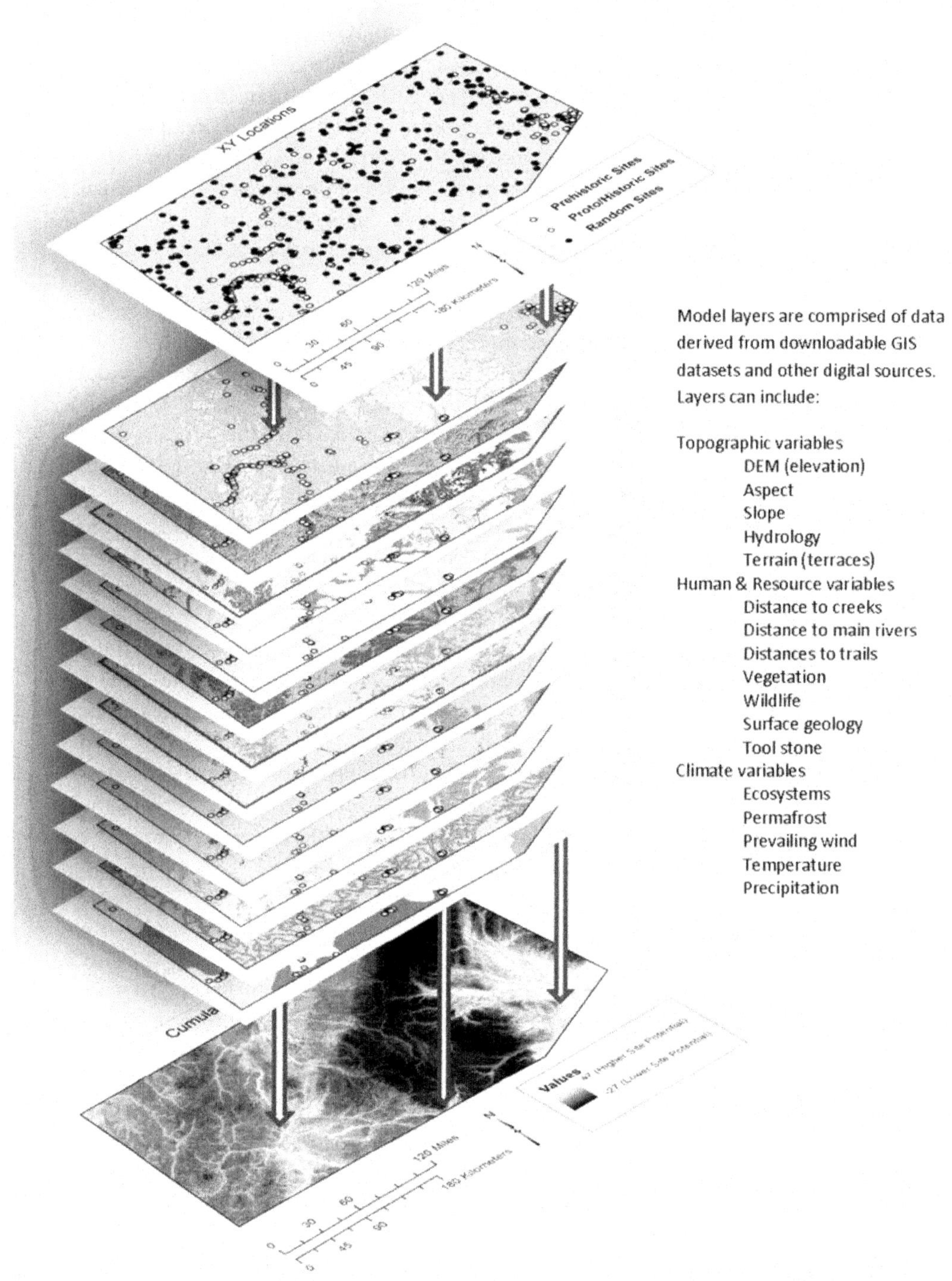
XY Locations
Prehistoric Sites
Proto/Historic Sites
Random Sites
120 Miles
180 Kilometers
Values
Model layers are comprised of data derived from downloadable GIS datasets and other digital sources. Layers can include:
Topographic variables
DEM (elevation)
Aspect
Slope
Hydrology
Terrain (terraces)
Human & Resource variables
Distance to creeks
Distance to main rivers
Distances to trails
Vegetation
Wildlife
Surface geology
Tool stone
Climate variables
Ecosystems
Permafrost
Prevailing wind
Temperature
Precipitation

Figure 27.2 Topographic, human, and climatic variables used in modeling archaeology across the interior Alaska landscape (courtesy of Carol Gelvin-Reymiller).

of harvest) may also help in detecting additional archaeological sites within the APE. Ethnographic data also aides in the interpretation of sites and artifacts on a variety of levels, addressing such topics as: (1) how a site or artifact was used; (2) how a site fits into Alaska Native and non-Native history; (3) whether a site's content can be applied to the explanation of the area's cultural history; and (4) if a site has religious or other significance not apparent from its physical attributes. The addition of ethnographic data will also enable the better development of historical and cultural context for a site,

Ethnographic and historic literature indicates that three main Athabascan linguistic groups inhabited and controlled large parts of this extended boundary, known as the Dena'ina, Ahtna, and Lower Tanana, which were all represented by smaller, seminomadic bands. Current archaeological and linguistic evidence suggests the Dena'ina have inhabited the southern foothills of the south-central and southwestern Alaska Range for perhaps the past 4,000 years, likely migrating from the Copper river drainage or Kuskokwim river drainage areas or possibly from the Tanana River area.[6] In contrast, the Ahtna and Lower Tanana linguistic stocks appear to have inhabited the regions of the Copper River and Tanana Valley since possibly the early Holocene[7] (see Figure 27.3).

For the purposes of this study, the Prehistoric Period is generalized as likely representing the period from 9000 bp to 1741.[8] This era roughly coincides with the establishment of an ecosystem similar to that found in the nineteenth/twentieth centuries, and ends at the historic period of direct contact with Russians and Euro-Americans.[9] In the northern part of the study region, the material cultural record appears to reach as far back as the Late Pleistocene, at Butte Lake.[10] In the southern part, the record appears to stretch back at least 7,000 years in the Jay Creek drainage.[11] The area was deglaciated by 9,000 years ago based on lake cores taken at four different lakes in 2014.[12] One objective of the study plan was to hold a regional elders' conference to inform Ahtna elders about the project. A regional elders' conference was held in the *Hwtsaay Hwt'aene* community of Cantwell. Archival and oral history sources were relied upon for the ethnogeography investigation; site investigations were not conducted except for an aerial reconnaissance of the study area for general orientation. The method included contemporary interviews with Ahtna Natives whose traditional territory included the study area, archival research focused upon pertinent written and photographic records, and transcription, translation, and analysis of oral history tapes from decades past – some in the Ahtna language, and some in English.

During the 2013 field season the study team collected data on Alaska Native culture and history in the study area, with the interviews and transcripts collected, translated, and transcribed primarily between February and August of 2013. Interviewees were asked questions to elicit information about past and present land use, cultural sites and their history, and in particular traditional cultural properties (TCP). The ethnogeography investigation involved: a regional elders' conference, analysis of archived Ahtna language interviews, analysis of archived English language interviews, contemporary English language interviews, place name mapping and ethnogeographic analysis, and trail mapping.

Audio collections identified as pertinent to the project were those of the Alaska Native Language Center Archive (ANLC) at the University of Alaska, Fairbanks, and

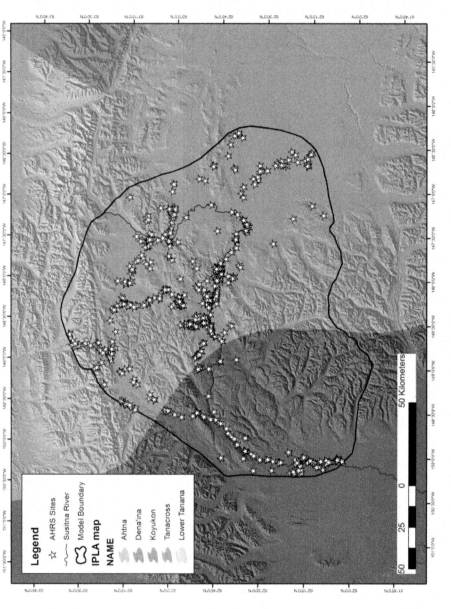

Figure 27.3 Map of the linguistic families: Western Ahtna (in the center to lower right); Koyukon (in the upper left boundary); Dena'ina (in the center to lower right); Tanacross (in the upper right corner); and Lower Tanana (across the upper boundary). The model area is outlined in black with the known archaeological sites depicted with white stars. Map created by Gerad Smith, adapted from M. E. Krauss, *Alaska Native Languages: Past, Present, and Future.* Alaska Native Language Center Research Papers No. 4. Fairbanks, AK: Alaska Native Language Center, University of Alaska, 1980. PO Box 757680, Fairbanks, AK 99775–7680. Permission to use by the State of Alaska.

those at the Ahtna Heritage Foundation's *C'ek'aedi Hwnax* archives. The inventory began by first identifying audio recordings by individuals well-informed about Western Ahtna history and culture – such as Jake Tansy, Henry Peters, Morrie Secondchief, Fred Ewan, and Jim Tyone. Audio recordings were then grouped by content or genre: place names, land use, history and events, and mythic stories. Often a single recording had a number of different segments – each concerning a separate genre. The third step was to categorize each recording according to its relevance. Recordings were ranked to focus on Western Ahtna place names and travel and provide intensive and objective documentation of Hwtsaay Hwt'aene territory.

Recorded stories pertinent to the upper Susitna River from Ahtna narrators Jim Tyone, Jack Tyone, John Shaginoff, Henry Peters,[13] Jake Tansy, Morrie Second-chief, Fred Ewan, and Fred John were evaluated, along with the few known Shem Pete recordings and narrative segments that pertain to the Talkeetna Mountains and the upper Susitna River. Audio recordings by Dena'ina elders Shem Pete, John Shaginoff, and others that relate to traditional Dena'ina territory have been identified but not translated or transcribed.

Oral history tapes and transcripts pertaining to the project area, in English but spoken by Ahtna elders, were sought and reviewed for their pertinence to the project area. Most of the material is from well-known bodies of work, though the data in many cases were never fully utilized. The fieldwork of Frederica de Laguna and Catherine McClellan in the 1950s and 1960s[14] formed a foundation for the Susitna data collection. Reckord[15] and West[16] were closely consulted. All reports, tape recordings, interview transcripts, and field notes produced by Bureau of Indian Affairs (BIA) investigators were reviewed for the Susitna ethnogeography investigation. Peter Dessauer and David Harvey's investigation of the Valdez Creek mining district produced a collection of eighteen audiotapes that includes interviews with several Ahtna elders who grew up at Valdez Creek.[17] These tapes were inventoried and selected portions were transcribed by the ethnogeography team. In the 1990s the Institute for Social and Economic Research (ISER), in conjunction with the Copper River Native Association (CRNA), recorded interviews with individuals discussing Ahtna subsistence patterns. The study team inventoried these recordings and transcribed those relating to the project.

The ethnogeography investigation also included interviews with living Ahtna elders and soon-to-be-elders to help identify potential TCPs in the study area, and to help inventory and evaluate cultural sites addressed by the archaeological investigation. The process required the development of an interview protocol, identification of individuals to be interviewed, and then interviews with those individuals about contemporary land use and the cultural landscape. The Ahtna Lands Committee, the director of the Ahtna Heritage Foundation, and the Ahtna Tribal Conservation District were contacted for assistance in developing the interview protocol and selecting interviewees. The protocol was designed to record Ahtna perspectives on the significance of activity sites, burials, sacred or spiritual sites, avoidance sites, and traditional use areas of contemporary, historic, or prehistoric age. The interview format was semi-structured, meaning the same open-ended questions were asked of each respondent. This helped standardize the description of Ahtna traditions, customs, and practices, and contributed to the development of a regional overview of

Ahtna land and activities from the late nineteenth century through the present. It was understood that answers to some of the questions could involve privileged cultural property. The interviews were conducted in accordance with the National Academy of Science's Principles for the Conduct of Research in the Arctic. Research guidelines adhere to principles of informed consent, confidentiality of personal information, community review of draft findings, and the provision of copies of research products including audio recordings and project reports to studied communities.

Thirteen interviews were conducted during July and August of 2013 in both Ahtna and English. These took place primarily in Cantwell at respondents' homes, local restaurants, or at the Native Village of Cantwell office. During them, interviewees described a variety of different types of sites including: subsistence sites used for hunting, fishing, gathering, and trapping; villages, hunting camps, fish camps, trapping cabins, and stop overs; trails or routes; sites that have to do with supernatural phenomena such as giant fish; geographic features and historical sites. All of these sites have place names – most in the Ahtna Language. In the text of this report Ahtna words are in italics and Ahtna place names are labeled with a number corresponding to the Ahtna Place Names List to be updated.[18]

The study plan identified three datasets to be developed for trails: one based on Bureau of Land Management (BLM) trail data, one based on field observations of the archaeological crews, and one (expected to be a foot-trail map) based on the ethnogeography investigation. As part of the ethnogeography investigation, 'routes' by four or five Ahtna speakers were mapped. A route is an ordered sequence of places on trails (usually by foot, at times by boat). Details about how trails are named and embedded in the Ahtna place names system were further investigated. For example, Ahtna 'stream-trails' are the most significant and are generally referred to simply by stream name. Investigations to date have noted 192 trails. The trail inventory is being assembled as a table and as maps, and will include plots of routes used by the last three generations of *Hwtsaay Hwt'aene* from the community of Cantwell.

In addition to analyzing and compiling primary and secondary ethnographic and linguistic data particular to the area of research, a specific effort was made to incorporate as much of that data as possible into digitally projected form. Much of the data being collected describes ancient names and stories of actual geographic landmarks. Additionally this often includes descriptions of prehistoric, protohistoric, and historic use of these places by native informants and Euro-American immigrants.

This resulted in updating the location of previously recorded Ahtna geographic place names based on more precise data, and adding new place names which hadn't been added previously been incorporated. These were projected as vector points in an ArcGIS® 10.2 geodatabase feature class (see Figure 27.4). In addition, points which referred to lakes and rivers were drawn as a line feature class.

In addition to the place names data, narratives also included discussion of various overland and water travel systems. These were depicted as line features which tried to mimic the most likely travel route between two described points, and also polygon features, which captured an array of place names described in a single story or narrative by an informant. At the time of writing, 42 trail systems, ten place name arrays, 197 new Ahtna place names, and 673 lakes and rivers had been geo-referenced (see Figure 27.5).

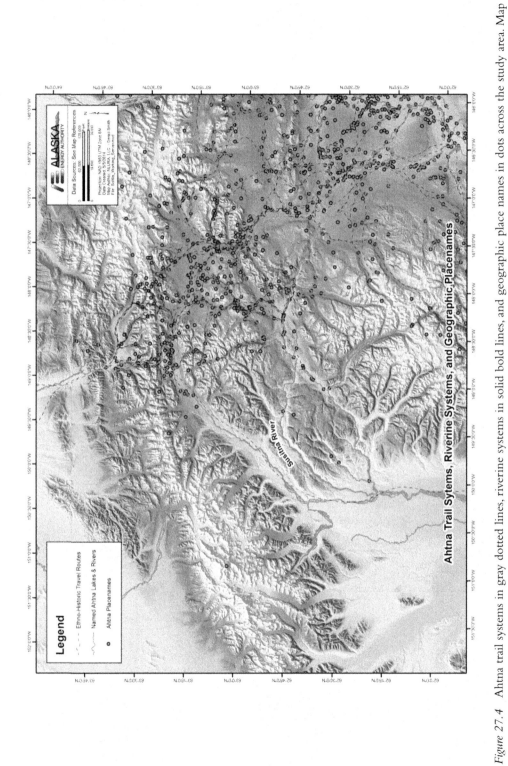

Figure 27.4 Ahtna trail systems in gray dotted lines, riverine systems in solid bold lines, and geographic place names in dots across the study area. Map created by Gerad Smith; permission to use by J.E. Kari.

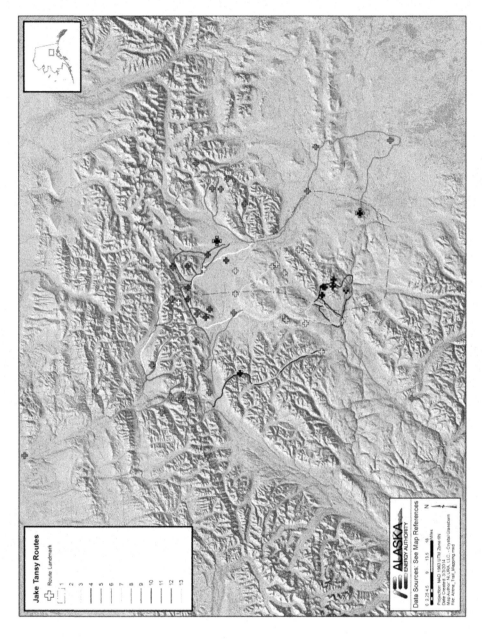

Figure 27.5 Western Ahtna routes and landmarks within and around the study area that have been geo-referenced and mapped into GIS. Map created by Gerad Smith; permission to use by J. E. Kari.

Results

The purpose of the archaeological and ethnogeographical programs of the study was to determine if correlations exist between prehistoric, protohistoric, historic, and ethnohistoric site locations and various ecological datasets in order to facilitate archaeological search strategies and inform spatial behaviors among site groups. Geospatial modelling efforts in the interior has introduced fine-grained methods with strong results.[19] The unique methods utilized in this study were first explored and developed in the Yukon–Tanana Uplands[20] and primarily build upon methods developed by Ben A. Potter, Carol Gelvin-Reymiller and Ben A. Potter, Hays et al., and Dave Zeanah et al.[21] An initial, course-grained exploratory GIS model was developed in April 2012 by archaeologist Gelvin-Reymiller to facilitate the first year of archaeological exploration in this region. This approach was what was available during that initial phase of exploration in an area where the accuracy of reported site locations could not be ascertained. After the 2012 field season, actual site locations were determined to deviate as much as 650 ft from their archived locations.

A fine-grained model was developed by archaeologist Gerad Smith in April 2013, and was used in part to inform target areas for further exploration. At the end of the 2013 field season, a large percentage of previously known sites had been relocated and locations refined, and used to test the model's applicability. In March of 2014 funds became available to combine the existing ethnohistoric dataset with the GIS model. But first, the dataset needed to be transferred from mainly paper maps, texts, translations, recordings, and interviews.

The Ahtna Place Names Lists assembled as a draft in the 1980s by Jim Kari[22] was revised and updated (including map locations) by the study team in 2013, resulting in a total of 2,744 records for the entire Ahtna region. The number of records was increased by 21 percent for three sections relevant to the project: the Nenana River (nineteen additional records), Susitna River (twenty additional records) and Gulkana River (ten additional records). Currently there are 721 records pertaining to the study area.

In addition to place names in the Ahtna language, current records include locally used English names not officially on maps such as 'Glacier Stream', 'Four Mile Lake', 'Moose Meadows', and 'Wolf Point'. While the geographic coverage of such unofficial place names is uneven, these locally used terms afford a sense of how functional place-naming continues on the current landscape, especially in the hands of Cantwell Ahtna people.

How GIS was critical to this case study

GIS provides the best database for languages linked to the landscape. The directional dimension of Western Athna and Northern Athabascan languages relies on clear description of features, resources, watersheds, and landmarks in a specific order. The repetition of specific words, such as resource procurement place names, were key to the archaeological success of the project. Kari explains, 'The Athabascan riverine directional system is the organizational intersection between the geography, the lexicon, and the grammar.'[23] GIS proved to be the most robust database where the people and the language are inextricably linked to the land. The archaeological evidence corroborates this connection to certain resources and areas. But the evidence is sparse compared to the linguistic data that inform which directions people traveled, the time of year, the type of resource harvest, and even ancient battle grounds. To have a tool that can combine the archaeological and linguistic datasets is invaluable to researchers in Alaska.

The following translation directly resulted in the identification of a cultural resource site rediscovered by archaeological helicopter survey, 'We had traps set and snares on the mountain sides there for ground squirrel.'[24] In lower elevations where caribou migrate linguistics data, now available in a geodatabase, identified a resource rich area. Archaeological survey focused in a lake system: Deadman Lake and Big Lake, originally known as 'Kacaagh xu' (Deadman Lake area). Several previously undiscovered sites were found in and around this watershed. What's significant is that is same area was surveyed in the 1980s and very few sites were identified. The difference is our team had the geo-referenced ethnohistory that identified this area as resource rich. Ground survey revealed a high density of surface lithic scatters resource sites.[25]

A third example highlights the spatial and temporal nature of GIS, in this case deep history. The name *Nac' a[e]leuut Na* translates to 'food is brought back stream'.[26] This Western Ahtna word is a direct link to the deep past. The 'food' referenced here refers to caribou that are known to aggregate in large herds during the summer months. For the last 9,000 years the people of this region have been sustained by this important resource. Not only is the meat necessary to sustain a family through the winter but the hides, antlers, and bones also provide essential materials for tool and clothing manufacture.

Responsible management of any resource whether natural, cultural, or a combination of the two requires a spatial geodatabase. Regardless of the datum used to map data collected in the field it has been invaluable to manage those data in a robust database. Files can be edited down to fine-grained accuracy in a geodatabase and uploaded to a GPS unit for real-time field information.

Conclusions: advancing CRM with GIS

Spatial and temporal datasets by definition require a tool that can manage large areas and topics through time. GIS has become that software tool and database manager that can handle field data, analyze trends in real time, produce reports, model landscapes, or geo-reference oral histories. The uses are infinite and have become a standard in natural and cultural resources. Where CRM stands to gain is in the streamlining of field-to-analysis-to-reporting phases of all project management. Big projects to small projects can be simply set up and managed as geodatabase files. Firms with available resources have begun to devote entire server structures to handle only GIS files and programs. The result has been overall positive for the CRM industry.

The study team used oral histories and other ethnogeographic information to incorporate place names, routes, trails, and other traditionally recognized features into a GIS geodatabase, allowing correlation of ethnohistoric datasets with prehistoric archaeology datasets. The ethnographic record indicates that indigenous groups migrated in annual, repetitive patterns across the landscape, and that these patterns were dependent on game location and proximity to enemy territory. Despite oral histories about hostilities, the archaeological record reflects similar artifacts, houses, and subsistence strategies among the three groups. A total of 68 known AHRS sites were rerecorded, and an additional 82 new sites were recorded. Together with the three new sites found in 2012, the site inventory in the portion of the direct APE surveyed thus far currently totals 167 AHRS sites.

Notes

1 J. M. Hays, P. M. Bowers, C. M. Mobley and T. Brelsford, *Revised Study Plan*. Report Prepared for the Alaska Energy Authority by Northern Land Use Research, Inc., Fairbanks, AK: Charles M. Mobley and Associates, and URS Corporation, 2012.

2 G. H. Bacon and C. E. Holmes, *Archeological Survey and Inventory of Cultural Resources at Fort Greely, Alaska, 1979*. Final Report. Submitted to Alaska District, US Army Corps of Engineers, 1980; J. P. Cook (ed), *Pipeline Archeology*, vol. 1, Fairbanks, AK: University of Alaska Institute of Arctic Biology, 1977; E. J Dixon, G. S. Smith and D. C. Plaskett, *Procedures Manual/Research Design Subtask 7.06: Cultural Resources Investigation for the Susitna Hydropower Project*. Alaska Power Authority. Submitted to Terrestrial Environmental Specialists, New York: Phoenix, Contract No. 218-102, 1980; J. E. Dixon, W. Andrefsky, C. J. Utermohle, G. S. Smith and B. M. Saleeby, *Susitna Hydroelectric Project: Cultural Resources Investigations 1979–1985,* appendix D (parts 1, 2 and 3), vols. 3, 4 and 5, Fairbanks, AK: University of Alaska Museum, submitted to Alaska Power Authority, 1985; J. E. Dixon, W. Andrefsky, C. J. Utermohle, G. S. Smith and B. M. Saleeby, *Susitna Hydroelectric Project: Cultural Resources Investigations 1979–1985,* appendix D (part 2), vol. 4, Fairbanks, AK: University of Alaska Museum, submitted to Alaska Power Authority, 1985; C. E. Holmes, *Archeological Reconnaissance Report for Fort Wainwright, Fort Greely, and Fort Richardson Withdrawal Lands, Alaska,* Report prepared for 172nd Infantry Brigade, 1979; A. D. Shinkwin and J. S. Aigner, *Historic and Prehistoric Land Use in the Upper Tanana Valley: Report on the Archaeological Survey along the Alaska Highway Pipeline from Delta Junction to the Yukon Border,* Fairbanks, AK: University of Alaska, submitted to the Northwest Pipeline Co., 1979.

3 This section was originally prepared for the Alaska Energy Authority, see: J. M. Hays, C. Gelvin-Reymiller, P. M. Bowers, C. M. Mobley and T. Brelsford, *Cultural Resources Study,* Report prepared for the Alaska Energy Authority by Northern Land Use Research, Inc., Fairbanks, AK: Charles M. Mobley and Associates, and URS Corporation, 2013.

4 J. E. Kari, 'A Case Study in Ahtna Athabascan Geographic Knowledge', in D. M. Mark, A. G. Turk, N. Burenhult and D. Stea (eds), *Landscape in Language, Transdisciplinary Perspectives*, Amsterdam: John Benjamins, 2011, 248.

5 J. E. Kari, 'Ahtna Geographic Names: A Case Study in Alaska Athabascan Geographic Knowledge', presented at the Landscape in Language Workshop, Albuquerque, NM, and Chinle, AZ, 2008; J. E. Kari, *Place Names Maps for Ahtna, Inc.*, Alaska Native Language Center, UAF. Compact disc with 17 PDF files, 2012.

6 J. E. Kari and J. A. Fall (eds), *Shem Pete's Alaska: The Territory of the Upper Cook Inlet Dena'ina*, Fairbanks, AK: Alaska Native Language Center, University of Alaska; and Anchorage, AK: CIRI Foundation, 1987.

7 J. E. Kari, *Ahtna Travel Narratives: A Demonstration of Shared Geographic Knowledge among Alaskan Athabascans,* Fairbanks, AK: Alaska Native Language Center, 2010.

8 Alaska Department of Natural Resources, Office of History and Archaeology (ADNR, OHA), *Standards and Guidelines for Investigating and Reporting Archaeological and Historic Properties in Alaska,* Historic Preservation Series No. 11, Anchorage, AK: Alaska Department of Natural Resources, 2013; Alaska Heritage Resources Survey, http://dnr.alaska.gov/parks/oha/ahrs/ahrs.htm, accessed January 8, 2014.

9 N. H. Bigelow, 'Late Quaternary Vegetation and Lake Level Changes in Central Alaska', PhD dissertation, Department of Anthropology, University of Alaska, Fairbanks, 1997; D. H. Mann, A. Crowell, T. D. Hamilton, and B. Finney, 'Holocene Geologic and Climatic History around the Gulf of Alaska', *Arctic Anthropology* 35, XXXX, 112–131; O. K. Mason and N. H. Bigelow, 'The Crucible of Early to Mid-Holocene Climate in Northern Alaska: Does Northern Archaic Represent the People of the Spreading Forest?', *Arctic Anthropology* 45, 39–70.

10 R. C. Betts, *Archaeological Investigations at Butte Lake, Alaska: An Inquiry into Alaskan Notched Point-Microblade Assemblages,* Fairbanks, AK: University of Alaska, Department of Anthropology, Geist Fund Report 91, 1987.

11 Dixon et al., *Susitna Hydroelectric Project.*

12 N. H. Bigelow, J. Reuther, M. Woller and K. Wallace, *Holocene Landscape and Paleoenvironments,* Report prepared by the University of Alaska, Fairbanks, 2015.

13 H. Peters and J. Peters, *Nay'nadełi I'ghaan Dghat'aen'den (The War at Nay'nadełi),* Alaska Native Language Center, 1977.

14 F. de Laguna, 'The Ahtna of the Copper River, Alaska: The World of Men and Animals', *Folk,* 11–12, 1969–70, 17–26; F. de Laguna, 'Sites in Ahtna Territory', manuscript on file at Alaska Department of Fish and Game, Division of Subsistence, Anchorage, AK, 1970; F. de Laguna and C. McClellan, 'Ahtna', in J. Helm (ed.), *Subarctic,* Handbook of North American Indians, vol. 6, ed. W. C. Sturtevant, Washington, DC: Smithsonian Institution Press, 641–63; C. McClellan, 'Introduction: Athabascan Studies', *Western Canadian Journal of Anthropology* 2, 1970, pp. vi–xix; C. McClellan, 'Feuding and Warfare among North-western Athapaskans', in A. M. Clark (ed), *Proceedings: Northern Athapaskan Conference, 1971,* vol. 1, Ottawa: National Museums of Canada, 1975, 181–258.

15 H. Reckord, *That's the Way we Live: Subsistence in the Wrangell-St. Elias National Park and Preserve,* Occasional Paper No. 34, Anthropology and Historic Preservation, Fairbanks, AK: Cooperative Park Studies Unit, University of Alaska, 1983; H. Reckord, *Where Raven Stood: Cultural Resources of the Ahtna Region,* Occasional Paper 35, Anthropology and Historic Preservation, Fairbanks, AK: Cooperative Park Studies Unit, University of Alaska, 1983.

16 C. West, 'Inventory of Trails and Habitation Sites in the Ahtna Region', manuscript on file, Anchorage, AK: Alaska Department of Fish and Game Division of Subsistence, 1973.

17 P. F. Dessaur and D. W. Harvey, *An Historical Resource Study of the Valdez Creek Mining Company District, Alaska–1977,* Anchorage, AK: US Bureau of Land Management, 1980.

18 Kari, *Ahtna Geographic Names.*

19 G. S. Smith, 'Highland Hunters: Resource Use in the Yukon-Tanana Uplands', Master's thesis, Department of Anthropology University of Alaska, Fairbanks, 2012; B. A. Potter, *Site Location Model and Survey Strategy for Cultural Resources in the Alaska Railroad Northern Rail Extension Project Area.* Northern Land Use Research Inc.s submitted to ICF Consulting Services, LLC, 2006; C. Gelvin-Reymiller and B. A. Potter, *Site Location Model and Survey Strategy for Cultural Resources in the White Mountain National Recreation Area and Steese National Conservation Areas,* submitted to the Fairbanks District Office, Bureau of Land Management, 2009; J. D. Reuther, J. S. Rogers, C. Gelvin-Reymiller, A. S. Higgs, C. Wooley, J. Baxter-McIntosh, R. C. Bowman and P. T. Hall, *Results of the 2012 Phase I and II Cultural Resources Survey of the Proposed Donlin Gold Natural Gas Pipeline*

Study, Northern Land Use Research, Inc., submitted to the Alaska Office of History and Archaeology, Alaska State Historic Preservation Office, Alaska Division of Parks and Outdoor Recreation, and the Bureau of Land Management, 2013.

20 Smith, *Highland Hunters*.

21 Potter, *Site Location Model and Survey Strategy*; Gelvin-Reymiller and Potter, *Site Location Model and Survey Strategy*; Hays et al., *Revised Study Plan*; Hays et al., *Cultural Resources Study*; J. M. Hays, C. M. Mobley, W. E. Simeone and J. E. Kari, *Cultural Resources Study: Study Plan*, Section 13.5, Initial Study Report prepared for the Alaska Energy Authority by Northern Land Use Research, Inc., Charles M. Mobley and Associates, and URS Corporation, Fairbanks, 2014; D. W. Zeanah, J. A. Carter, D. P. Dugas, R. G. Elston and J. E. Hammett, *An Optimal Foraging Model of Hunter-Gatherer Land Use in the Carson Desert*. Silver City, NV: US Fish and Wildlife Service, US Department of the Navy, and Intermountain Research, 1995.

22 Kari, *Ahtna Geographic Names*.

23 Kari, *Ahtna Travel Narratives*, 129.

24 Kari, *Ahtna Travel Narratives*, 64.

25 Hays et al., *Cultural Resources Study*.

26 Kari, *Ahtna Travel Narratives*, 69.

28

'MULTIPLICITY EMBARRASSES THE EYE'

The digital mapping of literary Edinburgh

James Loxley, Beatrice Alex, Miranda Anderson, Uta Hinrichs,
Claire Grover, David Harris-Birtill, Tara Thomson,
Aaron Quigley, and Jon Oberlander

Literature, geocriticism and digital opportunities

There has long been a deep intertwining of the concepts, experiences and memories of space and place and the practice of literature. But while it might be possible to conduct a spatially aware critical analysis of any text, not all texts manifest such self-conscious spatial awareness. Literary history, nevertheless, is rich with genres and modes that do, from classical pastoral and renaissance estate verse to metadrama, utopian writing and concrete poetry. Any critic seeking to give an analytical account of such writing will find it hard to overlook its immersive engagement with space and spatiality. And literary criticism has also enriched its vocabulary with concepts drawn from a range of modern and contemporary theoretical sources. Mikhail Bakhtin's notion of the chronotope, he suggested, named 'a formally constitutive category of literature', marking an irreducible spatiality (intertwined, for Bakhtin, with temporality) which was yet manifest only in particular, historically and generically specific, configurations.[1] Michel de Certeau developed a very different approach, distinguishing space from place in a distinctive fashion that has had a significant influence on literary critics.[2] Yi-Fu Tuan's own conceptualisation of this distinction has also had a literary critical resonance.[3] Henri Lefebvre's account of the 'production of space', with its conceptual triad of 'spatial practice', 'representation of space' and 'representational space', has also exerted its pull.[4]

Recently, however, literary critical interest in spatiality has reached a new intensity. No single label, let alone conceptual orientation, covers the range and kinds of work being undertaken. Where practitioners and observers have attempted definition, they have of necessity had to think inclusively. So Robert Tally, one of the most influential current critics working in this area, has sought to cast the net widely. As he says:

> I consider spatial literary studies – whether doing business as geocriticism, literary geography, the spatial humanities, or using some other moniker – as a multiform critical practice that would include almost any approach to the

text that focuses attention on space, place, or mapping, whether within the confines of the text, in reference to the outside world, or some combination of the two. What Edward W. Soja has termed the real-and-imagined places of literature, criticism, history, and theory, as well as of our own abstract conceptions and lived experience, these constitute the practical domain for spatial literary studies.[5]

For Tally, geocriticism itself names 'something like a general comportment toward the text, rather than a discrete methodology with its own set of rules and conventions'.[6] While his is not the only possible understanding of what either 'geocriticism' or 'spatial literary studies' might be, it is one that manages to grasp both the centrifugal and centripetal forces at work in current research in the field. And while Tally is obviously alert to the great differences between – to cite his examples – 'using geographical information systems (G.I.S.) to chart a novel's character or plot trajectories along the physical topography of a given region' and 'examining the concepts of *deterritorialization* and *reterritorialization* in theorizing matters of poststructuralist geophilosophy', he is right to seek to maintain a dialogue between them.

Central to the geocritical approach taken by Tally and others (particularly Bertrand Westphal, some of whose work Tally has translated into English[7]) is the notion of mapping. Literary texts have a cartographic dimension, to which a geocritical approach is attuned and which it seeks to bring out. Here, geocriticism perhaps insistently literalises what has been a sometimes metaphorical approach to cartography as a way of accounting for, or making sense of, a literary text's spatiality. This is an approach that chimes with long-term tendencies in the influential critical work of Franco Moretti. Moretti's own sense of the explanatory power of cartographic representation, first thoroughly evident in his *Atlas of the European Novel, 1800–1900*, has provoked and complemented his interest in the usefulness of computational methods in literary analysis, the practice of 'distant reading' with which his name is now definitively associated.[8] The convergence of the cartographic and the computational demonstrated by Moretti is part and parcel of a broader interest in such possibilities, visible in different ways in Ian Gregory and David Cooper's *Mapping the Lakes*, Barbara Piatti's *Literary Atlas of Europe*, Shelley Fisher Fishkin's collaborative *Digital Palimpsest Mapping Project* and the 'z-axis' work of the *Modernist Versions Project*, to name only four recent examples.[9]

It is possible, too, that digital approaches might offer solutions to geocritical problems which are insoluble in other ways. Tally himself has raised what, from one perspective, is an insuperable limit to Westphal's project:

> How does one determine exactly which texts could, in the aggregate, reasonably constitute a meaningful body of material with which to analyze the literary representations of a given geographical site? ... With certain cities, such as Paris, London, Rome, or New York, the almost mythic status of these places and the seemingly innumerable textual references to them render any geocritical analysis, at least those laying claim to a kind of scientific value, impossible. As Westphal admits, 'to attempt to undertake a full-scale geocritical analysis of those hotspots would be madness.' A geo-centered

method, if it aims truly to avoid the perception of bias, seems somewhat doomed from the start.[10]

There is here an echo of the modern and postmodern experience of the cityscape – a space or place too densely and variously populated to map or hold in a single prospective view.

But perhaps peeking beyond the horizon of possibility imagined here need not be 'madness' after all. Text mining and data visualisation technologies open up the possibility of reading very large corpora for their geocritical significance, or at least of creating the conditions for more thoroughgoing geocritical exploration to take place. This is a way of thinking about the relationship between literature and cartography at several different levels – not just the 'internal' map of a literary work, or the literary use of non-literary locations, but also the ways in which multiple texts might meaningfully coincide or vary in the way that they engage with the same loci. Where smaller scale studies might focus most on the former possibilities, the larger scale aggregation and alignment of literary representations of place offers opportunities for interaction and analysis that might well lead us to wonder about what 'full-scale geocritical analysis', and the attendant qualifying notion of 'scientific value', can actually mean.

The Palimpsest project: mapping literary Edinburgh

The Palimpsest project, undertaken at the universities of Edinburgh and St Andrews in 2014–15, provides an example of this larger scale digital analysis. The project was conducted by an interdisciplinary research team of literature and informatics scholars, including specialists in text mining, geoparsing, data visualisation and computer–human interaction. Taking up the challenges posed by Tally, the Palimpsest team sought to devise a way in which one could digitally map narrative representations of a city, in this case Edinburgh, translating a literary critical approach to place into a digitally intelligible model.

The self-conscious 'literariness' of Edinburgh, and its existing history of literary tourism, make it an ideal case for this type of research. It stands rather overtly as one of those 'real-and-imagined places of literature' that Tally describes:[11] a city that has been extensively reimagined through narrative and prides itself as a literary locale. In the 1840s, a 60-metre tall monument to Sir Walter Scott was erected, which now looms over the city's central train station, itself named after one of Scott's novels. Edinburgh was already regarded by the nineteenth century as a city defined by, and imagined through, its literary spaces. Laurence Hutton's *Literary Landmarks of Edinburgh* begins with the claim: 'No city in the world of its age and size – for Athens is older and London is larger – is so rich as Edinburgh in its literary associations, and no citizens anywhere show so much respect and so much fondness for the history and traditions of their literary men'.[12] He continues to marvel that this interest is not just found in the educated classes, but 'among the more poorly housed and the less educated classes, in whom one would least expect to find it'.[13] His opening portrait of Edinburgh is a city in which ordinary, everyday life is suffused with literary memory, even through its dirtiest pubs and its smallest wynds. This literary spatial memory stretches in Hutton's narrative from the seventeenth century onward, beginning with William Drummond's 'Hie Schule', built in 1567, and leading to Dr John Brown's mid-nineteenth-century Rutland Street home.

Hutton's approach to the city is still reflected in Edinburgh literary tourism. Visitors can take literary tours, walking past the homes of great authors such as Robert Burns or Arthur Conan Doyle, sitting in pubs visited by Johnson and Boswell, or stopping at the cafés in which J. K. Rowling wrote the first Harry Potter novel. Most of these tours approach Edinburgh as the real place that nurtured and inspired great works of literature, although more recently some take visitors past Edinburgh locations that are imagined in literary works, such as the tours of Irvine Welsh's Leith or locations that feature in Ian Rankin's Rebus novels. In 2004, Edinburgh was the first city to win a UNESCO World City of Literature designation, and while its literary tourist industry continues to grow, the focus of most tours remains on landmarks and topographical routes, including limited literary content.

The Palimpsest project wanted to instead offer a different experience of literary Edinburgh – a more text-centred experience, that would enable users to explore narratives from different periods clustered at one location, or narratives that span locations across the city. Building on findings from a prototype developed in 2012 from an idea by Miranda Anderson, the project team aimed to gather a more expansive dataset by mining several large collections of digitised text for works set in Edinburgh. We envisioned two visualisation tools through which end users could explore our database: an interactive map of Edinburgh, featuring narrative extracts set in locations around the city, and a complementary mobile application that would allow users to move through narrative imaginings of the city *in situ*. The database interface and suite of visualisations was released online under the name LitLong: Edinburgh.[14] Rather than using off-the-shelf software, the team developed these tools specifically for the Palimpsest project; however, many of their features draw on familiar visualisations, such as Google Maps, GPS navigation, word clouds and histograms.

The question of which texts would form the dataset for LitLong, the 'meaningful body of material' to which Tally points, was left, at least initially, to the algorithmic processes described in the next section.[15] However, human curation was required to ensure the selected texts met our literary critical criteria, and these criteria were devised prior to the text mining, in order to guide the computing processes. We were looking for 'Edinburgh-centric' works, which either belonged to a recognisably literary genre, such as the novel or short story, or had strong narrative or locodescriptive components – both memoirs and travel journals, for example, were included. We chose the use and frequency of place names as our primary marker in defining an 'Edinburgh-centric' work, and our gazetteer of Edinburgh place names guided our text searches, geolocation processes and shaped the end visualisations.

Text analysis and the geo-location of literary place

The text processing work carried out for Palimpsest involved three main steps: (i) the creation of an Edinburgh gazetteer; (ii) retrieval and ranking of Edinburgh-specific literature candidates; and (iii) textual analysis of the Edinburgh-centric literature.

Each of these tasks presented conceptual and practical challenges. There is no freely available gazetteer which includes all the Edinburgh place names the use of which we wanted to capture. These place names have different granularity, from area names (*Portobello, Cramond*), through street names (*The Royal Mile, Cockburn Street*) to open spaces (*The Meadows, Princes Street Gardens*), buildings (*Craigmillar Castle, Holyrood Palace*), statues and monuments (*Greyfriars Bobby, The Scott Monument*) etc. Therefore, a prerequisite for geo-referencing was to create an Edinburgh gazetteer by aggregating information from a variety of different sources. For street names we used OS Locator (OSL), for building-level information we used the Canmore site records database from the Royal Commission on the Ancient and Historic Monuments of Scotland (RCAHMS). For other information from area names through to pub names, we used an Edinburgh subset of Open Street Map (OSM). The aim was to create a gazetteer which could be used both as a place name lexicon when identifying potential place names in text and as a gazetteer for geo-referencing, i.e. assigning coordinates to recognised place names.

The aggregation process involved converting records from the three sources into a common XML format followed by a data clean-up stage to discard records which might trigger faulty recognition of place names in text. For example, RCAHMS has records for places with generic names such as *Station House* or *Barracks*, as well as records for residential houses with names such as *Bonny Views*. OSM has records for numerous modern-day businesses such as *Bay of Bengal* (a restaurant) and *Blossom* (a guest house). We attempted to exclude records such as these semi-automatically but the final gazetteer still contains many questionable Edinburgh place names, e.g. *Alien Rock* (a climbing centre), *Alpine Garden* (part of the Royal Botanic Gardens Edinburgh), *Beach House* (generic descriptor) and *The Waiting Room* (a pub). The presence of this kind of record in the gazetteer, however, does not seem to have had too deleterious an effect on place name recognition and subsequent geo-referencing. There are some place names which occur in the Palimpsest books for which none of the three sources has a record. These are mostly historical forms of modern place names or spelling variants (for example, *Cowgate-port, Nor' Loch, Edinboro*). For cases where such an omission has been observed, we have manually added appropriate records. The final version of the Edinburgh gazetteer contains 13,064 records corresponding to 10,204 unique place names.

The aim of the retrieval and ranking component is to identify in the pool of accessible literature those works which are likely candidates for being Edinburgh-specific and rank them. The goal was to uncover items of literature which would not immediately come to mind when being asked to name literature set in Edinburgh. We processed five major literary collections containing over 388,000 books in total, including world public domain works from HathiTrust, the British Library Nineteenth Century Books collection, out-of-copyright Project Gutenberg books, the Oxford Text Archive data and works from the National Library of Scotland.

In order to retrieve candidates of Edinburgh-specific literature, all of the literary data was indexed using Indri 5.6 and ranked using a set of 1,633 Edinburgh place name queries. We used the Indri inference network language model based ranking approach.[16] In our case, the ranking score of a document is computed by combining the score for the location query retrieved from the content of a book with a score based on information in the metadata of the book. For example, the ranking is increased given the presence of a set of favoured Library of Congress codes (including PR, DA, PZ, PN and PS) as well as given a list of relevant subject terms (edinburgh, scotland, literature, fiction, novel, poetry, poem, story, stories, drama, novella, english, biography, ballads, ballad, scottish). This is to allow documents with such metadata information to appear higher in the ranking. At the same time, the ranking score is down-weighted for ambiguity of Edinburgh place names in order to push documents which mention place names most likely not referring to a location within Edinburgh, like *Trinity*, down the list. The output of the document retrieval component is a set of ranked Edinburgh-specific candidate documents per collection. The ranked output was visualised using a curation tool developed by the SACHI group at the University of St Andrews. The curation tool was used for manual curation in order to guarantee that the final Palimpsest data set is of high recall as well as of high precision.

During the project, we fine-tuned the ranking component based on feedback from the curators after a two-week pilot curation phase. We considered additional ambiguous place names identified by the curators, removed documents containing non-literary title words (e.g. dictionary, catalogue, etc.) and ensured that the place name *Edinburgh* or one of its variants (e.g. *Edinburrie*, *Embra*, etc.) occurred at least once in the document. Alex et al. showed that these three measures lead to a small improvement in the mean average precision (MAP) of the ranking on a test set created during the pilot.[17] Most importantly, however, they resulted in a large reduction in the number of ranked documents (60 per cent) needing curation, which considerably reduced the workload of the curators. Since we conducted this work, Ted Underwood has published a methodology and code for identifying genre within the HathiTrust data.[18] Information on the genre (if not already available in the metadata) would considerably improve the quality of the ranked output as much of the manual curation of the ranked output was to differentiate between fictional and non-fictional works containing Edinburgh-based locations.

Using the optimised retrieval and ranking component, a total of 33,277 ranked documents were presented to the curators. Documents were ranked per collection as the type of metadata information available differed considerably. As a result of time constraints and evaluating the candidates further down the list in the ranked output, the decision was made only to curate the top 10 per cent per collection manually. This resulted in 503 out-of-copyright documents which were considered to be part of the Palimpsest corpus and therefore contained an Edinburgh setting. A further 43 documents from modern authors for which we received permission from publishers were also added to this corpus.

The text mining part of the system is done using a Palimpsest-adapted version of the Edinburgh Geoparser.[19] This contains two main components, a text mining pipeline for recognising place names and other entities in text and a geographic ambiguity resolution component which chooses between competing interpretations of place names (i.e. competing geographic coordinates) given their textual context.

The text mining pipeline first converts an input text into a common XML format and then each stage of processing incrementally adds annotations into the mark-up. First the text is segmented into paragraphs which are tokenised to add word and sentence elements. Words are part-of-speech tagged and lemmatised and then Named Entity Recognition (NER) is performed using hand-written rule sets combined with lexical look-up. For place name recognition, extensive lexicons of place names both from the UK and the rest of the world are used, and in the Palimpsest system this stage is augmented to include a lexicon of Edinburgh place names derived from the Edinburgh gazetteer.

The output of the text mining contains named entity annotations for dates, person names and place names. This is input to the geo-resolution step which looks up the place names in one or more gazetteers and ranks the results to arrive at the most probable interpretation given the context of the document. In Palimpsest, look-up in the Edinburgh gazetteer is done before look-up in more general Ordnance Survey and Geonames gazetteers which the system accesses via Edina's Unlock Places web service. Ranking uses heuristics combined with weighting of information such as geographic feature and size. We assume that a degree of geographic coherence holds within documents in that the relevant text is more likely to mention many places in a single area rather than a set of geographically unrelated places. To model this, proximity between gazetteer records for all the places mentioned in the document is strongly weighted to ensure that all locations mutually constrain one another to be as close together as possible. Thus the highest ranked interpretation of *Haymarket* will be the one in Edinburgh in a document that contains many Edinburgh or Scottish place names rather than the one in London in a document with more London or English place names.

The results of geo-resolution are added as XML annotations in the document and all that remains is to mark up the immediate context of each place name for display in the Palimpsest interfaces. We call the context surrounding a geo-referenced Edinburgh place name mention a Palimpsest snippet. In the final system implementation, we set this context to be the sentence containing the location as well as the previous and following sentence without crossing paragraph boundaries.

The Palimpsest snippets were also ranked by an 'interestingness' score (i-score). This was inspired by work on automatic prediction of text aesthetics and interestingness.[20] The aim is to rank snippets per document to give those snippets where the Edinburgh place name is not just a mention in passing more importance and therefore make them appear earlier on in the user interfaces. We compute this score by checking for a number of features, including snippet length, the presence of multiple Edinburgh-based locations in snippet, the presence of at least one Edinburgh-based location (excluding variants of Edinburgh), an adjective or adverb appearing in the snippet, the presence of different forms of certain verbs (be, do, say or go) and word repetition within the snippet. The i-score is computed by treating each of the features equally and can range between a value of 0 and 1 where 1 represents snippets for which all features apply and 0 those where none of the features apply.

The output of the text processing components is fed into a database which provides the input data for the user interfaces. It comprises of over 550 literary works mentioning 1,600 unique Edinburgh locations mentioned in more than 47,000 literary excerpts. This is an especially rich, large-scale dataset for a geocritical project, and constitutes a start, at least, on the work of gaining an effective mapping of the kind of literary 'high place' mentioned by Westphal and Tally.

Visualising literary place

The accessibility and utility of such a dataset, however, depends on its user interfaces. The study of geographic space and place from a literary perspective seems to automatically call for some sort of visual tools – call them maps – that facilitate explorations as well as the communication of patterns. Canonically, geographic locations are mapped to 2D space based on their unique latitude and longitude in order to explore or analyse spatial relations that would be otherwise impossible or, at least, difficult to decipher. Geospatial data is unique in that it comes with an inherent position which can be utilised in visual representations. In contrast, data extracted from literary texts such as the characteristics of the chosen language, applied grammatical structures or more content-related themes and relations between literary characters are more abstract – a range of different types of visual mappings may be plausible to visualise this sort of data. For instance, a group of literary characters could be represented as dots positioned in a single large circle with connecting lines representing their relations. When dealing with place names in a literary text one often intuitively thinks of these locations in terms of their geospatial meaning. Visualising literary space is challenged by this notion of abstract text on the one hand, and inherent geospatial meanings that invite conventional geospatial mapping on the other.

The visualisations and interactive interfaces we designed as part of the Palimpsest project – which were published online under the more easily pronounceable title of LitLong – are based on the idea of making the meaning of place in Edinburgh literature explorable for different audiences and in different contexts, once again reflecting the sheer multiplicity of literary interest and experience provoked by the city. Researchers, for example, may want to apply an analytical perspective to explore the data in depth from different perspectives focusing on authors, titles, themes and genre, publication year, or particular place name mentions as an entry point. In contrast, a general-interest audience may want to explore literature related to selected books or well-known neighbourhoods in Edinburgh. General-interest audiences may include visitors who wish to explore how famous places such as the Royal Mile have been mentioned in literature; people living in the city may experience known and familiar locations in a new way and with fresh eyes by exploring related literary work – as Renton describes it in *Trainspotting*: 'They say you have to live in a place to know it, but you have to come fresh tae it tae really see it.'[21] Interviews we conducted with literary scholars early on in the project indicated that in-situ explorations are of interest to academic scholars who may want to experience the places mentioned in literature themselves to facilitate interpretation.

To address these different potential exploration scenarios we developed two different visual interfaces that can be considered a first approach to explore this design space of visualising the literary layer of a city. The Location Visualiser is a visual web-interface that allows the exploration of literary snippets related to places in Edinburgh from a birds-eye point of view. The LitLong app is a mobile application that runs on a smart phone, and shows corresponding literary snippets as people explore Edinburgh in-situ, while walking through the city.

The Location Visualiser

The Location Visualiser in LitLong is a web-based interface that provides a general overview of place name mentions in the final literary works we included in our dataset through the text mining and editing processes described in the previous section.

The interface consists of three main components: a map showing the real-world place name mentions included in the literary works, a timeline, showing the distribution of literature over time, and a book list, listing the literary works, their corresponding author, publication year, and a link to the digitised version of the book (Figure 28.1). All three views are interlinked: interacting with one automatically updates the others. Various search filters are provided to enable more targeted explorations by keyword, place name or author. The Location Visualiser is implemented in JavaScript and PhD using standard libraries such as D3.js (for the general visualisation components) and Leaflet.js (for the map view). In the following we describe the different entry points the Location Visualiser facilitates into the Palimpsest literary collection and dataset.

One can start to explore data in the Location Visualiser with the map view. Here, place name mentions are presented on a conventional geospatial map based on their latitude and longitude. Place mentions in close proximity are shown as clusters to avoid clutter in frequently mentioned areas. Individual location mentions are shown as a quill symbol and location mention clusters are shown as filled blue circles with a number representing the amount of unique place names they represent. For example, Figure 28.2 shows four clusters of location mentions. Hovering over a cluster shows the geospatial area that it encompasses and a word cloud listing all corresponding place names with font sizes indicating their frequency of mention.

On demand, the word cloud also provides a glimpse of the literary context that the cluster encompasses. This begins to convey something of the context in which locations in this particular area were mentioned (see Figure 28.3).

The inspection of location clusters from this high-level point of view provides an idea of the literary topology of Edinburgh in terms of the popularity of certain areas in and around the city within English literature. Place names referring to locations in the inner area of the city of Edinburgh are quite frequent, whereas places outside the inner-city area are mentioned only in a few selected literary works (visible in the cluster of seven mentions). Clusters with fewer than 20 location mentions will directly display the corresponding literary snippets, instead of showing an overview of place names or keywords. Users can browse these snippets one by one; for each snippet the book title, author, and publication year is provided and identified place names are highlighted within the snippet (see Figure 28.4).

Zooming into the map enables a more fine-grained view of literary traces in and around the city. Clusters are broken down and details of the literary topology become visible (see Figure 28.5). The higher the zoom level, the smaller the geospatial areas and range of place names that location clusters encompass (see Figure 28.6).

Interacting with the map (i.e. zooming and panning) updates the other views as well as the potential filter options. The map acts as a location filter and the numbers of locations and authors are directly adjusted accordingly. Similarly, the booklist and timeline view are updated to show only titles that include place names included in the currently visible map section.

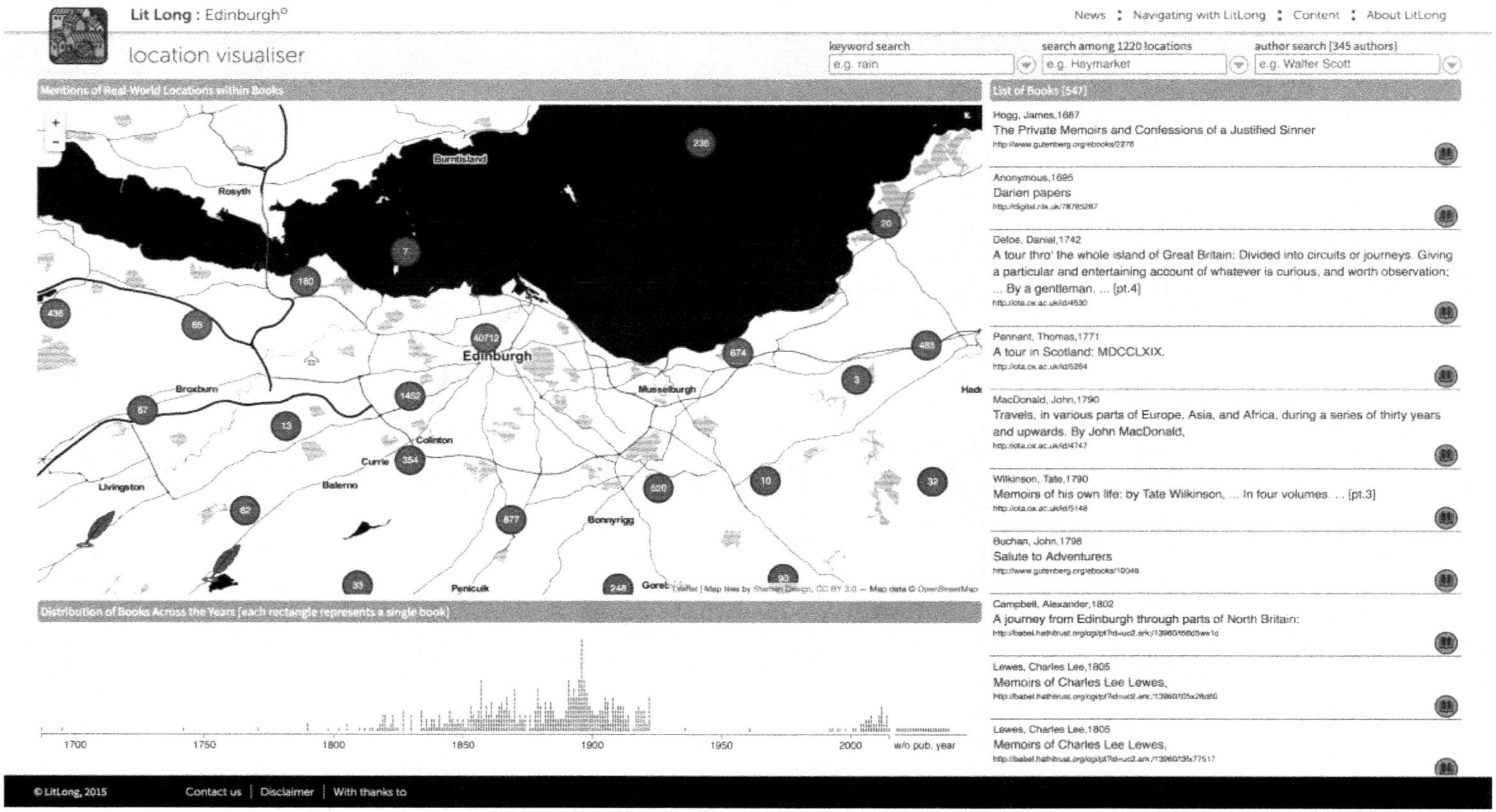

Figure 28.1 The Location Visualiser interface.

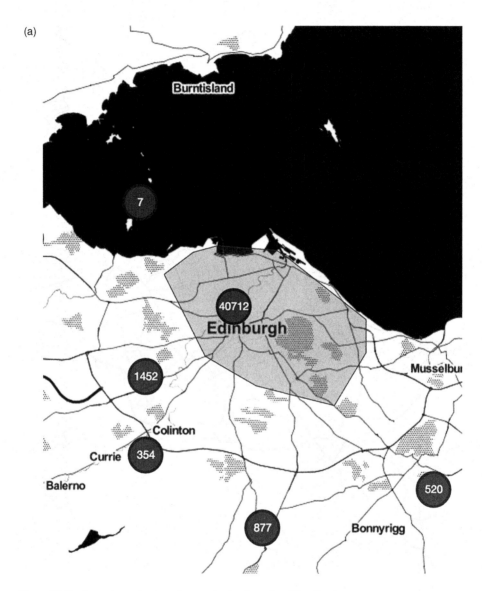

Figure 28.2 Location mention clusters in the Location Visualiser.

(b)

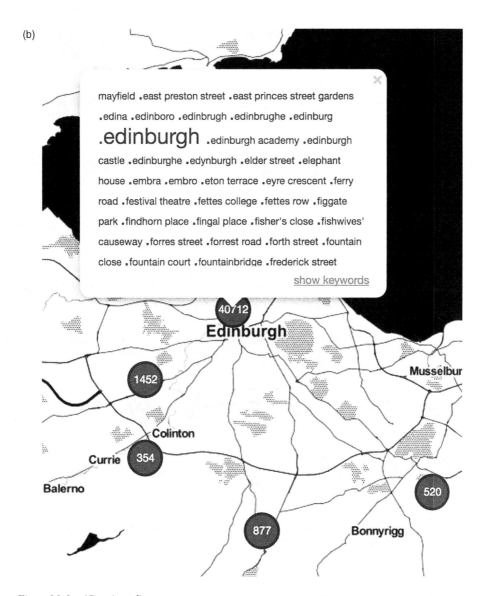

mayfield .east preston street .east princes street gardens
.edina .edinboro .edinbrugh .edinbrughe .edinburg
.edinburgh .edinburgh academy .edinburgh
castle .edinburghe .edynburgh .elder street .elephant
house .embra .embro .eton terrace .eyre crescent .ferry
road .festival theatre .fettes college .fettes row .figgate
park .findhorn place .fingal place .fisher's close .fishwives'
causeway .forres street .forrest road .forth street .fountain
close .fountain court .fountainbridge .frederick street

show keywords

40712
Edinburgh

Musselbur

1452

Colinton

Currie 354

Balerno

520

877
Bonnyrigg

Figure 28.2 (Continued).

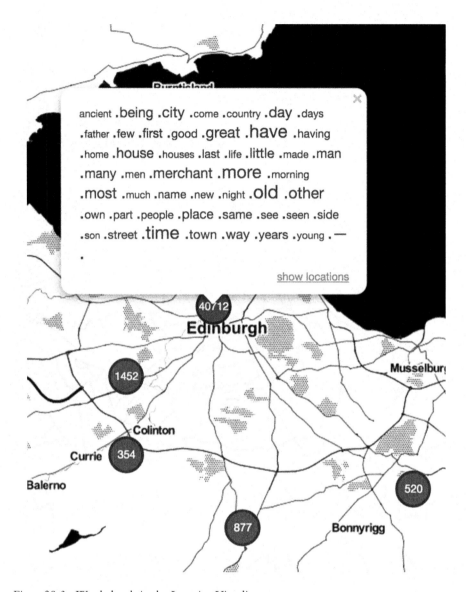

Figure 28.3 Word clouds in the Location Visualiser.

The dataset can also be explored on a book–by–book basis. The book list view simply lists each book included in our collection, including the paragraphs extracted from the book which contain Edinburgh place name mentions always corresponding to the area shown in the map as described above (see Figure 28.7).

Hovering over a book item in the booklist highlights its corresponding place name mentions in the map (see Figure 28.7). Again, multiple location mentions in close proximity are clustered, depending on the map's zoom-level. Selecting a book from the list via mouse click adds its location mentions as a permanent layer to the map. This can facilitate the comparison of selected literary works and their place name mentions (see Figure 28.7).

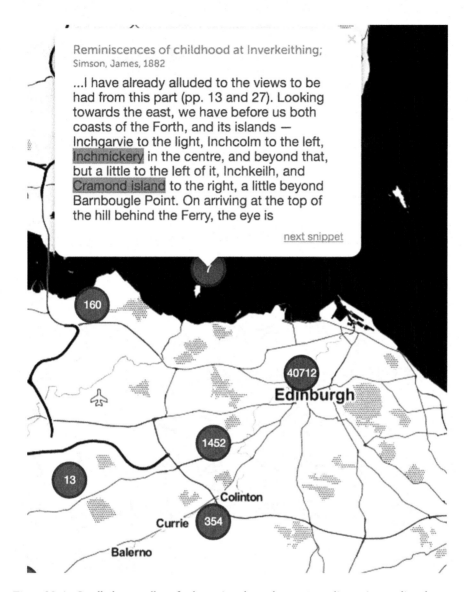

Reminiscences of childhood at Inverkeithing;
Simson, James, 1882

...I have already alluded to the views to be had from this part (pp. 13 and 27). Looking towards the east, we have before us both coasts of the Forth, and its islands — Inchgarvie to the light, Inchcolm to the left, Inchmickery in the centre, and beyond that, but a little to the left of it, Inchkeilh, and Cramond island to the right, a little beyond Barnbougle Point. On arriving at the top of the hill behind the Ferry, the eye is

next snippet

Figure 28.4   Small clusters allow for browsing through corresponding snippets directly.

The open-ended exploration approaches facilitated by the map and book list view are enhanced by a filtering mechanism that enables a targeted search of the collection by keyword, place name, and/or author. For example, entering an author of interest updates all views to only include books by this particular author. Autocomplete mechanisms are in place to provide direct-feedback on the availability of this particular author name in our dataset. Alternatively, a list of authors can be browsed to find authors of interest (see Figure 28.8). Here, font sizes indicate the number of Edinburgh-related snippets included in the authors' works. Equivalent selection mechanisms are available for the location and keyword search. The dropdown menus not only facilitate targeted search but can also convey an idea of the range of location

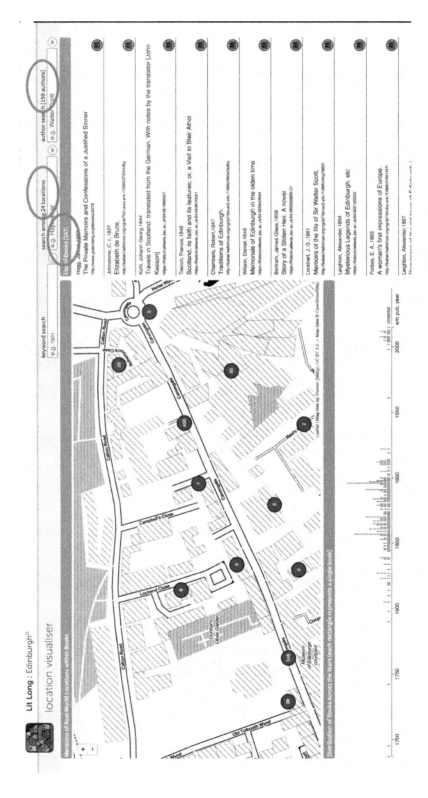

Figure 28.5   Zooming into the map provides details about literary mentions of Edinburgh's Royal Mile area.

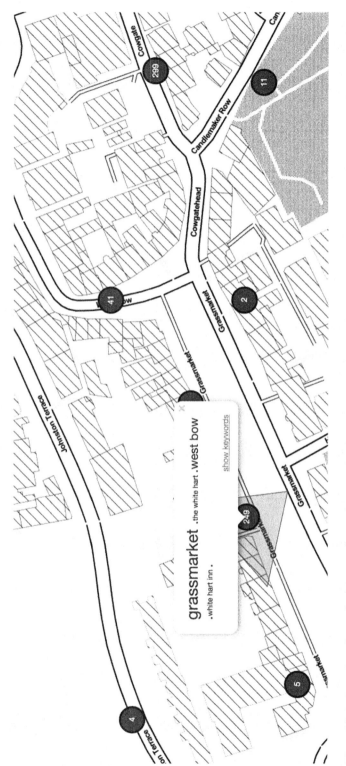

Figure 28.6 Location clusters become smaller as the zoom level increases.

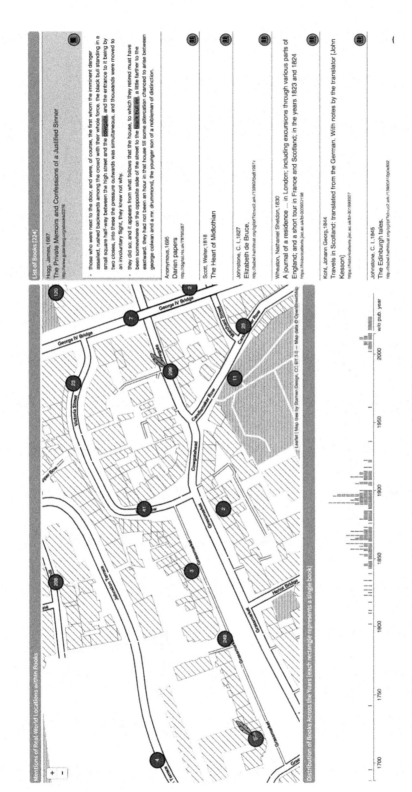

Figure 28.7 Book list view with the selected book's location mentions highlighted.

names and authors that are available as well as the types of keywords that are included in the snippets of selected authors or locations. This augments the more specific exploration of particular location clusters in the map view, by providing an idea of keywords, location names, and authors corresponding to the entire map section currently in view.

The iOS app

The LitLong mobile app (suitable for Apple iPhones and iPads) is the mobile counterpart of the Location Visualiser, providing opportunities to browse literary extracts while moving through the city of Edinburgh. It uses built-in location services of a mobile phone (GPS), to trigger location-specific requests to the LitLong database. The app was created in XCode, Apple's development environment. This enabled use of software development kits (SDKs) such as a map toolkit. The map

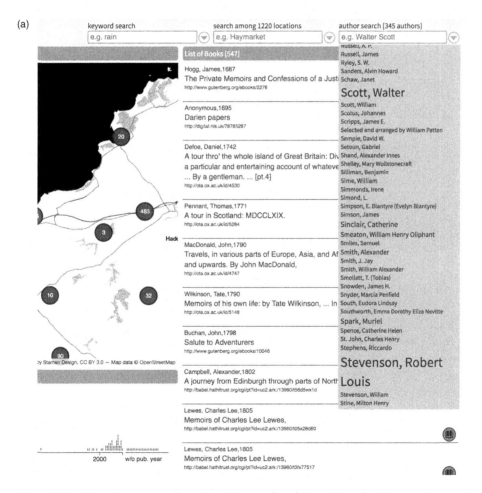

Figure 28.8 Drop-down menus provide a glimpse of available authors, location mentions and contextual keywords.

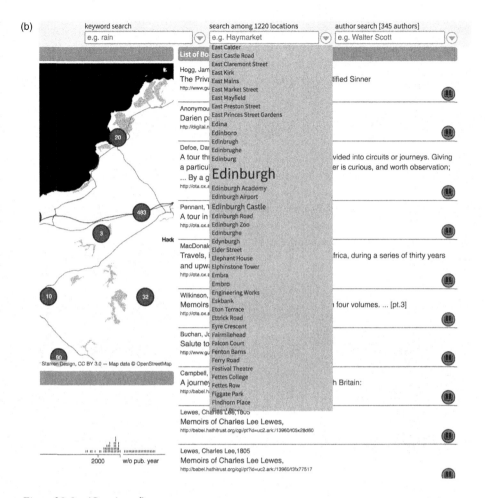

Figure 28.8   (Continued).

toolkit allowed incorporation of Apple maps into the app and placing pins in the map at specified latitude and longitudes (lat-longs), which allows the user to feel comfortable and familiar with the LitLong app environment.

As it is not assumed that the user will always have connectivity to the internet, the data required in the app is stored inside the app itself rather than relying on a database accessed via the internet. This created both technical opportunities and challenges. Storing the data in the app enables quick local searching of data from nearby locations without the need to wait for the request to be sent to the server and then receive the required information back. However, as iOS apps require any data inside an app to be loaded only when the app is open, and the dataset used is quite extensive, the loading of the data had to be streamlined. The initial load data was reduced to only the data required for app setup (such as lat-longs, location names and number of extracts at each location), enabling the pin locations of nearby books to be dropped

(a)   (b)

Figure 28.9   Screenshots of the LitLong iOS app: a) splash screen; b) the main view.

on the map in less than one second from initial launch. Then when more information from that location is required, such as the text extracts from books and their associated metadata, the data can be loaded into the app on request. To split the data up in this way json files with the data for each location were stored and loaded on request.

App operation is simple, and deliberately intuitive. On tapping the app launch icon a splash screen is shown (see Figure 28.9a). The user is then presented with a map and text boxes which show book information. The map can be used in two modes: either the user's current location serves to organise and select information, or the user taps on a specific book location shown with pen nibs on the map (see Figure 28.9b for a screenshot of the interface). The selected information shows the location at the very top, then the title, author, year and a link directly to the original full text (if available) which if tapped opens in a web browser. The extract itself appears in a scrollable text field. If there is more than one extract at that location then the user can go through these by using the blue left and right arrows by the text.

If a pen–nib is tapped then information about that location is shown in a pop-up (see Figure 28.10a), with the name of the location and the number of extracts at that

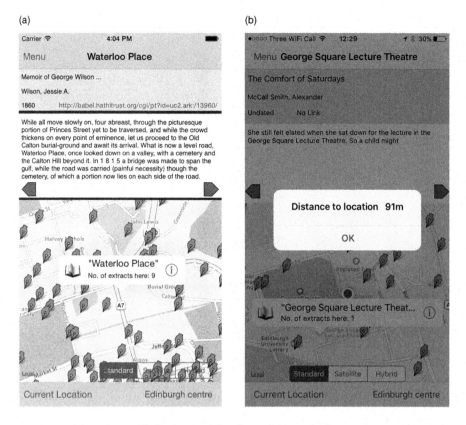

Figure 28.10 Screenshots of the types of information available in the LitLong iOS app when a book location is selected.

location. Then if the user taps the information (i) button the distance from the user to that location is shown (see Figure 28.10b). The map can be scrolled through to a different area by tapping and dragging, and zoomed in and out of by tapping with two fingers and pinching. The user can also snap either to their current location by pressing the relevant button in the bottom left of the screen, or to the centre of Edinburgh by pressing the button in the bottom right. To further improve the browsing locations of interest, a maximised view of the map can be selected by going into the menu which can be accessed either by swiping in from the left or by pressing the 'Menu' button on the top left (see Figure 28.9b).

Unembarrassing the eye

In his account of the presencing of place in literature, Sten Pultz Moslund, who has also been influenced by phenomenological and cognitive linguistic accounts, argues that topopoetic readings need to pay attention to the ways in which 'the earth of the place juts through the cultural world of the novel'.[22] This is not simply a one-way dynamic, as Moslund further describes: 'Topopoetically, we approach the novel and its signifiers, not as standing *for* the place, . . . but as standing *in* that very place . . . The landscape in the work, or the place, seems to open up in front of us, behind us, above us, and beneath us.'[23]

Reciprocal shaping occurs between the cultural and physical aspects of a place. Linguistic representations map on to underlying physical features and processes in ways that function practically within a society and that are based on characteristics in ourselves and in the world. Yet even 'factual' accounts of places are necessarily coloured by sociocultural and cognitive biases. A fictional text's use of real-world place names makes the narrative a form of counterfactual scenario; an 'as if' account, that emerges through an author's (and their readers') drawing on and adding to the previous usages and associations of the place and its name. This means that there is always both continuity and difference between the accounts, which creates persisting and shifting patterns whose own continuities and divergences provide meaningful insights and potential inspiration.

Our initial explorations were driven by a general curiosity around the ways in which this key geocritical dimension of literary works might be made visible and explorable through digital means and methods. The creation of the database, visual-isations and app have shown that it is possible to build what a number of scholars have termed a 'macroscope'. Tim Hitchcock has recently given this term a new twist, stressing not just the enlightening force of the large scale but equally the illuminating 'power of the particular'.[24] Such a machine combines high-level and large-scale explorations of literary works with the capability to attend to particular works, authors or locations. Our visualisations have focused on allowing users to pick their own path through the data, and to pursue alignments along a number of axes, such as place name, work, author or keyword. These interactions involve either actual or virtual placement within a map of Edinburgh, but they don't easily amount to a totalising view of the terrain in its literary significance. Our maps, in other words, do not provide a single plane within which all of the data is visibly arrayed.

There are costs involved in this approach. The collections of digitised texts on which we have drawn are not comprehensive, despite their scale; at the same time, the difficulty that machine reading experiences in tracking inference or weak impli-catures limits the extent to which the variety of ways in which place names can be contextualised or can be effectively mapped. This means that, to some extent, the large-scale approach has not made quantitative or statistical analysis any easier – as it is currently configured, LitLong does not readily permit users to gain a definitive, distantly read overview of spatial or temporal patterns of association and usage. Instead, the use of geolocation and its expression in cartographic form makes it pos-sible to disassemble texts into smaller units, our snippets, which can then be reassem-bled into new combinations on the basis of their geographical identity or contiguity. In its current form, LitLong offers a 'generous interface' – to use Mitchell Whitelaw's term (2012) – which furnishes its users with a rich experience of the particulars of literary place name usage, rather than a means of distant reading which meets the aspirations for that kind of analysis expressed most forcefully by Moretti.[25] As a mac-roscope, it privileges the singular encounter with the extract. It thus makes possible a range of new geocritical perspectives on the literature of single city, but it doesn't seek to establish a single or overall view. Indeed, it is as open to use by writers, readers and visitors as it is to academics – perhaps even more so.

Although our capacity to interpret literary place is not yet extended by these new media in the kind of panoramic or macroscopic way envisioned by some theoretical digital humanities' texts, the mining and visualisation of digitised texts allows both for new perspectives and for a continuation of the active reading practices which already inform scholarly and creative writing. Using LitLong it is possible to see, rather more immediately than otherwise, across the range and spread of place name usage associated with different authors – Walter Scott and Irvine Welsh, for example. The geolocated extracts also illuminate the diverse range of ways in which place names can operate across literary texts: as a grammatical entity of discourse; as a functional role in the story structure; as a means of achieving an aesthetic effect; as a representation of a thematic element or of a semantic complex.[26] The juxtaposition of the geolocated fragments of texts, like quotes in critical arguments or literary allusions, whilst not equivalent to nor a replacement for in-depth analysis of whole texts, can itself enable creative and scholarly insights.

In addition, our data could readily underpin further visualisations that might open up other lines of geocritical enquiry. For example, how do particular real-world place names mentioned in literary works relate to each other, beyond their geospatial attributes? Are certain locations frequently mentioned in relation to each other? How do the linear structure and temporal aspects of a narrative relate to the concept of place and space? And, in terms of context, how are particular place mentions represented in terms of surrounding contextual and grammatical structures? How can we visualise qualitative and topological differences across particular place name mentions (e.g. the mention of a city, neighbourhood, road, or building)? New visualisation approaches are needed to address such questions, some of which may branch off from the concept of geospatial maps and towards more abstract visualisations where the place names are represented, for example, according to their appearance and proximity to other location mentions within the narrative. Similarly, contextual relations between place and, for example, emotion could be opened to exploration via alternative visualisation techniques.[27]

Looking down on the city of Edinburgh from Calton Hill in his *Picturesque Notes*, Robert Louis Stevenson gives voice to the anxiety about informational superabundance that Westphal suggests will always defeat the attempt at geocritical analysis of culturally overdetermined sites. 'It is the character of such a prospect,' he says, 'to be full of change and things moving. The multiplicity embarrasses the eye; and the mind, among so much, suffers itself to grow absorbed with single points.'[28] Perhaps, with the advent of interfaces and forms of working in which close and distant reading might be usefully combined, it is no longer the case that the rich multiplicity of a site's literary geography need embarrass either the writer's or the critic's eye.

Notes

1 M. M. Bakhtin and Michael Holquist, *The Dialogic Imagination: Four Essays*, Austin, TX: University of Texas Press, 1981.
2 Michel de Certeau and Steven Rendall, *The Practice of Everyday Life*, Berkeley, CA: University of California Press, 1984.

3 Yi-Fu Tuan, *Space and Place: The Perspective of Experience*, Minneapolis, MN: University of Minnesota Press, 1977.

4 Henri Lefebvre, *The Production of Space*, Oxford: Blackwell, 1991.

5 Robert Tally, 'Textual Geographies: The Real-and-Imagined Spaces of Literature, Criticism, and Theory', *Reconstruction* 14, 2014.

6 Tally, 'Textual Geographies', 2.

7 Bertrand Westphal and Robert Tally, *Geocriticism: Real and Fictional Spaces*, New York: Palgrave Macmillan, 2011; Bertrand Westphal, *The Plausible World: A Geocritical Approach to Space, Place, and Maps*, Basingstoke: Palgrave Macmillan, 2013.

8 Franco Moretti, *Atlas of the European Novel, 1800–1900*, London: Verso, 1998; *Distant Reading*, London: Verso, 2013; *Graphs, Maps, Trees: Abstract Models for a Literary History*, London: Verso, 2005.

9 See *Mapping the Lakes: A Literary GIS* www.lancaster.ac.uk/mappingthelakes (accessed 27 January 2017); *A Literary Atlas of Europe* www.literaturatlas.eu/en (accessed 27 January 2017); Shelley Fisher Fishkin, '"Deep Maps": A Brief for Digital Palimpsest Mapping Projects (DPMPs, or "Deep Maps")', *Journal of Transnational American Studies* 3, 2011; 'The Modernist Versions Project', <http://web.uvic.ca/~mvp1922/>.

10 Robert Tally, 'Foreword', in Westphal, *Geocriticism*, p. xii.

11 Tally, 'Textual Geographies', 2.

12 Laurence Hutton, *Literary Landmarks of Edinburgh*, New York: Harper & Brothers, 1891, p. xiii.

13 Hutton, *Literary Landmarks of Edinburgh*.

14 James Loxley, Beatrice Alex, Miranda Anderson, David Harris-Birtill, Claire Grover, Uta Hinrichs, Jon Oberlander, Lisa Otty, Aaron Quigley, James Reid, and Tara Thomson. LitLong: Edinburgh, <http://litlong.org>, 2015 (accessed 27 January 2017).

15 Tally, 'Foreword', in Westphal, *Geocriticism*, p. xii.

16 T. Strohman, D. Metzler, H. Turtle, and W. B. Croft, *Indri: A Language-Model Based Search Engine for Complex Queries* (extended version), CIIR Technical Report, 2005.

17 Beatrice Alex, Claire Grover, Jon Oberlander, Ke Zhou and Uta Hinrichs, 'Palimpsest: Improving Assisted Curation of Loco-Specific Literature', in *Proceedings of DH2015*, Sydney, 2015.

18 Ted Underwood, 'Understanding Genre in a Collection of a Million Volumes', Interim Report, December 2014, <http://dx.doi.org/10.6084/m9.figshare.1281251> (accessed 27 January 2017).

19 See Beatrice Alex et al., 'Adapting The Edinburgh Geoparser for Historical Georeferencing', *International Journal of Humanities and Arts Computing* 9, 2015, 15–35.

20 D. Ganguly, J. Leveling, and G. J. F. Jones, 'Automatic Prediction of Text Aesthetics and Interestingness', in *25th International Conference on Computational Linguistics* (COLING 2014), 23–9.

21 Irvine Welsh, *Trainspotting*, London: Jonathan Cape, 1993, 228.

22 Sten Pultz Moslund, 'The Presencing of Place in Literature: Toward an Embodied Topopoetic Mode of Reading', in Robert Tally (ed.), *Geocritical Explorations: Space, Place and Mapping in Literary and Cultural Studies*, New York: Palgrave Macmillan, 2011, 29–43, at 38.

23 Moslund, 'The Presencing of Place in Literature', 39.

24 Tim Hitchcock, 'Big Data, Small Data and Meaning', *Historyonics*, 9 Nov. 2014; <http://historyonics.blogspot.co.uk/2014/11/big-data-small-data-and-meaning_9.html> (accessed 27 January 2017).

25 Mitchell Whitelaw, 'Towards Generous Interfaces for Archival Collections', *Comma*, 2012, 123–32.

26 Miranda Anderson and James Loxley, 'The Poetics of Place-Names in Digitised Literary Edinburgh', in David Cooper, Christopher Donaldson, and Patricia Murrieta-Flores (eds.), *Literary Mapping in the Digital Age*, London: Routledge, 2016, 47–66.

27 See e.g. the essays in Christian Nold, *Emotional Cartography: Technologies of the Self*, s.l.: s.n., 2009.

28 Robert Louis Stevenson, *Edinburgh: Picturesque Notes*, London: Seeley, Jackson, & Halliday, 1879, 31.

INDEX

Chapter-based case studies are indexed under place names where applicable with cross-references provided from subjects.